MANAGING TOURISM AND HOSPITALITY SERVICES

Theory and International Applications

D1404282

To my wife Lin and children Jillian, Benjamin, Joshua, Krystin and Jeremy for their support
and encouragement in this project
Bruce Prideaux

To all the Pearce boys for their ability to amuse and distract
Gianna Moscardo

And, to Barbara
Eric Laws

MANAGING TOURISM AND HOSPITALITY SERVICES

Theory and International Applications

Edited by

BRUCE PRIDEAUX
GIANNA MOSCARDO
ERIC LAWS

www.cabi.org

CABI is a trading name of CAB International

CABI Head Office
Nosworthy Way
Wallingford
Oxfordshire OX10 8DE
UK

CABI North American Office
875 Massachusetts Avenue
7th Floor
Cambridge, MA 02139
USA

Tel: +44 (0)1491 832111
Fax: +44 (0)1491 833508

Tel: +1 617 395 4056
Fax: +1 617 354 6875

E-mail: cabi@cabi.org
Website: www.cabi.org

E-mail: cabi-nao@cabi.org

A catalogue record for this book is available from the British Library, London, UK.

Library of Congress Cataloging-in-Publication Data

Managing tourism and hospitality services: theory and international application / edited by B. Prideaux, G. Moscardo, E. Laws.
    p. cm.
  Includes bibliographical references and index.
  ISBN-13: 978-1-84593-012-7 (alk. paper)
  ISBN-10: 1-84593-012-6 (alk.paper)
  1. Hospitality industry--Management. 2. Tourism--Management. I. Prideaux, B. (Bruce) II. Moscardo, Gianna. III. Laws, Eric, 1945- IV. Title.

  TX911.3.M37M323 2005
  647.94'068--dc22   2005016925

ISBN-10: 1 84593 012 6
ISBN-13: 978 1 84593 012 7

Typeset by SPi, Pondicherry, India.
Printed and bound in the UK by Biddles Ltd, King's Lynn.

Contents

Contributors

Anderson, B., *International Graduate School of Management, University of South Australia, GPO Box 2471, Adelaide, SA 5001, Australia.*

Brown, M., *Tiscover AG, Travel Information Systems, Maria-Theresien-Strasse 55-57, A-6020 Innsbruck, Austria.*

Buhalis, D., *Centre for eTourism Research (CeTR), School of Management, University of Surry, Guildford GU2 7XH, UK.*

Carlsen, J., *MUI Chair in Tourism & Hospitality Service, Co-director, Curtin Sustainable Tourism Centre, Curtin University of Technology, GPO Box U1987, Perth, WA 6845, USA.*

Clark, S., *Ex Manager, Strategic Planning Tourism, Queensland, Australia. Email: stephen@ goodthinking.com.au.*

Cooper, M.J., *International Cooperation and Research, Ritsumeikan Asia Pacific University, 1-1 Jumonjibaru, Beppu-shi 874-8577, Japan.*

Deery, M., *Centre for Hospitality & Tourism Research, Victoria University, PO Box 14428, Melbourne City, MC 8001, Australia.*

Diamantis, D., *Les Roches Management School, Switzerland.*

Erfurt, P.J., *Ritsumeikan Asia Pacific University, 1-1 Jumonjibaru, Beppu-shi 874-8577, Japan.*

Getz, D., *Haskayne School of Business, University of Calgary, Canada.*

Hudson, P., *JMC Holidays, UK.*

Hudson, S., *Haskayne School of Business, 2500 University Drive NW Calgary, Alberta T2N IN4.*

Jago, L., *CRC for Sustainable Tourism, C/- Centre for Hospitality and Tourism Research, Victoria University, PO Box 14428, Melbourne City MC, Victoria, Australia 8001.*

Kandampully, J., *Professor of Services Management, 265 J Campbell Hall, 1787 Neil Avenue, Ohio State University, Columbus, OH 43210-1295, USA.*

Kandampully, R., *265 J Campbell Hall, 1787 Neil Avenue, Ohio State University, Columbus, OH 43210-1295, USA.*

Karcher, K., *Tiscover AG, Travel Information Systems, Maria-Theresien-Strasse 55-57, A-6020 Innsbruck, Austria.*

Khan, M., *Room 565, Hospitality Program, Dept of Management, School of Business, Howard University, 2600 6th Street, NW, Washington, DC 20059, USA.*

Kim, S.S., *Department of Hospitality & Tourism Management, Sejong University, Seoul, Korea.*

Komppula, R., *Finnish University Network for Tourism Studies, University of Joensuu, PO Box 111, FIN-80101 Joensuu, Finland*

Krebs, L., *Department of Geography, University of Waterloo, Waterloo, Ontario, Canada N2L 3G1.*

Laws, E., *Adjunct Professor, James Cook University, Cairns, Queensland, Australia. E-mail: e.laws@runbox.com*

Le Pelley, B., *Guernsey Planning Department, UK. E-mail: barbara.lep@ guernsey.net*

MacLeod, M., *Land Economy Research, Scottish Agricultural College, Craibstone Estate, Aberdeen AB21 9YA, UK.*

Miller, G.A., *University of Surrey, UK.*

Moscardo, G., *School of Business, James Cook University, Townsville, QLD 4811, Australia.*

O'Neill, M., *Dept of Hotel and Restaurant Management, College of Human Sciences, 328B Spidle Hall, Auburn University, Auburn, AL 36849, USA.*

Pegg, S., *School of Tourism & Leisure Management, Faculty of Business, Economics & Law, Ipswich Campus, The University of Queensland, 11 Salisbury Road, Ipswich, QLD 4305, Australia.*

Pearce, P.L., *Tourism Program, James Cook University, Townsville, Australia.*

Pettit, T., *Civic and International Manager, Canterbury City Council, UK. E-mail: william. pettit@canterbury.gov.uk.*

Prideaux, B., *James Cook University, PO Box 6811, Cairns, Queensland 4870, Australia.*

Renolds, R., *Embry-Riddle Aeronautical University, College of Business, 600 S. Clyde Morris Blvd, Daytona Beach, FL 32114, USA.*

Rhoades, D., *Embry-Riddle Aeronautical University, College of Business, 600 S. Clyde Morris Blvd, Daytona Beach, FL 32114, USA.*

Santos-Arrebola, J.L., *Catedratico de Universidad, University of Malaga, Spain.*

Scott, N., *School of Tourism and Leisure Management, University of Queensland, Ipswich Campus, 11 Salisbury Road, Ipswich, Queensland 4305, Australia.*

Suh, J.-H.K., *School of Tourism & Leisure Management, Faculty of Business, Economics & Law, Ipswich Campus, The University of Queensland, 11 Salisbury Road, Ipswich, QLD 4305, Australia.*

Uysal, M., *Virginia Polytechnic Institute and State University, Dept of Hospitality and Tourism Management, 355 Wallace Hall, Blacksburg, VA 24061-0429, USA.*

Varini, K., *Ecole Hoteliere Lausanne, Switzerland.*

Yu, X., *Department of Management/Tourism, Monash University, Berwick Campus, Victoria 3805, Australia.*

Waguespack, B., *College of Business, 600 S. Clyde Morris Blvd, Daytona Beach, FL 32114, USA.*

Wall, G., *Department of Geography, University of Waterloo, Waterloo, Ontario, Canada N2L 3G1.*

Weiler, B., *Department of Management/Tourism, Monash University, Berwick Campus, Victoria 3805, Australia.*

Williams, F., *Land Economy Research, Scottish Agricultural College, Craibstone Estate, Aberdeen AB21 9YA, UK.*

List of Figures

List of Tables

1 Quality and Service Management Perspectives

Eric Laws, Bruce Prideaux and Gianna Moscardo
James Cook University, Australia

Introduction

Managing Tourism and Hospitality Services is the result of extended discussions between the three editors about their own research interests, and between them and colleagues in many countries about activities they have been engaged in. It became apparent that there are some important convergences in tourism and hospitality research, particularly as it relates to the study of service management in these still new and still rapidly developing sectors. In this book, the editors have presented a range of current research which individually records the commitment and application of the contributors, but taken together the collection of work provides a benchmark of current understanding, and examines the range of research methods being applied to further deepen the understanding of tourism and hospitality service management research. It is not our belief that this book is a definitive statement of research into this area, rather we hope that it will inspire present and future researchers to consider how to further advance the frontiers of tourism and hospitality research.

The overall aim of the various research projects which form the collection of work in this book is to enhance understanding of quality management in tourism and hospitality. This introductory chapter now briefly describes the structure of the book, before providing an initial review of the evolution of tourism and hospitality management research.

The Structure of this Book

Managing Tourism and Hospitality Services is organized in six parts. The 28 chapters deal with a wide range of issues, providing analyses of international tourism and hospitality management practices from many sectors of the industry, and utilizing an interesting selection of research methodologies and conceptual approaches. As the editors show in detail in the review and synthesis of the concluding chapter of this book, the work presented here makes a substantial contribution to the better understanding of current tourism and hospitality management and emergent research capabilities, while identifying some gaps and the need for further research in the future.

Part I deals with the core issue for tourism and hospitality managers of customer satisfaction. The five chapters examine some specific examples and draw together a range of theoretical and methodological approaches to customer satisfaction research and management. This theme of customer satisfaction is taken up in many of the subsequent chapters in this book.

Structural issues are the main focus of chapters in Part II. The three chapters dealing with competition and collaboration, both of which are strongly characteristic of the industry. The resultant tensions provide the dynamic context for managerial strategy while managers deal with the realities of designing and operating the complex socio-technical organizations delivering tourism and hospitality services.

The six chapters in Part III build on the understanding of customer satisfaction and the functioning of industry relationships by reporting and critically analysing examples of improvements to specific tourism and hospitality services. Part IV presents six chapters which focus attention on the experiences of those who work in the industry, their interactions with clients, and ways of managing them more effectively. A range of important ethical as well as practical and theoretical topics are raised and examined.

Research methods are the particular focus of Part V. The seven chapters provide examples of current research projects and evaluate a variety of methodologies. It is hoped that readers will feel encouraged to adopt a more varied approach to the design of their own future research as a result of reading some of the innovative thinking incorporated here.

Part VI contains one chapter which concludes *Managing Tourism and Hospitality Services*. In this the editors summarize, map and synthesize the analyses and findings of our 48 contributors, and identify some priorities for future research in this challenging and rapidly evolving industry.

Service Quality in Tourism and Hospitality Management

It has been suggested that service research has moved on its from its original concerns with distinguishing the study of service issues from those confronting manufacturing sectors (Fisk *et al.*, 1993; Laws, 2000). In part, second generation research is concerned with identifying and defining the distinguishing operational characteristics of the various service subsectors, but although researchers have been very active in describing the relevant features of tourism and hospitality, we have not yet reached a consensus.

For tourism, research must encompass the impacts of tourist activities on staff and destinations, and consider how the complex structure of the industry mediates both tourist satisfaction and destination impacts. In relation to hospitality, the scale is smaller and the boundaries of research can usually be confined to the interactions between guests and the staff who serve them in the context of particular models for each hotel or restaurant. This may account for the significantly greater volume of service quality oriented studies of hospitality operations, and there is therefore much for tourism specialists to learn from their hospitality-focused colleagues. In many instances, investigation of a research question, and particularly attempts to develop theory, may require a research design that examines aspects of both tourism and hospitality rather than attempting to make fundamental distinctions between these subsectors.

The rationale for the theme of service quality in this book is that most sectors of the tourism and hospitality industry have regularly experienced a high incidence of complaints (Pearce and Moscardo, 1984), including low standards during the journey between home and destination, poor accommodation, poor resort location and associated difficulties. A Consumers Association report discussed in Laws (1997) surveyed 11,500 British members asking them to rate the tour operators and countries they had patronized in the year to September 1996. The key criterion was 'whether they would definitely recommend them to a friend who wants to take the same sort of holiday'. Swiss Travel Service was the only operator of the 51 in the survey to gain a 'definitely' or 'probably' recommendation from all Consumer Association respondents who had used the company. Poor accommodation was the main source of dissatisfaction; other concerns related to representatives, brochure accuracy and changes to the arrangements once booked. Amongst the major tour operators' clients, the proportion surveyed who would 'definitely recommend' a particular tour operator ranged from only 48% for Thomson to a low of 25% for Airtours.

Earlier, the Chief Executive of British Airways had expressed the challenge of managing quality in the service sector in the following terms:

> Why not merely run an airline which is so good that it never has any problems? May I assure you that we are in a service business, and service businesses deal with people. There is never one perfect set of answers for dealing with people problems, otherwise they would not be people. What makes service businesses so interesting and so complex is that their prime stake in trade is people relations, and we are expected to handle those relations in the hurly burly of commerce, not in the quiet professionalism of a therapist's room.
>
> (Marshall, 1986, p. 10)

Much empirical research shows that the tourism industry is complex (Ashworth and Tunbridge, 1990; Leiper, 1990; Brown, 1998). However, it also highlights the relationships between the many organizations contributing to the products tourists purchase from the industry (Morgan, 1994; Buhalis, 2000), and focuses on the dynamics underlying its changing practices (Hall, 1995; Faulkner and Russell, 1997; Lew, 1999; Buhalis and Laws, 2001).

Hudson and Shephard (1998, pp. 61–62), have argued that 'service quality has been increasingly identified as a key factor in differentiating service products and building a competitive advantage in tourism'. They demonstrate how the attributes which consumers and producers consider important may be identified and quantified. In a review of PhD research by mature candidates in Britain, Baum (1998, p. 467) commented that 'there was a noticeable recent focus on research with a focus on service quality'. Nevertheless, tourism service quality remains rather under-researched. For example, Laws et al. (1999) identified only eight titles dealing with quality management aspects, out of a total of 380 books on tourism published in the decade since 1989. Furthermore, Harrington and Akehurst (1996, p. 135) commented that much of the research to date has been prescriptive and has lacked a focus on 'the extent to which quality has been effectively incorporated as a strategic concern in service organizations'.

The Quality of Service Experiences

The process by which consumers understand quality is often regarded as a comparison of the service standards expected when purchasing a service, compared to their perceptions of service experiences, although there are some limitations to the applicability of the model (Yusel and Yusel, 2001). Consumer satisfaction is the outcome when expectations are matched by service experience, conversely, dissatisfaction occurs when there is a mismatch, and expectations are not fulfilled by the service delivered (Engel et al., 1986). The psychological consequences of this meet the conditions for dissonance described by Festinger (1957) and Brehm and Cohen (1962).

Harrington and Akehurst (1996), in a detailed review of 21 leading articles, identified a wide range of dimensions used in definitions of quality. In his benchmark study of products and services, Garvin (1988) classified quality in five ways. Transcendent quality varies between individuals and over time, and can be understood in the common phrase 'I know it when I see it'. An approach relying on the measurable features of the product, the expert view of quality leads to design specification and technical drawings. User-based quality, while in part based on individual judgement, is also the basis of consumer legislation which introduced the test of merchantability, requiring goods sold commercially to be fit for their purpose: the classic test was that a bucket should not leak. Manufacturing quality is concerned to minimize deviations from the standards set in the producer's technical specifications. Goods meeting internal specifications therefore conform to the manufacturer's requirements, whether or not customers are satisfied. The fifth suggested classification is value-based quality. Commenting on value-based quality, Garvin (1988, p. 44) noted that 'it seems to be difficult to determine a generally valid link between price and quality'. Each component of the definition of value-based quality is relevant. Value is generally regarded as meaning the delivery of more of some desired attributes of the service than the customer expected. In the short term this may occur as the outcome of deliberately under-promising, or it may result from higher than normal performance in the service delivery system.

The longer-term significance is that it embraces the view that customers' expectations of service standards are not static over time.

Gronroos (1990) has made an important distinction between two approaches in analysing the quality of services; technology-driven and fitness for use and customer-driven definitions.

Technical Approaches to Production-oriented Service Quality

The challenge for service managers is to design a service delivery system which combines maximizing customers' judgements that the service experienced is satisfying, with technical efficiency in the use of resources to create it (Ramaswamy, 1996).

One strategy which managers often adopt in their search for consistent service is to eliminate employee discretion and judgement whenever possible (Sasser et al., 1978). It relies on the specification of tasks to a defined standard of performance. Increased standardization implies a reduction in the discretion allowed to individual employees; however, this often contradicts service sector clients' expectations of being treated as individuals, with needs that may vary during the many events of which a service is composed. Efficiency goals may clarify performance targets for staff, but can conflict with the customers' expectation of warm and friendly service. Underlying this approach are the twin assumptions that consumers experience a service as a series of events, while managers see the service as a set of elements which require skilled coordination and resource control, in delivering specified standards to clients. These assumptions are considered more fully in the discussion of blueprinting that follows.

Commenting on technical performance goals, Locke and Scweiger (1979) identified seven important characteristics of effective management programmes. They suggested that the goals set must be specific, accepted, cover important job dimensions, be reviewed, with appropriate feedback, be measurable and challenging, but attainable. Hollins and Hollins (1991) also advocated a process of continuous improvements, relying on a view which under-

lies service blueprinting that customers experience the service as a chain of events.

Chase (1978) noted that the technical approach works quite well in the manufacturing sector and hypothesized that it should be effective for low contact services. The meaning of low contact services is that interaction between staff and clients is minimized by the design of the service.

Customer-oriented Service Quality

The second quality approach discussed by Gronroos (1990) was fitness for use. This can best be understood in terms of customers' expectations of satisfaction, against which they evaluate their subsequent individual experiences during the service. Marketing theory argues that customers' experiences with any purchase give rise to outcomes for them varying from satisfaction to dissatisfaction. This reflects a divergence from the standards of service which clients had anticipated, as the following abbreviated quotations indicate: 'The seeds of consumer satisfaction are planted during the prepurchase phase of the consumer decision process' (Wilkie, 1986, p. 558). It is against this individual benchmark that tourists measure the quality of their service experiences.

> Satisfaction is defined as a postconsumption evaluation that the chosen alternative is consistent with prior beliefs and expectations (with respect to it). Dissatisfaction, of course, is the outcome when this confirmation does not take place.
>
> (Engel et al., 1986, p. 155)

Gronroos (1990) argued that service quality comprises the two fundamental components discussed above, technical quality ('what' is delivered) and functional quality ('how' the service is delivered), but he also noted an important third component – the organization's image or brand strengths.

Consumer Involvement

Consumers' degrees of interest and 'involvement' in purchasing particular products or services range from low to high. Involvement is likely to be high when the purchase has functional and symbolic significance, and entails some financial risk (Cohen, 1986; Asseal, 1987). Laws (2004) argued that four features of holiday travel suggest that many tourists experience a high degree of involvement in choosing their holiday:

- Holidays are expensive.
- Holidays are complex both to purchase and experience.
- There is a risk that the resort or hotel may not prove satisfying.
- The resort or hotel reflects the holiday maker's personality.

In the case of journeys by air, low involvement passengers may be satisfied when an airline provides an on-time flight with reasonable standards of comfort and catering. Any service enhancements such as a sophisticated entertainment system or fine meals are received with pleasure. In contrast, a high involvement passenger expects enhanced service as a minimum requirement, and looks for additional evidence of superior service such as the latest style of seating or enhanced facilities at the airport.

The Organizational Significance of Service Failure

Dissatisfaction amongst many consumers is a serious matter to the firm providing a service, as the implication is that customers will take their future business elsewhere. They are also likely to discuss their negative experiences with many other people, thereby further undermining the company's credibility in its marketplace (Fornell and Wernerfelt, 1987). However, a converse view of complaints has been suggested by Lyons (1996) who discussed how to analyse the factors leading customers to complain.

Organizations incur costs from dealing with the direct consequences of any service failure, but implementing a quality control system to minimize problems also imposes costs (Bitner et al., 1990; Leppard and Molyneux, 1994; Bejou and Palmer, 1998). These costs result from actions taken to get a service right from the start, auditing that it is correctly delivered, and the expenses of responding to any failure. Further costs are incurred in implementing preventative measures to reduce future dissatisfaction, including the redesign of service delivery systems or training and motivational programmes for staff. The two bases for managers of minimizing service failures are found in the technical aspects of service, and in understanding their customers' concerns.

Researching Customer Satisfaction

Chase (1978) posed the focal service marketing question: where does the customer fit in a service? During the mid-1980s a team of three researchers developed a way of researching service quality which became highly influential. SERVQUAL measures perceptions of service quality on five dimensions (reduced from ten original items): tangibles; reliability; responsiveness; assurance and empathy (Parasuraman et al., 1988). The survey instrument seeks to identify positive and negative gaps in the firm's performance on the five service quality dimensions through two sets of 20 statements which compare customers' expectations and their perceptions of the firm's service performance, rated on a 7-point Likert scale (see Table 1.1).

SERVQUAL has been criticized both for its underlying gap approach, including its core constructs of consumer satisfaction, expectations and quality (Chadee and Mattsson, 1996), and its methodology (Brown et al., 1993; Teas, 1994; Johns, 1999). Some researchers even question the continuing use of SERVQUAL:

> At best, it can be argued that SERVQUAL is applicable to contexts close to its original setting, that is, appliance repair, retail banking, long distance telephone . . . it is questionable . . . whether it is measuring service quality at all.

> (Robinson, 1999, p. 29)

Nevertheless, it has been applied to tourism in a number of studies, e.g. Mok and Armstrong (1996), Tribe and Snaith (1998) and Saleh and

Table 1.1. General service gaps.

1. Differences between consumer expectations and management perceptions of consumer expectations
2. Differences between management perceptions of consumer expectations and service quality specifications
3. Differences between service quality specifications and the service actually delivered
4. Differences between service delivery and what is communicated about the service to consumers
5. Differences between consumer expectations and perceptions of the quality of the service received; depending on the size and direction of the other four gaps

Source: Parasuraman *et al.* (1985).

Ryan (1992). Many contemporary researchers investigating the related issues of service quality and the ways in which customers experience service episodes continue to refer their work to the SERVQUAL model, either by directly employing some or all of its constructs, or by explicitly attempting to differentiate their analysis from what has become the benchmark of modern service management research. Although it has been subjected to severe criticism, SERVQUAL continues to serve researchers well in two important respects:

- It highlights unequivocally the centrality of quality in service research and management.
- It emphasizes the complexity of managing service experiences.

Investigating Service Design Through Blueprinting

Shostack (1984) introduced service blueprinting as a management tool. Her approach had three elements: (i) a time dimension, enabling the researcher to follow the customer's progress through the service delivery process; (ii) the main functions of the service, clarifying their interconnectedness; and (iii) performance standards for each stage of the process.

Service blueprints can be used to identify failpoints, the parts of a service which are most likely to cause errors (George and Gibson, 1988), providing the diagnostic capability of the service blueprinting method. Berkely (1996, p. 152) recommends blueprinting as

> one of the most sophisticated and promising approaches to service design . . . it provides service designers with a way to visualise service processes and to identify opportunities for improvement.

Blueprinting a service shows that in many instances little of the service is actually visible to the consumer. Shostack called this phenomenon the service iceberg, and stressed that the implication is that all aspects of the service design have to be managed from the perspective of how they impinge on customers' experiences.

As each of the events in a service is actually composed of many steps (Berkely, 1996), the amount of detail in service designs can be overwhelming: Schmenner (1995) identified 19 separate steps involved in the write-up of an auto repair order, itself shown as a single event in a blueprint. The issue for a researcher is to decide on the appropriate level of detail to enhance understanding of the service.

Mapping Tourism Services

Service maps add complexity back into the basic blueprinting concept, with additional information layers (or levels) which record the interactions between customer and contact staff, between contact staff and support staff, and between staff and managers, who may be remote from the service delivery location. Service mapping

> visually defines a service system, displaying each sub-process within the sequence. . . . The map should revolve around the explicit actions the customer takes to receive the service. . . . The specific contacts the customer has with contact personnel are mapped, as are the internal services (invisible to the customer) that support contact services.
>
> (Berry, 1995, p. 86)

Shostack and Kingman-Brundage (1991) have together generalized the management procedures needed for service development, emphasizing the iterative nature of defining services, analysing the data, synthesis and drawing conclusions. Their joint view is that blueprinting and its developments contribute to the master design of the service, and facilitate improvement and redesign as a result of continually increasing knowledge. Commenting on this, Gummesson (1993, p. 191) noted:

> The strengths of the procedural models . . . is . . . that they directly emanate from empirical material on service development where blueprinting was applied. It is in part inductive research and an application of grounded theory.

Senior and Akehurst (1990) further developed blueprinting in trying to understand customers' perceptions of a service system, or their experiences of using it. They emphasize service events from the customers' perspectives, understood through interviews, focus groups and participant observation techniques. Perceptual blueprinting can be used to analyse

> unstructured problem situations in which unpredictable human behaviour is a determining influence on the success or failure of a system. . . . Systems are coexisting technical and social systems which cannot be treated in isolation, yet design efforts often concentrate so much on the hard technical aspects that they neglect the soft social and less mechanical aspects.
>
> Senior and Akehurst (1990, p. 8)

This is particularly helpful, because it is widely accepted that customers' perceptions of service events differ, and that individual quality judgements are based on the divergence of the service experiences from service anticipated. Perceptual blueprinting has some of the characteristics of iterative or action research, in which managers are interrogated about the operational meaning (and validity) of their clients' commentary on the existing service delivery system. Subsequent phases explore the specification of managerial priorities, and the remedial actions to be taken in redressing the failpoints identified earlier.

Overall, blueprints and service maps 'present marketers with a new tool for strategic management of service details' (Kingman-Brundage, 1989, p. 30), enabling management to make decisions on service system design, marketing, quality control, human resource and technological management. Complexities are simplified, clarifying service functions and their interrelationships in a useful way to management (Mattsson, 1985), and helping employees to understand their impact on the customer's experience.

The significance of this was shown in Laws (2004, p. 21).

> The distinguishing features of its service styles are the power base on which an organization's image and its brands are built: these are the equity it has acquired with its customers, and they are the foundation for continuing client relationships. Therefore, the particular way in which the organization presents its service must be consistent, but that style must also evolve over time to remain appealing to consumers in the face of its competitors.

Researching Tourism and Hospitality Service Management

To the extent that an objective of this book is to contribute to theory building in hospitality and tourism, a discussion of research assumptions, principles and methods is now required. The process of deduction develops conclusions from what is already (assumed to be) known and accepted as existing principles. According to Ryan (1995) deduction is an inferential process based on reasoning from initial sources. In certain ways the existing theories applied to hospitality, and particularly to tourism are inadequate, particularly in explaining its complexity and the dynamics of the industry, suggesting the need for inductive theory building. Induction develops new propositions to explain a particular set of facts or observations.

One of the researcher's challenges is to distinguish pre-understanding from understanding. Pre-understanding refers to insights into a specific problem or social environment that the researcher carries before starting a research programme; this paradigm base is the conceptual input. Understanding refers to the insights gained by the researcher during a study; and is therefore theory output (Gummesson, 1991, p. 12), potentially this has the ability to modify or refute the original paradigm. In more general terms, May (1993, pp. 20–21) has noted the iterative nature of theory:

> Theory informs our thinking which, in turn, assists us in making research decisions and sense of the world around us. Our experience of doing research and its findings, in turn, influences our theorising . . . the issue . . . is not simply what we produce but how we produce it. An understanding of the relationship between theory and research is part of this reflexive process which focuses not just upon our abilities to apply techniques of data collection but to consider the nature and presuppositions of the research process in order that we can sharpen our insights into the practice and place of social research in contemporary society.

Kuhn (1970) has explained the importance of the paradigm on which any research is based. A research paradigm is the framework of concepts and assumptions that underpin the researcher's thinking and, importantly, these are normally shared by most, if not all, people in a research community (those undertaking research into particular problems at one time). In other words, the prevailing paradigm may inhibit the further development of theory.

A paradigm is 'a set of assumptions about the world which is shared by a community of scientists investigating the world' (Deshpande, 1983, p. 101). Bogdan and Biklen (1982, p. 30) defined a research paradigm as 'a loose collection of logically held together assumptions, concepts and propositions that orientate thinking and research'.

From the foregoing it can be argued that both the theoretical orientation of a researcher and the methodologies he adopts are derived from the paradigm held. However, much of the research in this book includes exploration of new situations such as evidence of consumer dissatisfaction, disrupted service delivery systems, negative destination impacts of tourism and the complex nature of hospitality and tourism industry relationships, leading to revision of the pre-understanding on which the initial enquiry was based through the development of new understanding (Gummesson, 1991). Thus, the paradigms underlying much contemporary research are called into question, notably in the deterministic approaches often taken towards service management, and in terms of the inability of existing theory to deal with the conditions of complexity and change which characterize much of tourism.

Another problem is that academic researchers give too little consideration to the significance of pre-understanding in choosing their research methods (Gummesson, 1991). He describes the hermeneutic spiral, recommending an iterative process where the researcher develops a different level of pre-understanding with each stage of the research. An iterative research design can assist to explore the perspectives of various sectors of the tourism industry.

Despite the impressive growth of the industry (and the study of it) noted above, research tends to be ad hoc and to deal with a limited set of issues, utilizing tools which are themselves questionable if understanding of the key issues facing the industry is to be advanced.

Qualitative Research

Research methods have often been polarized, with individual projects and researchers espousing either qualitative or quantitative approaches (Neuman, 1994). Although quantitative methods dominate (Walle, 1997), both are widely used in social science research. Increasingly, researchers employ a combination of the two methods to maximize benefits from a particular research project (Yin, 1994). Weissinger et al. (1997) and Riley and Love (2000) are amongst many who have argued the benefits of qualitative research, the latter noting Cohen's assessment (1988) that much of the seminal work in tourism was initiated through qualitative research.

The field of inquiries for which case studies are well suited is broad, and it encompasses most aspects of concern to contemporary tourism researchers. The employment of case studies as a research method has been championed by a number of researchers including Yin (1994), Gummesson (1991) and Perry and Coote (1994). Case studies have the advantage that they can embody several methodologies to investigate contemporary phenomenon in their real-life context, often in situations where the boundaries between the phenomenon and the context are not clear (Yin, 1994). Prideaux (2000) noted that many investigations into tourism development adopt this approach to research. Yin (1994, p. 13) identified the four core components of case study-based research as:

- investigation of a contemporary phenomenon within its real-life context;
- when boundaries between phenomenon and context are not clearly evident;
- multiple sources of evidence are used;
- they are part of a comprehensive research strategy, not just a data collection tactic or a design feature.

Similarly Jorgensen (1989, p. 19) has noted that

> the case studied may be a culture, society, community, subculture, organization, group, or phenomenon such as beliefs, practices, interactions. . . . Case studies stress the holistic examination of a phenomenon, and they seek to avoid the separation of components from the larger context to which these matters may be related.

However, the ability to form general conclusions from a range of observations is often regarded as the basis of scientific methodology (Kuhn, 1970) as scientific understanding advances on the interrogation, refinement and possible refutation of existing theory. Thus, knowledge is usually considered to be built on testable hypotheses. This is the basis of a major stream of criticism directed at case study-based research, arguing that its findings are limited by being specific to that case.

Case studies are recommended to investigate research questions characterized as 'how' or 'why' (Yin, 1994, p. 6). As a range of evidence and also different research methods often occur in one case study, the research strategy should include means to verify and validate the qualitative analysis, so that the findings of a case study will be more convincing and accurate (Jick, 1979). Denzin (1978, p. 291) defined triangulation as 'the combination of methodologies in the study of the same phenomenon'. The metaphor is based on navigational practice, multiple view points result in greater accuracy in locating an object. Both across method and within method triangulation can improve researchers confidence in their results. Glaser and Strauss (1967, p. 7) suggest that multiple scales or multiple comparison groups can be used to develop more confidence in emergent theory.

New Generations of Service Research

The originator of the 'moments of truth' concept, Normann (1991) drew attention to what he regarded as an important new generation in service research in his thorough survey of the service management literature. While the first generation had distinguished service activities from other sectors, Normann argued that this is giving way to a second generation of research focused particularly on service relationships, behaviour during service transactions and the design of services to optimize the moments of truth. The argument is that each of the moments of truth when the customer interacts with the service organization is an event which customers use to judge the overall quality of the service. It is therefore also a proper focus of management (and research) attention.

The foundations for an understanding of service quality are based on the 'emerging service paradigm'. In this way of thinking, service managers seek 'a balance between human input and technology, between costs and income, and finally between quality and productivity' (Gummesson, 1993, p. 40).

This approach is paradigmatic as it is dependent on a new style of management and an organizational climate which actively supports the philosophy of service quality as a major company objective. In particular, it suggests the need to empower customer contact staff, and to do so by focusing the organization's resources and its managers' skills on satisfying (legitimate) customer expectations, and fostering a culture of continuing quality improvements.

Tourism Service Systems

There is a general consensus in the research community that tourism services are complex, and that any element can contribute to the success or failure of a service. The complexity of tourism services can be appreciated using perspectives from systems theory. This concept argues that selected inputs are combined in a series of processes with the intention of producing calculable outputs (Lorenz, 1993), each process stage adding accumulating value to the service. Efficiency in the system's operation can therefore be evaluated by measuring outputs against the inputs required to produce them, by examining the quality of those outputs, and by considering the way each process contributes to the overall service. Checkland and Scholes (1990) and Kirk (1995) have noted that although systems thinking has mainly been applied to 'hard' engineering situations, where outcomes are unambiguous and highly predictable, the concept can be applied in situations where human behaviour is a significant factor in business activities which combine social and technical processes. This confronted the difficulty that in ill-defined problem situations it was not possible to answer the questions, 'what is the system, and, what are its objectives?' Explaining the way in which progress was made, Checkland and Scholes (1990) identified one feature which all had in common, 'They all featured human beings in social roles, trying to take purposeful action'.

A critical factor in many services is that the variety of tasks involved calls for a team-based approach. Consequently, it has been pointed out that 'teamwork is the focus of service quality programmes in several firms known for their outstanding customer service' (Garvin, 1988). Wisner (1999) studied transportation quality improvement programmes, and placed importance on finding the root causes of quality problems, employee empowerment, and setting quality goals and standards. He showed that it is effective for managers to involve and support employees in a continuous improvement process and to stress the importance of role behaviours that allow the programmes to succeed. Wisner also noted a strong correlation between quality programmes and performance elements such as customer service, on-time deliveries, competitiveness, customer complaints, future growth expectations, employee productivity and sales.

Mattsson (1985) distinguished two types of relationships essential to a firm's success. Vertical relationships describe the relation between a firm and its customers. Horizontal relationships exist between a firm and others supplying it. Porter (1985) stressed the importance of sound industry relationships, Buhalis and Laws (2001) have edited a collection of studies examining key aspects of channel management in the tourism and hospitality industry. More recently, research has focused on the special management characteristics of service organizations (see Laws, 2004, for further discussion), particularly service encounters, service design, service quality and customer satisfaction, internal marketing and relationship marketing. Together, they represent a new approach to management which Gummesson (1991) argued is sufficiently different from earlier approaches to merit recognition as a paradigm shift.

Much current thinking about tourism is hindered by a mechanical and linear approach which probably stems from two root causes:

1. The 'first generation' approach to services noted by Normann (1991) persists, its attraction to many managers and researchers lies in its reference to experience transferred from the manufacturing sector where management decisions about design and manufacturing control result in logically predictable outcomes. Much of the current thinking about tourism service quality reflects themes in economic theory which exhibit a preference for mathematical analysis of a set of forces tending to stability and equilibrium, in contrast to the heterogeneous, dynamic forces tending to greater diversity and increasing complexity in tourism which can probably be more realistically modelled through chaos theory (Faulkner and Russell, 1997; Gleick, 1987; Waldrop, 1992).
2. Modern mass produced goods and the processes of their production do not have the equifinality which characterizes transactions in tourism service systems. Equifinality is a key concept in systems theory, which recognizes

that given inputs into complex biological or social transactional processes may result in differing outcomes (Bertalanffy, 1968). The lack of relative certainty for tourism quality arises from human involvement in the service delivery processes, both as consumers and as producers, further compounded by the roles of individual expectations and perceptions in service judgements making consensual evaluation of service quality problematic.

Summary

Two primary functions can be identified for service sector managers. One is fundamentally concerned with designing and resourcing an appropriate delivery system that also defines the parameters for service encounters between staff and customers. The second function is concerned with staff selection and training, and beyond that, the development of an organizational culture which empowers staff to solve problems on behalf of customers, within the company's cost or profit policies, and rewards them for contributing to customer satisfaction. The first management function, service design, underpins successful service delivery. Successful design minimizes dysfunction, and optimizes the second managerial objective, effective service transactions, thus maximizing the likelihood of providing satisfying experiences for customers (see Laws, 2004, for a fuller discussion).

References

Ashworth, G.J. and Tunbridge, J. (1990) *The Tourist Historic City*. Belhaven, London.

Asseal, H. (1987) *Consumer Behaviour and Marketing Action*. Kent Publication Co, Boston, Massachusetts.

Baum, T. (1998) Mature doctoral candidates: the case in hospitality education. *Tourism Management* 19(5), 463–474.

Bejou, D. and Palmer, A. (1998) Service failure and loyalty: an exploratory empirical study of airline customers. *Journal of Services Marketing* 12(1), 7–22.

Berkely, B. (1996) Analysing service blueprints using phase distribution. *European Journal of Operational Research* 88(1), 152–164.

Berry, L.L. (1995) *On Great Service: A Framework for Action*. Free Press, New York.

Bertalanffy, L. (1968) *General Systems Theory*. Brazillier, New York.

Bitner, M.J., Booms, B.H. and Tetreault, M.S. (1990) The service encounter: diagnosing favorable and unfavorable incidents. *Journal of Marketing* 54(January), 71–84.

Bogdan, R. and Biklen, S. (1982) *Qualitative Research for Education: An Introduction to Theory and Methods*. Allyn & Bacon, Boston, Massachusetts.

Brehm, J.W. and Cohen, A.R (1962) *Explorations in Cognitive Dissonance*. John Wiley & Sons, New York.

Brown, M. (1998) *Defining Heritage Tourism: Implications for Marketing and Impact Assessment*. Discussion paper at TTRA Conference, Fort Worth.

Brown, T., Churchill, G. and Peter, J. (1993) Improving the measurement of service quality. *Journal of Retailing* 69(1), 127–139.

Buhalis, D. (2000) Marketing the competitive destination of the future. *Tourism Management* 21(1), 97–116.

Buhalis, D. and Laws, E. (eds) (2001) *Tourism Distribution Channels: Practices, Issues and Transformations*. Continuum, London.

Chadee, D. and Mattson, J. (1996) An empirical assessment of customer satisfaction in tourism. *Service Industries Journal* 16(3), 305–320.

Chase, R.B. (1978) Where does a customer fit in a service operation? *Harvard Business Review* 56(6), 137–142.

Checkland, P. and Scholes, J. (1990) *Soft Systems Methodology in Action*. John Wiley & Sons, Chichester, UK.

Cohen, J.B. (1986) Involvement, separating the state from its causes and effects. Quoted in Wilkie, W.L. *Consumer Behavior*. John Wiley & Sons, Chichester, UK.

Cohen, E. (1988) Traditions in the qualitative sociology of tourism. *Annals of Tourism Research* 15, 29–46.

Denzin, N. (1978) *The Research Act*. McGraw-Hill, New York.

Deshpande, R. (1983) Paradigm lost: on theory and method in research in marketing. *Journal of Marketing* 47(Fall), 101–110.

Engel, J.F., Blackwell, R.D. and Miniard, P.W. (1986) *Consumer Behaviour*. Dryden Press, New York.

Faulkner, H.W. and Russell, R. (1997) Chaos and complexity in tourism: in search of a new perspective. *Pacific Tourism Review* 1(2), 93–102.

Festinger, L.A. (1957) *A Theory of Cognitive Dissonance*. Stanford University Press, Stanford, California.

Fisk, R., Brown, S. and Bitner, M. (1993) Tracking the evolution of services marketing literature. *Journal of Retailing* 69(1), 61–91.

Fornell, C. and Wernerfelt, B. (1987) Defensive marketing strategy by customer complaint management: a theoretical analysis. *Journal of Marketing Research* xxiv, November, 337–346.

Garvin, D.A. (1988) *Managing Quality: The Strategic and Competitive Edge*. Free Press, New York.

George, W.R. and Gibson B.E. (1988) Blueprinting: a tool for managing quality in organisations. *QUIS Symposium,* University of Karlstad, Sweden, August.

Glaser, B. and Strauss, A. (1967) *The Discovery of Grounded Theory: Strategies for Qualitative Research*. Aldine, Chicago, Illinois.

Gleick, J. (1987) *Chaos: Making a New Science*. Heinemann, London.

Gronroos, C. (1990) *Service Management and Marketing: Managing the Moments of Truth in Service Competition*. Pearson Education, New York.

Gummesson, E. (1991) *Qualitative Methods in Management Research*. Sage, London.

Gummesson, E. (1993) *Quality Management in Service Organisation: An Interpretation of the Service Quality Phenomenon and a Synthesis of International Research*. ISQA, Karlstad, Sweden.

Hall, C.M. (1995) In search of common ground: reflections on sustainability, complexity and process in the tourism system – a discussion between C. Michael Hall and Richard W. Butler. *Journal of Sustainable Tourism* 3(2), 99–105.

Harington, D. and Akehurst, G. (1996) An exploratory investigation into managerial perceptions of service quality in UK hotels. *Progress in Tourism and Hospitality Research* 2(2), 135–150.

Hollins, G. and Hollins, B. (1991) *Total Design: Managing the Design Process in the Service Sector*. Pitman, London.

Hudson, S. and Shephard, G. (1998) Measuring service quality at tourist destinations: an application of importance-performance analysis to an Alpine ski resort. *Journal of Travel & Tourism Marketing* 7(3), 61–77.

Jick, T. (1979) Mixing qualitative and quantitative methods: triangulation in action. *Administrative Science Quarterly* 24(4), 602–611.

Johns, N. (1999) Quality Management. In: Brotherton, B. (ed.) *The Handbook of Contemporary Hospitality Management Research*. John Wiley & Sons, Chichester, UK, pp. 333–349.

Jorgensen, D.L. (1989) *Participant Observation: A Methodology for Human Studies*. Sage, London.

Kingman-Brundage, J. (1989) *Blueprinting for the Bottom Line in Service Excellence: Marketing's Impact on Performance*. AMA, Chicago, Illinois.

Kirk, D. (1995) Hard and soft systems: a common paradigm for operations management? *International Journal of Contemporary Hospitality Management* 7(5), 13–16.

Kuhn, T.S. (1970) *The Structure of Scientific Revolutions*, 2nd edn. The University of Chicago Press, Chicago, Illinois.

Laws, E. (1997) *The Inclusive Holiday Industry: Relationships, Responsibility and Customer Satisfaction*. Thomson International Business Press, London.

Laws, E. (2000) Service quality in tourism research: are we walking tall (yet)? *Journal of Quality Assurance in Tourism and Hospitality* 1(1), 31–56.

Laws, E. (2004) *Improving Tourism and Hospitality Services*. CAB International, Wallingford, UK.

Laws, E., Buhalis, D. and Craig-Smith, S. (1999) A structured bibliography of tourism books. *Asia Pacific Journal of Tourism Research* 3(2), 47–63.

Leiper, N. (1990) *Tourism Systems*. Massey University Press, Massey, New Zealand.

Leppard, J. and Molyneux, L. (1994) *Auditing Your Customer Service*. Routledge, London.

Lew, A.A. (1999) Tourism and the Southeast Asian crisis of 1997 and 1998: a view form Singapore. *Current Issues in Tourism* 2(4), 304–315.

Locke, E.A. and Scweiger, D.M. (1979) Participation in decision making, one more look. In: Staw, B.M. (ed.) *Research in Organisational Behaviour,* Vol. 1. JAI Press, Greenwich, Connecticut.

Lorenz, E. (1993) *The Essence of Chaos*. University of Washington Press, Seattle, Washington.

Lyons, J. (1996) Getting customers to complain. *Australian Journal of Hospitality Management* 3(1), 37–50.

Marshall, C. (Sir) (1986) The airlines and their role in tourism developments in the United Kingdom. *Proceedings of the Prospects for Tourism in Britain*. Financial Times Conferences, London, pp. 10–15.

Mattsson, L. (1985) An application of a network approach to marketing: defending and changing market positions. In: Dholakia, N. and Arndt, J. (eds) *Alternative Paradigms for Widening Market Theory*. JAI Press, Greenwich, Connecticut.

May, T. (1993) *Social Research Issues, Methods and Processes*. Oxford University Press, Oxford.

Mok, C. and Armstrong, R. (1996) Sources of information used by Hong Kong and Taiwanese leisure travellers. *Australian Journal of Hospitality Management* 3(1), 31–35.

Morgan, M. (1994) Homogeneous products, the future of established resorts. In: Theobald, W. (ed.) *Global Tourism: The Next Decade*. Butterworth Heinemann, Oxford.

Neuman, W. (1994) *Social Research Methods: Qualitative and Quantitative Approaches*, 2nd edn. Allyn & Bacon, Needham Heights, Massachusetts.

Normann, R. (1991) *Service Management: Strategy and Leadership in Service Businesses*. John Wiley & Sons, Chichester, UK.

Parasuraman, A., Zeithmal, V.A. and Berry, L.L. (1985) A conceptual model of service quality and its implications for future research. *Journal of Marketing* 49, 41–50.

Parasuraman, A., Zeithmal, V.A. and Berry, L.L. (1988) SERVQUAL: multiple item scale for measuring consumer perceptions of service quality. *Journal of Retailing* 64(1), 12–40.

Pearce, P. and Moscardo, G. (1984). Making sense of tourists' complaints. *Tourism Management* 5(1), 20–23.

Perry, C. and Coote, L. (1994) Process of a case study research methodology: tool for management development? *Paper at the National Conference of the Australian–New Zealand Association of Management,* pp. 1–22.

Porter, M. (1985) *Competitive Advantage*. Free Press/Macmillan, New York.

Prideaux, B. (2000) The Role of the Transport System in the Growth of Coastal Resorts – An Examination of Resort Development in South East Queensland. PhD thesis, Department of Tourism and Leisure Management, The University of Queensland, Ipswich, Australia.

Ramaswamy, R. (1996) *Design and Management of Service Processes*. Addison-Wesley, Reading, Massachusetts.

Riley, R. and Love, L. (2000) The state of qualitative tourism research. *Annals of Tourism Research* 27(1), 164–187.

Robinson, S. (1999) Measuring service quality, current thinking and future requirements. *Marketing Intelligence and Planning* 7(1), 21–32.

Ryan, C. (1995) *Researching Tourist Satisfaction*. Routledge, London.

Saleh, F. and Ryan, C. (1992) Conviviality: a source of satisfaction for hotel guests? An application of the SERVQUAL model. In: Johnson, P. and Thomas, B. (eds) *Choice and Demand in Tourism*. Mansell, London.

Sasser, E.W., Olsen, P.R. and Wycoff, D.D. (1978) *Management of Service Operations*. Allyn & Bacon, Boston, Massachusetts.

Schmenner, R. (1995) *Service Operations Management*. Prentice-Hall, Englewood Cliffs, New Jersey.

Senior, M. and Akehurst, G. (1990) The perceptual service blueprinting paradigm. *Proceedings of the Second QUIS Conference*. St John's University, New York, pp. 177–192.

Shostack, G.L. (1984) Designing services that deliver. *Harvard Business Review* 62(January–February), 133–139.

Shostack, L. and Kingman-Brundage, J. (1991) How to design a service. In: Congram, C. and Friedman, L. (eds) *The AMA Handbook of Marketing for Service Industries*. AMA, New York.

Teas, K. (1994) Expectations as a comparison of standards in measuring service quality, an assessment and reassessment. *Journal of Marketing* 58(1), 132–139.

Tribe, J. and Snaith, T. (1998) From SERVQUAL to HOLSAT: holiday satisfaction in Varadero, Cuba. *Tourism Management* 19(1), 25–34.

Waldrop, M. (1992) *Complexity: The Emerging Science and the Edge of Order and Chaos.* Simon &
    Schuster/Penguin, London.
Walle, A.H. (1997) Quantitative versus qualitative tourism research. *Annals of Tourism Research* 24(3),
    524–536.
Weissinger, E., Henderson, K.A. and Bowling, C.P. (1997) Toward an expanding methodological base in
    leisure studies: researchers' knowledge, attitudes and practices concerning qualitative research. *Loisir
    y Société* 20(2), 434–451.
Wilkie, W.L. (1986) *Consumer Behaviour.* John Wiley & Sons, New York.
Wisner, J. (1999) A study of successful quality improvement programs in the transportation industry.
    Benchmarking: An International Journal 6(2), 147–163.
Yin, R.K. (1994) *Case Study Research: Design and Methods.* Sage, London.
Yusel, A. and Yusel, F. (2001) The expectancy–disconfirmation paradigm: a critique. *Journal of Hospitality
    and Tourism Research* 25(2), 107–131.

2 Convention Delegates – The Relationship Between Satisfaction with the Convention and with the Host Destination: A Case Study

Leo Jago and Marg Deery
Victoria University, Australia

Introduction

The convention industry is one of the fastest growing industries within tourism today and contributes significantly to the Australian economy. Recent estimates of the industry's value suggest that the Business Events industry is worth approximately AUS$7 billion annually in direct expenditure from both domestic and international markets (Johnson *et al.*, 1999). Attractive convention destinations are perceived as providing lucrative tourism dollars for the host nation's economy (Upchurch *et al.*, 1999) and many countries now actively seek larger shares of this burgeoning sector. McCabe *et al.* (2000, p. 7) state that Australia and the UK are 'the only two countries in the world to have two cities in the top 20 convention cities (London, Edinburgh, Sydney and Melbourne)'. With the success of the 2000 Olympics, Australia has become, a favoured convention destination, and the challenge for the industry's leaders is to determine ways of maintaining this favoured status.

While much of the convention literature provides ample information on the selection of convention sites, little is offered in the way of understanding delegate satisfaction with conventions and host destinations. This chapter seeks to investigate the attributes of successful conventions as perceived by convention delegates. It is argued that satisfaction with a convention will lead to favourable perceptions of the host destination and likely repeat visitations and recommending behaviour. A case study is then used to explore the themes emerging from the literature to test their saliency. Melbourne, which has a thriving convention and exhibition industry and hosts substantial numbers of both international and domestic conventions and meetings, was chosen as the research site for the case study.

This case study uses data from 13 major conventions held in Melbourne, Victoria, over a 4-year period and qualitative data gained through 19 in-depth interviews with international delegates at two Melbourne international conventions. Quantitative data were collected from both domestic and international delegates, with a total of 889 delegates being surveyed.

Why host conventions?

Since the middle of the last century, there has been a growing need for businessmen and professional people to come together to discuss key issues, increase their knowledge of their industry, negotiate with their partners, or to exhibit their wares. The convention and meeting industry provides an effective means of communication. The US Department of Commerce (1991) ranked conventions, expositions, meetings and

©CAB International 2006. *Managing Tourism and Hospitality Services: Theory and International Applications* (eds Bruce Prideaux, Gianna Moscardo and Eric Laws)

incentive travel as a single industry and seventeenth among all US private sector industries. Besides being an important industry in itself, providing significant employment and economic benefits for host destinations, staging meetings and conventions, is considered to be 'an effective mechanism in re-imaging a city for both residents and outsiders in a positive and dynamic way' (Kim, 1998). The growth in the convention industry has increased the level of competition between venues, and in the importance of the quality and service provided by these venues.

Attributes of conventions

The attributes of a convention can be considered from three main perspectives: (i) those of the association, (ii) the delegate and (iii) the destination itself. An association is primarily an organized and structured collection of people with similar interests, which can range from professional associations to religious and social groups. Overall, conventions can be separated into three major categories, which are associations (i.e. professional, social or religious), corporations and government departments. All associations, from small regional ones to large international organizations, at some time or another, need to schedule meetings. It is generally agreed that the association market represents two-thirds of the industry spending (Shure, 1993; Abbey and Link, 1994). The corporate market represents 26% of the total meeting and convention industry (Meetings and Conventions, 1998; Meetings Market Report, 1998) and includes a range of meeting requirements, from board meetings to training seminars to product launches and trade fairs. Government organizations, another significant organizer of conventions, may hold meetings for a variety of reasons, including dissemination of information to the public, intergovernmental communication or training and planning.

Site selection criteria

In examining previous research into the issues relating to convention delegates' perceptions of successful conventions and convention des-

tinations, a number of themes evolved. These include site selection (e.g. Bonn et al., 1994; Crouch and Ritchie, 1998; Oppermann, 1998; Upchurch et al., 1999; Nelson and Rys, 2000; Crouch and Louviere, 2002), satisfaction with convention facilities (Shaw and Lewis, 1991; Rutherford and Umbeit, 1993; Oppermann and Chon, 1997; Rittichainuwat et al., 2001) and the influences of convention participants within convention decision making (Montgomery and Rutherford, 1994; Clark et al., 1997; Oppermann and Chon, 1997; Baloglu and Love, 2001). Crouch and Ritchie (1998), in developing a conceptual model of convention site selection, provide a sound overview of the convention literature.

In organizing a convention, one of the key criteria for success is to attract delegates by selecting appealing convention destinations and providing an interesting programme. The characteristics of the association and the purpose of the meeting, determine the type of convention that is to be staged. Choi and Boger (2002) investigated the relationship between association characteristics and site selection criteria, finding differences among associations by age, size and budget. In the UK, research (Right Solution, 1998) indicated that most organizers considered several venues before making a decision on a particular site, and provided information on the average number of delegates attending meetings and the average duration of such events. The importance of service qualities required by event organizers in the USA has been examined by Renegan and Kay (1987), who assessed the characteristics that meeting planners use to select a meeting facility (Shaw et al., 1991; Strick et al., 1993; Bonn et al., 1994). Meeting planners' perceptions have been highlighted by Upchurch et al. (1999) while Oppermann and Chon (1997) considered the convention participation decision making process.

Other studies, such as that by Crouch and Ritchie (1998), provide information on the priorities for site selection by associations. These priorities have been divided into four main groups: (i) accessibility, (ii) local support, (iii) extra-conference opportunities, and (iv) accommodation facilities. The extra-opportunities dimensions include entertainment, shopping, sightseeing, recreation and professional opportunities. These perceptions, however, are only from one perspective, that of the associations and their meeting planners.

Convention destination criteria

The next perspective is the destination for conventions. In order to promote a convention destination, it is important that delegates have sufficient time and opportunity to explore the destination, which, it is hoped will lead to a positive attitude towards the destination. This in turn should encourage repeat visitation and positive word-of-mouth (WOM) recommendation. While there has been an overall rise in the number of conventions, generating more income for local economies, participants to the event are becoming time-poor, having only limited time for other activities before and after the event (Rittichainuwat et al., 2001). The implication of this requires further research.

In the USA, there has been a significant increase in the number of destinations promoting themselves as convention centres, mainly because the industry generates direct spending of AUS$85 billion, pays over AUS$12 billion in tax and supports 1.6 million jobs (Deloitte and Touche, 1995). Clark and McCleary (1995) note that hosting a convention can generate millions of additional dollars for the local hospitality industry. Several studies (McGuiness, 1982; Sternlieb et al., 1983; Dean, 1988; Peterson, 1989; Elwood, 1992; Buchbinder, 1994; Judd, 1995) have indicated that cities of all sizes and attributes have been developing centres to attract conventions, stimulate growth and ensure economic stability. Fenich (2001) explored the way city policymakers can compare themselves with other cities or centres and identify their strengths and weaknesses. Fenich's review of the literature indicated that the most common attractiveness attributes across all studies were destination services, city vitality, city image, regional lifestyle and reputation.

Destinations, in order to promote themselves effectively, need to develop a brand/image/profile. To encourage repeat visitation and enhance WOM recommendations, they also need to ensure users' satisfaction with convention and destination facilities (as detailed by Shaw and Lewis, 1991; Rutherford and Umbeit, 1993; Rittichainuwat et al., 2001). Oppermann and Chon (1997) provide insights into the key ingredients of the convention industry and suggest a list of important attributes for convention destinations. While both the Crouch and Ritchie (1998) and Oppermann and Chon (1997) research are useful frameworks for study, neither has been empirically tested.

The perceptions and requirements of delegates may differ from those of the organizers. Robinson and Callan (2001) considered whether gaps exist between the attributes employed to assess the quality and desirability of a UK conference venue between the perceptions of conference organizers and the conference delegates. They found, in their preliminary study, that convention delegates placed greater emphasis on the quality of the product, the level of safety at a venue and a destination and the need for additional social activities within the time constraints of the convention.

Satisfaction Research

Satisfaction with conventions

In determining the role of delegate satisfaction in the success of a convention, it is important to explore the satisfaction literature. In relation to delegate satisfaction, it is argued here that satisfaction with the attributes of the convention and the convention destination will lead to repeat visitation and recommending behaviour. Thrane (2002) found that higher levels of intentions to recommend were associated with higher levels of satisfaction. Research into the determinants of satisfaction is abundant and ongoing. Satisfaction is a complex concept, explored through its component parts (attributes), and as an overall concept. A number of researchers have investigated a range of satisfaction antecedents. These include equity (Oliver and Swan, 1989), disconfirmation (Davis and Heineke, 1998), attribution (Oliver and DeSarbo, 1988), expectations (Wirtz and Bateson, 1999) and specific aspects of the consumption experience (Jones and Suh, 2000).

The literature tends to link satisfaction with the attributes of the convention facility with that of the destination. The links between choosing a convention facility and a destination, therefore, are strong. Oppermann (1996) summarizes the findings of previous research into the convention location attributes that are perceived, by meeting planners, as leading to successful conventions. Table 2.1 provides an overview of these findings.

Satisfaction with convention destinations

In a later study by Oppermann and Chon (1997), some attention is given to the perceptions of delegates in relation to conventions and host destinations. Their research, which presents a conceptual model, argues that there are four key elements in the delegate's decision to attend a convention. These are the association or convention factors, the personal or business factors, the location factors and the intervening opportunities. The location factors are of greatest relevance to the current discussion, with issues such as transport and climate

being critical dimensions in the delegate's decision making process. These proposed factors, however, are untested and, as such, cannot be verified from earlier studies. The literature on the perceptions of convention delegates to the convention destination, therefore, is limited and warrants further investigation.

In order to gain a closer understanding of the destination attributes that enhance convention delegate satisfaction, it is useful to examine the tourism destination literature. As indicated earlier, there is a significant amount of literature on destination choice (e.g. Judd, 1995; Sirakaya et al., 1996; Oppermann and Chon, 1997; Pearce, 1997; Crouch and Ritchie, 1998; Fenich, 2001), but research relevant to the current discussion is found largely in the tourist destination satisfaction literature. Kozak and Rimmington (1999) examined the satisfaction levels of tourists on 24 attributes of destinations. Those attributes receiving the highest levels of satisfaction included the friendliness of local people, value for money, attitude of staff, safety and security, local transport services and the natural environment. Other items providing satisfaction for tourists included the food, shopping facilities and the nightlife and entertainment.

Table 2.1. Meeting location attributes: a comparison of association meeting planner survey results.

Fortin et al. (1976)	ASAE (1992)	Edelstein and Benini (1994)	Oppermann (1996)
Hotel service	Quality of service	Availability of facilities	Meeting rooms/facilities
Air access	Meeting room facilities	Access to location	Hotel service quality
Hotel rooms	overall	Transportation costs	Hotel room availability
Conference rooms	Overall affordability	Distance from attendants	Clean/attractive location
Price level	Sleeping room facilities	Climate	Safety/security
Hospitality	Location image	Recreational facilities	Air transportation access
Restaurant facilities	Dining/entertainment	Tourist attractions	Food and lodgings costs
Personal safety	Air transportation	Mandated by by-laws	Overall affordability
Local interest	Exhibit facilities	Location image	City image
Geographic location	Highway accessibility		Transportation costs
Hotel info/assistance	Geographic rotation		Restaurant facilities
Local availability	Recreational facilities		Exhibition facilities
Tourism features	Climate		Scenery/sightseeing opportunities
Transport facilities			Climate
Previous experience			Nightlife

Source: Oppermann (1996, p. 177).

Satisfaction with pre-, post- and during convention activities

A number of convention delegate activities that provide delegate satisfaction with the convention destination, emerge from the literature. What is highlighted, from the limited previous research, is the lack of time that delegates have to undertake other activities such as shopping or sightseeing. For example, Rittichainuwat *et al.* (2001) found that association member delegates spent either no extra days (38%) or 1–2 days (46%) either before or after the conference. These restrictions on time have implications conference planners and for tourist destination marketeers and will be discussed later.

The importance of shopping as a tourist activity has received attention in recent research. Master and Prideaux (2000) found shopping and the convenience of shopping hours provided high levels of satisfaction for Taiwanese tourists to Australia. Turner and Reisinger (2001) have also provided greater understanding of the importance of shopping as a tourist activity. They argue that, in both international and domestic tourism, the second most important item in tourist expenditure is shopping (accommodation being the first). They also suggest that 'although shopping is seldom mentioned as a primary reason for travel, it is perhaps the most universal of tourist activities' (Turner and Reisinger, 2001, p. 15). Their research confirms the importance of shopping as an activity providing tourist satisfaction, as well as an activity that contributes significantly to the economy. Shopping is an obvious area for promotion by convention planners; the use of promotional material in conference satchels is indicative of the importance of this activity.

In a similar vein, the work by Bramwell (1998) is of relevance to this discussion. Bramwell's study investigates the level of tourist satisfaction with attributes of a city, in this case, Sheffield. Bramwell also found that shopping was a key attribute leading to tourist satisfaction. This attribute was followed by satisfaction with the countryside, sports facilities and activities, friendliness, entertainment, public transport, cultural activities, cleanliness and attractiveness of the city. Bramwell's study also provides information on the ways in which cities can become more attractive tourist destinations through the enhancement of various tourist 'products' such as sporting and cultural facilities and activities.

Finally, other studies that provide insight into satisfaction with a tourist destination focus on attributes such as the destination as a cultural experience. Research by Reisinger and Turner (1997a,b) examine satisfaction with the cultural aspects of Indonesian and Thai inbound tourism to Australia and suggest a high level of satisfaction with the cultural experience and with the destination. Master and Prideaux (2000) found that Taiwanese tourists to Queensland were highly satisfied with the destination and also that the tourists were prepared to experience a different culture within Australia. Chaudhary (2000) explores the pre- and post-trip perceptions of foreign tourists about India as a tourist destination. Chaudhary found high tourist satisfaction with India on the following dimensions: rich cultural heritage; variety of arts; good transportation facilities; and hospitality to tourists. On the other hand, issues of safety and tourism services were areas of satisfaction not met. All these studies provide evidence of the importance of the cultural aspects of a destination in developing tourist satisfaction.

Ultimately, however, in searching the literature for findings on convention delegate satisfaction with convention destinations, little has been unearthed. Research such as that by Oppermann and Chon (1997), which investigates the elements of destination branding, provides a springboard for similar research into the role of conventions in building destination loyalty. With the growth of interest in the concept of destination branding, the potential to brand a destination as a convention city is significant. This study, in a very exploratory way, attempts to investigate the aspects of Melbourne as a convention and tourist destination that provide satisfaction.

Case Study

A case study approach was used to explore the themes emerging from the literature. The case study combines qualitative and quantitative methods to build an understanding of convention delegate perceptions of successful conventions and of the destinations. The study obtained quantitative data from 889 convention delegates at a number of different types of conferences. In conjunction with this collection of quantitative data, a total of 36 in-depth interviews were conducted with representatives from 9 international associations, 8 professional conference organizers (PCOs) and 19 convention delegates. Whilst the research was predominantly Melbourne-based, interviews were held with PCOs from Sydney and Brisbane to achieve a more national, standardized approach to the research. The case study, therefore, addresses the themes taken from the literature in order to test their saliency.

The case study research site

Melbourne, the capital city of Victoria, Australia, was chosen as the research site for this case study, because a suite of research projects had been undertaken that could be woven together to provide a more comprehensive case study. Melbourne has a thriving convention and exhibition industry with a dedicated exhibition and convention centre as well as over 200 venues that host exhibitions, conventions and meetings. The city hosts substantial numbers of both international and domestic conventions and meetings and, as stated in the introduction, is perceived as one of the key convention destinations in the world.

Influences for delegates attending the convention

Content and networking opportunities

The literature suggests that one of the key motivations for convention delegate attendance at a conference is the opportunity to network and the content of the conference. The empirical findings from this research support the literature as to the key drivers: 'Usually it's because of the continual academic update. Every year there's something new, so I try to keep up with it.'

This finding supports the work of Rittichainuwat et al. (2001) who found education to be the most significant motivator for conference attendance. An important reason for delegates to attend was the networking opportunities available. The delegates felt that there were many benefits to be gained from meeting other people working in the same or similar fields as them and that a convention was a perfect opportunity to do so. Most associations hold conventions on a regular basis; therefore, delegates were likely to renew acquaintances with other delegates that they had met at prior conventions. In this increasingly 'time-poor' work environment, a concentrated educational tool such as a convention, is becoming more important.

Another key driver for motivating convention delegate attendance is the appeal of the destination.

> I do a lot of research into. . . . And I had never been to Australia before and so I thought it would be a good opportunity. I was funded to go which helps, particularly for this distance. The location is very important – I always like to be somewhere I haven't been before.

> Very beautiful and clean city with extremely friendly people. Nicest city I have ever visited. I love it!

The opportunity to discover a new city through attendance at a conference is obviously very important to convention delegates and one component that destination managers should use to attract future visitation.

Similarly, the opportunity to network and to make new business and research partnerships, appears to have increased in importance over the years. This finding is in keeping with Oppermann and Chon (1997) who argued that peer recognition, professional contacts, being part of the global community and enhancing personal interactions are important motivators for delegate attendance.

Drivers of convention delegate satisfaction

In managing the satisfaction of convention delegates, an issue to be addressed is managing the expectations and perceptions of delegates in relation to particular attributes of conventions. In surveying the delegates, the questionnaire was prepared by the research of Lee and Park (2002), Robinson and Callan (2001) and Oppermann (1996). The international delegates stated that they were satisfied with the convention if the following criteria were met:

- a well-organized convention;
- appropriate educational material covered;
- networking opportunities provided;
- the venue to be large enough to fit the number of delegates in comfortably;
- the venue to be easy to move around in;
- to be able to find accommodation close to the convention venue;
- well-connected transport links to a destination;
- easy communication with the convention organizers, particularly through the Internet.

As one delegate stated:

> The organization and facilities have been tremendous. The organization is outstanding. There is enough space – other conferences have been terrible, but everything is sorted here.

As indicated here, most items relate to the venue, but there are also components of the destination that delegates need to be satisfied with. In managing convention delegate expectations, therefore, there are certain venue facilities that need to be provided. The overall organization of the convention is important. In fact, a general comment in relation to satisfaction of delegates was provided by another delegate:

> I would recommend Australia as a conference destination, because the organization of the facilities in Australia is exceptional. Other conferences, say in the UK, you can't go where you want and you have to queue.

Satisfaction with Melbourne as a tourist destination

Satisfaction with the convention often has the flow-on effect of providing overall satisfaction with the destination for the delegate. The over-all satisfaction level is based on the experience of food and beverage, the culture, the shopping, having good access to transport and feeling safe within the environment. Not only is it important to manage the quality of the conference experience but also to determine the attributes of a conference destination that lead to delegate satisfaction. In surveying the delegates, a large number (over 70%) were satisfied with Melbourne as a tourist destination. Many respondents stated that Melbourne was perceived as a modern, western city with good transport links. It was also seen to be a beautiful city with good food, beer and wine.

Australia as a destination was a strong influence on people attending the conference, as it was an opportunity to come here, although the time and cost to travel, and the jetlag made repeat visits difficult.

Other attributes of a city as a tourist destination were found to be important for satisfied convention delegates. Melbourne has many attributes that provide convention delegates satisfaction. Some of the more interesting attributes coinciding with previous research findings are those of the importance of food and shopping: 'wonderful restaurants, great shopping, art galleries, museums, entertainment'.

However, it was also noted that many of those being interviewed could not respond to the question of what attracted them to the city, as many had not had sufficient time to explore the city. This is important for convention organizers to take into consideration when planning conventions.

As Turner and Reisinger (2001) argue, shopping is a key component of tourist activity and government agencies such as Tourism Victoria and the City of Melbourne have made this a strong element of their marketing campaign for Melbourne. Similarly, restaurants and eating out is a key platform for the marketing of Melbourne and aspects such as the cosmopolitan and sophisticated nature of dining in Melbourne were expressed in the data. The importance of this city aspect to tourist is confirmed in the work by Lee and Park (2002) and Kozak and Rimmington (1999).

One of the key attributes of the destination, as perceived by the convention delegates, was the friendliness of the people. This attribute was confirmed in the qualitative interviews with the international delegates who were very pleasantly surprised at the multicultural and tolerant nature of Melbourne residents: 'Friendly place to move around, even as a lone female traveller'. Although, one delegate commented: 'Too cold, people unfriendly, everybody dark in attitude. They need to lighten up and stop thinking they are the centre of the universe.' However, this attitude was in a very small minority of respondents.

In much of the research on satisfaction with tourist destinations, the friendliness of the local people is an important contributor. According to the interviews with the international delegates, not only were the local people seen as friendly, but they were also perceived as sophisticated and cosmopolitan.

> I think one thing I didn't appreciate until I got here was the mixture of cultures and I don't think that was in the information – I think it's a great bargaining point.

> Great facilities and walking around.

Melbourne was compared by many of the European delegates to European cities and the cultural activities of Melbourne perceived favourably. Reisinger and Turner (1997a,b), Chaudhary (2000) and Master and Prideaux (2000) confirm the importance of cultural activities in the tourist experience. The delegates were impressed with Melbourne's culture including art, history, antiques and architecture, e.g. 'Lots of interesting cultural things to do, architecturally stimulating'.

Specific attributes of the city such as its safety and cleanliness, appear to be important in providing satisfaction to tourists. Choi and Boger (2002) and Nelson and Rys (2000) found a similar level of the importance of safety for convention delegates. The qualitative interviews following the collection of the open-ended question data confirmed the high level of safety that tourists to Melbourne perceived.

> I knew it was going to be a large city, a good place for my wife to do things by herself. In some cities, she doesn't really feel comfortable going out, I knew she would feel comfortable here.

With a growing number of dangerous destinations, this is an attribute that Melbourne should promote.

The issue of prior experience or familiarity with the destination was stated as a reason for rating Melbourne in the way it was rated. Many of the respondents stated that they knew Melbourne, enjoyed it and were keen to revisit the city. Bowen's exploration (2001) of the antecedents of consumer satisfaction with long-haul destinations confirms the importance of prior experience in satisfaction with a destination. Similarly, Oppermann's research of meeting planners' decisions argues for the importance of prior experience. Again, this aspect is important for tourism planners who should highlight the benefits of familiarity with a satisfactory destination.

Finally, it should be noted that over 22% of respondents did not answer the satisfaction question indicating that they had not had sufficient opportunity to actually see Melbourne in order to form an opinion. This was reinforced in the depth interviews where delegates indicated that because they were 'time-poor', they often did not get a chance to even see the host city during a convention. The trend is to fly in at the start of the convention and then to leave as soon as the last session is over. There is often limited opportunity for pre- and post-touring activities. It is now becoming difficult to justify additional time outside the convention to experience the host city. Delegates expressed a great interest for experiencing the host city, but needed to do this as part of the convention rather than before and after. Conference organizers and city marketeers could use this information in their bid to gain greater conference delegate satisfaction as well as providing opportunities to 'showcase the city'. Given that the city is an important motivator for attending the convention, it is important to provide an opportunity to actually see the city during the visit in order to enhance the overall experience and improve the likelihood of WOM recommendation for other conventions or subsequent visits.

Conclusion

This chapter has attempted to provide greater understanding of convention and destination attributes that create convention delegate satisfaction. The findings provide a means of understanding the convention delegate and the importance of the convention destination to the delegate. Convention attributes that lead to delegate satisfaction include the content of the convention, the opportunities for networking, the facilities and space within the convention centre, as well as the proximity of accommodation to the convention venue. Attributes of the destination that create delegate satisfaction include the safety of the location, the culture and cultural activities, the food and the opportunities and facilities for shopping. Of equal importance in determining delegate satisfaction is the prior experience of the destination.

These findings have ramifications for government tourism agencies and convention organizers. The importance of specific convention attributes provides a focus for convention centres and PCOs to address for improved conventions. These findings also provide the basis for delegate boosting, a priority for many convention and visitor bureaux. In particular, it is important to factor other social activities into the convention in order to 'showcase' the destination. Convention delegates, otherwise, will not have the time to see the destination. In relation to the convention destination, cities that provide a safe environment, particularly for the increasing number of female convention delegates, will ensure their continuance as convention destinations. Good shopping facilities, a wide range of restaurants and friendly people will also ensure this. The marketing strategies for cities such as Melbourne, therefore, could benefit from the findings of this and other studies, particularly those related to destination branding. Future research, in fact, should focus on the link between the satisfaction with convention attributes and satisfaction with the convention destination. To date, the research in this area is limited and demands further inquiry.

References

Abbey, J. and Link, C. (1994) The convention meeting sector – its operation and research needs. In: Ritchie, J. and Goeldner, C. (eds) *Travel, Tourism and Hospitality Research: A Handbook for Managers and Researchers,* 2nd edn. John Wiley & Sons, New York, pp. 273–284.

American Society of Association Executives (ASAE) (1992) *Association Meeting Trends.* ASAE, Washington, DC.

Baloglu, S. and Love, C. (2001) Association meeting planners' perceptions of five major convention cities: results of the pre-test. *Journal of Convention & Exhibition Management* 3(1), 21–31.

Bonn, M., Brand, R. and Ohlin, J. (1994) Site selection for professional meetings: a comparison of heavy-half vs. light-half association and corporation meeting planners. *Journal of Travel & Tourism Marketing* 3(2), 59–84.

Bowen, D. (2001) Antecedents of consumer satisfaction and dissatisfaction (cs/d) on long-haul inclusive tours – a reality check on theoretical considerations. *Tourism Management* 22, 49–61.

Bramwell, B. (1998) User satisfaction and product development in urban tourism. *Tourism Management* 19(1), 35–47.

Buchbinder, S. (1994) Second tier advantage. *Association Management* 6(3), 29–36.

Chaudhary, M. (2000) India's image as a tourist destination – a perspective of foreign tourists. *Tourism Management* 21(3), 293–297.

Choi, J. and Boger, C. (2002) State association market: relationship between association characteristics and site selection criteria. *Journal of Convention & Exhibition Management* 4(1), 55–73.

Clark, J. and McCleary, K. (1995) Influencing associations' site selection process, *Cornell Hotel and Restaurant Quarterly* 36(2), 61–68.

Clark, J., Evans, M. and Knutson, B. (1997) Selecting a site for an association convention: an exploratory look at the types of power used by committee members to influence decisions. *Journal of Hospitality & Leisure Marketing* 5(1), 81–93.

Crouch, G. and Louviere, J. (2002) A review of choice modelling research in tourism, hospitality and leisure. In: Mazanec, A., Crouch, G., Ritchie, J.B. and Woodside, A. (eds) *Consumer Psychology of Tourism, Hospitality and Leisure,* Vol. 2. CAB International, Wallingford, UK, pp. 67–86.

Crouch, G. and Ritchie, B. (1998) Convention site selection research: A review, conceptual model and propositional framework. *Journal of Convention & Exhibition Management* 1(1), 49–69.

Davis, M. and Heineke, J. (1998) How disconfirmation, perception and actual waiting times impact on customer satisfaction. *International Journal of Service Industry Management* 9(1), 64–73.

Dean, A. (1988) Urbane and lively stimulus to revival, Riverside Convention Centre. *The AIA Journal* 1, 1–5.

Deloitte and Touche (1995) *The Economic Impact of Conventions, Expositions, Meetings and Incentives Travel*. Deloitte and Touche, Parsippany, New Jersey.

Edelstein, L. and Benini, C. (1994) Meetings Market Report (1994) *Meetings & Conventions* 23, 60–82.

Elwood, P. (1992) Second to none. *Association Meetings* 4(4), 19–25.

Fenich, G.G. (2001) Towards a conceptual framework for assessing community attractiveness for conventions. *Journal of Convention & Exhibition Management* 3(1), 45–65.

Fortin, P., Ritchie, J. and Arsenault, J. (1976) *A Study of the Decision Process of North American Associations Concerning the Choice of a Convention Site*. Laval University, Quebec City, Canada.

Johnson, L., Foo, L. and O'Halloran, M. (1999) *Meetings Make their Mark: Characteristics and Economic Contribution of Australia's Meetings and Exhibitions Sectors*. Occasional Paper No. 26, Bureau of Tourism Research, Canberra.

Jones, M. and Suh, J. (2000) Transaction-specific satisfaction and overall satisfaction: an empirical analysis. *Journal of Services Marketing* 14(2), 147–159.

Judd, D. (1995) Promoting tourism in US cities. *Tourism Management* 16(3), 175–187.

Kim, Y. (1998) The perceptions of convention professionnals toward the convention industry in Korea. *Journal of Toursim Research* 22(2), 99–106.

Kozak, M. and Rimmington, M. (1999) Measuring tourist destination competitiveness: conceptual considerations and empirical findings. *International Journal of Hospitality Management* 18, 273–283.

Lee, T.-H. and Park, J.-Y. (2002) Study on the degree of importance of convention service factors: focusing on the differences in perception between convention planners and participants. *Journal of Convention & Exhibition Management* 3(4), 69–85.

Master, H. and Prideaux, B. (2000) Culture and vacation satisfaction: a study of Taiwanese tourists in Southeast Queensland. *Tourism Management* 21, 445–449.

McCabe, V., Poole, B., Weeks, P. and Leiper, N. (2000) *The Business and Management of Conventions*. John Wiley & Sons, Milton, Australia.

McGuiness, D. (1982) Convention centres: too much of a good thing? *Planning* 48(November), pp. 13–17.

Montgomery, R. and Rutherford, D. (1994) A profile of convention-services professionals. *Cornell HRA Quarterly*, December, 47–57.

Nelson, R. and Rys, S. (2000) Convention site selection criteria relevant to secondary convention destinations. *Journal of Convention & Exhibition Management* 2(2/3), 71–83.

Oliver, R.L. and DeSarbo, W.S. (1988) Response determinants in satisfaction judgments. *Journal of Consumer Research* 14(4), 495–507.

Oliver, R.L. and Swan, J.E. (1989) Consumer perceptions of interpersonal equity and satisfaction. *Journal of Marketing* 53(2), 21–35.

Oppermann, M. (1996) Convention cities – image and changing fortunes. *The Journal of Tourism Studies* 7(1), 10–19.

Oppermann, M. (1998) Perceptions of convention destinations: large-half versus small-half association meeting planners. *Journal of Convention & Exhibition Management* 1(1), 35–48.

Oppermann, M. and Chon, K. (1997) Convention participation decision-making process. *Annals of Tourism Research* 24(1), 178–191.

Pearce, D. (1997) Competitive destination analysis in Southeast Asia. *Journal of Travel Research* 35(4), 16–24.

Peterson, D. (1989) *Convention Centres, Stadiums, and Arenas*. Urban Land Institute, Washington, DC.

Reisinger, Y. and Turner, L. (1997a) Cross-cultural differences in tourism: Indonesian tourists in Australia. *Tourism Management* 18(3), 139–147.

Reisinger, Y. and Turner, L. (1997b) Tourist satisfaction with hosts: a cultural approach comparing Thai tourists and Australian tourists. *Pacific Tourism Review* 1(2), 35–45.

Renegan, L. and Kay, M. (1987) What meeting planners want: The conjoint-analysis approach. *The Cornell Hotel and Restaurant Administration Quarterly* 28(21), 66–80.

Right Solution (1998) *The UK Conference Market Survey 1998*. Right Solution, Eastcote, Middlesex, UK.

Rittichainuwat, B.N., Beck, J. and Lalopa, J. (2001) Understanding motivations, inhibitors, and facilitators of association members in attending international conferences. *Journal of Convention & Exhibition Management* 3(3), 45–62.

Robinson, L.S. and Callan, R.J. (2001) The UK conference and meetings industry: development of an inventory for attributional analysis. *Journal of Convention & Exhibition Management* 2(4), 65–79.

Rutherford, D. and Umbeit, W. (1993) Improving interactions between meeting planners and hotel employees. *Cornell HRA Quarterly,* February, 68–80.

Shaw, M. and Lewis, R. (1991) Measuring meeting planner satisfaction with hotel convention services: a multi-variate approach. *International Journal of Hospitality Management* 10(2), 137–146.

Shaw, M., Lewis, R. and Khorey, A. (1991) Measuring meeting planner satisfaction with hotel convention services: a multi-variate approach. *International Journal of Hospitality Management* 10(2), 137–146.

Shure, P. (1993) Annual spending of $75 billion supports 1.5 millions jobs. *Convene* 8(6), 36–41.

Sirakaya, E., McLellan, R. and Uysal, M. (1996) Modelling vacation destination decisions: a behavourial approach. *Journal of Travel & Tourism Marketing* 5(1–2), 57–75.

Sternlieb, G., Burchell, R. and Listokin, D. (1983) *The Effect of Convention Hotel Development at the Great Island Site on the Economy of Atlantic City.* CUPR, New Brunswick, New Jersey.

Strick, S., Montgomery, R. and Grant, C. (1993) Does service sell the site: a meeting planner's perspective. *Journal of Travel and Tourism Marketing* 2(1), 87–93

Thrane, C. (2002) Music quality, satisfaction and behavioural intentions within a jazz festival context. *Event Management: An International Journal* 7(3), 143–150.

Turner, L. and Reisinger, Y. (2001) Shopping satisfaction for domestic tourists. *Journal of Retailing and Consumer Services* 8, 15–27.

United States Department of Commerce (1991) *U.S. Industry and Trade Outlook.* United States Department of Commerce, Washington, DC.

Upchurch, R., Jeong, G., Clements, C. and Jung, I. (1999) Meeting planners' perceptions of site selection characteristics: the case of Seoul, Korea. *Journal of Convention & Exhibition Management* 2(1), 15–35.

Wirtz, J. and Bateson, J.E.G. (1999) Introducing uncertain performance expectations in satisfaction models for services. *International Journal of Service Industry Management* 10(1), 82–99.

3 Issues Pertaining to Service Recovery in the Tourism and Leisure Industries

Shane Pegg and J.-H.K. Suh
The University of Queensland, Australia

Introduction

Since the early 1970s, the services sector has become the dominant sector of most industrialized economies (Ghobadian *et al.*, 1994). Given this dominance, it is not surprising to note that the delivery of a superior service quality is not just a key consideration but, in fact, is a prerequisite these days for business success (Bettencourt and Gwinner, 1996; Eccles and Durand, 1998). Despite this apparent recognition of the importance of service quality to businesses however, most tourism and leisure companies today are failing to satisfy the basic needs and wants of their customers (Reid and Bojanic, 2001; Suh, 2003, unpublished thesis). Whilst part of the failure relates to the ever-increasing levels of consumer sophistication that have become a feature pervading nearly all markets today it has, nevertheless, also much to do with how operators manage the delivery of services (Smith *et al.*, 1999; Reid and Bojanic, 2001). Three possible explanations for this include viewing the customer as a cost and not an investment, being insufficiently aware of the rising expectations of customers and failing to define customer satisfaction in a way that links it to financial results (McCarthy, 1997). Whatever the cause, service quality, and the critical components of it, can no longer be simply ignored (Suh, 2003, unpublished thesis).

As such, they demand our attention and thus serve as a basis for this case study's exploration of service recovery in the tourism and leisure industries.

Forces of Change in the Tourism and Leisure Services Industries

The services industry is currently facing an increasingly challenging business environment (Gardenne, 2000). Economic growth, higher disposable incomes and technological changes have fed the exponential growth of services and thus intensified competition (Kandampully, 2002). Adding fuel to the fire so-to-speak is the fact that the rate of change and level of competition are increasing as globalization and deregulation proceed.

Within the context of the broader environmental trends, several issues and trends are critical to understanding hospitality and tourism marketing (Gardenne, 2000; Reid and Bojanic, 2001). For example, a decrease in customer loyalty is a key feature of the hospitality and tourism markets, particularly in the Australian-Pacific Region, as they move towards maturity (Zeithaml and Bitner, 1996; Javalgi and Moberg, 1997; Gremler and Brown, 1999). In this context, customer loyalty is the process of building repeat purchase activity among buyers

(Schmid, 1997). Traditionally marketing communications focused on the product-service offering and the atmosphere enjoyed by the customer. More recently many hospitality and tourism organizations have focused on price with the consequential outcome being heavy price competition and much discounting of costs for various services. However, as noted by Reid and Bojanic (2001), competition on price is a short-term strategy that seldom builds customer loyalty. Therefore, companies are launching customer loyalty schemes, such as frequent flyer programmes and tie-ins to travel-related services, as a means of securing customer loyalty. The principles of such schemes are to identify frequent users; recognize their contribution to organizational success; and reward them with awards and incentives that effectively increase their loyalty to the service provider (Bejou and Palmer, 1998; Reid and Bojanic, 2001).

Consumer Expectations and Service Quality

Customers must be viewed as the judges of service quality, because their evaluations will impact on the outcomes important to service providers, including positive endorsement of a product and/or service by way of word-of-mouth (WOM) and, of course, return patronage. Hence, customers' perceptions of service quality, rather than technical quality, are important to market success and thus, to the bottom line. Similarly, the gap between expectations and service performance is the primary indicator of overall service quality (Wuest, 2001).

If service quality exceeds expectations, customers are delighted; if it conforms with their expectations, they may be satisfied; and if it is less than their expectations, they will be dissatisfied. Hence, it is far easier to please customers with low expectations than those with high expectations (Folkes, 1994; Wuest, 2001).

Customers' evaluations of service quality and perceptions of satisfaction differ widely because their perceptions rely on the way the service complies with their expectations (Wuest, 2001). The two main factors that introduce difference in customers' evaluations

of service quality are effectively their perceptions and expectations.

Service providers establish service standards to guide staff in practice and also act in the assessment of performance. However, service standards have to be considered as changing benchmarks because consumers' expectations tend to increase as they become accustomed to organizational efforts to achieve a competitive edge over other providers, such effects, including the provision of optional services (Wuest, 2001).

Benefits of good service quality

Service quality and customer satisfaction are key concerns of service providers today and are considered strategic concerns (Harrington and Akehurst, 2000). The basic assumption being that customer satisfaction drives profitability and thus business success (Storbacka et al., 1994; Johnston, 2001). Benefits to be derived from improvements in service quality and customer satisfaction include:

- Financial success and competitiveness (Ghobadian et al., 1994);
- WOM endorsement (Reisinger, 2001);
- Enhanced customer loyalty (Lee and Cunningham, 2001);
- Reduced operational costs (Ghobadian et al., 1994).

Implementation of Service Quality Strategies

An organization can take a passive or proactive approach to service quality. A passive approach is appropriate if service quality is not considered a major source of service differentiation or competitive advantage. In this approach, customer dissatisfaction is avoided by ensuring hygiene factors like tours departing on time or cleanliness of facilities (Ghobadian et al., 1994). However, for many businesses, service quality is considered a primary driver of business performance. For example, Javalgi and Moberg (1997, p. 165) stated that 'providing excellent customers service is often the key factor that builds competitive advantage for service providers'. Therefore, a strategic or proactive approach is appropriate to supporting a corporate image built around quality (Ghobadian et al., 1994).

Significantly, a strategic quality programme requires that management has a clear understanding of the organization's service quality definition and vision, customers' expectations, perceived quality, measures of quality and generic determinants of quality (Rust and Oliver, 1994). Conceptual models are also an important consideration, as they help to identify gaps and improvement opportunities (Parasuraman et al., 1985).

Service failure and service recovery

For many reasons, including avoiding wastage and ensuring customer satisfaction and a good reputation, companies aim to deliver a satisfying service each and every time. Nevertheless, factors such as the heterogeneity of service delivery arising from human involvement and varying customer expectations make service failure inevitable (Johnston, 1995). Service failures typically result from fail points in the service delivery process (Shostack, 1984). There are essentially three main categories of service failures:

- *System failures*: failures in the core service offering of the firm.
- *Customer needs failures*: failures based on employee response to customer needs or special requests.
- *Unsolicited employee actions*: actions, both good and bad, of employees that are not expected by customers (Reid and Bojanic, 2001).

Blanding (1992) has argued that added to these must be those circumstances where customers wrongly perceive a failure, perhaps due to misplaced expectations, those cases in which customers are at fault themselves, and where unavoidable impacts from the external environment cause dissatisfaction or service failure (Blanding, 1992).

A number of authors have recognized that service recovery strategies are particularly important to customer service management (Fornell and Wernerfelt, 1987; Bitner et al., 1990; Berry and Parasuraman, 1991; Keaveney, 1995). Hence, service recovery has become a strategic matter that is important to the differentiation of service offers and to the success of the business (Lewis and Spyrakopoulos, 2001).

However, it should be noted that there have been few theoretical or empirical studies of service failure and service recovery issues undertaken to date in the tourism and leisure industries (Suh, 2003, unpublished thesis). Perhaps one reason for this is the inherent difficulty in studying a procedure that is triggered by a service failure and therefore difficult to study in a field or replicate in a clinical environment (Smith et al., 1999).

Ultimately, the benefits of service recovery are directly linked to organizational growth and survival. Substantial cost benefits and increased profits arise from retaining existing customers, due to a lower cost of retention versus recruitment, existing customers being more receptive to marketing efforts, taking up less staff time due to asking less questions and being more familiar with procedures and employees, and importantly, being less price sensitive (Reichheld and Sasser, 1990).

Employees also benefit from good service recovery, both from having done a good job and often from the psychological effects that follow from the empowerment and training that usually are included as part and parcel of the service recovery processes. Benefits from good service recovery include better morale and work satisfaction which benefit the employer through better service to customers and reduction in the turnover of valuable trained employees (Lewis and Clacher, 2001).

Despite the clear benefits of service recovery, many service recovery efforts fail. Ideally, service recovery is a formal process, rather than an ad hoc process or even a complaint handling process (Lewis and Spyrakopoulos, 2001). Such a system is composed of multiple components, only one of which is the actual service recovery transaction. The outcomes of an effective service recovery system are the identification of service problems, effective resolution of those problems and significantly, staff acquisition of new skills and insights from the recovery experience (Zemke, 1995).

An Analysis of Service Quality Recovery Systems

Participants for this research study were 11 managers of service-based businesses operating in the tourism and leisure industries in the southeast Queensland region. The region encompasses two key coastal regions with the Sunshine Coast having a number of beach resorts catering for predominantly the domestic market. The Gold Coast, on the other hand, is developing into an international mass market for Asian tourists with a strong emphasis on shopping, theme parks and nightlife rather than a focus on the beaches themselves. The data were collected using a semi-structured interview with prepared open-ended questions that involved a face-to-face encounter between the researcher and the interviewees. In its simplest sense, interviewing is a way of generating empirical data (Holstein and Gubrium, 2002). The interviewees were identified using a snowball technique (Bouma, 2000). All but three of the participants were male. Almost half of the participants were aged between 26 and 35 years. Only two were aged over 45 years and three less than 25 years. Of all those interviewed, the lowest position held was that of supervisor, while one respondent was an owner-manager and another a consultant. The remaining participants identified themselves as holding the position of manager. All participants had been with their current employer for more than one year, while only two respondents had been with the same company for more than 15 years.

Importance of service recovery

All participants reported that service recovery was important to their organization. One respondent highlighted the fact that the degree of importance was related to the market segment, with service recovery being most important for inbound guests. Since all organizations are operating in competitive markets and all position themselves to one degree or another according to service quality, this finding is to be expected.

A number of factors were perceived by the participants to be driving the elevated recognition of service recovery, with each participant mentioning one to three factors. Good reputation, speedy correction of problems, organizational learning, recruiting new customers, profitability and valuing guests all received mention. Although customer satisfaction was on the minds of each of those interviewed, it was only recognized as important by a small minority of respondents. By far the most salient reason for service recovery being important was retention of customers, in what is currently a very competitive marketplace. As stated by one respondent: 'Customers are so important to our businesses. Unhappy customers who leave without having their problems fixed not only tell others of their problems, but importantly, don't come back.' This identified concern is in line with previous research findings that satisfaction with service recovery has an enormous impact on customers' future behaviour (Eccles and Durand, 1998).

The high importance placed on service recovery by the organizations involved in this study is consistent with the literature that claims service recovery is important for establishing a competitive edge in service delivery, for supporting a market position and for ensuring profitability (Johnston, 1994, 2001). Retention of customers is widely contended in the literature as an important benefit of service recovery, especially since complaining customers are often the organization's most loyal customers (Ranaweera and Neely, 2003).

Satisfaction with service recovery

All respondents mentioned they were satisfied with their organization's service recovery efforts, although few mentioned detailed effects of such despite prompting from the interviewer. Those who were willing to make comment usually referred to one aspect of their organization's service recovery. For example, speediness of resolution was mentioned as highly important by several respondents, reflecting research findings that quick resolution is important to customers (Bettencourt and Gwinner, 1996; Boshoff and Leong, 1998). One participant reported that all problems were solved, while others referred to their high occupancy or customer retention rate as being evidence of good service recovery, showing evidence of evaluating success in terms of direct or indirect outcomes. One manager reported his hotel had sufficient resources to achieve recovery: 'Yes, we have the resources around us to maintain guest satisfaction'. This is consistent with the literature that indicates that appropriate systems, processes and staff need to be in place to achieve excellent service recovery (Zemke, 1995).

The business with the least number of employees of all the organizations surveyed in this study, a family-owned gym, showed a proactive approach to problem identification and resolution, in that public relations strategies were used to prevent problems occurring in the first instance. The respondent stated: 'We spend a lot of time talking to people. This public relations prevents problems from occurring.' This proactive approach is evidence of best practice service recovery, which is very much focused on the prevention of service failures (Zemke, 1995; McDougall and Levesque, 1998). In this particular business, the managers interviewed noted that the face-to-face resolution of complaints was also regarded internally as evidence of good service recovery. This approach reflects a strong relationship marketing approach to neutralize local business competition. This connection between service recovery and building relationships with customers is also mentioned in the literature as being a key consideration for any business operation (Storbacka et al., 1994; Durvasula et al., 2000).

Use of formal service recovery processes

All organizations reported that they had formal service recovery processes in place. Some of the smaller organizations had no written procedures, while the larger ones had manuals to guide staff and written rules of thumb about appropriate compensation. However, it was reported that in the smaller establishments, the small staff numbers and closeness between staff and management resulted in verbal transmission of information and on-the-job training in acceptable service recovery tactics.

Provision for higher-level staff to become involved in recovery or follow up, handling complaints on the spot and recording complaints were key themes of service recovery mentioned by all respondents. One restaurant manager reported: 'Staff listen to the customer carefully and fix the problem as soon as possible ... if the customer is still unhappy the supervisor or manager can look after that'. Importantly, staff are part of the basic service product, but services can vary in interpersonal contact level from low to intensive contact. Thus, service providers behaviour, emotions, skills, knowledge and the way they perform the service, impact on customers' evaluations of the service and their satisfaction with it (Bitner, 1992; Johnston and Clark, 2001). It is thus important that staffs are responsive, caring and skilled. This in turn creates a need to choose employees with good interpersonal skills that are capable of showing empathy with the customer's situation and training, managing, controlling and motivating them well (Johnston and Clark, 2001; Reisinger, 2001b).

Empowerment of staff

All except two of the respondents claimed that their organizations had empowered staff to take control of issues impinging upon service quality standards. For example, a manager from a 5-star hotel reported: 'We believe in empowering our associates with the knowledge and tools to assist our guest to the best of their abilities'. Most of the organizations empowered their staff to choose the way to solve the problem and one manager from a large hotel pointed out that mistakes were not punished, but seen as learning experiences for staff: 'They are taught that if they make a wrong decision ... it is a lesson on what to do the next time'. In two of the smaller establishments, front-line staff gathered complaints only and the manager of a restaurant within a 4.5-star hotel claimed that while empowerment was desirable, it was limited by some staff being either short-term or casual.

The empowerment of staff to solve problems is desirable because such a process usually results in speedier and more convenient solutions for customers (Boshoff and Leong, 1998). The tactic of not punishing staff for mistakes encourages them to make their own decisions and learn from their mistakes and is a necessary consideration for effective empowerment (Korczynski, 2002).

Responsibility for service recovery

All but one of the interviewees attributed ultimate responsibility for service recovery to management. For example, a respondent stated: 'We always have a duty manager … the hotel assistant manager or the front office manager'. While it is rational that ultimate responsibility be placed in the hands of managers, this may reflect a reticence to devolve responsibility to empowered staff. A fitness centre did distribute responsibility to appropriate staff and managers, reflecting a philosophy of the person closest to the problem solving the problem. The respondent stated that trainers, sales staff, group fitness instructors and supervisors/managers were all responsible for service recovery outcomes.

Formal training in service recovery

While all organizations offered some form of training in service delivery, several of the smaller organizations did not implement focused training in service recovery. Within those organizations identified as having training tactics focusing on service recovery, learning on the job from real incidents was a strong theme, as was formal instruction. For example, one manager explained: 'We have several in-house courses on guest service, as well as daily briefings'. Those who do not have formal training relied on general training in service delivery, usually undertaken off the job. For example, the accommodation group management relied on a restricted license course offered by the Real Estate Institute of Queensland.

Evaluation of outcomes of service recovery

Most of those interviewed stated that their organization conducted evaluation of the outcomes of service recovery. However, examination of responses indicated that comments supported evaluation of outcomes in only four cases. Of these, one encouraged feedback, two used managerial review and one a formal monitoring strategy. The respondent from the latter organization stated: 'We actively promote feedback and measure success on a monthly basis'. This approach reflects best practice as various researchers (Carr, 1994; Chebat and Kollias, 2000) have found that supervisors' supportive behaviours, providing useful information, giving feedback, fair evaluations of performance and their direct stimulation of service-related behaviours were all positively related to service outcomes. In two cases the respondent appeared to have misunderstood the meaning of the question and referred to evaluation of customers' problems. When the question was restated by the interviewer, the response was that little was done in this regard within their organization. Evaluation of the outcomes of service recovery is thus a weakness in the service recovery programmes of the organizations taking part in this study. Without an evaluation programme organizations will not be able to detect faulty recovery strategies, since many customers may not actively or formally complain.

Linking of service recovery outcomes to planning

Only three of the participants claimed or indicated that their organizations linked service recovery outcomes to planning in consideration of financial or marketing factors. One front office manager for a 4.5-star hotel mentioned: 'If a trend is forming, we can clearly look at it and take action accordingly'. However, most participants tended to believe that successful service recovery would tend to lead to success in marketing and thus, to the achievement of a profit.

This finding is not surprising since the literature reports a general weakness in this area (Zemke and Bell, 2000). In general, organizations appeared to assume that excellent service recovery is linked to organizational success. There are of course practical difficulties in assessing the opportunity cost of service recovery and comparing it to the benefits received by the organization. This, as well as a general level of formal data gathering and evaluation within smaller organizations, may limit practice.

Discussion

The main purpose of this study was to examine the role that service recovery has for service operations seeking to maintain or enhance service delivery systems and more particularly, service quality standards. Analysis of the data revealed that all respondents considered service recovery to be an important consideration for operations. Significantly, it was customer retention that was identified as the primary motivator for improving or enhancing service quality systems within their respective employing organizations. Of particular interest was the fact that all but one of the respondents in this study attributed ultimate responsibility for service recovery to management with line staff perceived to have only a minor role to play in such an activity.

Employee empowerment

Employee empowerment is a tactic currently used widely by service organizations to cope with change in the environment and to support service quality and service recovery initiatives. The importance of empowering employees for service recovery is mentioned widely in the literature and is considered important by many successful organizations. For example, Boshoff and Leong (1998, p. 24) state: 'Once a service failure has occurred, customers prefer to deal with staff who are empowered to solve their problem quickly'. All the organizations investigated in this study implemented service recovery strategies. More importantly, each had a clear understanding of the value of service recovery with respect to being competitive and for surviving in the competitive service sector market, view that is considered imperative by many authors (Keaveney, 1995; Smith et al., 1999;

Lewis and Spyrakopoulos, 2001). All the respondents interviewed indicated that their organization empowered employees to some degree, i.e. the study found that formal empowerment policies were in place in the larger organizations and informal practices tended to predominate in the smaller organizations. Significantly, the informal practices were consistent with the management style in these organizations, which featured a strong reliance on horizontal communication and personal relationships with the customers. Significantly, the use of empowerment in these operations is consistent with the literature that considers empowerment essential for good service recovery (Boshoff and Leong, 1998).

While all the organizations involved in the study recognized the importance of organization policies, systems and procedures supporting service recovery, and the importance of training and empowering staff, one restaurant manager highlighted however the difficulty in empowering staff when many were part time or casual and therefore might not remain long with the organization. Indeed, the literature supports the notion that staff turnover would present a threat to the development of the skills and attitudes required for excellent service recovery and that staff turnover does result in a loss of valuable skills and expertise. In part, this problem arises from broader labour market trends (Gardenne, 2000). Nevertheless, the link between staff retention and training for empowerment are serious considerations, since the service provider's skills, motivations and attitudes greatly affect customers' evaluations of service quality (Reisinger, 2001a). Hence, it would appear in the organization's best interests to implement human resource management policies to retain staff, to support service recovery and employee empowerment strategies wherever possible (Korczynski, 2002). It would also appear that empowerment itself might help also to solve employee commitment problems (Carr, 1994). Service quality, service recovery and empowerment are all products of the organization's polices, systems, processes and procedures which must be optimized and coordinated to produce the best service outcomes. In other words, the organization must offer a complete and consistent service experience (Andreassen, 1999, 2001). However, empowerment is not an end in itself. It serves to contribute to service quality and service recovery, while good service quality, in turn, reduces the demand for service recovery.

Linking service quality evaluations to strategic planning

All organizations showed general weaknesses in the areas of evaluating outcomes and linking evaluation of outcomes to strategic planning. These processes are difficult to achieve, due to the difficulties in measuring costs and outcomes (Zemke, 1995). Nevertheless, these weaknesses are of great concern, since weaknesses in the evaluation of outcomes and communication may result in resource wastage in inefficient or unneeded activities and in lost opportunities to fine tune the service recovery process (Miller *et al.*, 2000; Marmourstein *et al.*, 2001). Moreover, lack of a link to strategic planning may mean that the strategy of the organization is not supported sufficiently by service recovery processes (Zemke, 1995; Zemke and Bell, 2000).

Implications for practice

As implied by the literature review and the study findings, service recovery and service quality must be seen as important elements of an organization's strategy and should be subject to strategic planning (Zemke, 1995, 2000). It is important for managers to recognize the causal link between policies, systems, processes, including employee empowerment, on one hand, and good service quality and good service recovery on the other (Miller *et al.*, 2000). Hence, efforts must be made to link the outcomes of service recovery to strategic and operational planning, so that service recovery can be aligned with corporate strategy and wastage eliminated.

To achieve the best organizational performance managers should treat the organization as an open system. This requires consideration of the interaction and impact of external and internal factors and system wide optimization to achieve the required level of service quality and service recovery (Lewis and Spyrakopoulos, 2001). This open system approach encompasses the consideration of customers' needs and wants and other impacts on customers' expectations.

Since commitment is essential to the successful implementation of service quality initiatives and the associated marketing tactics, the first step to improving service quality must be to consider how to ensure the commitment and support of those involved (Marmorstein *et al.*, 2001). This by necessity involves consideration of organizational culture, human resource management and change management in the case of staff and in some markets where relationship marketing is important, marketing communications to ensure the support of valued customers.

Service recovery should produce effective and reliable solutions that are consistent with customers' needs and expectations. Service should be one-stop, timely and convenient. Moreover, since the customer is often an active and important participant in the service process and would appear to form both passive and active expectations before, during and after service delivery, it is important to manage expectations at all times. For example, education of the consumer and the drawing of attention to pleasing aspects, such as freshly laundered linen, should optimize customer satisfaction and increase the chance of repeat business and good WOM (Webb, 2000).

Since reliability is more important than compensation for service failure points, it is important to improve service delivery systems first before establishing favourable service guarantee systems (Marmorstein *et al.*, 2001). In this context, empowerment must be considered when planning the systems, processes and procedures of service recovery. Organizational systems and functions, such as human resource management and especially employment practices, must be considered with empowerment in mind (Lewis and Spyrakopoulos, 2001).

Businesses differ across a number of dimensions, rendering impossible the application of standard solutions for service recovery.

Hence, managers should adapt theory to the situation of the business, adjusting strategies and tactics and the level of formality and empowerment (Bowen and Lawler, 1995). For example, smaller businesses should consider leveraging close connections with customers and the shorter communication channels within the organization to achieve more personalized service failure prevention and recovery.

Despite publicity about the service recovery paradox, organizations should not at any time seek to create service failures so they can impress customers with recovery actions (Swanson and Kelley, 2001). However, since most customers do not complain (Zemke and Bell, 1990), a negative impact could occur on the organization's reputation due to the service failures. Moreover, it is not certain that the service recovery paradox holds in all situations or that the impression created by good service recovery will overcome the negative effect of service failure on long-term customer commitment. In fact, findings on the existence of the paradox have been challenged by more recent research (Andreassen, 2001). Therefore, organizations should seek to proactively avoid service failure, thereby saving on service recovery expenses.

Recommendations for future research

While a considerable body of theory and research exists on the related areas of service quality, service recovery and empowerment, there are still many gaps in knowledge. For example, with respect to a greater understanding of customers' thought processes and reactions to service recovery. In general therefore, more work is needed on how consumers form expectations and how they react to different service recovery tactics. In addition, since linking service recovery outcomes with planning is seldom done, research needs to be carried out into the barriers to implementation of this important aspect of service recovery and, in turn, its direct impact on service quality.

This particular study provided some insight into the use of both formal and informal service recovery/staff empowerment approaches within the various service sector businesses.

However, little objective data were found as to the relative effectiveness of these types of strategy. Moreover, little hard data appear to be available on the effectiveness and outcomes of service recovery strategies for tourism and leisure services, either gathered by individual businesses or available in the literature. Hence, further research is needed on an organizational, industry specific and regional basis.

There are also a number of gaps and points of disagreement in the service quality literature with regard to measurement and customer psychology. For example, the SERVQUAL tool for measuring customer satisfaction is criticized in terms of its dimensions and for its focus on the disconfirmation of expectations, while there also exists a need to understand more about the expectation formation aspect of the disconfirmation paradigm. It is not well enough known how customers define their standards and parameters for evaluation and what they understand of their role during service delivery (Webb, 2000). Hence, there remains a need for more research, especially with regard to particular industries and service situations, such as those found in the tourism and leisure industries.

Finally, and despite the breadth of research related to business operations in recent years, there has been little research about how organizations actually define their service standards and determine parameters for evaluating customer satisfaction. There has also been limited research undertaken with respect to what they understand of their role during the service delivery process (Suh, 2003, unpublished thesis). Hence, there remains a need for more research in this area, especially with regard to particular industries and service situations, such as those found in the tourism and leisure industries. For instance, despite the substantial importance of services to national and regional economies, research has shown that service recovery is generally not well carried out nor are service recovery outcomes positively linked to strategic planning (Zemke, 1995; Smith et al., 1999; Suh, 2003, unpublished thesis). Yet service recovery is exceedingly important for operators such as those found in the tourism and leisure industries since the complex and variable nature of service delivery will almost certainly result in customers perceiving problems with service delivery (Bell and Ridge, 1992; Hoffman *et al.*, 1995; Leversque and McDougall, 2000).

Conclusion

The tourism and leisure industries are a mixture of service and physical product offerings and despite the involvement of different businesses, a region is usually judged on the overall impression of the visitor or tourist. As such, the tourism and leisure industries rely very heavily on the development of positive perceptions by the people providing the services to tourists, such as service staff in restaurants, hotels, fitness centres and so on (Reisinger, 2001a). Hence, service quality is important to the marketing of services in any circumstance and, more so, is particularly important for any region specializing in tourism and leisure service offerings.

A customer-focused company which delivers excellent service quality, and which recognizes the critical importance of appropriate service recovery processes, will more often than not meet or exceed customer expectations. Continuous improvement is implied by the trend towards higher expectations within customers (Smith *et al.*, 1999; Reid and Bojanic, 2001). Good performance therefore has two main elements: having systems, processes and procedures that deliver on organizational goals and having marketing and planning functions that can discover what customers want and transpose those wants into strategic marketing plans. Hence, planning and coordination; continuous quality improvement strategies like total quality management, development and deployment of human resources; and learning and feedback systems all contribute to service quality and service recovery performance (Lovelock *et al.*, 1998). Importantly however, service quality advocates hold that quality must be built into *every* component of a service system (Fitzsimmons and Fitzsimmons, 2001). Thus, to improve service quality it is paramount for tourism and leisure operations to examine all the steps involved, including the critical steps involving service recovery (Kandampully, 2002).

References

Andreassen, T.W. (1999) What drives customer satisfaction with complaint resolution. *Journal of Service Research* 1, 324–332.

Andreassen, T.W. (2001) From disgust to delight: do customers hold a grudge? *Journal of Service Research* 4(1), 39–49.

Bejou, D. and Palmer, A. (1998) Service failure and loyalty: an exploratory empirical study of airline customers. *Journal of Services Marketing* 12(1), 7–22.

Bell, C. and Ridge, K. (1992) Service recovery for trainers. *Training and Development* 46(5), 58–62.

Berry, L.L. and Parasuraman, A. (1991) *Marketing Services: Competing Through Quality.* Free Press, New York.

Bettencourt, L.A. and Gwinner, K. (1996) Customization of the service experience: the role of the frontline employee. *International Journal of Service Industry Management* 7(2), 3–20.

Bitner, M. (1992) Managing the evidence of service. *Quality in Services (QUIS-3) Conference.* Karlstad Univesity, Sweden.

Bitner, M., Booms, B. and Tetreault, M. (1990) The service encounter: diagnosing favourable and unfavourable incidents. *Journal of Marketing* 54(1), 71–84.

Blanding, W. (1992) 10 Reasons why manufacturers and service organizations have customer service quality problems. *Tapping the Network Journal* 2(2), 7–13.

Boshoff, C. and Leong, J. (1998) Empowerment, attribution and apologising as dimensions of service recovery: an experimental study. *International Journal of Service Industry Management* 9(1), 24–47.

Bouma, G.D. (2000) *The Research Process*, 4th edn. Oxford University Press, Oxford.

Bowen, D. and Lawler, E. III (1995) Empowering service employees. *Sloan Management Review* 36(4), 73–84.

Carr, C. (1994) Empowered organizations, empowering leaders. *Training and Development* 48(3), 39–44.

Chebat, J. and Kollias, P. (2000) The impact of empowerment on customer contact employees' role in service. *Journal of Service Research* 3(1), 66–81.

Durvasula, S., Lysonski, S. and Mehta, S.C. (2000) Business-to-business marketing: service recovery and customer satisfaction issues with ocean shipping lines. *European Journal of Marketing* 34(3–4), 433–452.

Eccles, G. and Durand, P. (1998) Complaining customers, service recovery and continuous improvement. *Managing Service Quality* 8(1), 68–71.

Fitzsimmons, J.A. and Fitzsimmons, M.J. (2001) *Service Management: Operations, Strategy, and Information Technology*, 3rd edn. McGraw-Hill, New York.

Folkes, V.S. (1994) How consumers predict service quality. In: Rust, R.T. and Oliver, R.L. (eds) *Service Quality: New Directions in Theory and Practice*. Sage, London.

Fornell, C. and Wernerfelt, B. (1987) Defensive marketing strategy by customer complaint management: a theoretical analysis. *Journal of Marketing Research* 24(4), 337–346.

Gardenne, D. (2000) *Brave New World: How Can Business Meet New Challenges in the 21st Century?* Inaugural Professorial Lecture (6 September), Central Queensland University, Rockhampton, Queensland, Australia.

Ghobadian, A., Speller, S. and Jones, M. (1994) Service quality: concepts and models. *International Journal of Quality and Reliability Management* 11(9), 43–66.

Gremler, D.D. and Brown, S.W. (1999) The loyalty ripple effect: appreciating the full value of customers. *International Journal of Service Industry Management* 10(3), 271–293.

Harrington, D. and Akehurst, G. (2000) An empirical study of service quality implementation. *The Service Industries Journal* 20(2), 133–156.

Hoffman, K.D., Kelley, S.W. and Rotalsky, H.M. (1995) Tracking service failures and employee recovery efforts. *Journal of Services Marketing* 9(2), 49–61.

Holstein, J.A. and Gubrium, J.F. (2002) The active interview. In: Weinberg, D. (ed.) *Qualitative Research Methods*. Blackwell, Oxford, pp. 112–126.

Javalgi, R.R. and Moberg, C.R. (1997) Service loyalty: implications for service providers. *Journal of Services Marketing* 11(3), 165–179.

Johnston, R. (1994) *Service Recovery: An Empirical Study*. Warwick Business School, Warwick, UK.

Johnston, R. (1995) Service failure and recovery: impact, attributes and process. *Advances in Services Marketing and Management* 4, 211–228.

Johnston, R. (2001) Linking complaint management to profit. *International Journal of Service Industry Management* 12(1), 60–69.

Johnston, R. and Clark, G. (2001) *Service Operations Management*. Financial Times/Prentice-Hall, London.

Kandampully, J. (2002) *Services Management: The New Paradigm in Hospitality*. Pearson Education Australia, Frenchs Forest, New South Wales, Australia.

Keaveney, S.M. (1995) Customer switching behavior in service industries: an exploratory study. *Journal of Marketing* 59(2), 71–82.

Korczynski, M. (2002) *Human Resource Management in Service Work*. Palgrave, New York.

Lee, M. and Cunningham, L.F. (2001) A cost/benefit approach to understanding service loyalty. *Journal of Services Marketing* 15(2), 113–130.

Levesque, T.J. and McDougall, G.H.G. (2000) Service problems and recovery strategies: an experiment. *Canadian Journal of Administration Sciences* 17(1), 20–37.

Lewis, B.R. and Clacher, E. (2001) Service failures and recovery in UK theme parks: the employees' perspective. *International Journal of Contemporary Hospitality* 13(4), 166–175.

Lewis, B.R. and Spyrakopoulos, S. (2001) Service failures and recovery in retail banking: the customers' perspective. *International Journal of Bank Marketing* 19(1), 37–47.

Lovelock, C.H., Patterson, P.G. and Walker, R.H. (1998) *Services Marketing: Australia and New Zealand*. Prentice-Hall, Sydney, Australia.

Marmorstein, H., Sarel, D. and Lassar, W.M. (2001) Increasing the persuasiveness of a service guarantee: the role of service process evidence. *Journal of Services Marketing* 15(2), 147–159.

McCarthy, D.G. (1997) *The Loyalty Link: How Loyal Employees Create Loyal Customers*. John Wiley & Sons, New York.

McDougall, G.H.G. and Levesque, T.J. (1998) The effectiveness of recovery strategies after service failure: an experiment in the hospitality industry. *Journal of Hospitality and Leisure Marketing* 5(2/3), 27–49.

Miller, J.L., Craighead, C.W. and Karwan, K.R. (2000) Service recovery: a framework and empirical investigation. *Journal of Operations Management* 18(4), 387–400.

Parasuraman, A., Zeithaml, V. and Berry, L. (1985) A conceptual model of service quality and its implications for future research. *Journal of Marketing* 49(2), 41–50.

Ranaweera, C. and Neely, A. (2003) Some moderating effects on the service quality-customer retention link. *International Journal of Operation & Production Management* 23(2), 230–248.

Reichheld, F.F. and Sasser, W.E. (1990) Zero defections: quality comes to services. *Harvard Business Review* 68(5), 105–111.

Reid, R.D. and Bojanic, D.C. (2001) *Hospitality Marketing Management*, 3rd edn. John Wiley & Sons, New York.

Reisinger, Y. (2001a) Concepts of tourism, hospitality and leisure services, In: Kandampully, J., Mok, C. and Sparks, B. (eds) *Service Quality Management in Hospitality, Tourism and Leisure.* Haworth Hospitality Press, New York, pp. 1–14.

Reisinger, Y. (2001b) Unique characteristics of tourism, hospitality and leisure services. In: Kandampully, J., Mok, C. and Sparks, B. (eds) *Service Quality Management in Hospitality, Tourism and Leisure.* Haworth Hospitality Press, New York, pp. 15–50.

Rust, R.T. and Oliver, R.L. (1994) Service quality: insights and managerial implications from the frontier. In: Rust, R.T. and Oliver, R.L. (eds) *Service Quality: New Directions in Theory and Practice.* Sage, London, pp. 1–20.

Schmid, J. (1997) Loyalty marketing: boom or bust. *Target Marketing* 20(8), 34–37.

Shostack, G.L. (1984) Designing services that deliver. *Harvard Business Review* 62(1), 133–139.

Smith, A.K., Bolton, R.N. and Wagner, J. (1999) A model of customer satisfaction with service encounters involving failure and recover. *Journal of Marketing Research* 36(3), 356–372.

Storbacka, K., Strandvik, T. and Gronroos, C. (1994) Managing customer relationships for profit: the dynamics of relationship quality. *International Journal of Service Industry Management* 5(5), 21–38.

Swanson, S.R. and Kelley, S.W. (2001) Attributions and outcomes of the service recovery process. *Journal of Marketing Theory and Practice* 9(4), 50–65.

Webb, D. (2000) Understanding customer role and its importance in the formation of service quality expectations. *The Services Industries Journal* 20(1), 1–21.

Wuest, B.S. (2001) Service quality concepts and dimensions pertinent to tourism, hospitality and leisure services. In: Kandampully, J., Mok, C. and Sparks, B. (eds) *Service Quality Management in Hospitality, Tourism and Leisure.* Haworth Hospitality Press, New York, pp. 51–64.

Zeithaml, V. and Bitner, M.J. (2000) *Service Marketing: Integrating Customer Focus Across the Firm,* 2nd edn. Irwin McGraw-Hill Publishing, New York.

Zemke, R. (1995) *Service Recovery: Fixing Broken Customers.* Productivity Press, Portland, Oregon.

Zemke, R. and Bell, C. (1990) Service recovery: doing it right the second time. *Training* 27(6), 42–48.

Zemke, R. and Bell, C.R. (2000) *Knock Your Socks Off Service Recovery.* AMACOM, New York.

4 Is Near Enough Good Enough? Understanding and Managing Customer Satisfaction with Wildlife-based Tourism Experiences

Gianna Moscardo
James Cook University, Australia

Introduction

The opportunity to view or interact with wildlife is a major component of tourism and recreation and it has been the topic of much academic and management attention. Much of this attention, however, has focused on how to manage the encounters between tourists and wildlife so as to minimize the negative impacts of the tourism on the wildlife. This reflects the fact that many wildlife encounters are conducted within the boundaries of protected natural areas and in many countries encounters with wildlife in any location are regulated by government wildlife agencies. Thus decisions about the nature of many wildlife-based tourism (WBT) experiences are made by protected area managers rather than tourism managers. Not surprisingly the core theme in the literature to date has been the ecological sustainability of current wildlife tourism practices and several authors have noted that the public sector managers involved in WBT rarely consider it as a tourism service. The tourists are not seen as customers and little attention is paid to their satisfaction or perceptions of the quality of the WBT experiences offered (Schanzel and McIntosh, 2000; Miller and McGee, 2001).

This chapter attempts to complement the existing focus on the ecological sustainability of WBT with an emphasis on the importance of understanding tourist satisfaction for the long-term success of this type of tourism service. The chapter outlines a conceptual model that combines aspects of service with constructs related to the interaction between humans and animals. The aim of the model is to suggest a set of attributes that contribute to tourist satisfaction in WBT experiences. It is envisioned that a better understanding of the relevant attributes and their relative effects on overall satisfaction should assist tourism managers in improving the quality of those service attributes that are under their control.

What is known about wildlife-based tourism experiences?

Only a handful of published studies that have investigated wildlife tourist satisfaction at particular sites or for particular activities exists. Table 4.1 contains a summary of the key findings of these studies with regard to the factors significantly related to overall satisfaction. As can be seen in this table some consistent factors emerge:

- the variety and number of animals seen;
- getting close to the wildlife and/or seeing the wildlife easily;

Table 4.1. Summary of factors related to satisfaction with wildlife-based activities.

Study	Factors contributing to satisfaction
Duffus and Dearden (1993) Whale watching tours on Canada's Pacific Coast – Killer Whales	Seeing whales Getting close to whales Seeing displays of whale behaviour Seeing coastal scenery Having a naturalist/crewmember to answer questions Seeing other marine mammals
Davis *et al.* (1997) Whale Shark Tours in Western Australia	Being close to nature Seeing large animals Seeing many different types of marine life Excitement Learning about the marine environment Adventure Underwater scenery Freedom Relaxation Being with friends
Leuschner *et al.* (1989) (Specialist) Birdwatchers in Virginia, USA	Seeing species not previously seen Seeing many different species Seeing rare or endangered species
Foxlee (1999) Whale watching in Hervey Bay, Australia	Numbers of whales seen Distance from whales Whale activity Information available about whales Information available about other marine life The style in which information was presented
Hammitt *et al.* (1993) Wildlife viewing in the Great Smoky Mountains National Park, USA	Seeing many different kinds of wildlife Seeing black bears Seeing white-tailed deer Seeing a larger number of animals First-time visitors Using binoculars/telescopes to see wildlife Taking photographs If numbers seen matched expected numbers
Tourism Queensland (1999) Whale watching in South-east Queensland, Australia	Number of whales seen Travel groups other than families Repeat visitors Domestic visitors On board commentaries Smaller boats
Schanzel and McIntosh (2000) Penguin viewing in New Zealand Note: The setting provides a series of covered trenches and camouflaged viewing hides which allow visitors to move around within the penguin nesting area with minimal disturbance to the birds.	Natural habitat and behaviour Proximity to the penguins Educational opportunities Innovative/novel approach Fewer other people present Presence of infant penguins

- seeing large, rare or new species;
- the natural setting itself;
- the provision of interpretation/education about the wildlife or the setting;
- features of the visitors themselves such as previous experience, travel party and origin.

Many of the studies reviewed in Table 4.1 were focused on a single type of wildlife viewing activity or a specific setting. Moscardo et al. (2001) report on an alternative approach which asked respondents to describe their best and worst wildlife experiences while on holidays. The results of this critical incidents approach confirmed the importance of variety, close contact, rare or new species, the natural environment and education. Feeding and touching animals also emerged as a factor contributing to the quality of the experience (although only for 14% of the sample). The investigation of worst wildlife experiences indicated that close contact with wildlife can also be a problem with 37% of respondents reporting being attacked, harassed or frightened by wildlife. Additional sources of concern revealed in these worst experiences included the welfare of the wildlife, poor animal enclosure conditions, poor quality or limited visitor facilities, bad weather and poor staff.

Another source of information on visitor satisfaction can be found in surveys and observations of visitors in zoos, aquaria and other captive settings. Reviews by Kreger and Mench (1995) and Bitgood et al. (1988) suggest the following factors are associated with visitor interest and enjoyment:

- Being able to get close, touch or feed animals.
- Educational shows and/or demonstrations.
- Pleasant natural outdoor settings.
- Naturalistic enclosures.
- Being able to easily see wildlife.

In addition to these factors several authors have noted that aspects of the wildlife are also related to visitor interest and enjoyment. Bitgood's team (1988) noted that infant animals and large animals attract visitor attention and infants also appear to create excitement and enthusiasm, while Broad (1996) reported that visitors to the Jersey Zoo most enjoyed primates, bears and baby animals. After a sub-

stantial review of the literature and additional research focused on most liked and disliked animals, Woods (2000) provided a set of features that were associated with greater preference for, and interest in, particular types of wildlife. According to this review:

- Larger animals are preferred over smaller ones.
- Animals perceived as intelligent are preferred.
- Colourful, graceful and soft/fluffy animals are attractive to humans.
- Animals which are considered to be dangerous to humans are generally disliked but some predators, particularly big cats and crocodiles, attract attention.
- Animals perceived as similar in appearance or behaviour to humans are preferred.

Some animals also appear to attract human attention because of their cultural associations or iconic status. Animals such as bears, eagles, wolves, turtles and whales are used as symbols in various cultures for concepts such as freedom, strength and intelligence.

Existing models of, and conceptual approaches to, wildlife-based tourism

The first and most prolific author to focus on the nature of the relationship between humans and wildlife was Kellert (1980, 1986, 1993). Much of Kellert's research has been concerned with understanding the different values humans associate with wildlife, cross-cultural differences in these value systems and the implications of these value orientations for wildlife conservation efforts. Of importance to the present discussion is his assertion that both culture and experience with wildlife play important roles in influencing human preferences for different animals. Kellert is also associated with the biophilia hypothesis which proposes that humans are instinctively drawn to wildlife regardless of the values they associate with them (Kellert and Wilson, 1993).

Another commonly used concept in research on wildlife viewing is recreation specialization. Duffus and Dearden (1990) first introduced the concept from recreation to apply specifically to non-consumptive wildlife interactions. The basic argument in this case is that wildlife viewers can be placed on a continuum ranging from a novice or generalist to an expert or specialist. Wildlife viewers at different stages of specialization will have different requirements and expectations and different factors will contribute to their satisfaction. Hvenegaard (2002) provides a review of the research that has subsequently applied this concept to wildlife viewing. The main conclusion of this review is that while in many studies significant relationships have been found between level of specialization and response to the experiences, consistent patterns have yet to emerge. That is, specialization appears to be associated with different requirements in different settings.

A more recent model has been put forward by Reynolds and Braithwaite (2001). This model uses two key dimensions to map WBT experiences – the effect on the wildlife and the richness or intensity of the experience. The former refers to the impacts of the tourism activity on the target wildlife, while the latter is a summary of various elements including authenticity, exhilaration and uniqueness. While the primary goal of this model is to determine the appropriate form of tourism activity for different wildlife and environments, Reynolds and Braithwaite recognize that additional factors may be necessary to understand the success of the experience in terms of visitor satisfaction. Specifically they suggest the type and length of interaction and the popularity of the species as two such factors.

A Mindfulness Model of Wildlife-based Tourism

In 1996, the author introduced the concept of mindfulness/mindlessness to the area of heritage attractions (Moscardo, 1996). This concept was taken from social psychology where it had been used to explain a large variety of everyday behaviours (Langer, 1989). The mindfulness theory proposes that in any given situation a person can be mindful or mindless. Mindfulness is a state of active cognitive or mental processing. Mindful people are paying attention to the information available in the environment around them, reacting to new information and learning. Mindless people, on the other hand, follow established routines or scripts for behaviour and pay minimal attention to the environment and new information. It is important to stress that mindlessness and mindfulness refer to different ways of thinking, not just different amounts of thinking. Langer and her associates have shown that people can be mindless even in quite complex situations and can perform complex tasks with minimal processing of new information. Further research has demonstrated that in many situations, including tourism and leisure experiences, mindfulness is preferred. Mindfulness is associated with positive perceptions of personal control, excitement, learning and satisfaction. By way of contrast, mindless visitors are more likely to report boredom, a lack of control and interest in the experience and dissatisfaction (see Moscardo, 1996, 1999; Langer, 1989, for a review of this research and more detailed discussions of the concept).

One of the major reasons for studying service quality and consumer satisfaction is because many researchers believe that these two concepts contribute to repeat purchase, word-of-mouth (WOM) recommendations and customer loyalty (Yuksel and Yuksel, 2001; Tian-Cole et al., 2002). As mindful visitors are not only more likely to be satisfied but also to remember the service experience, it is argued that it is in the interests of the service provider to encourage mindfulness. In the case of WBT experiences mindful visitors are also more likely to respond to conservation messages and minimal impact guidelines providing an extra incentive for WBT managers to encourage this mode of cognition.

What then are the conditions that contribute to mindfulness? It can be argued that there are two steps involved in encouraging mindful visitors: (i) you must capture their attention, and (ii) you must encourage them to engage in more active processing of the available information. Thus there are two sets of factors associated with mindfulness: (i) those that attract visitor attention, and (ii) those that hold that attention and encourage active cognitive processing. Attention is a basic concept in psychology and there have been very many studies into what captures attention. Several features of an object or a physical setting can automatically attract attention. These are:

- extreme stimuli – very large, very colourful, and very loud things attract attention;
- movement and contrast;
- unexpected, novel and surprising things;
- things which have personal significance;
- things which have the potential to be dangerous.

Features associated with active mental processing include:

- variety or change in an experience;
- personal control or choice;
- personal relevance and/or importance;
- opportunities to interact with objects and people;
- multi-sensory experiences.

In addition to these features there are also a number of setting conditions that can hinder

mindfulness and these include fatigue, disorientation, crowding, sensory overload and safety concerns. Further there are features of the individuals that can interact with the setting conditions to influence mindfulness. These include motivation or interest in the object or setting, previous experience with the activity, existing levels of knowledge about the activity and social group interaction (see Moscardo, 1996, 1999, for further details).

Figure 4.1 takes the mindfulness concept and applies it to the WBT experiences. The model incorporates predictions from a mindfulness approach with what is known about the features associated with visitor satisfaction from previous wildlife viewing research. The model consists of five main sets of factors – characteristics of the visitors, characteristics of the wildlife setting conditions, the nature of the interaction between the visitors and the wildlife and the outcomes. The visitor characteristics which are predicted to be important based on the work of Kellert and research

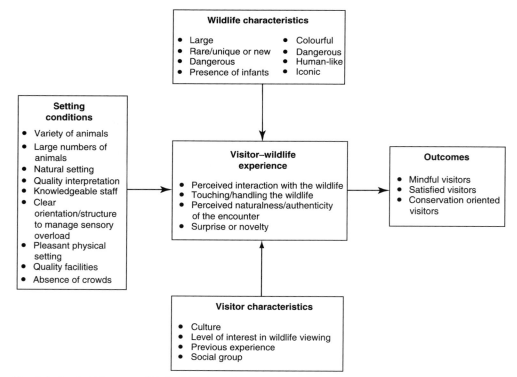

Fig. 4.1. A mindfulness model of wildlife-based tourist experiences.

into recreation specialization, are cultural background, level of interest in wildlife viewing, and level of experience with wildlife viewing. Although these factors are expected to be related to satisfaction there is insufficient evidence to make more detailed predictions. Given the more substantial data available on preferences for wildlife, it is easier to make more detailed predictions in this area of the model. Thus the model includes a list of characteristics which should encourage greater visitor attention and contribute to satisfaction. In the same way the model lists a set of features for the both the setting and the interaction experience which should encourage mindfulness and through that, satisfaction.

The initial version of the model is based on the results of published research and reviews of relevant concepts and theoretical frameworks. But the available published research is limited in quantity and is particularly dominated by studies of whale and bird watchers. These limitations are apparent in the nature of the model outlined in Fig. 4.1 which includes many variables without specific predictions. This is a preliminary framework which provides an initial selection of factors which are expected to be related to satisfaction based on either the mindfulness theory, the previous research or both. In order to develop this model and further explore tourist satisfaction in this sector the author has been involved in a three year research project jointly funded by the Cooperative Research Centres for Reef, Rainforest and Sustainable Tourism. The research team has collected survey data from more than 4000 visitors at more than 15 different locations around Australia. Table 4.2 summarizes the sites and experiences that have been included in the project to date.

Collecting the tourist data

Two main methods have been used to collect the data. In the first case research assistants have conducted the surveys on-site, usually at an exit point or on the return leg of a tour. A systematic sampling frame is established based on the number of tourists in the area or the tour and used to select potential respondents. Respondents who agree to participate are given a self-completion survey form and asked to

return it to the research assistants before leaving. This technique has resulted in an overall average response rate of 84% (range from 63% to 97%). In those settings where the flow of visitors is small the tour operator or site staff have been enlisted to hand out the surveys at the end of the experiences to all visitors. Visitors who agree to participate, complete the survey and return it to the research team using the stamped addressed envelopes provided. To date the surveys have been conducted in English only.

The tourists who participated

The sample used for the analyses reported here was 4147 and a demographic profile is given in Table 4.3. As can be seen the sample is composed of a range of visitors in terms of age, gender, travel party, usual place of residence, previous WBT experience and interest in viewing wildlife while on holidays. Two points about the results in Table 4.3 are worth noting. First, for the majority of respondents viewing wildlife is a part of a larger holiday experience rather than the primary motivation. Secondly, despite this many visitors had participated in a variety of WBT experiences in the previous 12 months. In particular there were high levels of participation in captive wildlife experiences and in visits to places where wildlife might be seen.

The Results

Tourists' satisfaction with the wildlife-based services on offer

Overall there was a high level of satisfaction with the WBT experiences available. Nearly one-third of those surveyed (30%) gave their wildlife experience a score of 10 out 10, with 85% giving it a score of 8 or higher on a scale from 1 to 10 (the mean was 8.0, with a standard deviation of 2.0). These high scores were reflected in high numbers of tourists who would definitely recommend the experiences to others (78%) and who intend to repeat the experience (55% would definitely repeat and 27% would repeat if they returned to the region). It is also important to note the high correlations between overall satisfaction and intention to recommend

Table 4.2. The settings studied.

Setting	Target species	Interpretation	Structure
Flinders Chase National Park, Kangaroo Island, South Australia (*n* = 361) A relatively remote national park with several places where wildlife populations gather. Sample included independent visitors and those on a tour.	Fur seals Kangaroos Koalas Magpie geese Platypus	Signs at major viewing areas, ranger led tours and commentary by bus drivers	Minimal
Rainforest Habitat, North Queensland, Australia (*n* = 564) A captive setting offering a series of large walk through aviaries and outdoor naturalistic enclosures.	Rainforest birds Kangaroos Koalas Crocodiles Butterflies	Signs and tours	Pathways determined for visitors
Northern Wet Tropics Rainforest, Australia (*n* = 487) These visitors were surveyed at a major gateway to the region and asked about their experiences in the national parks and other rainforest sites in the region.	Numerous	Signs at some sites	Minimal
Day trips to the Great Barrier Reef and Islands, Australia (*n* = 742) Visitors were surveyed on a variety of tour operations at two major ports.	Fish Coral Sea birds Other marine species	Nature guides provided by the operators	Substantial with itineraries organizing the experience for visitors
Seaworld, Gold Coast, Australia (*n* = 296) Theme park with a major emphasis on marine wildlife.	Marine mammals Polar bears	Signs, talks and shows	Substantial
Lady Elliott and Musgrave Islands, Southern Great Barrier Reef, Australia (*n* = 249) Surveys were conducted with visitors staying on the island resort and those on day trips.	Seabirds Turtles Coral Fish Marine species	Signs, talks and tours	Moderate
Atherton Tablelands, Australia (*n* = 176) Surveys were conducted through accommodation providers in this tropical rainforest region. Many of the accommodation providers advertise opportunities to view wildlife, especially birds.	Birds Kangaroos Rainforest species	Some signs provided at sites	Minimal
National parks in New South Wales and Victoria, Australia (*n* = 362) Visitors were surveyed at a variety of places where kangaroos are often seen. The focus of this survey was on kangaroo viewing.	Kangaroos	Some signs provided at some sites	Minimal

Table 4.2. *Continued*

Kangaroo Island, South Australia (*n* = 262) Visitors were surveyed on the ferry as they left the island which is promoted as a wildlife destination. Most wildlife viewing opportunities are unstructured.	Sea lions Seals Kangaroos Koalas Whales Penguins Echidna Platypus Magpie Geese Cockatoos	Some signs and guided tours provided at various locations	Minimal
Melbourne Zoo, Australia (*n* = 322)	Numerous	Substantial	Substantial
National Park Ranger led penguin viewing tours Kingscote, Kangaroo Island (*n* = 137) Tours involve rangers leading groups of visitors on an evening walk around the small coastal township where penguins nest.	Penguins	Pre-tour briefing and ongoing commentary	Ranger led and organized
Guided penguin viewing tours, Granite Island, South Australia (*n* = 189) As above only the location is much closer to urban areas on the mainland.	Penguins	Pre-tour briefing and ongoing commentary	Ranger led and organized

(Spearman's rho = 0.312) and repeat (Spearman's rho = 0.219) the experiences. These correlations confirm the importance of understanding the factors that contribute to overall satisfaction for service managers.

Factors significantly related to satisfaction with wildlife-based tourism services

Several different types of analysis were conducted to explore the relationships between various factors and overall satisfaction with the wildlife-based experience. Table 4.4 presents the results of *t*-tests and one way analyses of variance that indicated a significant relationship with satisfaction where the *p* level was set at 0.01. In addition to these mean difference tests, a number of correlations were also computed between variables measured with rating

scales and overall satisfaction. These analyses are summarized in Table 4.5.

With regard to the visitors' characteristics the results indicated that level of interest in seeing wildlife and social group were significantly related to overall satisfaction. The variable of country of residence was also significantly related to satisfaction lending some support to the prediction that culture is also an important factor. Although a viable alternative explanation is that of language with the most satisfied groups being those for whom English is the main language. Previous experience with the activity was not related to satisfaction. In terms of the features associated with the visitor wildlife experience, perceived interaction with the wildlife, perceived naturalness of the encounter, touching the wildlife and how surprising the encounter was, were all significantly positively related to overall satisfaction.

The results for the setting conditions supported the predictions of the model with

Table 4.3. Demographic profile of the sample ($n = 4147$).

Demographic characteristic	Sample %		
Age			
<21 years	5		
21–30 years	22		
31–40 years	24		
41–50 years	19		
51–60 years	16		
>60 years	14		
Gender			
Female	43		
Male	57		
Travel party			
Alone	6		
Spouse/partner only	33		
Family group	31		
Friends	15		
Other	15		
Travelling with children[a]	27		
Travelling as part of a tour group[a]	19		
Usual place of residence			
Australia	57		
UK/Ireland	13		
USA/Canada	12		
Other Europe	10		
Asia	4		
New Zealand	3		
Other	1		
Previous WBT experience			
Number of visits in the last 12 months	(0)	(1–5)	(>5)
• Zoos/wildlife parks	20	74	6
• Commercial wildlife tours	61	37	2
• Places where wildlife are often seen	21	61	18
• Places specifically to see wildlife	37	55	8
Interest in viewing wildlife while on holidays			
The opportunity to see wildlife is one of the most important factors in my travel decisions	20		
The opportunity to see wildlife is included in my travel decisions	49		
Viewing wildlife is not part of my travel decisions but I enjoy seeing wildlife while doing other things	30		
Not interested in seeing wildlife/I avoid wildlife on holidays	1		

[a]Additional questions.

regard to the variety of animals seen, with settings offering a few species associated with higher score than settings offering a single species. The results also indicated that settings offering many species were associated with lower satisfaction scores confirming the importance of managing information over-load. In the same vein settings offering some degree of structure were more positively rated than those with less or no structure. A clear relationship was also established between the provision of quality information or interpretation and overall satisfaction. Further it was found that captive settings were associated

Table 4.4. Factors significantly related to satisfaction with WBT.

Feature	Mean satisfaction scores (std dev.)	t or F value	Probability (p)
Setting characteristics			
Captive versus	8.7 (1.4)	$t = 7.92$	<0.001
Non-captive	8.0 (2.1)		
Focus on			
Single species	8.1 (1.8)	$F = 14.62$	<0.001
A few species	8.3 (1.7)		
Many species	7.9 (2.2)		
How many animals were seen?			
1 or 2	7.7	$F = 3.92$	<0.01
3–5	8.0		
6–10	8.1		
11–20	7.9		
Lots/many/more than 20	8.2		
Independent visits	7.9 (2.1)	$t = -6.75$	<0.001
Structured visits	8.5 (1.7)		
Visitor characteristics			
Country of residence			
Australia	8.2 (1.9)		
New Zealand	8.3 (1.8)		
Asia	7.6 (2.3)	$F = 5.78$	<0.001
USA/Canada	8.0 (2.1)		
UK/Ireland	7.9 (2.1)		
Other Europe	7.7 (2.2)		
Other	7.6 (2.2)		
Travel party type			
Alone	7.8 (2.2)	$F = 8.14$	<0.001
Spouse/partner only	8.0 (2.1)		
Family group (includes children)	8.4 (1.8)		
Friends	7.6 (2.2)		
Family and friends	8.3 (1.9)		
Other	8.1 (1.9)		
Male	7.9 (1.9)	$t = -3.00$	<0.01
Female	8.2 (2.0)		
The opportunity to see wildlife is			
One of the most important factors in holiday choice	8.2 (2.1)	$F = 8.52$	<0.001
A factor in holiday choice	8.1 (1.9)		
Not a factor in holiday choice but nice to see	7.8 (2.1)		
Encounter characteristics			
Animal was unaware of visitors	8.0 (2.0)	$F = 4.59$	<0.01
Animal was aware but did not respond	8.1 (1.8)		
Animal seemed to respond or interact	8.4 (1.9)		
Touched the wildlife	8.4 (1.7)	$t = -4.32$	<0.001
Did not touch	8.0 (2.0)		

with higher satisfaction scores than settings where the wildlife were seen in their natural environment. It is important to note that captive settings provide much more interpretation and structure than non-captive settings and offered more variety of wildlife. This would seem to indicate that these setting conditions (structure, interpretation and variety) are more important than the natural environment alone.

Table 4.5. Factors correlated with satisfaction.

Factors[a]	Pearson correlation with overall satisfaction ($p < 0.001$ for all results)
How much the visitor learnt about the wildlife	0.58
How exciting the encounter was	0.33
How natural the encounter was	0.25
How unexpected the encounter was	0.14
Satisfaction with the variety of wildlife	0.51
Satisfaction with the number of wildlife seen	0.56
Satisfaction with the quality of facilities	0.30
Satisfaction with information on wildlife	0.27
Satisfaction with how close able to get	0.48
Satisfaction with quality of natural environment	0.32

[a]The first five factors were measured on a scale from 0 (not at all/none) to 10 (very/many). Other factors were measured on a scale from 1 (not at all) to 5 (very) and these ratings were not collected at all sites.

While a significant relationship was found between the number of animals seen and satisfaction, it was not a simple linear relationship. Highest levels of satisfaction were reported by those who saw lots of/or many animals and those who saw three to ten animals. No significant relationship was found between satisfaction with wildlife experiences and how close visitors were able to get to the wildlife. These two results were initially surprising given the high correlations between overall satisfaction and satisfaction with these two factors. Further investigation of the relationships between these variables confirmed that there were positive and statistically significant relationships between how close visitors reported being able to get to the wildlife and their satisfaction with this distance ($r = 0.157$), and the number of animals the visitors report seeing and how satisfied they were with this setting condition ($r = 0.113$). In those settings where it was possible to see a variety of species the respondents were also asked what animals they expected or hoped to see. Fifteen per cent of the sample at these places could not list any animals they might see and only 17% could list more than two animals. The majority of visitors appeared to have only limited knowledge of the potential wildlife viewing possibilities. Given that visitors had only limited expectations about what they are going to see it seems that expectations for numbers and distance are established by the tour or attraction staff at the start of the expe-

rience. Clearly it is important that staff give accurate and realistic information about what is likely to happen early in the experience.

Satisfaction with the quality of the facilities and the state of the natural environment was also positively associated with overall satisfaction. The questionnaire included a question asking the respondents to list the number of other people present at their wildlife encounters. This question was included as a measure of the influence of crowding on overall satisfaction. No significant relationship was found between the number of other people reported and overall satisfaction. It is important to note, however, that 56% of the sample reported being with less than ten other people and a further 20% reported being with between 11 and 25 people. Thus the present range of sites did not allow for a complete test of this variable.

Most memorable wildlife seen

At those sites with the possibility of viewing more than one wildlife species respondents were asked to list the animals they saw and to identify the most memorable. They were then asked to give a description of this animal. Table 4.6 lists the most commonly mentioned wildlife at each of the relevant sites. The following were the ten most commonly given descriptions of the most memorable wildlife encountered:

Table 4.6. Most memorable wildlife encountered.

Site	Most memorable wildlife	Respondents at the site %
Wet Tropics Region	Kangaroo	12
	Spider	11
	Crocodile	10
Melbourne Zoo	Elephants	14
	Seals	13
	Gorilla	8
Great Barrier Reef day trips	Large fish	20
	Turtles	12
	Coral	11
Seaworld	Dolphins	47
	Polar bears	37
	Seals	9
Lady Elliott and Musgrave Islands	Turtle	44
	Fish	14
	Manta rays	10
Atherton Tablelands	Birds	12
	Frogs	9
	Snakes	7
Kangaroo Island	Sea lions	26
	Seals	21
	Kangaroos	19

- beautiful (27% of the respondents);
- big (26%);
- cute (22%);
- sleek, fast or graceful movement (21%);
- unique/rare/unusual (18%);
- colourful (15%);
- interesting (13%);
- intelligent (11%);
- dangerous (10.5%);
- small (8%).

The results confirm the principles set out by Woods (2000) and as predicted by the mindfulness model.

The relative importance of features of wildlife-based tourism services

The previous sections have confirmed that many of the factors set out in the mindfulness model were significantly related to overall satisfaction with the WBT experience. While this information is in itself of value to managers it is also important to assess the relative contribution of each of these factors to overall satisfaction. In order to investigate these a number of multiple regression analyses were conducted. Multiple regression is a technique that provides information on the relative contribution of different variables to a single target or dependent variable. As with all statistical techniques multiple regression has some limitations. The first of relevance to the present discussion is that categorical variables such as the characteristics of the wildlife cannot be included in the analyses. Further, only predictor variables that are not highly correlated with each other can be included. In the present case there were high correlations between the ratings of satisfaction with the various setting conditions and so a series of analyses were conducted with different sets of these factors. The summary of the results of these analyses is contained in Table 4.7.

These results show us that two consistently important factors from those analysed were the amount visitors believed they had learnt about the wildlife and the presence of teenage children in the travel group. The number of wildlife seen was also a significant variable in two of the analyses. Finally the results indicated that the best predictors of overall satisfaction were satisfaction with how close the

Table 4.7. Results of multiple regression analyses for satisfaction with wildlife experiences.

Overall results	Significant factors	T	p
$R^2 = 0.465$ $F = 84.2$ $P < 0.001$	Satisfaction with variety of animals seen How much was learnt about the wildlife Satisfaction with quality of environment Number of teens in the travel party Reported number of wildlife seen	12.0 6.8 3.0 2.6 2.2	0.0001 0.0001 0.01 0.01 0.05
$R^2 = 0.538$ $F = 56.6$ $P < 0.001$	Satisfaction with number of animals seen How much was learnt about the wildlife Number of teens in the travel party Whether or not touched the wildlife Satisfaction with quality of visitor facilities Reported number of wildlife seen	10.3 7.0 3.2 2.9 2.9 2.4	0.0001 0.0001 0.01 0.01 0.01 0.05
$R^2 = 0.426$ $F = 120.5$ $P < 0.001$	Satisfaction with how close able to get to wildlife How much was learnt about the wildlife Number of teens in the travel party	13.8 9.3 2.4	0.0001 0.0001 0.05
Other variables included in the analyses that were not included in the final equations	How far visitors travelled to get there Perceived interaction with wildlife Previous experience with site How close visitors reported getting to the wildlife How often the wildlife had been seen before How natural the encounter was The number of children under 12 years in the travel party		

visitors were able to get to the wildlife, satisfaction with the variety of wildlife seen and satisfaction with the number of wildlife seen. It should be remembered, however, that these were all highly correlated with each other.

Conclusions

Implications for service management

First, the results of surveys conducted with more than 4000 tourists at 12 different Australian WBT sites confirmed the importance of overall satisfaction for customer loyalty with significant positive correlations between overall satisfaction and intention to recommend and repeat the experience. High overall satisfaction was also found to be associated with high ratings of satisfaction with various features of the experience including satisfaction with the number and variety of wildlife seen and how close visitors were able to get to the wildlife. These variables were also highly correlated with each other. This phenomenon has been noted in previous

research (Yuksel and Yuksel, 2001). It was also found that stronger relationships existed between overall satisfaction and satisfaction with the number of wildlife seen and how close the visitors were able to get than between overall satisfaction and how close the visitors reported getting and how many animals they reported seeing. As the visitors expressed very limited expectations for these variables it seems that expectations for these variables are set in the early stages of the actual experience. The lesson here for service management is clear – visitors need to be given accurate and realistic expectations early in their experience.

The need for good quality information in WBT experiences is also reinforced by the consistent finding that the amount that visitors believed they had learnt about the wildlife was a major contributor to overall satisfaction. Quality interpretation is clearly a critical service component for this type of tourist activity. The provision of interpretation for visitors with limited English language skills is also an area that many WBT tours and attractions could develop to improve service and experience quality.

There has generally been a belief in the literature in this area that visitors would prefer to see wildlife in their natural environment or non-captive settings (Moscardo et al., 2001). The research reported here, however, suggests that higher satisfaction was likely in captive settings. Captive settings provided several features also predicted by the mindfulness approach to be important for visitor satisfaction including interpretation, the ability to view a range of different species and some degree of structure which helps visitors deal with sensory overload. Managers of non-captive settings need to think about the way in which visits and/or tours are structured and organized. The provision of good quality interpretation including information on how to structure a visit may be especially important in non-captive settings.

The survey data revealed several characteristics that were related to visitors' perceptions of wildlife species as memorable. These included both characteristics of the wildlife themselves such as movement, size and colour, as well as several features that were more human perceptions such as the animal being intelligent, unique and interesting. Interpretation that stresses these characteristics where appropriate may be useful in enhancing visitors' experiences.

Finally, the quality of the facilities and settings provided for visitors were significantly related to overall satisfaction. Although these features were not as important as some of those already mentioned, they should not be ignored. Much of the management literature related to WBT has focused on the wildlife and the present results show that there are significant and substantial contributions also made to overall satisfaction by service conditions.

The mindfulness model revisited

These results represent a first attempt to explore the complex set of relationships that operate in this particular type of tourism. The data includes many more open-ended questions including best features of the experience and suggested improvements that have yet to be analysed. This initial attempt does, however, provide support for further development of the model. Major goals of the research programme

are to conduct further analyses on this survey data-set and to enhance this data with a broader and more international selection of sites. Two further goals include exploring the link between satisfaction and conservation attitudes and to determine what elements contribute to effective or quality wildlife interpretation.

Some implications for the design and management of wildlife-based tourism experiences

Three core principles can be derived from the mindfulness concept and model. The first of these is variety. It is important that WBT managers do not rely solely on the passive viewing of wildlife, but offer a range of different styles of activity to support and enhance the wildlife viewing experience. Several zoos in the USA have begun to design 'immersion' experiences which include:

- well-designed naturalistic enclosures with hidden barriers;
- an array of static and interactive educational displays within the exhibit areas;
- self-guided and guided trails through the exhibit areas;
- models and artefacts such as skins to touch;
- audio-visual displays.

In such settings visitors can do more than simply view the wildlife. Another similar example can be found on a wildlife viewing day tour offered in Alaska which included artefacts such as skins and casts of prints and skulls for visitors to feel and smell and invited visitors to assist the guides in a number of activities related to recording wildlife sightings, preparing binoculars and handing out educational information. Another way to design variety into WBT experiences is to include more than one species in the programme, although including too many species can create overload.

In these examples of variety a number of the activities included in the programme provide opportunities for guests to participate in a range of activities rather than simply view the wildlife. Participation is the second core mindfulness principle. Participation not only encourages guests to get physically and mentally active, it also gives guests some sense of control over what is happening. Control is the third principle for encouraging mindfulness. Another way to enhance participation and control is to help guests develop their wildlife spotting skills with briefings and introductory sessions.

In those settings where many species are likely to be seen, control can also be enhanced by giving assistance to guests to make choices so that they are not overwhelmed by the options available. Options for providing this type of guest service include developing brochures or maps with suggested itineraries or routes and providing themed self-guided or guided tours that select a subgroup of species related to the theme. Such options could also have the benefit of encouraging repeat visitation over time.

Acknowledgements

The questionnaire for this research project was designed with input from Paul Reynolds, formerly of the Southern Cross University and Barbara Woods from James Cook University. The author is especially grateful for their contribution to the development of this project.

References

Bitgood, S., Patterson, D. and Benefield, A. (1988) Exhibit design and visitor behaviour: empirical relationships. *Environment and Behaviour* 20(4), 474–491.

Broad, G. (1996) Visitor profile and evaluation of informal education at Jersey Zoo. *Journal of Wildlife Preservation Trusts* 32, 166–192.

Davis, D., Birtles, A., Valentine, P., Cuthill, M. and Banks, S. (1997) Whale sharks in Ningaloo Marine Park. *Tourism Management* 18(5), 259–271.

Duffus, D.A. and Dearden, P. (1990) Non-consumptive wildlife-oriented recreation: a conceptual framework. *Biological Conservation* 53, 213–231.

Duffus, D.A. and Dearden, P. (1993) Recreational use, valuation, and management of Killer Whales (*Orcinus orca*) on Canada's Pacific coast. *Environmental Conservation* 20(2), 149–156.

Hammitt, W.E., Dulin, J.N. and Wells, G.R. (1993), Determinants of quality wildlife viewing in the Great Smoky Mountains National Park. *Wildlife Society Bulletin* 21(1), 21–30.

Hvenegaard, G.T. (2002) Birder specialization differences in conservation involvement, demographics, and motivations. *Human Dimensions of Wildlife* 7(1), 21–36.

Kellert, S.R. (1980) *Public Attitudes Toward Critical Wildlife and Natural Habitat Issues*. US Government Printing Service, Washington, DC.

Kellert, S.R. (1986) Social and perceptual factors in the preservation of animal species. In: Norton, B.G. (ed.) *The Preservation of Species: The Value of Biological Diversity*. Princeton University Press, Princeton, New Jersey, pp. 50–73.

Kellert, S.J. (1993) Values and perceptions of invertebrates. *Conservation Biology* 7(4), 845–855.

Kellert, S.J. and Wilson, E.O. (1993) *The Biophilia Hypothesis*. Island Press, Washington, DC.

Kreger, M.D. and Mench, J.A. (1995) Visitor-animal interactions at the zoo. *Anthrozoos* 8(3), 143–158.

Langer, E. (1989) *Mindfulness*. Addison-Wesley, Reading, Massachusetts.

Leuschner, W.A., Ritchie, V.P. and Stauffer, D.F. (1989) Opinions on wildlife: response of resource managers and wildlife users in the south-eastern United States. *Wildlife Society Bulletin* 17, 24–29.

Miller, K.K. and McGee, T.K. (2001) Toward incorporating human dimensions information into wildlife management decision-making. *Human Dimensions of Wildlife* 6(3), 205–222.

Moscardo, G. (1996) Mindful visitors. *Annals of Tourism Research* 23(2), 376–397.

Moscardo, G. (1999) *Making Visitors Mindful*. Sagamore, Champaign, Illinois.

Moscardo, G., Woods, B. and Greenwood, T. (2001) *Understanding Visitor Perspectives on Wildlife Tourism*. Wildlife Tourism Research Report Series: No 2. CRC for Sustainable Tourism, Gold Coast.

Reynolds, P.C. and Brathwaite, D. (2001) Towards a conceptual framework for wildlife tourism. *Tourism Management* 22, 31–42.

Schanzel, H.A. and McIntosh, A.J. (2000) An insight into the personal and emotive context of wildlife viewing at the Penguin Place, Otago Peninsula, New Zealand. *Journal of Sustainable Tourism* 8(1), 36–52.

Tian-Cole, S., Crompton, J.L. and Willson, V.L. (2002) An empirical investigation of the relationships between service quality, satisfaction and behavioral intentions among visitors to a wildlife refuge. *Journal of Leisure Research* 34(1), 1–24.

Tourism Queensland (1999) *1998 Whale Watching Survey: Research Findings*. Available at: www.tq.com. qep/research/whalrsch/index/htm

Woods, B. (2000) Beauty and the beast: preferences for animals in Australia. *Journal of Tourism Studies* 11(2), 25–35.

Yuksel, A. and Yuksel, F. (2001) Measurement and management issues in customer satisfaction research: review, critique and research agenda – Part 1. *Journal of Travel and Tourism Marketing* 10(4), 47–80.

5 Management of Tourism: Conformation to Whose Standards?

Noel Scott
University of Queensland, Australia

Introduction

This chapter provides a case study of the development of 'Schoolies Week' on the Gold Coast. The case study traces the development of Schoolies Week from its origins in the early 1970s through to the most recent attempts to better manage it, thus investigating issues of innovation and responsible management. Within this setting, the issue of who owns Schoolies Week and whose values should be used in better management is discussed.

The management of quality tourism presupposes agreement about which standards constitute quality. Many managers appear to follow a simple definition of quality as conformance to pre-specified standards (Lewis and Booms, 1983) where the standards might be derived from customers' expectations (Zeithaml and Bitner, 1996, p. 117). However, this is more problematic in tourism than in other industrial activities. Tourism is a partially industrialized activity (Leiper, 1990) and involves a number of 'common ownership' goods. These may be aspects of the destination environment that are attractions to visitors (e.g. National Parks, unique landforms), or derived from the social or cultural heritage of the destination. They may also be associations with the destination that have a special meaning for the visitors. Consequently, several groups have stakes in the way tourism oper-

ates and hence in the quality of the tourism experience.

In the case examined here, it has become a custom for school-leavers completing their final year of high school to visit the Gold Coast in Australia and celebrate for a week in a festival atmosphere known as Schoolies Week. This festival exists on the Gold Coast, in part due to the ability of previous generations of Queenslanders to engage in deviant sexually related behaviour. The Gold Coast is familiar with controversy, beginning with 'pyjama parties' in the 1950s, the wearing of bikinis on Gold Coast beaches in the 1950s and 1960s and later topless bathing. These are all related to issues of sexual licence, riotous behaviour and deviancy and Schoolies Week is no different.

The Schoolies festival affects Schoolies themselves, residents, other tourists (both actual and potential) and the different groups of tourism operators and businesses and it is therefore not surprising that Schoolies Week has become a contentious issue. Each year it is associated with numerous reports of crimes by and against Schoolies and sometimes deaths. Also the activities of Schoolies including drunk and disorderly behaviour have affected the image of the Gold Coast as a family destination. Since 1995, the Gold Coast City Council (GCCC) and more recently the Queensland State Government has provided entertainment activities and support for Schoolies in order to better manage Schoolies Week. However, there is a need to balance these interventions against the 'common ownership' reasons for existence of Schoolies Week. This chapter then examines the history and development of Schoolies Week, analysing the reasons for its success and motivations of Schoolies in attending it.

The Schoolies Week festival developed spontaneously and organically and is one of the few 'rites of passage' remaining for Australian teenagers. In some ways this explains the success of the festival. However, the celebrations of young people are noisy and sometimes riotous. In fact the Gold Coast as a tourist destination has traded on the image of youth, sex and partying since the 1950s. Thus specification of goals for quality management of Schoolies Week is less consensual than might otherwise be thought. There are conflicts of values between stakeholders that are not well addressed by standard business quality management theory.

The following material is drawn from the author's doctoral research and involves in-depth qualitative interviews with stakeholders connected with the historical and current development of Schoolies Week. A triangulation approach was used to collect data. An interview protocol was developed as the basis for discussion with respondents. Respondents were chosen initially from industry experts but thereafter a snowball sampling procedure was used. Additionally, respondents were self-chosen through response to publicity about the research study. Data was also drawn from archival records such as newspapers, government reports and the writings of other academics. Where respondents to the research are quoted, they are identified by a code for confidentiality purposes.

Schoolies Week History

Schoolies Week is a major annual tourism phenomenon in Australia involving students who have completed Year 12, the final year at high school. Similar activity has been identified in the USA where it is called 'graduation week' (USA Student Travel, 2002). In Australia, a number of studies have examined Schoolies Week primarily from a risk man-

agement perspective aimed at behaviour of young people which might endanger themselves or others during Schoolies Week (Gillespie et al., 1991; Ballard et al., 1998; Winchester et al., 1999; Jansen, 2000, unpublished thesis). A number of studies have also examined Schoolies Week from an economic perspective and as a tourism product (Faulkner, 1999; Raybould and Scott, 2001).

Schoolies Week activity is found in several places around Australia. It has been noted in Western Australia where it is associated with problem behaviour (Curd, 1997). In Queensland, there are five government recognized Schoolies Week locations (Gold Coast, Stradbroke Island, Sunshine Coast, Airlie Beach, Whitsundays and Magnetic Island, Townsville). All popular Schoolies Week destinations are seaside destinations.

Schoolies Week has been discussed as a 'rite of passage' associated with identity formation and transition between youth and adulthood (Wyn and White, 1997).

> The rite of passage of 'Schoolies' week occurs over several weeks in November–December, the summer holiday period which immediately follows the Australian school-leaving examination, the Higher School Certificate. School students, predominantly from New South Wales and Queensland, but also from Victoria, converge on the Gold Coast.

> (Winchester, et al., 1999, p. 59)

While it may be argued that a 'rite of passage' associated with transition to adulthood is a characteristic of many human societies, there are a number of factors that have changed the nature of this experience and increased the number of teenagers undertaking it (Gillespie et al., 1991; Irwin, 1995; Bartsch, 2002; Bell and Crilley, 2002). At one time the rites of passage of young adults in Australia took the form of debutante balls.

> So yes you still have your debutante balls in the country. They are not as prolific as they used to be when the girls were presented to the Mayor or to the Bishop. That's why they were called coming out balls because this is a person now. As a young woman who was able to be married I suppose is the main part. I tell you if you go back further its a

recognition that this person has finished their schooling and is looking for suitors to get married. (Respondent 1)

However, the debutante ball was overtaken by a number of social and economic changes in the 1960s and 1970s. These changes have been associated with the 'baby boom' after the Second World War, a term describing an increase in fertility rate in countries such as Australia, the USA and Canada during the period 1946–1962 (Light, 1988; Moses, 1999; Anisef and Axelrod, 2001). This baby boom resulted in a demographic peak in the population profiles of the developed world, with far-reaching implications for many of the social services offered by these Governments. This 'baby boom' generation entered secondary school between 1960 and 1976 and offered the potential to increase the numbers of high school-leavers. Additionally, the changes may be associated with the introduction of the contraceptive pill into the Western world.

At the same time there was an increasing emphasis on higher education by governments in Australia. Due to rapid technological and scientific advancement after 1945, there was a demand for increased numbers of workers with special skills along with a greater percentage of the population in clerical, administrative and professional positions (Logan and Clarke, 1984). This is reflected in the growth of student numbers in Year 12 in Queensland.

The school-leavers of the 1970s entered a social climate far more liberal and permissive than that of their parents. The 'swinging sixties' and the later protest movements against Vietnam in the late 1960s and early 1970s (Baker, 1992) are indicative of a changing society. Other indicative trends in Australian society were the first women's liberation organization formed in Sydney and Adelaide in 1969, the publication of *Portnoy's Complaint* in 1970 despite censorship laws, and also in 1970 an organization called 'Campaign against Moral Persecution' (CAMP), was founded to promote homosexual law reform. These changes in permissiveness were symbolized by the increase in display of long hair among teenage males.

These social changes were further compounded by two other events in the early 1970s. First, the age of majority in Australia was reduced from 21 to 18 in 1973, and secondly, free tertiary education was introduced in 1974 as a policy initiative of the Whitlam Federal Labour Government. One consequence of the first was to reduce the drinking age from 21 to 18 years and the effect of the second was to increase the affordability of university education. Taken together, these events are considered to have led to a large and increasing pool of Year 12 students not immediately occupied in seeking work after completing Year 12 and who were more likely to experiment with previously 'forbidden' activities. Additionally, these Year 12 students completed school in a social environment where the thrill of the debutante ball had faded.

However, these changes do not explain why Schoolies Week became associated with the Gold Coast in particular. This is discussed in the next section.

Schoolies Week on the Gold Coast

There were a number of factors that predisposed the Gold Coast to be the primary location of Schoolies Week. The Gold Coast in the 1960s was already an important holiday destination for Queenslanders and increasingly for the interstate market. Part of its attraction was the association of the Gold Coast with sexual freedom. The Gold Coast has a history of association with marginal sexual behaviour. One early entrepreneur, Bernie Elsey, built the Beachcomber hotel in 1956. At the Beachcomber, he introduced 'pyjama parties' as an activity for his guests and they became very popular. These dances ran for around 12 months until a woman wrote to a Brisbane newspaper complaining that it was immoral for teenagers to dance in pyjamas at a holiday hotel (Elliott, 1980, p. 99). However, by this time, the Gold Coast had developed a reputation. The Gold Coast also hit the headlines in the 1950s when fashion designer Paula Stafford popularized the bikini on Surfers Paradise beaches and again associated the Gold Coast with an image of liberal sexuality.

For young people, the Gold Coast in the 1970s had an additional attraction. It was strongly associated with beach culture (Lencek and Bosker, 1998). The beach was popularized as the 'centre of the world' for teenagers in the popular literature.

> It was the only thing that mattered to Gabrielle Carey and Kathy Lette's 1970 surfie chicks in Puberty Blues: 'Rain, snow, hail, a two-hour wait at the bus stop, or being grounded, nothing could keep us from the surf. Us little surfie chicks, we flooded onto the beach. We flooded onto the beach.'

(Drew, 1994, p. 106)

Surfing and surfing music were associated with a revolution in teenage habits and activities.

> A local surfing culture developed on the Gold Coast based on a mix of rock n' roll music from the United States, beach parties and teenage revolt. 'Gidget goes Hawaiian' in 1959 and Patricia Thompson as 'Little Pattie' pioneered a new outdoors model for the popular girl stereotype. Both showed how the young in Australia could get it together and have fun. Surfing and surfing music caused a revolution in teenage habits.

(Drew, 1994, p. 113)

This again highlights that the growth of 'countercultural' values, of 'doing your own thing', anti-authoritarianism, spontaneity, rejection of discipline and the values of the older generation, challenged the existing order in the 1960s and 1970s (Huntsman, 2001, p. 98). Clearly then, the Gold Coast tourism sector has for many years had multiple stakeholders with divergent standards and contradictory goals.

The reduction in the age of majority from 21 to 18 and subsequent reduction of the legal drinking age had an impact of the Gold Coast youth market as well. Up to the 1960s, the Gold Coast had later hotel drinking hours (till 10 p.m.) than other areas such as New South Wales, adding to the attraction of the Gold Coast (McRobbie, 2000, p. 123). The reduction in drinking age meant that drinking venues were able to access a larger youth mar-

ket. Drinking at the Broadbeach Hotel Beer Garden and Public Bar became popular with 17–18-year-old youths especially since at the time liquor licensing laws were not well enforced. Alexander McRobbie, a historian and journalist of long standing confirmed on the Gold Coast: '"Schoolies" started around the Broadbeach Hotel which had offered student packages and was in financial problems in late 1974' (20 November 2001, personal communication).

The Party

In the early 1970s, the Gold Coast was a major venue for youth activities related to the beach and drinking. The primary origin of these youths was Brisbane and surrounding areas with some interstate holidaymakers as well. This was facilitated by the availability of family 'weekenders' on the Gold Coast owned by Brisbane residents who tended to have above average income. Because of this, after completion of Year 12 many students in the 1970s holidayed on the Gold Coast. Thus during this period, the Gold Coast developed as a place for youths to holiday but this appears to have been a spontaneous and unorganized activity.

However, a number of people interviewed in this research claim to have been involved in the creation of Schoolies Week as a mass event. KK, a solicitor and writer, who lives on the Gold Coast asserts that a series of beach parties in and around houses in Broadbeach during the period from December 1974 to January 1975 led to the first Schoolies party. This involved a group of school students from private schools in Brisbane who had completed Year 12 in 1974 and were holidaying at a friend's 'weekender'. KK also provided the names of two other people who also attended these parties: JN (a Brisbane-based biologist) and DC (a Brisbane-based solicitor and law firm partner). I also spoke independently to a woman on the Sunshine Coast who provided support for the information provided by KK, JN and DC.

In 1974, KK had attended a number of private schools in south-east Queensland and had an extended network of friends and acquaintances. This group of friends all finished secondary school in 1974. In November and December 1974, KK, JN and DC and a group of others who had a common interest in surfing were staying in a house on the beach at Broadbeach in Hedges Avenue owned by JN's mother. Broadbeach is located about 4 km south of Surfers Paradise on the Gold Coast. Mrs N is described as 'ahead of her time' and a 'liberal woman'. She allowed the group of Year 12 students to use her house on the Gold Coast with little or no adult supervision, which was quite unusual for the times.

A number of parties were held over the 1974/75 Christmas break, and in the two subsequent years, the parties again took place regularly right through the year. During this time other Year 12 students still at school found out about these parties and began to attend. This may be interpreted as the process of diffusion of an innovation occurring (Rogers, 1983). Diffusion of an innovation occurs within a social system through communication between members. As might be expected, the idea of a great party at the beach was tremendously exciting and the news spread quickly across a group of high school students who knew each other through sports, parties and other social interaction.

Soon students were renting houses in the area in order to join in what became a larger celebration. Over that time numerous students from other private schools became involved. KK attended similar celebrations between 1975 and 1979 after which he did not feel himself part of the 'scene' anymore. However, by 1979 the tradition of Year 12 students drinking and celebrating over the Christmas period was well established.

The tradition of attending became commonly known amongst people leaving Brisbane schools and interviews conducted with school-leavers from 1982 and 1984 support this (S1 and S2). Christian outreach groups such as 'Rosies' became involved in the mid-1980s as a result of the growing reputation of Schoolies Week. Rosies was formed when one priest was told of the emergent festival by parents.

When Father PC was ordained in Melbourne, he came up to Queensland (in the mid-80s) and was teaching at Iona College. Parents used to come to him and say we don't want our kids going down to 'Schoolies' because of the reputation that it had at this time. (R1)

As a result, there appears evidence to indicate that a series of parties among teenagers during 1974–1979 was a trigger for the evolution of Schoolies Week. The early Schoolies Week was not an organized and commercial event. Instead it was a spontaneous group activity over an extended period that developed through a process of communication and diffusion into a cultural event, part of the structure of the youth 'rite of passage'.

Commercialization of Schoolies Week on the Gold Coast

The growth of student numbers attending this unorganized Schoolies Week continued in the 1980s and by 1989 students in Sydney were travelling to the Gold Coast. At that time the founder of Sports Break Travel was a tourism operator who sold holidays to the sports market, specifically 'End of Season Footy Trip' package holidays to Australian Rules football teams in Sydney. In 1989, his dentist asked him during a 'check-up' if he could arrange a holiday for his teenage son. This was because by this time, accommodation providers on the Gold Coast were actively avoiding providing accommodation to 'Schoolies'. Accommodation operators considered Schoolies poor tenants because they often 'wrecked' their rooms, were noisy and would invite others into their rooms to sleep. However, because his company Sports Break Travel had access to a bank of accommodation previously providing accommodation for 'rowdy' groups of footballers, he was able to provide accommodation for Schoolies (O1).

Schoolies proved to be a growth market for Sports Break Travel and a separate company was started, Break free Holidays, focused on the Schoolies market. This company has proved successful and the sales of Schoolies Week accommodation and later, packages including entertainment, increased as shown in Fig. 5.1. Over the 1980s Schoolies became focused on Surfers Paradise since most of the

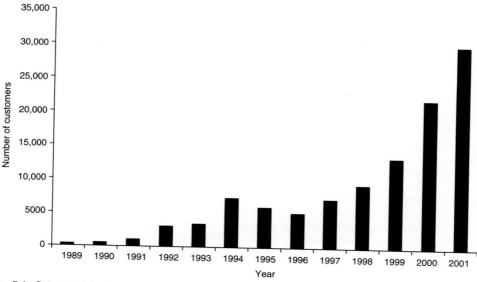

Fig. 5.1. Sales of Schoolies accommodation by Breakfree Holidays, 1989–2001. Source: Breakfree Holidays.

commercial accommodation was there. For the same reason most of the accommodation offered by Breakfree Holidays was located in Surfers Paradise.

After 1991, Breakfree Holidays began to advertise in New South Wales and Victoria. However, interstate sales increased slowly. In 1995, Schoolies Week received significant negative publicity due to a civil disturbance in Cavil Mall purportedly caused by drunken 'Schoolies'. Following this, the GCCC became much more active in the planning and management of Schoolies Week. In 1996, the GCCC provided entertainment for Schoolies Week and in 1997 a GCCC Schoolies Week officer was appointed. Thereafter, Schoolies Week was increasingly organized, an official media spokesman provided by the GCCC and numerous innovations introduced to reduce harmful behaviour by 'Schoolies'. In 2001, a competitor to Breakfree, Teenbreak, began selling Schoolies Week packages.

The Schoolies Week festival has become a focus for State Education, Health and Police Departments who provide educational material about Schoolies Week in schools across Queensland. One particular problem associ-ated with Schoolies Week is predatory sexual behaviour by older males. In 2001, Schoolies Week was estimated to be worth AUS$12.5 million in direct expenditure in a study conducted as part of this thesis (Raybould and Scott, 2001, 2003).

A Government Review

The Schoolies Week festival was characterized by a number of incidents including some violence. In the major Queensland daily newspaper, Schoolies Week was described as 'an orgy of violence and stupidity' (*Courier Mail*, 6 January 2003). Many commentators indicated that most of these incidents appear to have been perpetrated by a number of older non-school-leavers. After the 2002 festival, the Queensland Government undertook to review Schoolies on the Gold Coast. This review involved public consultation in February 2003 and evoked considerable public comment and divergent opinion. Interestingly, there was little involvement of school-leavers in these discussions.

Discussion

The history of Schoolies on the Gold Coast raises a number of issues related to the topic of this book. The recent history of the festival indicates that Schoolies Week has developed as a commercial festival and thus should be subject to better management. However, the emergent purpose of Schoolies Week was as a celebration and this has traditionally involved drinking and some deviant behaviour. Indeed, the festival developed on the Gold Coast in a fashion similar to other examples of then deviant behaviour found on the Gold Coast over the last 50 years. The management of the festival to quality standards imposed by a local council or the State Government challenges this 'reason for existence'. The festival is a 'rite of passage' and celebration of independence and adulthood. It exists because trends in wider society have changed the nature of this transition and eliminated some prior alternatives.

For policymakers the difficulties of Schoolies Week relate to enforcement of standards. The issue of management of the festival arose from problems of crime and violence. In closed venues such as stadia and concert halls there is some control of participants. However, in Schoolies Week, the activities take place in common areas such as the city mall or on the beach. Here, visitors who are not Schoolies have right of access. Additionally, much of the alcohol consumption and unruly behaviour by Schoolies occurs in apartment rooms or in hotels.

For tourism operators on the Gold Coast, Schoolies Week occurs in a traditional low occupancy period and so is useful economically. However, there is also some evidence that the activities of Schoolies Week are impinging on the wider image of the Gold Coast as a family holiday destination. Also there is considerable variation in the benefit derived from Schoolies Week by different types of operators. Tour operators and more expensive restaurants derive little income from Schoolies while apartments and hotel operators are able to charge higher prices to a captive market.

For the community of the Gold Coast, Schoolies is a festival attended by local school-leavers as well as by visitors from other parts of Queensland and interstate. The local community has responded to the growth of Schoolies through both local government and volunteer programmes. The Gold Coast City Council provides a programme of activities for Schoolies and also organizes several hundred volunteers to provide support and help to distressed Schoolies.

So how does a tourist destination manage such issues? Clearly there are social values and commercial interests involved as well as issues of crime and police enforcement. This chapter highlights these issues in order to focus attention on the nature of destination management and development of tourism quality standards that appear to differ from the more distinct and clear-cut issues faced by most commercial hospitality or tourism enterprises. Quality management requires careful specification of and conformation to standards but the issue is whose standards?

Schoolies Week is an interesting case and would benefit from longitudinal research to examine the impact of any new government policy introduced. More generally, it raises the issue of development of quality standards for destinations. In this chapter, issues related to the experience of one type of visitor have been discussed. The Gold Coast is one of Australia's largest holiday destinations and receives many other types of visitors, both domestic and international. Developing quality standards for such heterogeneous travellers is a topic requiring further research.

References

Anisef, P. and Axelrod, P. (2001) Baby boomers in transition: Life-course experiences of the 'class of '73'. In: Marshall, V.W., Heinz, W.R., Kruger, H. and Verma, A. (eds) *Restructuring Work and the Life Course*. University of Toronto Press, Toronto, pp. 473–488.

Baker, A. (1992) *What Happened When: A Chronology of Australia from 1788.* Allen & Unwin, Sydney.

Ballard, R., Curd, D. and Roche, A. (1998) The meaning, madness and the magic of 'Schoolies Festival'. Paper presented to APSAD National Conference, Sydney.

Bartsch, P. (2002) Rite of passage. *Courier Mail*, 22 August, p. 15.

Bell, B. and Crilley, G. (2002) An application of the CERM performance indicators program to benchmarking in the Australian caravan and tourist park sector. Paper presented to CAUTHE conference: Tourism and Hospitality on the Edge, Bureau of Tourism Research, Perth.

Curd, D. (1997) *Alcohol, Safety and Major Public Events.* Queensland Police Service, Brisbane.

Drew, P. (1994) *The Coast Dwellers.* Penguin Books, Ringwood, Victoria, Australia.

Elliott, J. (1980) *Southport-Surfers Paradise.* Gold Coast Publications, Southport, Australia.

Faulkner, B. (1999) *Economic Impact of 'Schoolies' on the Gold Coast Economy.* Centre for Tourism and Hotel Management, Griffith University, Gold Coast, Australia.

Gillespie, A., Davey, J., Sheehan, M. and Steadson, D. (1991) Thrills without spills: the educational implications of research into adolescent binge drinking for a school based intervention. *Drug Education Journal of Australia* 5(2), 121–127.

Huntsman, L. (2001) *Sand in our Souls: The Beach in Australian History.* Melbourne University Press, Melbourne.

Irwin, S. (1995) *Rites of Passage: Social Change and the Transition from Youth to Adulthood.* UCL Press, London.

Leiper, N. (1990) Partial industrialisation of tourism systems. *Annals of Tourism Research* 17(4), 600–605.

Lencek, L. and Bosker, G. (1998) *The Beach: The History of Paradise on Earth.* Viking Pengiun, New York.

Lewis, R.C. and Booms, B.H. (1983) The marketing aspects of service quality. In: Berry, L., Shostak, G. and Upah, G. (eds) *Emerging Perspectives on Services Marketing.* American Marketing Association, Chicago, Illinois, pp. 99–107.

Light, P.C. (1988) *Baby Boomers.* W.W. Norton, New York.

Logan, G. and Clarke, E. (1984) *Education in Queensland: A Brief History.* Department of Education, Queensland, Brisbane.

McRobbie, A. (2000) *20th Century Gold Coast People.* Gold Coast Arts Press Centre, Surfers Paradise, Australia.

Moses, N. (1999) Born at the right time: a history of the baby boom generation. *Canadian Review of Sociology and Anthropology* 36(1), 145–147.

Raybould, M. and Scott, N. (2001) *Schoolies' Week Gold Coast 2001: Report of The Results of a Visitor Survey and Estimation of Economic Impacts.* Cooperative Research Centre for Sustainable Tourism, Griffith University, Gold Coast, Australia.

Raybould, M. and Scott, N. (2003) School's out forever: A study of the Gold Coast 'Schoolies' festival. In: McCabe, V. and Hobson, P. (eds) *Proceedings of the CAUTHE Annual Conference Riding the Wave of Tourism and Hospitality Research.* CAUTHE, Coofs Harbour, Ipswich, Australia.

Rogers, E.M. (1983) *The Diffusion of Innovations*, 3rd edn. Free Press, New York.

USA Student Travel (2002) Graduation Week. *USA Student Travel*.

Winchester, H.P.M., McGuirk, P.M. and Everett, K. (1999) Celebrations and control: Schoolies Week on the Gold Coast Queensland. In: Teather, E. (ed.) *Embodied Geographies: Spaces, Bodies and Rites of Passage.* Routledge, London.

Wyn, J. and White, R. (1997) *Rethinking Youth.* Allen & Unwin, Sydney.

Zeithaml, V.A. and Bitner, M.J. (1996) *Services Marketing.* McGraw-Hill, New York.

6 Tiscover – Development and Growth

Dimitrios Buhalis,[1] Karsten Kärcher[2] and Matthew Brown[3]
[1]University of Surrey, UK; [2]Tiscover AG Travel Information Systems, Austria;
[3]Tiscover AG, Austria

Explaining Destination Management Systems

Destinations emerge as amalgams of products, facilities and services that satisfy the need for travelling and generate the motivation to visit. Destinations, therefore, comprise the 'total tourism product' or the 'total travel experience'. Managing destinations is a really difficult task that requires bringing all local actors and stakeholders together. Planning, management, marketing and coordination of destinations are being undertaken by either the public sector (at national, regional or local level) or partnerships between stakeholders of the local tourism industry. They undertake mass media advertising; provide advisory services for consumers and the travel trade; produce and distribute brochures, leaflets and guides both at destinations and at the places of origin of the tourists; and finally they have the strategic responsibility of the entire destination (Mill and Morrison, 1985; Cooper, et al., 1998).

Information communication technologies (ICTs) gradually penetrate the entire range of strategic and operational management of the tourism industry and destinations are not an exemption (Buhalis, 2003). In the last 10 years destination management organizations (DMOs) have gradually been realizing the potential opportunities emerging through ICTs and use technology in order to improve their function and performance as well as for communicating their marketing message globally (Buhalis, 1997). Both technological enablers and demand drivers propel the development and realization of destination management systems (DMSs) around the world.

DMSs typically include information on attractions and facilities and often incorporate the ability to undertake some reservations. DMSs are usually managed by DMOs, which may be private or public organizations, or a combination of both. DMSs provided new tools for destination marketing and promotion, as they use ICTs to disseminate information and to support a reservation function for products and facilities for specific destinations. There are many definitions, but in essence a DMS is a collection of computerized information about a destination, that is interactively accessible. Gradually DMSs moved to transactions and e-commerce, enabling local organizations to accept bookings through a DMS. There is an increasing literature on DMSs, although there is still limited agreement on the role and functionality of a DMS (Archdale et al., 1992; Vlitos-Rowe, 1992; Buhalis, 1993, 1994, 1995, 1997, 1998; Sheldon, 1993, 1997; Archdale, 1994; O'Connor and Rafferty, 1997; Cano and Prentice, 1998; Frew and O'Connor, 1998, 1999; Pollock, 1998a,b, 1999; Wöber, 1998; WTO, 1999, 2001).

This case study addresses a number of service management areas. It demonstrates how emerging ICT solutions facilitate the e-commerce in the tourism. Tiscover is an innovative service management as it is addressing a number of markets and stakeholders both in the forms of business to consumer (B2C) and business to business (B2B). As an aggregator and retailer of tourism products for the destinations it covers, Tiscover provides a wide range of information and services to the public. As a distributor, it enables tourism suppliers to promote their products directly to the consumer and also to other intermediaries through onward distribution. It also allows DMOs to distribute information and augment their service and products influencing consumer choice. Tiscover also supports backward distribution by feeding products in other web portals and therefore it supports B2B service management with its partners that procure and represent tourism products through Tiscover.

The Strategic Role of Destination Management Systems

ICTs, and DMSs in particular, can support destinations to strengthen their competitiveness as they enhance the ability of destinations to satisfy the information and reservation needs of individual and institutional buyers efficiently. This is achieved by providing appropriate and accurate information online and by developing supplementary distribution channels for local tourism products, which become critical for the destination's future attractiveness (Buhalis, 2003).

A number of DMSs are now online and there are considerable benefits evident. World Trade Organization (WTO, 1999, 2001) suggests that the major advantages of the Internet for destinations are to:

- increase business for the destination and the local suppliers;
- generate revenue for the DMO, through reservations and value added services;
- improve communications and relationships with both individual travellers and targeted groups;

- reduce costs associated with communications as well as printing, mailing and distributing brochures;
- create good public relationships with/for the destination, the DMO and other local organizations.

The strategic management and marketing of destinations resides with public tourist organizations, namely, National and Regional Tourism Boards. Naturally, therefore, the majority of the DMS developments hitherto have been led by public tourist organizations. DMSs facilitate this function by administrating a wide range of requests and by providing information to an ever increasing tourism supply, in an efficient and appropriate way. E-commerce also emerged, with a number of DMSs moving to fully transactional and functional websites that can support the entire range of purchasing requirements on a B2B and B2C basis. Destinations can also take advantage of the database marketing techniques, by identifying and targeting profitable market niches and by tailoring market-driven products for particular customers.

Thus, ICTs provide a way to improve the accessibility of, and the quantity and quality of information on the destination's facilities while they present travellers with options in minimizing their search costs (Sheldon, 1993). Moreover, at the organizational level, DMSs provide the strategic infostructure for DMO to coordinate their activities. They provide tools to distribute information and bring together all stakeholders in a networked environment. DMSs therefore emerge as the strategic tools that support the interface between destination tourism enterprises (including principals, attractions, transportation and intermediaries) and the external world (including tour operators, travel agencies and ultimately consumers) (Buhalis, 2000, 2003).

In the 1990s, a number of DMSs gradually emerged for destinations around the world. Tiscover in Austria and Gulliver in Ireland led these developments and gradually other destinations including Singapore, Australia, Holland and Jersey followed their example. The following paragraphs explain the development of Tiscover as one of the world leaders in the DMS world. Interestingly Tiscover has adapted a dual role, namely a traditional DMS for the Tyrolean Tourism Board and also a technology/software supplier/application service provider for other destinations in Austria and overseas.

Tiscover's Background and Development

The Travel Information System (TIS) GmbH was formed in 1991 to promote tourism in the Tyrol region of Austria. TIS was first launched on the Internet in February 1995 as one of the first-ever travel websites. Tiscover became a publicly listed company (Tiscover AG) in 2000, a year which also saw the launch of Tiscover's WAP service, offering accommodation bookings across mobile phones.

The Tiscover portals allow consumers to research destinations the way they choose. The portals feature in-depth tourist information for each destination and country, currently providing content on over 3200 tourist regions, towns and cities. They offer at-a-glance guides to top tourist attractions and cultural events, coupled with real-time online bookings and reservations for thousands of accommodation providers. Tiscover AG shareholders are the State of Tirol (90%), the Bank

of Austria (3%), Bayerische Hypo- und Vereinsbank AG (1%) and Swarovski AG (6%), a multinational precious stones manufacturer. Tiscover now operates portals in several countries with a particular focus at present on Germany, Austria, Switzerland, Italy and the UK, with further countries to join.

Tiscover is one of the leading DMS providers, operating the world's largest family of destination portals. Rated one of the top travel websites, Tiscover has developed its brands in Europe, attracting partnerships with market dominating Internet Service Providers (ISPs), AOL and T-Online. It also established partnerships with key travel portals, including ebookers.com, HolidayAutos, Avis, Travelchannel.de, Start.de and Lycos.

The system gradually establishes a family of destination tourism portals operated in partnership with a number of central European DMOs. The Tiscover partner sites include the country portals www.tiscover.com, www.tiscover.de, www.tiscover.ch and www.tiscover.at. In addition to the Tiscover country portals, where all partners cooperate, each destination can also present itself independently, using identical technology but appearing with a completely different look and feel (e.g. www.austria.info (Fig. 6.1 left) vs. www.tiscover.at (Fig. 6.1 right) and www.tirol.at vs. www.tiscover.at/tirol). This enables them to reinforce their branding and maintain their individuality.

Fig. 6.1. Comparison of www.austria.info and www.tiscover.at.

Hence, Tiscover is creating a community-based approach to tourism marketing that encourages healthy competition within a framework of cooperation. This 'co-opetition' allows destination-marketing organizations to establish and position themselves without the hefty costs associated with building a technical system and an online user base and brand from scratch. This is an example of co-opetition at its best, as system and online marketing and distribution costs and risks are shared, but the unique identities of the destinations are preserved.

Figure 6.2 highlights the entire range of stakeholders, customers and suppliers of Tiscover and demonstrates that the system is emerging as an infostructure for destination-based information. At the same time Tiscover emerges as both a technology supplier and a new type of intermediary, empowering B2B and B2C transactions.

Technological Innovation

Tiscover operates a system with over 100 servers located in the data centre. In the field of hardware, Tiscover relies on SUN Microsystems and Compaq including:

- server with SUN Solaris, Linux, MS Windows XP/2000 and NT;
- over 100 SUN and Compaq servers;
- SUN 6800 Fire as database server (up to 24 processors);
- a total of about 100 GB RAM;
- 2 terabyte disk space;
- storage area network;
- redundant systems.

More redundant systems are operated for the Tiscover Office Management tools:

- Router (Cisco Router 3640);
- Firewall (Cisco Secure Pix Firewall, Checkpoint Firewall-1);
- Load balancing system;
- Web server (Apache, iPlanet, MS IIS);
- Application server with Macromedia JRUN and/or Navision Axapta.

For the OM tool Address/CRM, Microsoft Navision (Damgaard) Axapta's process logic was used and the software modified to meet the demands of the tourist marketplace.

Tiscover's database system for Office Management is an Oracle 8i Enterprise Server which is hosted on a SUN Fire 6800. SUN Fire's SPARC3 processor and Solaris operating system provide enhanced performance and scalability. Oracle is the leading seller of database management software and supports even highest data volume transaction rates.

All servers operate on a 24-h/day in the Tiscover data centre. This enables regular system control and maintenance; low cost for operation, IT and EDV experts; top quality and service by Tiscover; and easy data integration into Internet partners (e.g. AOL, T-Online). Advantages: Updates are made in the data centre and not at the customer which reduces costs considerably. Operation in the data centre is only interrupted during maintenance work (updates, etc.) and it is kept to an absolute minimum.

For its DMO partners, Tiscover provides a powerful yet standardized Application Service Provider (ASP) solution to support the marketing and sales processes of DMOs. The decentralized maintenance approach of Tiscover meets the need for constantly updated tourist information and works on the basis of an extranet. Every single tourist information provider, be it a small guest house or a large local tourist office, may update and extend their range of products, inventory, prices, seasons and tourism information directly, 24 h a day. All that Tiscover customers need is a PC with a browser and Internet access. *No further investments are required* in hardware, software, operating systems, Internet servers or firewalls.

The ASP (Application Service Provision) model provides a number of advantages, including:

- low investments in hardware;
- high-performance server and network;
- low operating and maintenance cost, since no regular on-site service is required as with client/server models;
- smooth 24/7 operation;
- problem-free integration of updates without technical adaptations on-site;
- problem-free integration of the client's offers and information into Tiscover's current and future network of marketing partners;

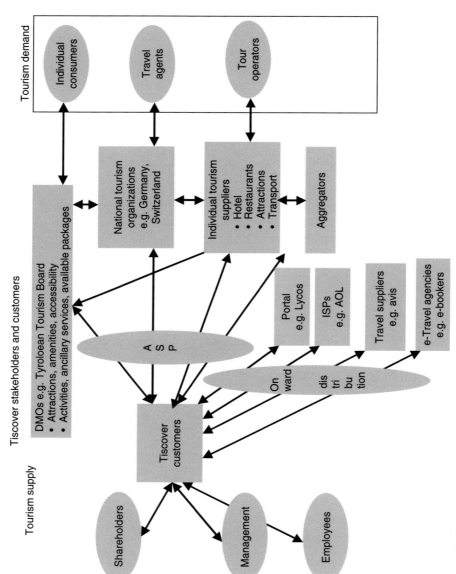

Fig. 6.2. Range of stakeholders, customers and suppliers of Tiscover.

- clients can use the system from various locations and/or everywhere there is Internet access;
- one-source data strategy, using centralized data management based on the industry's leading technology (Sun Solaris mainframe server, Oracle database, Linux operating system).

Every year Tiscover invests millions of euros to offer the most advanced Internet technology, and customers and partners are always and *immediately upgraded* to the most recent system version, without having to purchase system (software, hardware and network) upgrades. In early 2002, the system Tiscover2002 was introduced as the 7th generation of the Tiscover online platform. The new system allows an easier and faster data maintenance and provides individual design options for partner hotels opening up new possibilities in online marketing. Another novelty is a number of integrated overall solutions that can be tailor-made to fit the requirements of tourist organizations and call centres. Tiscover's Office Management tools include the Booking Centre, Room Information and Address/CRM and comprise back-office solutions designed to optimize the internal business processes.

E-commerce and the Growth of Bookings

Marcussen (2005) suggests that (Table 6.1) online travel sales increased by as much as 40% from 2003 to 2004 and reached €18.2 billion in the European market in 2004 – or 7.6% of the market (up from €12.9 billion or 5.5% in 2003). A further increase of about 28% during 2005 to about €23.3 billion may be expected (9.5% of the market). The European online travel market could reach €28.3 billion or 11.3% of the market by 2006. The UK accounted for 37% of the European online travel market in 2004, with Germany in second place at 20%. The ten new EU member countries have been included in the European online travel market and contributed a little under 2% to the total in 2004, after growing quickly during 2004. The direct sellers accounted for 66%

Table 6.1. Trends in overall online travel market size – Western Europe 1998–2006.

Year	Market (billion €)	Internet sales (billion €)	Internet sales in % market	Internet sales increase %
1998	218	0.225	0.1	NA
1999	231	0.8	0.3	255
2000	247	2.5	1.0	211
2001	244	4.9	2.0	97
2002	242	8.6	3.5	75
2003	237	12.9	5.5	51
2004	240	18.2	7.6	40
2005	244	23.3	9.5	28
2006	249	28.3	11.3	22

Note: Each year's actual average exchange rates have been applied for 1998–2004.
Source: Marcussen (2005), available at: http://www.crt.dk/uk/staff/chm/trends.htm accessed on 5 October 2005.

of online sales in the European market in 2004, more than ever before. In 2004, the breakdown of the market by type of service was as follows (with 2003 brackets):

- Airtravel: 57.6% (58.0%)
- Hotels: 16.1% (17.0%)
- Package tours: 15.6% (15.3%)
- Rail: 8.8% (7.7%)
- Rental cars: 1.9% (1.9%)

It is quite evident, therefore, that online bookability is now a crucial part of tourism websites and it is fully functional with Tiscover. The Tiscover booking engine allows direct online booking of products and packages and offers the possibility to make advance payments via the Internet. Tiscover and its partners are thus already present in the growing trend of online transactions in the travel market. The portals also feature weather reports, and feeds from webcams positioned in popular tourist areas. This is of particular importance due to the significance of snow conditions for ski destinations such as Tirol. The live destination portals, in Austria, Germany and Switzerland, are popular, with over 35 million visitors in December 2004. The country portals are estimated to have attracted 55 million online visits and 300 million page views during 2004.

On 13 January 2003, the online booking platform drew record traffic to its sites. With around 1.5 million page impressions Tiscover logged a new traffic record. At peak times, roughly 1000 visits per minute were tracked to Tiscover-branded sites. The reason for this substantial increase in traffic is attributed to the fact that more and more consumers – especially winter guests and last-minute bookers – are doing their travel research and bookings online. The great number of travel-related requests and bookings is also credited to the high market acceptance of Tiscover 2002. With many new functionalities, a consumer-friendly navigation and easy online bookability, Tiscover meets the Web users' demands for in-depth information and customer service.

Table 6.2 and Figs 6.3–6.5 demonstrate the growth of visits to Tiscover as well as reservation requests and page views, demonstrating clearly the growth rate.

SWOT Analysis

Tiscover has a number of strengths and weaknesses and faces several opportunities and threats in the workplace.

Strengths

The key strength of Tiscover is its technology. The risks surrounding the implementation of a new technology in a region are substantially reduced due to the fact that the Tiscover solution will use an existing technology and existing platforms, based on an available technology that is now in its 7th generation and used by

Table 6.2. Summary of visits, page views and bookings/enquiries – Tiscover-branded sites.

Year	2000	2001	2002	2003
Visits (in millions)	29.7	53.5	57	44.6
Page views (in millions)	134	198	225	246
Bookings/ enquiries	533,000	765,000	870,000	1,194,000

thousands of customers. There is no risk of the technology becoming outdated, as a region will automatically benefit from Tiscover ASP-based technology updates at no extra cost. Through close collaboration with local partners, Tiscover also provides customer support and training all year around.

Onward distribution and partner marketing is an additional key strength. The Tiscover model has attracted cooperation with market-dominating ISPs, search engines and travel portals such as AOL, T-Online, ebookers.com, HolidayAutos, Avis, Travelchannel.de, Start.de and Lycos. This allows destination-marketing organizations and suppliers to benefit from even more distribution channels and increased levels of traffic, offering the opportunity to reach new customers, throughout the world. Onward distribution is fast becoming a major determinant of visibility and competitive advantage.

Customers will increasingly demand better and more destination information from the online systems that they use. This should mean that with the technological advances that Tiscover undertakes, and their ability to provide destination information in a consistent manner, they enhance their competitive position.

Weaknesses

The system rigidity of the Tiscover system can be seen as a drawback. The system was built in Austria with the Austrian market in mind. This has proved somewhat problematic in accommodating overseas markets with differing social, economic and geographical profiles. The variations can be designed around the existing system but this takes resources, costs that Tiscover will have to absorb. In addition, as Tiscover is primarily owned by the Tyrolean Tourism Board, it is often seen with scepticism by competing local destinations as they often fear that its parent organization may influence the visibility of other destinations.

Opportunities

The rapid growth on e-tourism provides clear opportunities for Tiscover. The organization is therefore expecting to benefit from:

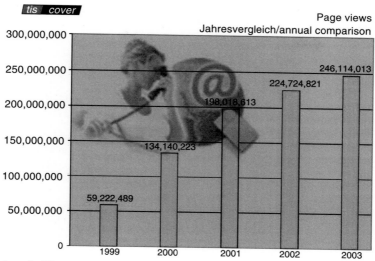

Fig. 6.3. Page views for Tiscover.

- the growth of Internet access across European Union (EU) markets enabling customers to book online either directly on Tiscover or on partner sites;
- the demographic progress of the Internet generation to professional occupations leading to an increase in online spending;
- wireless technological advances leading to an increase in the use of online travel systems;
- the digital interactive television (iDTV) uptake.

In addition, as more DMOs appreciate the emerging need to use ICTs strategically, there is a promising demand for Tiscover services on a global level.

Threats

Conflict

World travel will continue to be affected by political and military actions around the world, in the short and medium term. This may however lead to an increase in EU-based travel for EU citizens, in markets where Tiscover has a strong presence. The use of the Tiscover system will allow

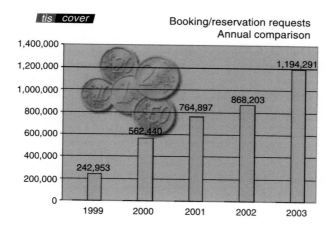

Fig. 6.4. Booking and reservation requests for Tiscover.

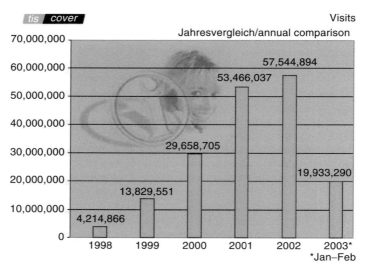

Fig. 6.5. Visits to Tiscover. Source: Tiscover AG (http://www.abouttiscover.com/unternehmen/statistik...
2.html?_h = daten).

accommodation suppliers to adjust their product rapidly to the changing political climate without the cost of expensive brochure changes.

A number of competitors emerge in the marketplace aiming to supply ICT systems to DMOs such as World.Net and Integra compete with Tiscover in the UK market and offer a DMS, which is designed around the requirements of particular destinations. This is, however, a stand-alone solution, and is implemented for specific tourism boards. Whilst it does not address onward distribution and marketing issues. On top of the ICT suppliers, several DMOs decide to develop their own DMS internally.

The Future for Tiscover

The future of Tiscover seems bright and several key strategies are implemented to address that. There exist growing expectations from con-sumers and DMOs in regard to functionality and content. Consumers are demanding ever-more access to better and wider information on a destination. They demand accurate real-time information regarding the destination, commu-nications to it, facilities, events, weather and bookable accommodation, presented in an attractive and user-friendly way. Technological

innovation is also a strategic priority. The development of both the depth and the breadth of the products and destinations featured in Tiscover will ensure that Tiscover should also remain a market leader in the design and sale of travel systems. This is because they innovate and produce systems at the leading edge of technology, with features demanded by cus-tomers and required by DMOs.

International market expansion is critical for Tiscover's future. Tiscover is expanding out of its home market of Austria and already has a presence in Italy, Germany, Switzerland and the UK. Ambitious plans for expansion outside of the EU are showing promise and are evi-dence of Tiscover's drive to gain lucrative over-seas market share.

A number of new products are also being developed currently. Using the technology base that Tiscover has developed, as well as the human capital they have acquired, Tiscover has expanded its booking system projects with the development of Mytraveldream. Mytraveldream is a unique auction system for accommodation that has a database containing over 30,000 accommodation suppliers in 15 countries and is a move to tap into the increasing lucrative mar-ket of last-minute bookings.

Finally, partnerships with onward distribu-tors will be a key to the future success of Tiscover.

Tiscover has successfully sought partnerships with organizations to help better understand markets and tailor products. In addition, it expands its value chain through onward distribution channels. Cooperation already exists between Tiscover and AOL, T-Online, ebookers.com, HolidayAutos, Avis, Travelchannel.de, Start.de and Lycos. Future cooperation with these organizations as well as new partners should see Tiscover continue to gain from these partnerships and to expand its role as an infostructure for all of its stakeholders.

Conclusion

The market will increasingly demand better and more destination information from the online systems, which should mean that Tiscover should remain a market leading product. Tiscover is a well-established enterprise. TIS GmbH was launched in 1991 to promote tourism in the Tyrol region. This maturity is represented by the launch of the 7th generation online platform 'Tiscover2002' in early 2002. The online tourism market is expanding rapidly and this will represent a solid growth in income for Tiscover from their licensed products, commissions on travel product sales and the sale of new systems to DMOs. One can expect further growth in the market when the world political situation stabilizes and economies expand.

Tiscover has also embarked on a drive to win market share in lucrative overseas markets. As technology progresses Tiscover invests heavily to produce the most advanced Internet technology, and offers customers and partners immediate system upgrades whilst developing new concepts in the distribution of accommodation as well as developments in its traditional supply systems. At present Tiscover has a unique business model and aims to be a key player in the e-tourism arena of the future.

Service management is of critical importance to Tiscover if it is to satisfy all its stakeholders and achieve its strategic objectives. By ensuring that customer care is maintained at the highest level, Tiscover has managed to grow dynamically. It is a major priority that both individual consumers, purchasing their tourism products, as well as for professional organizations, that use Tiscover to promote/distribute their products or for enriching their own offering, are recipients of exemplary and honestly priced services. As there is a proliferation of services and offerings in the marketplace, Tiscover has identified service management as an ongoing strive for excellence that will differentiate the company to allow them to enhance their competitiveness.

References

Archdale, G. (1994) Non European initiatives and systems. In: Schertler, W., Schmid, B., Tjoa, A. and Werthner, H. (eds) *Information and Communications Technologies in Tourism. Conference proceedings ENTER 1994, Innsbruck 12–14 January*. Spinger-Verlag, Vienna, pp. 56–63.

Archdale, G., Stanton, R. and Jones, G. (1992) *Destination Databases: Issues and Priorities*. Pacific Asia Travel Association, San Fransisco, California.

Buhalis, D. (1993) Regional integrated computer information reservation management systems as a strategic tool for the small and medium tourism enterprises. *Tourism Management* 14(5), 366–378.

Buhalis, D. (1994) Information and telecommunications technologies as a strategic tool for small and medium tourism enterprises in the contemporary business environment. In: Seaton, A. (ed.) *Tourism-The State of the art: the Strathclyde Symposium*. John Wiley & Sons, Chichester, UK, pp. 254–275.

Buhalis, D. (1995) The impact of information telecommunication technologies on tourism distribution channels: implications for the small and medium sized tourism enterprises' strategic management and marketing. PhD thesis, Department of Management Studies, University of Surrey, Guildford, UK.

Buhalis, D. (1997) Information technologies as a strategic tool for economic, cultural and environmental ben-
    efits enhancement of tourism at destination regions. *Progress in Tourism and Hospitality Research*
    3(1), 71–93.
Buhalis, D. (1998) Strategic use of information technologies in the tourism industry. *Tourism Management*
    19(3), 409–423.
Buhalis, D. (2000) Marketing the competitive destination of the future. *Tourism Management* 21(1),
    97–116.
Buhalis, D. (2003) *eTourism: Information Technology for Strategic Tourism Management*. Prentice-Hall,
    London.
Buhalis, D. and Laws, E. (2001) *Tourism Distribution Channels*. Continuum, London.
Cano, V. and Prentice, R. (1998) Opportunities for endearment to place through electronic visiting: WWW
    homepages and the tourism promotion of Scotland. *Tourism Management* 19(1), 67–73.
Cooper, C., Fletcher, J., Gilbert, D., Shepherd, R. and Wanhill, S. (1998) *Tourism: Principles and Practice*.
    Longman, London.
Frew, A. and O'Connor, P. (1998) A comparative examination of the implementation of destination mar-
    keting system strategies: Scotland and Ireland. In: Buhalis, D., Tjoa, A.M. and Jafari, J. (eds)
    *Information and Communications Technologies in Tourism. ENTER 1998 Conference
    Proceedings*. Springer-Verlag, Vienna, pp. 258–268.
Frew, A. and O'Connor, P. (1999) Destination marketing system strategies: refining and extending an assess-
    ment framework. In: Buhalis, D. and Scherlter, W. (eds) *Information and Communications
    Technologies in Tourism. ENTER 1999 Conference Proceedings*. Springer-Verlag, Vienna,
    pp. 398–407.
Marcussen, C.H. (2005) Trends in European Internet distribution of travel and tourism services. Available at:
    http://www.crt.dk/uk/staff/chm/trends.htm accessed 5 October 2005.
Mill, P. and Morrison, A. (1985) *The Tourism System: An Introductory Text*. Prentice-Hall, Upper Saddle
    River, New Jersey.
O'Connor, P. and Rafferty, J. (1997) Gulliver-distributing Irish tourism electronically. *Electronic Markets*
    7(2), 40–45.
Pollock, A. (1998a) Creating intelligent destinations for wired customers. In: Buhalis, D., Tjoa, A.M. and
    Jafari, J. (eds) *Information and Communication Technology in Tourism. ENTER 1998 Conference
    Proceedings*. Springer-Verlag, Vienna, pp. 235–247.
Pollock, A. (1998b) New technologies as help for integrated quality management. In: *European Tourism
    Forum. Conference Proceedings*, Vienna, 1–3 July, pp. 78–87.
Pollock, A. (1999) Marketing destinations in a digital world. *Insights*, May, A149–A158.
Sheldon, P. (1993) Destination information systems. *Annals of Tourism Research* 20(4), 633–649.
Sheldon, P. (1997) *Information Technologies for Tourism*. CAB International, Wallingford, UK.
Vlitos-Rowe, I. (1992) Destination databases and management systems. *Travel and Tourism Analyst* 5,
    84–108.
Wöber, K.W. (1998) Improving the efficiency of marketing information access and use by tourist organiza-
    tions. *Information Technology and Tourism* 1, 23–30.
WTO (1999) *Marketing Tourism Destinations Online*. World Tourism Organization, Madrid.
WTO (2001) *eBusiness for Tourism: Practical; Guidelines for Destinations and Businesses*. World
    Tourism Organization, Madrid.

7   Co-branding in the Restaurant Industry

Maryam Khan
Howard University, Washington, USA

Introduction

Branding has become a powerful marketing force in the hospitality industry. Today branding has become so popular that the concept of a brand has become synonymous with the word 'hotel' or 'fast food' in the minds of the consumers across the global. For example, the chain of hotels and the name 'Hilton' and fast food giant 'McDonald's'. Branding is defined as a name, term, symbol, design or a combination of these factors to position the identity of a product or service in the minds of the consumers. Several types of brands have been identified, e.g. umbrella branding and sub-branding, ingredient branding, family brands, individual brands, proprietary branding and co-branding.

Co-Branding

Definition

Co-branding also called co-location, is the practice of locating two or more brands at one operation. Strategically, co-branding can command more power by bringing in different brands, which have acquired consumer loyalty, recognition, business experience and/or convenience, at one site. Co-branding is a form of cooperation between two or more brands with

significant customer recognition, in which all the participants' brand names are retained.

Types of co-branding

According to Blackett and Boad (1999), co-branding can be of different types. The most common ones include the following:

1. *Value endorsement co-branding* is evident where the level of cooperation is specifically designed to include endorsement of one or both brand values and positioning. The participant companies cooperate because they have, or want to achieve, alignment of their brand values in customer's mind.
2. *Ingredient co-branding* is possible where a brand supplies its product as a component or supplementary branded product. For example, sale of Taco Bell's sauce in retail market and use of Starbucks coffee by United Airlines. The inclusion of the product or the ingredient greatly enhances the value of the product or services provided by one brand.
3. *Complementary competence co-branding* is between two powerful and complementary brands involving a range of tangible or intangible components. For example, this can be between two strong brands like McDonald's and Walmart.

Prerequisites of co-branding

Conditions that contribute to the success of co-branding include: (i) both brands are easy to identify based on their product or trademark; (ii) both brands provide different variety of items, which are considered to be the best value for the price; (iii) there is enough demand for both brand products on a regional, national or international level; (iv) there is a symbiotic relationship between the two brands; (v) brands are compatible and complementary, but not competing with each other; (vi) both brands should have identical personality characteristics; (vii) both brands should bring different products and/or services; and (viii) brands should be aligned vertically and not horizontally. From the consumers' point of view both brands should be considered as united, monolithic entity and not two separate brands running side by side.

Examples of co-branding

Co-branding, because of its various advantages, is becoming very popular in the hospitality industry. Co-branding can be between hospitality and non-hospitality related businesses. It is now becoming common between one or more non-traditional types of businesses such as between retail stores, convenience stores, truck stops, educational institutions, stadiums, airports, hospitals, bookstores, coffee shops and theme parks. The popularity of co-branding is evident by the number of units planned in the restaurant sector alone. Baskin-Robbins and Dunkin' Donuts have plans for at least 1000 sites. Texaco has plans for 500 America's Favorite Chicken restaurants at its service stations. Subway Sandwiches and Salads opened over 1700 outlets in convenience stores, and Taco Bell have over 1500 restaurants in gas stations alone. Other combinations exist between hotels and restaurant businesses. Carlson Hospitality Worldwide has launched triple-branded complexes that fuse its Country Inn and Suites, Italianni's and Country Kitchen concepts at one location. Blimpie International, Baskin-Robbins and Dunkin' Donuts have entered into a co-branding test agreement.

A common example of co-branding is the food/fuel dual concept. McDonald's Corporation signed deals with petroleum companies to develop food and fuel locations. A similar deal was signed between KFC and Chevron Corporation. Within restaurant business, Yum Corporation offers all three of its own sibling brands under one roof, in addition to serving Pepsi drinks, which belongs to its parent company. This provides a variety of menu items, which attracts a larger group of diners, particularly families. For example, KFC, Pizza Hut and Taco Bell offer chicken, pizza or taco items to family members who would prefer different menu items. KFC can be regarded as a destination purchase while Taco Bell brand can be an impulse purchase.

In order to be successful, co-branding requires some type of synergy between brands whether it is in menu, customer base or convenience. Nathan's Famous collaborated with 60 Miami Subs and also serves Arthur Treacher's menu items. Twistee Treat chain wanted to open a unit at an East Coast airport, but needed a menu other than what they had. So they joined with Gourmet's Choice Coffee Company. They both came up with shared menu items containing sandwiches in addition to their menu items. Synergies can also be related to customer demographics. For Taco Time, which is traditionally reported to be more female-skewed business attracted more male customers by co-branding with A & W Restaurants. Similarly, Smoothie King, which attracts a health-conscious customer, attracted other customers when it combined with Maggie Moo's super-rich ice cream business. Some synergies can be based on the seasonal appeal of certain products. For example, Fenders, the frozen custard chain desired to have a concept with year-round appeal since their business is slow during winters. They selected Cousins Subs to complement their sales.

Breyer's Ice Cream Parlor and Oreo Cookies came up with Oreo's Ice Cream, which is another example of co-branding. Yorkshire Global Restaurants, Inc. combined A & W, and Long John Silver's concepts to form a unique co-branded concept. This is considered as a method of stepping into a relatively mature market thereby assuring sales and profit growth. Similarly, Subway Sandwich and Little

Caesars Pizza co-branded together to increase sales. Long John Silver's, a prominently fish food operation teamed with TCBY Enterprises Inc., the ice cream and frozen yogurt chain, and Moxie Java, a coffee chain. Opening a restaurant that combines the three concepts under one roof provides a combination of menu which includes signature items consisting of batter-dipped fish, frozen dessert and upscale coffees. The tripartite operation allows customers to select a meal that includes entrée, dessert and beverage under one roof.

It has become very common for hotel chains to collaborate with full-service restaurant or fast food establishment in the vicinity so that their guests can receive room service deliveries. Also several restaurant chains such as McDonald's and KFC have arrangements to share space inside hotels, providing familiar branded menu items to guests. Similarly Starbucks Coffee is served to Marriott and United Airlines' guests. Putting strong brands together makes co-branding successful and attractive. 'McDonald's 3'n1' restaurant in Lincoln, Nebraska, combines unique dining experience for those who enjoy table service with those who want traditional McDonald's experience. It offers a variety of menu items and conveniences including Sandwich & Platter Shop and Bakery & Ice Cream Shop menus. This restaurant serves breakfast, lunch and dinner. There can be unique and interesting combinations in hospitality co-branding that provides mutual benefits, some examples of which are shown in Table 7.1.

Advantages of co-branding

1. A co-branding deal by collaboration efforts offers the increased possibility of a new source of income. This has been evident even when well-recognized brand names join forces. For example, Subway Sandwich and Little Caesars Pizza reported increased sales up to 100%.
2. Brand entry is possible into new markets in regions or countries where it was not possible to access on solo basis, which were out of reach. Co-branding with a well-established local brand could maximize the chances of success in market penetration. This is true for brands entering countries or regions where there is a strong compatible local brand.
3. Businesses can offer their consumers different promotions, package-deals and other benefits at a reduced cost. Hotels co-branding with airlines, cruise lines, credit card or insurance companies were able to provide added benefits to their customers.
4. Both brands can minimize the expenditure required to enter new markets since the arrangement calls principally for sharing. Going in together can save by merging storage areas, common areas and washrooms. There are other synergies that contribute to cost savings.
5. Two or more companies by going together can avoid certain barriers to restrictions imposed by local laws, state legislation or other obstacles. For example, some places have restriction on the number of new outlets, or have minimum requirements for investment. On these occasions a company may prefer an existing business and go with co-branding. Convenience and grocery stores are good examples since they are already located at choice places and it is easier to go with a restaurant operation at such locations. On the flip side, poor performing locations such as gas stations can benefit by having a brand name restaurant or grocery outlet.
6. It reduces the risks associated with getting into a new market without reducing the rewards or potential return on investment. It amounts to the reduction of the risk for failure. Also, there is a reduction of retaliation from other competitors. When going with an established brand, other competitors will be careful in retaliation to an existing business. An example is the White Castle chain of restaurants in the USA, with a strong reputation for hamburgers. With changes in consumer tastes and responding to the competition they wanted to add a chicken menu item. They could have developed their own, but decided not to, since it would dilute their reputation for hamburgers. Evidently, they decided to co-brand with Church's Chicken brand.
7. Since the investment is comparatively less, the possibility of faster returns exist in co-branding. The new synergy of two well-recognized brands provides for favourable consumer response and instant performance in the marketplace. This may have taken longer with

Table 7.1. Examples of special co-branded operations.

Brand 1	Brand 2	Special/value-added features
Taco Time	Subway and A&W	Combined menu choices; attracted both male and female consumers; increased meal time offerings
Breyer's Ice Cream Parlor	Oreo Cookies	Oreo cookies ice cream – combining two strong product brands
Marriott	Starbucks Coffee	Offering of a popular coffee product by an international hotel chain
Several Hotels	Kinkos	Providing enhanced business services to hotel guests
Choice Hotels International – Econolodge	Proctor & Gamble – Mr Clean	Housekeeping staff gets certification after training – guests consider the hotel chains to have clean, comfortable rooms – franchisees happy with this arrangement
Howard Johnson International	Crayola	Kids Go HoJo and Crayola Kids – Crayola Kids Magazine with four-pack Crayola Crayons to families with kids – give impression of kids and family friendly hotels
KFC	Taco Bell and Pizza Hut	Variety of menu choices – appeal to families with different menu preferences as well as convenience
McDonald's	Disney	Attract children at a major theme park and familiarity with different characters
Le Cordon Bleu	Teflon	Well-known French culinary academy with a leading French cookware manufacturer
TGIFridays	ESPN	TV campaign shows sports anchormen eating at TGIFridays restaurant
New World Coffee & Bagels	Carvel Ice Cream	Match fills in the gap during the seasons and part of the day
McDonald's	Delray Farms Facilities, Inc.	A combination with grocery store providing foods to shopping clients
Dunkin' Donuts	Home Depot	Home improvement workers who visit early morning can start with breakfast
Winchell's Donut House	Lucy's Laundry Mart	Having donuts and coffee while getting laundry
Dunkin' Donuts	Stop & Shop Supermarkets	Attracting shopping customers throughout the day

increased investment in case the brands were going solo.

8. It is relatively easy to get financial help for a co-branded business, since the investment and risks required are relatively low. Financial institutions consider such risks favourably when strong brands are involved. Also, since there are shared expenses, the prospects for getting good interest on loans are possible.

9. There is an enhanced perception of quality when brands combine creatively. For example, a franchise steak house in Ritz Carlton hotels will give the perception of quality since the steak house is associated with a quality hotel brand. For consumers there is an immediate perception of quality associated with familiar brands.

10. One of the greatest benefactors of technology is co-branding. Increased specialization has led to unique collaboration between hospitality businesses and credit cards or reservation systems. One company's investment in technology can benefit other or there can be a mutual sharing of investment in technology.

11. Co-branding can also be used for introducing as well as field-testing an entirely new brand. This can become the preliminary stage for a longer-term marketing plan. Either one or both of the partners may be new trying to test a new market and to gain consumer confidence without investing a lot of resources. This can be a strategy to see how a product and service can survive or compete within existing markets.

12. Co-branding can also be used for the reinforcement of messages provided by advertisement. For example, Subways have an advertising campaign regarding the caloric value of their meals and weight loss. This message is already there and a co-brand can focus on other aspect of their menu or product thereby tagging along to the message that is already conveyed.

13. In oversaturated markets such as fast food restaurants in the USA, co-branding provides another opportunity to introduce existing concepts. When hotels decide to give up their breakfast offering by providing a doughnut or coffee shop within their premises, new locations become available to fulfil that function. An example can be Starbucks or Krispee Donuts outlets found in many hotels.

14. A new concept can emerge by co-branding which can have its own distinct identification. At times when a brand has a lot of 'look alikes' co-branding can provide an opportunity to revamp and emerge as a distinctive new brand.

15. Co-branding can enrich relationships between two brands. Some corporations have benefited by using co-branding to know more about other businesses leading to further cooperation or joint ventures. This can also be true for purveyors of selected equipment or products, which have joined hands with hospitality operations.

16. With collaboration values of two or more brands can be exchanged or adapted. Whether these values are in strategy, marketing, human resources or operations, they can be of mutual benefit.

17. Joint research and development activities can also be facilitated by co-branding. It creates an atmosphere of mutual understanding and respect and can lead to research, which can be beneficial for the co-branded business. Some corporations have large research and development departments, which can be used by co-branded partners.

18. Co-branding provides opportunity for one partner to talk to the consumers of other partner, for example, the collaboration between hotels and car rental companies. Both have access to the consumers and can learn from the likes and dislikes of the consumers.

19. Non-traditional collaboration can take place by co-branding. Thus retailers, super markets, gas stations and restaurants are finding it to be of immense value. Similarly, hospitals, nursing homes, theme parks and attractions, transportation companies, hotels and resorts are coming up with co-branding alliances. More of such alliances will become evident with time.

20. Safety is considered one of the major benefits of co-branding in many locations. Being in the midst of other businesses and having continuous flow of traffic makes these sites to be relatively safe. Traditional restaurants that have experienced problems due to insecurity are finding co-branded locations attractive for future growth.

21. Finally, co-branding can also be used to revitalize a brand, which is in its later stages of life cycle. Restaurants whose concepts need change can try co-branding and enter with a rejuvenated image and concept.

As evident, co-branding provides a lot of opportunities and it is successful if one or more of the above-mentioned advantages are utilized. It is not possible to fully utilize all the benefits but the survival of co-branding depends on the judicial use of these advantages. It mostly depends on how well the brands complement each other and how well they fit into the entire realm of business venture.

Disadvantages of co-branding

Co-branding can be a powerful and useful tool if utilized in a right way. On the other side of the equation, because of improper use it can lead to chronic problems, which are discussed in the disadvantages of co-branding. Co-branding should not be considered a method of getting rewards without any efforts. There are considerable risks to all parties that their brand reputation is at stake and in many instances this can backfire. It all depends on how well suited the partners are. Some of the risks and pitfalls are discussed in the following list:

1. Co-branding should not be used as a method of expecting rapid return on investment. Time should be given for the relationship to build like any other business.

2. The success of co-branding depends on compatibility between the two brands. The culture, attitude and values of both brands should coincide in order to have a successful relationship. Even smaller conflicts and friction points can lead to failures. The desire on part of one brand to have more control can lead to disagreements.

3. Overextending a brand by co-branding can also prove detrimental. As the name indicates, co-branding works well when both brands are compatible for the business. Sometimes brands would like to overextend and get into areas where they do not belong. It was reported that the co-branding between Rally's Hamburgers and Green Burrito did not work well due to their price differential. A person seeking a 99-cent hamburger did not care for a burrito selling for US$3.50. Also, Rally's double drive-through layout encouraged customers to eat in their cars. While it was easy to eat hamburgers in a car, it was awkward to eat burrito dripping all over.

4. Changes in the strategy, positioning or marketing of one brand may have an impact on another. With changes in leadership there may be a significant shift in strategy, which can have an adverse impact on the other brand. Co-branding does not work when intentional or unintentional abrupt shift in relationship is involved.

5. Changes in financial status of one brand or both brands can have an adverse effect on the relationship. Bankruptcies by one brand can have disastrous impact from the business as well as consumer point of view. Failure of one brand to meet its financial targets or goals may lead to abrupt dissolution of co-branding agreement. Other financial problems may be related to how bills will be paid for shared goods, services, cleaning, promotion, etc. Also keeping records using common cash registers can be a sticking point.

6. Mergers and takeovers, which are very common in businesses, can also have an impact on co-branded partners. The brighter side of the mergers and acquisitions is the possibility of buying different brands and combining to form more exciting co-branded products or services. If one partner gets involved in a merger or is a victim of takeover, then this relationship is in jeopardy of continuing. Unfortunately, these are very unpredictable events and can hardly be avoided. It is much more serious if the company taking over is already involved in co-branding with other partners. This leaves limited choices for the existing partner.

7. Public opinion, consumer attitudes and changes in society can all have an impact on one party or the other. For example, the use of beef items by one restaurant brand can lead to protest by consumers thereby affecting the sales of the other co-branded partner.

8. Brand identity and individuality can be lost if co-branding is not followed appropriately. For example, Taco Time and A&W restaurant units share a long counter and cash registers but their signage inside and out gives both names equal weight and importance. Consumers may identify the brands as a hybrid of two brands rather than two brands existing simultaneously. There should be differentiation in marketing aspects including signs, logos, slogans, staff uniforms, colours or other identification features. Co-branding should not result in dilution or disappearance of the identity of original brand. If this happens then it defeats the purpose of co-branding.

9. Brand incompatibility can occur if sibling brands are used. There is a tendency of the owner of several brands to combine two siblings into co-branding. Although this has worked very well for Yum Brands such as Taco Bell, KFC and Pizza Hut to get involved into co-branding this may not work for others. For example, Burger King and Haagen-Daz belonged to the same group of companies. It was not possible to co-brand these two brands since the consumer profiles were entirely different for both these brands. Tapping into an existing consumer base should not be at the cost of taking consumers away from one business or the other. Thus incompatibility of brands can lead to failure of this relationship.

10. There are operational aspects such as deliveries, inventory keeping, incompatible accounting systems and sale of one brand or the other, which may cause confusion and friction.

11. Above all, legal issues may create several problems. When two brands are involved, the legal question as to who will be the host becomes a point of contention.

As in the case of advantages not all disadvantages may be present in co-branded units. So far it has worked very successfully for majority of the operations. Problems reported were minor and mostly related to logistics such as how to share a drive-through, preparation and service issue. Evidently, benefits far outweigh the disadvantages of co-branding.

Research on co-branding

Although there is much published about brands and branding, research related to co-branding is still in the infancy stage. But several reports and articles dealing with co-branding can be found in trade magazines and journals. Attempt is made to illustrate a cross section of the research done in this field as well as some reports related to co-branding.

Of the many ways the branding phenomenon has emerged through the foodservice industry, none has been more widely implemented than co-branding, particularly in the quick-service restaurant (QSR) sector. A study to determine if there is qualitative and quantitative value from co-branding between hotels and restaurants found that hoteliers believe that their guests are more satisfied with a nationally branded restaurant compared to the independent restaurant. It was reported that both hotels and restaurants benefit from an increase in operating performance from co-branding. A hotel can experience increases in average daily rate and occupancy, while a restaurant can gain an average of a 57% increase in revenues. Thus, both operations could benefit greatly from co-branding in terms of profits, revenues, operating efficiencies and customer loyalty, if the strategy is implemented properly (Boone, 1997).

In a study by Hahm (2001), relationships among implicit and explicit requirements and the timing of co-branding entry were reported. It also found that restaurateurs who were not satisfied with prior sales performance were more likely to invest in the co-branding concept. Investors in co-branding ventures were usually satisfied with the performance of their co-branded restaurants.

Pairing up with complementary concepts has a synergistic effect that can cut overhead and maximize traffic and sales. Co-branding offers a concept with a weak day-part a chance to pair up with a concept strong in that time slot, such as Wendy's increasing breakfast sales due to Tim Hortons' Donuts store. With multiple concepts, operators have the ability to please more people, and thus capture more customers (Tasoulas, 2000). With results as good as they are, chains plan to increase co-branding efforts. Many businesses seem to be expanding and co-branding seems to be the way to do it (Bertagnoli, 2000). The success of co-branding, which is a type of cooperation between two or more brands in which participants' brand names are retained, depends upon the creation of a seamless logic running through the offer, which allows the consumer to easily understand the benefits (Blackett and Russell, 1999).

Adding a fast food franchise to an already successful convenience store franchise is becoming more appealing to numerous storeowners, since it was reported that fast food is now the second-most purchased category in convenience stores (Cleaver, 1996). Consumers are particularly attracted to co-branding due to its brand awareness. Price is another consideration when buying co-branded items whether by impulse or destination purchase. Brand awareness and price-fairness concepts were found to play significant roles in the customer-value process (Oh, 2000). Consumers' brand selection process, purchase behaviour and their impact on brand management are least understood in the hospitality literature (Laroche and Parsa, 2000). Many hospitality companies prefer to develop and manage multiple brands for growth purposes (Lewis and Chambers, 1989). Brands with market-share leadership tend to occupy the top group when measured for intention to purchase.

Case Study – McDonald's and Gas Stations

One of the primary examples of co-branding is the alliance between Oil companies and McDonald's restaurant chains. McDonald's have worked with different oil companies including Exxon, Amoco, Mobil and Citgo for co-branding relationship. In light of the above discussion on co-branding, this case study is designed to portray a major co-branding effort between well-known corporations.

History

It was in the early 1990s when McDonald's decided to pioneer a new format for developing a restaurant, convenience store and fuelling facility at one location. It was mainly considered from the point of view of the convenience of the consumer, who can get food, branded fuel and convenience-store items by making one stop. By co-developing the sites or the existing sites, McDonald's was able to accomplish this idea. Although the idea was simple, McDonald's was faced with several challenges including the site and building design, mutually satisfactory business terms, contracts, marketing support systems, construction support, accounting, and so on. All these are important aspects of franchising their business. It was on 6 May 1993 that McDonald's opened its first co-branded unit in collaboration with Texaco, in Arkansas. Consumer enthusiasm and success of this experiment eventually led to the development of more than 400 co-branded units in the USA.

Concept

Brands used are well known to the consumers, who have to stop at the gas stations, whether local or interstate, at all times. It was reported by McDonald's that they received positive feedback from numerous surveys and focus group discussions involving their consumers. The majority of the consumers favoured the idea of McDonald's and gasoline co-branding.

They loved 'one-stop shopping' where they can get food as well as convenience-store items while they stop for filling gas. These locations are easy to get to, easy to use, fast/efficient and saves time. It was also reported that these co-branded sites fit well in small towns where customers not only value the convenience but also perceive its presence as community recognition by the outsiders. In addition, these co-branded units were bringing in business from outside the community in addition to the local business. It was also shown that the customers' cross-purchase utilization of the various businesses at these sites increased dramatically.

The instant recognition of two well-known brands can be a major factor in the success of co-branding. The consistent quality, convenience, cleanliness, comfort and ambience all contribute to the appeal of the co-branded operations at these locations. Customer-satisfaction ratings were reported as very high at co-branded sites, for both the site as a whole and each of the separate businesses. In addition, future repurchase intentions were reported to be very high.

Benefits

Mutual benefits as reported in this chapter were commonly attributed for the win–win situation for McDonald's, oil companies, as well as for the consumers. Other benefits listed by McDonald's include: (i) for urban/suburban concept, each party benefits from leveraged capital, due to shared land, development and construction costs; (ii) considerable savings result in investment and operating costs; (iii) shared operating expenses; (iv) better access to prime estate and the ability to intensify its use; (v) access to well-organized engineering department at McDonald's thereby providing site layouts, building blueprints, interior space planning, code requirements and other needed documents; (vi) proven development process supported by real estate and construction professionals; (vii) combined marketing resources such as advertising at national, regional and local levels; (viii) advertising and promotion help; (ix) complementary day-parts, since gas and convenience store are mostly busy during traffic hours and McDonald's can provide lunch and breakfast traffic; (x) both partners can expect a greater return on their respective investments than in a stand-alone gas station facility; and (xi) through effective marketing each party can potentially benefit from the increased traffic generated by both partners.

Market criteria

McDonald's wanted to work with these oil companies so that they can have successful partnership with them in order to bring their offering to markets, which are considered too small for it to have a free standing restaurant. The market criteria for a co-branded facility are not different from a traditional McDonald's restaurant. They would like to be as close to the customers as possible, whether the consumer is close to home or is travelling on interstate highways. Particularly in rural areas with small population, it was worthwhile for McDonald's to go with co-branding with well-branded partners. The concept developed is very simple and flexible to allow the oil partner to size the convenience store and fuelling facilities to meet the needs of the marketplace. For McDonald's, the concept involved a limited core menu, with a customer seating area and drive-through window service. From the operations point of view, there are two operations working simultaneously at the site. While each operation is independent of the other, operators can and do work together to optimize sales. Cross-marketing promotions help in increasing consumer counts. Market research done by McDonald's identifies which markets will be beneficial. In some instances, the oil partners may consider retrofitting an existing building in conjunction with McDonald's. Both partners work together to create a floor and site plan that allows both to function efficiently. McDonald's already has ready-made floor plans that can be used. McDonald's allows convenience store and restaurant each to offer their own coffee and fountain drinks. McDonald's is tenant, and oil partner provides facilities such as restrooms, HVAC, electrical, parking and yard lights. McDonald's makes contribution for defined leasehold improvements. Normally the lease is for 10–20 years with different 5-year options. Real estate costs are shared between the parties, typically 50/50, based on circumstances and type of co-branded units. The rent is based on an annual minimum, plus a percentage of sales. Convenience is the major determining criteria for selecting new store locations. All costs associated with acquiring, developing and operating the site are shared and split based upon each partner's usage.

Future of Co-branding

Co-branding, particularly in hospitality industry definitely has a bright future. Irrespective of how an economy is doing, businesses will continuously be looking for innovative methods and co-branding seems to be a logical answer. The increasing cost of real estate, the demand for convenience by consumers, increased use of technology, joint ventures, alliances and mergers, will all contribute to the future demand for co-branding. Also service industry is booming worldwide and co-branding has been successfully and extensively tried in this industry. With several major parent companies such as Tricon Global Restaurants owning KFC, Pizza Hut and Taco Bell, co-branding will become a normal way of combining two or more units. In short, co-branding has a potential for further growth and development as reported by Blackett and Boad (1999). Also, it will find applications in 'brand extension' activity. Co-branding can facilitate the worldwide penetration into saturated markets, which may become the faster, economical and safer method of conducting business. Larger retail chains, supermarkets and malls will have more co-branded outlets in the near future. Thus all indications are that co-branding is here to stay.

References

Bertagnoli, L. (2000) The buddy system. *Restaurants & Institutions* 110(29), 79, 82–84.

Blackett, T. and Boad, B. (1999) *Co-branding: The Science of Alliance.* St Martin's Press, New York, 142 pp.

Blackett, T. and Russell, N. (1999) Two brands are better than one: why co-operation makes sense. *Brand Strategy* (September), 8–11.

Boone, J.M. (1997) Co-branding – a preliminary study. *Cornell Hotel and Restaurant Administration Quarterly* 38(5), 34–43.

Cleaver, J. (1996) Teaming up for one-stop convenience. *Franchise Times* 2 December (7), 3–33.

Hahm, S.P. (2001) Co-branding as a market-driven strategic financial investment option in the hospitality industry. PhD dissertation. Virginia Polytechnic Institute and State University, Blacksburg, Virginia.

Laroche, M. and Parsa, H.G. (2000) Brand management in hospitality: an empirical test of the Brisoux-Laroche Model. *Journal of Hospitality and Tourism Research* 24(2), 199–222.

Lewis, R.C. and Chambers, R.E. (1989) *Marketing Leadership in Hospitality.* Van Nostrand Reinhold, New York.

Oh, H. (2000) The effect of brand class, brand awareness, and price on customer value and behavioral intentions. *Journal of Hospitality and Tourism Research* 24(2), 136–162.

Tasoulas, M.A. (2000) Grab your partner: market report on co-branding. *Restaurant Business* (May), 79–88.

8 Airline Service Quality in an Era of Deregulation

Dawna Rhoades, Rosemarie Reynolds
and Blaise Waguespack, Jr
College of Business,
Embry-Riddle Aeronautical University, USA

Introduction

The airline industry, both domestically and internationally, has always been treated as a special case in the world of business, even by individuals and governments that normally espouse the virtues of free markets and deregulation. This special status is based on its importance to national defence, economic development and national pride (Kane, 1998). In times of war, many nations rely on their civilian fleet of aircraft to provide the additional lift capability necessary to deploy troops and equipment as rapidly as possible. Therefore, a healthy, viable domestic system of carriers is considered an essential part of any national defence strategy. Furthermore, while the nature of the relationship between air transportation and national economies is not always clear, the impact of air transportation on economic development cannot be denied. The Air Transport Action Group (2000) reported that the world's airlines carried over 1600 million passengers in 1998 and transported almost 40% of the world's manufactured exports. Worldwide, airlines employed over 28 million people and produced over US$1360 billion in annual gross output. The aviation industry is also a key component of the travel and tourism industry that supported roughly 192 million jobs in 1999 and generated an estimated US$3550 billion in revenue.

Of course, international airlines do more than transport passengers and cargo, the carriers also 'carry the flag' of the respective nations around the world. This factor should not be underestimated as a driver of individual and government perception. When the bankruptcy and subsequent grounding of the Swissair fleet forced the Swiss football team to fly Aeroflot to the qualifying match in Moscow, one article reported this event as a 'further humiliation for the Swiss flag carrier' (Hall *et al.*, 2001).

In spite of these arguments for special status, in the late 1960s and early 1970s, the weight of opinion began to shift away from the tight international and domestic regulation of aviation; domestic deregulation and international liberalization came to be seen as the best means of lowering fares, increasing air traffic and providing consumers with greater choices. In the case presented here, we will explore the reasons behind the move towards deregulation and liberalization, review the effects on airline service quality at both the domestic and the international level, and discuss efforts to address service and safety quality issues in the new cost-conscious environment facing today's airlines.

Changing Domestic Industry

During the 1930s and 1940s, national governments around the world intervened to ensure the development and survival of viable domestic air transportation systems. Whether intervening directly by assuming full or partial ownership of national air carriers, as was common in Asia and Europe, or indirectly through subsidies as in the USA, all governments felt that it was necessary to establish a system of tight regulation in air transportation. Governments, through their designated agencies, allocated routes, established fares, controlled entry and exit into the market and enforced standards on safety and service quality (Sinha, 2001; Rhoades, 2003). In this system of tight domestic and international regulation, carriers had only one avenue for differentiating themselves from competitors – service quality.

By the early 1970s, there were an increasing number of studies that argued that regulation forced competition based solely on service, and thus created fares that in many cases were 50% higher than comparable intrastate (unregulated) fares. In addition, studies suggested that regulation forced carriers to accept uneconomical load factors, raised labour costs, protected inefficient carriers and prevented the establishment of economies of scale that would allow carriers to reduce unit costs (Caves, 1962; Jordan, 1970; Kahn, 1971). In 1978, the USA became the first nation to deregulate its domestic market. New Zealand followed in 1983 and Australia in 1990. The European Union (EU), through a process referred to as liberalization, removed competitive barriers over a period of 10 years through a series of three legislative packages passed in 1987, 1990 and 1993.

Effects of deregulation

The expectation was that deregulation would increase the number of carriers and lower fares in domestic markets. Evidence prior to 2001 indicates that deregulation did not significantly increase the overall number of carriers in the Australian, New Zealand or European markets, although fares did fall in several cases with the entrance of a new carrier. Unfortunately, these new entrants generally did not survive for long (Sinha, 2001). The

Australian market experienced a growth of 66% and an average airfare drop of 41.3% in the year following deregulation, but both numbers have fluctuated in the years since as carriers have started up and failed (Forsyth, 1991). Recent entrants to the Australian market include Impulse Airlines (recently acquired by Qantas), VirginBlue (owned by Richard Branson of Virgin Atlantic) and Australian Airlines (a low-cost subsidiary of Qantas). In Europe, the McKinsey Consulting Company expects that 2001 and 2002 would be a turning point for European low-cost carriers which appeared set to increase their overall share of the intra-European market from 7% to 14% over the next 5 years (Binggeli and Pompeo, 2002). The Boston Consulting Group predicted that German low-cost carriers would achieve a 25% market share on routes to European and German destination in 2003. The low-cost market share of British and French carriers is predicted to be even higher at 55% and 30%, respectively (Flottau, 2003). Overall, low-cost European carriers increased capacity by nearly 50% between mid-2001 and mid-2002 and are set to continue to expand into major carriers' markets where a company like Ryanair may have a seat-mile cost that is half of their major carrier rivals (Sparaco, 2002; Matlack et al., 2003). The volatility of the current business climate in the European airline industry can also be highlighted by recent industry restructuring that began in 2001, which has seen the emergence of 22 new entrants, while a record 40 carriers, many of them small-sized companies, ceased operations (Sparaco, 2002).

In the USA, where the market has experienced the longest sustained period of deregulation, airfares fell an estimated 33% in real terms between 1976 and 1993 in large part due to the number of start-up carriers entering the market. At the same time, over 200 new entrants started up and failed since 1978 in the USA (Rosen, 1995). However, changing market conditions, which preceded the events of 11 September 2001, do not look favourable for new start-ups at this time. With the forces of economic instability, the openness of Internet distribution systems and the pricing information now in the consumer's hands, along with major corporate customers controlling air transport expenses (a major source of airline revenue), airlines face a difficult operating environment that has led to the bankruptcy of at least two major airlines, United Airways and US Airways. While a favourable market position is forecasted for low-cost airlines (Southwest, JetBlue, AirTrans), the US industry will have to undergo a restructuring period to adapt to changing market forces (Velocci Jr, 2002).

Trends in US service quality

The effect of deregulation on airline service quality has not been widely studied and there are few empirical studies examining the pre- and post-deregulation levels of service quality, although there is a general consensus in the USA that service quality has declined significantly (Kahn, 1990). Prior to the 1978 US deregulation of the airline industry, service standards were set by the Civil Aviation Bureau. Delivering quality was a matter of conforming to standards. Since deregulation, defining airline quality has become more problematic. By and large, surveys of frequent flyers have been used by such organizations as the *Frequent Flyer* magazine or Condé Nast to rank airlines on issues considered key to customer satisfaction such as on-time performance, airport check-in, schedule, seating comfort (Glab, 1998). While such surveys are an interesting source of information, it is difficult to compare across surveys or even to examine individual airline performance across time (Rhoades and Waguespack, 2001).

The US Government began publishing the *Air Travel Consumer Report* in 1987. This report includes information on on-time performance, flight problems, denied boardings, fare complaints, mishandled baggage and other forms of customer complaint. One of the first attempts to use these data to examine airline quality was the *Airline Quality Rating* (AQR) report, which was first released in 1991. The AQR was a weighted measure of 19 factors including airline safety measures, service factors (taken from the *Air Travel Consumer Report*) and financial performance measures. This measure was criticized on a number of counts including the negative

weighting it assigned load factor, the failure to address service factors such as seat comfort and prices, and the difficulty in sorting out the effects of safety, service and financial performance on airline quality. The AQR was recently changed to address these concerns (Bowen and Headley, 1999; Rhoades and Waguespack, 2001).

The data reported in this study of service quality also come directly from the *Air Travel Consumer Report*. These data are systematically collected each month from US carriers and can be compared across years. Since the data are reported in raw form, the study has normalized it by the total number of departures recorded for each carrier in that year. Table 8.1 examines the trend for the ten major US carriers. The numbers represent the total number of service problems from the above categories per yearly departures, a measure of service 'disquality' per departure. As the data indicate, service quality improved for the industry as a whole from 1987 to 1993 then began to decline dramatically reaching levels in 2000 that led many in the USA to call for re-regulation of the industry and the passing of 'passenger bill of rights' legislation. While the effort to pass legislation has stalled in the USA, the movement has gained support in Europe with the European Commission (EC) moving forward with legislation, which would increase the compensation levels owed to customers when facing service difficulties, such as denied boardings, is expected to pass in 2003 (Baker and Field, 2003). Evidence from a similar study of service and safety quality conducted on US national and regional carriers found that there is a significant level of variation in service levels within this group of carriers. Some carriers posted service levels better than their major counterparts while others demonstrated a serious inability to achieve even the average service quality level of their peers (Rhoades and Waguespack, 2001).

The two studies cited above deal with basic service, i.e. the ability to ticket passengers correctly, check them in and fly them and their baggage from point A to point B on time. The studies do not address the issue of amenities such as meals, frequent flyer programmes, legroom or entertainment. However, as noted above, domestic air transportation is

Table 8.1. Total quality rates for major airlines.

Airlines	1987	1988	1989	1990	1991	1992	1993	1994	1995	1996	1997	1998	1999	2000	2001
Alaska	0.4793	0.3907	0.3799	0.3810	0.3048	0.3535	0.3054	0.3269	0.3908	0.5184	0.5113	0.5175	0.4174	0.2603	0.2164
America West	0.6631	0.6654	0.5399	0.6910	0.5054	0.3549	0.3693	0.3991	0.4296	0.4148	0.2943	0.3411	0.4087	0.6144	0.3932
American	0.8078	0.6497	0.5851	0.5444	0.3799	0.4424	0.4149	0.3664	0.3965	0.4430	0.3843	0.3614	0.4162	0.4481	0.3573
Continental	0.6017	0.4785	0.4945	0.4192	0.3905	0.4781	0.4482	0.4649	0.3320	0.2949	0.2799	0.3116	0.3507	0.4435	0.3681
Delta	0.6252	0.5970	0.5710	0.5006	0.4435	0.4858	0.4634	0.4364	0.4657	0.5235	0.4534	0.4443	0.4758	0.4847	0.4035
Northwest	0.6457	0.6240	0.5508	0.5281	0.4072	0.4157	0.4072	0.4239	0.4637	0.4034	0.4571	0.5216	0.3879	0.4326	0.3345
Southwest	0.8212	0.4943	0.3621	0.3030	0.3070	0.3063	0.3003	0.3395	0.3362	0.3110	0.2838	0.3446	0.3366	0.4167	0.3845
TWA	0.5218	0.4374	0.6046	0.6177	0.4927	0.5427	0.3353	0.4134	0.4703	0.4674	0.4234	0.4626	0.4756	0.5804	
United	0.4928	0.4990	0.6029	0.5605	0.5095	0.5097	0.5241	0.4882	0.4650	0.6169	0.5958	0.7507	0.6745	0.6242	0.4737
US Airways	1.0052	0.8152	0.5770	0.3924	0.3414	0.4003	0.3596	0.4057	0.3520	0.3949	0.3236	0.3277	0.3955	0.3697	0.2941
Industry average Quality by year	0.6664	0.5651	0.5278	0.4938	0.4082	0.4289	0.3928	0.4064	0.4102	0.4388	0.4007	0.4383	0.4339	0.4675	0.3584
Confidence interval Upper limit	0.7859	0.6568	0.5900	0.5789	0.4639	0.4836	0.4445	0.4432	0.4504	0.5091	0.4771	0.5348	0.5024	0.5488	0.4142
Lower limit	0.5469	0.4734	0.4636	0.4087	0.3525	0.3743	0.3410	0.3696	0.3700	0.3686	0.3243	0.3418	0.3654	0.3861	0.3025

increasingly forecast to be the domain of the low-cost, no-frills carriers, where consumers are willing to trade service features for price benefits. International service though, due to the long times involved in travelling, continues to strive for higher levels of service amenities, but even these amenities are coming under increasing financial scrutiny (Piling, 2003).

Changes in the International Air Transport Industry

The international system that emerged in air transportation after the end of the Second World War was in many ways regulated tighter than domestic aviation. In the absence of a multilateral system governing air service rights, governments negotiated on a one-to-one basis for the right to fly passengers and cargo between their home markets and other nations. These bilateral air service agreements designated the routes to be flown, carriers eligible to fly and frequency of flights to be allowed. Any changes in the agreed system required carriers to petition their government to reopen negotiations with the other nation involved. Since reciprocity or the exchange of rights was considered a guiding principle of air service agreements, no country would agree to increase the rights of one nation's carriers without receiving similar rights for its own carriers. In this system, the International Air Transport Association, a trade association composed of international carriers, set fares and established the technical means of cooperation between carriers. Fares for a given route were set to ensure that carriers made money; revenue sharing was employed to ensure that carriers profited equally from the carriage of passengers on that route (Graham, 1995; Toh, 1998). These fares and arrangements were acknowledged by national governments within their approved bilateral air service agreements.

Having deregulated its domestic markets, the USA began to pursue an international policy that was aimed at eliminating what it perceived as the key barriers to free market international aviation. To achieve its vision, the USA began to negotiate a series of so-called open skies bilateral agreements that remove restrictions on pricing, capacity and routes (Rhoades, 2003). The first such agreement was signed with the Netherlands in 1992; however, the open skies movement did not gain momentum until 1997 when some 15 nations joined the open skies regime. By the end of 2001, 56 nations had signed open skies agreements with the USA. One key element not included in US open skies agreements is cabotage (also known as the 'Seventh Freedom'), which is the right of a 'foreign' carrier to transport passengers or cargo between two points within another country. Europe also began to move towards the creation of a single aviation market that would eventually permit a carrier established in an EU country to offer service between any two points in Europe (including two domestic points within another EU country) while allowing the market to determine price and capacity. The Association of European Airlines (AEA) has recently proposed extending the single European aviation market across the north Atlantic creating a Transatlantic Common Aviation Area (TCAA), a single common aviation market between Europe and the USA (Association of European Airlines, 1999; Flottau and Taverna, 2002).

While many countries have entered into open skies treaties, there are still other countries and airlines who have complained about the process. To these critics, the open skies process was just another artificial trade barrier as the treaties tended to be affirmed at the same time that an airline alliance was seeking US anti-trust immunity. The complaint is that the open skies treaties do not allow cabotage, foreign ownership or effective foreign control of domestic airlines; they simply create more opportunities for collusion between airlines by opening up the possibility of anti-trust immunity (Walker, 1998). At the end of 2002, the European Court in a ruling stated that portions of the open sky treaties signed by individual member states were in fact illegal. While a period of uncertainty has been introduced, it is expected that the EC will receive a mandate to negotiate on behalf of all EC members (Field, 2003). The impact of this ruling could hasten the creation of a TCAA and possibly open the US market for cabotage and foreign ownership of airlines (Flottau and Taverna, 2002).

Effects of liberalization

A recent report has concluded that average fares to open skies countries have declined by 20% since 1996 (US Department of Transportation, 2000). In Europe, evidence indicates that liberalization has increased the number of cross-border routes served as well as the frequency of flights offered on all intra-EU routes. According to a study conducted by the Civil Aviation Authority of Great Britain, fares have declined on routes served by three or more carriers (Abbot and Thompson, 1989; Civil Aviation Authority, 1995; Humphries, 1996; Morrell, 1998).

Although the number of cross-border routes served and the frequency of flights offered have increased, at least one important goal of liberalization has not been fully realized – to increase competition by encouraging new carriers to enter international markets and existing carriers to add new routes. In fact, most international carriers have chosen not to serve additional markets directly but to enter into a variety of alliance relationships with other carriers in an attempt to service the largest number of destinations most frequently. Three issues may account for an airlines choice of alliances over direct entry. Firstly, the use of alliances reduces the cost of entry into new markets. Secondly, alliances allow carriers to 'serve' markets that may not otherwise generate enough traffic to be profitable. Thirdly, carriers are often reluctant to invest in new routes when there is uncertainty about government reactions to increased competition with national carriers.

As Table 8.2 indicates, the number of airline alliances has increased dramatically since 1994.

By far, the overwhelming alliance activity engaged in by the airlines is known as code sharing. Code sharing occurs when two airlines agree to offer a flight in which each carrier operates its own separate leg of the journey. For example, a US and a British carrier may agree that on a flight from Chicago to London, the US carrier will fly the Chicago–New York leg and transfer passengers in New York to the British carrier who will then fly the New York–London leg of the journey. Code sharing allows airline to 'serve' many destinations without actually flying to them, therefore eliminating the need for local facilities, personnel, landing slots, etc. Many of these destinations may also not generate enough traffic to fill the aircraft of major international carriers, thus making them uneconomical to serve. When code sharing is combined with arrangements that allow carriers to utilize the baggage handling, check-in and maintenance facilities of alliance partners, it can result in major cost savings. Alliances that coordinate on computer reservation systems and marketing may also generate more passenger traffic and revenue. This can be done through the coordination of prices, take-off and land schedules and joint marketing efforts. In order for this level of coordination to take place between 'competitors', national governments must waive many of their policies relating to competition (or anti-trust as it is called in the USA). The US government actually ties anti-trust immunity to the signing of open skies agreements. The EC has tied approval of alliances largely to the relin-

Table 8.2. Alliance summary 1994–2001.

	1994	1995	1996	1997	1998	1999	2000	2001[b]
Number of alliances	280	324	389	363	502	513	579	548
With equity stakes[a]	58	58	62	54	56	53	–	–
Without equity	222	266	327	309	446	460	–	–
New alliances	21	34	26	56	84	79	72	79
Number of airlines	136	153	159	177	196	204	220	163

Source: *Airline Business*, June 1994–June 2001.
[a]Equity calculations change beginning in 2000.
[b]The drop in total alliances and airline is largely attributable to the end of the qualifier alliance and the bankruptcy of Swissair and Sabena.

quishment of landing slots at key European airports (Rhoades, 2003).

The other notable trend in airline alliances has been towards the formation of the so-called mega-alliance, a wide-ranging agreement between multiple carriers to cooperate on everything from code sharing to maintenance to facility sharing. Table 8.3 shows the current membership in the four mega-alliances (Ott, 2002). These mega-alliances, formed by the airlines in the late 1990s to provide a global air transportation network to their customers, are themselves branded entities with the exception of Wings which is the unofficial name assigned in the industry to the Northwest–KLM alliance. An ongoing issue with these mega-alliances is the constant evolution of the alliance members (Ott, 2002; Baker and Field, 2003). As alliance members must constantly react to various economic, regulatory and competitive forces both locally and globally, this puts a strain on any alliance relationships. With the worldwide deregulation trend accelerating, and therefore the potential for airline consolidation increasing, the control and ownership of national airlines also impacts on alliance formation. For

example, in 1999, Air Canada faced the prospect of takeover by Canadian Airlines (which has since folded) that would have moved the airline from the Star Alliance to the Oneworld grouping. As this article is being prepared, Qantas, which is a member of Oneworld, is attempting to acquire a large stake in Air New Zealand, a Star member, which would effectively force Air New Zealand to exit the Star Alliance. In the USA, an announced domestic code-sharing agreement among Delta, Northwest and Continental may have an unknown impact on the SkyTeam and Wings alliance.

International alliance quality

While the strategic alliance may allow an airline to reduce costs and serve markets without an actual presence, it does generate several problems. One major problem relates to the ability of the carrier and alliance to brand themselves in the eyes of the travelling public. A more critical problem involves the ability of

Table 8.3. International mega-alliances.

	Oneworld	SkyTeam	Star	Wings
	Aer Lingus	Aeromexico	Air Canada	KLM
	American Airlines	Air France	Air New Zealand	Northwest
	British Airways	Alitalia	All Nippon Airways	Continental[a]
	Cathay Pacific	Czech Airlines	Austrian Airlines	
	Finnair	Delta Air Lines	bmi, British Midlands	
	Iberia Airlines	Korean Air	Lauda Air	
	LanChile		Lufthansa Airlines	
	Qantas Airways		Mexicana	
			SAS	
			Singapore	
			Thai Airways	
			United Airlines	
			Varig	
Annual Pax (m)	227.5	220	302	110
Fleet	1974	1224	2123	1276
Destinations	563	507	700	531

Source: Alliance membership, Ott (2002), 'Alliances may be fewer, but savings will improve', *Aviation Week and Space Technology*, November 18, 65–68. Alliance performance data – Star Alliance factsheet (2003); Northwest Investor Report (2003); Continental Investor Report (2003); SkyTeam Communications (2003).
[a]Data for Continental combined with Northwest (NW)/KLM information. While not an official member of Wings, the broad code-share agreement with NW does increase the access and reach of Wings.

alliance partners to coordinate service quality across the different carriers.

Coordinating alliance branding

For many airlines, the move into a global alliance brings a brand dilemma to the forefront (Piling, 2001). While the airline is often tied to its national identity, the airline wants to project a global image. Therefore, the airline has to project two brand images at once, the 'home' national brand and the global alliance brand. The goal of many alliance-branding efforts is to assure the global air traveller that a certain level of quality, efficiency and service exists across the alliance. So, while national identities are not likely to disappear and be replaced by a true global alliance brand identity, the global alliance brands are developed as one way of representing the alliance's quality to the passenger.

Coordinating alliance quality

Since alliances involve structurally and legally independent firms, cross-alliance teams are frequently used in an attempt to ensure quality of lateral/cross-airline processes. In addition, a uniform awareness of organizational culture plays an important role in airline and alliance quality efforts (Ainsworth et al., 2001).

Cross-alliance teams

The use of cross-alliance teams is expected to generate effects similar to cross-functional teams, which have linked to innovation (Sethi et al., 2001), product quality (Sethi, 2000), collaboration (Freedman, 2000) and organizational commitment and shared identity (Irvine and Baker, 1995). However, as Freedman (2000) pointed out, simply creating such cross-alliance teams is not enough to ensure quality across the alliance. Careful consideration must be given to such factors as team composition, team leadership and team contextual variables. Composition is particularly critical because team members must not only be proficient in their own specific task, but also be able to work as part of a team, e.g. have teamwork skills.

Several attempts have been made to clarify 'teamwork' and the skills involved therein.

Although there are a variety of different approaches to defining teamwork, almost all definitions emphasize collaborative effort and communication in order to build trust and cooperation (Brown, 2002). A variety of skills have been identified as prerequisites for teamwork. These include: interpositional knowledge, or knowledge of teammate roles, tasks and informational requirements; the ability to adapt to unpredictable situations; a willingness to monitor each other's behaviour; the ability to provide feedback and motivational reinforcement, structure and organization for each other; assertiveness; and conflict resolution skills (Cannon-Bowers and Salas, 1998). Thus, careful selection and appropriate training are required to ensure that cross-alliance teams have the necessary knowledge and skills to perform their quality assurance functions effectively.

Team leadership is critical in that the team leader impacts not only the team's performance in terms of effectiveness but also influences such factors as team mood, cohesion and commitment (Komaki et al., 1989; George, 1995; Korsgaard et al., 1995). Team contextual variables cover a gamut of issues within the areas of the organizational context and team boundaries – particularly the degree of integration and differentiation (Sundstrom et al., 1990), the nature of the industry, the degree of environmental turbulence and the designs of the team member's respective organizations. These issues will influence such factors as the amount and type of support for the team, the amount of autonomy given to the team, the permeability of the boundary between the team and other organizational units, the organizational climate and the availability of dependable measurement systems for providing feedback to the team (Keller, 1994; Eisenhardt and Tabrizi, 1995).

Creating culture

A second critical consideration in assuring alliance service quality is organizational culture. Research in acquisitions and mergers has consistently shown that cultural clashes are one of the primary causes for integration failures (Hall and Norburn, 1987; Buono et al., 1989). Thus, Levinson and Asahi (1995) noted that interorganizational learning in strategic alliances requires attention not only to structural and technological factors but also to cultural factors. Ainsworth *et al.* (2001) found that beyond the specific airline operations background, the one 'mandatory element' of an alliance executive's background is cultural sensitivity.

Larsson and Lubatkin (2001) examined 'cultural clashes' in 50 mergers, and concluded that social controls, such as training, cross-visits, retreats, celebrations and similar socialization rituals, were the most effective method of creating a joint organizational culture. Thus, while cross-alliance teams may be one method of working to ensure intra-alliance quality, it may also be desirable to ensure that the cultures of the alliance partners with regard to quality 'fit' and if they do not, to institute a definite programme of interorganizational learning in order to develop a joint culture that emphasizes quality.

Conclusion

The world's airlines are being asked to choose whether they will compete as low-cost, no-frills carriers or as traditional full-service carriers. In domestic markets around the world, consumers are increasingly choosing low-cost carriers. These consumers want low prices but they also expect good basic service. On the other hand, international long haul travellers continue to prefer the traditional carrier with all the amenities that they have come to expect from such carriers. Meeting these expectations in the complex environment of the strategic alliance has challenged the ability of airlines to work together in cross-alliance teams. It has also made it essential that airlines examine the quality culture within their own carrier and between the carriers within their alliance.

References

Abbott, K. and Thompson, D. (1989) *Deregulating European Aviation: The Impact of Bilateral Liberalization.* Center for Business Strategy Working Paper Series No. 73, London.

Ainsworth, G., Bell, M., Kaufman, E., Kemp, L. and Tallents, A (2001) The global challenge. *Airline Business* (August), 80–84.

Association of European Airlines (1999) *Towards a Transatlantic Common Aviation Area: AEA Policy Statement.* Association of European Airlines.

Baker, C. and Field, D. (2003) Global shifts. *Airline Business* (January), 52–54.

Binggeli, U. and Pompeo, L. (2002) Hyped hopes for Europe's low-cost airlines. *McKinsey Quarterly* 4.

Bowen, B.D. and Headley, D. (1999) *Airline Quality Rating 1999.* W. Frank Barton School of Business, Wichita, Kansas.

Brown, J.A. (2002) Group level contextual performance: is it teamwork? *Proceedings of the Southern Management Association 2002.* Atlanta, Georgia, pp. 189–195.

Buono, A., Weiss, J. and Bowditch, J. (1989) Paradoxes in acquisition and merger consulting: thoughts and recommendations. *Consultation: An International Journal* 8(3), 145–159.

Cannon-Bowers, J.A. and Salas, E. (1998) Team performance and training in complex environments: recent findings from applied research. *Current Directions in Psychological Science* 7, 83–87.

Caves, R. (1962) *Air Transport and Its Regulators: An Industry Study.* Harvard University Press, Cambridge, Massachusetts.

Continental Investor Report (2003) Available at: www.continental.com

Civil Aviation Authority (1995) *CAP 654 The Single Aviation Market: Progress So Far.* Civil Aviation Authority, London.

Eisenhardt, K.M. and Tabrizi, B.N. (1995) Accelerating adaptive processes: product innovation in the global computer industry. *Administrative Science Quarterly* 40, 84–110.

Field, D. (2003) US mulls implications of open skies renunciation. *Airline Business* (January), 13.

Flottau, J. (2003) EasyJet takeover of DBA far from certain. *Aviation Week and Space Technology* (February), 38.

Flottau, J. and Taverna, M.A. (2002) European court sets stage for airline metamorphosis. *Aviation Week & Space Technology* (November), 24–25.

Forsyth, P. (1991) The regulation and deregulation of Australia's domestic airline industry. In: Button, K.J. (ed.) *Airline Deregulation: International Experience*. David Fulton, London, pp. 48–84.

Freedman, A.M. (2000) Multigroup representation: representative teams and teams of representatives. *Consulting Psychology Journal: Practice and Research* 52(1), 63–81.

George, J.M. (1995) Leader positive mood and group performance: the case of customer service. *Journal of Applied Psychology* 25, 778–794.

Glab, J. (1998) A personal approach. *Frequent Flyer* (June), 24–28.

Graham, B. (1995) *Geography and Air Transport*. John Wiley & Sons, New York.

Hall, P. and Norburn, D. (1987) The management factor in acquisition performance. *Leadership and Organization Development Journal* 8(3), 23–30.

Hall, W., Grant, J., Done, K. and Cameron, D. (2001) Swissair Grounding Causes Travel Chaos. October 2.

Humphries, B. (1996) The UK Civil Aviation Authority and European Air Services Liberalization. *Journal of Transport Economics and Policy* 3, 213–220.

Irvine, D. and Baker, R. (1995) The impact of cross-functional teamwork on workforce integration. *International Journal of Conflict Management* 6(2), 171–191.

Jordan, W.A. (1970) *Airline Regulation in America: Effects and Imperfections*. Johns Hopkins University Press, Baltimore, Maryland.

Kahn, A.E. (1971) *The Economics of Regulation*. John Wiley & Sons, New York.

Kahn, A.E. (1990) Deregulation: looking backward and looking forward. *Yale Journal of Regulation* 7, 325–354.

Kane, R.M. (1998) *Air Transportation*, 13th edn. Kendall/Hunt Publishing, Dubuque, Iowa.

Keller, R.T. (1994) Technology-information processing fit and the performance of R&D project groups: a test of contingency theory. *Academy of Management Journal* 37, 167–179.

Komaki, J.L., Desselles, M.L. and Bowman, E.D. (1989) Definitely not a breeze: extending an operant model of effective supervision to teams. *Journal of Applied Psychology* 74, 522–529.

Korsgaard, M.A., Schweiger, D.M. and Sapienza, H.J. (1995) Building commitment, attachment, and trust in strategic decision-making teams: the role of procedural justice. *Academy of Management Journal* 38, 60–84.

Larsson, R. and Lubatkin, M. (2001) Achieving acculturation in mergers and acquisitions: an international case survey. *Human Relations* 54(12), 1573–1607.

Levinson, N. and Asahi, M. (1995) Cross-national alliances and interorganizational learning. *Organizational Dynamics* 24(2), 50–63.

Matlack, C., Weber, J. and Zellner, W. (2003) In fighting trim: european carriers are leaner than their US rivals. *Business Week* (April), 50.

Morrell, P. (1998) Air transport liberalization in Europe: the progress so far. *Journal of Air Transportation World Wide* 3, 42–60.

Northwest Investor Report (2003) Available at: www.ir.nwa.com

Ott, J. (2002) Alliances may be fewer, but savings will improve. *Aviation Week & Space Technology* (November), 65–67.

Piling, M. (2001) Identity parade. *Airline Business* (April), 66–71.

Piling, M. (2003) Smarter service. *Airline Business* (January), 36–39.

Rhoades, D. (2003) *Evolution of International Aviation: Phoenix Rising*. Ashgate Publishing, Aldershot, UK.

Rhoades, D. and Waguespack, B. (2001) Airline quality: present challenges, future strategies. In: Butler, G.F. and Keller, M.R. (eds) *Handbook of Airline Strategy: Public Policy, Regulatory Issues, Challenges, and Solutions*. McGraw-Hill, New York, pp. 469–480.

Rosen, S.D. (1995) Corporate restructuring: a labor perspective. In: Cappelli, P. (ed.) *Airline Labor Relations in the Global Era: The New Frontier*. ILR Press, Ithaca, New York.

Sethi, R. (2000) New product quality and product development teams. *Journal of Marketing* 64(2), 1–14.

Sethi, R., Smith, D. and Park, W. (2001) Cross-functional product development teams, creativity, and the innovativeness of new consumer products. *Journal of Marketing Research* 37(8), 73–85.

Sinha, D. (2001) *Deregulation and Liberalization of the Airline Industry: Asia, Europe, North America, and Oceania*. Ashgate Publishing, Aldershot, UK.

SkyTeam Communications (2003) *SkyTeam Transatlantic Cooperation Generates Greater Benefits for Customers and Member Airlines: Revenue Projection of Approximately USD 100 million Highlights Continued Growth* (May 22).

Sparaco, P. (2002) Low-cost carriers steal the European show. *Aviation Week & Space Technology* (November), 59–61.

Star Alliance Factsheet (2003) Available at: www.staralliance.com

Sundstrom, E., DeMeuse, K.P. and Futrell, D. (1990) Work teams: applications and effectiveness. *American Psychologist* 45, 120–123.

Toh, R.S. (1998) Towards an international open skies regime: advances, impediments, and impacts. *Journal of Air Transportation World Wide* M3, 61–70.

US Department of Transportation (2000) *International Aviation Developments: Transatlantic Deregulation – The Alliance Network Effect*. Department of Transportation, Washington, DC.

Velocci, A.L. Jr (2002) 'Can majors shift focus fast enough to survive?' *Aviation Week & Space Technology* (November), 52–54.

Walker, K. (1998) Lifting the 7th veil. *Airline Business* (October), 73–76.

9 Service System: A Strategic Approach to Innovate and Manage Service Superiority

Jay Kandampully and Ria Kandampully
Ohio State University, USA

Introduction

The increasing importance and growth of tourism and hospitality services as a major global industry has been of interest to academics and practitioners alike. Today, firms compete on the basis of services provided, not on the basis of physical products (Gronroos, 2000). The competitive advantage of the service component within the hospitality and tourism offer has become increasingly evident as customers increasingly perceive little to differentiate between the myriad of comparable product offerings. For example, to a tourist, there are limited differences between one hotel and the other, or one tour operator and the other. While their product offerings are largely similar, within their services there may be considerable difference – not in *what* is being offered, but in terms of *how* it is being offered. This *how* is the true outcome experience of the service that manifests true value to the customers.

Advances in information technology (IT) have not only reduced the life cycle of services, since service features are often emulated, but have also assisted in their innovation and efficiency. The global marketplace and the changing nature of business demands that hospitality and tourism firms interact with their customers and business partners using technology to provide services and information instantaneously across international borders. Essentially, such service interactions relate to 'high-touch' (traditional face-to-face interaction) and 'high-tech' (those interactions that take place over a long distance via a technology interface). Moreover, services, whether provided face-to-face or at a distance, form a required component of almost every hospitality and tourism business enterprise, and essentially constitute the factor determining the firm's success in the global marketplace.

Changing Marketplace

The emergence of the global marketplace has compelled the hospitality and tourism industry to transform itself into a truly customer-focused business enterprise – irrespective of the products and services sold. Services have thus become the recognized value assessment variable for predicting a hospitality or tourism firm's success. Moreover, services have become the uncompromisable core component of hospitality and tourism business and, from a management perspective, they have evolved to assume a strategic function. There has thus been a shift from production orientation to service orientation – essentially transforming hospitality and tourism into a service business. Hospitality and tourism firms' service function is concerned with almost every activity or component of the firm, and includes: people, process or physical evidence (both tangible and intangible evidence representative of the firm from the customer's perspective); internal and external customers; and the various networks, alliances and partners (Kandampully, 2002a). Indeed, external relationship networks have become an essential prerequisite if hospitality and tourism firms are to acquire the capabilities and knowledge required to serve the holistic needs of customers.

Service leaders successfully introduce products and services to the market far in advance of customer expectation. Moreover, in the customer's mind, a firm maintains its market-leadership position by continuing to operate at the cutting-edge and by extending conventional parameters. Service firms today are expected to delight customers with their creativity and innovation. Thus, in operational terms, innovation can be translated as a firm's foresight to 'think for the customer' by creating services that 'drive' the marketplace in offering superior value to the customer (Kandampully, 2002a). Thus to stay ahead in competition, hospitality and tourism firms must constantly innovate and manage the services they offer. Furthermore, as the core benefit of business, services should maintain their central position by ensuring a meticulous focus on quality and value. This central position of services as the benchmark within hospitality and tourism businesses necessitates a holistic and strategic perspective of services, and one that renders them capable of interlinking with all other activities of the business. The increasing use of technology to support various business activities has made it possible to maintain standards, and to coordinate and support activities throughout the organization.

Technology has traditionally been viewed as the key to productivity in manufacturing industries. However, in recent years, technology has assumed greater significance in service industries such as hospitality and tourism. Technology should be used as a tool, implemented to enhance the effectiveness of employees and the system, and ultimately to reflect on customer satisfaction (Bensaou and Earl, 1998). Technology, Berry (1995) argues, should be the servant not the master, and

engender its users with more control in achieving what they wish to accomplish. Technology, thus, is not intended to replace labour input, but to offer support and to elevate the competitive advantage of hospitality and tourism organizations by enhancing their employees' capacity to offer superior service. Market competition has thus forced hospitality and tourism firms to incorporate modern technology into their key offerings to discerning customers, who have little product loyalty. To do otherwise is to risk losing out to competitors who have adapted their strategies to the technology-based competitive environment (Bitner et al., 2000; Olsen and Connolly, 2000).

Moreover, information and its timely access through technology are often crucial to the effective functioning of the various internal activities in hospitality and tourism firms, factors that may be deemed to be particularly pertinent in nurturing employee empowerment. Hospitality and tourism firms can effectively utilize IT to support instantaneous access to information and, essentially, to motivate and energize hospitality and tourism employees to embrace empowerment and perform at exceptional levels of service by facilitating action in any given situation – to serve both internal and external customers. IT presents service firms with the opportunity to store digital information. Such digital information has become a powerful tool in the workplace by enabling junior members of a hotel or tourism firm to assume responsibility, and to make on-the-spot decisions without the need to consult senior management. Junior members of staff who are equipped with both decision making information and customer information will be able to modify the firm's service offer to meet customer-specific requirements without delay. IT will also assist the sharing of important information between different units of a multi-unit firm, different departments of a hotel or a tourism firm, and between different levels of staff; this can effect faster and better decision making throughout the organization.

Customer data collection and its dissemination to various hotels of an international hotel chain has become common practice in endeavours to enhance customer service. At La Mansion del Rio Hotel in San Antonio, Texas, USA, employees are trained to gather information about customer preferences for their database; this is further analysed and utilized in customer-focused initiatives throughout the hotel (Peppers and Rogers, 2000, p. 115). IT, thus, represents a new addition to the list of skills traditionally required from hotel and tourism employees. Within this technology-oriented new hospitality and tourism business environment, it is thus not experience, but immediate access to information at all functional areas of the firm that will prove invaluable to employees in the delivery of exceptional service.

To survive and prosper in this new global marketplace, it is therefore imperative that hospitality and tourism firms continually innovate the services they offer while they simultaneously manage the quality of services valuable to the customers – every time all the time. This, however, not only requires a strategic focus, but a collective orientation. In this chapter, we discuss the use of a 'service system' capable of bringing together the internal activities of the organization and under a focus of superior service delivery (Kandampully and Duddy, 2001). The benefit of the service system, according to them, is the outcome of the collective efficiencies of three strategies: (i) service empowerment; (ii) service guarantees; and (iii) service recovery. A cohesive service system that permeates the conceptual and operational interrelationships of the entire organization will not only help the firms to excel in service delivery, but the outcome will prove difficult for other organizations to emulate, thereby proffering a competitive advantage.

Service Empowerment

Over the last three decades, both theory and practice have concluded that *people* are the key to both creating and sustaining an organization's quality of service. According to Peters and Austin (1994, p. 98), irrespective of where the technology leads, quality comes from people. Schneider (1994) similarly expresses the view that 'the people make the place'. Many researchers and practitioners have likewise identified the crucial role of the 'people' factor in organizations (Albrecht and

Zemke, 1985), particularly in relation to the customer's perception of enhanced *service value*. Such perceptions are increasingly recognized as central to an organization's continued success (Henry, 1994). For example, Crosby and Stephens (1987) found that the personal contact of the service provider was the strongest influence on overall customer-service satisfaction. Moreover, there is increasing acknowledgement that service value is associated not with production, but with what the customer receives. Exceptional service, or service that leads to customer delight, requires organizations to ensure a continuous transformation of service – not in terms of *what* is being offered, but rather *how* it is being offered. The role of service personnel has, thus, become an increasingly important construct in the customer's perception of service value (Grieves and Mathews, 1997).

In recent years, empowerment has emerged as the new orthodoxy of managing human resources and has been promoted, at least by its proponents, as central in extricating an employee's potential resourcefulness by enabling them to assume increased responsibilities, and to be more accountable for their actions (Keenoy, 1990). Empowerment encourages employees to exercise initiative and to use their imagination in every aspect of their day-to-day work, to improve or better their work, and rewards them for taking self-directed action. Customer requirements frequently extend beyond departmental boundaries, rendering it necessary for employees to operate across functional boundaries.

Lawler (1992) presents a strong conceptual argument that advocates employee involvement as a prerequisite to the concept of empowerment. He believes that in organizations where employee involvement in empowerment is the norm, it would have a direct effect on four organizational performance variables, such as cost and productivity, quality, speed in responding to customer requests and innovation. Additionally, when employees are engaged in decision making, the result is often enhanced employee commitment to addressing the needs and objectives of the organization.

Underlying empowerment is the premise that an employee's values will be in line with those of the organization. Organizations must be prepared to allow employees the freedom to act and to make decisions based on their own judgement. For example, if a service employee is empowered, then that employee must be allowed to decide how best to deal with the needs of the customer, and should assume accountability and responsibility for dealing with problems of customer complaint and operational bottlenecks. Clearly, empowerment would allow the flexibility necessary to respond quickly to the needs of customers.

Moreover, empowerment provides the flexibility and confidence that allows individuals to be more imaginative in creating new solutions that meet customers' needs (Antonacopoulou and Kandampully, 2000). This implies that rules and regulations to be followed should not govern employees' actions. Empowerment is essentially the opposite of doing things by the book. At times, it is often seen that service personnel are willing to do the unusual to meet the needs of the customer. However, organizational rules and procedures commonly impinge on the willingness of employees to go beyond their job task to serve customers' needs.

One of the most cited service organizations, with reference to their management style, is Nordstrom's rulebook. Nordstrom is a department store chain based in Seattle, USA. Nordstrom's management philosophy encourages the development of a strong service culture. Its salespeople focus their attention, not on sales, but in forming long-term relationships with individual customers by personal follow-ups and an unusual degree of personal catering. The business culture presents them with the ideal opportunity to take the initiative in developing the customer relationship. Nordstrom has relatively few rules and regulations; it relies on the leadership of the store and the departmental heads to instill the primary values of service-oriented selling into all new employees. An excellent example of this is Nordstrom's employee handbook. It reads just this:

> *Use your own good judgment in all situations*
>
> *There will be no additional rules.*
> *Please feel free to ask your department manager, store manager or division general manager any question at any time.*

There are two dimensions to empowerment: (i) organizational and (ii) personal. Giving employees overt permission and encouragement to work creatively is in the customer's best interests. Management's responsibility is to support their employees' efforts and to treat them as management requires their customers to be treated. Employees in such situations need to be rewarded in a timely fashion and applauded for their initiatives, triumphs and achievements. This issue also implies a culture that encourages employees to experiment with new ideas (service innovation), and to be afforded mistakes when their intentions are for the right reason, thus providing the opportunity to learn and improve. Such a culture is comparable to the image of the 'Learning Organization' (Antonacopoulou, 1998).

There are several examples of organizations which reflect this philosophy. One such example is the SAS Airline. In his book *Moments of Truth,* Carlzon (1989), CEO of SAS Airline, recounts how his organization was forced to readjust its systems and policies to empower employees. An organization's rules, regulations, policies and structures are set in place to assist their employees to be able to serve the customers better; if they are not, then one has to redesign those which restrict an employee's opportunity to offer an exceptional quality of service. It should not be necessary for an employee to work against the system in meeting a customer's special needs.

Another example is Federal Express, which is one of the most talked-about organizations in the international arena. It is their management philosophy and organizational culture which impresses most. Federal Express is a high-involvement, horizontally coordinated organization that responds to customers with empowered employees who are encouraged to use their judgement above and beyond the rulebook. In 1990, Federal Express became the first service organization to win the highly coveted Malcolm Baldridge National Quality Award. The company's motto is 'People, service and profits'. Their organization's strengths are embedded in their ability to manage their business through self-managing work teams, where managers and workers receive bonuses through profit-share schemes. Under these circumstances, empowered employees work creatively and flexibly to serve the individual and often diverse needs of their customers.

A pay cheque might keep a person on the job physically, but it will not keep a person on the job emotionally. Service leaders such as 'Ritz-Carlton Hotels' clearly communicate the firm's commitment: trust in every employee and pride in the dignity of every employee's contribution to the organization and the value they offer to customers. Ritz-Carlton proclaims that 'We are Ladies and Gentlemen Serving Ladies and Gentlemen.' This unique statement, known as the 'Credo of Ritz-Carlton', is today synonymous with trust and superior service – both within customers and employees – rendering it the most valuable and marketed commodity of their organization (Kandampully, 2002a).

These examples indicate how empowerment can represent not merely another fad superficially applied, but a central characteristic of a hospitality and tourism company's ethos and culture. It is argued here that the empowerment orientation of a firm should extend the concept of flexibility to encompass more than those aspects normally considered people-related. Service empowerment will prove effective only if the firm's internal supporting systems engender sufficient flexibility to permit empowered employees to undertake creative modification (service innovation) of their job tasks – and to therefore deviate from the firm's standard processes and systems – for the benefit of the customer (Hamel and Prahalad, 1989, p. 67). By nurturing service empowerment, managers are essentially creating competitive intelligence within all employees and at every level of the organization to build the firm's competitive advantage (Hamel and Prahalad, 1989, p. 67). Empowerment should thus permeate all functions and activities of the firm if its true potential is to be realized.

Empowerment per se may not prove effective unless management shifts its mindset to acknowledge that it is the contribution of the human mind (knowledge) that will play a major role in tomorrow's service industries (Peters, 1994). Indeed, every enterprise today, whether we are referring to a hospitality, tourism or computer software business, will operate in the global market and an age of

technology and knowledge; hence, the 'creativity' of the people within the organization is more valuable than 'experience' in the innovative world of business. Business success will depend on an organization's ability to imagine and/or create a need (Pilzer, 1990). It can therefore be argued that innovation in services reflects the creativity of the human mind (knowledge). It is, indeed, progress into the unknown – through new knowledge – that will enable an organization to attain wealth and the all-important competitive advantage (Kelley, 1997). It is the people within a service organization who create and innovate an organization's service offer, as service differentiation comes from people and their contribution to the infinite field of knowledge.

In the past, labour represented, and was considered by management to be the inevitable cost incurred in the production of goods and services. However, according to the present understanding of 'resources', labour is valued not in terms of physical assistance, but in terms of mental contribution. The labour within an organization or country is no longer a designated *cost* but a valuable *resource*. The true economic value of a person is primarily attributed to his or her knowledge and creative skills (Kandampully, 2002b). This view is highlighted by Moody (1991) in the *New York Times Magazine* with his assertion that 'Microsoft's only factory asset is the human imagination'. Hamel and Prahalad (1989, p. 67) suggest that managers nurture and develop competitive intelligence at every level of the organization in order to build the firm's competitive advantage. A similar view is held by SONY's chairman, Morita (1988), who indicated that it is not the manual labour of employees that allows a company to dominate the global market, but the contributions of the employees' minds.

Empowerment, as discussed here, is beyond the concept of a single strategy; it is the concept of creating a thinking and creative mind within the organization. Hence empowerment should be viewed as only one part of a holistic service strategy, since empowerment alone may not prove sufficient to proffer the firm a competitive advantage unique in the marketplace. Service firms not only have to create new and innovative services and convince customers to use them, but also need to acquire instantaneous feedback of their changing needs. More pertinently, ensuring that the innovative and creative services of the firm are supported by a superior quality of service – every time all the time – is imperative. The concepts of service guarantees and service recovery can be effectively employed to achieve such a result.

Service Guarantees

If a firm is to gain market leadership in this hypercompetitive global market, it must innovate and offer new services far in advance of customer request. It is therefore essential that managers adopt strategies that will entice customers to use the services on offer. Whether it is a new service or existing service, customers understand that they take a higher risk in choosing a service because of the intangible nature of its outcome and the fact that:

- services cannot be tested;
- services cannot be returned;
- services cannot be reworked.

Customers subsequently perceive a greater risk when buying hospitality and tourism services than when buying products (Zeithaml, 1981). It is thus evident that, to attract prospective customers and maintain market leadership, hospitality and tourism firms are required to reduce customer-perceived risk. In the past few years, service guarantees have gained considerable support and recognition among practitioners and academics as a unique and effective strategy in reducing customer risk. Moreover, service guarantees will not only help eliminate the perceived risk of customers, but also assist the firm to:

- reinforce the service promise;
- enhance immediate customer feedback;
- identify fail points in the organization;
- communicate service standards to both internal and external customers;
- increase customer satisfaction;
- develop a service-oriented culture;
- communicate their commitment to the consistent quality of their service offering.

A service guarantee, from the perspective of the customer, thus has the potential to help firms manage many internal and external factors more effectively than ever before. It has been established that hospitality and tourism firms that assume the commitment to offer service guarantees command a substantially greater market share (Sowder, 1996), enabling them to enhance the value of their offer and to gain a premium price for their services (Hart, 1988). For example, Promus Hotel Corporation's 100% satisfaction guarantee elevated their 'Hampton Inn' hotels to the top of the service league. PULSE research shows that 84% of companies communicate their dedication to quality to their customers through service guarantees (Hill, 1994). Similarly, research conducted by Sowder (1996) and Evans et al. (1996) shows that service guarantees provide a powerful competitive advantage to hospitality and tourism firms that are capable of delivering on their promise.

Hart (1990, 2000) suggests that there are some key attributes that a service guarantee should possess. They should be: (i) unconditional; (ii) easy to understand and communicate; (iii) easy to invoke; (iv) easy to collect; and (v) they should be meaningful and offer real value to the customer. Additionally, since it may be difficult to predict exactly how a customer will respond to a guarantee, a firm should be willing to alter its service guarantees as it learns of its customers' reactions to them. Thus, from a marketing perspective, a service guarantee has the potential to influence customers to avail themselves of the services on offer, in the knowledge that at least they have the option of receiving a refund of the payment should the outcome not meet their requirements. To obtain monetary reimbursement is not the reason that a customer purchases such services. The 'true' intention of most customers is to receive a service.

Service guarantees provide customers with a source of reliable information that outlines the various specifications of the service that they can expect to receive from the firm (Maher, 1991). Moreover, Maher is of the view that service guarantees constitute a double-barrelled device, informing customers what to expect while, simultaneously, ensuring that the services delivered are commensurate with the firm's service promise (standards).

Moreover, a service guarantee constitutes a hospitality and tourism organization's 'blueprint' for service, which defines the service promise to its internal and external customers simultaneously (Kandampully, 2001). Service guarantees not only set the criteria by which customers evaluate the quality of service they receive, but they clearly establish the standard to which every member of the organization must adhere to match customers' expectations. This offers a very clear focus to employees, allowing them the opportunity to go beyond their job to think for the customer, and to creatively innovate and render services far in advance of customers' expectations. It is the creative 'thinking for the customer' that provides engenders employees with pride and satisfaction in their job, and helps them develop the all-important relationship with the customer that leads to long-term loyalty.

The firm's service guarantee is thus not merely a strategy, but will percolate through every level of the organization to become the firm's service culture. A service guarantee will therefore assist the organization in its metamorphosis to a service-oriented culture, where every employee takes pride in upholding the firm's promise to its customers and transforms every moment-of-truth to a memory of superior experience.

Service Recovery

Through numerous studies, researchers such as Parasuraman, Berry and Zeithaml have clearly demonstrated that service reliability is at the heart of excellent service, and is considered the core attribute of good service by most customers. Breaking the service promise is the single most important way in which service firms fail their customers (Berry et al., 1990). Therefore, consistent superior service without failure represents, for the customer, the firm's adherence to its service promise. However, given the high involvement of the human element in services, at both the production and consumption stage, mistakes are inevitable,

albeit not intentional. Developing service systems with the expectation of producing superior service every time is unreasonable as 'zero defects' approach to services may not be entirely tenable.

The relative flexibility inherent to services that lends itself to creative modification to ensure that the needs of individual customers are met equally renders it susceptible to possible failures. It is therefore imperative that service managers with this knowledge prepare for corrective action well before mistakes occur. It is this preparedness that sets a firm apart from the others. Preparation, not only for services but also for correction, clearly reconfirms the firm's competency and commitment to its customers. Moreover, it is when mistakes do happen, that the firm's true service orientation is made explicitly clear to the customer (Zemke and Bell, 1990; Oliver, 1997).

If, however, a firm fails to rectify its mistakes immediately following a service failure, it has, in effect, failed to regain customer confidence, and the situation could clearly lead to negative word-of-mouth communication (Berry and Parasuraman, 1992). In not recovering from service failure, the firm essentially communicates to the customer that it has failed twice – described as 'double deviation' by Bitner et al. (1990). Customers are, in fact, seldom unhappy about service mishaps, but are unhappy when the service organization is unwilling to claim responsibility for the mishap and, more importantly, when the service provider is unable to undertake immediate corrective action to recover from the failed service. Thus it is not the service failures that upsets the customer, but the way in which the firm handles the failure (Tax and Brown, 1998). Research clearly indicates that, irrespective of the nature of the failure experienced, customers remain loyal to the service firm provided that an effective recovery is executed Kelley et al. (1993).

While the primary purpose of service recovery is to return the aggrieved customer to a state of satisfaction, the firm is able to actualize the true benefit of recovery only if it utilizes the information to make changes so that service offered in the future will meet customers' expectations without failure. Hence, it is suggested that every service failure/recovery experience trigger an organization-wide learning process, and effect correction and improvement of the organization's people, systems and procedures. Moreover, technology can effectively help both inter- and intra-organizational learning so that employees are instantaneously updated with new information (knowledge) across international borders. Knowledge-empowered employees can therefore utilize their creativity to make continuous changes in the standards and procedures, and satisfy customers' changing needs. In this age of information, technology not only supports every employee by providing access to the firm's collective knowledge, but also facilitates interdependency between the three strategies (service empowerment, service guarantees and service recovery). The collective focus of the three independent but interrelated strategies is referred to here as a 'service system' (see Kandampully and Duddy, 2001). Knowledge sharing using IT and interdependent strategies, we argue, will prove crucial if hospitality and tourism organization are to create an environment conducive to innovation, and to maintain the quality of services they offer.

Conclusion

It is this collaborative interdependency which proffers the service system the potential to strengthen the firm's service culture and competency while, at the same time, rendering it difficult for competing organizations to emulate. The benefit of the service system is embedded in its ability to facilitate the ongoing process of innovative rejuvenation of the service offered, thus helping the firm to maintain its market leadership. Firms that seek to maintain consistent market leadership in this new age of technology and a global market economy value both their internal and external customers.

A service system helps the entire organization to focus on the customer; and, in so doing, it recognizes the innovative ability of every employee that makes up the organization. Adopting the service system clearly indicates a firm's commitment and trust in its employees which, in effect, nurtures the pride and ownership that motivates employees to go beyond their job tasks and creatively modify (innovate) services to meet customers' individual needs. In the competitive world of hospitality and tourism business, the use of IT and the subsequent access to knowledge/information can represent a powerful contributing factor to employee creativity. Moreover, it is this creativity that manifests within each individual employee and their job tasks that can propel hospitality and tourism organizations to market leadership. It is the creative service that ultimately imparts the uniqueness of a firm's offer, and the service system that helps to render it possible.

References

Albrecht, K. and Zemke, R. (1985) *Service America: Doing Business in the New Economy.* Dow Jones-Irwin, Homewood, Illinois.

Antonacopoulou, E.P. (1998) Developing learning managers within learning organizations. In: Easterby-Smith, M., Araujo, L. and Burgoyne, J. (eds) *Organizational Learning: Developments in Theory and Practice.* Sage, London.

Antonacopoulou, E.P. and Kandampully, J. (2000) Alchemy: the transformation to service excellence. *The Learning Organization* 7(1), 13–22.

Bensauou, M. and Earl, M. (1998) The right mindset for managing information technology. *Harvard Business Review,* September–October, 119–128.

Berry, L.L. (1995) *On Great Service: A Framework for Action.* Free Press, New York.

Berry, L.L. and Parasuraman, A. (1992) Prescriptions for a service quality revolution in America. *Organizational Dynamics,* Spring, 5–15.

Berry, L.L., Zeithaml, V.A. and Parasuraman, A. (1990) Five imperatives for improving service quality. *Sloan Management Review,* Summer, 29–38.

Bitner, M.J, Booms, B.H. and Tetreault, M.S. (1990) The service encounter: diagnosing favorable and unfavorable incidents. *Journal of Marketing* 54, January, 71–84.

Bitner, M.J., Brown, S.W. and Meuter, M.L. (2000) Technology infusion in service encounters. *Journal of the Academy of Marketing Science* 28, 138–149.

Carlzon, J. (1989) *Moments of Truth*. Harper & Row, New York.

Crosby, L.A. and Stephens, N. (1987) Effects of relationship marketing on satisfaction, retention, and prices in the life insurance industry. *Journal of Marketing Research* 24, November, 404–411.

Evans, M.R., Clark, J.D. and Knutson, B.J. (1996) The 100 percent unconditional money back guarantee. *Cornell HRA Quarterly*, December, 56–61.

Grieves, J. and Mathews, B.P. (1997) Healthcare and the learning service. *The Learning Organization* 4(3), 88–98.

Gronroos, C. (2000) *Service Management and Marketing: A Customer Relationship Management Approach*. John Wiley & Sons, Chichester, UK/New York.

Hamel, G. and Prahalad, C.K. (1989) Strategic intent. *Harvard Business Review*, May–June, 63–76.

Hart, C.W. (1988) The power of unconditional service guarantees. *Harvard Business Review*, July–August, 54–62.

Hart, C. (1990) An objective look at unconditional service guarantees. *The Bankers Magazine* November/December, No. 6, 80–83.

Hart, C. (2000) Uncovering customer value – extraordinary guarantees. *Marketing Management* 9(1), 4–5.

Henry, W.J. (1994) The service employee's pivotal role in organizational success. *Journal of Services Marketing* 8(4), 25–35.

Hill, F. (1994) Making your quality initiative successful: the human side of quality. *CMA Magazine* 68(4), 27.

Kandampully, J. (2001) Service guarantee: an organization's blueprint for assisting the delivery of superior service. In: Kandampully, J., Mok, C. and Sparks, B. (eds) *Service Quality Management: In Hospitality, Tourism and Leisure*. Haworth Hospitality Press, New York, pp. 239–253.

Kandampully, J. (2002a) *Services Management: The New Paradigm in Hospitality*. Pearson Education, French's Forest, Australia.

Kandampully, J. (2002b) Innovation as the core competency of a service organization: the role of technology, knowledge and networks. *European Journal of Innovation Management* 5(1), 18–26.

Kandampully, J. and Duddy, R. (2001) Service system: a strategic approach to gain a competitive advantage in the hospitality and tourism industry. *International Journal of Hospitality and Tourism Administration* 2(1), 27–47.

Keenoy, T. (1990) HRM: a case of the wolf in sheep's clothing. *Personnel Review* 19(2), 3–9.

Kelley, S.W., Hoffman, D.K. and Davis, M.A. (1993) A typology of retail failures and recoveries. *Journal of Retailing* 69(4), 429–452.

Kelley, K. (1997) New rules for the new economy. *Wired*, September, 140.

Lawler, E.E. III (1992) *The Ultimate Advantage: Creating the High Involvement Organization*. Jossey Bass, San Francisco, California.

Maher, D. (1991) Service guarantees double-barrelled standards. *Training* 28(6), 22–25.

Moody, F. (1991) Mr. Software. *New York Times Magazine*, 25, August, 56.

Morita, A. (1988) *Made in Japan: Akio Morita and SONY*. Signet Books, New York, 165 pp.

Oliver, R.L. (1997) *Satisfaction: A Behavioural Perspective on the Consumer*. McGraw-Hill, New York.

Olsen, M.D. and Connolly, D.J. (2000) Experience-based travel. *Cornell Hotel and Restaurant Administration Quarterly* 41(1), 30–41.

Peppers, D. and Rogers, M. (2000) *The One-to-One Manager: Real-World Lessons in Customer Relationship Management*. Capstone Publishing, Oxford, UK.

Peters, T. (1994) *Crazy Times Call for Crazy Organizations: Tom Peters Seminar*. Macmillan, London, p. 10.

Peters, T. and Austin, N. (1994) *A Passion for Excellence: The Leadership Difference*. Random House, New York.

Pilzer, P.Z. (1990) *Unlimited Wealth: The Theory and Practice of Economic Alchemy*. Crown Publishers, New York.

Schneider, B. (1994) HRM – a service perspective: towards a customer-focused HRM. *International Journal of Service Industry Management* 5(1), 64–76.

Sowder, J. (1996) The 100% satisfaction guarantee ensuring quality at Hampton Inn. *National Productivity Review*, Spring, 53–67.

Tax, S.S. and Brown, S.W. (1998) Recovering and learning from service failure. *Sloan Management Review*, Fall, 75–88.

Zeithaml, V.A. (1981) How consumer evaluation process differ between goods and services. In: Donnelly, J. and George, W. (eds) *Marketing of Services: Proceedings of the American Marketing Association Conference*. Chicago, Illinois.

Zemke, R. and Bell, C. (1990) Service recovery: doing it right the second time. *Training*, June, 42–48.

10 Marketing Tourism Online

Lorri Krebs and Geoffrey Wall
University of Waterloo, Canada

Introduction

Marketing tourism via the Internet is a complex exercise with its own peculiar challenges. Tourism itself cannot be reduced to one specific product or service, nor does the Internet simply replicate the potentials of any one specific promotional medium or advertising venue. As society has evolved, changes have occurred in lifestyles and spending patterns and, in conjunction with technological advancements, such as those in transportation and information technology, have combined to shape current travel patterns. Competition to attract tourists has also changed from trying to stimulate people to engage in travel, to trying to capture an increase in market share. Growing number of tourism professionals are turning increasingly to the Internet in the hope that it will give them an edge in their attempts to compete for market share.

At the same time, many businesses remain unconnected to the Internet as scepticism regarding the effectiveness of adopting the Internet as a marketing medium is still prevalent among many tourism operators. Cited as being 'too much trouble' or 'too expensive', the Internet and its role in marketing remain a mystery for some who might be able to benefit from its use.

There are still many unknowns and uncertainties surrounding the marketing of tourism businesses through the Internet. Many operators of tourism enterprises grapple with their annual marketing budgets and face decisions whether or not to invest more in marketing through the Internet, and to what extent might they engage in e-commerce. Gaps exist in the knowledge requirements felt to be associated with adopting this technology, including how to justify the expenditures required to establish and maintain a presence on the Internet. For those still not comfortable with computers, or perhaps for the technologically challenged, the idea of marketing their business using the Internet may seem to be out of reach. Thus, although literature on the use of the Internet in tourism is growing rapidly, because the technology is changing continually and because of the lack of quality information on Internet use by both suppliers and tourists, there is an ongoing need to share current information and experiences.

This chapter explores both the supply and demand sides of the marketing of tourism through the Internet. The suppliers are those tourism businesses that provide information on the Internet. If there was no tourism-related information on the Internet, then potential or actual tourists would not be able to use the Internet as an input into their decision making. Potential and actual tourists constitute the demand side and they may access information on the Internet prior to, during or after their travel is undertaken. There are also intermediaries, such as travel agents, who may choose to have a presence on or access information from the Internet. Thus, a comprehensive understanding of Internet use in tourism requires a holistic perspective, including an appreciation of the roles of numerous players.

This contribution consists of two main components. It will begin with a general discussion of Internet use in tourism through an examination of literature on the use of the Internet by suppliers, tourists and travel intermediaries. This will be followed by a case study on Internet use in Banff, Alberta, Canada. The case study is used to illustrate how a major tourism destination that is a small community within a National Park with significant restrictions on further development, brings together both large and small tourism enterprises successfully and markets to attract approximately 4.6 million annual visitors. The use of the Internet by visitors to Banff will also be examined.

Suppliers and Tourists

Both marketing and tourism researchers have traditionally focused separately on either the supply or the demand side both in general and specifically, with respect to Internet use. The majority of academic studies of Internet use have investigated the demand side, i.e. the uses of the Internet by tourists (Aroch, 1985; Crouch, 1994; Lee, 1996; Klaric, 1999; McCabe, 2000). However, there has been a call for a more integrated approach to tourism research (Jamal and Hollinshead, 2001) to provide a greater understanding of particular issues by exploring them from more than one perspective. The use of the Internet as a marketing tool, then, should be explored from multiple perspectives. For example, as indicated above, use of the Internet in tourism depends on the fact that suppliers have an online presence. However, it would be insufficient to only examine the supply (the presence of suppliers on the Internet) without considering aspects of demand (Internet use by potential and actual tourists) and, accordingly, both are considered in this chapter.

Suppliers

Examples of products or services that are aspects of tourism supply include hotels, attractions, airlines, car rental companies and entertainment outlets. However, because this chapter examines uses of the Internet, supply can be extended to include destination marketing organizations, governments, Internet service providers, Web browsers, online travel agencies and other online travel intermediaries (although intermediaries will also be considered separately below). According to Smith (1994), supply-side research has typically centred in one of three perspectives: (i) a comprehensive planning approach; (ii) a product-specific analysis or (iii) the development of supply-side statistical measures (Smith, 1994). This, however, appears to be an unnecessarily narrow perspective for there is a plethora of research on service quality, aspects of employment in tourism, resource evaluation and other topics. Nevertheless, the supply-side of tourism has not been a strong aspect of academic research on Internet use. On the other hand, there is a wide variety of industry research which includes and even emphasizes Internet use in tourism (Ference, 1996; Evans, 1998; O'Connor, 1999; WTO, 1999). Much of this research has been undertaken from a marketing perspective, with an economic focus (Kotler et al., 1993; Ference, 1996; Seaton and Bennett, 1996). This literature is drawn upon to provide insights on Internet adoption and use by tourism suppliers.

Airlines were among the first tourism businesses to offer use of the Internet to their customers to facilitate planning a trip or reserving a seat and, most recently, purchasing a ticket online (Lipman, 1998). As a result of their early adoption of the Internet, much of the published literature uses the experiences of the airlines in case studies (Lee, 1996; Sheldon, 1997; Lafferty and van Fossen, 2001), although the majority of these case studies pertain to the use of central reservation systems and not specifically to the use of the Internet as a marketing tool. Most of the data on e-commerce in the tourism industry has also been generated from business conducted through airlines. *The New York Times* reported that airline tickets are still the dominant product in e-commerce transactions (Hansell, 2001). However, there are ongoing debates about the reliability of online statistics (Schonland and Williams, 1996; Sora and Natale, 1997).

The Internet can add immense marketing power to both small and large tourism businesses (Milne, 1996). One large company, the National Car Rental Company, was on the brink of bankruptcy, but attributes its recent successes to the use of information technology, especially the Internet (Greenfield, 1996). Smaller tourism businesses can also benefit from the Internet by aligning themselves with larger firms or organizations to gain a presence on the Web (Marcussen, 1997). The hotel sector, from small bed and breakfasts to international hotel chains, regularly use the Internet to enable customers to book rooms and many have reciprocal links with government and tourism organization's Web pages (Yoakhum, 1998). It has been shown that many tourism establishments, such as hotels, are putting a larger proportion of their marketing budgets into Web pages on the Internet (Sheldon, 1997; O'Connor, 1999). Promoting tourism on the Internet has also been discussed by Hanna and Millar (1997) and they have offered suggestions on Web page composition, managerial issues (such as ensuring that online information is kept up to date) and information content.

In spite of the seeming advantages of being able to contact millions of potential customers in their own homes, many tourism suppliers have been cautious in spending money to setting up a Web presence. Suppliers have commonly exhibited an interest in the demographics of Internet users (Marcussen, 1997). While suppliers see marketing, including use of the Internet, as a means of achieving an increase in business activity (Churchill, 1991), ultimately it is economics, or increased profits generated through the Internet, that interests them. However, in terms of return on investment, it has been difficult to gauge the economic effects in actual monetary figures (Vellas and Becherel, 1999). Connolly et al. (1998) revealed that not all shoppers use the Internet for the actual purchase of a product or service even though information ascertained on the Web may have been the influencing factor. A Commerce Net-Nielsen survey found that 53% of Internet users used the Web to reach a purchase decision, yet only 15% completed their purchase online (as reported by CyberAtlas.com, 1998). The volume of e-commerce has been particularly difficult to measure accurately, let alone predict (Loader, 1997). Thus, the most difficult obstacle for many suppliers is to justify the expenditure when they are unable to quantify the results. Calantone and Mazanec (1991, p. 110) noted that tourism is one of the last industries to experience the change from a seller's to a buyer's market. As a result, marketing techniques have been slower to advance and have focused too long on influencing customers rather than developing an explanatory model of travel decision making and testing its applicability.

The above circumstances give rise to the main concern which is a lack of clarity on exactly how the Internet can be used by suppliers to persuade customers to choose their product. Vellas and Becherel (1999, p. 115) have stressed the importance of obtaining a deeper understanding of the behaviour of potential e-commerce users in the tourism industry. Clearly, simply having a website does not ensure the generation of more business. Consequently, there is a need to examine the demand side to gauge the extent to which tourists and potential tourists are using the Internet and why. Before this topic is addressed, the use of the Internet by travel intermediaries will be considered briefly.

Intermediaries

Intermediaries include travel agents and tour operators. Travel agents can play a key role in influencing a traveller's choice of destination by marketing and selling the products or services of tour operators (Milne, 1996). The Ecotourism Working Group (1995) suggested that the most important actors in international nature tourism are the tour operators. Research in Canada has shown that 50% of vacationers seek the advice of travel agents in making their airline selections and that 66% of those seeking tour packages are strongly influenced by travel agent recommendations (Milne, 1996).

It is not only some of the suppliers who have been reluctant to embrace the Internet. Typically, travel agents have been opposed to the increasing use of the Internet for tourism purposes. Fearing that the Internet would reduce and eventually eliminate the need for travel agents, the Internet was not initially embraced by this segment of the tourism industry. The Internet has been viewed by them as being a competitor for reserving and purchasing travel and not as an information supplement. Travel agents have traditionally relied heavily on brochures in their marketing strategies and were not quick to employ the Internet. Since many people pick up brochures prior to making decisions on a destination to visit, they are seen as being a very important resource. However, travel agencies could certainly benefit from the Internet if they were to use it as an additional information source, for example to gain familiarity with a region. It has been shown that 'the ability of travel agents to act as information brokers is limited by an agent's knowledge of a region' (Wilkinson, 1991, p. 39). There is an opportunity to access travel pages online and to look up destination alternatives, different prices and rack rates for hotels and airlines. The fear is that potential customers are then able to use the Internet as leverage with the travel agency networks (Walle, 1996).

In order to deal with competition from the Internet, many travel agencies are opting to set up an Internet presence of their own to provide services for their clients. By joining the Internet, travel agencies may reduce the loss of market share among those who would prefer to book travel using this medium. The Internet also allows travel agents to find travel opportunities for specific market niches quickly and easily. For example, the Internet provides the ability for a travel agent (or a golfer) to search for all holidays catering to golfers. With online travel databases such as *Golfis* or *Lanier's Golf Guide online*, destinations that may have been previously unknown to a travel agent or potential tourist become new possibilities.

Tourists

In order to study demand, the tourists or potential tourists themselves must be considered.

Demand is more widely researched than supply. Pearce (1993, p. 113) indicates that tourism demand is 'the outcome of tourists' motivation, as well as marketing, destination features and contingency factors such as money, health and time relating to the traveller's choice behaviour' (Pearce 1993, p. 113). Baloglu and McCleary (1999) define potential tourists as 'people who engage in information searches about destinations'. Such information searches may include use of the Internet. Demand emanates from all types of tourists, although its consequences may differ, and considerable information is available on tourist typologies, satisfaction, values and motivations. Many opportunities exist to explore Internet uses as a part of this research and such studies have become more pervasive in recent years.

In service industries, one way of defining success is achievement of satisfaction by the consumer (Fornell *et al.*, 1996). Furthermore, one of the key factors in determining tourist satisfaction has been the quality of information sources available to them. Although the Internet is rarely discussed specifically in this literature on expectations and satisfactions, the fact that information sources play a crucial role in tourists' decision making is a good indicator of the need for further research on this topic.

Hanna and Millar (1997) have identified three categories of Internet uses related to travel:

1. Tourists planning a trip – seeking information on air routes and accommodations, distances between cities and towns and attractions, locations of local information centres, and other related topics.
2. Travel agents seeking information for their clients – this has been discussed above in relation to intermediaries.
3. Those who emigrated from the region and use information to 'keep in touch and as a promotional brochure for their friends'.

Studies that profile the pleasure traveller have also begun to explore Internet use. Bonn *et al.* (1999) determined that the pleasure traveller who uses the Internet is generally college-educated, less than 45 years of age, stays at commercial lodging establishments and spends more money each day when travelling than the average traveller. Japanese foreign independent travellers (FITs) use the Internet most often in pre-trip planning to gain as much information as possible on the destination. On the other hand, the traditional Japanese group tour market will most likely use a travel agent when making tour plans and not consult the Internet to assist with destination decisions.

Understanding how a potential visitor responds to destination images is crucial to studies of motivation and the decision-making process (Dann, 1996). Based on the fact that motives determine what is desired as an outcome of a decision, it is believed that the affective appraisal of alternative destinations can occur well before the final decision stage (Gartner, 1993, p. 196). Motives for travel have been shown to be affected by various modes of information dissemination and advertising (Dann, 1996; McWilliams and Crompton, 1997). Thus, exposure to information about a type of trip or a particular destination prior to making the decision can affect the actual choice. Thus, it is important to examine the effects of the people's choices of destinations. In fact, recent studies concerning the affective components of images have been examining the Internet as one factor among many (Dann, 1996). This is a departure from traditional motivation studies that have employed simple word descriptors in questionnaires (Dann, 1996).

The search for more information about travel, whether it is to research a destination, book a trip or just check availability, is clearly one of the motivations behind current Internet use (Walle, 1996). Hanna and Millar (1997) revealed that although a relatively high number of users accessed travel pages, low numbers of users actually accessed the reservation pages. They concluded from these results that many Internet users at that time still preferred to use their travel agents for making bookings (Hanna and Millar, 1997).

Summary

In summary there is growing interest in the use of the Internet in tourism from both supply and demand perspectives. Just as the Internet is a novel form of information technology, and its use is evolving rapidly in tourism, so, inevitably, research on the Internet and its actual and potential uses by all those involved in the industry lag both the phenomena itself and the needs of tourism enterprises. Futhermore, a holistic perspective requires that one address the activities of suppliers and intermediaries as well as the tourists. In order to ground the general discussion in the use of tourism in a specific place, aspects of Internet use in Banff, Alberta, Canada, will now be discussed.

Use of the Internet in Banff, Alberta

The town of Banff is one of the most important tourist destinations in Canada. Since the focus of this chapter is with broad aspects of the use of the Internet in tourism, Banff is an appropriate location to explore Internet use as it is an important destination for both international and domestic tourists. Visitors to Banff National Park reached 4,678,000 in 2001. Banff National Park covers an area of 6641 km^2 but the town of Banff, where the majority of accommodations and tourists are located, is only 4.84 km^2. There are 7135 residents of Banff and more than 1500 businesses are registered as being active in the area. In the winter season, the majority of visitors are skiers and snowboarders.

In order to explore the use of the Internet as a marketing tool, surveys and interviews were conducted over the course of a winter tourist season (December–March 2002) with both tourists and suppliers. Examples of tourism suppliers are car rental companies, hotels and destination marketing organizations such as Ski Banff and Banff/Lake Louise Tourism Bureau. In Banff there are three main 'suppliers':

1. Ski Banff, which promotes skiing at three world-class ski resorts in the area.
2. Banff National Park, the marketing of which is controlled at the national level by the federal government of Canada.
3. Banff/Lake Louise Tourism Bureau (BLLTB) which represents every business in Banff.

The third 'supplier', BLLTB, is of particular interest here because it represents more than 1500 business members and provides them all with some form of Internet presence. Since there is no Chamber of Commerce or other business organization in town, all have become members of BLLTB. Every member has been provided with an Internet link on the main BLLTB website so that there is complete participation from the supply perspective.

Most of the winter visitors to Banff were found to originate from Canada, closely followed by USA, and then UK, Germany, Australia, China and New Zealand in that order. There are also small numbers of visitors from many other countries. As indicated above, the primary activities and/or reasons for travelling to Banff in the winter season were skiing/snowboarding, but some came for sightseeing, conferences or weekend getaways to relax in a mountainous environment.

When examining effectiveness of marketing tools, one is trying to understand their influences upon decision making with an intention, ultimately, to use this information to match supply and demand. Many models and theories related to decision making have been proposed but they all include the information source or sources as a key variable or component. For example, one may be interested in whether a particular advertisement, book or experience influenced the decisions of potential or actual visitors. Similarly, for this discussion, the role of the Internet in these decisions is the focus of attention. More specifically, the extent to which the Internet is perceived as being an

important information source by winter tourists to Banff is the topic of concern here.

In order to address this question, a survey of visitors to Banff was undertaken: 202 completed an in-depth questionnaire and 68 participated in informal interviews in various locations throughout the town of Banff. The survey of visitors was conducted between December 2001 and March 2002 as a means to explore in what capacities tourists are using the Internet. Are they accessing the Internet for e-commerce (to actually purchase something), to make reservations, as a means of making comparisons (to compare possible destinations or the options within a destination, or the means of getting to a destination), as an information source to embellish their knowledge of the area, product or service, or to communicate with someone who has been there or used the product (through chat rooms or e-mail)? The first step was to examine the sources of information that tourists used most often and also to determine their Internet use. It is necessary to make a distinction between the two because there are many reasons for using the Internet that are not connected with tourism. Figure 10.1 shows the sources of information that the respondents regularly draw upon in connection with tourism. It indicates that all of the respondents to this survey used the Internet as a source of information. Friends (or by word of mouth), television, magazines, brochures and travel catalogues were used by successively smaller proportions of respondents. Less than half of the respondents used travel agents. Television use included

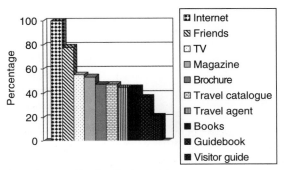

Fig. 10.1. Sources of information used by Banff winter visitors.

more than commercials as many informants indicated that they gained information from travel shows.

Equally important in examining whether or not the Internet is used is learning *how* and *when* it enters into tourists' decision-making processes. Mackay and Fesenmaier (1998) broke down travel planning into five stages:

1. No intention to travel.
2. Preplanning a trip.
3. Finalizing travel plans.
4. Reserving and/or purchasing a travel product.
5. Decisions made on a trip.

The level of Internet use of Banff winter tourists for each of these five stages of travel is presented in Fig. 10.2. High levels of Internet use were found among Banff winter visitors in all stages of travel. Internet use is most frequent during the preplanning stage, suggesting that information searches are a frequent Internet use activity. Some people are still reluctant to actually purchase travel items via the Internet and this was the phase in which the Internet was least used among this group of tourists. However, the Internet was still used to actually purchase travel products by almost 70% of respondents. Respondents frequently indicated in conversation that they liked sites that allowed them to check availability, make reservations and pay, and a majority performed monetary transactions over the Internet (engaged in e-commerce).

Many respondents indicated they have visited travel websites when they had no intention to take a trip. This is less common with other

marketing media. For example, requesting brochures or travel catalogues in the absence of an intention to take a trip would be unusual, and seeking information from a travel agent with no trip intention is unlikely behaviour.

It is apparent that people look for different types of information from the Internet depending upon their stage of travel. Eight types of information were generally sought from the Internet:

1. General information about a destination.
2. Accommodation.
3. Attractions.
4. Transportation.
5. Events.
6. Cultural information.
7. Website links.
8. Types of travel (e.g. skiing).

When tourists had no intention to take a trip, they mostly sought general information about a destination. During preplanning, accommodation information became very important as well. When finalizing travel plans, respondents considered accommodation information to be the most valuable, followed closely by general information, transportation and event information. As the respondents moved to the purchasing point, transportation was deemed to be most important followed closely by accommodation and attractions. While on a trip, tourists continued to place a high value on general information, but accessed cultural information as well.

Overall, general information was of primary importance and categories of travel were viewed as being least important, followed by Web links, events and cultural information –

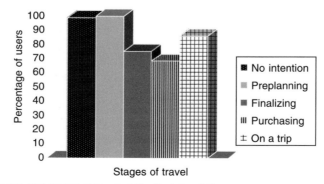

Fig. 10.2. Internet use and stages of travel of Banff winter visitors.

on a scale of 1 (the most important) to 7 (the least important) – Fig. 10.3.

Having looked briefly at how Banff winter tourists are using the Internet and the types of information they are seeking, we will draw our attention back briefly to the supply side. So what is the role of the suppliers? Why is it necessary to examine supply at all? The most obvious answer is that there have to be websites to use for the potential or actual tourist to use the Internet for tourism-related purposes. In a marketing context, suppliers are usually attempting to communicate with a particular target or market. Thus, suppliers should know why they wish to use the Internet, who they wish to communicate with, and what information they wish to convey. At first sight, this may seem to be simple but, when asked, it was found that many suppliers had not previously thought seriously about these questions and had difficulty in answering them.

In Banff, most of the business operators, especially the smaller or newer ones, felt they needed Internet presence. However, it was often perceived as being too expensive to have a website designed and many felt that they did not understand the process sufficiently and so were hesitant to get involved. Only one supplier who had a website had actually thought carefully about what they hoped to gain from the Internet; that was the BLLTB. Their main objective for developing the website was to avoid personal contact by potential or actual

visitors with the Bureau. The site was intended to be used for information only and to provide information tourists may want, in particular, links to their members' (local businesses) own sites. In fact, if someone does contact the Bureau with a question, the Bureau will update the website to include the answer so that they will not receive further inquiries about it.

Suppliers really control use in the sense that if it is not available, it cannot be used. From advertising and marketing perspective, if a supplier wants to increase market share, the Internet should be included and budgeted for in their marketing plans, particularly if they wish to attract frequent Internet users, such as most skiers. To neglect the Internet as an advertising medium is to ensure that a certain, but unknown, percentage of potential tourists will not visit or use the tourism product or service. Tolerance for non-representation is low among many Internet users. There is a prevalent attitude among many potential tourists that suggests that they will not stay at a property that has no presence on the Internet. They will choose a different product or service that can be accessed via the Internet – perhaps even regardless of which tourism product or service was their original intention when they initially went online. Thus, the referrals from friends and relatives are not as effective in influencing decision making if the potential tourist cannot access and corroborate similar information online. Thus, among Banff skiers,

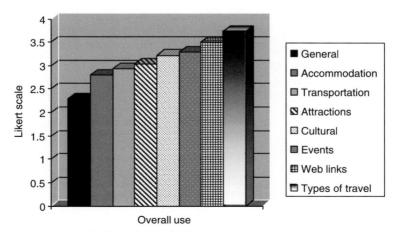

Fig. 10.3. Importance of type of information available.

recommendations by friends were often put aside if they could not book online.

It is possible to conclude from the Banff case study that most suppliers in this tourist town have a Web presence and almost all winter visitors are Internet users. Of course, the situation may be different among tourists who visit at other times of the year, among other market segments and in different destinations. It appears that the Web is an effective means of providing information to tourists, although there is still reluctance among some users to pay through the Internet and, thus, become fully involved in e-commerce. Since potential tourists have to look actively to acquire information, it is unlikely that the Internet can be used successfully to lure a new market segment. However, if suppliers wish to increase market share in existing market segments, they should be willing to invest resources into their websites. Failure to have a Web presence can discourage potential purchasers, especially highly educated, high-spending tourists, such as Banff skiers, who are frequent users of the Internet.

Conclusion

It is necessary to examine how innovations affect current systems to identify the changes occurring as a result of adoption of new technology. The Internet represents 'the emergence of a new medium, mixing forms of communication which were previously separated in different domains of the human mind' (Castells, 2000, p. 392). The Internet has been called 'a new form of orality expressed by an electronic text' (Castells, 2000, p. 392). Marketing through the Internet requires a different strategy than with traditional media. The Internet does not target and overtly contact specific people since the user initiates the interaction (Walle, 1996). Current 'outbound Internet tactics are primarily intended to mass market and promote products to all interested Internet users' (Walle, 1996).

This chapter has explored how the Internet is becoming intertwined in many facets of tourism. Goeldner et al. (2000) acknowledge that the Internet is both an information source and a means of making transactions: 'Consequently, the Internet is a new marketing medium. It has the advantage that it can be used by virtually everyone in the tourism industry from the largest operator to the smallest.' It provides the opportunity to inform, motivate and provide contacts that are often used to evaluate destination alternatives and make choices.

This chapter has examined the Internet and the role it is playing in tourism marketing. The use of the Internet by tourism suppliers, travel intermediaries and tourists has been reviewed and a case study of Banff, Alberta, has been outlined. A common feature throughout these discussions has been an emphasis on the role of the Internet as an information source and a marketing tool. While the effectiveness of brochures in marketing destinations has been documented (Wicks and Schuett, 1991; Goossens, 1994) and the influences of friends and relatives are not disputed (Gitelson and Kerstetter, 1994), the full effects of the Internet on decision making are only just beginning to be discovered.

It is also important to appreciate that the Internet may be used differently by different market segments. If potential tourists have specific expectations of the form and contents of a worthy website and their criteria are not met, then the website will be ineffective in promoting the destination or business (Murphy, 1999). On the other hand, it may be possible to attract large number of tourists to an area or attraction as a result of having an Internet 'link'. If the particular tourist supplier is not prepared for a sudden influx of customers, it may result in dissatisfaction among clients and the risk of damage to the resource on which the supply is based through overbooking, environmental degradation, insufficient supplies and related management challenges. Since there is a lack of conclusive evidence concerning who is using the Internet and to what end, it is possible that an inappropriate target market may be reached (Loader, 1997). For example, Milne (1996, p. 122) noted that 'the socio-economic profile ascribed to eco-alternative travellers' are the same as for Internet users. As many 'eco' vacationers have certain expectations about appropriate group sizes and behaviour (Ecotourism Working Group, 1995), could there be a potential problem with controlling the Internet 'masses' that may be attracted to this form of tourism?

Regardless of such uncertainties, the Internet does appear to be an effective means of marketing various types of tourism. The Banff case study illustrates the pervasiveness of Internet use among both suppliers and tourists in some markets. It is likely to continue to be an important means of information exchange between suppliers and tourists for the foreseeable future. As such, Internet use needs to be understood by tourism suppliers and marketeers and merits further research.

References

Aroch, R. (1985) Socio-economic research into tourist motivation and demand patterns. *Tourist Review* 40(4), 27–29.

Baloglu, S. and McCleary, K.W. (1999) A model of destination image formation. *Annals of Tourism Research* 26, 868–897.

Bonn, M.A., Furr, H.L. and Susskind, A.M. (1999) Predicting a behavioural profile for pleasure travelers on the basis of Internet use segmentation. *Journal of Travel Research* 37(4), 333–346.

Calantone, R.J. and Mazanec, J.A. (1991) Marketing management and tourism. *Annals of Tourism Research* 18, 101–119.

Castells, M. (2000) *The Rise of the Network Society*. Blackwell, Oxford.

Churchill, G.A. (1991) *Market Research: Methological Foundations*. The Dryden Press, Chicago, Illinois.

Connolly, D.J., Olsen, M.D. and Moore, R.G. (1998) The Internet as a distribution channel. *Cornell Hotel and Restaurant Administration Quarterly* 39(4), 42–54.

Crouch, G.I. (1994) Promotion and demand in international tourism. In: Crotts, J.C. and van Raaij, W.F. (eds) *Economic Psychology of Travel and Tourism*. Haworth Press, New York, pp. 109–125.

Dann, G.M.S. (1996) Tourist images of a destination – an alternative analysis. In: Fesenmaier, D.R., O'Leary, J.T. and Uysal, M. (eds) *Recent Advances in Tourism Marketing Research*. Hayworth Press, New York, pp. 41–55.

Ecotourism Working Group (1995) *Ecotourism as a Conservation Instrument?* Research reports of the Federal Ministry for Economic Cooperation and Development, Vol. 117. BMZ, Cologne, Germany.

Evans, M. (ed.) (1998) *World Travel and Tourism Development*. Issue 3. THG International Publishing, Chicago, Illinois.

Ference, W.C. (1996) *Online Travel Marketing Services in Canada. Report and Analysis*. Canadian Tourism Commission, Montreal, Canada, p. 118.

Fornell, C., Johnson, M.D., Anderson, E.W., Cha, J. and Bryant, B.E. (1996) The American customer satisfaction index. *Journal of Marketing* 60(1), 7–18.

Gartner, W. (1993) Images formation process. *Journal of Travel and Tourism Marketing* 2(2/3), 191–215.

Gitelson, R.J. and Kerstetter, D. (1994) The influence of friends and relatives in travel decision-making. *Journal of Travel and Tourism Marketing* 3(3), 59–68.

Goeldner, C.R., Ritchie, J.R.B. and McIntosh, R.W. (2000) *Tourism: Principles, Practices, Philosophies*. John Wiley & Sons, New York.

Goossens, C. (1994) External information search: effects of tour brochures with experiential information. *Journal of Travel and Tourism Marketing* 3(3), 89–107.

Greenfield, D. (1996) Or overhaul. *Operations Research Management Science* (April), 12–14.

Hanna, J.R.P and Millar, R.J. (1997) Promoting tourism on the Internet. *Tourism Management* 18(7), 469–470.

Hansell, S. (2001) Web sales of airline tickets are making hefty advances. *New York Times*, online issue.

Jamal, T. and Hollinshead, K. (2001) Tourism and the forbidden zone: the underserved power of qualitative inquiry. *Tourism Management* 22, 63–82.

Klaric, Z. (1999) Impact of distance and availability of information on travel to conflict regions – example of Croatia. *Turizam* 47(1), 26–35.

Kotler, P., Haider, D.H. and Rein, I. (1993) *Marketing Places*. Free Press, New York.

Lafferty, G. and van Fossen, A. (2001) Integrating the tourism industry: problems and strategies. *Tourism Management* 22, 11–19.

Lee, C.K. (1996) Major determinants of international tourism demand for South Korea: inclusion of marketing variable. *Journal of Travel and Tourism Marketing* 5(1/2), 101–111.

Lipman, G. (1998) A global opportunity. In: Evans, M. (ed.) *World Travel and Tourism Development*, 3rd edn. THG Publishing, Chicago, Illinois, pp. 25–29.

Loader, B.D. (1997) *The Governance of Cyberspace: Politics, Technology and Global Restructuring.* Routledge, London.

Mackay, K.J. and Fesenmaier, D.R. (1998) A process approach to segmenting the gateway travel market. *Journal of Travel and Tourism Marketing* 7(3), 1–39.

Marcussen, C.H. (1997) Marketing european tourism products via Internet/WWW. *Journal of Travel and Tourism Marketing* 6(3/4), 23–34.

McCabe, S. (2000) The problem of motivation in understanding the demand for leisure day visits. In: Woodside, A.G., Crouch, G.I., Mazanec, J.A., Oppermann, M. and Sakai, M.Y. (eds) *Consumer Psychology of Tourism, Hospitality and Leisure.* CAB International, Wallingford, UK, pp. 211–226.

McWilliams, E.G. and Crompton, J.L. (1997) An expanded framework for measuring the effectiveness of destination advertising. *Tourism Management* 18(3), 127–137.

Milne, S. (1996) Tourism marketing and computer reservation systems in the Pacific. In: Hall, C.M. and Page, S. (eds) *Tourism in the Pacific.* International Thomas Publishing, London, pp. 109–129.

Murphy, J. (1999) Surfers and searchers: an examination of website visitor's clicking behaviour. *Cornell Hotel and Restaurant Administration Quarterly* 40(2), 84–89.

O'Connor, P. (1999) *Electronic Information Distribution in Tourism and Hospitality.* CAB International, Wallingford, UK.

Pearce, P.L. (1993) Fundamentals of tourist motivation. In: Pearce, D.W. and Butler, R.W. (eds) *Tourism Research: Critiques and Challenge.* Routledge, London, pp. 113–134.

Schonland, A.M. and Williams, P.W. (1996) Using the Internet for travel and tourism survey research: experiences from the net traveler survey. *Journal of Travel Research* 35(2), 81–87.

Seaton, A.V. and Bennett, M.M. (1996) *The Marketing of Tourism Products: Concepts, Issues and Cases.* International Thomson Business Press, London.

Sheldon, P. (1997) *Tourism Information Technology.* CAB International, Wallingford, UK.

Smith, S.L.J. (1994) The tourism product. *Annals of Tourism Research* 21(3), 582–595.

Sora, S.A. and Natale, S.M. (1997) Aspects of change for management in the Internet environment. *International Journal of Value-Based Management* 10, 213–219.

Vellas, F. and Becherel, L. (1999) *The International Marketing of Travel and Tourism. A Strategic Approach.* Macmillan Press, London.

Walle, A.H. (1996) Tourism and the Internet: opportunities for direct marketing. *Journal of Travel Research* 35(1),72–76.

Wicks, B.E. and Schuett, M.A. (1991) Examining the role of tourism promotion through the use of brochures. *Tourism Management* 11, 301–312.

Wilkinson, P. (1991) Travel agents as information brokers: the case of Anguilla & Dominica. *The Operational Geographer* 9(3), 37–41.

WTO (1999) *Marketing Tourism Destinations Online.* World Tourism Organization Business Council, Madrid.

Yoakhum, J. (1998) Information technology tightens up on room space. In: Evans, M. (ed.) *World Travel and Tourism Development*, Issue 3. THG International Publishing, Chicago, Illinois, pp. 290–293.

11 Guidelines for Professional Activity Services in Tourism – A Discussion About the Quality of a Tourist Experience Product

Raija Komppula
University of Joensuu, Finland

Introduction

The total demand and supply for nature-based activity services such as skiing, trekking and fishing has risen rapidly during the last ten years. Lapland is particularly well known as a nature-based adventure destination in several target groups: short Christmas packaged tours for British families, wilderness trekking for individual tourists and incentive-adventures for foreign and inbound tourists are an especially growing business. For Finnish companies, nature-based activities are an important means of corporate entertainment, and local businesses are, in many cases, the most important customer group for activity operators, especially outside the tourism peak seasons.

The number of businesses that specialize in nature- and adventure-excursions, fishing services and similar nature-based activities have increased significantly since 1993. In Lapland and a few skiing or other holiday centres in southern Finland most of the activity companies are small employing only the owners. Only a few operators employ staff in addition to the owner and these operators are usually restricted to serving a maximum of 50 customers at any one time. Almost a quarter of the nature-based activity operators do not have full-time personnel (Aalto *et al.*, 1999).

Many of the businesses providing these services are so-called rural tourism companies, which often operate on a part-time basis only. Generally, the hospitality, tourism and leisure industries have low entry barriers. Many new businesses are created as a result of identifying an opportunity following experiences of neighbours, or are built on the back of a hobby or an interest. For individuals with no business or industry background, many of the skills have to be learnt whilst 'on the job' (Morrison *et al.*, 1999, p. 128; Komppula, 2002). There is no legislation in Finland that regulates start-ups in the tourism industry, so it is possible to begin offering activity service without any professional training or experience.

These characteristics of the industry mean that it is difficult to guarantee the quality of these services. Nevertheless, nature-based activities are often marketed as unforgettable, memorable and unique experiences, which promise excellent product quality. While nature-based activities are most often the basis for incentive products, the quality demands for the products are high, in general.

The purpose of this chapter is first to briefly present the results of a tourism development project called the MONO project and then assess the results from a services perspective. The aim of the MONO project was to develop voluntary guidelines for the production of a range of nature-based activity services in order to help the service providers, intermediaries and customers in the production, purchase and evaluation of the products. After discussing the outcomes of the project the chapter examines the concept of tourist product followed by a presentation of a descriptive model of prerequisites for the customer-oriented tourist product. A short theoretical review on the service quality is then presented, after which the results of the MONO project are discussed in the light of these theories.

The MONO Project – Guidelines for Professional Activity Services in Tourism

In order to develop the quality of the nature-based activity service offering, a national project (the MONO project) was funded by the European Social Fund through the Administrative Board of South Finland, and conducted by South Karelian Fair Center Ltd during 2000–2002. The aim of this project was to develop voluntary guidelines for the activity operators in order to develop the quality and professionalism of these services. The project is discussed in detail in Komppula et al. (2002).

The problem for businesses within the field of activity services was seen to be the versatility of available products and the fact that there are no clear basic concepts to define the actual product. In addition, it was felt that there are no existing meters or systems, which would assess the functional quality of the product, the professional skills of the providers of the service, safety, environmental and consumer protection standards and the functional quality of subcontractor relationships.

The objective of the guidelines was to be as comprehensive as possible and to meet international standards while also providing practical instructions for the operator in service production. Snowmobiling and trekking/cross-country skiing product groups were chosen for the pilot products of the first stage of the development work. After the pilot stage, products based on adventures and experiences, riding and cycling and water activities were also examined.

The development of the guidelines was conducted by six product-based teams. The National Consumer Administration, the Ministry of the Environment, the Ministry of Education, the Finnish Forest Research Institute and several organizations representing each activity as well as numerous entrepreneurs from the industry were represented in the teams. The work was based on a workbook, which contained the appropriate legislation and the known practices in the field for each type of activity. A consultant, who led the teamwork, prepared the workbook. The work groups checked and specified the demands set for products, professional demands, guidelines for sustainable development, safety demands, guidelines regarding consumer protection and customer service expertise presenting these as clear instructions. The consultant in charge of the work, together with the project manager, drafted a final manuscript which was based on the workbooks and contained completed guidelines for professional activity services in each activity area.

The guidelines packages produced by the product teams consisted of 38 pages: 11 pages of definitions for concepts and terms, 21/2 pages of defining the professional qualifications for the activity sector, 3 pages of sustainable development, 7 pages of safety instructions, 1 page of consumer protection, business-to-business agreements and customer service expertise and 6 pages listing laws and other existing norms that regulate the activity service production.

In the definitions section, there are, definitions of activities, e.g. snow-mobiling routes, trekking routes, hiking routes and different kinds of cycling routes. The definitions indicate how easy or difficult the route as well as the type of facilities and services there are along the route (e.g. toilets, camp fires, shelters). Where internationally known and accepted definitions or national norms were identified, they are adapted as definitions. Otherwise, the definitions were created through teamwork. An important contribution of the definitions section was an agreement on the product definitions, for example, the difference between a snow-mobile safari and snow-mobile excursion is defined: an excursion is 1–3 h long guided trip and a safari is a more than 3 h guided tour with a destination and with at least one meal.

The minimum content of product specification is also defined, as well as equipment required for the activity. For each product group the 'demandness level' is defined and described. This description includes the level of difficulty of the activity and a description of how demanding a track or activity is. An example of an easy activity, in this case cross-country skiing, means a short track on open, even terrain, normal is a track on passable terrain, exacting means skiing in a variable terrain and very exacting means long term skiing in a variable terrain. For riding and cycling, the definitions also contain recommendations in relation to customers' capabilities. The definitions also contain recommendations for terms of cancellation as well as terms of payment. The following illustrates the type of definitions that were developed:

> LEVELS OF RIDING
> Easy: former experience of riding not required;
> Normal: some experience of riding required;
> Demanding: advanced skills of riding required;
> Extremely demanding: advanced skills and long experience of riding required.

The definitions section of each report offers an important contribution to the relationships between the customer and the service provider, especially in marketing. If all the counterparts use the same 'language' it is more probable that customers know what they can expect, which may reduce the risk of disappointment.

The legislation section comprised the last part of the report but it was the first part of the report written during the MONO project. The need for an in-depth review of legislation was important and highlighted the absence of legislation for a number of nature-based activities. As a consequence of this legislative deficiency, a number of activity-based operators have had to resort to borrowing guidelines from existing laws. As a consequence the great majority of entrepreneurs, most of whom were the pioneers in their fields, have experienced a difficult and time consuming task attempting to clarify legal requirements. It was obvious that a few entrepreneurs started building their facilities and business activities without sufficient knowledge of legal requirements and responsibilities. This has not posed a problem in the absence of accidents, but following an accident legal action to ascribe responsibility and claims

for compensations have posed considerable problems for operators.

Because a remarkable part of the legislation refers to safety requirements, consumer protection as well as indemnification regulations and the sections relating to consumer protection and business-to-business agreements are quite short. The safety section contains detailed recommendations on safety checks and guidance before and during the activity, recommendations on the number of guides per group and recommendations for rescue plans. Guidelines for professional demands and customer service expertise contain listings of skills and knowledge needed in different professional tasks in the activity industry.

Environmental responsibility and sustainable development had a central position in the objectives of the project. In the final publication guidelines on sustainable development concentrated mainly on ecological sustainability and, in particular, on the sustainable use of the natural environment. The chapter containing the guidelines included practical advice and examples for an entrepreneur to avoid actions that might spoil the environment. There is also one sentence about cultural and social sustainability: it is recommended that entrepreneurs not cause any inconvenience to local people in terms of their social, economic or cultural life.

These guidelines were launched for the industry during 2003. A new project with the objectives of training the entrepreneurs and teachers in the educational sector began at the beginning of 2003. In the first stage of the training project teachers of vocational education, consultants in the travel and tourism sector and the representatives of rural advisory centres are trained up for the basic principles of the MONO. These stakeholders are important intercessors of the guidelines in the industry. At the second stage specialists of the respective activities in the MONO will organize specialized courses for the entrepreneurs.

Nature-Based Activity Service – a Tourist Experience Product

Several definitions of the tourist product (Middleton, 1989; Murphy et al., 2000;

Middleton and Clarke, 2001), as well as the theory of service marketing (cf. Grönroos, 2000), emphasize the added value of the product, which emerges at each stage of the production process. The aim and the desired outcome for the customer is value, which at each given time is a subjective experience (cf. Gunn, 1994). This value has to be balanced against those sacrifices that the customer is willing to make in order to obtain a particular experience.

Particularly with holiday tourism, the customer hopes to have memorable positive experiences defined as events, which often follow each other as a process. The experiences may be singular, sudden or they may be continuous, like a travel experience. An emotional experience requires both physical and mental presence in order to come true. When buying an experience, a customer pays to be able to spend time and enjoy a series of memorable events, which the enterprises 'set on display' (Pine and Gilmore, 1999; Mossberg, 2001). According to Cho and Fesenmaier (2001), the most important challenge in travel and tourism marketing in the future is that of creating expectation of experience.

Because the emotional experience is subjective, it is not possible to produce emotional tourism experiences in enterprises. Edvardsson and Olsson (1999) (cf. also Edvardsson et al., 2000) argue that the service company does not provide the service but the prerequisites for the various services. The company sells opportunities for services, which are generated in partially unique customer processes. The central goal of service development is to develop the best and right prerequisites for well-functioning customer processes and attractive customer outcomes. The prerequisites for the service are the end-result of the service development process. The correct prerequisites can be described by a model with three basic components: (i) a service concept; (ii) a service process; and (iii) a service system (Edvardsson and Olsson, 1999).

The core of the tourist product, *the service concept*, consists of the idea of what kind of value the customer expects and how to create the prerequisites for this experience. In marketing terminology, the service concept is expressed in such a way that it evokes mental images of being able to gain, through a partic-

ular product, the very experiences and value that the customer expects from travelling. The service concept is based on the needs of the customer, which are based on the primary and secondary motives of the customer to travel (Komppula and Boxberg, 2002).

The description of the *service process* of the tourist product includes the definition of the formal product (cf. Kotler *et al.*, 1999; Komppula and Boxberg, 2002). For the customer, it is expressed in the form of a brochure or an offer. In the company and for the staff, the formal product might mean the determination and definition of the chain of activities in the customer process and the production process (Komppula and Boxberg, 2002). This chain can be illustrated as a service blueprint, which first of all charts those activities and processes (customer processes), which the customer goes through at different stages of the service (Zeithaml and Bitner, 2000, pp. 206–207).

The *service system* includes those resources available to the service process for realizing the service concept. This includes the involvement of the service company's staff, the customers, the physical and technical environment and the organization and control of these resources. The hospitality element of the tourist product is mainly produced by the staff and other customers. Freedom of choice and customer involvement are highly dependent upon the service process, the customer himself and the physical environment. All these together, the service concept, the service process and the service system create the prerequisites of the tourist experience, the augmented product, the very intangible expectations, which will or will not be fulfilled as the outcome of the customer process (Komppula and Boxberg, 2002).

For the customer, the tourist product is an experience based on his or her subjective evaluation, which has a certain price and which is the outcome of a process, where the customer exploits the services of those who offer them by taking part in the production process of the service himself or herself. Figure 11.1 illustrates the nature of the customer-oriented tourist product.

The underlying prerequisite for successful tourist product development is a continuous service system development, which involves

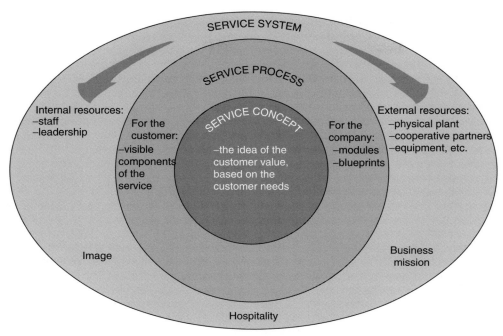

Fig. 11.1. Prerequisites for the customer-oriented tourist product. Source: Komppula and Boxberg (2002, p. 24).

continual development of the company strategy (Edvardsson *et al.*, 2000). So the 'augmented tourist product' mentioned by Middleton and Clarke (2001) (see also Lumsdon, 1997; Kotler *et al.*, 1999) is actually the company itself, its reputation and image. The corporate image refers to the kinds of ideas and impressions people have of the organization in general. The corporate identity is made up of the perceptions formed by external audiences of everything a company is seen to do. Branding does, at the level of the product, what corporate identity does at the level of the firm (Seaton, 1996, pp. 126–127).

The tourist product, which is created with these prerequisites may also be described as a service package, which consists of several molecules (Shostack, 1977). In the context of the tourist product, these are often called modules. The core of the product is formed by the service concept based on the needs of the customer, a description of the value, for which the enterprise creates the prerequisites with different activities. These activities form the service

process, in which the customer takes part. The parts of the chain are service modules produced by the tourist businesses. The customer experiences the product in that service environment and within the framework of that organization which the business has to offer and filters the experience through the expectations and mental images which he or she has had on the operator and other corresponding products. When a customer turns to the activity operator, he or she expects it to offer experiences, which are created together with the customer and businesses. The task of the operator is to provide the best possible prerequisites for the experience, an attractive idea and description of the product, successful service process and a reliable, functioning service system. The tourist experience product could be illustrated as in Fig. 11.2.

The customer-oriented model of the immediate prerequisites of the tourist product presented in Fig. 11.1 and the packaged tourist product presented in Fig. 11.2 may be applied to the description of the tourist product both in singular tourism businesses and in

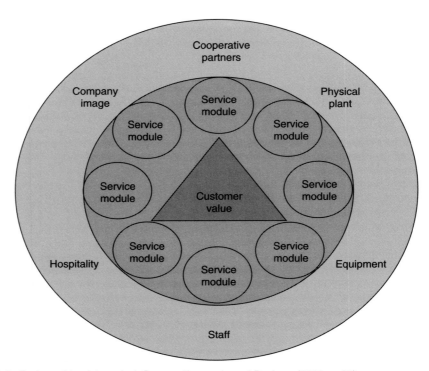

Fig. 11.2. Packaged tourist product. Source: Komppula and Boxberg (2002, p. 25).

tourist destinations. It is essential that the starting point for examination is always the value expected by the customer. This value may, however, be the outcome of several businesses or activities, even in many destinations, as is noted in the definition of the total tourist product put forward by Middleton.

A typical Finnish incentive product for foreign customers could take shape in the following manner. The service concept is created by a business customer's need to offer his or her staff an exclusive nature adventure experience, which rewards its participants mentally with the feeling of exceeding one's limits and indulges the customer with luxurious care afterwards. From this need, those businesses offering this tourist product start to outline those activities and processes, which would belong to the actual product. Each of these activities form their own module, for which a specific production plan and blueprint will be drafted, as with those activities which bind the modules together. The modules form an entity, which is implemented in an appropriate environment. Figure 11.3 illustrates the description of a product when the target customer group is, e.g. the male salesmen of a car factory.

The formal product of the same service concept, i.e. the service process, would seem quite different if the target group was, e.g. a senior club consisting of former female managers of a large bank. The service system and concept could be the same, but the activity models would emphasize far softer adventures.

The Quality of the Tourist Product

Through the years, researchers have been on a quest to identify the most significant components of service quality. The SERVQUAL battery developed by Zeithaml *et al.* (1990) has produced a generic measure of service quality

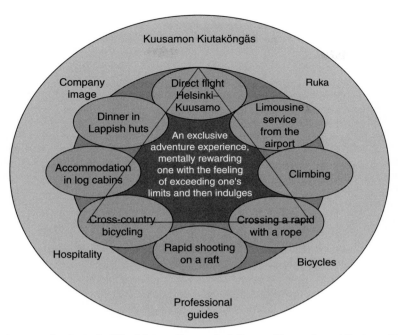

Kuusamon Kiutaköngäs

Company image

Direct flight Helsinki–Kuusamo

Ruka

Dinner in Lappish huts

Limousine service from the airport

An exclusive adventure experience, mentally rewarding one with the feeling of exceeding one's limits and then indulges

Accommodation in log cabins

Climbing

Cross-country bicycling

Crossing a rapid with a rope

Hospitality

Rapid shooting on a raft

Bicycles

Professional guides

Fig. 11.3. An example of a typical Finnish incentive product. Source: Komppula and Boxberg (2002, p. 33).

through an examination of 22 service items, which factor into five basic service dimensions: reliability, tangibles, responsiveness, assurance and empathy.

Reliability reflects the service provider's ability to perform service dependably and accurately, including 'doing it right the first time'. Tangibles consist of the appearance of physical facilities, equipment, personnel and communication materials. Responsiveness represents the willingness to help customers and provide prompt service. Assurance reflects the knowledge and courtesy of employees and their ability to inspire trust and confidence. Guests expect to feel safe in their transactions with employees. Empathy involves the caring, individual attention a firm provides for its customers (Parasuraman et al., 1988). Although the original SERVQUAL instrument has been challenged by a number of academic researchers, there have been many adaptations of the tool to suit specific operational characteristics of the hospitality environment. As a result, such terms as LODGQUAL, LODGSERV, DINESERV, HOLSAT and GROVQUAL have become common in the

industry (Knutson et al., 1991; Stevens et al., 1995; Tribe and Snaith, 1998; Augustyn and Ho, 1998; O'Neil, 2001).

Perceived service quality reflects the difference between the guest's expectations and the actual services performed. The extent to which expectations and service performance are similar or different influence the extent to which guests are satisfied or dissatisfied. A customer's expectations are derived partly from personal needs, previous experience of similar products and word-of-mouth (WOM) recommendation from others, as well as from marketing communication. Grönroos (1984) distinguishes three dimensions of perceived service quality: technical, functional and image-dimensions. Technical dimensions represent what the consumer actually receives from the service as a result of the interaction with the service provider. Examples include a restaurant meal or a hotel room. Functional quality represents the actual performance of the service, the manner in which the service provider delivers the service to a customer. Attitude, tact, skills, knowledge and friendliness are examples. They are seen subjectively by the customers. Together, technical quality and functional quality represent a bundle of goods and services that create an image.

In his later work, Grönroos (2000) has presented seven criteria for good perceived service quality, which he divides into three dimensions as illustrated in Table 11.1.

The guest's overall perception of service quality results from a variety of experiences with the service provider over a period of time. Service providers have to look not only at the on-site personal experience of the guest, but also at events that precede and follow. On this service, continuum services can be described as: those the guest experiences before entering the facilities of the service provider (these include customer information, reservations, hours, grounds); those the guest encounters while the service is actually being performed (including check-in/point of entry, payment terms, guest assistance, physical facilities, guest services, checkout/point of departure); and those that occur after the guest has departed (customer follow-up, complaint resolution, frequent guest incentives). Quality service emanates from total service commitment, which requires a commitment on all the levels

of the service provider organization. Everyone in the organization should work together towards the common goal of delivering quality service (Schlagel Wuest, 2001, pp. 57–64).

If we adapt the above discussion about service quality to the description model of prerequisites of customer-oriented tourist product as well as the model of a packaged tourist product, we may suggest the following: the quality of service concept evaluated before the experience refers to the image-dimension and image-related criteria of the tourist product. Outcome-related criteria are adapted during and after the service process. The quality of the service process evaluated refers to process-related criteria, which contain both technical and functional qualities. The service system quality is a combination of all the other dimensions, but the system quality especially reflects the overall commitment of the service provider to the good quality. Grönroos (1990) argues that excellent service quality cannot be provided without committed, dedicated and capable staff. This argument suggests that internal marketing and employee satisfaction are as vital to organizational success as is effective external marketing and functional and technical quality.

Table 11.1. The seven criteria of good perceived service quality.

1. **Outcome-related criteria**
   - *Professionalism and skills*: Customers realize that the service provider, its employees, operational systems and physical resources have the knowledge and skills required to solve their problems in a professional way.
2. **Process-related criteria**
   - *Attitudes and behaviour*: Customers feel that the service employees are concerned about them and interested in solving their problems in a friendly and spontaneous way.
   - *Accessibility and flexibility*: Customers feel that the service provider, its location, operating hours, employees and operational systems are designed and operate so that it is easy to gain access to the service, and that the services are adjusted to the demands and wishes of the customer in a flexible way.
   - *Reliability and trustworthiness*: Customers know that whatever takes place or has been agreed upon, they can rely on the service provider, its employees and systems, to keep promises and perform with the best interest of the customers at heart.
   - *Service recovery*: Customers realize that whenever something goes wrong or something unpredictable happens the service provider will immediately and actively take action to keep them in control of the situation and find a new, acceptable solution.
   - *Serviscape*: Customers feel that the physical surrounding and other aspects of the environment of the service encounter support a positive experience of the service process.
3. **Image-related criteria**
   - *Reputation and credibility*: Customers believe that the service provider's business can be trusted and gives adequate value for money, and that it stands for good performance and values which can be shared by customers and the service provider.

Source: Grönroos (2000, p. 81).

Discussion

The MONO project was initiated by practitioners who have not incorporated an understanding of any service quality or tourist product theory into their project plan. The goals of the project were based on obvious needs expressed by all the important stakeholders in the business: the service providers, intermediaries and the most important customer group, the business sector customers.

Nevertheless, the idea of the project seems to accept the description of the prerequisites for the customer-oriented tourist product. The idea of the service concept is illustrated by one typical activity operator from Eastern Finland who actively participated in the MONO process:

> Very often the business clients are looking for a product that is short (maximum a day), sharp and attractive. Sharp means that the idea has to appeal. If we think, for example, of a four hours canoeing trip, the activity itself is not yet attractive, but the idea comes from where the customer is going to canoe and why. The objective of the trip is as important as the activity itself. The presentation of the core product, the idea of the product, has to appeal. One can almost sell an old activity with a new presentation and a new aim, the same activity for a different reason, which then comes as a new activity.

This activity operator sells about 40% of its turnover directly to the corporate entertainment customers. About 40% of its income comes through intermediaries (Komppula, 2001, pp. 14–15).

The technical and functional dimensions of service quality played the most important role in the MONO project. Considerable attention was paid to safety regulations as well as to the efficiency and effectiveness of the implementation of the service process. The integration of the modules in the chain of activities in the service process guarantees the accessibility and flexibility and reliability and trustworthiness of the service and the business. Professionalism and skills were generally discussed from a technical point of view, but the interactive dimension of service quality (attitudes and behaviour) were also briefly discussed. Customer service expertise may have a central role in the follow-up project, once the training of the entrepreneurs begins.

The image-related criteria of service quality, reputation and credibility, as well as serviscape refer to the service system quality. The system includes the company's organization, including the service culture and employees, customers and the physical and technical resources. These components must form a whole and work together if the company is to be able to offer services that offer good quality. From the customer's point of view, most of those qualities that comprise the technical and functional dimensions of quality goods are qualities that they require to be granted as a 'normal' quality. High quality is something extra, which makes the product valuable. The above-mentioned entrepreneur states:

> The fact is that most of the products that sell well, are easy: cooking coffee and making sausages and pancakes by the fire. Behind all the product development procedures there is the underlying business mission: we must not be cheaper than others, not the most 'visible' in the market but the best in customer service. This indicates that the equipment does not have to be better, the places do not need to be better, but the customer service must be the best, because that is what the customer will remember. The customer needs to remember that he had a great time. Customer service means all the activities that aim at the best possible customer care during the customer process, including the pre-purchase phase and the presentation of the product in the brochures.

(Komppula, 2001, pp. 15–16).

It is easy to agree with Seaton (1996), who argues that the firm is just as much a product as the individual packages of offerings it makes.

It is reasonable to assume that the significance of sustainable development in the MONO project will not grow until matters that are 'closer' and more concrete from the point of view of the producers and clients are in good order in all enterprises. Not until the products are safe and comparable in relation to their technical properties everywhere, will 'higher' values such as sustainable development become a competitive advantage in an enterprise. The project manager of the MONO project has, during the process, stressed that the objective is not to create any kind of quality system, which could be audited by some kind of organization. The purpose of the project is to present the guidelines as a 'theory-in-use', which would create its own legitimacy through the demands of the customers. If the customer counterpart demands agreed qualifications and the businesses can provide the quality in practice, competition between the businesses will take care of the rest. Nevertheless, many stakeholders, especially educational organizations, have expressed an interest in creating these guidelines as a quality system with quality 'visible' badges or labels. It is an open question as to what the customers' opinions are, but the customers will decide if the MONO project will gain the legitimacy and if the guidelines will become a theory-in-use.

Conclusion

This case shows that tourist product quality is in practice (and in theory as well) often seen as a key to customer value. Several researchers, nevertheless, suggest that service quality is only one of a number of factors that influence value for the customer. Little research has been undertaken to understand the role that different value dimensions (such as functional value, emotional value, social value and epistemic or novelty value) play in the different situations (Soutar, 2001). In relation to tourist experience products, it may be that social and emotional aspects play more important roles than the technical and functional dimensions of service quality, which still seem to have a remarkable role in service quality models and theory. Understanding the customer needs and wants helps the service provider to offer the best possible prerequisites for the customer-oriented tourist product. By participating in customer processes, the customer hopefully may then experience the value proposed in the marketing of the tourist product.

In the MONO project, a sustainability dimension was also included. It must be noted that this dimension is not underlined in general service quality theories. The case shows that requirements of sustainability in tourism businesses are more common in strategic plans, business missions and marketing, than in practical actions. Sustainable development will become a competitive advantage in an enterprise, if it finds that sustainable development is a property of a product or the enterprise that affects its competitiveness in the market. Then an enterprise will attitudinally commit itself to the development of such property.

References

Aalto, K., Laiho, M. and Talonen, H. (1999) Matkailun ohjelmapalveluyritysten myynti-ja informaatiokana-vat. Loppuraportti 31.8.1999. *Tampereen yliopiston Liiketaloudellisen tutkimuskeskuksen julkaisuja* 9. Tampereen yliopistopaino, Tampere.

Augustyn, M. and Ho, S.K. (1998) Service quality and tourism. *Journal of Travel Research* 37 (August), 71–75.

Cho, Y.-H. and Fesenmaier, D.R. (2001) A new paradigm for tourism and electronic commerce: experience marketing using the virtual tour. In: Buhali, D. and Laws, E. (eds) *Tourism Distribution Channels: Practices, Issues and Transformations*. Bookcraft, Bath, UK, pp. 351–370.

Edvardsson, B. and Olsson, J. (1999) Key concepts for new service development. In: Lovelock, C., Vandermerwe, S. and Lewis, B. (eds) *Services Marketing: A European Perspective*. Prentice-Hall Europe, Berwick-upon-Tweed, UK, pp. 396–412.

Edvardsson, B., Gustafsson, A., Johnson, M.D. and Sanden, B. (2000) *New Service Development and Innovation in the New Economy*. Studentlitteratur, Lund, Sweden.

Grönroos, C. (1984) A service quality model and its marketing implications. *European Journal of Marketing* 18(4), 36–44.

Grönroos, C. (1990) *Service Management and Marketing: Managing the Moments of Truth in Service Competition*. Lexington Books, Lexington, Massachusetts.

Grönroos, C. (2000) *Service Management and Marketing: A Customer Relationship Management Approach*. John Wiley & Sons, Chichester, UK.

Gunn, C. (1994) *Tourism Planning*, 2nd edn. Taylor & Francis, New York.

Knutson, B., Stevens, P., Wullaert, C., Patton, M. and Yokoyama, F. (1991) LODGSERV: a service quality index for the lodging industry. *Hospitality Research Journal* 14, 272–284.

Komppula, R. (2001) New-product development in tourism companies – case studies on nature-based activity operators. Paper presented at the *10th Nordic Conference in Tourism Research*, 19–20 November, Vasa, Finland.

Komppula, R. (2002) Success in rural tourism micro—businesses–financial or lifestyle objectives. Paper presented at the *RENT XVI–Research in Entrepreneurship And Small Business Conference*, 21–22 November, Barcelona.

Komppula, R. and Boxberg, M. (2002) *Matkailuyrityksen tuotekehitys*. Edita Oyj, Helsinki.

Komppula, R., Juvonen, O. and Boxberg, M. (2002) Developing guidelines for professional activity services in tourism using a participatory approach – A Finnish Case Study. Paper presented at *ATLAS-Conference 2002*, 14–16 November, Estoril, Portugal.

Kotler, P., Bowen, J. and Makens, J. (1999) *Marketing for Hospitality and Tourism*, 2nd edn. Prentice-Hall, Upper Saddle River, New Jersey.

Lumsdon, L. (1997) *Tourism Marketing*. International Thomson Business Press, Oxford.

Middleton, V.T.C. (1989) Tourist product. In: Witt, S.F. and Moutinho, L. (eds) *Tourism Marketing and Management Handbook*. Prentice-Hall, Hempel Hempstead, UK.

Middleton, V.T.C. and Clarke, J. (2001) *Marketing in Travel and Tourism*, 3rd edn. Butterworth–Heinemann, Oxford.

Morrison, A., Rimmington, M. and Williams, C. (1999) *Entrepreneurship in the Hospitality, Tourism and Leisure Industries*. Butterworth–Heinemann, Bath, UK.

Mossberg, L. (2001) *Upplevelser och Marknadsföring*. DocuSys, Göteborg.

Murphy, P., Pritchard, M.P. and Smith, B. (2000) The destination product and its impact on traveller perceptions. *Tourism Management* 21, 43–52.

Parasuraman, A., Zeithaml, V. and Berry, L. (1988) SERVQUAL: a multiple-item scale for measuring consumer perceptions of service quality. *Journal of Retailing* 64(1), 12–40.

Pine, J. II and Gilmore, H.H. (1999) *The Experience Economy: Work is Theatre & Every Business a Stage*. Harvard Business School Press, Boston, Massachusetts.

Schlagel Wuest, B. (2001) Service quality concepts and dimensions pertinent to tourism, hospitality, and leisure services. In: Kandampully, J., Mok, C. and Spark, B. (eds) *Service Quality Management in Hospitality, Tourism and Leisure*. Hayworth Hospitality Press, New York, pp. 51–66.

Seaton, A.V. (1996) The marketing mix: the tourism product. In: Seaton, A.V. and Bennet, M.M. (eds) *Marketing Tourism Products: Concepts, Issues, Cases*. International Thomson Business Press, Falmouth, Massachusetts, pp. 112–134.

Shostack, G.L. (1977) Breaking free from product marketing. *Journal of Marketing,* April, 73–80.

Shostack, G.L. (1984) Service design in the operating environment. In: George, W.R. and Marshall, C. (eds) *Developing New Services*. American Marketing Association, Chicago, Illinois, pp. 27–43.

Soutar, G.N. (2001) Service quality, customer satisfaction, and value: an examination of their relationships. In: Kandampully, J., Mok, C. and Spark, B. (eds) *Service Quality Management in Hospitality, Tourism and Leisure*. Hayworth Hospitality Press, New York, pp. 97–110.

Stevens, P., Knutson, B. and Patton, M. (1995) DINESERV: a tool for measuring service quality in restaurants. *Cornell Hotel and Restaurant Administration Quarterly* 36(2), 56–60.

Tribe, J. and Snaith, T. (1998) From SERVQUAL to HOLSAT: holiday satisfaction in Varadero, Cuba. *Tourism Management* 19(1), 25–34.

Zeithaml, V.A. and Bitner, M.J. (2000) *Services Marketing: Integrating Customer Focus Across the Firm*, 2nd edn. Irwin/McGraw-Hill, London.

Zeithaml, V.A., Parasuraman, A. and Berry, L.L. (1990) *Delivering Quality Service: Balancing Customer Perceptions and Expectations*. Free Press, New York.

12 Tourism Development: Hard Core or Soft Touch?

Fiona Williams and Marsaili MacLeod
Scottish Agricultural College, UK

Introduction

The tourism product of an area is subject to the influence of many factors, but often it is the effectiveness with which factors are deployed rather than their abundance that are important considerations. It is the supply-side elements of tourism development, and in particular, approaches to management and marketing that provide the focus of this chapter. Through the medium of case studies, the authors explore how the motivations of tourists are encouraged (via promotion) and ultimately met (via provision) in terms of the supply-side of tourism. More importantly, what form does tourism development take in order to meet the requirements of tourists and is this development appropriate, in terms of scale and benefit to the rural locality?

A common research proposition is that small-scale endogenous tourism developments (that are characteristic of 'soft' tourism approaches) are more beneficial and appropriate in the periphery than large-scale developments controlled from the core (characteristic of 'hard' tourism). It is anticipated that peripheral areas (relative to core areas) will place greater reliance on natural and cultural features that necessitate 'softer' development for purposes of protection.

This chapter aims to investigate this proposition, by drawing upon empirical evidence from six European case-study regions (exhibiting varying degrees of peripherality), based on the findings of the EU FP5 project entitled, 'Aspatial Peripherality, Innovation and the Rural Economy (AsPIRE)'. The tourism product and its marketing and management are contrasted and compared with a view to examining how differential approaches to tourism development in rural areas reflect not only the natural and cultural assets associated with the rural product, but the nature and effectiveness of actors in the tourism realm. More specifically, the authors will attempt to:

- explore how the motivations of tourists are encouraged (via promotion) and ultimately met (via provision);
- establish the relationship between accessibility, and the type of tourism product available;
- examine the relationships between types of tourism and their access to vertical and horizontal networks.

Perspectives on Peripherality

The transition from an industrial economy towards a service economy presents new opportunities for tourism sector growth, particularly in rural and peripheral areas where returns from the traditional primary industries (e.g. farming and fishing) are limited or fluctu-

©CAB International 2006. *Managing Tourism and Hospitality Services: Theory and International Applications* (eds Bruce Prideaux, Gianna Moscardo and Eric Laws)

ating (Ravenscroft, 1994). It is widely acknowledged in literature that the tourism sector, through capitalizing on the natural environment, is one of few development opportunities open to rural areas, as they undergo a significant restructuring and diversification process (Swarbrooke, 1992; Butler and Hall, 1998; Bryden and Bollman, 2000; Wanhill, 2000).

Yet the competitiveness of tourism and other enterprises in peripheral regions has been historically constrained by a number of factors. A classification provided by Copus (2001) is a useful means by which to consider the spatial peripherality issues present in the tourism literature. Conventional concepts of peripheral disadvantage are classified into three broad groups: the causal, contingent and associated. Causal elements include increased travel or transport costs and the absence of agglomerative advantage, both as a result of remoteness relative to the main population centres or hubs of economic activity. Contingent elements of peripheral disadvantage are consequential of the causal elements, such as the high cost of service provision. Associated elements are connected with peripherality, although the causal links are less direct.

First, consider the causal elements of the classification in relation to tourism literature. There have been attempts to model transport mode selection (e.g. Mill, 1992) and identify common decision variables (e.g. availability, frequency, cost/price, speed/time and comfort/luxury). The inhibiting aspects of the distance decay function on travel decisions are incorporated in such models. For example, Prideaux (2000) concludes that increased distance generally leads to increased transport access costs and assumes greater importance within the total holiday cost. Absence of agglomerative advantage has also been cited as a barrier to tourism development in remote locations characterized by small and medium-sized enterprises (SMEs). Wanhill (1997) highlights a number of weaknesses in tourism SMEs that can be attributed to lack of agglomerative advantage. These include transactions and information costs prohibitive to obtaining knowledge, and supply dominated by family businesses with limited business skills.

Secondly, contingent elements include limited market opportunities or markets in decline, limited ability to appreciate market needs and demands, little statistical information or market research and a lack of strategic management (Wanhill and Buhalis, 1999). Finally, barriers 'associated' with peripherality include seasonality coupled with poor climate, a lack of tourist infrastructure, and that tourism alternatives are usually primary resource economies with small manufacturing bases.

Paradoxically, although weak characteristics have traditionally defined peripherality, the residual qualities have been recreated as a tourism product in recent years, to the point that distance itself may become a function of the destinations popularity. Underdevelopment has favoured the preservation of unique landscapes, environmental features, culture and tradition, which are being revalued in postmodern society. Embedded in peripheral localities are local identities which form the 'culture' or 'essence' of an area and effectively provide further resources available for development by local actors (Ray, 1999). These resources are inextricably linked with the local territory and can be strategically used to add value to local products and services, and to create positive images that motivate people to visit. Therefore, many of the conditions of marginal territories embody features which act as a product, and have the potential to be beneficial to tourism development. At the same time, reduced travel time and cost has deconstructed spatial notions of distance from the core.

Approaches to Development – the Product in the Periphery

Lying within the transformation of peripheral regions from zones of production to zones of consumption is a paradox: the modern tourist is now consuming the very qualities that make these localities peripheral (Gomez and Lopez, 2001). However, whilst peripheral areas may have tourism assets from which to harvest opportunities, 'the preconditions for effective peripheral area tourism development may contain within them the potential seeds for their destruction (or at least erosion): pristine environments can be sullied by tourism impacts'

(Slee, 2001, unpublished data). The type of tourism activity promoted can influence the effectiveness of peripheral localities in deriving benefits from this phenomenon. As such, the success of tourism in peripheral areas can be said to reflect both the strategic management of an appropriate tourism product, and the ability of the tourism sector to overcome the implicit challenges of inaccessibility.

In order to reduce such detrimental effects often associated with large-scale mass development, experts advocate soft tourism models (WTO, 1998, p. 131). Soft tourism emerged as one of the multiple forms of sustainable tourism in the late 1980s and early 1990s, particularly favoured by peripheral areas. Such models coincided with conditions of increased economic well-being coupled with decreased travel costs, and sensitivity to the detrimental effects of mass tourism on socio-cultural and environmental milieux. Soft tourism is characterized by small-scale endogenous development, comprising activity that makes use of local products, employs local people, does not place unacceptable burdens on the environment and respects local traditions and ways of life (Lane, 1994). Its antithesis is hard tourism, which is typified as large-scale developments, often controlled by external actors, with neither little cognizance of the impacts on local cultures and environments nor little connection to them (Slee, 1998). Such tourism systems are likely to be weakly connected to the local economy, due to the foreign business ownership, and supply chains. Relationships with external suppliers, distributors and retailers may result in 'leakages' from the local economy.

The advocacy of the soft tourism model has coincided with a growing interest in endogenous approaches to rural development, 'favouring local control and direction and more integrated strategies based on combined and sustainable economic, social and environmental development' (Bryden and Dawe, 1998, p. 5). Such development strategies utilize distinctive aspects of the economic, social and cultural environments in order to raise the profile of a locality whilst simultaneously linking people, products, innovation and investment to a particular place and encouraging a strong local participation in development (Ray, 1999). Such integrative strategies are characterized by

trust-based relationships between local tourism providers, consumers and institutions, and the use of place-based promotional schemes. This system is deemed beneficial for the area not least because, in terms of simple regional multiplier analysis, tourism enterprises that have strong local linkages tend to utilize, and offer the consumer, locally produced products and services. From the perspective of the tourist, locally embedded tourism provides interesting and educational product attributes, and a more authentic experience.

Proposition

The success of tourism in peripheral areas is dependent upon creating links with external actors, and in attracting international customers to the locality. Therefore, we expect effective tourism development in peripheral areas to utilize soft tourism approaches and to display not only strong local (or horizontal) networks within the locality, but strong external (vertical) networks to intermediaries, which have traditionally assisted with the movements of tourists. It is anticipated that hard tourism approaches, which are commonly exogenous in nature, are more likely to be dominated by external networks, with less integration into the locality. In such cases, external agents may control capital and expertise, with little financial benefit to the locality (Buhalis, 1999).

It is proposed, therefore, that small-scale endogenous tourism developments (characteristic of soft tourism approaches) are more beneficial and appropriate in the periphery than large-scale developments controlled from the core. Consequently it is anticipated that the tourism product in more inaccessible regions will demonstrate characteristics of 'soft' tourism, i.e. a dedicated product and specialized processes. Conversely, the tourism product in more accessible regions is likely to be characteristic of 'hard' tourism, exhibiting standardized processes and a generic product. Simultaneously (as shown in Fig. 12.1) it is expected that there will be greater local and external integration, through horizontal and vertical networks of the local tourism industry

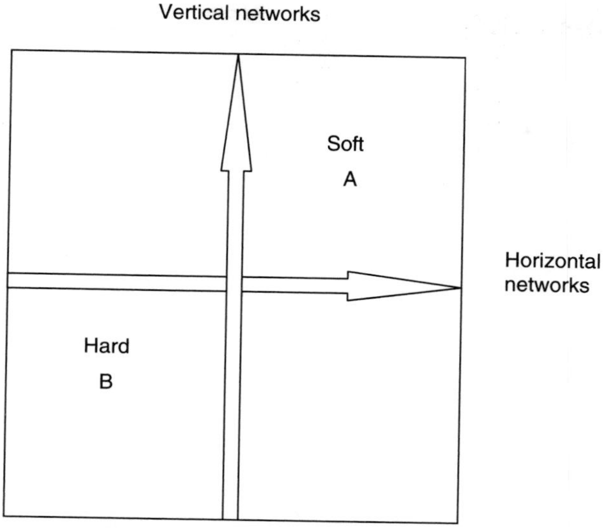

Vertical networks

Fig. 12.1. Diagrammatic summary of the research proposition.

in the more peripheral regions, relative to those with greater accessibility.

Methodology

In order to investigate these issues the authors draw upon empirical evidence from six European case-study regions (both peripheral and more accessible), based on the findings of AsPIRE.

The methodological instruments used are part of the AsPIRE project's integrated case-study work, which has been undertaken in six countries represented in the research team.[1] A broad research design was formulated that adopted common interview schedules for all of the case-study regions. This paper draws on data derived from four primary data collection instruments: (i) a visitor survey; (ii) intermediary survey; (iii) business survey; and (iv) organizational survey (Table 12.1).

Brief description of survey instruments

Two different but complementary surveys were carried out under a 'consumer' banner. Both surveys utilized a questionnaire used for face-to-face interviews. First, a visitor survey was conducted with 50 visitors in each study area. Consequently, this questionnaire was relatively short and the questions were largely closed. Both factual and perceptual information was sought from visitors with questions targeted at the collection of behavioural and attitudinal data and that for purposes of classification. Likert rating scales (relating to designative attributes of the areas) and verbal bipolar

[1] SAC, Aberdeen, Scotland (coordinator), TEAGASC Rural (Dublin) and National University of Ireland (Galway) (Ireland), University of Valencia (Spain), University of Patras (Greece), University of Dortmund (Germany), University of Helsinki (Finland).

Table 12.1. Type and number of interviews.

Survey type	No. of interviews
Visitor	300
Intermediary	23
Business	64
Organization	20

scales (relating to evaluative attributes of the areas) were included. There was limited information available regarding the numbers and nature of visitors to the study regions, i.e. there is no all-encompassing, coherent sampling frame. Hence the surveys were dependent on using a range of sample sources available in the study areas, namely visitor attractions, transport terminals and accommodation providers. These sample sources are obviously subject to seasonality constraints and visitor movements. A combination of quota and purposive sampling techniques were adopted. A distinction was made (as far as available information allowed) between different segments of the market and given the information available, an approximate representative (quota sample) was used. Interviews were 'staggered' as far as possible, in season and to encompass weekend and weekdays.

Secondly, an intermediary survey was utilized for interviews with those organizations who 'package' the study areas in some way, i.e. they act as an intermediary between the area and the potential consumer for purposes of tourism. As previously factual and perceptual information was sought from the survey. Information relating to those organizations offering packaged products within the study area was fragmented, hence a 'snowballing' sampling approach was adopted.

A face-to-face business survey of at least ten tourism service providers in each study region was undertaken and examined aspects of service provision, business relations, performance and market orientation. The organizational survey was designed to encompass both public/statutory, quasi-public, and third-sector organizations involved with the promotion and/or development of tourism in the study regions. The questionnaire was semi-structured consisting of open and closed questions. Some of the questions were attitudinal and involved Likert rating scales.

Results and Analysis

The case-study regions

A case-study region in each of the six participating countries was selected on the basis of a peripheral location relative to the European core (see Fig. 12.2). For purposes of the AsPIRE project a single Baseline Peripherality Indicator was developed, which enables the regions to be ranked according to accessibility within the European Union (EU). This indicator describes the peripherality of the study areas in conventional (and relative) terms as a function of potential accessibility to main centres of EU population, calculated from multimodal travel times.[2] Table 12.2 shows the indicator values for our study regions, standardized to the EU's average.

The regional scores highlight that Shetland (Scotland), in the upper northern part of Europe is the most peripheral of all the regions, the Spanish region of L'Alcoia is somewhat middling, whilst the regions of Clare (Ireland) and Rottal-Inn (Germany) are relatively more accessible. As such, softer tourism approaches were anticipated to be characteristic of Shetland, Evrytania and Keski-Soumi, whereas it was expected that more commercialized, generic tourism products would be increasingly found in L'Alcoia, Clare and Rottal-Inn.

Using this indicator as a basis for comparison, in the sections that follow we attempt to contrast and compare the product in the study regions and discuss the influence of accessibility/peripherality on the nature of the product and on its promotion, development and management.

Volume and value

The measurement of tourism is problematic. Harmonized tourism statistics and the development of integrated systems of tourism data collection, remain elusive – more so at the regional and local levels. Consequently, meaningful statistics as to the economic contribution of the tourism industry in the study areas are not readily available. However, the data in Table 12.3 can give us some indication of the tourism market in our areas and also the

---

[2] A detailed account of the indicator's calculation can be found in Spiekermann et al. (2002) Review of Peripherality Indices and Identification of 'Baseline Indicator'. http:// www.1sac.ac.uk/aspire.

Fig. 12.2. The case-study regions. Note: The region of L'Alcoia, Spain, forms part of the larger administrative region of Camp de Morvedre.

Table 12.2. Case-study region's baseline peripherality index score.

Country	Study region	Centroid	Baseline peripherality index score	
			Study region	National average
Scotland	Shetland	Lerwick	3	70
Greece	Evrytania	Karpenision	19	54
Finland	Keski-Suomi	Jyvaskyla	38	41
Spain	L'Alcoia	Alcoy	50	69
Ireland	Clare	Ennis	57	64
Germany	Rottal-Inn	Pfarrkirchen	61	123

Table 12.3. Volume of trips in case-study regions.

Indicator/study region	Trips (actual)				Trips (% total)	
	Domestic	International	Total	Region's % of total	Domestic	International
Shetland (2000)	37,743	9,435	47,178	0.23	80	20
Scotland (2000)	19m	1.7m	20.7m	–	91.8	8.2
Evyrtania (1998)	46,253	745	46,998	0.36	98.41	1.59
Greece (1998)	5.6m	7.5m	13.1m	–	42.8	57.2
Keski-Suomi (2000)	440,218	63,488	503,706	5.9	87.3	12.7
Finland (2000)	6.5m	2m	8.5m	–	77	23
L'Alcoia	n/a	n/a	n/a	n/a	n/a	n/a
Spain (1999)	6.9m	6.3m	13.2m	–	52.5	47.5
Clare (1999)	709,000	1,128,000	1,837,000	14.2	38.6	61.40
Ireland (1999)	6.6m	6.3m	12.9m	–	51.10	48.90
Rottal-Inn (2001)	127,324	5,235	132,559	0.12	96	4
Germany (2001)	90.2m	18m	108.2m	–	83.4	16.6

significance (or otherwise) of the tourism sector in the area, relative to the rest of the country. It is acknowledged that the years to which the data refer differ – where possible the most recent statistics available were utilized.

The relationship between peripherality and regional market share (within the national context) is not linear. The more peripheral regions of Shetland and Evrytania capture only a small percentage of the national market, as would be expected. Accessibility to Clare in Ireland (baseline 57) is increased by the proximity to Shannon International airport, which may have enabled it to capture such a large share of the national market. On the other hand, the most accessible region of Rottal-Inn has a very small market share, despite its greater accessibility (baseline 61). The type of visitor market is also contrasting: only 4% of Rottal-Inn's market is international, whereas 61.4% of Clare's visitors are international. Indeed, Table 12.3 illustrates that, in Clare and Shetland, the international market is proportionally greater than that for their respective countries. This is also reflected in the visitor survey (origin of visitors) as shown in Table 12.4.

Although an absence of comparable employment or expenditure figures for the tourism sector in the six regions makes it difficult to establish the economic importance of the

tourism industry, where figures do exist, they do not often reveal the true significance of the sector. For example, in Rottal-Inn 3.3% of the employees are directly employed in the tourism sector, but it is perceived locally to be 'one of the main economic pillars' (Bayer SLU, 1993, p. 59) of the county, having shown steady growth over recent years. As such, a more accurate assessment of importance of tourism sector to the local economy in our regions is captured by a comparative evaluation by local tourism organizations, as illustrated in Table 12.5.

The interviewees were asked to rank the importance of tourism as a sector on a scale of 1–5 (unimportant to very important). Five of the six regions considered the tourism industry to be important or very important in spite of vast variations in the volume of visitor traffic.

Table 12.4. Origin of visitors (visitor survey).

Study region	% of Sample	
	Domestic	International
Shetland	72	28
Evrytania	98	2
Keski-Suomi	94	6
L'Alcoia	98	2
Clare	24	76
Rottal-Inn	92	8

Table 12.5. The importance of tourism to the local economy.

Study region	Average score	Strategy to guide development
Shetland	4.0	3-year strategy tourism strategy. Also numerous individual projects ongoing, e.g. interpretation, access, signage
Evrytania	4.25	Regional promotion for Kapenisi/Evrytania: includes website creation and development of traditional products, cultural shows, etc.
Keski-Suomi	4.50	Recently completed tourism strategy
L'Alcoia	2.0	No dedicated tourism strategy
Clare	4.0	Strategic plan to 'generate tourist activity'
Rottal-Inn	4.0	County Development Concept 2006

This is also reflected by the provision of dedicated development strategies to guide tourism development, or as in the case of Rottal-Inn, as part of a wider area-based development strategy.

The one exception is the Spanish region of L'Alcoia, which forms part of one of three provinces in the Valencian region of Spain. This inland area, consisting of rugged, dramatic terrain is a sharp contrast to the sun and beach tourism of adjoining areas, which attract international visitors. As Tables 12.4 and 12.5 illustrate, tourism in the L'Alcoia area is not well developed: the region is dependent nearly entirely on domestic visitors, and there are no defined strategies to foster the growth of tourism. This is primarily because the area has been traditionally dedicated to agriculture and manufacturing, and the tourism industry is small and fragmented. The lack of statistics and the relative lack of importance attributed to the sector in this area are characteristic of the situation.

The results from the business survey also reveal differences in the state of the tourism industry. The small sample of tourism service providers (including accommodation and leisure services providers) revealed the majority of firms (55%) had been operating less than 10 years, and the average firm age was significantly lower within the relatively peripheral Scottish and Greek study areas, and less peripheral Spanish region. This may suggest tourism development is still in its infancy in these regions, as their ability to gain comparative advantage over other regions is impeded by distance costs.

The infancy of tourism development in the more peripheral regions, relative to the more established industry in Rottal-Inn and Clare, is also highlighted by business performance figures (Table 12.6). Both operational and financial indicators of performance were used to assess firm performance. A high proportion of firms reported growth across all measures, though less so in employment

Table 12.6. Tourism business performance.

Measure of performance	% of firms reporting growth in the last 5 years						
	Shetland	Evrytania	Keski-Suomi	L'Alcoia	Clare	Rottal-Inn	Total %
Employment	27	40	55	50	–	20	32
Profit margins	75	80	73	50	–	20	48
Total sales	86	80	82	50	–	40	54
Investments	86	60	55	50	–	–	39
Market extension	63	–	18	50	–	10	22
Total (No.)	11	10	11	8	11	10	61

Note: There are no data for Clare, due to firm confidentiality.

generation and market extension. The fact that a higher percentage of firms in Scotland, Greece and Finland reported growth in profit margins, sales and investments is indicative of the infancy of the firms, and the tourism development, in these regions.

Although it was expected that foreign ownership would be more pronounced within the more accessible regions of Germany, Ireland and Spain, this was in fact, not the case as businesses across all regions were predominantly created (66%) and managed (64%) by family owner-managers.

Further indication of the character of the supply-side of the product can be attained from consideration of the nature of the market that it is servicing. The main purposes of visits across all regions, as found in our visitor survey sample, are holidaying (overnight stays) (Fig. 12.3). The visiting friends and relatives (VFR) market is more pronounced in Keski-Suomi and Clare. Keski-Suomi, L'Alcoia, and the Rottal-Inn experience a larger number of day trippers. This is attributed to the nature of the attractions (particularly in Keski-Suomi) and in the cases of Rottal-Inn and L'Alcoia, their proximity to large centres of population: Munich, Passau and Salzburg to Rottal-Inn and the coastal markets in the areas adjacent to L'Alcoia. This highlights the advantage of local accessibility in developing a domestic market.

The majority of the respondents (on holiday) in the Scottish, Finnish, Spanish and German study areas were staying in one main location in the region and taking day trips. In the Irish and Greek areas half of the above respondents were touring in the region, staying in 2–3 (plus) locations.

Nature of the Product

The tourism product in all of the areas is similar in that it draws very much upon the natural and cultural heritage endowments of the case-study regions. For example the county of Rottal-Inn, situated on the Austrian border in south-east Germany offers a traditional farming landscape and culture, and also benefits from being part of a 'spa-triangle' in eastern Bavaria. The Shetland Isles (northernmost Scotland) have developed a specialist niche market that draws upon the abundant wildlife and birdlife on the islands. A combination of outdoor recreation and built heritage is evident in Co. Clare in the midwest of Ireland. The mountainous Greek area, Evrytania, has a product bias towards the provision of 'wilderness' sport.

The main features of each area utilized for tourism purposes (as stated by the various public sector organizations responsible for the development and promotion of tourism and also tourism intermediaries) are summarized in Table 12.7. The themes of landscape, the environment, natural and cultural heritage and outdoor recreation are common throughout and given the predominantly 'rural' status of the areas this is to be expected.

These themes are also reflected by business provision (Table 12.8). Firms were more likely to offer traditional hospitality, cooking and outdoor leisure recreation than relaxation

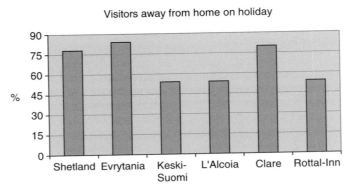

Fig. 12.3. Purpose of visit.

Table 12.7. Tourism themes and provision.

Themes/provision	Organizations	Intermediaries
Shetland	• Archaeology • Viking heritage • Wildlife (in particular birds and special interest) • Landscapes/seascapes	• Stopover/touring • Crafts • Wildlife
Evrytania	• Natural beauty (mountains, rivers, lakes) • Skiing • Alternative tourism (conferences, events) • Traditional local products	• Outdoor pursuits
Keski-Suomi	• Winter tourism • Tourist centres • Natural landscape • Sauna culture	• Outdoor pursuits
L'Alcoia	• Historic (Roman) heritage • Industrial archaeology • Natural heritage	• Mountains
Clare	• Marine (sea angling) • Open countryside: walking, cycling, equestrian • Heritage (indoor attractions)	• Golf • Landscape and heritage
Rottal-Inn	• Spa/health water • Regional culture and tradition • Attractive, varied landscape	• Wellness and beauty

Table 12.8. Services offered by tourism businesses.

	No. of firms offering tourism service							
Services offered	Shetland	Evrytania	L'Alcoia	Keski-Suomi	Clare	Rottal-Inn	Total	Total %
Relaxation and rest	2	2	4	6	8	3	25	40.3
Leisure and outdoor recreation	3	3	5	4	9	3	27	43.5
Sports and related activities	2	3	4	2	8	3	22	35.5
Cooking (cuisine)	2	2	11	7	1	6	29	46.8
Culture and tradition	5	–	3	2	9		19	30.6
Traditional hospitality	7	6	10	6	7	1	37	59.7
Other	4	2	4	–	–	6	16	25.8

and rest, sports and culture and tradition. The popularity of 'culture' in the case of Co. Clare reflects its strong international market.

Perceptions among tourism businesses of unique selling features of the areas are depicted in Table 12.9. Nature is considered the most important unique selling feature, whereas history and architecture are considered less important. Although only a minority of the business respondents stated that they offered cultural products and services, the overall significance of local culture and tradition to all six regions tourism products is well recognized.

In order to investigate the consumption of the product, visitors to the regions were asked to list their three main activities or pursuits whilst in the area. The numbers attributed to each activity are outlined in Table 12.10. The more popular activity categories of 'general touring/visits' and 'outdoor recreation' draw upon the unique selling features mentioned above in particular 'nature' and 'culture, tradition and heritage'.

Visitors were also asked whether they agreed or disagreed with a number of statements made about the product (Table 12.11). There was little variance in response between countries. An attractive natural landscape was attributed to all of the areas, as were friendly local people. Five of the areas (excluding Greece) could also be said to exhibit seasonality given a less appealing winter climate in these areas. The Greek area, Evrytania has a ski infrastructure that attracts a local winter market, thus helping to overcome the traditional off-peak season experienced elsewhere.

The statement about 'interesting wildlife' did differ quite significantly between the regions, being more of a feature in the more peripheral regions of Shetland, Evrytania and Keski-Soumi. This may hint at the development of niche markets in the more peripheral areas and the existence of unique resources upon which to draw.

Product Promotion

The main features of the areas utilized for purposes of promotion (by both the tourism organizations and intermediaries) are summarized in Table 12.12. Whilst at first glance the product in our areas has appeared very similar, the approaches to promotion of the destination area differ among the regions. This is, in part, attributable to a positive utilization of the distance/peripherality factor and product characteristics attributed to it. For example, organizational representatives in Shetland were keen to develop the evaluative aspects of the product in terms of the promotional message – remoteness, safety, escape, lack of pollution, tranquillity and other aspects of the product associated with distance from the core. The promotion of such attributes is designed to appeal to a high-earning, predominantly urban-based market both domestic and international.

The utilization of the peripherality 'factor' is also true of Evrytania. The Greek area possesses a strong image as a recreation/amenity area and as a producer of traditional and authentic products. A focus on alternative or

Table 12.9. Unique selling features identified by firms.

Unique selling features	No. of firms							
	Shetland	Evrytania	L'Alcoia	Keski-Suomi	Clare	Rottal-Inn	Total no.	Total %
Nature	9	10	9	10	11	6	55	88.7
History	4	3	3	4	4	1	19	30.6
Architecture	3	–	4	3	1	2	13	21
Culture/tradition/ heritage	8	5	3	7	8	4	35	56.5
Services and facilities	3	7	6	6	8	4	34	54.8
Other	8	–	2	1	1	2	14	22.6

Table 12.10. Visitor pursuits (no. of visitors).

Activities undertaken	Shetland	Evrytania	L'Alcoia	Keski-Suomi	Clare	Rottal-Inn	Total %
General touring/ visits	40	28	43	28	39	36	214
Recreational (outdoor)	20	2	18	23	50	44	157
Eating/drinking	3	10	11	11	24	8	67
Rest/relaxation	3	3	13	10	17	13	59
Shopping	3	1	0	4	7	1	16
Specialist nature	10	0	0	0	0	0	10
Photography/art	3	0	0	1	0	0	4
Total	82	44	85	77	137	102	527

Table 12.11. Visitor ratings of the tourism product.

Aspect of product	% of visitors to area agreeing with statement						
	Shetland	Evrytania	Keski-Suomi	L'Alcoia	Clare	Rottal-Inn	Mean %
Good recreational opportunities	62	84	84	54	72	70	71
Good sporting activities	24	90	72	38	60	44	55
Attractive natural landscape	96	84	96	100	98	92	94
Interesting industrial heritage	62	92	50	18	60	0	47
Appealing historic sights	94	86	52	44	96	74	74
Interesting local culture/ traditions	90	88	58	84	94	56	78
Friendly local people	94	92	92	96	96	90	93
Interesting wildlife	96	96	88	30	66	64	73
Appealing summer climate	62	100	88	96	56	92	82
Appealing winter climate	8	100	58	50	2	24	40

Table 12.12. Organization and intermediary promotional messages.

Promotional message	Organizations	Intermediaries
Shetland	• 'Stimulating mind, body and spirit' • Natural choice • Island of adventure • More than you'd ever imagined • Discovery, explore, freedom	• Coastlines and islands • Skeins and skerries
Evrytania	• 'The Switzerland of Greece' • Alternative forms of tourism • Adventure • Culture and tradition	• Land of adventure
Keski-Suomi	• Proximity to nature • Heritage: attractions based on tradition • High quality • Festivals of Moors and Christians	• Stories you can live by yourself
L'Alcoia	• A town to discover • Heart of the mountain • Natural resources – water, outdoor pursuits	• Heart of the mountain • Discovery
Clare	• Recreation and cruising, golf • Heritage – Bunratty Park • Wellness and health	• Explore the land of your ancestors
Rottal-Inn	• Nature and water • Varied landscape • Recreation	• Rural spa

adventure tourism in recent years has drawn upon the area's remoteness from major urban centres to assist in the development of the 'adventure' message.

The relatively less peripheral areas in Ireland and Germany draw upon natural resources and heritage, and products associated with 'rural'. Their relatively higher level of accessibility enables the regions to appeal to a less specialized, generic market. For example, the existence of Shannon airport in Ireland has been responsible for the tourist traffic to Co. Clare being dominated by large-scale American tours, attracted by golf and heritage. The German region of Rottal-Inn is striving to overcome its national perception of peripherality, through promoting its products to neighbouring Eastern European countries.

The role of external (vertical) linkages

Evidently place-specific products are important in all regions. Notwithstanding this, the extent to which the tourism industry is itself localized and integrated appears to vary.

In order to gain an insight into the linkages between consumer and place, organizations in the study areas were asked to agree/disagree (on a scale 1–4) with a number of statements made about the nature of the market and cooperation within the area. The average scores against each statement for each region are shown in Table 12.13. External linkages, through intermediaries providing customers to businesses, are particularly apparent in Clare. There is also evidence of intermediary activity in Shetland and Evrytania though this is not as pronounced – the independent market appearing more dominant in these areas.

The visitor survey also revealed evidence of prior bookings, for transport and accommodation, being made through intermediaries (operators) in Clare, and to a lesser extent in Shetland whereas in Evrytania, Keski-Soumi, L'Alcoia and Rottal-Inn prior bookings tended to be made directly with the provider. The role and significance of intermediaries emerged in

Table 12.13. Business relations.

Statements	Average score (1–5) by tourism organizations					
	Shetland	Evrytania	Keski-Suomi	L'Alcoia	Clare	Rottal-Inn
Tourism business in the area is largely a consequence of tour operators (based outside the area) bringing tourists to the area	2.7	2.8	2.5	1.3	3.0	1.25
Tourism business in the area is largely a consequence of independent travellers deciding to visit the area	4.0	3.75	2.5	3.0	1.0	3.4
Tourism businesses within the area collaborate together in order to gain mutual benefit from visitors	2.3	2.8	3.0	2.3	4.0	3.2
Tourism businesses within the area and public institutions cooperate in order to promote tourism to the area	2.6	2.0	3.0	2.0	4.0	3.0

the business survey: the majority of firms surveyed had arrangements with businesses outside of the region to regularly supply them with customers. For example, all of the firms interviewed in Clare had formalized contractual agreements with businesses (customers) outside the area to supply a specified number of tourists at predetermined prices. Such vertical linkages were also apparent in Shetland and Rottal-Inn. The only obvious exception to this was Keski-Suomi in Finland where few firms had contact with external businesses as a means to source custom.

To investigate the relationships operating within these various networks, intermediaries known to service the areas were asked to specify whether relationships with businesses were informal or formal. Relationships between businesses and intermediaries in Shetland, Evrytania, L'Alcoia and Rottal-Inn were all described as 'regular' and 'informal'. The Finnish intermediaries appeared divided in that half of the intermediaries described their business relationships in the previous manner and

the remainder described the relationship as a 'formalized contractual agreement'. All of the intermediaries sampled in connection with Clare stated that the relationship was wholly formalized, characteristic of a 'hard tourism' system. The intermediaries interviewed stated that they had working relationships with public institutions responsible for the promotion of tourism in the regions.

The level of internal (horizontal) linkages

There was, however, less consensus of opinion as to the extent of cooperation between indigenous tourism firms and institutions. Although it was hypothesized that such horizontal linkages would be a feature of all regions, and more so in the more peripheral regions, this was not the case. Only 20% of the firms surveyed stated that they, and other businesses in their region, had business relations with public institutions for the promotion of tourism. Furthermore, only a quarter of firms had informal relations with other businesses for the exchange of customers. The tourism organizations confirmed this finding, believing although there was some evidence that tourism businesses within the area collaborated, this was not ubiquitous (Table 12.13). The only exception was in Greece, where firms were more likely to collaborate on a range of promotional, sales and provision activities.

On the other hand, the findings from the business survey suggested that local linkages to the economy were more pronounced in the more peripheral regions. For example, 83% of firms in Shetland sourced their business inputs from within the region and from regular suppliers, whereas this was the case for only 36% of firms in Clare, and 40% of firms in Rottal-Inn. The latter two regions were more likely to use spot-trade, or external suppliers.

Development – the Influence of Peripherality

The perceived influence of location on the tourism product and its development and management is outlined in the charts and tables that follow. Table 12.14 contains a summary of the immediate effects of location as summarized by organizational representatives. The influences are considered to be both positive and negative and relate to the causal, contingent or associated aspects of peripherality. For example, many of the perceived barriers can be linked directly to increased travel cost or lack of agglomerative advantage. Equally the perceived benefits of location are characteristics that can be described as, contingent to, or associated with, peripherality.

Undoubtedly the location of the study regions has affected the management of the product. The maturity of the product and the way in which the product has developed also tell us something of the influence of access and location. Whilst at first glance the product attributes in the regions appears similar, the means by which they have been developed differ considerably. In Clare, the existence of Shannon International Airport has allowed the development of a high volume market, dominated by operators (of US and

European origin). However, this creates problems in terms of undesirable impacts, such as overcrowding and pressure on local utilities. A positive slant on this is the economic benefit to be derived from large-scale tourism activity. This said, it was acknowledged in the organizational survey that the distribution of these benefits among local businesses is unequal. The public sector organizations responsible for promotion and development are keen to distribute economic benefits more evenly between large and smaller providers (currently trade is dominated by large hotels and coach tours).

The other relatively more accessible region in the group is Rottal-Inn (Germany). Here the product has developed steadily over a period of three decades, focusing upon the themes of 'health and well-being' and servicing both operators and independent travellers. The dispersion of these visitors (and thus the benefits to be derived from them) is much dependent upon the motorization of tourists so once again attempts are being made to 'integrate' the product more fully into the wider economy of the area. The proximity of Rottal-Inn to potential markets in Austria and Czechia is also deemed to have potential for development. Thus whilst the cases in Ireland and Germany are at different stages of maturity they both show similar characteristics in terms of access to markets and the problems associated with this.

At the opposing end of the peripherality scale are Shetland and Evrytania. In both cases, the product is low volume and as we have seen draws upon the 'remoteness' of the regions in a favourable sense for purposes of promotion. Tourist infrastructure and service provision is deemed problematic in both areas, with the sustainability of wholly tourism businesses being questionable. Thus what has tended to evolve are more specialist products targeted to small-scale, niche markets. The nature of tourism in these areas appears more integrated with other sectors of the economy. Both areas have established links with intermediaries in recent years, for the provision of tourists. The intermediaries appear to be national to the regions, small-scale and specialist.

Issues of accessibility and characteristics 'associated' with peripherality play an impor-

Table 12.14. The influence of location on the tourism product and market.

Influence of location	Benefits	Problems
Shetland	• Little in the way of impacts as small volume • Location – remoteness, getting away, useful for developing niches • Community involvement (strong)	• Expensive to travel • Little in the way of sustainable business, i.e. stand-alone tourism • Lack of awareness (education among markets) relocation/access • Staffing problems • Landscape attraction (public good)
Evrytania	• Long staying tourism • Good horizontal networks and developing vertical networks • Strong image as a recreation area	• Low level of infrastructure and services • Remoteness from major urban centres
Keski-Suomi	• Potential domestic markets easily accessible • Natural landscape is the main attraction • Easier to get financial support (peripheral status)	• Foreign visitors use air/boat traffic – increases cost of the area • Unawareness of the area among potential markets
L'Alcoia	• Attractive natural landscape • Proximity to mass tourism in coastal areas (day-visitor market)	• Poor infrastructure: bottleneck roads
Clare	• Scenery is deemed to be attractive	• Uncertainty regarding the weather • Poor roads • Crowded facilities and short season • Trade dominated by large companies
Rottal-Inn	• Proximity of attractive foreign tourism destinations	• Emphasis on one area (Bad Birnbach, a natural spa)

tant role in the decisions of firms to locate and/or operate in a given area. Unsurprisingly, firms in the more accessible regions of L'Alcoia, Clare and Rottal-Inn were more likely to state that accessibility was an important aspect of their business location, whereas this was less important in the more peripheral regions (Table 12.15). A high percentage of firms stated that place-specific attributes, such as image, culture and landscape, were significant location factors. The extent to which such trade-offs in terms of business decisions pay dividends can also be considered from the perspective of consumer trade-offs and overall satisfaction with the product.

Tourist's perceptions of inaccessibility are sensitive to a range of factors; origins, destinations, impedance, types of transport or cost. Table 12.16 shows the extent to which visitors agreed with statements pertaining to travel to the regions. The perceptions largely agree with our baseline indicator of peripherality presented in Table 12.2. The most peripheral of our areas, Shetland, was considered to be the least accessible according to visitors and consequently the most expensive to travel to. Although the majority of visitors surveyed in Clare were of international origin, compared to Shetland the area was not considered overly expensive to access.

It is also useful to consider visitor perceptions of aspects of the product once in the regions. In other words having made the trip (albeit lengthy and/or costly or otherwise) did particular product attributes meet their expectations? Visitors were asked to assess the expense, value and quality of the goods/services within the region. What we assume from the results in Table 12.17 is that the visitors to Shetland were content with the tourism

Table 12.15. Important aspects of business location.

Aspect of region	% of firms stating that the factor is decisive to business location					
	Shetland	Evrytania	Keski-Suomi	L'Alcoia	Clare	Rottal-Inn
Accessibility	25	50	27	60	100	57
Regional image	58	80	18	40	73	71
Local culture	58	20	27	40	82	85
Landscape and nature	83	80	54	60	100	100

product in spite of relatively greater expense to travel to the islands.

Measuring visitor satisfaction is only one means of viewing 'success', but is deemed crucial to the ongoing, positive development of a tourism product. The positive evaluations (of value and quality) evident in Table 12.17 are surely an encouraging sign for the study regions, particularly for those with dual high counts. It would appear that a great deal has been done to overcome the barriers associated with a peripheral location and that there are positive practices attributable to these areas.

Conclusions and Recommendations for Further Research

In order to investigate the management, marketing and development of tourism in peripheral areas, this paper has drawn upon empirical evidence taken from six European case-study regions, all exhibiting varying degrees of conventional peripherality. The emphasis has been upon the relationship between accessibility and the type of tourism product available and also

the relationship between the product and forms of vertical and horizontal networks.

Comparable data in official statistics are effectively not available, therefore a 'true' contrast in terms of the economic contribution of tourism to the economies of our study regions is very difficult to determine. This also begs the question as to how the measurement of 'successful' tourism can be undertaken in a meaningful way. Existing indicators tend to focus on the economic impacts of tourism, yet the social, cultural and environmental impact is of equal importance to the sustainability and longevity of the industry; hence should be incorporated into any measure of 'success'. The perceived importance of the sector in the local economy was ascertained (according to public sector organizations), indicators of the performance of tourism businesses were sought as was the satisfaction of visitors as to particular aspects of the product. The results across the three surveys were largely consistent in their assessment of the areas. In five of the six regions tourism was considered to be an important sector. This was particularly marked in terms of the three more peripheral areas of the group and a higher percentage of

Table 12.16. Visitor perceptions of accessibility and cost (no. of visitors).

	Accessible	High travel costs
Shetland	26	35
Evrytania	41	13
Keski-Soumi	45	19
L'Alcoia	40	5
Clare	46	15
Rottal-Inn	47	5

Table 12.17. Visitor opinion of goods and services (no.of visitors).

	Expensive	Good value	Quality
Shetland	23	40	44
Evrytania	16	30	40
Keski-Soumi	24	28	35
L'Alcoia	4	40	38
Clare	20	36	45
Rottal-Inn	6	35	41

firms in these areas also reported growth in profit margins, sales and investments. Visitor satisfaction appeared high in terms of value for money and quality and did not vary greatly between more or less peripheral regions in spite of perceptions of higher travel costs to the less accessible of the areas.

Maintaining the proposition that 'soft' is better in the case of tourism development in peripheral regions, we have attempted, by comparing the tourism product and its promotion, to draw out those characteristics associated with soft tourism. All of the regions capitalize to varying degrees on the natural and cultural resources present in the areas – these resources forming the basis of the tourism product. What has been more challenging to establish is the degree to which this cultural and natural heritage is embedded in the locality, is linked with the local territory and portrays a local identity. However, within the results there are signs that some of our areas have a 'softer' approach to development. For example, the nature of the market, particularly in terms of volume did differ considerably, with Clare having a particularly large volume of visitor traffic in season, with the ensuing overcrowding and negative impacts. Shetland and Evrytania had much lower visitor numbers and had developed a very specific product to their areas, such as wildlife tourism and adventure tourism, respectively.

Within the various products, the utilization of the regions' 'peripherality' differed considerably and the influence of 'peripherality' for the product and its promotion became more apparent as the 'pictures' of our areas evolved. The two relatively (to the group) more accessible areas (Rottal-Inn and Clare) tended to play up the accessibility aspects of the area through proximity to main markets (as in the case of Rottal-Inn) or transport infrastructure (as with Co. Clare). Conversely, the more peripheral Shetland and Evrytania used the characteristics of the regions' associated with peripherality (and perceived distance from the core) to add value to the product (particularly in terms of product promotion).

The various networks operating in the regions also indicated at the validity of our summations, though not conclusively. For example, the existence of strong, formalized vertical networks in Clare was particularly prominent. In Shetland and Evrytania there was evidence of some vertical linkages with consumers via intermediary activity, though this was far less pronounced and of a predominantly informal nature. Stronger horizontal networks and collaborative activity were apparent in the Greek area but there was little evidence of this elsewhere, despite an acknowledgement of the need to integrate the product more fully into the locality (as in Clare and Rottal-Inn).

The question remains as to the causal elements of these relationships. Is a tourism sector that is small-scale, integrated and endogenous in nature, a consequence of a focused management effort in terms of destination strategy and development or is it simply the only, viable approach available to remote and peripheral areas?

The evidence presented is largely anecdotal and less in the way of quantified per se, but as we have seen the complexities of the variables and relationships between them make this a particularly challenging task. A conclusion that can be drawn from the work is that despite evidence of conventional peripherality, the associated development barriers, and a similar product base in all regions, the more peripheral areas appear to be performing equally as well as those more accessible areas. Can we therefore assume that there are aspects of management that compensate for disadvantage? Whilst the AsPIRE project has touched on some of these issues, i.e. governance, social capital, information technology, it is clear that the complexities and disparities of these phenomenon are not yet fully understood and a great deal of work remains to be done. The authors believe that this work provides a springboard to further investigation that may consider specific aspects of linkages and hard/soft approaches to development within the tourism context. Indeed the subject matter lends itself to more rigorous qualitative analysis that can be afforded by other disciplines such as sociology and cultural geography.

Acknowledgement

The research on which this chapter is based forms part of the AsPIRE (Aspatial Peripherality Innovation and the Rural

Economy) project, which was funded by the EU Fifth Framework (LIFE) Programme (Contract No QLK5-2000-00783). The research partnership comprises the Scottish Agricultural College, TEAGASC (Dublin), National University of Ireland, Galway, University of Valencia, University of Patras, University of Dortmund and the University of Helsinki.

References

Bayerrisches Staatsministerium fur Landesentwicklung and Umweltfragen (1993) Inselgutachten der Landesplanung. In: Bayern – Rottal, Konzepte und Streategien zur Entwicklung eines Teilraumes, Munchen (Bayerrisches Staatsministerium fur Landesentwicklung and Umweltfragen), 213 pp.

Bryden, J. and Bollman, R. (2000) Rural employment in industrialised countries. *Agricultural Economics* 22(2), 185–197.

Bryden, J. and Dawe, S.P. (1998) Development strategies for remote rural regions: what do we know so far? Paper presented at the *OECD International Conference of Remote and Rural Areas – Developing through Natural and Cultural Assets*, Albarracin, Spain, November, 5–6.

Buhalis, D. (1999) Limits of tourism development in peripheral destinations: problems and challenges. *Tourism Management* 20, 183–185

Butler, R. and Hall, C.M. (1998) Conclusion. In: Butler, R., Hall, C.M. and Jenkins, J. (eds) *Tourism and Recreation in Rural Areas*. John Wiley & Sons, New York, pp. 249–258.

Copus, A.K. (2001) From core-periphery to polycentric development: concepts of spatial and aspatial peripherality. *European Planning Studies* 9(4) 539–552.

Gomez, M.B. and Lopez, P.F. (2001) Tourism, territory and marginality: principles and case studies. Paper presented at the *Annual Conference of IGU Commission on Evolving Issues of Geographic Marginality in the Early 21st Century World* (July), Stockholm.

Lane, B. (1994) What is rural tourism? *Journal of Sustainable Tourism* 2(1), 7–21.

Mill, R.C. (1992) *The Tourism System: An Introductory Text*, 2nd edn. Prentice-Hall International, Upper Saddle River, New Jersey.

Prideaux, B. (2000) The role of the transport system in destination development. *Tourism Management* 21, 53–63.

Ravenscroft, N. (1994) Leisure policy in the new Europe: the UK Department of National Heritage as a model of development and integration. *European Urban and Regional Studies* 1(2), 131–142.

Ray, C. (1999) Endogenous development in the era of reflexive modernity. *Journal of Rural Studies* 15(3), 257–267.

Slee, B. (1998) Soft tourism: can the Western European model be transferred into Central and Eastern Europe. In: Hall, D. and O'Hanlon, L. (eds) *Rural Tourism Management: Sustainable Options International Conference Proceedings*, 9–12 September, Ayr, UK, 481–496.

Swarbrooke, J. (1992) Towards sustainable rural tourism: lessons from France, Tourism Intelligence Papers, A-65, November, *Insights*, ETB.

Wanhill, S. (1997) Peripheral area tourism: a European perspective. *Progress in Tourism and Hospitality Research* 3, 47–70.

Wanhill, S. (2000) Creative innovations in attraction development. Paper presented at the *9th Nordic Tourism Research Conference* (October), Bornholm, Denmark.

Wanhill, S. and Buhalis, D. (1999) Introduction: challenges for tourism in peripheral areas. *International Journal of Tourism Research* 1, 295–297.

WTO (1998) *Guide for Local Authorities on Developing Sustainable Tourism*. WTO, Madrid.

13 Quality Management for Events

Donald Getz[1] and Jack Carlsen[2]
[1]University of Calgary, USA; [2]Curtin University, Australia

Introduction

This chapter explores the meaning and management of quality for events, including a discussion of quality standards and quality management methods. A case study is presented to illustrate the use of quality evaluation methods, particularly service mapping.

Event 'quality' can be conceptualized as the amalgam of programme and service delivery as presented to consumers. It requires skilful management of the interactions among the setting (venues, decoration, atmosphere), people (guests, staff, volunteers and participants), management systems (e.g. health, security and communications) and the event programme (whether a competition, celebration, entertainment, education or business). To a large degree event quality is dependent upon organizational and personnel quality, as it is difficult to imagine a high-quality event being produced by incompetent organizers.

Quality control is a fundamental responsibility of event managers and should consist of the setting of quality standards, customer and market research, evaluation and control mechanisms and continuous improvement systems (including benchmarking, and staff and volunteer training), all within a customer-oriented culture (Getz, 1997). Each event and event-producing organization must consider the meaning and importance of quality as applied

to their specific type of event and its key goals. To the owners and managers of events, adopting quality standards and management should lead to continuous improvement, better performance in terms of achieving the event's goals and fewer problems. Tourism-oriented events will gain from heightened appeal, as the tourism industry wants better events to attract and satisfy specific market segments. Quality standards can also provide assurance to customers that basic services will be provided at least to a reasonable standard, and that they do not have to fear for their safety or health.

Those who fund events (government agencies at various levels), or sponsor them commercially, will associate quality standards with risks. In other words, top-ranked or certified events should be better able to use the money wisely and therefore provide the desired return on investment. Governments at all levels have an important stake in many festivals and events, both directly (when funded or produced by an agency) or indirectly (because events reflect upon the place in which they are held). When the perspective of external stakeholder groups is taken, event impacts become a measure of quality.

Although each event must assume responsibility for its own quality management, increasingly there are collective initiatives being taken by professional associations and industry groups to develop quality standards and related event accreditation programmes. For example,

Carlsen (2001) reported on the approach taken by the event industry in Western Australia. The Canadian province of Quebec has adopted quality standards for event organizations, and a collaboration between the tourism ministry in the province of Ontario and Festivals and Events Ontario is developing even more comprehensive standards (Getz, 2003, unpublished report).

Dimensions of Quality for Events

Table 13.1 summarizes the ensuing discussion in which three major dimensions of event quality are examined; the organization, its personnel and management systems; programme and service quality (including the setting); and impacts.

Organizational quality

Generic quality assurance programmes, such as the widely employed ISO 9000 series, focus upon the organization itself by prescribing standard processes and management systems. ISO 9000 places the emphasis on adoption of policies, procedures and management systems and documenting everything to do with provision of quality products or services. This was

the approach taken in Western Australia and Quebec.

Event managers are increasingly required to be certified by professional bodies such as the International Festivals and Events Association, International Special Events Society, the Convention Industry Council or the International Association of Exhibition Managers. Unfortunately, many small event organizations cannot afford to help their managers get formal, event-related education or certification, and many people in the industry have migrated into it from other backgrounds. The main challenge, therefore, is to ensure that all event staff and volunteers are well trained and competent in fulfilling their specific, assigned tasks.

As indicated in Table 13.1, organizational quality standards should begin with philosophy and values, and cover all management systems including human resources. For tourism-oriented events, a separate set of 'tourism readiness' standards will apply, such as procedures for greeting and orienting visitors and policies covering price and packaging.

Service quality

Organizations and personnel are means towards the end of producing a great customer

Table 13.1. Main dimensions of event quality.

1. Organizational and personnel quality
   - philosophy and values (including a code of ethics; environmental and social responsibility; consumer orientation; leadership; being a learning organization; stakeholder participation)
   - management systems in place and documented: business and strategic planning; site planning; organization and coordination; risk and security; health and safety; financial controls; human resource management and specifically training; service quality; marketing and communications; impact assessment and evaluation
   - staff and volunteer competence: evidence of training programmes and professional certification; performance evaluation
   - a separate set of 'tourism readiness' standards and criteria should apply to those events with a tourism orientation
2. Service and programme quality
   - tangibles, including the 'hygiene factors' (health, cleanliness, safety, security, comfort, information, signage, crowd control), accessibility and setting
   - reliability, responsiveness, assurance, empathy (how services are delivered)
   - programme (determined either by expert judges or customer satisfaction)
3. Impacts
   - evidence of impact assessment and forecasting (ecological, environmental, economic, social and cultural)
   - green operations implemented (in itself this is a graduated compliance system)

experience. The way a visitor experiences an event can be described mostly as a 'service encounter'. The well-known SERVQUAL model (Zeithaml et al., 1988) adds considerably to service quality management by highlighting the dimensions of quality that are important to consumers. Getz (1997, p. 177) applied these to events, as illustrated in Table 13.2. The 'tangibles' consist of the setting (venues or site), equipment, food and beverages, the appearance of staff and volunteers and communications about the event. All events have to satisfy the tangible 'hygiene' factors (cleanliness, safety, comfort and essential services).

Programme quality from the consumer's perspective is certainly implicit in designations like the annual Top 100 Events in North America (by the American Bus Association). However, other criteria might apply, such as judgements regarding the event's tourist attractiveness or recognition for long-term success.

'Programme quality' refers to the event as performance. It is more difficult to judge, especially if artistic or cultural in nature. Consumer satisfaction measures are useful (e.g. what was your overall level of satisfaction with this event?), as are the evaluations of other stakeholders including the tourism industry (e.g. how would you assess this event in terms of its tourist appeal and satisfaction of visitor needs?), professional artists or cultural interpreters (e.g. how would you rate this event's artistic programme in terms of cultural authenticity and artistic merit?) and those who fund the event (e.g. did it meet your expectations and requirements?).

Bowdin and Church (2000) equated quality at events with meeting customer needs and measures of customer satisfaction. They argued that quality programmes have costs, but they are quickly recovered by the event organization – first by reducing waste and

Table 13.2. Service quality elements for events.

1. Tangibles	• the 'hygiene' factors (safety, health, comfort, convenience)
	• appearance and cleanliness of all venues and equipment
	• appearance of symbols, logos and other representations of the event
	• hours of operation
	• physical accessibility (including for special needs)
	• waiting times and conditions (queuing)
2. Reliability	• absence of problems (getting it right the first time)
	• accuracy (e.g. of information, money handling, food service)
	• running programmes on time
	• honouring promises
	• consistent treatment of all guests
	• different standards of service are clear to all patrons
3. Responsiveness	• prompt service when needed and asked for
	• returning calls; following up on all requests
	• readiness of staff and volunteers to give service (empowerment!)
	• accessibility of staff and assistance when needed by guests
	• coordination of efforts (teamwork)
4. Assurance	• competence of staff and volunteers; display of knowledge and skills
	• courteous service to all
	• security (absence of real and perceived threats; confidentiality)
	• credibility (honest and trustworthy staff and volunteers; reputation of the organization and the event)
	• communication (listening to customers; accurate, understandable and on-time information; assuring guests that problems and queries will be handled in a timely, effective manner)
5. Empathy	• caring (customers feel they are cared about)
	• individualized attention (e.g. for tour groups and special needs or requests)
	• approachability (guests feel comfortable asking for help)

Source: adapted by Getz (1997) from Zeithaml et al. (1988).

failures, and second by reducing quality inspec-
tions and evaluations over time.

Impacts

Events are globally valued for their economic
benefits, and event managers might be
tempted to stress their success in attracting
tourists and generating favourable publicity for
the destination or host community. This is a
legitimate measure of event quality, but should
be carefully balanced through conducting benefit–cost evaluations that also consider the
often-intangible social, cultural and environmental impacts. More and more events are
becoming 'green' through recycling, reducing
and reusing practices, and this introduces a
whole new set of quality standards.

Review of Related Research

Numerous events conduct visitor studies, but very
few academic studies of event quality have been
published. A notable exception is that of the
Dickens on the Strand Festival in Galveston,
Texas, which has been studied systematically.
The early research (Ralston and Crompton,
1988) examined service quality within the context of reliability, tangibility, responsiveness,
assurance and empathy, and identified high- and
low-ranked items through a series of statements
presented to visitors. Crompton and Love
(1995) concluded that the tangible dimension
was most important at Dickens on the Strand,
specifically ambiance, sources of information at
the site, comfort amenities, parking and interaction with vendors. Actual performance measures
were found to be substantially better predictors of
quality than importance assigned by customers
to various service attributes and various disconfirmation operationalizations, which incorporated
expectations of service quality. They concluded
(Crompton and Love, 1995, p. 19): 'It appears
that respondents either did not form meaningful
expectations or, if they ever formed, did not use
them as criteria against which they measured
performance to determine quality'. The authors
recommended that different measures of quality
be employed in event evaluations. Also, they

suggested that importance measures were of
practical value to managers.

Love and Crompton (1996, unpublished
data) also used research at the Dickens festival to
test the hypothesis, based on the works of
Herzberg (1966) that some event elements are
'dissatisfiers' which can undermine the visitor
experience, while others are 'satisfiers' which
provide benefits. 'Dissatisfiers' are like
Herzberg's 'maintenance' factors – they must be
provided to expected levels of quality, but in
themselves do not satisfy visitors. The
researchers argued that most of the physical factors at events, such as parking, rest rooms and
information, are dissatisfiers, while ambiance,
fantasy, excitement, relaxation, escape and
social involvement are satisfiers. High-quality
events must meet expectations in both categories, but they are non-compensatory in that a
single or small number of attributes can determine perception of overall quality. Tentative
support for this model was confirmed, and the
researchers believed that certain attributes were
perceived to be of so poor or high quality that
visitors disregarded or discounted other attributes in giving their overall appraisal.

Baker and Crompton (2000) argued that
'quality' is an output of the event management
system (i.e. the opportunity provided to event
guests), whereas 'satisfaction' is an 'outcome'
equated to 'quality of experience'. The satisfaction or experiential outcome is not fully
controllable by event producers because of
external influences. From the responses of a
sample of 524 festival-goers they identified
four 'quality of opportunity domains':
(i) generic features of the event; (ii) specific
entertainment features; (iii) information; and
(iv) comfort amenities. Information and comfort amenities were called 'hygiene' factors,
and they can provoke dissatisfaction if poor,
but not add to overall satisfaction if exception-
ally good. Generic and entertainment features
of the event were found to be more likely to
generate increased satisfaction and motivate
return visits or positive word-of-mouth (WOM)
recommendations. The authors recommend
that event organizers evaluate both the quality
of the performance and visitor satisfaction.

Saleh and Ryan (1993) found that quality
of the music programme is the most important
service factor in attracting people to jazz festi-

vals. Overall satisfaction levels affected the intention for repeat visits. Similarly, Thrane (2002) explored the link between satisfaction and future intentions of festival-goers. The study took place in Norway. He and students conducted interviews asking for performance ratings concerning music quality, plus an overall satisfaction rating and future intentions regarding repeat visits and giving positive recommendations about the event. Analysis of results suggested that music quality affected overall satisfaction which in turn affected the intention for repeat visits. However, regarding the potential for recommending the festival to others, music quality had both a direct and indirect affect (as mediated by overall satisfaction). The most important conclusion is that event managers must try to improve programme quality (in this case music) and be concerned with other factors that shape overall satisfaction.

Stiernstrand (1997), in Sweden, determined that high perceived quality of 'essential services' (i.e. hygiene factors) did not translate into repeat visit intentions, but low perceived quality of essential services would result in lower repeat visitation. For tourists, who often seek novelty, low satisfaction ratings would definitely result in low repeat visits, but high ratings did not necessarily translate into repeat visits. Price, accessibility and weather were also found to be important factors – in addition to perceived service quality – in explaining satisfaction with events.

Case Study

This case study was first documented by Getz et al. (2001) and has been updated for this book by way of an interview with the general manager. The researchers evaluated service quality using triangulation (direct observation, participant observation and visitor survey) and employed service mapping as an analytical and management tool.

The Margaret River Masters is an annual professional surfing event, which is part of the World Qualifying Series (WQS) linked to the World Championship Tour (WCT). Many of the world's top male and female surfers

compete, alongside numerous local and other Australian surfers, thus ensuring that the event will attract keen interest among the large Australian surfing community. Margaret River itself is an attractive destination for residents of Perth, a large city some 3–4 h drive to the north.

In 1998 attendance was free of charge, so it is difficult to know exactly how many attended, but organizers announced a crowd of 4500–5000 on the final Sunday of the meet. Competitions ran over an entire week, culminating in the women's finals on Saturday, the 4th April and men's finals on Sunday. Observations and surveys were only completed only on these two days when it was known that the largest audiences would be present.

Methods and analysis

Three evaluation methods were simultaneously employed: direct observation; participant observation; and a visitor survey. The direct observation involved checklists covering observations of attendance, crowd behaviour and visitor characteristics. The same nine observers also kept diary notes that were afterwards transcribed by each observer into a narrative of their experience and assembled into a composite (see Table 13.3). Then a service map (based on Bitner, 1993) was prepared from the composite notes. Because of the details involved, the map was subdivided into two sections covering: (i) approach, site orientation and departure, and (ii) on-site experiences. Analyses of the map, narratives and composite notes, are complementary. On its own, the map provides a clear picture of the sequence of visitor movements surrounding the event, including the range of on-site experiences, together with interactions with setting and staff or volunteers. But it does not provide essential details such as notes on quality, problems observed or even potential areas of improvement.

Visitor flows and actions were first assessed (see Fig. 13.1). The sequence can be interpreted in the context of anticipation, arrival and orientation that mark all visits to attractions or new areas. Event mangers can enhance their customers' experiences by maximizing anticipation of an enjoyable experience (through

Table 13.3. Example of diary notes at the surfing event.

1. Approach to site
   Signage and access to the parking area was adequate, but there were both vehicles and pedestrians using the same narrow entrance to the car park. This was not only causing delays for vehicles but was also potentially dangerous for pedestrians. There was also a heavy vehicle wetting down the road at 8:30 a.m. and this also caused minor delays.
2. Parking area
   The parking was not in marked bays, but there are attendants to give direction to parking areas. They also maintain a presence there all day, which provides some security for parked vehicles. Leaving the parking area required a steep walk to the site, which some would find arduous.
3. Enter site
   No sense of arrival or welcome statement at the main entrance to the event, which was disappointing. Some banners/signage at the entry point along the road would be appropriate, perhaps with some information handouts and audio commentary.
4. Information search
   No signage on site as to direct access to main viewing, beach or VIP areas. Programmes were available in the VIP area, and an update of the surfing heat winners and progress was displayed on a board OUTSIDE of the VIP area. There was no dedicated information centre, but the commentary on each heat was enough to give spectators information on the surfing, provided it was audible.
5. Seating/comfort
   Seating in the viewing area was in short supply, and seats were difficult to find and keep. As soon as one person vacated a seat, someone else would occupy it. This was a problem around meal times, when visitors wanted to sit and eat. Viewing from the seating was inadequate, with people standing along the front of the marquee disrupting the view of those seated behind. The grandstand provided good viewing of the surfing, but seating was uncomfortable and difficult to access when the grandstand was full. There was also the risk of sunburn sitting in the uncovered grand stand – it should be covered in case of rain as well.
6. Food and beverage
   Food service was adequate at most times during the event and food quality was acceptable. Pricing of food was reasonable, but there was some evidence of over-pricing of sponsors' products (Coke products, Emu Bitter and Southern Comfort). This impeded enjoyment and discourages consumption of beverages as prices were about double normal bottle shop prices. The range of beverages was also limited to sponsors' products only so, for example, flavoured milk was not available. This appears to be a monopolistic approach to beverage provision at the event.
7. Viewing competition
   The commentary enhanced viewing, although the commentators did not always know who was competing, and sometimes were a bit 'over the top' with their off-hand comments. However, a major problem exists with the lack of a PA system in the VIP area, and there was inadequate commentary in those areas. This was a source of frustration and annoyance, that people in these areas were not informed of the progress of heats. Other areas such as the car park and the beach had good audible PA systems. Binoculars certainly enhanced viewing of the event, and should be available to VIPs or at least recommended to all visitors to the event. People standing along the front of the marquee disrupted viewing of the event in the VIP area.
   There were some disruptions to the power supply, but were quickly resolved. A major problem exists with the cordless microphones used during the presentation ceremonies. The signal was frequently lost, or broken up, so that speeches were inaudible. This was especially annoying during the winner's speeches on both days, and all winners need to be briefed on speaking clearly into the microphone. The presentation and speeches should be the highlight of the event, but were very flat on both days.
8. Toilet break
   Toilets were adequate most of the time, although by Sunday afternoon the toilet in the VIP area was wet and smelly, and may not have been cleaned all weekend.

Table 13.3. – *Continued*

9. Special elements

The VIP area has already been described. There were VIP areas for sponsors, which seemed like a double standard. There was also an ad-hoc VIP area set aside for surfing administrators, using a roll of plastic barricade material. This segregation also seemed unnecessary, and left the VIP area feeling like a VUP (very unimportant persons) area.

10. Depart site/leave area

Leaving the site and the car park was easy, with parking attendants and police directing traffic on to Caves Road. Traffic along Caves Road was heavier than normal, and combined with the trucks and local traffic to make driving fairly hazardous.

communications), facilitating an efficient and smooth arrival and providing a user-friendly orientation through information, signage or greeters. The design of the site can also contribute by providing an obvious and attractive entrance (both physical, as in a gateway, and symbolic as with signs, greeters, decorations or other visual cues). Of critical importance is the direction of visitors to important areas, in this case viewing, vendors and sponsors' facilities, the stage with scoreboard and the VIP area.

Figure 13.2 details the customer actions associated with on-site experiences. These are non-sequential because visitors were free to come and go from the site, choose their viewing spots (with the exception that the VIP area was restricted to pass holders) and make use of toilets, vendors, sponsors' booths and promotions. VIP pass holders had the greatest number of options, as they could also enjoy all the public areas.

Physical evidence of service quality was evaluated, revealing a number of good points, problems or potential problems and suggestions for improvements. No major problems were observed, and in fact the audience on both Saturday and Sunday enjoyed fine weather and good surfing within a relaxed atmosphere. Specific observations are shown on the map, covering the following topics: signage and access; entrance; information and signage on-site; site layout and aesthetics; seating and viewing; toilets; cleanliness; public safety; communications with audience; food and beverages; other vendors; officials and police; parking; security; information; announcers; sponsors; and staff contacts.

Overall, there was some confusion as to who was staff (owing to a lack of obvious uniforms or badges), and between the various vol-

unteer and staff groups (e.g. security, uniformed police, parking crew, clean-up crew, food servers and other vendors, management staff). Unclear staff/volunteer identification might have accounted for a noted absence of staff where and when they were expected.

Visitor surveys were conducted, taking the form of a direct disconfirmation, self-completion questionnaire, on which 21 items were provided. These covered the degree of visitor satisfaction or dissatisfaction on a 5-point scale with physical elements of the site (i.e. parking, access, cleanliness, food and beverages, personal comfort, safety, seating, signs and directions, toilets, viewing and overall satisfaction with the site), the staff (helpful, knowledgeable, presentable, available, approachable/friendly/pleasant, overall satisfaction with staff) and 'other' (souvenirs, crowd behaviour, running on time, the surfing competition, hours of competition).

Detailed results of the visitor survey have been reported elsewhere (Carlsen, 2003) but the highlights are worth noting here. Of 500 questionnaires distributed over two days, a total of 239 useable responses were obtained (48%). In many cases the forms were picked up immediately, but others were held on to by event-goers who did not complete or return them to the researchers. An effort was made to distribute a questionnaire to everyone within a selected area at the predetermined times. Respondents were gender balanced (51.5% male), mostly young (59.4% aged 16–25 years, and only 3.3% aged 45 or over) and mostly from Western Australia. However, 22% were from out of the state or country.

Visitors' overall perceptions of the site were positive, with a total mean score of 3.74 out of 5, and the 'overall' rating of the site was

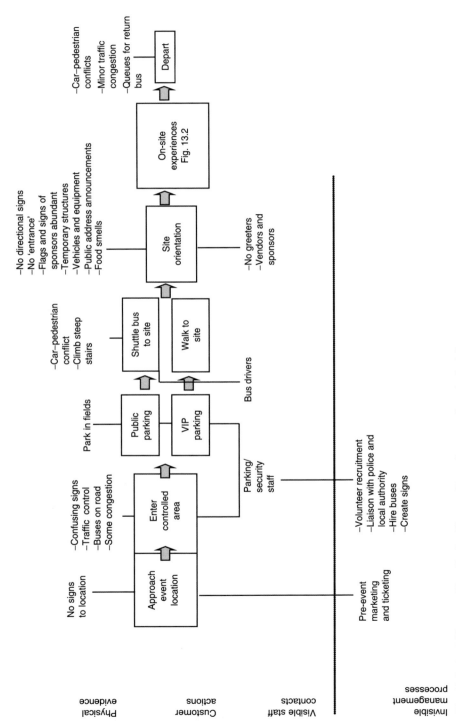

Fig. 13.1. 1998 Margaret River Surfing Masters Stage 1: approach and orientation.

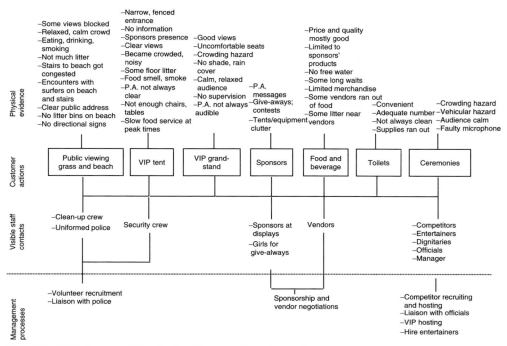

Fig. 13.2. 1998 Margaret River Surfing Masters, Stage 2: on-site visitor experiences.

4.09. The lowest means were recorded for parking (3.30), toilets (3.41) and viewing the event (3.41). Safety ranked the highest (4.25). Looking at individual responses, 15% were clearly dissatisfied with personal comfort and 21% were dissatisfied with seating. Regarding staff, the 'overall' rating was a mean of 3.94, and none of the items rated 4 or higher, or lower than 3.84. Ten per cent were dissatisfied with the availability of staff. The 'overall' mean for the 'other' items was 4.06, with only one item yielding a mean of less than 4.0 – souvenirs were thought to be inadequate, attracting a mean of 3.69.

Despite the fact that the event ran behind schedule and the waves were relatively small, clearly most respondents were at least satisfied with the event. One key measure of satisfaction was the finding that 77% of respondents intended to return next year, while fully 88% indicated a readiness to recommend the event to others. In fact, 53% had attended the event previously.

In addition to completing log books, the observers also made periodic notes, in assigned locations covering the entire site, on the following: attendance; gender and approximate age (by categories) of event-goers; types of groups (e.g. family, friends, alone); 'involvement' (anticipation, arousal, action or aggression); expenditure (evidence of spending on sponsors' products or others); and environment (evidence of impacts, including litter or vegetation trampling).

While this technique is potentially very accurate on some points, there is also a risk of bias, especially on interpreting crowd mood. Basically this was a fairly passive, well-behaved crowd, and observers summarized the most frequent state of involvement as being 'arousal'. This can be interpreted to mean that the audience was paying attention to the competitive surfing.

Management implications

The surfing event appeared to be a success from the points of view of both spectators and observers. There were no major problems observed, and analysis of the visitor survey revealed a fairly high level of overall satisfaction. However, several issues and potential problems that should be dealt with to improve future events were recorded.

Overall visitor experiences and service could be improved by providing more visible and welcoming staff/volunteers. Readily identifiable uniforms and badges should be worn by all 'event staff' so that visitors know who to approach for information and assistance. A central information point and better directional and informational signage (both to and on the site) are required. A few technical problems interfered with the public address announcements and awards presentations, and these can easily be fixed.

Food and beverage service should be expanded and improved, particularly for peak times. Litter prevention and trash removal needed improvement, as did maintenance of the toilets. The site appeared to be at or near its maximum capacity during the Sunday finals of the competition, with crowding posing potential safety problems and interfering with visitor enjoyment of the competition and awards ceremonies. A full separation of vehicular and pedestrian traffic might not be possible, but should be attempted.

Reassessment of the free-admission policy is one approach to the crowding problem. More visitors might be willing to pay for reserved seating and VIP treatment, including larger or more tents for covered dining. But this in itself would not solve the difficulty of controlling access to an otherwise open park and beach area. Expansion or redesign of the site might be a better option, with the aim of providing for more viewing areas. Relocation of some of the sponsors and vendors' equipment would help.

There are some indications that the service quality feedback provided to the event organizers has had the effect of improving visitor experiences, based on observations of the event and visitor surveys in 2003. The event continued to grow in profile and popularity between 1998 and 2003, and attracted a new title sponsor on a lucrative 3-year arrangement from 2002. The event is now referred to as the Salomon Masters at Margaret River with the global adventure sports company providing a new chapter in the sponsorship story of the event (Carlsen, 2003). Accompanying this new arrangement came a need to present an even more professional and successful event to ensure optimization of the event experience not only for visitors, but sponsors and participants as well.

It appears from a visitor survey in 2003 that satisfaction levels with the event are increasing, with some 82.1% of respondents either satisfied or very satisfied with the event experience (based on a sample of 112 visitor and participant responses). Further inferences can be drawn from the finding from the same survey that 92% of respondents intended to return to the event next year and that the 'loyal' participants in previous events remains high – with 46.9% of respondents in 2003 attending previously. In terms of other concerns identified in the 1998 studies, there have been several improvements including:

- Event staff are now issued with shirts and identification.
- Audio-visual and technical problems have been fixed.
- A wider range of food and beverage is now available, although food quality remains an issue.
- The site is now secured and illegal access is restricted.
- An admission fee to cover the cost of the shuttle bus from the off-site public car park has been introduced.
- The main viewing area is undercover, making the event more enjoyable even in bad weather.

Overall, it has been interesting to note how systematic observation and recording of event visitor experiences and impressions has led directly to management decisions which have improved the quality of the event.

Conclusion

Event 'quality' management is a complex issue, commencing with the realization that it embodies dimensions of organizational, service and programme quality as well as event impacts. Multiple stakeholders, including customers, can have different perspectives on the meaning and measurement of quality. Quality standards, either for individual events or across the event industry, must encompass all these elements.

Researchers have demonstrated several important facts about the experience and perceptions of quality at events. First and foremost, it is the programme itself that motivates and satisfies visitors. This helps to explain why service quality failures do not seem to detract from overall enjoyment, nor will they necessarily generate low satisfaction ratings.

Service quality at events can also be evaluated objectively by skilled observers such as staff or external researchers. Ideally, multiple methods and measures will be used. Service mapping is a very useful evaluation tool that can lead directly to development of service blueprinting and standards, or can be used to evaluate the existing quality specifications. This technique also has value as a check against visitor comments that might tend to be skewed towards the negative or positive.

References

Baker, D. and Crompton, J. (2000) Quality, satisfaction and behavioral intentions. *Annals of Tourism Research* 27(2), 785–804.

Bitner, M. (1993) Managing the evidence of service. In: Scheuing, E. and Christopher, W. (eds) *The Service Quality Handbook*. Amacom, New York, pp. 358–370.

Bowdin, G. and Church, I. (2000) Customer satisfaction and quality costs: towards a pragmatic approach for event management. In: Allen, J. *et al.* (eds) *Events Beyond 2000: Setting the Agenda, Proceedings of a Conference on Event Evaluation, Research and Education*. University of Technology, Sydney, pp. 186–200.

Carlsen, J. (2000) Events industry accreditation in Australia. *Event Management* 6(2), 117–121.

Carlsen, J. (2003) Riding the wave of event sponsorship: sponsorship objectives and awareness at the Margaret River Masters Surfing Event. In: Braithwaite, R.W. and Braithwaite, R.L. (eds) *Riding the Wave of Tourism and Hospitality Research, Proceedings of the CAUTHE Conference 2003*. Southern Cross University, Lismore, Australia

Crompton, J. and Love, L. (1995) The predictive validity of alternative approaches to evaluating quality of a festival. *Journal of Travel Research* 34(1), 11–24.

Getz, D. (1997) *Event Management and Event Tourism*. Cognizant Communication, New York.

Getz, D., O'Neil, M. and Carlsen, J. (2001) Service quality evaluation at events through service mapping. *Journal of Travel Research* 39(4), 380–390.

Herzberg, F. (1966) *Work and the Nature of Man*. World Publishing, New York.

Ralston, L. and Crompton, J. (1988) *Motivation, Service Quality and Economic Impact of Visitors to the 1987 Dickens On The Strand Emerging from a Mail Back Survey*. Report # 3 for the Galveston Historical Foundation. Department of Recreation and Parks, Texas A&M University, College Station, Texas.

Saleh, F. and Ryan, C. (1993) Jazz and knitwear: factors that attract tourists to festivals. *Tourism Management* 15, 289–297.

Stiernstrand, O. (1997) *Service Quality in Event Tourism*. European Tourism Research Centre, Ostersund, Sweden.

Thrane, C. (2002) Music quality, satisfaction and behavioural intentions within a jazz festival context. *Event Management* 7(3), 143–150.

Zeithaml, V., Berry, L. and Parasuraman, A. (1988) Communication and control processes in the delivery of service quality. *Journal of Marketing* 52, 35–48.

14 CAVIAR: Canterbury and Vladimir International Action for Regeneration – A Case Study of Techniques for Integrated Marketing, Service Quality and Destination Management

Barbara Le Pelley[1] and William Pettit[2]

[1]Guernsey Planning Department, UK; [2]City Council Canterbury, UK

Introduction

The success of any project depends on the interest and commitment of the people involved. This case study of international links between two World Heritage status cities presents the economic partnership between Vladimir in Russia and Canterbury in the UK and demonstrates how techniques and know-how have been successfully transferred across different cultural backgrounds and legislative systems. The case study explains the conceptual framework for the actions undertaken and assesses how the techniques learnt have been adapted by the Vladimir City Administration and by businesses in Vladimir to develop a sound basis for a sustainable heritage tourism industry in the city.

Background to the Case Study

A link between the city of Vladimir, 120 miles (190 km) north-east of Moscow and Canterbury, 60 miles (95 km) south-east of London, has existed since the mid-1980s when the 'Three Towns Association' linking Canterbury and Vladimir with Bloomington-Normal, Illinois, USA, was established. The link was initially cultural, leading to the exchange of artists, musicians, theatre groups

and so on, although a limited amount of educational links also occurred through student exchanges. In 1994 the Mayor of Vladimir, Igor Shamov, sent, via the Three Towns Association, an open letter to the Tourism Officer of Canterbury City Council asking for assistance in redeveloping the tourism industry in Vladimir. Particular assistance was sought for help in finding suitable partners to take this work forward.

Historically, tourism had been one of the most important sources of income for Vladimir. It is one of Russia's oldest towns and preceded Moscow as the nation's capital. A wealth of historic monuments dating from the 12th and 13th centuries, frescoes, rare wall paintings and icons are the main attractions for heritage tourism. A total of 1,050,000 tourists came to Vladimir in 1989 but by 1995 this had fallen to 125,000, primarily due to the many political and economic problems in Russia resulting from the break-up of the Soviet Union (see Fig. 14.1).

Under the former State-controlled economy individual freedom to travel was restricted. Trade unions and various government agencies controlled and paid for the cost of transportation to and accommodation in Vladimir for the majority of visitors, who came from the Soviet republics and the Russian Federation. With the move towards a market-controlled economy following the break-up of

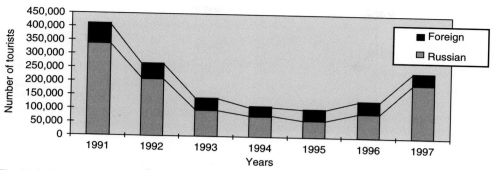

Fig. 14.1. Tourist arrivals in Vladimir, 1991–1997.

the Soviet Union these organizations reduced the scale of their operations and the number of tourists fell rapidly. Although domestic tourism had been the main source of Vladimir's visitors, there had also been a significant market in foreign tourists (70,000 in 1991) from more than 25 countries, including the USA and Japan. Even though this market also declined it was not, proportionately, as steep a decline. This foreign market, together with the revival of trade from Russia and the Commonwealth of Independent States (CIS), was seen as the nucleus for reviving the city's tourism industry, but in the new free-market economy the city needed to learn how to market itself and to provide the quality experience foreign tourists expected, skills which had been unnecessary under a State-controlled economy.

Before any meaningful practical advice could be given by Canterbury, it was necessary to visit Vladimir to assess what was already established and what potential there was for re-establishing a thriving tourism industry. The authors visited Vladimir, on behalf of the City Council in 1996. As a result, the Canterbury and Vladimir International Action for Regeneration (CAVIAR) project was born. Its purpose was to devise a Heritage Tourism Development Plan for Vladimir.

Theoretical Overview

Providing practical assistance to Vladimir posed an interesting theoretical challenge. The destination management techniques widely referred to and accepted in the literature (Butler, 1980; Ryan, 1993; Russell and Faulkner, 1998) implicitly assume the existence of an underlying free-market economy, within which the tourist exercises free choice between competing destinations. In turn, the element of competition and the destination's position in the destination development life cycle elicits a well-documented range of actions and market responses. The state-controlled economy under which Vladimir had until recently been operating did not offer that element of free choice. A major consequence was that the city's decision makers had not had to concern themselves with matters such as profit, price and quality. How then to position Vladimir as a destination, in order to advise on appropriate techniques?

Vladimir had to be conceived, from a historical perspective, as two markets: the free-market nucleus of foreign visitors, which conforms to the 'Exploration' stage of the Irridex – destination development model (Le Pelley and Laws, 1998) and for which tried-and-tested management responses are known and secondly, the state-controlled domestic market, which did not fit the destination development model. The sudden and rapid decline of Vladimir's state-controlled domestic tourism sector, as a result of factors beyond the city's control, can be conceived as being comparable to the sudden collapse in western economies of a subsidized industry such as shipbuilding, forestry or coal mining when government decisions suddenly withdraw support for that industry causing the region's economy to go into steep decline. In the West, tourism is often seen as an alternative economic generator in such circumstances.

In Chemainus on Vancouver Island in Canada, for example, the final closure of the timber industry and the construction of a new highway, bypassing the town, resulted in severe decline with the very real prospect that the town would fail. This crisis led the residents to fight back, by deliberately turning the town into a visitor attraction based on a spectacular trail of murals depicting its former industry (Kotler et al., 1993). Ironically, Vladimir was in the position where a sudden, unforeseen decline in the state-controlled tourism industry was to be replaced by the development of a free-market tourist industry! Again, Canterbury's experience would be invaluable to Vladimir. Canterbury City Council had gained considerable experience of using tourism as an economic regenerator through its work in reviving the seaside towns of Herne Bay and Whitstable (Le Pelley et al., 2002).

The example of Chemainus demonstrates a practical application of the concept of community-driven tourism planning described by Murphy (1985), whereby ideas initiated by interested members of the community are brought before a larger forum for deliberation and a consensus is reached on actions to be undertaken. This approach is now widely adopted by communities in British Columbia working within the Provincial Government's Community Tourism Action Programme. A development of this concept had already been tested in Canterbury through the setting up of the Canterbury City Centre Initiative, a stakeholder-benefits approach to tourism management in a historic city (Laws and Le Pelley, 2000). This had demonstrated that a community-driven approach could be adapted and was as applicable to a mixed-economy European historic city as it was to rural communities in British Columbia. Could the community-driven approach also be applicable to a large Russian city which had, until recently, not experienced a free-market economy and had been subject to significant top-down control by the state? Given that Vladimir had very few resources available to it, other than the enthusiasm and commitment of the City Administration and key tourism entrepreneurs, it was worth a try.

The initial fact-finding visit to Vladimir (funded by the British Council) was to be for 5 days, at the end of which the Russians were expecting to be presented with a report setting out recommendations for action. To achieve this, a rapid understanding was needed of Vladimir's destination 'hardware' (accommodation, attractions, transport, public realm) and 'software' (interpretation, standard of visitor services, marketing). Some information was already available in the form of a SWOT (strengths, weaknesses, opportunities, threats) analysis carried out by consultants but this needed to be updated. Again, British Columbia's Community Tourism Action Programme provided a useful model. Its instructions demonstrate how communities themselves can gather sufficient background information to make informed choices, identify actions and agree who will undertake them. Using this model, the City Administration was asked to make an informed assessment of Vladimir as a destination, prior to the fact-finding visit. This assessment would be used to structure the visit.

Vladimir – the Regional Context

Vladimir is a large historic city with a population of more than 300,000 located about 120 miles (190 km) north-east of Moscow with reasonable road and rail links (by Russian standards) to the capital. It is an industrial city producing tractors, electric motors and a wide range of consumer goods and agricultural products. In addition, Heritage tourism is a main attraction to the region. Vladimir is a key city of Russia's world famous 'Golden Ring' – a group of 16 historic towns to the east of Moscow.

Suzdal, about 20 miles (30 km) north of Vladimir is the nearest Golden Ring town and has the well-deserved status of a City-Museum, with a vast range of religious buildings and a fine open air museum of wooden buildings. The richness and diversity of Suzdal's ecclesiastical heritage defies description. The White Monuments of Vladimir and Suzdal (churches, cathedrals and monasteries) were inscribed on the UNESCO World Heritage List in 1994. The Vladimir-Suzdal Museum Reserve now cares for the majority of the historic and cultural monuments which are the main tourist attractions in the city and region.

Although it is administratively independent from Vladimir, Vladimir and Suzdal are effectively one tourism 'product' and the authorities of both towns are beginning to collaborate on restoration and promotional programmes, the most significant of which is the Moscow–Suzdal–Vladimir tour. Thus, Vladimir is able to gain from its fortunate location within easy travelling distance of Moscow, the gateway to Russia.

Vladimir – the City Context

Vladimir was founded around 990 AD. It was rebuilt in the middle of the 12th century and became the capital of Russia and its seat of Christianity, a status the city retained for 150 years. Vladimir's monuments and other places of interest are concentrated in the 12th-century core of the city, which is 120 acres (48 ha) in extent within the ramparts. The white stone monuments of the pre-Mongolian period include two cathedrals and the only remaining City Gate. There is also a substantial monastery (once used as the local KGB headquarters) and numerous churches. In addition to the historic, archaeological and cultural monuments, the city tourist product consists of restaurants, hotels and tourist companies specializing in folklore and traditional crafts. About 5 miles (8 km) from the city in a remote spot near the village of Bogolyubovo stands the beautiful and imposing Church of the Intercession on the Nerl. Although access to the church requires a lengthy walk across open meadows, it remains an essential attraction for most visitors to Vladimir.

Prior to the break-up of the Soviet Union care of the monuments was funded by the State. They have now become the responsibility of either the religious institutions that were their original owners, or the Vladimir City Administration. This has created a conflict of interest in respect of the ecclesiastical monuments that are again being used for religious purposes which restricts their availability for tourist visits. The Vladimir-Suzdal Museum Reserve has now accepted that tourism is an

important part of its function, as has the Department of Historic Centre Reconstruction.

Considerable upgrading and refurbishment is needed to bring the city's infrastructure up to date. About 11,400 persons live in the historic core of the city, through which the main through road passes creating a traffic problem. There is insufficient parking for tourists. The state of building dilapidation and inadequate infrastructure standards illustrated in Tables 14.1 and 14.2 provides an inkling of the scale of problems facing the City Administration, which is why a significant taxable contribution from tourist industry profit is sought.

Vladimir Tourism Development Analysis

During the fact-finding visit everything about Vladimir's tourism industry was assessed from basic visitor facilities, such as public toilets (practically non-existent), to street lighting and signposting, including the requirement for a tourist information centre and the safeguarding of the built heritage. Two seminars were held with the Vladimir City Administration and local businessmen. The first was in the form of a workshop facilitated by the authors, whereby consensus on what were the strengths and weaknesses of the Vladimir City product was sought. The second introduced the concept of 'Getting it Right', developed by the English Historic Towns Forum (EHTF) in 1994 (updated in EHTF, 1999), an integrated approach to destination management in which the whole city is regarded as the tourist product and those responsible for various aspects

Table 14.1. Tenure of buildings in the historic core of Vladimir.

Tenure of buildings	Number
Municipal buildings	294
Private dwelling houses	218
Municipal dwelling houses (dilapidated)	133
Historic and architectural monuments	105
Federal monuments	(41)
Local monuments	(64)

Barbara Le Pelley and William Pettit

Table 14.2. Infrastructure problems in the historic core of Vladimir.

Infrastructure problem	Extent of problem
No direct water supply	58% of buildings
No connection to main sewerage	40% of buildings
No natural gas supply	90% of buildings
Reduced capacity of electricity supply	23 of the 36 electricity sub-stations cannot be used because of their poor condition
Inadequate heating	68% of houses are still heated by the traditional stove

are encouraged to recognize the links between their responsibilities and work together.

The example of the Canterbury City Centre Initiative (Laws and Le Pelley, 2000) was drawn on to demonstrate how the links between 'hard' and 'soft' tourism infrastructure can be recognized and managed sustainably in support of a heritage tourism destination. The importance of understanding the symbiotic relationship between individual businesses and the environmental quality of the setting within which they operate in the public realm was demonstrated. Also explained were the benefits of working in partnership, the importance of quality service standards and the supportive role of marketing. This seminar helped the Vladimir City Administration and the businessmen to focus their attention on the opportunities and threats affecting Vladimir's tourism industry.

The remainder of the fact-finding visit concentrated on assessing the tourist 'hardware' – hotels, tourist attractions and Suzdal, a unique experience, which confirmed the City-Museum's strategic marketing significance for Vladimir. The 'software' of tourism was further assessed through individual interviews with the operators of tourism businesses. These investigations updated the SWOT analysis and

enabled a number of conclusions to be reached about Vladimir and its potential for tourism development. Table 14.3 shows the main reasons for the decline in tourism in Vladimir.

The findings of the SWOT Analysis were confirmed as a useful guide for future action (see Fig. 14.2).

A report summarizing the findings of the fact-finding visit and outlining recommended actions was presented to the Vladimir City Administration's Department of International Relations, Economic Development and Tourism. The department was also given a selection of the tourist and destination management literature commonly available to tourist destinations in the West. This was all subsequently translated into Russian and used to inform the development of a conceptual model for the development of Vladimir's tourism industry. The key conclusions reached for developing assistance for Vladimir are shown in Table 14.4.

Establishing the CAVIAR Project

In January 1997, a detailed report entitled 'Working with Vladimir' was presented to the

Table 14.3. Causes of decline in Vladimir's tourism.

Political instability	• Unstable political situation in Russia from 1991
Inadequate infrastructure	• Inadequate physical infrastructure compared with world standards
	• Lack of modern, comfortable means of transport
Poor standard of the tourist product and its interpretation	• Poor quality hotels which did not meet modern standards and foreign tourist demands
	• Lack of world standard tourist services
	• Lack of large-scale advertising and promotion of the Vladimir tourism product
	• Lack of interesting events and actions organized for tourists

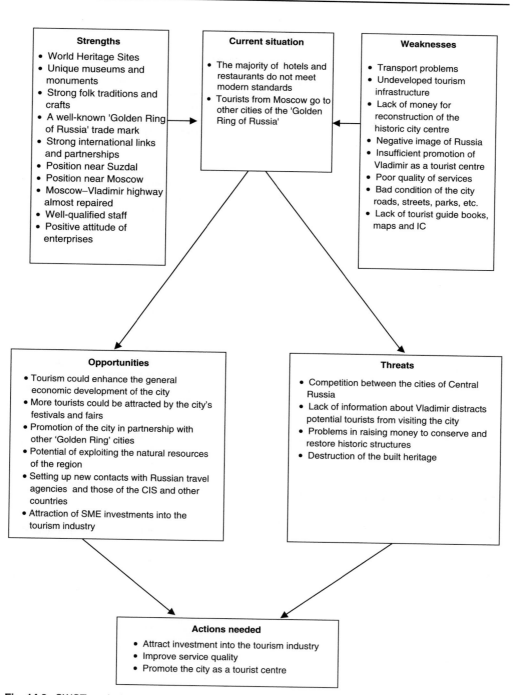

Strengths
- World Heritage Sites
- Unique museums and monuments
- Strong folk traditions and crafts
- A well-known 'Golden Ring of Russia' trade mark
- Strong international links and partnerships
- Position near Suzdal
- Position near Moscow
- Moscow–Vladimir highway almost repaired
- Well-qualified staff
- Positive attitude of enterprises

Current situation
- The majority of hotels and restaurants do not meet modern standards
- Tourists from Moscow go to other cities of the 'Golden Ring of Russia'

Weaknesses
- Transport problems
- Undeveloped tourism infrastructure
- Lack of money for reconstruction of the historic city centre
- Negative image of Russia
- Insufficient promotion of Vladimir as a tourist centre
- Poor quality of services
- Bad condition of the city roads, streets, parks, etc.
- Lack of tourist guide books, maps and IC

Opportunities
- Tourism could enhance the general economic development of the city
- More tourists could be attracted by the city's festivals and fairs
- Promotion of the city in partnership with other 'Golden Ring' cities
- Potential of exploiting the natural resources of the region
- Setting up new contacts with Russian travel agencies and those of the CIS and other countries
- Attraction of SME investments into the tourism industry

Threats
- Competition between the cities of Central Russia
- Lack of information about Vladimir distracts potential tourists from visiting the city
- Problems in raising money to conserve and restore historic structures
- Destruction of the built heritage

Actions needed
- Attract investment into the tourism industry
- Improve service quality
- Promote the city as a tourist centre

Fig. 14.2. SWOT analysis.

Table 14.4. Developing assistance for Vladimir.

Issue	Assistance needed from Canterbury
Marketing and customer care skills	• The previous reliance on 'guaranteed' organized sector bookings has removed any need to develop marketing and customer care skills. • The standards of customer care and of hotel accommodation expected by Western tourists are not well understood in Vladimir. Support for small and medium-sized enterprises (SMEs) and business training in quality service standards is needed. • All aspects of visitor services need to be developed. Vladimir would benefit from the customer care initiatives and techniques which the Canterbury City Centre Initiative is promoting amongst businesses in Canterbury. • A tourist information centre (TIC) needs to be established, together with training in TIC management.
Environment	• It is vital to safeguard the whole built heritage of the city, consisting of historic buildings and wooden vernacular architecture, not just the World Heritage sites. Canterbury's experience and excellence in historic building conservation techniques will be invaluable to Vladimir. • Attention needs to be given to environmental issues: water quality, vehicle emissions and the public realm.
The role of the public and private sectors	• The concept of building a partnership between the public and private sector is new to Vladimir and much more than a single seminar is needed. • It is apparent that much could be gained by a study tour to Canterbury and nearby UK tourist towns to give the Russians vital first-hand experience of the standards required and the potential of the private sector.

Policy Committee of Canterbury City Council. As well as giving background details on Vladimir, its similarities and links with Canterbury and a summary of the exploratory work which had been undertaken during the fact-finding visit, it also outlined the framework for a potential bid to the Know-How Fund in the context of the United Kingdom Foreign and Commonwealth Office's Local Government Technical Links Scheme, to help to fund the proposed assistance to Vladimir. Approval was sought from the City Council to proceed with an application. Financial assistance from the Fund would be essential to enable the project to proceed but the City Council would, itself, need to set aside some funding for the project. The City Council agreed to proceed with the project and a partnership agreement was signed between the two City authorities in July 1997 (see Fig. 14.3).

The CAVIAR Project

The application to the Know-How Fund was approved in June 1998 and a timetable was drawn up for the programme of work which would result in the delivery of the CAVIAR project. The primary input was to be the transfer of expertise from Canterbury City Council and Canterbury City Centre Initiative to meet the skills needs of the Vladimir City Administration and the city's tourism industry. The Know-How Fund stipulated that it wished to monitor the project and would require a formal report, through which it would assess the project's success.

Particular staff and consultancy skills which were to be made available to Vladimir by Canterbury through the CAVIAR Project included:

Formal Declaration of Intent July 1997

The formal signing of this partnership agreement between Canterbury and Vladimir cements the friendship which has developed between our towns over the last 12 years and marks the beginning of a new phase in our relationship. The future focus will be on economic partnership in addition to the valuable social and cultural contacts which have already been of great benefit to both our towns.

We sign this Protocol d'Accord on behalf of both our cities in the sincere belief that working together and opening our eyes to each other's cultural and economic activities will benefit both our cities and assist in the continuance of a peaceful relationship between our countries.

Igor Shamov
Mayor of Vladimir

Colin Carmichael
Chief Executive
Canterbury City Council

Fig. 14.3. Partnership agreement.

- a commitment to local government and business partnerships through networking and networking development (Canterbury City Centre Initiative);
- identifying short- and medium-term market opportunities within a long-term development plan;
- teamworking skills and teamwork development;
- providing business help and advice to assist with running a Visitor Information Centre;
- wider understanding of historic town management issues (through links with other networks of historic towns, such as the English Historic Towns Forum and the Euroregion Historic Towns Association);
- strategy development;
- specialist conservation, tourism, economic development and local authority management expertise.

Inputs to the project from Vladimir, which were expected to contribute to the success of the project, were:

- The experience and commitment of officials of Vladimir City Administration;
- The language resources of Vladimir City Administration (most participants had an excellent command of English);
- The tourism experience of Vladinvesttour (a Vladimir tourism promotion company with strong commitment to the project).

The main intended outputs of the project were:

- compilation and physical production of a tourism development strategy document for Vladimir;
- implementation of the strategy;
- sharing of Canterbury's tourism industry experience;
- transfer of technical skills;
- establishment of a public/private partnership – the Vladimir City Initiative;
- delivery of Customer Care training to key Vladimir entrepreneurs for eventual cascading to staff in Vladimir;
- transfer of specific expertise in the management of Visitor Information Centres.

The project phases are shown in Table 14.5.

Achievements of the CAVIAR Project

Successes

The key output of the CAVIAR project was to be the strategic development of Vladimir's tourism industry through the sharing of tourism expertise. There is clear evidence that this was achieved, both in increased visitor numbers and in development of the industry:

- Vladimir City Administration, assisted by a tourism and business student at the Vladimir State University developed the SADT-Model tourism development plan, entitled the 'Strategic Plan of Tourism Development in Vladimir'.

Table 14.5. Project phases.

Project phase	Timetable
Inauguration of CAVIAR project	June 1998
Study tour to Canterbury by Vladimir City Administration officials and representatives of the newly established Vladimir City Initiative	October 1998
Local consultation in Vladimir on the development of a tourism strategy. Begin cascaded delivery of 'customer care' training	Winter 1998/99
Canterbury City Council officers visit Vladimir to finalise the CAVIAR project and assess the effectiveness of 'customer care' training	May 1999
Know-how Fund report produced in Canterbury and agreed with Vladimir	June–July 1999
Final report submitted to Know-how Fund	October 1999

- The Vladimir City Initiative public/private sector partnership was established. This very strong partnership demonstrated significant practical application in Vladimir of the ideas gained through the CAVIAR project study tour to Canterbury. Its partners included:

  - all relevant departments of Vladimir City Administration;
  - the Vladimir-Suzdal Museums Reserve;
  - the manager of the 'Golden Ring' complex;
  - tourism companies;
  - vladimir State University;
  - a representative from the Russian International Academy of Tourism.

- There was enormous enthusiasm in Vladimir for applying the customer-care skills and improved standards of service delivery learnt from the techniques in Canterbury. A major cascading exercise to businesses unable to go on the study tour was undertaken. It was also evident in many locations that an openness of presentation and merchandizing was being introduced as a direct result of the visits undertaken during the study tour to Canterbury.
- A Tourist Information Centre was opened in the main museum in Vladimir which took many of its ideas for imaginative exhibits, historical interpretation and open, customer friendly displays from the Canterbury district and other Kent TICs included in the study tour. Visitor numbers to the museum increased by 20–25% in 1999.
- An information centre was opened in Suzdal.
- Information provision was made available through the use of video, a website, e-mail and fax (the Moscow–Suzdal–Vladimir tour

is now heavily marketed through the Internet).
- The Vladimir City Administration instituted consultation with residents in small, local focus groups which enabled them to be part of the destination development process.
- The Vladimir City Administration recognized the importance of tourism in its own right and established a specific budget for tourism development.
- There was recognition that the main beneficiaries of the project were the citizens of Vladimir in general. Although individual organizations and businesses may have benefited from the application of knowledge gained for the CAVIAR project, the total benefit to the community was greater than the sum of its parts.
- An unexpected beneficiary was Canterbury City Council. It learnt how to organize a 'City Day' from the Russians and also greatly increased its expertise in working with different administrations.

Disappointments

Inevitably, there were disappointments and misgivings that such an ambitious programme could be achieved. These were to a large extent overcome by the commitment and enthusiasm of one man, the Managing Director of Vladinvesttour, who proved both a stimulus to the confidence of the emerging Vladimir City Initiative and also made a significant contribution to the development of inbound tourism to Vladimir from Moscow and the other Golden

Ring cities, e.g. the 'Discover Russia through its people' promotion. The crucial contribution of such a project champion when times get difficult has been observed in many other successful partnerships. The United Kingdom Civic Trust regards such Civic Champions as crucial to the success of voluntary partnerships and now runs free training courses to enable individuals to fulfill their potential.

The CAVIAR project was unable to complete all the tasks envisaged at the outset. Difficulties arose towards the end of the project period because of delays in establishing a new Tourist Information Centre in Vladimir. It was not possible, for example, to deliver on-site training of TIC staff, since they had not been recruited. It is hoped that this can be a major element of a future bid. During phase 3, it became apparent that there had been difficulties in Vladimir in the production of a visitor guide and map of the city. By the time the difficulties emerged, it was too late to help within the terms of the CAVIAR project. Although the CAVIAR project was delayed in its approval phase, the implementation period was roughly as planned, but delivered a year later than originally envisaged. This delay appears not to have had any adverse effect on the value of the project. Indeed, it may be argued that the additional time enabled the Vladimir City Initiative

to achieve a level of cohesion, increasing the ability of members to benefit from the study tour to Canterbury in October 1998.

The Know-How Fund assessors felt that the work targets set for the project had been largely achieved and concluded that 'overall it seems as though the Project has been a success'. They added, 'We hope that both Canterbury and Vladimir will continue to collaborate and that the foundations laid by the Project will be sustained and built upon'.

The Importance of the SADT Tourism Development Model

The SADT Tourism Model was one of the key outputs of the project. It demonstrates the important contribution marketing and services management skills can make in creating a successful destination (see Figs 14.4 and 14.5). The main aim of the model is to create a modern, competitive tourism industry in Vladimir and to determine the actions the City Administration should take to achieve:

- budget efficiency;
- social efficiency;
- economic efficiency;
- financial efficiency.

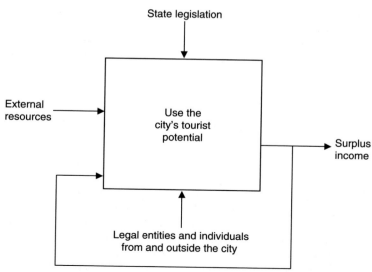

Fig. 14.4. SADT conceptual diagram.

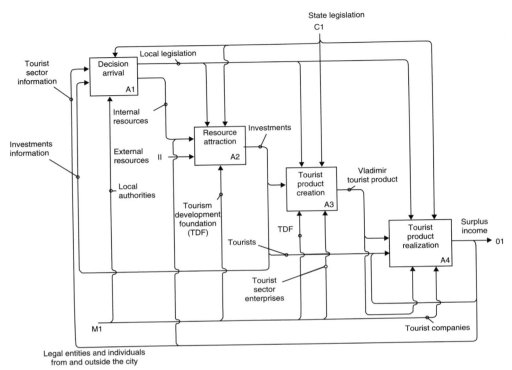

Fig. 14.5. SADT Tourism Development Model. @ Normal:

Its importance as the underlying conceptual framework for the major achievements gained in Vladimir cannot be overestimated. Unlike the soft, open systems models more generally conceived in western destinations, whereby tourist satisfaction and environmental quality are stated to be key objectives as well as financial returns for the destination, the SADT model focuses primarily on determining how and through whom Vladimir can achieve the economic investment it needs. The Concept Diagram for the two-part model, first of all, identifies the combination of State legislation, external resources, legal entities and individuals from inside and outside the city, which is needed to unlock the city's tourist potential and generate the surplus taxable income needed to develop the industry. Next, the SADT model itself conceptualizes who should be involved at each phase of developing the destination, the linkages between them and the outcomes at the four key development stages:

- decision arrival;
- resource attraction;
- tourist product creation;
- tourist product realization.

The model also recognizes the importance of developing a legislative framework within which the tourism industry should operate and the need to regulate such aspects as health and safety standards and quality standards. It is evident that the Russians gained a clear understanding of the requirement to work at a number of different levels in achieving an integrated tourist product. Practically, the conceptual aspects are then translated into an Implementation Plan and a frank Market Segment Analysis to guide marketing efforts (Tables 14.6 and 14.7) Very few destinations in the West have such a sophisticated, or single-minded conceptual framework for developing their tourism industry.

Table 14.6. Strategic plan for tourism in Vladimir.

Strategic Plan for Tourism Development in Vladimir
Tourism Development Project

Project tasks and aims
- to create a modern competitive tourism industry in Vladimir
- to achieve: budget efficiency; social efficiency; economic efficiency; financial efficiency

Aims	Short term (under a year)	Medium term (under five years)	Strategic (more than five years)
Social	Employment provision		
		Development of tourism business activity	
			Creation of favourable living and working conditions for city residents, increasing their living standards
Economic	Development of the city's infrastructure		
	Increase in attracting investment to the city		
	Maximize economic opportunities from tourism		
	Evaluation of required capital and operating costs	Realization of investment projects	Creation of competitive tourism industry
Budget		Increase the city's profitable budget	
Financial		Creation of a self-financing tourism industry based on project management	Increased income for tourism enterprises; increased currency returns

Actions
The Project tasks identify the actions the City Administration needs to take:
- Carry out market research, form a marketing strategy and create a favourable image for the city
- Regular monitoring of tourism industry enterprises
- Draft local legislation to regulate enterprises working in the tourism industry
- Create a favourable investment climate and attract financial resources for tourism
- Develop a mechanism for coordinating the activities of state, municipal and non-governmental institutions working in the sphere of tourism
- Train tourism personnel and improve the quality of tourism services

Critique and Conclusions on the CAVIAR Project

The CAVIAR Project was ambitious in its aims and achieved considerable success. Building on the experience gained in Canterbury, it demonstrated that the community-based approach to tourism development could, indeed, be adapted to the circumstances pertinent to different cultures, different legislative systems and different types and sizes of tourist destinations. There was clear evidence that the economic and social aspects of tourism development were understood and acted upon. The SADT model did not, however, encompass the third key factor of sustainable tourism – the environment in general, even though the crucial importance of this had been stressed at the outset of the CAVIAR project and was demonstrated during the study tour to Canterbury. This is not a criticism of the very real achievements made but, rather, a reflection on the

Table 14.7. Vladimir target markets.

Type of tourism	Objective group	Age category	Interest in historic places	Readiness to spend money	Importance for the city	Seasonal indicators	Important notes
Cognitive Tourism	Russian tourists, people on holiday	Unlimited	Medium	Medium	Low	High tourist season (summer)	Seaside resorts show how to market to these tourists.
Cognitive Tourism	Schoolchildren from Russia and CIS	Under 17	High	Low	Medium	School holidays	These represent about 80% of all visits.
Cognitive Tourism	Archaeology students, Russian and foreign people interested in history	18–25	High	Low	High	Summer	There is a good potential to use these people as inexpensive labour for restoration of the city monuments.
Conferences, exhibitions	Russian and foreign companies representatives coming via travel agencies	35 and more	Medium (if well-developed infrastructure exists)	High (if there are no strict accommodation arrangements)	High (if there is well-developed economic cooperation)	Spring, autumn	This market is now being developed. Such customers could be very helpful in spreading information about the city.
Foreign tourist groups	Foreign tourists coming on day excursions by buses	50 and more	High	High	Low (good city coach stations and parking places needed)	High tourist season (summer)	This market is stable and consists of under 6% of all visits.
Foreign tourists from partner cities	Tourist with common interests coming via partnership committees and exchange programmes	Unlimited (depending on exchange program: sports, cultural, educational)	High	High	High	Summer, winter	It is very easy to define the size of this market and to forecast tourist flows.
Excursionists	Independent tourists and tourist groups with common interests coming from Moscow	35–55 (on the average)	High	High	High (good parking places needed to encourage travel by car)	May–September (Dacha time)	This group needs information about the city and an Information Centre.

priorities perceived by the Vladimir City Administration and the Vladimir City Initiative in striving to improve the city's economy with very limited resources.

As Akehurst (1998), referring to a similar project in the Polish city of Kalisz, points out:

> Outside experts cannot impose their thoughts and plans on the city and, rightly, the people of Kalisz would not allow this. These considerations also raise issues of whether western tourism planning concepts and procedures are appropriate within a developing economy. There is no easy answer to this, and indeed the only answer must be to listen carefully to what objectives are being sought and devise plans which are realistic and sympathetic to both people and environment in the attainment of those objectives.

So it is with Vladimir. Initial concentration on the marketing and service quality aspects of tourism is achievable and will generate surplus income. When you have to cope with making significant provision of the most basic infrastructure to improve the living standards of your people, the niceties of environmental management must wait their turn.

Recently, Vladimir appointed its first Tourism Officer who has approached Canterbury to discuss the possibility of collaborating on a 'Son of CAVIAR' project. This further evidence of the City Administration's support for tourism is welcome and will, hopefully, enable the tasks left over from the first project to be completed. Perhaps it will also enable the environmental aspects to be reconsidered and incorporated into the model. To do so, successfully, would provide additional evidence of the adaptability of a community-driven tourism development approach.

Acknowledgement

Many people in Canterbury and Vladimir were generous with their time and expertise in setting up and implementing the CAVIAR Project. Its success is a testimony to all who supported it.

References

Akehurst, G. (1998) Tourism planning and implementation in the Polish city of Kalisz. In: Laws, E., Faulkner, B. and Moscardo, G. (eds) *Embracing and Managing Change in Tourism*. Routledge, London.

Butler, R. (1980) The concept of a tourist area life cycle: implications for management of resources. *Canadian Geographer* 24(4), 5–12.

EHTF (English Historic Towns Forum) (1994) *Getting it Right: A Guide to Visitor Management in Historic Towns*. EHTF.

EHTF (English Historic Towns Forum) (1999) *English Tourism Council: English Heritage 'Making the Connections'*. EHTF.

Kotler, P., Haider, D.H. and Rein, I. (1993) *Marketing Places*. Free Press, New York.

Laws, E. (1995) *Tourist Destination Management*. Routledge, London.

Laws, E. and Le Pelley, B. (2000) Managing complexity and change in tourism: the case of a historic city. *International Journal of Tourism Research* 2(4), 229–246.

Le Pelley, B. and Laws, E. (1998) A stakeholder-benefits approach to tourism in a historic city centre: the Canterbury City Centre Initiative. In: Laws, E., Faulkner, B. and Moscardo, G. (eds) *Embracing and Managing Change in Tourism*. Routledge, London.

Le Pelley, B., Human, B. and Grant, M. (2002) Seaside town regeneration: Herne Bay and Whitstable. In: Laws, E. (ed.) *Tourism Marketing Quality and Service Management Perspectives*. Continuum, London.

Murphy, P.E. (1985) *Tourism a Community Approach*. Routledge, London.

Russell, R. and Faulkner, B. (1998) Reliving the destination lifecycle in Coolangatta – an historical perspective on the rise, decline and rejuvenation of an Australian seaside resort. In: Laws, E., Faulkner, B. and Moscardo, G. (eds) *Embracing and Managing Change in Tourism*. Routledge, London.

Ryan, C. (1993) *Recreational Tourism: A Social Science Perspective*. Routledge, London.

15 Emotional Labour and Coping Strategies

Barbara Anderson
University of South Australia

Introduction

Whether it is supermarket checkout operators bidding farewell to customers with the now hackneyed injunction to 'have a nice day' or businesses promising 'service with a smile', the importance of the emotional display of front-line service workers cannot be overstated. However, this type of emotion work, which has come to be known as emotional labour, is not without its human and economic costs. 'Burnout' has been identified amongst front-line service workers, resulting in a lowering of service quality and contributing to absenteeism and job turnover, which impacts on the service workers' potential earnings and organizational profitability.

In this chapter, the nature of the emotional labour which is 'performed' in the course of customer service work is discussed together with the strategies used by front-line service workers to cope with the emotional demands of this type of work. Based on the findings of four case studies, drawn from research carried out amongst Australian managers and workers in the Tourism and Hospitality industries, a number of strategies are suggested which organizations may wish to implement to support their staff in their customer service work.

Nature of Front-line Service Work

Front-line service work means that the service workers must become a 'one-minute friend' to each of their customers (Albrecht and Zemke, 1985, pp. 114–115). In the process of becoming this friend, service workers must manage their own emotions and emotional display in order to make the service encounter a pleasant experience for customers. The emotions that are masked are as much a consideration as those displayed (Rafaeli, 1989, p. 388; Rosenberg, 1990, p. 4).

Emotional Labour

In recent years, this practice of emotion management has become known as 'emotional labour' and a number of definitions of such labour have been proposed. In her pioneering work, Hochschild (1983, p. 7) uses the term emotional labour 'to mean the management of feeling to create a publicly observable facial and bodily display; emotional labour is sold for a wage and therefore has exchange value'. Morris and Feldman (1996, p. 987) define emotional labour as 'the effort, planning and control needed to express organizationally desired emotion during interpersonal transaction'.

©CAB International 2006. *Managing Tourism and Hospitality Services: Theory and International Applications* (eds Bruce Prideaux, Gianna Moscardo and Eric Laws)

Ashforth and Humphrey (1993, p. 90) describe emotional labour as 'the act of displaying the appropriate emotion (i.e. conforming with a display rule)'. These definitions highlight the effort involved in managing feeling and its display to correspond with occupational norms as well as the influence of employers in directing their employees' emotional display (Erickson and Wharton, 1997, p. 190).

Characteristics of Jobs Involving Emotional Labour

According to Hochschild (1983, p. 147), jobs involving emotional labour possess three characteristics:

- require face-to-face or voice-to-voice or facial contact with the public;
- require the worker to produce an emotional state in the client or customer;
- allow the employer to exercise some control over the emotional activities of employees.

Those who perform such jobs in the tourism and hospitality industries include tourist information officers, tour guides and drivers, front desk staff and concierges in hotels and waiting and bar staff in restaurants. Their face-to-face interactions with customers may often be regulated by organizational guidelines in order to produce positive experiences for their customers.

Regulation of Emotion

Employers use a variety of strategies to standardize the emotional display and actions of their front-line service workers. These strategies include the provision of scripts, ranging in complexity from simple instructions to detailed directions for more complex transactions (Leidner, 1999, pp. 87–88). The wearing of a uniform may perform a variety of functions. As well as being a sign of professionalism and a legitimization of the service workers' roles within the organization, uniforms can impact on the emotional display of the workers, as they are continually being made aware that

they are employees, fulfilling a particular role, and hence the need to behave accordingly (Easterling et al., 1992; Rafaeli and Pratt, 1993; San Filippo, 2001).

'Performance' of Emotional Labour

Emotional labour is performed in either of two ways:

- *Surface acting*: simulating emotions that are not really felt.
- *Deep acting*: attempting to experience the emotions to be displayed (Morris and Feldman, 1996, p. 990), citing Hochschild (1983). Indeed, the actor 'psychs' himself/ herself into the desired persona (Mann, 1997, p. 7).

Ashforth and Humphrey (1993, p. 90) suggest that:

> emotional labour can be considered a form of impression management to the extent that the labourer deliberately attempts to direct his or her behaviour toward others in order to foster both certain social perceptions of himself or herself and a certain interpersonal climate.... The labourer is viewed as an actor performing on stage for an often discriminating audience.

This view of emotional labour as a performance confirms the observation made by Hochschild (1983, p. 98) about the selection of Delta Airlines trainees:

> The trainees, it seemed to me, were also chosen for their ability to take stage directions about how to 'project' an image. They were selected for being able to act well – i.e. without showing the effort involved. They had to be able to appear at home on stage.

Consequences of the performance of emotional labour

While Hochschild (1983) concentrated on the deleterious or negative effects of emotional labour, subsequent writers have suggested that she has exaggerated the 'human' costs associated with this type of work (Seymour, 2000).

Emotional labour can be either positive or negative for workers depending on how it is performed (Kruml and Geddes, 2000).

However, of particular concern to both managers and service workers is one particular negative consequence known as burnout, defined by Maslach and Jackson (1981, p. 99) as 'a syndrome of emotional exhaustion and cynicism that occurs frequently among individuals who do "people-work" of some kind'. Schaufeli and Enzmann (1998, p. 19) note that there are numerous definitions of burnout. On the basis of their review of current literature of burnout, they have developed the following comprehensive definition:

> Burnout is a persistent, negative, work-related state of mind in 'normal' individuals that is primarily characterised by exhaustion, which is accompanied by distress, a sense of reduced effectiveness, decreased motivation, and the development of dysfunctional attitudes and behaviours at work. This psychological condition develops gradually but may remain unnoticed for a long time by the individual involved. It results from a misfit between intentions and reality in the job. Often burnout is self-perpetuating because of inadequate coping strategies that are associated with the syndrome.
>
> (Schaufeli and Enzmann, 1998, p. 36)

Although not substantiated by empirical evidence, burnout is thought to be likely to develop as a result of both surface and deep acting (Schaufeli and Enzmann, 1998, p. 127). However, there is evidence of a positive relationship between burnout and lack of social support, particularly from supervisors (Schaufeli and Enzmann, 1998, p. 82). Burnout has significant implications as it can lead to a deterioration in the quality of service provided and appears to be a contributor to job turnover, absenteeism and low morale (Maslach and Jackson, 1981).

Coping with the 'Performance' of Emotional Labour

Given the negative effects associated with the performance of emotional labour, it is important that service workers are able to cope adequately with the demands associated with this type of labour. The strategies used by individuals to cope with negative or stressful life events have a major influence on their physical and psychological well-being (Endler and Parker, 1990, p. 844). The importance of the use of appropriate coping strategies is highlighted in Schaufeli and Enzmann's definition (1998), which suggests that burnout is self-perpetuating if coping strategies are inadequate.

Coping strategies have been classified as being emotion-focused or problem-focused. Emotion-focused coping strategies include avoidance, minimization, distancing and wresting positive value from negative events. Some cognitive types of emotion-focused coping strategies result in a change in the way an encounter is construed, which is equivalent to reappraisal. Behavioural strategies which include engaging in physical exercise to take one's mind off the problem, having a drink, venting anger and seeking emotional support are also emotion-focused coping strategies. Problem-focused coping strategies include reducing ego involvement or learning new skills and procedures (Lazarus and Folkman, 1984, pp. 150–152).

Social support, 'information from others that one is loved and cared for, esteemed and valued, and part of a network of communication and mutual obligation' (Stroebe, 2000, p. 245), has been identified by Schaufeli and Enzmann (1998) as being very important in the prevention of burnout. Nevertheless, it should be said that studies have failed to demonstrate the buffer effect of social support in allowing workers with more support to cope better with their job demands (Schaufeli and Enzmann, 1998, p. 83).

In summary, front-line service work consists of a series of interpersonal transactions, during which, service workers must manage their emotions such that these transactions are pleasant for the customers and produce positive outcomes for their organizations. The acting abilities of these workers contribute to the success of these transactions. However, there are costs associated with such 'performances', one of which has been identified as 'burnout', which can be prevented by social support. A variety of emotional-focused or problem-focused strategies can be used by service workers to cope with the challenges of their work.

Case Studies

The four case studies presented are drawn from the results of a larger research project, 'Recognition and Management of Emotional Labour in the Tourism Industry', carried out by a research team at the University of South Australia, consisting of Chris Provis (project leader), Shirley Chappel and Barbara Anderson. The full report of the project, funded by the Co-operative Research Centre–Sustainable Tourism, is found in Anderson *et al.* (2002).

In this two phase qualitative study, carried out in 2001, two different methodologies, a focus group and semi-structured interviews, were used. These methodologies were thought to be the most appropriate to gather data as they provided not only a basic structure for the discussions in the focus group and interviews, but also the freedom to pursue any comments when considered appropriate. In the first phase, six managers from accommodation, hospitality, tourist information and transportation organizations participated in a focus group. The managers raised a number of issues associated with the performance of emotional labour, e.g. its consequences, and aspects related to selection and training. On the basis of this discussion, a series of questions about the performance of emotional labour were devised for managers and service workers. During the second phase, nine different organizations drawn from the same sectors in the Adelaide metropolitan area and four organizations in regional South Australia agreed to participate and a total of 45 semi-structured interviews were conducted. These interviews were generally carried out in the various workplaces and lasted approximately 30 min, due to time constraints on the inter-

viewees. The interviewees were not asked to provide any personal information, and in order to preserve their anonymity, all their names have been changed. A profile of the interviewees is provided in Table 15.1.

Some of the issues which were discussed are presented in the case studies which follow. Managers were asked about the manner in which they supported their staff in their customer service work and how their standards and norms for customer service were administered. Issues, such as the extent of organizational influence over expression and presentation, the support received from managers and co-workers and the strategies used to cope with this type of work were discussed with service workers.

It should be noted that the majority of workers were highly motivated and enjoyed their customer service work and accepted readily that emotion work was an integral part of their jobs.

Case study 1: accommodation

The interviewees were members of the front-office staff of a 4-star Adelaide hotel, which is part of a large international chain.

Lachlan, the manager, reported that the organization had standard operating procedures throughout the hotel chain for things such as processing credit card charges. However, with respect to the verbal interaction with guests, he said that:

> I'd rather that it was theirs, theirs alone,...if there is an issue with someone's greeting...I'd obviously take them aside, explain to maybe word it like this, but I wouldn't have them...reading the same thing out to every guest that comes in, not at all,...the interaction is definitely their own thing to do.

Table 15.1. Profile of interviewees.

Industry sector	Managers		Service workers	
	Male	Female	Male	Female
Accommodation	1	1	2	4
Hospitality	2	1	–	2
Tourist information	1	4	1	12
Transportation	3	–	3	8
Total	7	6	6	26

He supported his staff in their customer service work by being consistent in his praise and mentioned that sometimes he would do small things for them that they would not necessarily expect, for example, if working on night shift, he would buy food from the coffee shop. He maintained an open-door policy for the staff and also encouraged them to support each other.

Service workers

In discussing the organization's influence over their expression and presentation, interviewees indicated that they were free to be themselves, as reflected in the following comments:

> No, we don't have any scripts. Well normally when we're trained...they just normally let us know how, what appropriate terms to sort of use when we deal with guests...(Louise)

> It's my personal script, with [Hotel's] intertwinings...there are guidelines to follow, but it's up to you to put your personal flair on it... (Stuart)

Uniforms were provided which were generally popular:

> Yeah, I like to have the uniform, because you look more professional and, and you [are] actually representing our company. (Kate)

There was the proviso in that uniforms had to fit properly:

> My uniform doesn't fit me properly, it's not measured for individuals.... I've always felt really uncomfortable in my uniform. (Shannon)

The exhausting nature of front-line service work was also described clearly in the following comments:

> We have to like always be neat and tidy, try to have a smiley face all the time and things like that, but sometimes it is tiring to be smiling all the time ... (Kate)

> The hardest part is doing it all the time, one after the other, after the other,...saying the same thing over and over again. One of the hardest times would have to be Christmas and New Year, when you walk off the desk after 8 hours, just feeling like you could just go home and not talk to anyone ever again. (Shannon)

In recognition to the nature of front-line service work, the need for some formal type of support was mentioned:

> If you're in this sort of work, sort of environment, you sort of know already that that's what you sort of gonna get [sic], part of the job, so and I think they...should have, ..., psychologists, ..., you know, people have, they can't cope anymore, and they burst and, ..., so they should sort of maybe have a like psychologist or someone come in every three months or something and have a word to each one, say 'how are you going?' (Kate)

The following comments highlight the importance of having supportive managers and co-workers:

> I'd rather guests who's angry with me than ... someone I'm working with. Like I say, my boss start yelling at me, I think I'd get more emotionally upset about that than actual guest. (Kate)

> I feel that I can talk to someone who'll help me deal with that, as in my immediate manager above me, my front-office manager or I could talk with other staff that I'm on with...have a bit of a bitch about that person (guest)...but I feel that's, that's a good way of getting it off your chest...(Stuart)

The value of social support and a coping strategy, such as venting, were highlighted in the following comments:

> Oh yeah, you have to get things out of your system, otherwise you'll go crazy. I mean, if you keep everything inside you, sometime, you just burst, so I mean, I have done that with one of the co-workers... (Kate)

> I think we all sometimes...share it amongst ourselves, and that kind of makes us feel better too because we talk about...explain what's happened and then yeah, you kind of fell a bit better after that, you know... (Louise)

Case study 2: hospitality

This restaurant is located in a popular Adelaide seaside suburb. One manager, Michael, indicated that they did not have detailed rules as to how staff related to guests. Michael's only stipulation was that staff smiled when guests arrived and left the restaurant. The other manager, Claire, was most adamant in her view that 'no, no, no, goodness no, you've got to be individual…'. Both managers were supportive of their staff. For example, Michael indicated that when there were particularly difficult tables, he would not remove the waiting staff as it made them look like failures, but he would go to the table and act as a 'bit of a buffer'. Claire mentioned that:

> Part of my role also is not just to make sure the customers are happy too, it's also for the staff as well…to feel that they can…release with us.

She also mentioned the stresses associated with unsupportive management:

> It's not so much coping with the stress of the work environment, um, a lot of it actually reflects back to management, opposed to the job…how management push, how management treat the staff and that there perhaps isn't the support or it's like always pointing out the wrong thing, what you're doing wrong constantly, opposed to pointing out what's been wrong, but to rectify it and also to tell the positives as well, to encourage you, exactly, that's what tends to miss…

Claire acknowledged the 'performance' aspects of the work:

> It's like as soon as you enter the front-of-house where customers are, you're on stage, you perform, …it can be a good thing, it can be a bad thing, it depends as to what level.

Rhianna, the young service worker confirmed this concept of 'performance':

> As soon as you take the plates out the back or something, you just might have a sigh and say oh, you're tired, or you wish…the night was over or something like that, but as soon as you walk through the doors and back out there, it's got to change.

As far as her presentation and expression were concerned, Rhianna indicated that the uniform which she was wearing had to be neat and tidy and that the staff were allowed to be 'pretty individual with our characters, just not over the top'.

She indicated that colleagues would support each other:

> If there's a bad table and if there's two people working in a section, and if there's a bad

table, like we'll both know about, because we'll tell each other that they're not very nice or that they're giving you a hard time.

Rhianna also endorsed the value of talking with the rest of the staff at the end of the evening in these comments:

> I think its good to sit down and have a talk with everybody that you've worked with, at least five minutes, just to capture whatever happened or to fix anything that you think went wrong.

> If we finish at the same time, we'll have a drink and it's nice, nice relief too, you can just all sit around and then you can complain too, like you can say whatever you've got to say to them and get it all out…then you don't have to take it home to partners…

Case study 3: tourist information

Hannah, the manager of the tourist information centre in a popular seaside suburb, indicated that there were policies and procedures governing customer service. New staff went through inductions and the policies and procedures were regularly reviewed at staff meetings. As far as the expression of her staff, Hannah said:

> It's always important that… you always control yourself and basically, I guess, have a happy face.

She indicated that she was always willing to assist staff with difficult customers and recounted that:

> Other staff, I know at times, have actually heard a situation happening, and they've gone out to the reception area, so not in an obvious sense of, maybe stocked brochures or done something very discrete,…, just as more of a matter of support or maybe sort of assisted with an enquiry when they realise a person may actually be getting a little aggressive…

Service workers

With respect to the way in which they were presented at work, one interviewee recounted that:

I've started um, sort of full-time with the [organization], but for the last about 15–16 months, I've been a temp. and thus, had to fight to get a uniform, when I was given this position, because I say it as an important thing to identify me as part of a profession,…, going out and meeting with people, I just felt going in my own clothes, although I would wear businessy-clothes,…, people didn't necessarily see me as being well, I'm with the [organization]…I think it's a good way to identify us… (Skye)

…when the idea of a uniform was first voted, I thought no, I'm certainly not into the Chairman Mao-style of dressing. However, I spoke to my daughter-in-law and her mother, who are…reasonable Australians, and they both said they loved people in uniform because then you knew who to speak to, and I thought, oh, well, if it's good for the customers, then I'm happy to do it. (Sheena)

In discussing the extent of organizational influence over their expression at work, several service workers not only mentioned the policies and procedures for customer service but also their own personal service ethos:

I follow their policies and their guidelines, um, because I realise I'm representing [organization], um, I also um, have my own expectations of myself, how I should present myself to the general public and that's always…pleasant, helpful, friendly…. (Ailsa)

Well, I, my immediate reaction is 'not very much' but it may really be that its because my own expectations marry very closely with the organization, I don't notice. (Sheena)

In the ensuing discussion about scripts, Sheena indicated:

… I've got my own little scripts that I've created for myself, but they have an entertainment value for the customers,…no, we don't have scripted behaviours here.

Several interviewees reported 'psyching themselves up' at the beginning of a day and acknowledged the 'performance' aspect of their work:

Absolutely, I walk in the door, before I answer the phone, before I speak to anyone I say to myself, 'the sky is blue, I'm happy', so to that extent, say but I wouldn't bother to do, if I was just….sitting at the computer, but if I deal with people, if I want it to be a positive thing, I always tell myself 'life's good', something like that. (Sheena)

…I always say when you're out there, I always feel like, like you're an actress… The very minute I sit in the car, I have to say to myself 'you're going to work, you've got to concentrate about work', and so the minute I put the key in the ignition and I drive, I'm only thinking about work…by the time I've parked the car, opened the door, turned the alarm off, I'm ready. (Lucy)

With respect to support from colleagues, one interviewee indicated that:

We've got a very good system here…because the door is sort of close to the reception and its always left open…if they can hear that someone is getting angry or, or even just spending more time than is necessary…then, somebody will come up and say, 'oh, [name], there's a call for you, would you like to take it now?' (Lucy)

A combination of emotion-focused and problem-solving strategies were sometimes used to cope with difficult situations, for example:

If there's no other people in the centre, … by talking to the other staff, um, it then becomes a problem-solving session, where we look at strategies of how to deal with those situations,…, in the future, if they come up, so yeah, and I think just talking out the problem, um, just relieves the tension that I'd be feeling, but I think, well that's good… other people have listened to me and I think, oh yeah, and I've sort of got some positive feedback from them, so then everything's back on track. (Ailsa)

In other cases, strategies of distancing and reducing ego involvement could be used:

I start from the position, in my head, they're not angry with you, 'cause they don't know you,…I'm just there, I'm just available,…I also have a really clear plan of action, I'm not really foul-mouthed, but once I've dealt with it, I'd go out the back and when there's no one around I say something absolutely putrid, to help,… I've got no way of knowing how they've got to this point on that day, so, but, the least likely thing is that I've caused it, and the least likely, the least important person in their life is me, so, you know, let's not over-rate my role in this…it's really, really easy to put yourself at the centre of things, but in reality, you know, if they weren't born to you and they're not married to you, you're not really all that important to them, are you? (Sheena)

Case study 4: transportation

This transportation company was located in the city of Adelaide. The manager was based at the Head Office and the service workers were located in a branch office a short distance away, still within the centre of Adelaide.

With respect to the standards and norms for customer service, the manager, George, indicated that his organization was in the process of going through a refresher course with customer service techniques 'and just revisiting some of the things that we take for granted, fine-tuning the way we do our delivery'. He believed that it was very important to be able to share with other colleagues, 'to have that release'.

Service workers

With respect to the extent of the organization's influence on their expression at work, one interviewee commented that:

Since we've been taken over by [organization], we've been more, um been encouraged to be more standardized because then you sound more professional, but we are very much an individual office...we're allowed to be individuals, more so than if we worked somewhere like [organization] which is our head office. (Liana)

Another interviewee mentioned that:

You sort of gotta learn how to hold your own anger and your own problems aside to help others and to serve customers and to be that bright, chirpy, friendly consultant. (Rosie)

Indeed, another interviewee acknowledged the 'performance' aspect of her work:

I wanted to be an actress...my favourite course at school was drama, I love drama, so...as I said before you['re] sort of yelling and the next minute you'll pick up the phone and you'll be a totally different person, I think acting has a big part to play. (Rosie)

Another interviewee reported 'psyching themselves up' at the beginning of a day:

Of course, absolutely, yes, you have to, yes, I don't do it consciously though, I think it just happens, ...(Liana)

Uniforms were worn and were popular with the service workers:

My uniform? I like it...we look fresh and bright and sort of um, professional. (Liana)

...we all put our hand up to say 'yes', we, we want a uniform, because it's...a smart approach, a professional look, and um, we prefer to wear the uniforms. (Rosie)

The difficulties caused by the absence of a full-time manager in the office were discussed by several interviewees:

It would be a lot easier if he was in the back office here, you could say, 'look, we've got a customer out the front, who wants to speak to the manager, can you sort of head out, and help us out here?'...I feel that is the manager's role, they are to handle customer complaints and to a certain degree...I think we're taking on extra stress that really we shouldn't be taking on. Sort of aggravates us at times... (Rosie)

[It] probably unfairly puts staff under pressure, that's what it does. That's the frustrating thing, it shouldn't have to happen like that, there should be someone who can stop in. Probably there's, there's too much taken on board because of that, just by default. That shouldn't be the way it works. (Liana)

Service workers reported using a variety of strategies, such as distancing and venting, to cope with the challenges of their customer service work:

I have done it in the past, sometimes ohh, I just need to [take] a break from there, I'll go in the back and I'll take phone calls and I'll answer some faxes. (Andrew)

You share the experience whether it be with somebody or out here, against the wall.... Yeah, and then you swear and then you go back out and you smile again.... And you just laugh, because you think 'oh, I just swore at the wall'...you might say to your colleagues as well, I mean, that helps too, you just bounce something off them... and it's like, 'oh, I feel better now'... (Liana)

If I get a bit stressed...I guess I just step back and just go out, I will make myself a cup of coffee or something and then that's you know, a 2 minute break...and then, you know, the stress will be over...or if there's a problem, I'll just quickly talk about it with someone and then it's kind of over with. (Beth)

The importance of support of colleagues was readily acknowledged:

Oh yes, ...you really do need support of your fellow colleagues...to keep you sane and to help you through the hard times, yeah, I think we all look after each other fairly well here. (Rosie)

I find it really hard to deal with complaints.... I feel bad within myself...you take a 5-minute break...but that's where the work colleagues come in as well, 'cause we're such a close, close bunch. They...help...we talk each other through it as well...which is nice. (Rosie)

The adverse effects of the performance of emotional labour on social relationships if coping strategies are not effective were also mentioned:

Sometimes, I'll have the worst day at work, but I, I hold it all in, and I'll get home and I'll take it out on my partner.... Why did I do that? I'm like why, why? Maybe I should have just sat somewhere for ten minutes in the car before I got home and just sort of relaxed, just you know, not talked to anyone, just sat there quietly and sort of let it all just go. (Rosie)

There are a number of familiar themes running through these case studies which have been summarized in Table 15.2.

It can be seen from Table 15.2 that service workers in all case studies used a variety of

the emotion-focused (E/f) and problem-focused (P/f) coping strategies outlined by Lazarus and Folkman (1984) in the course of their customer service work. The importance of managerial and co-worker support, which could be construed as particular forms of social support, was widely acknowledged. Although the concept of burnout was not explicitly covered in this study, the exhausting nature of client service work was acknowledged in a number of case studies. The availability of social support may well be contributing to the prevention of burnout amongst these workers, as suggested by Schaufeli and Enzmann (1998). The suggestions made by Mann (1997) and Ashforth and Humphrey (1993) that workers 'psyched' themselves up or acted in their course of their employment were confirmed by the comments of a number of interviewees. However, in contrast to a number of organizations mentioned by Leidner (1999), there was no evidence of formal scripts being provided for staff. Individual expression was preferred by managers and workers alike, although some workers developed their own informal scripts or routines. Confirming the observation of San Filippo (2001), uniforms were widely acknowledged as a sign of professionalism.

Strategies for Managers

On the basis of this snapshot of front-line service work, it is possible to make a number of recommendations about the strategies which organizations may wish to implement to sup-

Table 15.2. Case study themes.

Case study no.	Use of coping strategies	Importance of manager support	Importance of co-worker support	Exhausting nature of work	Formal scripts	'Performance'	Uniforms
1	E/f	✓	✓	✓	x	–	✓
2	E/f	✓	✓	–	x	✓	✓
3	P/f and E/f	✓	✓	–	x	✓	✓
4	E/f	✓	✓	✓	x	✓	✓

Table 15.3. Organizational strategies to support front-line service workers.

Strategy	Implementation
Managerial support	• 'Open-door' policy: to foster good communication with staff
	• Positive, supportive supervision
Managerial and co-worker support	• Team meetings: to foster communication, problem-solving
	• 'Time-outs' allowed, when appropriate
Physical layout	• Staff not working in isolation in customer service areas
Training	• Customer service skills such as conflict resolution and communication skills
Job design	• Time divided between customer contact and 'back-office' functions

port their front-line service workers. These strategies and the manner in which they may be implemented are outlined in Table 15.3.

By the implementation of these strategies where appropriate, organizations will be able to provide supportive environments in which front-line service workers are able to 'perform' their customer service work. The negative effects of this potentially exhausting work can thereby be minimized, with consequent positive impacts on employee well-being and organizational productivity.

References

Albrecht, K. and Zemke, R. (1985) *Service America! Doing Business in the New Economy*. Homewood, Dow Jones-Irwin.

Anderson, B.A., Provis, C. and Chappel, S.J. (2002) *The Recognition And Management Of Emotional Labour In The Tourism Industry*. CRC-Tourism, Gold Coast, Australia, pp. 1–56.

Ashforth, B.E. and Humphrey, R.H. (1993) Emotional labour in service roles: the influence of identity. *Academy of Management Review* 18(1), 88–115.

Easterling, C.R., Leslie, J.E. and Jones, M.A. (1992) Perceived importance and usage of dress codes among organizations that market professional services. *Public Personnel Management* 21(2), 211–221.

Endler, N.S. and Parker, J.D.A. (1990) Multidimensional assessment of coping: a critical evaluation. *Journal of Personality and Social Psychology* 58(5), 844–854.

Erickson, R.J. and Wharton, A.S. (1997) Inauthenticity and depression. *Work and Occupations* 24(2), 188–213.

Hochschild, A.R. (1983) *The Managed Heart*. University of California Press, Berkeley, California.

Kruml, S.M. and Geddes, D. (2000) Catching fire without burning out: is there an ideal way to perform emotional labour. Emotions in the workplace. In: Ashkanasy, N.M., Hartel, C.E.J. and Zerbe, W.J. (eds) Quorum Books, Westport, Connecticut, pp. 177–188.

Lazarus, R.S. and Folkman, S. (1984) *Stress, Appraisal and Coping*. Springer, New York.

Leidner, R. (1999) Emotional labour in service work. *The Annals of the American Academy of Political and Social Science* 561(Jan), 81–95.

Mann, S. (1997) Emotional labour in organizations. *Leadership & Organization Development Journal* 18(1), 4–12.

Maslach, C. and Jackson, S.E. (1981) The measurement of experienced burnout, *Journal of Occupational Behaviour* 2, 99–113.

Morris, J.A. and Feldman, D.C. (1996) The dimensions, antecedents, and consequences of emotional labour. *Academy of Management Review* 21(4), 986–1010.

Rafaeli, A. (1989) When clerks meet customers: a test of variables related to emotional expressions on the job. *Journal of Applied Psychology* 74(3), 385–393.

Rafaeli, A. and Pratt, M.G. (1993) Tailored meanings: on the meaning and impact of organizational dress. *Academy of Management Review* 18(1), 32–55.

Rosenberg, M. (1990) Reflexivity and emotions. *Social Psychology Quarterly* 53(1), 3–12.

San Filippo, M. (2001) Dressed for success. *Travel Weekly* 60(60), 35–37.

Schaufeli, W. and Enzmann, D. (1998) *The Burnout Companion to Study and Practice: A Critical Analysis*. Taylor & Francis, London.

Seymour, D. (2000) Emotional labour: a comparison between fast food and traditional service work. *International Journal of Hospitality Management* 19, 159–171.

Stroebe, W. (2000) Social psychology and health. In: Manstead, T. (series ed.) *Mapping Social Psychology*, 2nd edn. Open University Press, Buckingham, UK.

16 Service Ethics for Ecotourism Guides

Guides

Xin Yu and Betty Weiler
Monash University, Australia

Introduction

According to role theory, roles define both the expectations for and the performance of behaviours corresponding to a particular job (Troyer *et al.*, 2000). Role theory has been underutilized in tourism research, and provides a valuable basis upon which to examine particular jobs in the industry, in this case, the job of a tour guide. This chapter commences with the study context and then reviews the literature on role theory in relation to tour guiding. This includes analysing and determining the reasons for change over time, differences in roles across a range of situations and organizations, relationships between individual role performance and organizational performance and mechanisms for improving individual performance. The chapter then presents an empirical study on the role of the guide on group tours from Mainland China to Australia, including descriptions of the samples, methods of data analysis and research findings. The study identifies the key roles tour guides of Chinese group tours need to play, the knowledge, skills and attitudes needed to fulfil these guiding roles, how visitors and tour guides perceive the importance of each role, how tour guides perform their roles and the impact of role performance on the visitors' guided tour experience with a focus on the role of cultural mediator. The chapter concludes with implications of the research findings and directions for future study.

Importance of Roles of Australian Tour Guides of Mainland Chinese Group Tours

Outbound travel by Chinese citizens has grown rapidly in recent years. In 2000, over 10 million Mainland Chinese travelled outside China. It is predicted that China will become the fourth largest country of tourist origin in the world by 2020 (World Tourism Organization, 1998).

For Australia, the annual growth rate of Chinese visitor arrivals was 38% for 2001. Similar growth is set to continue for at least the next 8 years, which is beyond the growth of any market. The latest forecasts from the Australian Tourism Forecasting Council (2002) indicate that the number of Chinese visitors to Australia will reach more than 1.4 million annually by 2012. As a point of comparison, this is double the number of tourist arrivals from New Zealand in 2001/02, Australia's largest current overseas market (Australian Bureau of Statistics, 2002). Clearly, the Australian government and industry see China as an important target market in need of strategic planning and marketing efforts.

It is the policy of the Chinese government that the development of Chinese outbound travel needs to be organized, planned and controlled (China National Tourism Administration, 2001). Control is achieved using a number of mechanisms such as the use of single-trip passports, limiting travel to designated destinations and restricting travel options through approved travel agencies and tour operators. By 2002, China had approved 22 destinations for outbound travel including Singapore, Malaysia, Thailand, the Philippines, Indonesia, Australia, New Zealand, South Korea, Japan, Vietnam, Laos, Cambodia, Brunei, Nepal, Hong Kong, Macao, Myanmar, South Africa, Turkey, Egypt, Malta and Germany. Australia was the first western country to be given approved destination status (ADS) that enables Chinese nationals to use ordinary passports and apply for tourist visas when wishing to visit Australia (Tourism Forecasting Council, 1999).

For the moment, ADS gives Australia a certain competitive advantage. However, that advantage could change in the likely event that ADS is granted to other major world tourist destinations in North America and Europe. Australia will then face stiffer competition in the emerging Chinese market. Naturally, the quality of the Chinese tourists' experiences will determine, at least in part, Australia's success in securing its market share (Yu et al., 2001).

Under the ADS scheme, Chinese holiday-makers must join an ADS group tour if they wish to visit Australia. These ADS group tours are fully inclusive, requiring a local guide for every group. As a result, tour guides looking after Chinese tour groups serve as the main point of contact between the destination and their Chinese clients. Most Chinese tourists are first-time visitors to Australia so their dependence on tour guides in brokering their intercultural experience is particularly high (Yu and Weiler, 2001). Thus, a tour guide for this market plays a central role in both facilitating an experience and determining the quality of the experience (Yu et al., 2001). However, despite the importance of the tour guide's job, little research has been conducted on tour guide's roles.

As mentioned in the introduction, a role is a set of expectations for behaviours corresponding to a position (Troyer et al., 2000). Roles can be used as the basis for job descriptions and for specifying organizational expectations and performance requirements (Welbourne et al., 1998), and have been recognized as central to understanding employee behaviour in organizations (Katz and Kahn, 1978). Role theory also suggests that an individual's role expectations are influenced by both the individual's personal attributes and the context of the position. Thus, employee performance will be a function of both the individual and the organization. Researchers have begun to recognize the importance of using roles as a way of conceptualizing and improving work performance (Ilgen and Hollenbeck, 1992; Jackson and Schuler, 1995).

A premise of this study is that tour guides escorting Chinese visitors in Australia play multiple roles. Using role theory, this study provides a systematic analysis of tour guides' role definitions and expectations, role dynamics, role performance, the impact of role performance on customer satisfaction and factors affecting role performance. Although there have been a few studies that have examined the role of the tour guide (Holloway, 1981; Cohen, 1985; Pond, 1993; Weiler and Ham, 2001), this study uses role theory not only to define the roles of tour guides but also to examine the actual role performance and factors affecting the role performance. It is also unique in its focus on the role of cultural mediation, a role that emerged as being particularly important in guiding groups of Chinese tourists in Australia.

The Contribution of Role Theory to Tour Guiding

According to role theory, the first step in analysing the roles that tour guides perform is to define tour guiding. As the job of a tour guide is considered semi-professional, the roles of tour guides have not been institutionalized and are subject to various interpretations (Holloway, 1981; Cohen, 1985). Thus we review the definitions of tour guides given by different stakeholders and sources.

Definitions of tour guides and guiding

The *Oxford Advanced Learner's Dictionary* (Hornby, 2000, p. 572) defines a guide as 'a person who shows other people the way to a place, especially somebody employed to show tourists around interesting places'. In this definition, providing direction is indicated as the primary role of a guide. This pathfinding role is the original function of a guide who acts as a geographical guide to offer directions (Cohen, 1985).

The International Association of Tour Managers (IATM) and the European Federa-tion of Tourist Guide Associations (EFTGA) define a tour guide as a person who guides groups or individual visitors from abroad or from the home country around the monuments, sites and museums of a city or region; to interpret in an inspiring and entertaining manner, in the language of the visitor's choice, the cultural and natural heritage and environment (European Federation of Tourist Guide Associations, 1998).

These industry bodies perceive the tour guide's role as providing not only direction but also cultural and environmental interpretation. It is implied that interpretation is a part of guiding. The practice of interpretation was originally used in the USA National Park Service, and then adopted by others in both the public and the non-public sectors (Pond, 1993). 'The goal of interpretation is to convey the magnificence of a place, inspire visitors and ultimately convince them of the need to preserve park lands' (Pond, 1993, p. 71). 'Interpretation provides the sociological, educational and cultural underpinning of guiding' (Pond, 1993, p. 71). Cohen (1985) posits that interpretation is the essence of the cultural-mediating role of tour guides. As a result, interpretation is increasingly recognized by tourism industry bodies and researchers as a key function of guiding (Cohen, 1985; Weiler et al., 1991; Pond, 1993; Gurung et al., 1996; Weiler and Ham, 2001).

In addition, the aforementioned definitions underline the multifaceted nature of the guiding job by categorizing tour guides based on the types of tours including inbound or domestic; the tour setting such as city or regional; the subject matter (e.g. cultural, natural heritage and environment) as well as the native language of the tour client.

As indicated in their organizational names, we can see that the IATM and EFTGA also distinguish between the job of a tour manager and a tour guide. Tour manager, often used interchangeably with courier, tour escort and tour leader, refers to a person who escorts the group during the entire trip, and is mainly responsible for managing the logistical aspects of the tour (Cohen, 1985). A tour guide, normally city-based, accompanies the group on day tours and sometimes on overnight tours. His or her major role is to provide the group with the information on the visited place(s). The tour guide might also undertake some of the administrative responsibilities of a tour manager (Holloway, 1981). However, in many cases, especially in non-urban areas, the roles of tour manager and guide are often merged and the differences between the two are blurred. For the purpose of this chapter, we define a tour guide as someone who plays the roles of both tour manager and tour guide.

This review of definitions of tour guides reveals that a tour guide's role can be multifaceted, including provision of direction and information on attractions and the visited region, facilitating understanding of the destination and its culture and managing the safety, security and control of the group (Schmidt, 1979; Holloway, 1981; Pond, 1993). The level of demand for each of these roles depends upon the nature of the group and the situation (Holloway, 1981). Based on existing definitions, we define a tour guide of inbound group tours as a person who leads groups from abroad to the important sites of a city or region, provides commentary and interpretation of cultural and natural attractions in the language of the visitors, facilitates tourists' experiences in the host country and manages the tour.

Role importance and dynamics

A recent study (Rodham, 2000) on role theory suggests that traditional approaches to the study of roles focus on descriptions of what role incumbents do but have not managed to capture their dynamic nature, i.e. how jobholders respond to the situation they are in and take on roles they feel to be compatible with that situation. Rodham's study demonstrates that roles can change when the situation changes, hence the dynamic nature of certain jobs or occupational positions.

In the case of tour guiding, Cohen (1985), in a seminal article, posits that the professional tour guide's role has moved away from its original role of pathfinder towards a mediatory role. This process of transition and professionalization is closely related to the development of tourism as a system and the emergence of institutionalized tourists on tours (Cohen, 1972). The guide's job, Cohen (1985) argues, has become more routinized, and tourists have become more experienced and demanding. Visitors ask for and expect an improved guiding service such as fuller information and interpretation of the sights.

Cohen's mediatory function of the tour guide includes two components, social mediation and cultural brokerage. Cultural brokerage is considered by Cohen as a primary role of the professional tour guide. A number of tourism researchers also acknowledge that tour guides assume the role of cultural mediator between the tourist and the sight (McKean, 1976; Nash, 1978; Schmidt, 1979; Holloway, 1981; Pearce, 1984; Cohen, 1985; Hughes, 1991; Bras, 2000; Smith, 2001; Yu et al., 2001). According to Cohen (1985), social mediating involves being a go-between, linking visitors to the local population and to tourist sites and facilities and making the host environment non-threatening for the tourist. We concur with many authors that social mediation is largely a part of cultural mediation especially when guiding inbound groups from another country.

Thus, key responsibilities of culture brokers include selecting and presenting culture, managing the intercultural differences between different cultural groups and facilitating tourists' intercultural experiences (Holloway, 1981; Cohen, 1985; Smith, 2001; Yu et al., 2001). Using communication as an agent, cultural interpretation may be the most important function of culture brokering (Cohen, 1985). It aims to convey the magnificence of a place, and ideally develops understanding, appreciation and protection of the visited area. Ultimately, interpretation inspires visitors, helps them connect with the place and generally facilitates the visitor's intercultural experience (Pond, 1993; Smith, 2001; Yu et al., 2001).

Employee and organizational role performance and their impact on customer satisfaction

In tourism, organizational performance can be measured in a number of ways such as years in the business, profit margins, customer satisfaction, customer loyalty, yield and reputation. The guide's role is seen largely as a means of satisfying customers, thereby achieving positive word-of-mouth (WOM) advertising and repeat purchase, all of which are measures of organizational performance.

Research on the contribution of tour guide performance to visitor satisfaction has been limited. A study of Australian nature-based guides found that guides were knowledgeable and perceived to be competent by visitors, but lacked key interpretive skills for delivering both commentary and minimal impact messages. In spite of this, the level of satisfaction among visitors with the guides' performance was high, as was the level of customer satisfaction with the tours (Weiler, 1999). More research is needed to establish whether there are clear links between quality guiding and visitor satisfaction, and between poor guiding and visitor dissatisfaction as well as to examine relationships between the guide's performance and other measures of organizational performance.

How to improve tour guides' role performance

According to role theory, an employee's attributes and perceptions as well as context or organization factors can affect his or her role performance (Welbourne et al., 1998). To improve a tour guide's role performance, first, a tour guide must have the required competence to accomplish guiding tasks. In other words, as a professional tour guide, one needs to have broad knowledge and good guiding skills (they must be able) and the right attitude to do their job (they must be willing) (Ap and Wong, 2001).

Second, the organization and context in which a guide works, such as his/her employer (e.g. tour operator) and the wider tourism industry must provide 'adequate resources' (i.e. material, instrument and social resources) (Heiss, 1990) for tour guides to enact their roles. For example, formal training helps guides understand and acquire the skills required to perform their roles. Employment practices that favour (e.g. pay more for) trained guides and workplaces that provide or support training and other forms of professional development help to improve tour guide performance. Other factors such as reasonable pay and fair working conditions (working hours and benefits) can also affect performance (Ham and Weiler, 2002).

Third, tour guides and their organizations should have consistent expectations of the guide's roles. Tour guides, like other service workers, are brokers between the organization and its customers. They can experience role conflict when confronted with competing demands from the two constituencies (Troyer *et al.*, 2000), for example, if tourists have been led to expect an experience different to what the tour operator and/or tourism industry can provide. Anecdotally, one can see examples of this in wildlife tour brochures featuring close-up photographs of nocturnal and/or rare wild animals, implying an experience the tour guide is most unlikely to be able to deliver. Tour descriptions depicting close encounters with indigenous people are often equally misleading, leaving the tour guide in the impossible position of trying to provide an experience within the constraints of the itinerary and without negatively impacting the natural and cultural environment. While the guide is not usually identified as the one responsible for delivering the product advertised, they are often the ones held accountable when the product 'fails' because they are the point of contact between the customer and the company.

Finally, organizations can affect the behaviour of employees at work by influencing work-related roles in many different ways including rewarding behaviours, requiring behaviours formally and informally recognizing behaviours and even punishing employees when behaviours are not enacted (Welbourne *et al.*, 1998). For example, promotion systems should reward individual tour guides for career development such as participating in training and acquiring new skills. For recogniz-

ing appropriate behaviours and eliminating inappropriate ones, the tourism industry can implement guide award schemes and guide certification, regulation, licensing and penalties for infringement.

The Empirical Study

One useful approach to role analysis is to examine role performance of employees by administering a questionnaire survey or conducting an interview that asks respondents (in this case, tour guides) to describe their own roles or those of others (Biddle, 1979). The remainder of this chapter presents an empirical study, which utilized the views of multiple stakeholders to identify role perception, competence and performance of tour guides of Mainland Chinese group tours in Australia. The study was done in two phases: a qualitative phase in late 2001 using semi-structured interviews, followed by a quantitative phase in late 2001 and early 2002 using self-completing questionnaires.

Sampling and data collection

Semi-structured interviews with tourism industry representatives were conducted in phase 1 of the study. The 20 informants interviewed included representatives of one inbound tour operator association, one tour guide association, one tourism training institution, five Chinese-speaking tour guides, seven ADS Australian inbound tour operators and five approved Chinese travel agencies (wholesalers) headquartered in Beijing. Sampling was purposive and, in the case of the Australian inbound tour operators, a census was attempted (i.e. the 30 approved tour operators were all contacted; however, only 7 granted the opportunity for a formal interview).

For the tour guide survey (phase 2), the researcher distributed approximately 100 questionnaires to tour operators and tour guides either in person or by mail, of which 31 completed questionnaires were returned.

For the tourist survey (the other half of phase 2), a list of ADS Australian tour operators (30) and a list of ADS Chinese travel agencies (21) were obtained. A random sample of tour operators was used to distribute questionnaires to Chinese visitors in ADS groups. In order to ensure an adequate sample size, the researcher also obtained permission from two hotels in Melbourne to access respondents; these two hotels accommodate most of the Chinese ADS groups that stay in Melbourne. In total, 495 questionnaires were collected, producing a useable response set of 461.

Method of data analysis

The data from phase 1 consisted of field notes and tape transcripts which were content-analysed and classified. In phase 2, although the main purpose of conducting the visitor survey and the tour guide survey was to examine tour guides' intercultural competence (see Yu, 2003a, unpublished thesis), certain sections of each questionnaire were related to tour guides' roles. Respondents of both the guide survey and the visitor survey were asked to rate the relative importance of several roles of tour guides. In addition, visitors were asked to answer three open-ended questions about their most memorable experience during their visit to Australia, what role, if any, their tour guides played in such experience and any other comments they would like to make. Responses to the open-ended questions provided insight into the expectations of roles of tour guides, perceived role performance and the impact of tour guides' role performance on respondents' guided tour experience in Australia. This chapter reports mainly the findings from the quantitative data analysis about the perceptions of the intercultural competence of tour guides reported separately in an unpublished PhD thesis (Yu, 2003a).

To analyse how industry representatives and visitors perceive the roles of tour guides, responses to the semi-structured questions in the in-depth interviews and responses to the open-ended questions were translated and transcribed, and inductive data analysis was used to process the data. This involved coding, data display and conclusion drawing and verification (Huberman and Miles, 1994). For example, when discovering units related to roles of tour guides, the researcher looked at words, sentences and paragraphs that carried similar meanings of different roles of tour guides, then sorted units into categories according to their common properties or elements. Five main roles (categories) were finally identified.

Several steps were taken to achieve the validity of the findings. First, the researcher inspected and compared all the data fragments (Glaser and Strauss, 1967) so that the full variation of the issues under investigation could be observed (Perakyla, 1997). Secondly, the researcher sought to 'overcome the temptation to jump to easy conclusions', and consequently to think critically in order to achieve objectivity (Silverman, 2000, p. 178). Thirdly, data were treated comprehensively to achieve integrated and precise results (Mehan, 1979). For example, the perceptions of roles of tour guides given by the industry representatives were compared with the findings from both visitor survey and guide survey, and integrated concepts were identified. Finally, the majority of responses to open-ended questions were tabulated to show strong tendency (Silverman, 2000). Statistical analysis was performed to compare how visitors and guides perceive the roles of tour guides.

As the following results reveal, the use of multiple data sources and multiple methods of collecting data proved to be valuable and, because the qualitative and quantitative data are in many cases consistent, enhanced the trustworthiness of the research findings. However, it must be acknowledged that there may be sampling error due to non-random sampling and a small sample size for the tour guides' survey.

Research findings

This section presents the findings from the empirical study regarding role perception (roles of tour guides defined by tourism industry representatives and perceptions of the importance of the roles of tour guides by tour guides and visitors) and role performance (the evaluation of role performance of tour guides, the impact of guides' performance on guided tour experiences, what tour guides need to have to fulfil their roles and how to improve their performance).

Roles of tour guides defined by tourism industry representatives

The interviews in phase 1 sought to define the roles of Chinese group tour guides from the perspective of industry representatives. The informants were asked to describe the most important roles played by a Chinese group tour guide. Five main roles (categories) were finally identified: 'provide information', 'be a cultural mediator', 'manage group itinerary', 'care for health and safety of group' and 'provide good customer service' (Yu, 2003b). Some examples from the interview transcripts are presented in Table 16.1.

The five roles of Chinese-speaking tour guides suggested by the tourism industry representatives are generally consistent with the findings from several previous studies on tour guides' roles. These previous findings are presented in Table 16.2.

Perceptions of respondents regarding importance of tour guide roles

Based on the important roles identified by tourism industry representatives and previous studies, the same five roles of Chinese-speaking tour guides were finally defined. In both the visitor survey and the tour guide survey, respondents were asked to rate the relative importance of these five roles by circling the number that best represented their view, from 1 (not at all important) to 7 (extremely important). An independent samples t-test was performed to compare the relative importance of the tour guides' roles rated by the visitors and by the tour guides. The results are presented in Table 16.3.

No results were statistically significant, suggesting that tourists and tour guides have similar perceptions of the five roles. Both tourists and tour guides typically perceive all five roles as either important (5) or very important (6). This is consistent with past studies that tour guides need to perform multiple roles. It is also interesting to note that the three parties – tourism industry representatives, Chinese tourists and tour guides – hold similar views on the relative importance of the roles Chinese-speaking tour guides need to play. All acknowledge the role of cultural mediation as important even though some tourism industry representatives note that being a cultural mediator is desirable but not easy to achieve.

Results from the three data sources reveal not only the perceived importance of tour guide roles but also insights into the meanings of some of the roles. Responses to open-ended questions in the visitor survey and the interviews with tourism industry representatives indicate a finer breakdown of the guide's roles as well as the dynamic nature of the job,

Table 16.1. Roles of tour guides (examples from interview transcripts).

Roles of tour guides	Transcripts
Provide information	The role of tour guides is to provide information (interview 1, transcript 71) and to reveal things so that visitors could draw inspirations from their experience. Visitors could bring home new ideas and new concepts (interview 5, transcript 18–20).
Be a cultural mediator	A qualified tour guide should be able to act as a bridge between two cultures and as a people-to-people ambassador (interview 2, transcript 147–149).
Manage tour itinerary	An important role of tour guides is to finish all activities in the itinerary (interview 8, transcript 4–5).
Care for health and safety	Tour guides need to make visitors feel secure in a non-Chinese-speaking country (interview 3, transcript 5–6).
Provide good customer service	Tour guides need to know how to help their clients in their best interest (interview 1, transcript 75–76) and look after the welfare of their clients including meals, accommodation, sightseeing and travel (interview 5, transcript 13–14).

Table 16.2. Roles of tour guides suggested by past studies.

Role categories	Schmidt (1979)	Holloway (1981)	Cohen (1985)	Hughes (1991)	Pond (1993)	Gurung et al. (1996)	Wong (2001)	Ham and Weiler (2002)
Provide information	Guide's presentation could make or break a tour	Information giver, fount of knowledge	Disseminate correct and precise information	Providing interesting commentary	Disseminating information	Provide quality of information	Communication	Communication
Be a cultural mediator	Buffer intermediary	Cultural mediator	Mediating encounters between cultures	Cultural brokers between group and the unfamiliar	Mediator, facilitate connections between people	Cultural broker, mediating encounters		
Manage tour itinerary	Condense itinerary to cover highlights	Organize programmes	Control of itinerary	Provide detailed itinerary	Control of group	Smooth accomplishment of the tour	Control of itinerary	Managing time
Care for health and safety	Safety and security		Offer security and comfort		Caretaker of details	Ensuring security and safety		
Provide good customer service		Caring for passengers' needs	Provision of services, to ensure hospitality		Serving travellers' needs	Provision of services	Customer relationship	Being personable and adaptable

Table 16.3. Perceived importance of tour guides' roles. (Independent samples test: tourist vs guides.)

Roles	Mean scores		SD			
	Tourist	Guide	Tourist	Guide	t-values	Significance
Give accurate and enjoyable commentary	6.3	6.0	1.1	1.0	1.8	0.1
Be a good cultural mediator	5.8	5.8	1.4	0.9	0.0	1.0
Provide good customer service	6.4	6.3	1.0	0.8	0.7	0.5
Manage group itinerary	6.1	6.0	1.2	1.1	0.2	0.8
Care for health and safety of group	6.4	6.3	1.0	0.8	0.3	0.8
N = 461 (tourist), N = 31 (guide)						

where performing one role often overlaps with another. For example, to be a good cultural mediator, the visitors expect a tour guide to be able to enhance visitors' understanding of the host society, cultural values and lifestyles, provide language interpretation, facilitate communication and initiate interaction between the locals and visitors. To deliver accurate and enjoyable commentary, according to tourism industry representatives, a tour guide is expected to be able to reveal things and make his or her audiences feel inspired. The responses to open-ended questions in the visitor survey indicate that visitors in particular expect the guide to provide good customer service by being caring, warm, helpful and patient. Finally, the visitors' expectations of the role of managing the tour itinerary include providing a variety of programmes or activities, following a logical route and providing detailed information on and advanced notice of changes to the itinerary. The guide is also expected to be sensitive to cultural differences when planning itineraries. In other words, there is a blurring not only between the roles of a tour manager (sometimes undertaken by a different person, especially in other types of tours) and the role expectations of the local guide but also in the role of the travel agent and the tour operator (responsible for itinerary planning). As we shall see in the next two sections, these expectations in some cases contribute to reductions in customer satisfaction. The problem is exacerbated by inadequate organizational and industry support, recognition and remuneration of guides.

Tour guides' role performance and its impact on visitors' guided tour experiences

Findings from the interviews indicate that tour guides on ADS tours are perceived to be performing well in many aspects of their roles: knowing their clients' language, having a good understanding of the culture of Mainland China, knowing how to help their clients in their best interest and dealing with clients' problems. Some are bilingual and bicultural, and can facilitate cultural understanding.

In one of the open-ended questions, respondents were asked to describe what role, if any, their guides played in their most memorable experience during their visit to Australia. The roles most frequently mentioned by respondents to the visitor survey as being performed adequately including being a good tour manager, being a cultural mediator and being personable. With respect to tour managing, visitors note that some guides did well at informing, giving directions, arranging the itinerary and solving problems. As a cultural mediator, some of the tour guides were seen to deliver culturally relevant commentary; to further visitors' understanding of Chinese and Australian cultures such as Australia's folklore, people and lifestyles; to broaden visitors' views; to link between Eastern and Western cultures; and to facilitate communication between visitors and locals. Respondents also commented on their guides as being personable, meaning that their guides were caring, warm, helpful, patient and loved their guiding job.

However, not all comments were positive. Both tourism industry representatives and visitors perceive the main weaknesses in the current performance of Chinese group tour guides to be inadequate knowledge about Australia, resulting in a lack of depth in guides' commentary. For example, the tourism industry representatives commented that some Chinese-speaking tour guides have limited knowledge of Australia, especially knowledge of tourism sites and culture, and they also are lacking in English language proficiency and guiding skills. Respondents of the visitor survey also acknowledged that guides should know their job better and make more of an effort in providing information on Australia's history, geography, culture and economic development and the country's position in the world.

The findings from the open-ended questions on the visitor survey describe the roles Chinese group tour guides play in more detail but are generally consistent with the opinions expressed by tourism representatives. However, these findings are somewhat different to research undertaken on nature-based guides in Australia, where their depth of knowledge was found to be one of their major strengths, while certain aspects of interpretation and communication were the areas where guides were underperforming (Weiler, 1999).

The role of cultural mediator was identified as important in previous studies and also recognized by respondents in phase 1 of this study. In phase 2, special attention was given to investigating the impact of the cultural mediator role on the tourists' overall guided tour experience. The following quotes (Yu, 2003a, p. 136) from the responses to the open-ended questions indicate that tour guides play an important role in cultural mediation, as they

- furthered our understanding of Chinese and Australian cultures;
- broadened our views, acted as a link between eastern and western cultures;
- enhanced our understanding and facilitated the communication between visitors and the locals.

What tour guides need to have to fulfil their roles and how to improve tour guides' performance

The findings also provide insight into the views of tourism industry representatives regarding the skills, knowledge and attitudes required by guides. The skills most frequently mentioned by respondents were people skills, problem-solving skills and communication skills. According to respondents, people skills refer to the ability to get to know their clients, to establish rapport with them (often in a very short time) and to develop an understanding of their background, including their expectations, interests and special requests. Problem solving refers to the ability to cope with the unexpected and to deal with emergencies. Communication includes the ability to understand and speak both Chinese and English, to present interesting commentary and to show respect for different cultures in both verbal and non-verbal communication.

Respondents also acknowledged that a tour guide needs to have a wide knowledge base including Australian history, geography, culture, people, places of interest, clients' culture and basic guiding procedures. This is the so-called 'broad knowledge' referred to by Ap and Wong (2001). They also need certain attitudes including a passion for tour guiding, commitment to work and willingness to resist unethical practices. Patience, flexibility and empathy are identified as important personal traits of tour guides.

The competencies that tourism industry representatives acknowledged as important for tour guides (in terms of knowledge, people skills and communication skills) are supported by the findings from both the visitor survey and the guide survey. Respondents of the visitor survey perceived people skills, or in other words, social and interpersonal skills as an important component of guide competence. The need for knowledge and communication skills was acknowledged by visitors, as they rated tour guides' cultural and language skills as two important elements of a tour guide's competence. The details of these finding are reported in an unpublished thesis (Yu, 2003a).

Factors that may be contributing to the underperformance of Chinese group tour guides in certain areas include lack of awareness of role expectations and lack of recognition and enforcement systems, as well as inadequate resources to support them in their jobs. According to the information collected from the interviews, there is not a strict entry qualification and standard for tour guiding in Australia. As a result, tour guides may not have clear role expectations, resulting in variable levels of professional performance among Chinese group tour guides. In addition, tour guiding is not regulated; tour guides are required neither to have a certificate nor to have a licence. The absence of reward, recognition and enforcement systems may be contributing to the neglect of some roles.

There is mounting evidence that tour guiding as a career is underrecognized, underresourced and underremunerated. In the case of ADS guides, some respondents claimed that tour guides escorting Chinese tour groups are paid at about one-third of the rate of pay of English- and Japanese-speaking tour guides. The seasonality and limited hours of tour operations in this market further reduces the income and employment benefits of guiding ADS tour groups. As discussed earlier in this chapter, poor remuneration and industry/government support can only exacerbate problems with poor performance.

Discussion and Conclusions

At the outset of this chapter, some benefits of using role theory as an analytical framework were outlined. In this study, it has helped to highlight some anomalies in the roles expected and performed by guides of Chinese tour groups in Australia. This includes the importance of duties associated with tour and group management, and the central role of cultural mediation. This suggests that a 'one size fits all' approach to job definition, recruitment and remuneration for tour guides may be inappropriate. Thus the findings from this study are of most use to travel companies involved with the China market. This section highlights the interpretation and implications of the research findings and identifies avenues for further research.

Discussion of findings in relation to role theory

The use of role theory in this study provides several important insights for the Australian government and tourism industry for better understanding role expectations of tour guides on Chinese tour groups (ADS groups) in Australia and ways of improving tour guides' performance. First, the role of the tour guide in guiding ADS groups is in some ways typical of other tour guide roles, i.e. it is multifaceted and dynamic. But in other ways, it is broader (e.g. to some extent, also performing the tour manager's role) and more demanding.

Secondly, there is some tension created by differences in role expectations between customers and employers, but this appears to be minimal. Nevertheless it is important to remain vigilant in ensuring that customers' role expectations continue to be consistent with those of employers. Tour itineraries that promise the unachievable put the guide in a difficult position and increase the chance of role conflict for the guide. Currently, the challenge of the guide's role comes less from this tension than from the gap between the customer's expectations of and dependency on their guides and the resourcing and support provided by employers and the industry in general.

Thirdly, guides of Chinese tours in Australia who are committed to their jobs are performing well in many areas, notably with respect to Chinese language and culture. Some were good at managing the tour and at cultural mediation, but could perform better in delivering commentary. The main concern of visitors was that the commentary lacked depth.

Finally, good guiding, particularly with respect to the cultural-mediation role, is contributing to customer satisfaction; but poor guiding practice, particularly with respect to unethical practice and depth of commentary, is contributing to customer dissatisfaction. Factors that may be contributing to poor performance include lack of broad knowledge and poor interpretation/communication skills. The tourism industry representatives interviewed in this study perceive guide performance to be generally good, with the main weakness being in 'content' knowledge. They may feel that acquisition of such knowledge and skills is the responsibility of individual guides and fail to see the need for supporting professional development, on-the-job training, better remuneration and reward for good practice. However, excellence in cultural interpretation and mediation will likely only be achieved with commitment and support from all parties: government, the tourism industry, employers and the guides themselves.

Implications of findings

The findings have implications for tour guide recruitment, employment, training and certification. With respect to recruitment, a basic entry qualification might be considered for recruiting Chinese group tour guides. In Australia, the competency standards of tour guides and the codes of conduct developed by Tourism Training Australia and China Inbound Task Force are useful starting points and should be used by inbound tour operators, tour coach companies and tour guides to make the members of the guiding community well aware of their role expectations.

In terms of employment practices and conditions, travel companies and tour operators may need to support their guides with adequate resources such as better minimum wages and training, thereby ensuring better performance of tour guides. The findings also point to the need for training to improve both the general knowledge and the interpretive communication skills of guides. Finally, a formal tour guide certification or licensing system would raise the recognition of the professionalism so that Chinese tour guides, and indeed all guides, can be rewarded according to their levels of qualification, and can see more incentives to improve their performance.

Directions for future study

The use of role theory highlights some directions for future research. First, although the emphasis in this study was not on role dynamics, it is clear from the findings that tour guides must adjust to particular situations and respond to differences in tour group members, employers and even environmental factors. The extent to which guides are recruited, trained and empowered to deal with such variations would be a fruitful avenue for further research.

Secondly, there is mounting evidence that the demands of tour guiding generally are much greater than in the past. Further research is needed to examine the impact of changing visitor expectations, industry trends (such as increased travel from new and emerging markets) and increased threats (such as litigation and terrorism) on tour guides' roles.

Thirdly, this study focused on the role of cultural mediation. There is scope for scrutiny of other aspects of tour guiding, including the guide's ability to handle logistical tasks such as time management, group management and health and safety issues; the style and quality of commentary, interpretation and involvement of visitors; the accuracy and authenticity of what is delivered; the guide's ability to respond to questions and adapt to the particular interests of the group; and so on.

Finally, future research should consider the use of multiple approaches and methods, including participant observation, which was beyond the scope of the present study. There is also a need for focused research at particular destinations, sites and attractions, and for experimental manipulation of tour guiding variables based on the research findings from this study.

Conclusion

This research points to the value of role theory as a framework for investigating visitor expectations and employee (tour guide) performance, and highlights the fruitfulness of further research of this nature in the wider tourism industry. In particular, this study links the role expectation and role performance of guides, and demonstrates the need for research linking role performance and organizational performance, including but not limited to visitor satisfaction.

References

Ap, J. and Wong, K. (2001) Case study on tour guiding: professionalism, issues and problems. *Tourism Management* 22, 551–563.

Australian Bureau of Statistics (2002) *Overseas Arrivals and Departures*. Australian Bureau of Statistics, Canberra, Australia.

Biddle, B.J. (1979) *Role Theory: Expectations, Identities and Behaviours*. Academic Press, New York.

Bras, K. (2000) *Image-Building and Guiding on Lombok: The Social Construction of a Tourist Destination*. Tilburg University, Amsterdam.

China National Tourism Administration (2001) '15-Year' Planning for China Tourism Development & 2015, 2020 Long-Term Targets. China National Tourism Administration, Beijing.

Cohen, E. (1972) Toward a sociology of international tourism. *Social Research* 39, 164–184.

Cohen, E. (1985) The tourist guide: the origins, structure and dynamics of a role. *Annals of Tourism Research* 12, 5–29.

European Federation of Tourist Guides Association (1998) *Information Brochure*. European Federation of Tourist Guides Association.

Glaser, B.G. and Strauss, A. (1967) *The Discovery of Grounded Theory: Strategies for Qualitative Research*. Aldine Publication, New York.

Gurung, G., Simmons, D. and Devlin, P. (1996) The evolving role of tourist guides: the Nepali experience. In: Bulter, R. and Hinch, T. (eds) *Tourism and Indigenous Peoples*. International Thomson Business, London, pp. 107–128.

Ham, H.S. and Weiler, B. (2002) Toward a theory of quality in cruise-based interpretive guiding. *Journal of Interpretation Research* 7(2), 29–49.

Heiss, J. (1990) Social Roles. In: Rosenberg, M. and Turner, R.H. (eds) *Social Psychology: Sociological Perspectives*. Transaction, New York, pp. 94–129.

Holloway, J.C. (1981) The guided tour: a sociological approach. *Annals of Tourism Research* 8(3), 377–402.

Hornby, A.S. (ed.) (2000) *Oxford Advanced Learner's Dictionary*, 6th edn. Oxford University Press, Oxford.

Huberman, A.M. and Miles, M.B. (1994) Data management and analysis methods. In: Lincoln, J.R. (ed.) *Handbook of Qualitative Research*. Sage, Thousand Oaks, California, pp. 428–444.

Hughes, K. (1991) Tourist satisfaction: a guided 'cultural' tour in North Queensland. *Australian Psychologist* 26(3), 166–171.

Ilgen, D.R. and Hollenbeck, J.R. (1992) The structure of work: job design and roles. In: Dunnette, M.D. and Hough, L.M. (eds) *Handbook of Industrial and Organizational Psychology*. Consulting Psychologists Press, Palo Alto, California, pp. 165–207.

Jackson, S.E. and Schuler, R.S. (1995) Understanding human resource management in the context of organizations and their environments. In: Spence, T.J., Darley, J.M. and Foss, D.J. (eds) *Annual Review of Psychology*, Vol. 46. Palo Alto, California, pp. 237–264.

Katz, D. and Kahn, R.L. (1978) *The Social Psychology of Organizations*. John Wiley & Sons, New York.

McKean, P.F. (1976) An anthropological analysis of the culture brokers of Bali: guides, tourists and Balinese. *Joint UNESCO/IBDR Seminar on the Social and Cultural Impact of Tourism*. Washington, DC.

Mehan, H. (1979) *Learning Lessons: Social Organization in the Classroom*. Harvard University Press, Cambridge, Massachusetts.

Nash, D. (1978) Tourism as a form of imperialism. In: Smith, V. (ed.) *Hosts and Guests: The Anthropology of Tourism*. University of Pennsylvania Press, Philadelphia, Pennsylvania, pp. 33–47.

Pearce, P. (1984) Tourist-guide interaction. *Annals of Tourism Research* 11, 129–146.

Perakyla, A. (1997) Reliability and validity in research based upon transcription. In: Silverman, D. (ed.) *Qualitative Research*. Sage, London, pp. 201–219.

Pond, K.L. (1993) *The Professional Guide*. Van Nostrand Reinhold, New York.

Rodham, K. (2000) Role theory and the analysis of managerial work: the case of occupational health professionals. *Journal of Applied Management Studies* 9(1), 71–81.

Schmidt, C. (1979) The guided tour. *Urban Life* 7(4), 441–467.

Silverman, D. (2000) *Doing Qualitative Research: A Practical Handbook*. Sage, Thousand Oaks, California.

Smith, V.L. (2001) The culture brokers. In: Smith, V.L. and Brent, M. (eds) *Hosts and Guests Revisited: Tourism Issues of the 21st Century*. Cognizant Communication Corporation, New York, pp. 275–289.

Tourism Forecasting Council (1999) *Forecast*. Tourism Forecasting Council, Canberra, Australia.

Tourism Forecasting Council (2002) *Forecast*. Tourism Forecasting Council, Canberra, Australia.

Troyer, L., Mueller, C.W. and Osinsky, P.I. (2000) Who's the boss? a role-theoretic analysis of customer work. *Work and Occupations* 27(3), 406–427.

Weiler, B. (1999) Assessing the interpretation competencies of ecotour guides. *Journal of Interpretation Research* 4(1), 80–83.

Weiler, B. and Ham, S. (2001) Tour guides and interpretation in ecotourism. In: Weaver, D. (ed.) *Encyclopedia of Ecotourism*. CAB International, Wallingford, UK, pp. 549–563.

Weiler, B., Johnson, T. and Davis, D. (1991) *Roles of the Tour Leader in Environmentally Responsible Tourism*. Eco-tourism (Incorporating the Global Classroom), Australian Bureau of Tourism Research, Canberra, Australia.

Welbourne, T.M., Johnson, D.E. and Erez, A. (1998) The role-based performance scale: validity analysis of a theory-based measure. *Academy of Management Journal* 41(5), 540–555.

Wong, A. (2001) Satisfaction with local tour guides in Hong Kong. *Pacific Tourism Review* 5, 59–67.

World Tourism Organization (1998) *Tourism: 2020 Vision – Executive Summary*. World Tourism Organization, Madrid, Spain.

Yu, X. (2003a) Conceptualizing and assessing intercultural competence of tour guides: an analysis of Australian guides of Chinese tour groups. Unpublished PhD thesis. Monash University, Melbourne, Australia.

Yu, X. (2003b) Chinese tour guiding in Australia: current status, issues and recommendations. In: Black, R. and Weiler, B. (eds) *Interpreting the Land Down Under: Australian Heritage Interpretation and Tour Guiding*. Fulcrum Publishing, Golden, Colorado, pp. 186–203.

Yu, X. and Weiler, B. (2001) Mainland Chinese pleasure travellers to Australia: a leisure behaviour analysis. *Journal of Tourism, Culture and Communication* 3(2), 81–92.

Yu, X., Weiler, B. and Ham, S. (2001) Intercultural communication and mediation: a framework for analysing intercultural competence of Chinese tour guides. *Journal of Vacation Marketing* 8(1), 75–87.

17 Effective Management of Hotel Revenue: Lessons from the Swiss Hotel Industry

Kate Varini and Dimitrios Diamantis
Les Roches Management School, Switzerland

Introduction

During the past few years, yield management has gained wide acceptance in both airline and hotel industries. It is widely used in the transport sector such as airline companies, and secondarily by the hotels, cruise lines and tour operators. The term yield originated in the airline industry means yield per available seat mile (Donaghy *et al.*, 1998). There are numerous definitions of yield management defined by researchers, academics and practitioners. Kimes (1989), from School of Hotel Administration, Cornell University, describes yield management as the process of allocating the right type of capacity or inventory unit to the right kind of customer at the right price so as to maximize revenue or yield. Donaghy *et al.* (1998) consider yield management to be a revenue maximization technique that aims to increase net yield through the predicted allocation of available capacity to predetermined market segments at optimum price. Lieberman (1993) describes yield management as the practice of maximizing profits from the sale of perishable assets, such as hotel rooms, by controlling price and inventory and improving service.

The purpose of this chapter is to discuss the skill set and requisites necessary to effectively manage revenue in different size hotels,

from an experience of the Swiss hotel industry. Empirical research indicated that because the 'Revenue Manager' position was relatively new to hotels, the evolution of the position was not yet complete; and therefore, hotels looked elsewhere, the airline industry for example, to obtain ideas. Further, the chapter also discusses the challenges that the revenue manager can face in terms of different products that will deliver in periods of high and low demand. Overall, the chapter highlights the pros and cons of having a revenue manager as well as the implication of such a role for an organization and consumers. It also reviews the role of small to medium enterprises (SMEs), discusses the status of tourism in Switzerland and presents the results of a survey conducted to the hotel managers in which their skills are evaluated.

Yield Management in Small to Medium Enterprises

Experts of yield management tend to suggest that collaboration among hotels in the same region or area would be the best solution for small to medium properties. Data on major events and conferences, guest segmentations and trends on buying behaviours can be shared among hoteliers. It would be even more effective with the collaboration of local government authorities such as a tourism board.

The other issue concerning yield management in small to medium hotels is the use of non-computerized yield-management systems. There are several effective ways to practice yield management manually such as a spreadsheet, which is used by a large number of hotels, especially in Europe. In the work of Donaghy (1999), a few worksheets have been developed, such as daily yield report, booking sheet, pricing sheet, overbooking sheet and demand chart. A structured yield-management system will significantly alter the traditional approach to accommodation management in various areas. There is a need to look at the hotel as a whole, integrating all the departments and all the personnel.

Donaghy *et al.* (1997) developed a ten-stage framework for the effective operation of a yield-management system, which is an appropriate approach for small to medium hotels. Further, a knowledge of market demand and the behaviour of consumers is equally important. Yield management in the hotel industry is a relatively reactive approach whereby the rates are effectively determined by the customers through their patterns of demand. Hotels constantly seek feedback from the market once a set of rates is thrown out into the market to determine the rate that customers are prepared to pay. Obtaining customer and market data is a difficult task and certainly costly. Due to limited market intelligence, hotel managers would be best to utilize available customer and market data. There are certain ways of doing that, for example, available information such as average length of stay, booking pace (the lead time from the reservation made to the actual check-in time), source of reservation, average room rate and customer preferences.

Market data are not difficult to gather if hotel managers are fully aware of trends in the area where the hotel operates. Events or exhibitions, local festivals, conventions and meetings and other activities would increase the demand for rooms throughout the year. A marketing task force could be established to assist hotel managers in this task. Customers today have a variety of ways to find and buy the rooms, thus purchasing behaviours should be monitored and analysed. Further, there is a need to focus on strategies to enhance customer value by clearly defining short-term versus long-term value proposition, and profit versus revenue.

The type of data on guest and market, as Donaghy *et al.* (1997) listed, should include areas such as booking cancellation, denials (guests who could not be accommodated), declines (guests whose enquiry did not result in a booking), no-shows (booked guests who did not arrive) and overbooking levels. All these areas of information should be served as the guidelines in the decision-making process. One of the ways to obtain customer and market data is the property-management system, where all the guest histories are kept and constantly updated. Many hotel chains have sound guest history systems incorporated within the property-management systems. However, revenue management (RM) is less popular in small and medium hotels for various reasons:

1. Small firms differ in their approach to innovation. Scarce resources limit funds for research into new markets, products and techniques thus creating a barrier to enhancing the acceptance and credibility required in order to implement RM techniques (Storey, 1994).
2. Under normal conditions, a hotel may need 20–30 days minimum a year where the demand exceeds the capacity and 100% occupancy is achieved. In the case of a smaller establishment, a greater number of sell-out nights may be required to make the investment in learning about the concept and updating the necessary skills worthwhile.
3. Until recently the large investment required to purchase a computerized RM system was out of the reach of small hotels. Moreover, systems were far too complex for a small-scale hotel operation.

In overcoming problems of this nature, RM in SMEs requires that someone oversees the revenue management daily, weekly and monthly tasks. With today's technology this could even be done remotely, by an external body.

Skill Set for Revenue Management

The level of competencies required for RM depends on the size and complexity of the hotel operation as well as the level of the revenue manager. In a small hotel the general manager may have the responsibility to manage revenue as well as many other tasks, and therefore cannot be expected to have a very specific level of competencies that may be required in a senior-level revenue manager managing the revenue of multiple, large city properties. The two main skills sets are: (i) managerial, and (ii) technical.

Skill set 1: managerial skills

Managerial and leadership skills are required in order to communicate and implement RM strategical decisions within all levels of the hotel organization. A first time implementation of RM in a hotel will require an ability to encourage and enforce change. An awareness of the criticality of support (especially that of top management) will ensure that the revenue manager will possess an ability to convince superiors and department heads of the importance of RM decisions via weekly or biweekly RM meetings.

A simple knowledge of human psychology will assist revenue managers in managing the inevitable conflict between different departments/divisions (mostly between sales and rooms) and assist in training staff and in evaluating customers perception of fairness and which communications may be required to ensure that a positive perception persists.

> RM meetings and day-to-day decision making can only be conducted effectively when all parties, with a stake in the decision(s), understand all the data being presented and who all share common goals, which should be RevPAR gains.
>
> Von Bahr-Lindmann (2000)

Regional revenue managers may need to be multilingual in order to carry out the workshops and trainings required in different locations.

A revenue manager must possess an ability for abstract thinking and be able to market and manage the booking situation on a daily evolving basis to minimize lost revenue opportunities and to turn undesirable booking requests into desirable ones, for example, moving a tentative group booking from a high-demand period to low-demand by offering rate incentives. The creation of different innovative products that will stimulate demand without generating any customer feelings of unfairness or profit erosion is required.

As variable pricing and restrictions will need to be applied, revenue managers need to have an idea of supply and demand economics, i.e. how changing price will affect demand for a particular class of room as well as how to set rates, how many to have as well as what restrictions to put in place. A knowledge of effective use of availability controls and revenue optimization is also required (not only on a one night, high-demand night but through low/high-demand times, optimizing on the low-demand night stay) as well as the ability to evaluate whether a booking at rack rate for one night will be accepted or a corporate rate for three nights. A revenue manager needs to be able to use dynamic pricing techniques to stimulate demand when required. This will require the use of the different distribution channels without jeopardizing current demand levels, avoiding cannibalization of business by giving guests with a high willingness to pay access to lower rates. An in-depth knowledge of what customers value and how much they might be willing to pay is required in order to price products effectively.

As the avoidance of profit erosion is a major factor in RM, managers making decisions regarding pricing of hotel rooms should be aware of their average fixed and variable costs per room available and the impact of an unsold room on hotel profitability. Also, managers need an awareness of how much profit contribution is required from rooms in order to succeed as a lodging organization. A revenue manager needs a solid commercial background, strong analytical skills and ability to make tactical decisions based on strategic analysis of overall demand situations in line with the systems in place at the hotel.

Revenue managers must practise revenue analysis and tracking and be able to use benchmarks to judge RM success, taking into account the competitor set as well as the hotels own performance data. There is a need to understand certain statistical methods to maximize revenue and use the analysis of data to identify critical dates (exceptions) as well as to apply local knowledge of demand factors not captured by historical statistics.

Skill set 2: technical skills

Managers of revenue need an understanding of the basic concept of RM, including a basic knowledge of certain statistical areas such as probability theory behind the concept as well as an understanding of RM in terms of numbers that relate to their hotel organization. Skills required include:

- A strong understanding of the rooms product. This will enable RM to determine which categories should be available and how to make inventory flexible ensuring optimization in high- and low-demand times.
- Managers should know when each type of customer books and at which level the hotel should be overbooked in order to fill the hotel to its capacity and avoid any spoilage or spillage of rooms. To do this, the RM will need to put in place procedures that will reduce the unpredictability of guest behaviour.
- A hotel manager must appreciate the value of variable pricing and be able to manipulate prices in order to manage demand and avoid revenue dilution.
- Different lengths of stay need to be managed with different availability controls. Understanding how to make duration more predictable can enhance these duration controls (Kimes, 1998).
- An understanding of the tools required to manage revenue, i.e. forecasting, overbooking, pricing strategy and information systems.
- An understanding of the different RM calculations and benchmarks used to analyse, monitor and measure performance.

A knowledge of how hotels operate and a very good understanding of the hotel market and hotel business in the surrounding area (region or city) is also essential. This could include information on competitors, events (national, regional and global) as well as sales and marketing initiatives and information on the economic environment.

As overbooking occurs when using RM, situations will occur where customers with reservations find themselves without a room at the hotel booked and must be 'walked'. Revenue managers need to create and enforce standards that cover aspects of who should be booked out/walked and how they should be walked. These standards or procedures should have the goal of minimizing customers' feelings of unfairness and subsequent loss of loyalty.

A good understanding of how to use database will ensure that managers can evaluate the importance of good data management. Systems need to be put in place to ensure the capture of plentiful, accurate and relevant data in a form that will allow optimum manipulation (essentially on customer booking patterns and demand patterns by market segment) to enable the production of forecasts to the highest degree of accuracy possible.

As the ability to accurately forecast demand directly affects the increase in revenues generated by the use of RM, revenue managers need to be able to reduce forecasting error by tracking and evaluating deviations and putting into place systems that increase the accuracy of forecasts. Forecast allows the computerized revenue management system (CRMS) to manage the hotels inventory of rooms via efficient rate allocation and inventory control often involving the central reservation system (CRS) and multiple distribution channels. If no CRMS is in place, the revenue manager must do this manually, identifying and carefully monitoring critical days that are not performing according to business as usual.

Depending on the degree of computerization, revenue managers will need varying levels of expertise in manipulating a property management system (PMS) and CRS. At the very least a revenue manager needs to be able to appreciate the value and applicability of CRMS. If using a CRMS, managers need to be able to monitor and evaluate the systems to ensure that agreed goals are met. Overrides should only be made in exceptional situations when the revenue manager has information that the system does not have access to. Electronic distribution channels' costs and sales need to be monitored and with the increase in global distribution system (GDS) activity, electronic marketing intelligence reports should be used to evaluate channel performance.

To manage revenue, varying levels of marketing knowledge are required at different levels of the organization, starting with a basic knowledge for hotel reservationists in order to code business efficiently and quote rates appropriately. In managing revenue, revenue managers need a good understanding of marketing theory and should be able to run training programmes for staff in the required basics. At senior level, the director of revenue will need to prepare and implement strategic sales plans and have a good understanding of pricing and positioning. In all cases, an ability to segment specifically for RM is required, i.e. in addition to segmenting customers by their needs, perceptions and reactions, customers need to be segmented according to their willingness to pay and booking behaviour. Extensive knowledge of competitors/marketing intelligence will assist in optimizing revenue.

A revenue manager needs to train, monitor and evaluate reservationists in order to ensure proper quoting for RM, so that customers understand why rates may change and what they have to do to have access to better rates. Incentives that reinforce the RM effort need to put in place in all areas where long-term revenues may be affected. An understanding of the group sales process will assist when sales performance is evaluated according to need periods and records of lost revenue opportunities (e.g. inquires that were not converted into sales). All performance measurement will need to evaluate external influences (i.e. economic or competitor factors) when rewarding revenue improvements and should not disregard customer loyalty levels. Last but not least, these factors depend on the setting in which they occur. In this case, the chapter will consider the case of Swiss tourism before moving to an assessment of the performance of Swiss hotel managers.

Tourism in Switzerland

Switzerland is a popular destination and recorded 11 million arrivals in 2000, an increase by 400,000 tourists since 1996 (WTO, 2001). Furthermore 46% of all travel by Swiss citizens is domestic.

One of the reasons for the nation's success to date can be attributed to government policy. Switzerland is able to pursue a tourism policy of clear differentiation with respect to larger competitors. The federal government's tourism policy is based on the brand 'Switzerland'. It is not merely a communication strategy, but really a question of a tourism policy vision, of managing the tourism country of Switzerland as a virtual company or a kind of 'Switzerland Tourism Holding'. This has reflected in good performance in terms of its tourism demand and supply.

According to the 'Economic policy guidelines for 1999–2003 going for growth', the governing principle represents a long-term concept, realizable along the following guidelines:

- an open economy and active partner at the international level;
- a competitive industrial and service centre;
- an economic centre endowed with substantial value-added potential;
- an innovative training and research centre;
- a country of social peace.

One of the objectives of tourism policy is to ensure that policy decisions in flanking or hierarchically superior policy areas are as tourism-friendly as possible. This 'cross-sectional' aspect of the tourism policy gives rise to difficulties due to conflicting objectives. Entrepreneurial activities in the field of tourism are shaped to a great extent by territorial organization and regional development policies. A cross section-orientated tourism policy also has to come to terms with the state as a regulatory authority. The Swiss federal government (Federal Council) published an action plan for improving the framework conditions of Swiss tourism in its report on tourism to the Parliament on 29 May 1996. The aim of this plan, which has already been implemented to some extent, is to dismantle restrictive regulations that stand in the way of tourism growth. This action plan was devised with the help of the government's interministerial Consultative Commission for Tourism.

Tourism demand performance: a consumer perspective

The economic performance in terms of the demand is outlined as follows:

- Domestic and international tourism are important factors in the Swiss economy generating revenue of 22.7 billion Swiss francs in 2000. Of this, 9.7 billion (or 43%) came from domestic tourism. Expenditure by foreign visitors in Switzerland added some 13 billion Swiss francs (4% of the GDP) as illustrated in Table 17.1.
- Expenditure by foreign visitors staying overnight in tourist accommodation establishments totalled 7.5 billion francs in 2000, of which tourists staying in hotels spent four-fifths as illustrated in Table 17.2.
- The economic downturn of the mid-1990s has been overcome. While at that time (the lowest point) only 75% of the Swiss population took trips involving three or more overnight stays, in 1998 it was nearly 80%. However, to date it has not been possible to regain the high levels seen in 1990 and 1992 as illustrated in Table 17.3.
- The picture was somewhat different when considering all trips of at least one overnight

Table 17.1. Swiss tourism revenue.

Total tourism revenue	1989	1994	1999	2000
From domestic tourists	7.1	9.0	9.4	9.7
From foreign tourists	9.9	11.4	11.8	13.0
Total	17.0	20.4	21.2	22.7
Tourism's share of Swiss GDP(%)	5.9	5.7	5.4	5.6

Note: in billion Swiss francs.
Source: Swiss Federal Statistical Office.

stay, nearly 85% of all persons spent at least one night away from home in 1998 with an average length of stay of 2.77 days as illustrated in Table 17.4.

Tourism supply performance: a hospitality perspective

The hotel industry is the major factor in Switzerland's tourism industry. As early as 1912, prior to the outbreak of the First World War, there were 211,000 hotel beds in Switzerland, and by 2000, this figure had risen to 259,700 (Table 17.5). The number has not significantly changed in recent years, but quality has been widely adapted to the changing demands of tourism.

Due to its seasonal nature, tourism statistics distinguish between existing, i.e. the total of all hotel beds in Switzerland and available hotel beds. Occupancy rates of hotels have increased since 1996 as illustrated in Table 17.6.

Case Study of Swiss Hotel Managers

Introduction

The chapter now discusses the qualitative analysis of four case studies of small to medium hotels. The properties are all located in the same region and vary from 2-star to 5-star hotels. The main objective of this analysis is to investigate the knowledge and understanding that hoteliers had of yield management and its application in their properties.

A questionnaire was developed for hotel managers in Switzerland with the aim of assessing the gap between their knowledge and skills required to effectively manage revenue. The questionnaire was tested at the end of a 5-day seminar on RM conducted by Ecole Hotelier de Lausanne. A group of 20 attendees agreed to fill in the questionnaire and gave helpful comments. As the questionnaires had to be translated into three languages, French, German and Italian, three personal interviews were conducted with hotel man-

Table 17.2. Tourism expenditure in Switzerland.

Overnight tourists year 2000	Expenditure for lodging	Expenditure for meals	Expenditure for incidentals	Total
In hotels	2959.7	1371.4	2020.7	6351.8
In vacation apartments	199.3	232.7	248.5	680.4
At camp grounds	22.5	46.1	48.6	117.2
In group accommodation	37.3	48.9	46.8	133.0
In youth hostels	8.9	8.4	4.5	21.9
With friends and relatives	–	–	–	185.9
Total	–	–	–	7490.2

Note: in million Swiss francs.
Source: Swiss Federal Statistical Office.

Table 17.3. Net travel intensity for trips of +3 overnight stays for selected years between 1990 and 1998.

1990	1992	1995/96	1998
83%	83%	75%	79%

Source: Institute for Public Services and Tourism at the University of St Gall.

Table 17.4. Key data for travel with at least 1 overnight stay.

Key figures	1995/96	1998
Net travel intensity in % (proportion of the population which had undertaken at least one trip)	79	84
Multiple travellers (with more than 1 trip in % of all travellers)	72	70
Gross travel intensity in % (number of trips per 100 inhabitants)	225	232
Travel frequency (number of trips per traveller)	2.85	2.77

Source: Institute for Public Services and Tourism at the University of St Gall.

Table 17.5. Swiss hotels and beds capacity.

Year	Number of hotels	Number of beds existing	Number of beds available
1990	6,700	269,800	222,600
1995	6,100	264,400	222,000
1999	5,800	259,500	219,600
2000	5,800	259,700	219,400

Source: Swiss Federal Statistical Office.

agers in order to verify the correctness and clarity of the translated text. The managers were observed as they filled in the question- naires and then gave their comments after they completed the questionnaire – all non- verbal communication such as sighs, pauses, etc. was noted. Some final changes were made to the questionnaire format.

Table 17.6. Swiss hotel occupancy.

Switzerland	1996	1998	2000
Supply available rooms	120,558	119,961	119,926
Supply available beds	220,548	219,412	219,394
Overnight stays in millions – Swiss	12.4	13.1	14.0
Overnight stays in millions – foreigners	17.3	18.7	19.9
Overnight stays in millions – total	29.7	31.8	33.9
Occupancy in % of available rooms	43.4	46.7	49.7
Occupancy in % of available beds	36.8	39.7	42.3

Source: Swiss Federal Statistical Office.

The population and response rates

The members of the Swiss Hotel Association constituted the population for this study. This provided a study group of managers with similar hotel culture in an area, Switzerland, known for its 'traditional' hotel-management methods. Based on data provided by the Swiss Hotel Association, 2485 hotels met these criteria. As the majority of hotels in the study can be classified as small (with an average of 38 employees), the questionnaire was directed to the general manager, revenue manager (non-existent in most cases) or the person in charge of sales or reservations. A letter from the President of the Swiss Hotel Association that endorsed the study accompanied the questionnaire, which was translated into the three official Swiss languages.

The questionnaires were sent out and returned over a 30-day period. In order to ensure the accuracy of the gap measurement, 15 questionnaires were also sent to European revenue managers at senior and middle levels. Four hundred and nine usable questionnaires were received back from the Swiss hotels with the breakdown by language as shown in Table 17.7.

Table 17.7. Questionnaire and response.

Language	Sent	Returned	Response rate (%)
French	559	69	12.3
German	1926	313	16.3
Italian	232	26	11.2

Generally, the response rate was higher for 4–5-star and city hotels.

All the 15 questionnaires sent to European revenue managers were returned completed and usable. The overall response rate to the Swiss questionnaire was 16.5%, a level common to surveys of this kind.

The respondents

The respondents comprise mostly managers with a professional hotel school background (65%) and a minority with a university degree (5%). In hotels with more than 200 rooms, the respondents all had higher levels of professional education. The questionnaires were filled in mostly by hotel owners/general managers (81%) but also by managers involved in 'rooms' areas such as reservations, RM, reception, rooms division, sales and marketing (9%). In the larger hotels, respondents tended to work more with sales and marketing departments, but overall, 'reception' was the main area of work contact. The managers surveyed had mostly been in the hotel industry for more than 5 years (68%), 57% of the sample declared a period of more than 9 years; 11% declared they had been in the hotel industry for less than 5 years. In general, managers described themselves as mostly all-rounders having expertise in operations rather than specific domains. The hotels with more than 100 rooms had managers with greater rooms expertise – the lower the standard/category of hotel, the greater expertise in food and beverage areas of the hotel. The managers in the study spent 38% of their time in operations with 34% dedicated to administration and

28% only dedicated to 'managing'. In small 3-star hotels (<50 rooms) managers spent even greater amounts of their time in operations. More administration and 'managing' is done in 4- and 5-star establishments with administration predominating in 5-star hotels. This appears to reflect a greater availability of time for analysis available to managers in larger, higher category hotels. Managers in small hotels spent most of their working time in operations and so would not have the time to dedicate to manual data collection for RM, making an affordable computerized system essential. Of the respondents, 89% declared that they were the ones setting rates, making them the principal controllers of revenue in the hotel.

The hotels in the survey

The level of hotel where these managers are employed comprises mainly of 3- and 4-star hotels (75%) with an annual revenue of more than 500,000 Swiss francs (87%). As 83% of respondents manage hotels with 100 rooms or less, the hotels in the study can be mostly considered as SMEs (Arthur Andersen, 1997). On the other hand, the hotels can be considered mostly small if an average of annual employees is used as a measure (the hotels have on average 38), as defined by the European Commission in 1996 (Thomas, 2000).

The location of the surveyed hotels was mostly in mountain areas (38.6%), the remainder were spread between city (15.6%), lake (18.8%) and other locations (25.9%). It should be noted that major cities in Switzerland such as Geneva and Lausanne could be classified also as 'lake' locations. Also, although in mountain areas, hotels cannot be strictly considered resorts as many meeting and forums are run in these mountain locations (e.g. World Economic Forum – Davos, a ski resort).

The hotels classified themselves as mostly independent (64%) with 25% declaring to be part of a voluntary chain, being run via a management contract or franchise agreement with over 50% open 12 months of the year.

Improved profits through RM requires that the hotels have 20–30 sell-out days (Varini, 2001). Of the hotels in the study, 82% affirmed to have more than 20 sell-out days

per year with 55% of their business at rack rates (fully yieldable). The hotels have the largest portion of their business coming from leisure customers, this is reflected in the average lengths of stay: in 40% of cases it was 1 to 2 nights; in 43% of cases, 3 to 5 nights; and in 15% of cases more than 5 nights.

Data analysis

The data were analysed using the competency framework developed. In some areas results were good, in others a broad gap in knowledge of requirements for RM is evident. The fact that most of the managers in small and medium hotels have been in the industry for more than 9 years, the period in which RM was developing, explains the lack of specific skills required to implement the concept effectively.

Evaluating Skill Set 1 – Leadership/Communication Skills

As the survey was directed at managers, it was assumed that they already have leadership skills in order to be able to carry out managerial tasks in their current position. The only skills measured in this survey are those of communication. The results in this area demonstrate an ability to encourage and enforce change (small enterprises lean towards change more easily than large ones). As the key controllers of revenue are mostly the owners or general managers, top management support becomes automatic and so therefore if they decide to embrace RM, decisions can be enforced easily. When asked what additional skills would be required to improve their performance, the majority of managers replied that staff training was a priority for them. They felt that it was important to keep their staff updated and hold meetings in order to share information. This confirms that they are aware of the need to convince key employees via regular meetings (Fig. 17.1).

The Swiss hotel managers demonstrated a great emphasis on customer-relationship management and so would therefore be sensitive to their customers of fairness when applying RM.

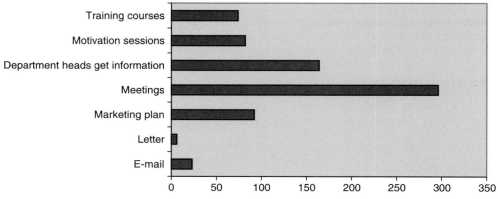

Fig. 17.1. How managers inform key selling staff of their strategic decisions.

Of the respondents, 60% state that once they have set their rates they monitor guest reactions to ensure rates are at the correct level. They also segment loyalty and frequency of stay that will enable them to give greater benefits to loyal customers when applying RM, thereby maintaining their long-term revenue stream. From a communication perspective, Swiss hotel managers do well, although when discussing market segmentation and loyalty later, the disadvantage of their overemphasis on customer loyalty will be discussed.

Skill set 1 – conceptual creativity

The correctness of pricing levels is an essential condition for effective RM. This can be evaluated by a number of different actions, i.e. closely monitoring competitors and analysing the evolution of demand by monitoring the pace of reservation and customer reaction. In high-demand periods this might even be done on an hourly basis. Of the Swiss hotel managers in the study, 52% evaluate their competitors' prices via reading their competitors' brochure once in a while (every few months) and, more frequently, browsing their competitors' website (daily to weekly) and 41.8% evaluate main rate decisions on a daily/weekly basis (41.8%).

When comparing the answers of the Swiss hotel managers to those of European revenue managers, it is apparent that although efforts are made to monitor the correctness of room rates, the monitoring process needs to be more widespread and more frequent in order that hotels have the knowledge to be able to react in a dynamic marketplace.

Product management

In a situation of oversupply, 73.35% of Swiss hotel managers would take short-term measures to increase occupancy rates. However, rather than selecting the best option such as creating options for new segments with appropriate restrictions in place (chosen by only 32.3% of Swiss hoteliers), they preferred to create a special offer with no restrictions. Depending on the offer, this could create revenue dilution where guests are willing to pay a higher rate but take up the special offer, causing less revenue to be generated than without the special offer. This type of promotion should not be offered to higher-paying guests because it may cause feelings of unfairness to be generated with a resulting damage to customer loyalty.

Skill set 1 – administrative

Almost 65% of the managers in the study are aware of their fixed costs. In fact when setting rates, cost is the major source of data that influences their pricing decision. Unfortunately what is not common knowledge among Swiss hoteliers is the impact of an unsold room on profitability, also known as profit erosion.

Monitor and evaluate performance with statistical analysis

Another area where a gap is apparent is in statistical analysis. The majority of hotels in the study did use statistics to evaluate hotel performance. The most used performance measure is the 'occupancy' calculation, which is carried out in 94% of the sample. The problem exists in the frequency of this calculation: 48% of respondents declared that this is done on a daily basis while 37% only do a monthly calculation. Seventy per cent of hotels also calculate average rate, revenue per available room/customer as well as average length of stay. To be effective, these statistics should be calculated on a daily basis.

To the detriment of potential hotel room revenue, the weakest area of statistical analysis found was in the areas most critical for forecasting, essentially, the forecasting required in order to manage overbooking effectively and the forecasting of unconstrained demand. On an average only 39% of the hotels produce the statistics required with a disappointing percentage gathering these statistics on the required daily basis (early departures 12.7%, denials 14.7%, no-shows 25.43%, booking pace 8.1%). Managers in the study did not feel that they need strong statistical skills, which emphasizes the lack of awareness of the importance of this skill.

Evaluating Skill Set 2 – the Technical

Hoteliers use forecasting and overbooking to optimize room revenue and carefully monitor guest reactions when changing their pricing policy. While they showed an understanding of the tools that exist, there was a lack of understanding of how a systematic approach, rather than one stemming solely from experience and intuition, can enhance RM efforts. As already mentioned, 94% of Swiss hoteliers carry out occupancy calculations with 70% also calculating RevPAR, thus demonstrating a wide knowledge of the basic statistics required to evaluate room revenue.

Although a basic understanding of the concept of RM exists (because basically hotel managers do it already intuitively), a clear understanding of how revenue can be optimized is lacking. The research demonstrates that on a scale of 1–24, 59% of Swiss hotel managers score 8 or less with 37.6% scoring 16 or less. A small portion of hotel managers (3%) obtained between 17 and 24 points. These highest-scoring hotels, without exception, are those with more than 20 sell-out days. These high scoring hotels are even spread throughout categories, sizes and locations.

The hotel operation and environment

It is assumed that the managers have this knowledge as they have been in the industry a number of years and have mostly graduated from hotel schools.

Data management – warehousing and mining

Not a great deal of physical data is currently being collected as managers rely on their years of experience rather than statistics. Reservation coding is done according to marketing type segmentation and other information such as booking pace and denial information is rarely collected.

If managers intend to implement RM, they must be aware that it is critical to have accurate and plentiful data. In small hotels collecting this data manually is not feasible, as managers do not have the time to dedicate to such a time-consuming task. Therefore, the question of data collection and manipulation relies on the availability of a simple computerized RM system that will soon be available within a price range small hotels can afford.

Once a system is available and appropriate segmentation is in place, managers must train reservation agents to code and accurately maintain guest history files scrupulously.

Managers must ensure that practices, such as checking in of no-shows by the night audit manager, are discontinued to allow accurate interpretation of the data by the system.

Forecasting

In general, accurate forecasting can be considered a key driver of RM. In Swiss hotels, the majority of managers carry out this task on a frequent basis but not in enough detail (see Fig. 17.2).

It can be seen that in Switzerland (CH), 'forecasting by day' (Fig. 17.2), is usually undertaken for the following 3 days, 10 days or month. European (EU) revenue managers forecast by day for the next 3, 10, 30 and in some cases 365 days, every day. This type of forecasting of course requires the use of a revenue management system (RMS) to produce such frequent and detailed forecasts. The RMS also uses large amounts of historical data in the forecast calculations and will usually forecast in detail such as by arrivals, day of the week, length of stay and market segment. In a hotel with ten market segments and three different lengths of stay, this may mean a total of 210 different forecasts redone on a daily basis for the next 365 or in some cases 550 days. Forecasting weekly is illustrated in Fig. 17.3.

Technology

As already mentioned, in order to manage revenue effectively, small and medium hotels need the skills and knowledge but also a simple, affordable RMS to manage the data required in this effort.

Market segmentation

The research has shown that market segmentation for RM should not be determined according to traditional marketing needs but necessarily by customer needs, and more importantly by booking behaviour and their willingness to pay. But only about 15% of Swiss hoteliers did use the latter criteria to segment their market compared with 7 out of 12 (58%) of the European revenue managers who were also surveyed. Collecting certain guest data such as length of stay, booking pattern, cost of servicing and additional revenue spent is crucial for RM. However, Swiss hotel managers focus more on collecting guest information for marketing objectives (e.g. demographic data) or for customer-relationship programmes (e.g. guest comments/complaints). Data relevant for RM are collected only to a minor extent (33%) compared to European revenue managers (65%). The information on booking behaviour together with details on a guest's willingness to pay is essen-

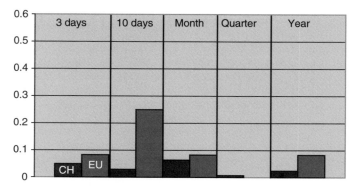

Fig. 17.2. Forecast daily for the next 3 days, 10 days, month, quarter and year.

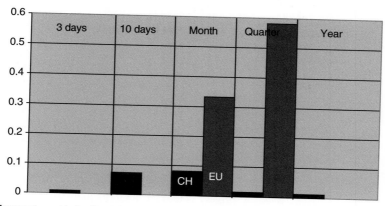

Fig. 17.3. Forecast weekly for the next 3 days, 10 days, month, quarter and year.

tial in order to be able to forecast and make decisions on whether or not to accept the earlier booking price-sensitive guest or to hold rooms for the guest willing to pay a higher rate but booking at the last minute.

The basis for the segmentation criteria

The hotels in the study place a great emphasis on segmentation by loyalty or frequency of stay. When RM is in place, loyalty is important but only when combined with a high willingness to pay. Ideally, customers should be segmented by their value (calculated over 12 months) rather than frequency and a non- or semi-yieldable category/segment created for the customers with the highest value. With RM, the number of guests in this category will be significantly lower as frequent guests with a medium to low value would be classified according to demand. The chart on the previous page demonstrates the difference in segmentation criteria and rates the criteria according to RM requirements. It can be seen that some European revenue managers are not segmenting correctly for RM.

Conclusion

Hospitality organizations have experienced significant challenges over recent years. Service quality, empowerment of employees and green issues are subjects that occupy their management practices. One of the challenging issues, however, centres on the daily management of such operations in periods of a high and low demand. The reaction of employees to these difficult times (low occupancy) as well as the management of the organization in busy periods (high occupancy) is a matter of a great concern.

This chapter discussed the skills required for an effective hotel manager. The most important factor in RM is the variability of occupancy rates over a 12-month period. RM has its biggest impact (in terms of increasing revenue) on the high-demand nights, when most of the hotel's revenue is earned. In general RM needs, and should be applied whenever the demand exceeds the capacity. Yield strategies need to be applied on those days where there are not enough rooms to accommodate all the demand. This is the case for trade shows, specific holiday seasons and any special events that affect the occupancies at the hotels. Ideal RM periods may be very short such as the high season for a seasonal ski resort in the Alps but every hotel should have some of these days during a year.

It is important to note that RM does not create demand or set rates, but can improve the hotel's bottom line by reducing the uncertainty involved in the hotel business. The notion of uncertainty in terms of the market is far greater in smaller firms (Storey, 1994). Scarce resources may lead to limited market information and promotion resulting in hotels concentrating on one or two markets and thus running the risk of losing a large part of their business because of an inappropriate choice of target market. If RM can help to reduce this uncertainty, business performance can be improved.

Specifically, this research has uncovered the urgent need for simple, inexpensive, computerized systems for small- and medium-sized medium category hotels to enable them to collect the critical data required for optimal product management, segmentation, forecasting and overbooking.

Swiss hotel managers need a greater understanding of the impact of the unsold room on hotel profitability and need to monitor their rates with greater frequency by conducting a detailed and frequent analysis of competitor activity as well as the testing of rates/products via different distribution channels. This is a time-consuming process, currently something that managers of small- and medium-sized operations do not have to spare. The utilization of an RM system could free up some of their time currently spent on simple forecasting, giving the opportunity to spend more time on statistical analysis of their operation, a skill that needs to be enhanced in order to optimize revenue.

The basic knowledge required to effectively manage revenue is most suitable for hotels that sell out more than 20 room nights per year. A subject of further research could investigate whether this is the reason for their success or that success has motivated them to seek ways to further optimize their performance.

References

Arthur Andersen (1997) *Yield Management in Small and Medium-sized Enterprises: Executive Summary. European Commission.* Arthur Andersen Tourism Unit, Brussels.

Donaghy, K. (1999) *Yield Management: Profitability Managing Room Sales.* West Strand Enterprises, Northern Ireland, UK.

Donaghy, K., McMahon-Beattie, U. and McDowell, D. (1997) Yield management practices. In: Yeoman, I. and Ingold, A. (eds) *Yield Management, Strategies for the Service Industries.* Cassell, London, pp. 183–201.

Donaghy, K., McMahon-Beattie. U., Yeoman, I. and Ingold, A. (1998) The realism of yield management. *Progress in Tourism and Hospitality Research* 4, 187–195.

Institute for Public Services and Tourism at the University of St Gall (2001) *Key Data on the Traveling Behavior.* University of St Gall, Switzerland.

Kimes, S.E. (1989) The basics of yield management. *Cornell Hotel and Restaurant Administration Quarterly* 30(3), 14–19.

Kimes, S.E. and Chase R.B. (1998) Strategic levers of yield management. *Journal of Service Research* 1(2), 156–166.

Lieberman, W. (1993) Debunking the myths of yield management. *Cornell Hotel and Restaurant Administration Quarterly* 34(1), 34–41.

Storey, D.J. (1994) *Understanding the Small Business Sector.* Routledge, London.

Thomas, R. (2000) Small firms in the tourism industry. *International Journal of Tourism Research* 2, 345–353.

Varini, K. (2001) Revenue management in small and medium-sized hotels: what are the basic conditions needed to successfully apply this concept in Switzerland? *Hotel & Tourismus Revue*, 10 May.

Von Bahr-Lindmann, K. (2000) Revenue Managers: Key Technical Competencies. MARKETMIX at: www.yieldmgt.com/newsletter.html

WTO (World Trade Organization) (2001) *Communication from Switzerland.* Available at: www.wto.org

18 Service Management in a World Heritage Area – Tourists, Cultures and the Environment

Malcolm Cooper[1] and Patricia Erfurt[2]

[1]Ritsumeikan Asia Pacific University, Japan; [2]University of New England, Australia

Introduction

This chapter provides a case study of the critical issues and interrelationships inherent in the management of tourism and hospitality services within a World Heritage environment, with special reference to backpackers visiting Fraser Island, Queensland, Australia. The study of island ecotourism provides a significant focus for the discussion of service quality that is the rationale of this book, in that it is a branch of tourism that is concerned with visitors experiencing natural environments without threatening their viability (Buckley, 1994). One of the most critical aspects of this focus is the part visitor culture and their attitudes towards such environments play in the overall ability of ecosystem and resort managers to ensure effective environmental protection while maintaining tourist flows (BTR, 1998). As a location for a case study of these impacts Fraser Island is unique, in that not only it is Australia's World Heritage listed and largest island ecosystem but also one of its oldest Island resorts. Government, tour operators and resort owners have developed ecotourism strategies that have significant implications for the environment of the Island, but these depend on acceptance by the visitor for much of their efficacy.

It is not only the culture of visitors (including a significant number of backpackers) that has a significant bearing on the nature and success of these strategies, but also of the service providers that has a definite impact. To this end, the present study found that there is a very apparent dichotomy between strategy and practice in relation to environmental protection through ecotourism on the part of the managing authorities. Perhaps not surprising therefore is an apparent unwillingness on the part of some visitors to conform to modes of behaviour that the management strategy espouses but that actual practice does not seem to enforce. So much so that, from the point of view of visitors the Queensland Parks and Wildlife Service (QPWS – management of the Island environment) appears to see visitors to the Island as a revenue-raising opportunity, rather than as groups who may be more able than most to understand the requirements of tourism in a fragile environment. Additionally, resort managers and transport operators are bound by permit regulations set by the QPWS, but can only oversee actual visitor activities where they are in close proximity to the tourist (as in tour groups). As a result there is a big gap in surveillance of actual behaviour with respect to most visitors.

The visitors also contribute to the problems of management, in that their culture of seeking low-cost access, their unregulated movement and activities and a certain disregard of the requirements of the management of tourism on the Island, make it difficult for service providers to ensure that a quality experience is delivered while ensuring that the environment (the tourism resource) is safeguarded. Consequently, some aspects of the environmental management of Fraser Island are made more difficult, and certainly the visitors do not gain a lot out of the ecotourism aspects of their experiences.

This case study goes some way towards meeting an urgent need for better understanding of tourism industry performance at the local and regional level in conditions of reduced local operator control over service outcomes. In order to provide data, local tourism operator and visitor surveys from the period 1998–2001 were reanalysed in order to gain a reliable indication of the issues associated with service quality relating to attractions visited on the Island, the attitudes towards that environment as expressed by backpackers and other tourists and the attitudes towards the tourist as expressed by QPWS personnel. These data are discussed below.

Service Management and the Ecotourist

Service management is the core focus of this book but it is not the function of this chapter to dissect its various ramifications. However, it is necessary at this point to provide a discussion of how service management and service quality are affected by the culture of visitors in general terms, before illustrating their interaction in this particular geographical area.

Service quality is the outcome of travel suppliers' activities and the judgement of tourists of their actual experiences (Laws, 2001). It comprises two fundamental components: (i) technical quality ('what' is delivered); and (ii) functional quality ('how' it is delivered), with an important subsidiary component, that of the deliverer's image (Gronroos, 1988). Within this framework quality means the totality of the attributes (and attribute values) of a service that have a bearing on its suitability for satisfying given needs and wants. These vary depending on the aspirations of the target group. Quality is therefore interpreted as meaning the perceived or experienced condition of a product, service or organizational outcome measured against the requirements of the target groups it is intended for.

Previous writers have noted that how a service or product is perceived will depend on two key factors: its stimulus of the consumer, and the consumer's own personal and group characteristics (personal history, culture, socio-economic status – Laws, 1986; Wilkie, 1986; Ziethmal et al., 1988; Harington and Lenehan, 1996). Throughout the literature on customer satisfaction, the issue of which external stimulus consumers choose to operate on, and which of their personal and/or group characteristics comes into play in the intermediation processes that they engage in has been a major preoccupation of researchers. In summary, it is generally accepted that consumers reach a judgement about the quality of a service or product actually experienced by measuring that against their perceptions of how that service should be.

To be able to deliver on the promise of environmental management through quality services to tourists in an island setting of the type represented by Fraser Island then will be dependent on the objective facts of those services (incidence, duration, method of delivery, rules of engagement, quality of information and/or physical presentation), and on the personal characteristics of visitors. Effective management of the tourism and environmental product of the island depends upon striking the right balance between service quality and environmental protection. It is to this requirement that we now turn.

Fraser Island Ecotourism: a Case Study

Fraser Island ecotourism falls within the trend to new forms of tourism that offer specialized products to smaller, segmented niche markets (Oppermann and Chon, 1997; Weaver, 1998). These include greater involvement with host communities, sustainable products with a strong emphasis on environment, culture and education and visitor experiences that are personalized, specialized, interactive, meaningful and flexible (Orams, 1995; Cooper, 2001). Within this, changing tourist attitudes have recently given rise to an increasing demand for environmental education, ecotourism and other nature-based opportunities (Oppermann, 1994). This has been especially important amongst backpackers, one of the major groups of Fraser Island tourists (Cooper et al., 2001).

The Australian Conservation Foundation (ACF), in its Tourism Policy (ACF, 1994), specified six characteristics that it considered essential to ecotourism:

1. Visitation to enjoy nature, wildlife, culture and archaeology.
2. A high degree of interpretation.
3. High quality, low-impact design in all infrastructure.
4. Promotion of conservation knowledge and ethics.
5. The provision of net benefits to environmental protection.
6. The provision of net benefits to indigenous communities and other affected communities.

These defining characteristics broadly follow the minimalist impact definition of ecotourism (Whelan, 1991; Figgis, 1993; Weiler, 1993), with the addition of environmental education and cultural appreciation (Ceballos-Lascurain, 1987; Hall, 1994), and have been adopted in the main by responsible Australian State and National Government agencies in specifying appropriate ecotourism *strategies*. According to Buckley (1994), however, *in practice* both the tourism industry and the government agencies have been inclined to focus on the product side and to treat ecotourism as identical to observing nature, rather than as a means of educating visitors about that environment or actively protecting it.

By doing this, it is possible to promote more intensive visitation in national parks, for example, by giving the 'being in nature' (e.g. camping) experience a veneer of respectability as ecotourism (Jenkins and McArthur, 1996). The tourists feel actively part of environmental protection without actually having to do something, and this enables them to suspend disbelief at increasing numbers of fellow visitors and

a lack of real engagement with the ecosystem being observed (Wheeller, 1993). But as Pearce and Moscardo (1985) pointed out, using the attraction of nature-based tourism as a justification for increasing visitor numbers, without appropriate planning and the matching of particular types of visitors with particular environments, can put at risk the very attractions that are supposed to benefit from this 'low impact' form of tourism.

As a result, the 'reality' of the ecotourism experience is largely of the presentation of natural attractions as a means of selling a tourism *product* rather than of ensuring sustainable impact on the environment from tourism. In this frame, the dominant marketing images are of pristine destinations rather than a more sophisticated account of the ecotourism experience that includes minimal-impact behaviour (Jenkins and McArthur, 1996). The central theme of this chapter is that this is in fact what has happened on Fraser Island, especially with respect to 'Backpacker' tourism. Backpackers and other groups of 4-Wheel Drive (4WD) tourists actually consume the environment rather than protect it. A result, the QPWS is faced with considerable environmental pressure from the very visitors who might have been expected to be predisposed towards environmental protection. Support for the strength of this assertion is to be found in the results of surveys of backpacker visitors to Fraser Island carried out by both the department and the private operators, as reported below.

Fraser Island: a description

Over 120 km long and an average of 15 km wide, Fraser Island is the largest sand island in the world. It is remarkable for its 90 km long surf beach, its chain of unique perched lakes, its vast sand-blows and unique vegetation. There is prolific wildlife, mostly nocturnal, with the local wild dog (dingo) considered to be the most pure strain in Australia. A unique species of tortoise can be found in many of the freshwater lakes. Access to Fraser Island is via vehicular barge, aircraft, cruise vessels, private boats or on commercial tours. Roads on the

Island are mainly sandy tracks, many of which may only be negotiated by 4WD vehicles.

Fraser Island is part of an area known as The Great Sandy Region of Queensland. In terms of naturalness, this region ranks higher than other comparable areas in Queensland (DoEH, 1998). Much of the Great Sandy Region is World Heritage Area and Fraser Island is also a National Park. These natural attributes and World Heritage listing have attracted domestic and international visitors in increasing numbers. Some of them seek uncontrolled access while others seek a high level of comfort.

Fraser Island visitor surveys: exposing a dichotomy between service culture and actual impact on the environment

The following comments were derived from surveys carried out by the QPWS and the City of Hervey Bay Tourism and Development Board, during the period 1998–2001. The objectives of these surveys were:

1. To identify where and how visitors acquire information about the recreational opportunities on and the environment of Fraser Island and what they did with it.
2. To ascertain how the National Parks and Wildlife appear to expect visitors to act within that environment, and the level of service to be supplied.
3. To identify the level of awareness of the importance of the Fraser Island environment amongst visitors, and the factors that might impinge upon this awareness.

The methodology and results of the individual surveys have been reported on elsewhere (Cooper, 2001; Cooper et al., 2001) and need not be repeated here. Approximately 800 visitors were contacted during the 4 years of the surveys (a survey was not conducted in 2002). Each respondent was asked to comment on several aspects of their experience; ranging from sources of information about Fraser Island, through their length of stay in Australia, to the type of experience they had on Fraser Island, and how they interpreted the need to protect the World Heritage environment that

they found themselves in. The ecotour company Top Tours, along with other similar companies, also conducts surveys of visitors. These surveys are carried out on a regular basis as a check on the content and acceptability of their tours, including the effectiveness of pre-tour information sessions and the quality of service provided. The following discussion summarizes the results of all these surveys with respect to service quality on the Island.

Table 18.1 summarizes the general characteristics of the respondents. No attempt has been made to differentiate the results by year. There was a strong bias in the data towards youth (majority being under 25), gender (59% female to 41% male) and European respondents (88%), these being characteristic of backpackers to the Island. With respect to Hervey Bay, some 1 million visitors are accommodated each year, and of these, over 120,000 were backpackers in 2001.

Table 18.1 also suggests that overseas tourists tend to visit Fraser Island fairly early in their stay in Australia, and indicates that Fraser Island is very high on a tourist's list of possible Australian destinations either before or shortly after arrival. There is therefore at least sufficient information getting through to visitors to alert them to the desirability of visiting the Island, if not to its environmental fragility.

The surveys identified that the major reasons for choosing to visit Fraser Island were environmental in nature (Table 18.2 – on average 64% of total visitors), being a mixture of undifferentiated 'environment', 'sand island/National Park' and a 'different' experience (which involved in the most part the type of natural experience not found in their home environments). Subsidiary reasons such as 'word-of-mouth' (WOM) propaganda may also have contained an environmental message important in persuading respondents to visit the Island. A significant minority of 14% of the respondents explicitly chose the Island to indulge in 'sand driving', which suggests that their information about the Island included the knowledge that off-road driving was possible and indeed desirable as a past-time.

The reasons why respondents chose 4WD camping tours as their preferred way of visiting Fraser Island are noted in Table 18.3. As might be expected the most important

Table 18.1. General characteristics of survey respondents.

Characteristic	No. of respondents	%
Gender		
Male	318	41.1
Female	457	58.9
Age		
<20	49	6.3
20–25	526	67.9
26–30	118	15.2
>30	69	8.9
No response	13	1.7
Country of origin		
Australia	28	3.6
New Zealand	7	0.9
USA/Canada	21	2.7
UK	395	50.9
Germany	104	13.4
Other Europe	180	23.2
Japan	21	2.7
Other Asia	7	0.9
No response	13	1.7
Median length of stay		
<1 month	21	2.7
1–3 months	298	38.4
4–6 months	76	9.8
7–12 months	288	37.5
>1 year	35	4.5
No response	55	7.1
Total respondents	775	100.0

Source: Cooper *et al.* (2001).

reasons were cost (25% of respondents), followed by freedom and flexibility to decide on the nature of the tour and stopping places (24.1%), acting on a recommendation as the best way to see the Island (15.2%) and the

Table 18.2. Reason for choosing to visit Fraser Island.

Reason	Frequency	%
Environment	208	26.8
Sand Island/ National Park	194	25.0
Sand driving	111	14.3
Word of mouth	105	13.5
New/different	104	13.4
No response	53	6.8
Total	775	100.0

Source: Cooper *et al.* (2001).

chance to have a significant group experience (13% – safety, size, etc.). Of minor importance was 'adventure', while the opinions of other backpackers, the need for a permit and the actual mode of transport (4WD) appeared to have little effect on the decision. Age of respondent plays a part in this though: with cost and the recommendations of peers being most important to younger respondents; freedom and flexibility being important across the board; and group experiences being relatively more important to older respondents.

Impact on the Island

On obtaining tours or barge permits, most visitors are given printed guides to the National Park. Presumably, the assumption is that they will then understand the nature of the Island's environment. No further information or training is given by QPWS, but backpackers do get short (25 min) 'dos and don'ts' video presentation about driving and camping on the Island at their hostel prior to the trip, and maps and park guides are made available to other visitors (Table 18.4). Table 18.5 reveals that few of the respondents actually read the QPWS guides made available to them on Fraser Island's ecosystem and how to behave within it, although some 70% indicated that they had received a copy. It would appear that these guides are certainly not read in their entirety, being either thought to be not applicable to the

Table 18.3. Reason for choosing off-road vehicle travelling on Fraser Island.

Reason	Frequency	%
Cost	194	25.0
Freedom and flexibility	187	24.1
Adventure	49	6.3
Group experience	104	13.4
4WD experience	21	2.7
Recommended as best	118	15.2
Flexibility	62	8.0
Other backpackers	28	3.6
No response	13	1.7
Total	775	100.0

Source: Cooper *et al.* (2001).

Table 18.4. Sources of information on Fraser Island.

Source	Sunmap (%)	Type supplied Park guide/itinerary (%)	Video/other (%)	None (%)
Hostel	5.0	–	90.0	5.0
Tour hire company	55.0	20.0	10.0	15.0
Permit centre	–	100.0	–	–
Other location	20.0	20.0	–	60.0

Source: Cooper *et al.* (2001).

particular situation (of 4WD) or thought to be not particularly useful when gaining actual information on the Island. This point is further explored.

Surprisingly, the surveys also showed that most accommodation houses do not provide detailed information on Fraser Island with the tours they book or recommend. Only 10% provided this service. Instead, visitors obtain their information about Fraser Island from permit providers (QPWS) as they land on the Island or from vehicle hire companies and from other miscellaneous sources. While a majority (55%) of vehicle hire companies gave out documentation such as the guides published by Sunmap (Queensland Government visitor maps with limited descriptions of attractions) or specific attraction itineraries for their vehicles (20%), these were considered to be too general by respondents.

In combination, therefore, most visitors receive at least a Park Guide/itinerary and a Sunmap product to use on their trip, but these do not include comprehensive information about the environment and how to minimize impact on it. QPWS rangers instead are placed

in a position of having to clean up after visitor use, rather than being employed to educate and control. Visitors, especially those in 4WD vehicles with difficulty but only sporadically, are made to adhere to environmental guidelines. The upshot of this is the record of vehicle accidents, sand dune degradation, littering and camp site destruction that gave rise to the attempt at understanding visitor impact embodied in the surveys undertaken by the Government (DoEH, 1998).

Respondents were also asked to rate the information and service received on a 5-point scale, ranging from very good to not graded. Table 18.6 details the results. It is obvious that respondents rated the generalized destination information service obtainable from tour companies and by WOM prior to their visit very highly, but the information on how to drive on the Island and the environmental impact information was rated less important. Indeed, the published park guides supplied to backpackers appear to be disregarded almost completely.

Table 18.5. Use of guides.

Guide	Respondents (%)
Supplied	
Yes	70.5
No	29.5
Read	
All	7.1
Part	24.1
None/not considered useful	60.8

Source: Cooper *et al.* (2001).

Controlling service quality in relation to the environment

There seems no doubt that the managers of the important Fraser Island environment will face increasing pressure from visitors for the foreseeable future. There also seems no doubt, from the information presented here, that visitors are in fact interested in the protection of the environment they have come to see. But, just at the point where they might become a useful resource with respect to environmental conservation many of them are let loose in off-

Table 18.6. Rating of information received.

Source	Level of satisfaction				
	Very good	Good	Satisfactory	Poor	Not graded
Hostel	5.0	20.0	45.0	15.0	15.0
Tour hire company	45.0	25.0	10.0	20.0	–
Permit centre	–	10.0	25.0	10.0	55.0
Park guide	5.0	10.0	20.0	–	65.0
Sunmap	45.0	25.0	10.0	5.0	15.0
Travel guides	30.0	25.0	20.0	15.0	10.0
Word of mouth	50.0	25.0	15.0	–	10.0

Source: Cooper *et al.* (2001).

road vehicles, without adequate education and control, to make their own way. Park guides to conservation and behaviour are essentially disregarded. Also, while camping grounds are marked on maps and visitors receive information about how to behave, they are not always well policed, leading to littering and other forms of environmental degradation.

Small wonder then that in this situation visitors to the Island take full advantage of the implied freedom and flexibility to indulge themselves. Impacts range from 'sand and bush bashing' to an almost complete disregard of environmental protection instructions (signage). In fact, it has been noted by Park Rangers that various groups have appeared to disregard signs just because they were in English and not in their native language, despite understanding the message!

This dichotomy essentially comes about because service providers are not in fact requiring visitors to take the task of environmental protection seriously. Quality of service with respect to the environment would dictate that this situation not to be allowed to occur, but the QPWS appears to be caught in a dilemma of its own making. The culture of 'sand and bush bashing' is allowed to continue, while the department makes considerable amounts of money from the sale of permits to visit the Island.

The local company Top Tours has long advocated controlled access to the environment through structured tours, and has found that there is in fact increasing demand for this solution to the above paradox. However, a more radical solution may be found in making

environmental protection the core of a visit to the Island, restricting 'sand bashing' and other recreational pursuits to very tightly controlled areas as a reward for success in a programme of rehabilitation. Quality assurance through restriction of allowable activities may seem draconian, but may just be the only safe path to maintaining services, and indeed access to the environments the visitor has come to experience. The practice of enrolling visitors as volunteers in environmental rehabilitation and education programmes is not new in Europe and the USA, and should therefore be somewhat familiar to the majority of visitors to the Island.

The propensity for backpackers at least to act on WOM suggestions from their peers and acquaintances could assist in this change of approach by Park Managers. The key would be to excite sufficient numbers of visitors to see the experience of being actively involved in rehabilitating and conserving a World Heritage value environment as an important part of the desired level of service in relation to the visit. An on-site education campaign, plus documents to sign up to before obtaining a permit, plus appropriate entries in guidebooks such as Lonely Planet, plus advance notice in the hostels on the Australian backpacking circuit, would fit with the way in which many visitors access and process information, while appealing to their wish to be involved in a more effective way.

Visitor programmes such as that being advocated here have the advantage that reducing environmental impact is forcefully pointed out to the visitor as a condition of their permit to land. Training in acceptable methods of waste disposal, in the conditions for driving and camping, and information on how to respect approved sites for recreation/camping would form part of that permit. While there would need to be spot-checks by rangers, this would be no more onerous for departmental resources than the current system of clean-up after the event. Of direct benefit to environmental managers, however, would be the possibility of active environmental rehabilitation. Visitor 'volunteers' made responsible for the revegetation and/or clean-up of a particular area as a condition of entry could gain both environmental 'credits' (which might be recognized in some way in relation to the cost of permits) and worldwide recognition for their efforts through appropriate publicity.

Conclusion

This discussion has identified that there is a lack of enforcement of minimal impact practices for backpackers travelling to Fraser Island. Travellers appear to be perceived as short-term visitors on a recreational day pass, and inherent in this perception (of revenue) is an ambivalence that remains tolerant to independent and often uncontrolled access to fragile areas. What is needed is a strategic approach to service quality that targets the needs of visitors and encourages them to adopt minimal impact practices. To achieve the level of service quality that truly incorporates willing visitor participation requires reinventing ecotourism on Fraser Island so

that it incorporates environmental rehabilitation. Ecotourism operators such as Top Tours have long advocated controlled access through structured tours, and are finding that there is increasing demand for this product. For the independent visitor, service providers should be required to further restrict independent access to 4WD vehicles on sand dunes and/or the QPWS should allow more access to ecotourism operators that place minimal impact, rehabilitation and protection works in the heart of their product.

This chapter has discussed the effect of the failure to insist on truly effective service quality with respect to the environment by the managers of the Fraser Island World Heritage Area which, when coupled with a laissez-faire culture towards the environment on the part of visitors, has resulted in considerable management problems in the Park. For the Park authorities service quality must be two-way, and incorporate adherence to their own set standards just as much as the persuasion of clients (visitors) to do the right thing by the environment. As a possible solution, it is recognized that visitors from Europe and the USA are generally familiar with volunteer-based rehabilitation programmes, and those run in Australia by organizations such as the Australian Trust for Conservation Volunteers are finding that international tourists are becoming their main market. These products could easily be accommodated within the time frames of most visitors, and could considerably reduce the dichotomy between expressed service and actual service to the Fraser Island environment.

References

Australian Conservation Foundation (ACF) (1994) *Tourism Policy*. ACF, Sydney.

Buckley, R. (1994) A framework for ecotourism. *Annals of Tourism Research* 21(3), 661–669.

Ceballos-Lascurain, H. (1987) The future of ecotourism. *The Mexico Journal* (January), 13–14.

Cooper, M. (2001) Backpackers to Fraser Island, why is ecotourism a neglected aspect of their experience? *Journal of Quality Assurance in Hospitality & Tourism* 1(4), 45–59.

Cooper, M., Abubakar, B. and Rauchhaupt, P. (2001) Eco-tourism development into the new millennium on Fraser island: tour operator's perspectives. *Tourism* 49(4), 359–367.

Department of Environment & Heritage Queensland (DOEH) (1998) *Final Report of the Review of Tourism Activities in the Great Sandy Region*. DoEH, Brisbane.

Figgis, P.J. (1993) Eco-tourism: special interest or major direction? *Habitat* 21(1), 8–11.

Gronroos, C. (1988) Service quality: the six criteria of good perceived service quality. *Review of Business* 9, 10–13.

Hall, C.M. (1994) Ecotourism in Australia, New Zealand and the South Pacific: appropriate tourism or a new form of ecological imperialism? In: Cater, E. and Lowman, G. (eds) *Ecotourism: A Sustainable Option?* John Wiley & Sons, Chichester, UK, pp. 137–157.

Harington, D. and Lenehan, T. (1996) *Managing Quality in Tourism*. Oak Tree Press, Dublin, UK.

Jenkins, O. and McArthur, S. (1996) Marketing protected areas. *Australian Parks and Recreation* 32(4), 10–17.

Laws, E. (1986) Identifying and managing the consumerist gap. *Service Industries Journal* 6(2), 131–143.

Laws, E. (2001) Distribution channel analysis for leisure travel. In: Buhalis, D. and Laws, E. (eds) *Tourism Distribution Channels*. Continuum, London, pp. 53–72.

Oppermann, M. (1994) Regional aspects of tourism in New Zealand. *Regional Studies* 28, 155–167.

Oppermann, M. and Chon, K.-S. (1997) *Tourism in Developing Countries*. International Thompson Business Press, London.

Orams, M.B. (1995) Towards a more desirable form of ecotourism. *Tourism Management* 16, 3–8.

Pearce, P. and Moscardo, G. (1985) Conservation and the tourism justification. *Habitat* 13(3), 34–35.

Weaver, D. (1998) Deliberate ecotourism in the South Pacific. *Pacific Tourism Review* 2(1), 53–66.

Weiler, B. (1993) Guest editor's introduction. *Tourism Management* 14(2), 83–84.

Wheeller, B. (1993) Sustaining the ego. *Journal of Sustainable Tourism* 1(2), 121–129.

Whelan, T. (1991) Ecotourism and its role in sustainable development. In: Whelan, T. (ed.) *Nature Tourism: Managing for the Environment*. Island Press, Washington, DC, pp. 3–22.

Wilkie, W.L. (1986) *Consumer Behaviour*. John Wiley & Sons, New York.

Ziethmal, V.A., Berry, L.A. and Parasuraman, L.A. (1988) Communication and control processes in the delivery of service quality. *Journal of Marketing* 52(April), 35–48.

19 The Relationship Between Airline Cabin Service and National Culture: A Cabin Crew Perspective

Bruce Prideaux[1] and Seongseop Kim[2]

[1]James Cook University, Australia; [2]Sejong University, South Korea

This chapter examines aspects of service quality from the perspective of cabin crew's need to be aware of cross-cultural differences that may be encountered in the airline cabin service environment of international airline operations. In the competitive international aviation environment, inflight service standards are an important element of an airline's ability to gain and retain customers. Recognizing that cross-cultural differences exist and instituting strategies to meet customer's specific cultural requirements in areas such as food and beverage service is an important issue for airline planners. However, airlines have to balance passenger's expectations of high levels of inflight service and any specific cultural requirements they may have with the demand by the same passengers for low airfares, particularly those travelling in economy class. To achieve an acceptable level of service against the often conflicting personal needs of passengers as well as the need for airlines to contain costs, airlines utilize a range of strategies based on the standard of food and beverage service, provision of inflight entertainment, cabin furnishings, availability of amenities during flights and the standard of service offered by cabin crews. By their nature services such as food and beverage service, provision of inflight entertainment, cabin furnishings and availability of amenities during flights constitute the hardware

of service because of the fixed and preplanned nature of this category of service. The standard of service offered by cabin crews constitutes the software side of cabin service. However, the delivery of inflight service by flight attendants is limited by the service hardware provided by the airline often leaving attendants with little scope to meet particular passenger needs once a flight has commenced. It is against these predetermined service standards that flight attendants must attempt to meet passenger's service expectations.

During flights, the cabin crew is responsible for caring passenger's safety and comfort and duties include a range of obvious activities such as food and beverage service and other less-obvious duties ranging from assisting in medical emergencies to responding to persons or incidents that may affect the safety of the aircraft and its passengers. In any typical flight it can be expected that the cabin crew will have to attend to passengers from a range of cultural backgrounds and perform their role in a manner that is culturally sensitive. Yet in many nations, the concept of a national culture based on a common ethnicity or religious affiliation is changing rapidly. Many European nations as well as the USA, Canada and Australia have a growing proportion of immigrants and as a consequence passengers' ethnicity may not be a good guide to passengers' nationality or culture. However, passenger expectations of service standards and their personal patterns of behaviour may exhibit a cultural element that may lead to differing and at times possibly conflicting sets of expectations between passengers. In these circumstances flight attendants are required to demonstrate a high level of cultural awareness while refraining from placing their personal cultural interpretations on the actions of passengers.

In common with other businesses, airlines recognize that delivering quality service is an essential strategy for success and long-term survival in the contemporary business environment (Parasuraman et al., 1985; Reichheld and Sasser, 1990; Zeithaml et al., 1990; Laws and Ryan, 1992; Laws, 1997). Powell (1995), for example, has argued that service quality has emerged as an irrepressible, globally pervasive strategic force in recent decades while Ghobadian et al. (1994, p. 55) have stated that service quality is the major strategic variable in the battle for market share. To emphasize this point Ghobadian et al. (1994, p. 55) state that 'excellence of service is the critical corporate priority'. According to Zeithaml et al. (1996) managers must understand the impact that service quality has on corporate profits. While airlines have recognized this business imperative they also need to contain costs in a competitive international aviation environment while offering service that at least equals if not betters their competitors.

The importance of service is widely acknowledged (Laws, 1986, 2003; Zeithaml et al., 1990; Kandampully, 2002) but is not something that can be implemented easily and successfully without a great deal of planning and training. In the airline environment, the hard wiring of service is determined by a variety of factors including cost, length of journey, competition for other carriers on a particular route and the expectations of customers. Inflight entertainment must cater for a wide variety of tastes including children and adults thus limiting or requiring editing of the range of movies shown. Food service is another area that requires considerable planning. As airlines rarely carry extra meals, decisions on the mix of dishes available can be critical on flights

where there are passengers from a number of cultural backgrounds. Meeting passengers' expectations in what for some may be a stressful environment may be the difference between a pleasant travel experience and a poor travel experience.

Service is to some extent an intangible because expectations differ between individuals and what is acceptable to one person or even group based on cultural affinity may be unacceptable to other individuals and groups. In an airline setting, it is not always possible to anticipate the diversity of requirements although airlines do attempt to meet dietary requirements. Viewing an airline cabin from a host–guest perspective it is apparent that while the airline does have responsibility for attempting to provide service that meets some national culture requirements there should also be the expectation that passengers will recognize that they also have a responsibility to be respectful guests and not expect what cannot be sensibly provided. In an airline setting, passengers are able to purchase superior service by purchasing business or first class seats but this depends on the individual's ability to pay.

Zeithaml et al. (1990, p. 20) defined service quality as 'the extent of discrepancy between customers' expectations or desires and their perceptions'. This conceptualization is based on the expectancy/disconfirmation paradigm. Key expectancy disconfirmation is comprised of two processes: (i) formation of expectations; and (ii) disconfirmation of these expectations. Participant expectations serve as standards or reference points against which the service performances are judged. Hence, if the service performs as expected, the expectation is confirmed. Conversely, if the service performance is not as expected, then the expectation is disconfirmed. Measurement may be difficult where customers do not share a cultural homogeneity and expectations differ because of cultural differences. In some cases these difference may lead to incidents of air rage (Barron, 2002).

Culture can be viewed from three perspectives: (i) national culture, which may identify one national group from another; (ii) regional culture, which refers to the locality of upbringing (e.g. cities or farming communities); and (iii) personal culture, which is a reflection of the family and community values that an individual acquires as they develop from childhood to adulthood. National culture refers to cultural traits that differentiate the members of one nation from another and may include religion, language, dress, cuisine and customs. Thus national culture is a measure that allows others to identify a person as belonging to a particular national culture. In countries such as Korea, the USA, China and Australia, as in many countries, there are distinctive regional cultures that include city culture as well as rural area culture and while individuals raised in both settings share the same national culture they may view the world from different perspectives according to the region they live in. Individual culture embodies the national culture as well as habits, attitudes and perspectives that are moulded by the family and the community an individual is raised in. In a broad sense, culture may be described as the collective mental programming of people in an environment and everything that people have in common (Hofstede, 1980). It is possible to discern other aspects of culture aside from the geographical perspective outlined thus far. Master and Prideaux (2000) identified an ideological perspective that includes norms, values, beliefs and customs that underlie and govern conduct in a society as well as a material aspect that affects behaviours such as what to eat, where to travel, what to buy and how to behave while travelling. Irrespective of geographical location, members of society usually acquire culture during early childhood and as they grow the cultural environment in which they live is enriched and values and mores are reinforced through shared life experiences. Other factors that influenced the individual include their immediate and extended family structure, the social groups to which they belong and the professions they interact with.

Tourists bring with them their cultural values and behaviours and they may be identified according to national cultural values which are expressed as social behaviours, attitudes, perceptions, needs, expectations and experiences as well as their regional and personal values including beliefs, norms, motivations and verbal or non-verbal communication patterns (Burns and Holden, 1995; Fridgen, 1996). As a result, the behaviours and actions of tourists are influenced by the individual's national culture as well as regional and personal cultures. While it is often possible to group persons by their national cultures, it may be difficult to group them by their regional and personal cultures. Furthermore, the behaviours of individuals that are regarded as appropriate in one cultural setting may not be acceptable in another cultural setting (Pizam and Sussmann, 1995) leading to confusion for both hosts and guests. It is within this multi-layered dimension of culture that airline cabin crew must attempt to provide a high and consistent standard of service.

In an airline cabin, the cabin crew encounters passengers from a range of national cultures and an ability to understand cross-cultural differences in tourist behaviour or attitudes is of considerable importance. Research into cross-cultural issues has become recognized as an important field of study and a number of specific areas of research have emerged. One group of studies has compared tourists from different countries (Huang et al., 1996; Armstrong et al., 1997; March, 1997; Iverson, 1997; Sussmann and Rashcovsky, 1997; Thompson and Cutler, 1997; Kim and Lee, 2000), while a second group of studies has examined tourists of different nationalities from the viewpoint of service providers and guides (Pizam and Sussmann, 1995; Pizam and Jeong, 1996). A further group of studies have examined host–guest differences (Reisinger and Turner, 1997, 1998, 2002), while the final group of studies has analysed organizational behaviours in the specific areas of the tourism industry such as hospitality sector (Jansen-Verbeke and Stell, 1996; Gilbert and Tsao, 2000; Master and Prideaux, 2000). As a result of this research, a range of differences between tourists from various national groups have been identified leading to the development of strategies that have been suggested as tools to enhance tourist satisfaction. The research discussed in this chapter focuses primarily on how differences between national groups of airline passengers impact on the standard of service able to be offered by the cabin crew.

Research conducted in the past has identified significant differences between tourists based on nationality particularly in the areas of motivation and travel-related variables (see Huang *et al.*, 1996; Armstrong *et al.*, 1997; March, 1997; Iverson, 1997; Sussmann and Rashcovsky, 1997; Thompson and Cutler, 1997; Reisinger and Turner, 1998, 2002; Kim and Lee, 2000; Master and Prideaux, 2000; Kozak, 2001; Kim *et al.*, 2002). These and other studies have confirmed that it is useful to segment tourists by nationality and establishing specific marketing strategies for each national market. To date most of the studies cited were conducted in a Western setting and there remains a gap in the literature of studies in Asian and importantly in multinational settings that include both Western and Asian tourists.

To identify areas where national culture may effect the level of service able to be offered by cabin crew within the constraints of the cabin hardware that has been provided by the airline, the investigators selected Korean Airlines as a representative airline based on the fact that the airline employed Korean nationals as cabin crew on international services which carried a wide range of Asian and European passengers. The passenger mix was of particular interest as it included Asians who display wide differences in national culture as well as non-Asians. The researchers divided airline passengers into five major national cultural groups: Japanese, Korean, Chinese, American and South Asian (Malaysian, Philippines, Indonesian) while recognizing that there could be wide differences between regional and personal cultures within each group. These factors were discounted for the purposes of this research, as they required a level of investigation that was required to fulfil the aims of this research. Cabin crews operating international flights rather than domestic flights were selected for investigation because of their high level of exposure to the demands of passengers on international flights. The investigators selected a group of 15 items that reflect the behaviour patterns of airline passengers belonging to the five national groups and were developed from structured interviews with female and male cabin crew employed by Korean Airlines. Each of these employees had 3 or more years' service as international cabin crew, giving them considerable experience in observing cultural differences between passengers. To confirm the structure of the survey and

validate the cultural items to be surveyed, a pilot study was conducted on 20 international cabin crew. Several items were reworded as a result.

The survey was conducted by three interviewers, themselves Korean Airlines cabin crew, who distributed questionnaires to cabin crew who had at least 2 years' experience on international services. A response rate of 84.8% based on 250 surveys was achieved. Because of missing data 12 questionnaires were excluded.

A 7-point Likert-type scale [strongly disagree (1), neutral (4), strongly agree (7)] was employed to elicit respondents' views on their agreement–disagreement with statements describing passenger behaviour. Respondents were asked to indicate their views on the 15 items for each of the five national categories of passengers. The majority of respondents were female (72.2%), and most were members of either the under 30 (46.4%) or 30–39 (46.9%) age groups. The respondents were well educated with almost all having completed junior college, graduate school or university (94.3%). Over half of the respondents (55.4%) had 5+ years' experience working for Korean Airlines and most had experienced most of the 60 air routes operated by Korean Airlines.

A general linear model (GLM) with repeated measures was used to analyse the results that are displayed in Table 19.1. The GLM is a suitable method when the same individuals are measured two or more times for a series of continuous dependent variables (Tabachnick and Fidell, 1996). Each respondent in this study was measured five times on the same dependent variables. Significant differences were observed for all 15 items indicating a wide variety of responses that do not necessarily follow any pattern except to reflect the cultural behaviour of each national group for each item.

Results

The findings, illustrated in Table 19.1, indicate that there are significant differences in behaviour between the national groups confirming previous research (Rokeach, 1973; March, 1997; Kim and Prideaux, 2003). Based on these results, examples of which are highlighted

Table 19.1. Results of GLM (general linear model) with repeated measures for comparison of behaviours of airline passengers by cultural backgrounds (n = 200).

Behaviour	Five different national groups					Within-subject one-way ANOVA F-value	P-value
	Japanese	Korean	Chinese	American	South Asian		
1. Tend to be favourable to flight attendants	5.67	3.77	3.77	3.92	4.46	188.2	0.000
2. Tend to like reading books, magazines and newspapers	4.63	4.26	4.02	4.77	3.42	64.9	0.000
3. Tend to be noisy	2.82	4.93	5.47	3.01	3.80	389.8	0.000
4. Tend to stare at passengers or flight attendants	3.93	5.48	5.25	2.71	4.32	425.3	0.000
5. Tend to move to a vacant seat	2.98	5.76	4.85	3.51	3.61	399.2	0.000
6. Tend to ask for gifts provided by the airline company	2.37	4.45	4.42	3.85	3.84	100.7	0.000
7. Tend to follow the guidance of attendants	5.63	4.10	4.28	4.88	4.10	82.2	0.000
8. Tend to actively complain to flight attendants about inconvenience in a plane	3.74	4.80	4.59	5.39	3.04	220.0	0.000
9. Tend to show high expectations of service quality	3.67	5.10	4.55	4.16	4.04	103.1	0.000
10. Tend to like purchasing duty-free products	5.34	5.85	4.74	2.51	2.73	310.5	0.000
11. Tend to write a protest letter without any hesitation when unsatisfactory service is provided	2.30	3.87	3.70	4.96	2.22	51.8	0.000
12. Tend to not express direct dissatisfaction when unsatisfactory service is given	6.16	3.19	4.00	3.55	3.98	31.5	0.000
13. Tend to hinder work of flight attendants due to frequent demands	3.20	4.20	4.59	3.15	3.25	109.8	0.000
14. Tend to say 'thank you' or to express gestures of 'thank you' when help is offered by flight attendants	6.16	3.62	4.53	5.80	4.91	190.7	0.000
15. Tend to ask for more drinking water and food	2.00	4.25	4.55	4.05	3.85	234.5	0.000

Source: Kim and Prideaux (2003).

in the following discussion, it is possible to develop profiles of passengers according to their national culture with the proviso that national culture is only part of a mosaic of cultural attributes that each person exhibits, the others including regional and personal culture as well as ideological and material perspectives of culture. Results do indicate specific patterns of service expectations in aspects such as duty-free purchases, expectations of the availability of inflight reading materials and requests for additional food and beverages. Knowledge of the types of services likely to be requested allows airlines to anticipate these requirements and build these into destination-specific service standards perhaps on a route-by-route basis.

It is apparent that on flights to and from Japan there will be considerable behavioural differences between Korean and Japanese passengers that may lead to a level of discomfort for each respective group. Thus while Korean passengers tend to be noisy and not follow directions of cabin crew, Japanese passengers are more likely to be quiet and respectful. On flights to China, cabin crew can expect both Chinese and Korean passengers to be noisy, stare at other passengers and complain to cabin crew.

Moreover, if the flight has a number of American passengers, cabin crew can expect these passengers to require reading matter, be relatively quiet, keep to themselves and follow the directions of cabin crew. They are also more likely to complain about poor service by writing a letter but also express their thanks for service that is given by cabin crew.

Respondents reported that Japanese passengers were more likely to treat attendants with respect, while Chinese, Korean and to a slightly smaller extent US passengers were less likely to respect attendants. American followed

by Japanese and Korean passengers indicated a preference for reading material. From an airline perspective, this may be expensive to offer because of the need to carry a range of magazines in different languages although the variety and quantity required will be dictated by the particular countries serviced on each flight. In respect to in-cabin behaviour Koreans and Chinese were more likely to move to a vacant seat than other nationalities and were the least likely to follow the guidance of cabin crew, and were more likely to ask for gifts provided by the airlines company. Japanese passengers on the other hand were the least likely to ask for gifts and were more likely to follow the directions of cabin crew than Koreans, South Asians and Chinese, with obvious implications during emergency situations.

This research highlights the types of problems that cabin crew face daily in the discharge of their duties. Competitive pressures ensure that airlines are very conscious of the need to balance passenger's desire for comfort and quality service with the same passenger's demand for airline seats that are as low-cost as possible. As a consequence, some of the trade-offs taken may reduce the overall level of passenger satisfaction with the service hardware of the airline cabin. It is the cabin crew who must work within these constraints to make each passenger's trip as pleasant as possible. Knowledge of the potential cross-cultural dimensions of passengers based on their national culture is an essential part of the job of cabin crew, particularly when each flight will be unique in the composition of passengers carried. This knowledge, either acquired on-the-job or through formal training, is an important aid to enhancing passenger service standards despite the fixed constraints of the cabin hardware.

References

Armstrong, R.W., Mok, C., Go, F.M. and Chan, A. (1997) The importance of cross-cultural expectations in the measurement of service quality perceptions in the hotel industry. *International Journal of Hospitality Management* 16(2), 181–190.

Barron, P. (2002) Air rage: an emerging challenge for the airline industry. *Asia Pacific Journal of Transport* 4, 39–44.

Burns, P.M. and Holden, A. (1995) *Tourism: A New Perspective.* Prentice-Hall, Englewood Cliffs, New Jersey.

Fridgen, J.D. (1996) *Dimensions of Tourism.* AHMA, East Lansing, Michigan.

Ghobadian, A., Speller, S. and Jones, M. (1994) Service quality concepts and models. *International Journal of Quality & Reliability Management* 11(1), 43–66.

Gilbert, D. and Tsao, J. (2000) Exploring Chinese cultural influences and hospitality marketing relationships. *International Journal of Contemporary Hospitality Management* 12(1), 45–53.

Hofstede, G. (1980) *Culture's Consequences: International Differences in Work-Related Values.* Sage Publications, Beverly Hills, California.

Huang, J.-H., Huang, C.-T. and Wu, S. (1996) National character and response to unsatisfactory hotel service. *International Journal of Management* 15(3), 229–243.

Iverson, T.J. (1997) Decision timing: a comparison of Korean and Japanese travellers. *International Journal of Hospitality Management* 16(2), 209–219.

Jansen-Verbeke, M. and Stell, L. (1996) Cross-cultural differences in the practices of hotel managers: a study of Dutch and Belgian hotel managers. *Tourism Management* 15, 544–548.

Kandampully, J. (2002) Innovation as the core competency of a service organization: the role of technology, knowledge and networks. *European Journal of Innovation Management* 5(1), 18–26.

Kim, C. and Lee, S. (2000) Understanding the cultural differences in tourist motivation between Anglo-American and Japanese tourists. *Journal of Travel and Tourism Marketing* 9(1/2), 153–170.

Kim, S.S. and Prideaux, B. (2003) A cross-cultural study of airline passengers. *Annals of Tourism Research* 30(2), 489–492.

Kim, S.S., Prideaux, B. and Kim, H. (2002) A cross-cultural study on casino guests as perceived by casino employees. *Tourism Management* 23, 511–520.

Kozak, M. (2001) Comparative assessment of tourist satisfaction with destinations across two nationalities. *Tourism Management* 22, 391–401.

Laws, E. (1986) Identifying and managing the consumerist gap. *Service Industries Journal* 6(2), 131–143.

Laws, E. (1997) *The Inclusive Holiday Industry, Relationships, Responsibility and Customer Satisfaction.* Thomson International Business Press, London.

Laws, E. (2003) *Improving Tourism and Hospitality Services.* Thomson Learning, London.

Laws, E. and Ryan, C. (1992) Service on flights, issues and analysis by use of diaries. *Journal of Travel and Tourism Marketing* 1(3), 61–72.

March, R. (1997) Diversity in Asian outbound travel industries: a comparison between Indonesia, Thailand, Taiwan, South Korea and Japan. *International Journal of Hospitality Management* 16(2), 231–238.

Master, H. and Prideaux, B. (2000) Culture and vacation satisfaction: a study of Taiwanese tourists in Southeast Queensland. *Tourism Management* 21, 445–449.

Parasuraman, A., Zeithaml, V. and Berry, L. (1985) A conceptual model of service quality and implications for future research. *Journal of Marketing* 49, 41–50.

Pizam, A. and Jeong, G. (1996) Cross-cultural tourists behavior. *Tourism Management* 17(4), 277–286.

Pizam, A. and Sussman, S. (1995) Does nationality affect tourist behavior? *Annals of Tourism Research* 22(4), 901–917.

Powell, T.C. (1995) Total quality management as competitive advantage: a review and empirical study. *Strategic Management Journal* 16, 15–37.

Reichheld, F. and Sasser, W. (1990) Zero defections: quality comes to services. *Harvard Business Review* 68, 105–111.

Reisinger, Y. and Turner, L. (1997) Cross-cultural differences in tourism: Indonesian tourists in Australia. *Tourism Management* 18(3), 139–147.

Reisinger, Y. and Turner, L. (1998) Cross-cultural differences in tourism: a strategy for tourism marketers. *Journal of Travel and Tourism Marketing* 7(4), 79–106.

Reisinger, Y. and Turner, L. (2002) Cultural differences between Australian tourist markets, Pt 1. *Journal of Travel Research* 40(3), 316–327.

Rokeach, M. (1973) *The Nature of Human Values.* Free Press, New York.

Sussmann, S. and Rashcovsky, C. (1997) A cross-cultural analysis of English and French Canadians' vacation travel patterns. *International Journal of Hospitality Management* 16(2), 191–208.

Tabachnick, B.G. and Fidell, L.S. (1996) *Using Multivariate Statistics,* 3rd edn. HarperCollins College Publishers, New York.

Thompson, C. and Cutler, E. (1997) The effect of nationality on tourist arts: the case of the Gambia, West Africa. *International Journal of Hospitality Management* 16(2), 225–229.

Zeithaml, V., Berry, L.L. and Parasuraman, A. (1990) *Delivering Quality Service: Balancing Customers Perceptions and Expectation.* The Free Press, New York.

Zeithaml, V., Berry, L.L. and Parasuraman, A. (1996) The behavioral consequences of service quality. *Journal of Marketing* 60, 31–46.

20 Considerations in Improving Tourism and Hospitality Service Systems

Eric Laws
James Cook University, Australia

Introduction

The market environment for tourism services is highly competitive and very dynamic. New destinations and new tourism products result in constantly expanding opportunities for travellers, and they come from new as well as established countries of origin. Established tourism enterprises and destination areas therefore face competition from a stream of new businesses, which are able to employ the latest advances in tourism management without the drag on innovation of existing resources and staff who are used to doing things a certain way. The response to competition, even for the most effective of established providers, must be constant efforts to improve existing services. Effective managers are always asking questions about what makes their service successful or unsuccessful.

This chapter focuses particular attention on the challenges of improving the interactive aspects of services, these are widely regarded as important for customers, staff and organizations, as the following quotation indicates:

The direct contacts between the customer and an employee of the service firm are referred to as the service encounters or moments of truth. These are natural opportunities emerging in the production/delivery process; for example, the interaction between a doctor and a patient, a bank manager and a client, a flight attendant and a passenger. Both the doctor, the bank manager and the flight attendant become part-time marketeers: the customer becomes a co-producer and a prosumer (the terms *pro*-ducer and con-*sumer* as suggested by Toffler, 1980). Looking at it from the opposite angle the term part-time employee can be used to signify the customer's role. If the customer does not cooperate ... the services cannot be properly produced and delivered.

(Gummesson, 1990)

Service Management

The delivery system specifies the service to be produced, but as Schmenner (1995, p. 19) points out, 'it needs to be synchronized with the service task and the service standards so that the service encounter (SE) remains a pleasurable one for all concerned'. George and Kelly (1983) have examined the sequence involved in the process of managing services, again emphasizing the central role of the encounters between staff and customers, as shown in Table 20.1.

Table 20.1. Steps in managing services.

1. Orchestrate the encounter.
   - Access, buyers' needs, expectations, knowledge of evaluative criteria
   - Process, technical expertise, manage interactions, elicit customer participation
   - Output, satisfying service purchase experience
2. Quality assessment using established expectations as the basis for judgement.
3. Educate buyers about the unique characteristics of the service.
4. Emphasize organizational image and communicate the image attributes of the firm and its service.
5. Encourage satisfied customers to communicate to others.
6. Recognize contact personnel's role.
7. Involve customers during the design process.

Source: George and Kelly (1983).

Staff Influence on Service Satisfaction

A frequent theme in services management literature is that service experiences are significantly influenced by the interactions between staff and customers. Managerial decisions about the characteristics of the services offered are dependent on the way individual employees interpret service design and performance criteria. Furthermore, service delivery entails interaction with the customer, and its quality therefore depends partly on gaining their cooperation. The view that service quality is produced in the interaction between a customer and elements in the service organization has been referred to as 'interactive quality' (Lehtinen and Lehtinen, 1982, cited in Ryan, 1995). However, quality derives not only from the interaction of customers with staff, but also the way that customers interact with each other. Familiar examples are the difficulty for the courier and the dissatisfaction which all other passengers experience when one client on a coach tour is consistently late in returning to the vehicle after sightseeing stops, or the group of people partying energetically in the hotel room next to yours.

A related problem is that customers' behaviour and perceived attitudes can please or distress staff. Supportive customer behaviour has been shown to correlate positively with job satisfaction and performance, whereas instrumental behaviour by passengers has negative outcomes for staff. Instrumental behaviour has been defined as 'telling staff how to perform their tasks'. Its dysfunctional results can be minimized by 'decoupling' the service, that is, by 'redesigning it to minimize encounters' (Bowen and Schneider, 1985, p. 133). However, this approach has been criticized as inappropriate in tourism because it reduces human interactions and responsiveness. Saleh and Ryan (1992) have emphasized the expressive nature of the delivery of the service, i.e. the ability to empathize with the customer as indicated by their term, 'the conviviality of the service'. Since customers have few ways to judge the quality of the service, interactions with staff are a primary factor in determining customer satisfaction (Bitner *et al.*, 1994).

Dyadic and Multiplex Service Interactions

Much of the service literature is concerned with an interaction in which one client is served by one contact person representing the company. Such analyses have traditionally been centred on dyadic interaction at the point of sale (Evans, 1963; Olshavsky, 1973). However, in tourism services the presence of other people is common, and sometimes become a significant factor in a client's experiences. Service transactions are performed in a public setting. Additionally, the service often affects more than one client, and they interact with each other. Table 20.2 identifies four types of interaction that can occur during service episodes.

Table 20.2. Interactions during services.

1. Service contact between staff and customers
2. Interaction between customers
3. Customer contacts with the firm's physical environment and resources
4. Customer interaction with the firm's processes and routines

Source: Bitner *et al.* (1990).

Taking the example of flights, during service delivery, cabin staff have a significant power differential over passengers based on their greater technical knowledge of the complex service delivery technology and their company's service design (or blueprint). This differential is further emphasized by the style differences between carriers, which means that passengers experienced on one airline, type of service or class may have misperceptions of another airline's practices. Furthermore, from the client's perspective, he or she is passing through a series of events that comprise the service, but each staff member provides a particular service on a repetitive basis. This point escalates in significance when routine service delivery is disrupted and passengers demand or expect particular responses to their own needs, or when they complain formally after such an occurrence.

Customer Participation in Services

A complicating factor is that customers have differing expectations of the service. 'Customer expectations and requests that exceed the firm's ability to perform account for 74% of the reported communications difficulties. This implies that ... even if the system is working at optimal efficiency, employees can expect to face a large number of communications difficulties' (Nyquist et al., 1985). The authors quoted above went on to identify nine service situations likely to cause problems for staff as shown in Table 20.3.

Table 20.3. Difficulties in dealing with customers.

1. Unreasonable demands
2. Demands against policy
3. Unacceptable treatment of employees
4. Drunkenness
5. Breaking social norms
6. Special needs customers – psychological, language or medical difficulties
7. Unavailable service
8. Unacceptably slow performance
9. Unacceptable service

Source: Nyquist et al. (1985).

The foregoing discussion has given additional emphasis to the role of contact staff in the satisfaction of clients. Complex service such as that provided during air travel or in a hotel is often designed to be delivered by teams of people with specialized skills such as check-in or inflight service. The service-management model proposed by George and Kelley (discussed above) therefore has to be enlarged to accommodate issues involved in the management of work teams, and their coordination. Many organizations have implemented programmes to help staff understand the ways in which their particular role contributes to the overall success of the enterprise. Lockwood et al. (1992, p. 328) have described how one hotel put on a programme called 'Together we care'. They comment wryly 'the company realized that, although together they might have cared, individually nobody gave a damn!' The significance of this has been underlined by Bitner et al. (1990, p. 71). 'Many times ... interaction is the service from the customer's point of view yet front-line employees are not trained to understand customers and do not have the freedom and discretion needed to relate to customers in ways that ensure effective service'.

Service Encounters

This emphasis on SEs reflects other writers' views. 'Since SEs are the consumer's main source of information for conclusions regarding quality and service differentiation, no marketeer can afford to leave the SE to chance' (Shostack, 1985). Similarly, Adams (1976) commented 'employees of service organizations are often as close to their customers psychologically and physically as to other employees. They are the organization's most immediate interface with the customer.'

These interactive aspects of SEs are significant at a more fundamental level: interactions with other people are basic human activities, and occupy a large part of our time. Poor SEs affect the quality of everyday life and staff may spend their entire working day in repeated SEs.

Taken together, this discussion demonstrates that the nature of the service interface and the quality of contact between clients and staff can enhance or detract from:

- achieving customer satisfaction;
- achieving staff satisfaction;
- accomplishing the organization's mission.

From the perspective of competitive marketing, an improved understanding of customers' participation in service events yields insights on how to manage those services to their greater satisfaction. This may have two beneficial effects: (i) it is likely to promote customer loyalty by encouraging repeat purchases from satisfied customers; and (ii) it may contribute to more refined positioning through product adjustment, client awareness and advertising appeals.

Service management requires a dual focus, on the underlying technology and the human interactions required to deliver satisfactory experiences to clients. Many tourism services are technologically complex, and few customers are able to judge the technical quality of the service experience, but they do make assessments of the skills and attitudes of staff. This implies that service quality is difficult to manage and that the method common in manufacturing, that of prescribing specific product attributes, cannot work for tourism services. In common with other services, tourism is put to the test in the interaction between client and the staff providing each aspect of the service package, whether this is check-in at the airport, the hotel or excursions. At these times, clients match what they experience to the standards, which they expected to enjoy.

The level of analysis for marketeers should include the transaction between the company, its staff and the clients. Lalonde and Zinszer (1976) found an emphasis in the empirical literature on the significance of 'the buyer/seller interface'. Czepiel et al. (1985) used the term 'service encounter' for this interface. Table 20.4 lists seven points distinguishing SE roles from other interpersonal transactions.

The SE is a process of people doing things together, continuously interpreting the situation and adjusting to each other. Much of the interaction is however guided by rules, which are largely unrecognized until something goes

Table 20.4. Service encounters.

1. SEs are purposeful.
2. SEs work, recognized as such by both parties.
3. SEs are a special type of stranger relationship.
4. SEs are limited in scope: they are focused by and limited by the functional requirements to areas of legitimate enterprise.
5. Information exchanges in the SE are limited to task-related matters.
6. The roles of both the client and the service staff are well defined.
7. During the service there is a temporary status differential between the client and the server.

Source: Czepiel (1985).

wrong. In other words, to paraphrase Czepiel, staff and client join in a dyad for the express purpose of creating a service. In doing so they each adopt situation-specific roles and behaviour. The framework for these purposeful roles is provided by management decisions determining the service delivery system, it is this system that distinguishes the outcomes for consumers and staff of one organization's market offering from those of its competitors (Bettencourt, 1997). The lines of reasoning summarized above led Shostack (1985) to argue that:

- The encounter can be controlled.
- It can be enhanced.

Further Discussion

One strategy that managers often adopt in their search for consistent service is to minimize employee discretion and judgement whenever possible (Sasser et al., 1978). This approach works well in the manufacturing sector and is also quite effective for 'low contact' services (Chase, 1978). It relies on the specification of tasks to a standard of performance required by management, thereby providing a basis for measuring the effectiveness of staff performing tasks. Increased standardization implies a reduction in the discretion allowed to individual employees; however, this contradicts service-sector clients' normal expectations of being treated as individuals, with needs which differ from those of other clients, and which may vary during the many events of which a service is composed. Efficiency goals may have the benefit of efficient use of resources and clarification of performance targets for staff, but the resultant mechanical style of service can conflict with the customers' expectations of warm and friendly service. Underlying this discussion are the twin assumptions that consumers experience a service as a series of events, while managers see the service as a set of elements that require skilled coordination and resource control, in delivering specified standards to clients.

The service performance is experiential, and as it involves the way in which a customer participates, he or she has the potential to help or hinder the process. The view that service quality is produced in the interaction between a customer and elements in the service organization has been referred to as 'interactive quality'. Supportive customer behaviour has been shown to correlate positively with job satisfaction and performance, whereas instrumental behaviour by customers has negative outcomes for staff.

The Servuction Approach

There is often more to the ways in which tourists 'participate' in the services they purchase than a passive acquiescence in the service delivery system, or an occasional dispute with staff or managers when some error occurs. The point at which a customer interacts with the organization has been recognized as a major organizational design variable (Chase and Tansik, 1983). Part of the problem is that services are delivered by people to other people, and this makes the staff – their appearance, attitudes, competencies and behaviour towards the customer, towards each other and towards their employer, a significant factor in the service experienced by a customer (Shostack, 1985). A major factor is that task uncertainty is greater when staff work in direct contact with clients. The interaction creates uncertainty for service employees primarily because clients' behaviour cannot be accurately predicted, yet staff have to communicate and interact with customers in performing their work. Similarly, Weitz (1981)

demonstrated that sales representatives who modify their approach contingent upon customers' behaviour are more effective. But in services the significance of effective interactions goes beyond delivery; it seems that the ability of workers to notice and understand customers' desires and respond to them appropriately is crucial (Solomon et al., 1982).

The term servuction has been coined for the involvement of customers in the production of service. 'Servuction refers to the production and delivery of services – the word is easily recognized as analogous to production. The word emphasizes an essential fact: 'services are different from products and should not be forced to borrow terminology from manufacturing' (Gummesson, 1990, p. 97). The real difference is the fact that the customer is involved in servuction process, therefore the 'service provider has less control over the environment and the behaviour of the actors'. He asks how the quality of cars would be affected if customers were allowed to wander around the factory. 'In participating in the servuction the customer helps, or makes difficult, the process. Consequently, servuction quality is partly the result of interaction and joint efforts between the customer and the service provider; it is a result of the division of labour' (Gummesson, 1990, p. 97).

If any of the moments of truth fail, a consumerist gap (Laws, 1986, 2004) opens, causing dissatisfaction. The result of any customer dissatisfaction is twofold for the organization: the costs of complaint handling, and the potential loss of future business both from the distressed customers and from others to whom they voice their dissatisfaction (Fornell and Wernerfelt, 1987). Sternlicht (2002) described The Sheraton Promise, a compensation programme for guests at any Sheraton in the USA or Canada who complain about one or more of ten problems (see Table 20.5). A variety of levels of compensation are to be provided, following an apology. Staff participate in a role-play training session where they practice making an apology and offering compensation.

Management discovers its failure to provide satisfaction by two feedback mechanisms: exit and voice. Voice occurs when a consumer expresses dissatisfaction directly to the firm.

Table 20.5. The main complaints from hotel guests.

1. Wrong type of room
2. Room not cleaned properly
3. Uncomfortable bed
4. No wake up call
5. Slow service
6. Noise outside the hotel
7. Errors in the bill
8. Slow check-in
9. Reserved room not ready

Source: Sternlicht (2002).

Hirschman (1970) has classified customers as alert or inert. Alert customers exit when they experience dissatisfaction, inert customers voice, but may exit. Exit is a corrective market mechanism, which should affect the firm's decision making. Successful firms are sensitive to exit!

Many of the models of marketing behaviour include a feedback loop (or loops), a mechanism by which consumers are able to express their opinions of a current market offering. The function is to allow the producer to modify future output to obtain a closer match to their wishes. The complaining customer can be regarded as providing feedback that directly attempts to change the firm's policies or behaviour, or to obtain compensation. Voice is more desirable than exit!

Service Standards

Underlying the investigation of the meaning to customers of their experiences is a view that this is useful to managers in developing a competitive position, and then maintaining the advantages gained. In essence, this chapter argues that an understanding of customer perceptions of service delivery is a necessary but insufficient condition for satisfactory management of consumer experiences. Equally important (but a secondary focus here) is an understanding of the organizational and technical realities, which underlie the service design or blueprint. But the blueprint for service enactment is drawn up in the context of two constraints. The general technical and regulatory factors under which businesses operate are the first constraint. Next, the blueprint for two companies operating in similar circumstances will differ, reflecting the corporate mission statement and its senior managers' understanding of the contingencies and conditions of a particular period. Many organizations attempt to measure service quality, but 'they look primarily at the end results . . . and tend to neglect the service components contributing to those end results' (Senior and Akehurst, 1990, p. 7). Similarly, in their preface Czepiel and the co-editors of a study of service systems identified an overriding question for those who manage or research service industries. 'What makes a SE good–good for the employee, good for the customer and good for the firm?' (Czepiel et al., 1985).

Quality Audits

Another important approach is to audit service systems for quality. 'A quality audit is a systematic appraisal of service quality. It offers a quick and effective means of assessing service quality from the point of view of the customer. . . . Quality audits have often been conducted by in-house personnel, particularly in large organizations such as hotel chains. However, in-house auditors quickly become familiar with the service standards of their organization. They may take some aspects of the service for granted and will also tend to emphasize the aspects of quality, which management regard as important rather than those that are significant to the customer' (Johns and Clark, 1993, p. 360). These authors have developed a method of tracing the customer's service experience as a journey through a series of events. Discussing museum service auditing, they identify the features noted in Table 20.6.

Service Problem or Service Crisis

Dissatisfaction with some elements of a complex service is probably a common occurrence in the tourism industry. In most cases,

Table 20.6. Features of museum service quality.

1. Extensive movement of people
2. Unpredictable flow and demand patterns
3. A need to help customers make decisions about what they want to see and in what detail
4. A comparatively long journey time during which services such as food, drink and toilet facilities will probably be needed
5. Commercial opportunities

Source: Johns and Clark (1993).

a service problem is not immediately a service crisis, although it may escalate into one; Basil Fawlty knew intuitively how to exacerbate his clients' and staff's concerns.

There are three phases to dealing with service problems. The immediate challenge is to recognize that a problem has occurred. The response should be to remedy the defect promptly and without drama. A clean fork can easily be substituted for a dirty one. But the defect is a service problem too. This is addressed by waiters who respond to the client, perhaps spending extra time with them or by suggesting an addition to the meal ordered, and if they have the authority, on a complimentary basis. The third phase is normally the responsibility of managers rather than contact staff, although many are empowered to offer compensation such as an upgrade, a glass of cognac or a voucher discounting any future purchase. Beyond that, the organization can learn from the customer's experience.

Fornell and Wernerfelt (1987) reported that in over half the cases, which they investigated by following up written complaints, employees' responses to the situation had aggravated the complaint. This is significant because an even greater proportion of complainants reported that they would tell others about the events when their complaint was unresolved. However, in few cases was there a need for financial compensation – it was more likely that the complainant wanted better communications and a more pleasant response to his problem.

Lewis and Morris (1987) have distinguished between individual complaint handling, determined by the long-term value of future purchases of an individual complainant

and that person's word-of-mouth (WOM) impact upon other consumers, and aggregate complaint analysis, identifying and resolving common consumer problems thus avoiding their recurrence, and typically calling for a change in the firm's marketing mix.

One of the most significant supplier responses to consumer discontent has been the widespread establishment within firms of formal organizational structures for consumer affairs. Typically, consumer affairs departments seek to improve relations with the consuming public and to make firms more responsive to the needs and grievances of consumers. They have the potential to improve the satisfaction of consumers in the marketplace, and offer significant opportunities for improving marketing effectiveness by improving the company's knowledge of its customers' service experiences and expectations. A report for the US Commission of Consumer Affairs (TARP, 1979) showed that complaining customers exhibit stronger brand loyalty than customers who did not complain and that loyalty could be strengthened further by the firm's complaint handling.

However, reliance on customers' unsolicited comments is subject to limitations such as those identified by Lewis and Morris (1987). They pointed to differences in personal behavioural characteristics tending to make complaints more or less likely, and addressed the organizational consequences of customer complaints, suggesting that interdepartmental communications might be suppressed because of various behavioural barriers in particular organizations. In particular, the higher the rate of consumer complaints, the more isolated is the complaint handling function likely to become.

Complaints are not always directed formally to the organization supplying a service. Many customers, whether dissatisfied or pleased with a service, discuss their experiences with friends, relatives or colleagues. The commercial significance of WOM communications in social interactions is that dissatisfied customers are likely to tell many friends and business colleagues about their (perceived) bad experiences (Stafford, 1966). They may thereby influence their contacts away from that supplier. However, if the dissatisfied client can be persuaded to direct his or her complaint to the company, it then has a second chance to put matters right, and in addition to placating one customer (and his travelling party), may also gain favourable WOM recommendations amongst the passenger's circle of influence.

The value of complaints lies both in their power as a communications device and as a means of giving the firm a chance to turn a dissatisfied customer into a satisfied and loyal customer (Fornell, 1981). The foregoing analysis suggests that marketing oriented managers should encourage complaining behaviour; but the key to long-term benefits from the strategy lies in effective analytical techniques as a basis to their response strategies.

The Costs of Quality Control

Three sets of costs are involved in quality control systems, shown in Table 20.7. It is a managerial prerogative to decide which of these should be emphasized.

Profit Impacts of Service Quality Control Measures

There is no doubt that relative perceived quality and profitability are strongly related:

> Whether the profit measure is return on sales or return on investment, businesses with a superior product/service offering clearly outperform those with inferior quality.
> (Buzzell and Gale, 1987)

Hollins and Hollins (1991) have also advocated a process of continuous improvements, relying on a view which also underlies service

Table 20.7. Costs of quality management.

1. Failure costs – errors, correction, checking, dealing with customers complaints, the costs of getting it wrong.
2. Appraisal costs – checking, inspection, quality audits, checking that it is right.
3. Prevention costs – planning training, good procedures, getting it right first time.

Source: Lockyer and Oakland (1981).

blueprinting that the service is a chain of events which the customer experiences. They regard the stage of designing the service is its managers' main opportunity to determine the characteristics of the service offered to customers. Zeithaml et al. (1996, p. 31) report that many organizations 'have instituted measurement and management approaches to improve their service. ... the issue of highest priority today involves understanding the impact of service quality on profit and other financial outcomes of the organization'. However, 'the link between service quality and profits is neither straightforward nor clear'.

An organization incurs costs from any service failure, but implementing a quality control system also incurs costs. These costs result from actions taken to get a service right from the start, auditing that it is correctly delivered and the expenses of responding to any failure (Lockyer and Oakland, 1981). From a managerial perspective, the techniques used in service blueprinting and consumerist gap studies (Laws, 2004) can assist in locating problems with an existing service delivery system, and it can also be helpful in evaluating the benefits of alternative remedial actions. Apart from the physical or psychic consequences for customers and staff of unsatisfactory services, the costs include disturbance in the running of departments and a reduction in future sales levels, resulting from dissatisfaction. Further costs are incurred in implementing preventative measures to reduce future dissatisfaction, including the redesign of service delivery systems or training and motivational programmes for staff.

Anderson (1988) discussed the importance of informal communications between individuals concerning their evaluation of service experiences, in contrast to formal compliments. He considers that the individual's degree of satisfaction is generally regarded as the antecedent of their product-related comments to colleagues. He further notes that there is a general consensus that satisfied and loyal customers engage in comment, but also empirical evidence indicates that dissatisfied customers are more vocal still.

'When service failures occur, the organization's response has the potential to either restore customer satisfaction and reinforce customer loyalty or exacerbate the situation and drive customers to a competing firm' (Bateson, 2002, p. 65). Fisk *et al.* (1993, p. 75) regard service recovery, the actions the organization takes in response to a service failure, as a research area of great importance. 'The service recovery paradox predicts that a customer's cumulative satisfaction with a service organization ... will increase when he or she is very satisfied with the organization's handling of a service failure.'

First or Second Generation Service Thinking

There is a general consensus in the research community that tourism services are complex, and that any aspect can contribute to the success or failure of a service. Despite this, many studies and management actions are hindered by inappropriate ways of thinking about services, and their complex nature. The 'first generation' approach to services discussed by Normann (1991) persists, relying on experience transferred from the manufacturing sector where management decisions about design and manufacturing control usually result in logically predictable outcomes. The weakness in the management and analysis of service organizations arises from themes in economic theory that rely on mathematical analysis of a set of forces tending to stability and equilibrium, in contrast to the heterogeneous, dynamic forces tending to greater diversity and increasing complexity in the market place (Gleick, 1987; Faulkner and Russell, 1997). These are inadequate to either describe or analyse tourism service quality issues fully, and imply that flexible, innovative management approaches are needed.

Marketing insights and methods play a central role in setting organizational resources to work towards achieving predetermined targets of turnover, growth, volume of business and so on. Organizational targets and the steps to reach them are usually specified in a business plan that shows how the organization intends to satisfy its objectives. These may be set out in a formal statement of its mission, the way in which it relates to society and reflect intelligence about emerging trends in the company's environment, and a detailed understanding of the company's own operational strengths.

Mattsson (1985) distinguished two types of relationship essential to a firm's success. Vertical relationships describe the relation between a firm and its customers. Horizontal relations exist between a firm and others supplying it. Porter (1985) stressed the importance of sound industry relationships. Buhalis and Laws (2001) have edited a collection of studies examining key aspects of channel management in the tourism and hospitality industry. More recently, research has focused on the special management characteristics of service organizations, particularly SEs, service design, service quality and customer satisfaction, internal marketing and relationship marketing. Together, they represent a new approach to management, which Gummesson (1990) argued is sufficiently different from earlier approaches to merit recognition as a paradigm shift.

A great deal of managerial effort is directed towards achieving improvements in the efficiency and effectiveness of organizations. It was noted earlier that one of the distinguishing characteristics of services is their dependence on direct contact between staff and clients in the delivery of the service. In contrast, the manufacturing of most products occurs 'offstage', remote from the view of customers. Although managers may wish to specify precise standards for their services, just as a production manager in a factory setting would be expected to, in reality each service transaction is itself a variable and the quality of the service is dependent on the interaction between staff and client in the context of the physical setting and the technical features of the service delivery system designed by its managers. Furthermore, the quality of the service provided is judged by each client. This is the basis for second generation service thinking, which emphasizes both that the organization should be designed around good service delivery and that its management should be constantly focused on quality issues, designing the system from that perspective.

An additional factor in many services is that the variety of tasks involved calls for a team-based approach. Consequently, it has been pointed out that 'team work is the focus of service quality programmes in several firms known for their outstanding customer service' (Garvin, 1988). Wisner (1999) studied transportation quality improvement programmes, and placed importance on finding the root causes of quality problems, employee empowerment and setting quality goals and standards. He showed that it is effective for managers to involve and support employees in a continuous improvement process and to stress the importance of role behaviours that allow the programmes to succeed. Wisner also noted a strong correlation between quality programmes and performance elements such as customer service, on-time deliveries, competitiveness, customer complaints, future growth expectations, employee productivity and sales.

Conclusion

The author's view is that interaction, consumer satisfaction, the design of the service and the way it is presented are components of the distinction customers make between one company and its competitors. The conclusion to draw from the preceding discussion is not that managers should maximize contact points, increase complexity or invest in the most luxurious service settings. Rather, deliberate decisions should be taken on each of these aspects to create a service balance which is appealing to target customers and which can be delivered by a particular organization reliably and profitably.

Once a service has been designed, managers face the challenges of ensuring that it is delivered to clients in a consistent way which yet recognizes their individual needs and concerns, but also can respond to service problems. By examining the factors influencing customers' changing satisfaction, another measure of the effectiveness of any quality control systems in place can be activated; and the benefits of additional quality control systems can be assessed. The appropriateness of the technical design of delivery systems can also be explored (as shown in Laws, 2004), and taken together with an understanding of the meaning to customers of their service experiences, this is helpful to managers seeking to develop a competitive position, then maintain the advantages gained.

References

Adams, J.S. (1976) The structure and dynamics of behaviour in organizational boundary roles. In: Dunette, M.D. (ed.) *Handbook of Industrial and Organizational Psychology*. Rand McNally, Chicago, Illinois.

Anderson, E. (1988) Customer satisfaction and word of mouth. *Journal of Service Research* 1(1), 5–17.

Bateson, J. (2002) Consumer performance and quality in services. *Managing Service Quality* 12(4), 206–209.

Bettencourt, L. (1997) Customer voluntary performance: customers as partners in service delivery. *Journal of Retailing* 73(3), 383–406.

Bitner, M.J., Booms, B.H. and Tetreault, M.S. (1990) The service encounter: diagnosing favorable and unfavorable incidents. *Journal of Marketing* 54(January), 71–84.

Bitner, M.I., Booms, B.H. and Mohr, L. (1994) Critical service encounters: the employees point of view. *Journal of Marketing* 58(4), 95–106.

Bowen, D.E. and Schneider, B. (1985) Boundary spanning role employees and the service encounter: some guidelines for management and research. In: Czepiel, J.A., Soloman, M.R. and Surprenant, C.F. (eds) *The Service Encounter, Managing Employee/Customer Interaction in Service Business*. Lexington Books, Lexington, Massachusetts, pp. 125–148.

Buhalis, D. and Laws, E. (eds) (2001) *Tourism Distribution Channels: Practices, Issues and Transformations*. Continuum, London.

Buzzell, R.D. and Gale, B.T. (1987) *The PIMS Principles*. Free Press, New York.

Chase, R.B. (1978) Where does the customer fit in a service organization? *Harvard Business Review* (November–December), 137–142.

Chase, R.B. and Tansik, D.A. (1983) The customer contact model for organizational design. *Management Science* 49, 1037–1050.

Czepiel, J.A., Soloman, M.R. and Surprenant, C.F. (eds) (1985) *The Service Encounter*. Lexington Books, Lexington, Massachusetts.

Evans, F.B. (1963) Selling as a dyadic relationship. *American Behavioural Scientist*, May, 76–79.

Faulkner, H.W. and Russell, R. (1997) Chaos and complexity in tourism: in search of a new perspective. *Pacific Tourism Review* 1(2), 93–102.

Fisk, R., Brown, S. and Bitner, M.I. (1993) Tracking the evolution of services marketing literature. *Journal of Retailing* 69(1), 61–91.

Fornell, C. (1981) Increasing the organizational influence of corporate consumer affairs departments. *Journal of Consumer Affairs* 15(Winter), 191–213.

Fornell, C. and Wernerfelt, B. (1987) Defensive marketing strategy by customer complaint management: a theoretical analysis. *Journal of Marketing Research*, 24(November), 337–346.

Garvin, D.A. (1988) *Managing Quality, the Strategic and Competitive Edge*. Free Press, New York.

George, W.R. and Kelly, T. (1983) *Personal Selling of Services: Emerging Perspectives on Service Marketing*. AMA, Chicago, Illinois.

Gleick, J. (1987) *Chaos*. Sphere Books, London.

Gummesson, E. (1990) Service design. *The Total Quality Magazine* 2(2), 97–101.

Hirschmann, A.O. (1970) *Exit, Voice and Loyalty: Responses to Decline in Firms, Organizations and States*. Harvard University Press. Cambridge, Massachusetts.

Hollins, G. and Hollins, B. (1991) *Total Design, Managing the Design Process in the Service Sector*. Pitman, London.

Johns, N. and Clark, S.L. (1993) The quality audit: a means of monitoring the service provided by museums and galleries. *Journal of Museum Managership and Curatorship* 12, 360–366.

Lalonde, B.J. and Zinszer, P.H. (1976) *Customer Service: Meaning and Measurement*. NCPDM, Chicago, Illinois.

Laws, E. (1986) Identifying and managing the consumerist gap. *Service Industries Journal* 6(2), 131–143.

Laws, E. (2004) *Improving Tourism and Hospitality Services*. CAB International, Wallingford, UK.

Lewis, R.C. and Morris, S.V. (1987) The positive side of guest complaints. *Cornell Hotel and Restaurant Administration Quarterly* 27, 13–15.

Lockwood, A., Gummesson, E., Hubrecht, J. and Senior, M. (1992) Developing and maintaining a strategy for service quality. In: Teare, R. and Olsen, M. (eds) *International Hospitality Management*. Pitman, London.

Lockyer, K.G. and Oakland, J.S. (1981) How to sample success. *Management Today*, July.

Mattsson, L. (1985) An application of a network approach to marketing: defending and changing market positions. In: Dholakia, N. and Arndt, J. (eds) *Alternative Paradigms for Widening Market Theory*. JAI Press, Greenwich, Connecticut.

Normann, R. (1991) *Service Management: Strategy and Leadership in Service Businesses*. John Wiley & Sons, Chichester, UK.

Nyquist, J.D., Bitner, M.J. and Booms, B.H. (1985) Identifying communication difficulties in the service encounter: a critical incident approach. In: Czepiel, J.A., Soloman, M.R. and Surprenant, C.F. (eds) *The Service Encounter*. Lexington Books, Lexington, Massachusetts.

Olshavsky, R.W. (1973) Customer–salesman interaction in appliance retailing. *Journal of Marketing Research* 10(May), 208–212.

Porter, M. (1985) *Competitive Advantage*. Free Press/Macmillan, New York.

Ryan, C. (1995) *Researching Tourist Satisfaction*. Routledge, London.

Saleh, F. and Ryan, C. (1992) Conviviality: a source of satisfaction for hotel guests? An application of the SERVQUAL model. In: Johnson, P. and Thomas, B. (eds) *Choice and Demand in Tourism*. Mansell, London, pp. 107–122.

Sasser, E.W., Olsen, P.R. and Wycoff, D.D. (1978) *Management of Service Operations*. Allyn & Bacon, Boston, Massachusetts.

Schmenner, R. (1995) *Service Operations Management*. Prentice-Hall, Englewood Cliffs, New Jersey.

Senior, M. and Akehurst, G. (1992) The perceptual service blueprinting paradigm. *Proceedings of the Second QUIS Conference*. St Johns University, New York, pp. 177–192.

Shostack, L. (1985) Planning the service encounter. In: Czepiel, J.A., Soloman, M.R. and Surprenant, C.F. (eds) *The Service Encounter*. Lexington Books, Lexington, Massachusetts, pp. 243–253.

Solomon, M.R., Surprenant, C., Czepiel, J.A. and Gutman, E.G. (1982) *Service Encounters as Dyadic Interactions: A Role Theory Perspective*. Working Paper 82, New York University, New York.

Stafford, J.E. (1966) Effects of group influence on consumer brand preference. *Journal of Marketing Research* 3, 68–75.

Sternlicht, B. (2002) Hotels pay back. *Business Traveler*, November, 16.

TARP (Technical Assistance Research Programs) (1979). *Consumer Complaint Handling in America: Final Report*. Office of Consumer Affairs, Washington, DC.

Toffler, A. (1980) *The Third Wave*. Pan Books, London.

Weitz, B.A. (1981) Effective sales interactions: a contingency framework. *Journal of Marketing* 45, 185–195.

Wisner, J. (1999) A study of successful quality improvement programs in the transportation industry. *Benchmarking: an International Journal* 6(2), 147–163.

Zeithaml, V., Berry, L. and Parasuraman, A. (1996) The behavioural consequences of service quality. *Journal of Marketing* 60, 31–46.

21 The Role of Research in Improving Tourism and Hospitality Services: Measuring Service Quality

Simon Hudson,[1] Graham A. Miller[2] and Paul Hudson[3]
[1]University of Calgary, Canada; [2]University of Surrey, UK; [3]JMC Holidays, UK

Marketing Research in Tourism and Hospitality

Research in tourism and hospitality marketing has matured over the past few decades, fuelled by a proliferation of texts and journals specifically related to the subject. In a critique of marketing research theory and methodology in the tourism industry, Baker *et al.* (1994) suggest that the tourism industry is progressing through the stages of the management development process to a true marketing orientation. The most important point of this evolution of management orientation is that the true marketing orientation is the most efficient, and the marketing research process is the key to that efficiency. Marketing research is only an input to management decision making, not a substitute for it. Tourism managers who understand this point will better meet their customers' demands for goods and services and simultaneously use fewer resources to provide those goods and services. Good research is the key to good customer service. If the research is not effective, efficient or accountable, then the tourism management decision process is at best not supported and at worst erroneously influenced.

Just as Baker *et al.* (1994) have provided a critique of tourism research, Morrison (2002) recently reflected on hospitality research. Despite acknowledging that over recent decades hospitality research has made considerable advancements, he highlights a significant degree of debate concerning the definitional, philosophical and conceptual dimensions of hospitality. Morrison's conclusions call for definitional precision for hospitality; a clearly articulated research philosophy locating hospitality as a specialist field of study within the social science landscape; an enhanced degree of research philosophy awareness by researchers; and the benefits of formulating and agreeing an internally valid conceptual framework. He presents a preliminary attempt to conceptualize hospitality research at the start of the 21st century, conceived as a fourfold circular model (see Fig. 21.1).

According to McIntosh *et al.* (1995), there are six reasons to conduct tourism and hospitality research:

1. To identify, describe and solve problems in order to increase the efficiencies of day-to-day tourism operations.
2. To keep tourism and hospitality firms in touch with their markets in terms of trends, changes, predictions, etc.
3. To reduce the waste produced by tourists and tourist organizations.

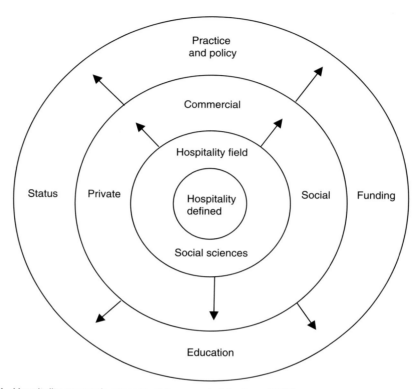

Fig. 21.1. Hospitality research conceptual framework (Morrison, 2002).

4. To develop new areas of profit in terms of finding new products, services, markets, etc.

5. To help promote sales in situations where research findings are of interest to the public.

6. To develop goodwill – the reason being that the public thinks well of firms that are doing research in order to meet consumers' needs better.

Unfortunately in tourism and hospitality, many smaller organizations feel that 'real' marketing research is a costly and time-consuming luxury only available to large companies with professional research staff, sophisticated computers and an almost unlimited budget. Other organizations see marketing research as something to be undertaken when a major event is about to occur – the introduction of a new product, the acquisition of a new property or a change in target markets. Its value then is recognized, but its ability to contribute to an organization's success on a day-to-day basis is often overlooked. Another common problem in the tourism industry is that organizations are not making full use of the information that already exists and is easily accessed. Sometimes information is available and studies are done, but the results are either ignored or not fully considered in the final decision-making process. It happens when the information is not in accord with the prevailing view of management or when the information has not been properly analysed and clearly presented.

Applied Research in Tourism and Hospitality

Most marketing research is classified as applied research, undertaken to answer specific questions. It differs from pure research (done by scientists at universities or by government authorities), which is aimed at the discovery of new information. Applied research in tourism and hospitality can be grouped into eight categories: (i) research on consumers; (ii) research on products and services; (iii) research on pricing; (iv) research on place and distribution; (v) research on promotion; (vi) research on competition; (vii) research on the operating environment; and (viii) research on a destination. Table 21.1 lists some of the typical research programmes undertaken within these categories.

This chapter focuses on the first category: research on consumers. The process by which customers evaluate a purchase, thereby deter-

Table 21.1. Applied research in tourism and hospitality.

1. Research on consumers.
- Identifying existing markets.
- Identifying potential markets.
- Identifying lapsed consumers.
- Identifying tourism constraints.
- Testing customer loyalty.
- Developing detailed consumer profiles.
- Identifying general trends in demographics and psychographics.
- Identifying changes in attitudes and behaviour patterns (generally).
- Identifying changes in attitudes and behaviour patterns (product-specific).
- Measuring consumer satisfaction.

2. Research on products and services.
- Measuring attitudes towards existing products or services.
- Identifying potential new products which may be at the end of their product life cycle.
- Identifying products that are considered acceptable substitutes/alternatives.
- Evaluating competitor's products.
- Evaluating consumer attitudes towards décor, presentation and packaging.
- Evaluating consumer attitudes about combinations of products and services (bundles of product attributes).

3. Research on pricing.
- Identifying attitudes towards prices.
- Testing attitudes towards packages and individual pricing.
- Identifying costs.
- Identifying costing policies of competitors.
- Testing alternative pricing strategies.
- Testing payment processes (credit cards, electronic funds transfer, etc.).
- Measuring willingness-to-pay.

4. Research on place and distribution.
- Identifying attitudes towards location.
- Identifying attitudes towards buildings/premises.
- Identifying attitudes on virtual sites.
- Identifying potential demand for product or services at other locations.
- Identifying cooperative opportunities for distribution of information or services.
- Identifying problems with the distribution system.

5. Research on promotion.
- Testing and comparing media options.
- Testing alternative messages.
- Testing competitor's messages and their effectiveness.
- Testing new communications options (Internet, e-mail, Web pages).
- Identifying cooperative opportunities.
- Measuring advertising and promotion effectiveness.

6. Research on competition.
- Measuring awareness.
- Measuring usage.
- Identifying levels of customer loyalty.
- Identifying competitors' strengths and weaknesses.
- Identifying marketing activities.
- Identifying specific competitive advantages (locations, suppliers, etc.).
- Identifying cooperative opportunities.

7. Research on the operating environment.
- Economic trends.
- Social trends.
- Environmental issues.
- Political climate and trends.
- Technological developments and their impact.

8. Research on a destination.
- Measuring residents' attitudes.
- Measuring relative competitiveness.
- Benchmarking.
- Measuring customer loyalty.
- Identifying tourism activities.
- Identifying spending patterns.
- Branding research.

mining satisfaction and likelihood of repurchase, is important to all marketers, but especially to services marketers because, unlike their manufacturing counterparts, they have fewer objective measures of quality by which to judge their production (Zeithaml et al., 1988; Brown and Swartz, 1989). The issue of measuring service quality has received increasing attention in recent years in the tourism and recreation literature (Crompton and Mackay, 1988; Crompton et al., 1991; Hamilton et al., 1991; Crompton and Love, 1995). However, to date only a few comprehensive attempts have been made to assess service quality in the tourism industry specifically (Chadee and Mattsson, 1996) and fewer still in tour operating (Hudson and Shephard, 1998). This chapter assesses the four main methods of measuring customer service quality, and then in a case study, compares these methods by measuring service quality for a medium-sized UK tour operator.

Measuring Service Quality

The two main research instruments that have been developed over the years to analyse the concepts of quality and consumer satisfaction in the service industry are: importance–performance analysis (IPA) and service quality (SERVQUAL). IPA is a procedure that shows the relative *importance* of various attributes and the *performance* of the firm, product or destination under study in providing these attributes. Its use has important marketing and management implications for decision makers, and one of the major benefits of using IPA is the identification of areas for service quality improvements. Results are displayed graphically on a two-dimensional grid; and by a simple visual analysis of this matrix, policymakers can identify areas where the resources and programmes need to be concentrated. Introduced over 20 years ago (Martilla and James, 1977), the use of IPA is well documented in the literature. Originally applied to the service department of an automobile dealer, the employment of this marketing technique has spread into various fields. It has been applied to the health care market (Cunningham and Gaeth, 1989),

dental practices (Nitse and Bush, 1993), banking services (Ennew et al., 1993), the hotel industry (Bush and Ortinau, 1986; Martin, 1995), adult education (Alberty and Mihalik, 1989), tourism policy (Evans and Chon, 1990) and tourist destinations (Hudson and Shephard, 1998).

Others have sought to modify or develop the technique. Easingwood and Arnott (1991) used a similar idea to present their survey-based study of generic priorities in services marketing. They employed two dimensions: (i) current effect on performance (similar to importance); and (ii) scope for improvement (related to performance). They also suggested an additional matrix of ease of change and sensitivity to change, to reflect the practicalities and constraints to improvement. Slack (1994) built on this idea by examining how the matrix could be modified to reflect managers perceived relationships between importance, performance and priority for improvement. Finally, in a study of health care services, Dolinsky (1991) extended IPA to include competitors' performance, concluding that inappropriate strategies may result if a competitive dimension is not included in the analysis.

The validity and reliability of IPA has been questioned (see Oh, 2001). The main limitations lie in the survey instrument itself. The Likert scale does not have the ability to distinguish between subtle differences in levels of importance and performance. It also does not take into account any relationship that might exist between the levels of importance and performance and the cost of that service. There are also problems associated with aggregating across all customers to generate measures of expectations and performance associated with either a single attribute or the overall service offering. In particular, it is possible that consumers who think that an attribute is important also perceive it to be poorly supplied, while those who think the same attribute is unimportant may perceive it to be well supplied. The comparison of means could reveal a close match on aggregated scores and yet there may still be a quality mismatch.

SERVQUAL is an instrument developed by Parasuraman et al. (1985), which focuses on the notion of perceived quality. It is based on the difference between consumers' expectations and perceptions of service. Exploratory research conducted in 1985 showed that consumers judge service quality by using the same general criteria, regardless of the type of service. Parasuraman *et al.* captured these criteria using a scale composed of 22 items designed to load on five dimensions reflecting service quality. The dimensions are: (i) assurance; (ii) empathy; (iii) reliability; (iv) responsiveness; and (v) tangibles. Each item is used twice: first, to determine customer's expectations about firms in general, within the service category being investigated; second, to measure perceptions of performance of a particular firm. These evaluations are collected using a 7-point Likert scale. According to the authors, the service quality is then the difference between customer's perceptions and expectations.

SERVQUAL is a concise scale, easy to use by managers, and is now referred to as a standard by other service researchers (Llosa *et al.*, 1998). The scale has been replicated in many different service categories so as to examine its generalizability. However, some of them show that conceptual and methodological problems exist regarding the measurement of perceived service quality and its true dimensionality. Cronin and Taylor (1994), for example, have argued that the mere fact of asking a respondent to mark his perceptions of performance already led him to compare mentally his perceptions and expectations. In other words, the estimation of perceptions might already include a perception minus expectation mental process. They suggest that just performance, or SERVPERF, is the measure that best explains total quality. Yuksel and Rimmington (1998) also suggest that performance is the only most reliable and valid measure of satisfaction. However, Parasuraman *et al.* (1993) answer these criticisms emphasizing that the critical indicator for a firm willing to improve its service quality is the amplitude and the direction of the gap between the expectation and the perceptions scores, not the perception itself. Tribe and Snaith (1997) also suggest that performance alone cannot give a full picture of satisfaction.

In its original form, the SERVQUAL instrument measured ideal expectations and perceptions. In response to certain criticisms regarding the measurement of expectations, a refined and more sensitive measure of expectations covering minimum and desired levels of service has been proposed by Parasuraman *et al.* (1994). However, Caruana *et al.* (2000) investigated the usefulness of the revised SERVQUAL instrument and concluded that the addition of minimum expectations has added little that is of incremental value to the measurement of service quality.

Other criticisms of SERVQUAL focus on the nature and number of dimensions. SERVQUAL replications, carried out in different service activities, show that the number of dimensions in the scale is not unique. For instance, Finn and Lamb (1991) found out that the dimensions change when customers estimate 'product' services (department stores) instead of 'pure' services (banks). The number of dimensions found in the different replications varies from three (McDougall and Levesque, 1992) to nine (Carman, 1990). Babakus and Mangold (1989) and Cronin and Taylor (1992, 1994) considered SERVQUAL as 'undimensionable' because they do not confirm the scale structure. Llosa *et al.* (1998) disagreed with the last criticism, but did find that the 22 items of the SERVQUAL scale do not clearly evoke, in respondents' minds, the five service quality dimensions. In fact, using a revised SERVQUAL scale, Parasuraman *et al.* (1994) moved away from their original five dimensions to three: reliability, tangibles and a single factor for responsiveness, assurance and empathy. More recently, Brady and Cronin (2001) found that the service quality construct conforms to the structure of a third-order factor model that ties service quality to distinct and actionable dimensions: outcome, interaction and environmental quality. In turn each has three subdimensions that define the basis of service quality dimensions.

A third major criticism of SERVQUAL is that information about importance is not gathered and integrated in the calculation of the quality score. Importance is recognized by many authors as relevant for the measuring of perceived service quality (Carman, 1990; Fick and Ritchie, 1991; Koelemeijer, 1991; McDougall and Levesque, 1992). However, the relative importance of each of the dimensions in contributing to overall quality of service is rarely addressed in SERVQUAL studies. Carman (1990) suggests that the original SERVQUAL model should have been expressed as:

$$Q = \sum Ii\ (Pi - Ei)\ \text{where } I \text{ is the importance}$$
$$\text{of service attribute } i$$

The equation shows that all three variables – importance, perceptions and expectations – are material and play different roles in evaluating overall quality. Thus, a user of these scales should collect information on all three variables, not just perceptions and expectations. This provides a clear list of priorities, ensuring service provider's focus on the most important aspects first. Following this procedure allows organizations to gain a comprehensive understanding of customer expectations, how the industry as a whole is performing against them, and what aspects of service are most important to the customers.

Attempts have been made to compare the relative predictive validity of these alternative measures for evaluating quality (Dorfman, 1979; Crompton and Love, 1995; Yuksel and Rimmington, 1998). In all three studies, the various methods (SERVQUAL, IPA, SERVPERF) were correlated with an overall measure of quality to find that measures of performance alone have higher predictive validity than do measures that incorporate expectations or preferences. They also found that the inclusion of importance weights did not improve the predictive validity of the measures. But the studies had limitations. The dependent variable itself was a performance-based measure and, as such, was more similar to the performance than to the disconfirmation measures. It is therefore not surprising that measures of performance had higher predictive validity than measures that incorporated expectations or preferences. In addition, all the studies asked respondents to comment on both importance and performance at the same time, whereas many believe that one interview should be conducted before the service experience, and another after the experience to avoid 'hindsight bias' (Weber, 1997; Llosa et al., 1998; Caruana et al., 2000).

Despite such attempts to find the 'right' measure for service quality, there still appears to be no consensus in either the leisure or the marketing literature on how evaluation of quality should be operationalized. Dorfman (1979) and Crompton and Love (1995) concluded that there is no single best way to measure recreational satisfaction acknowledging that the diagnostic potential of the SERVQUAL and IPA format has emerged as the primary rationale for preferring its use over the simple perceptions format.

Case Study: Measuring Service Quality in the Tour-operating Sector

In the tour-operating sector, customer research is still naive, with most tour operators relying upon traditional methods of customer feedback such as customer service questionnaires (CSQs) at the end of the holiday. Although such methods are important as they provide information about the customer's actual holiday experience, they are unable to provide a measure of their original expectations about their holiday. In fact, managers have revealed scepticism with regard to the precise usefulness of CSQs while nevertheless persisting with their use (Bowen, 2001). All major package holiday companies have spoken about the need to exceed customer expectations in order to deliver exceptional service. To do this successfully, they need to understand what customers expect from their holiday, rather than assuming that they already know it.

This study was an attempt to compare and contrast the various methods used to measure service quality by building on the literature reviewed above. Service quality and customer satisfaction for holidaymakers was measured using IPA and SERVQUAL. In addition, service quality was measured according to the formula recommended by previous service quality researchers (Carman, 1990; McDougall and Levesque, 1992; Martin, 1995; Heung et al., 2000), whereby the SERVQUAL gap between customers' expectations and perceptions is to be multiplied by how important customers rate each element of service. Finally, Cronin and Taylor (1994) suggest that just performance, or SERVPERF, is the measure that best explains total quality, so the results of performance only were analysed in order to compare with the other three formulas.

Based on the service quality models reviewed, a research programme was carried out in winter 1999/2000 for a medium-sized UK tour operator. The idea was to use the results to form an action plan of improvements for customers and allow the company to identify the key drivers of customer satisfaction. The aims were as follows:

- Understand what consumers expect from each individual aspect of their holidays.
- Understand what aspects are important to them.
- To examine each aspect of service delivery and identify the service quality gaps.
- To compare the different methodologies for calculating service quality.

Although most replications of SERVQUAL and IPA ask respondents to complete the survey in one interview, many authors recommend that one should conduct two interviews with a given respondent, one before the service experience and the other after the experience (Carman, 1990; Weber, 1997; Llosa et al., 1998; Caruana et al., 2000). So one month before they went on holiday, customers were asked to complete first the following questionnaire:

1. What is important to you? This asked respondents to rate on a 5-point Likert scale (ranging from extremely important to not at all important) 146 elements of their holiday. These elements represented the complete service delivery chain and included the usefulness of the brochure, getting to the airport, flights, representative, resort, accommodation and contacts with the tour operator at home.
2. What are your expectations? Respondents were then asked to rate on a 5-point Likert scale (ranging from definitely expected to definitely not expected) the same 146 elements of their holiday.

In a second questionnaire towards the end of their holiday, respondents were asked:

3. How did you find it? This questionnaire asked respondents to rate on a 5-point Likert scale (ranging from strongly agree to strongly disagree) the same elements of their holiday as measured in points 1 and 2 above.

The sample was drawn from the population of bookings taken for the upcoming winter season. A representative sample was chosen in terms of accommodation types and resorts in order to increase both the reliability and the validity of the research programme. Customers from all over the UK were asked in writing if they would like to participate in the panel and offered a £100 travellers cheque for participating. A total of 250 people were asked to participate in the study and the response rate was 88%. Because the scale dimensionality of SERVQUAL appears to have a weak standing and the five dimensions are not as distinct and independent as one would wish (Llosa et al., 1998), this study did not attempt to force the attributes into the five original SERVQUAL dimensions. Instead, the 146 elements were divided into 13 different dimensions reflecting various aspects of the holiday experience (see Table 21.2).

When the respondents had completed the questionnaires, a service quality score was calculated for each question, using the following four formulas:

1. Performance (P) minus Importance (I).
2. Performance (P) minus Expectations (E).
3. Performance (P) minus Expectations (E) multiplied by Importance (I).
4. Performance (P) only.

Results

Data were analysed using SPSS for Windows, and a service quality score was calculated for each dimension of the holiday experience. Table 21.2 compares the mean scores for expectations and performance (SERVQUAL), and the results clearly show a negative service gap in all dimensions. In fact, mean scores were significantly lower ($P < 0.05$) on performance for all dimensions except for the quality of the skiing and snowboarding.

According to the IPA (see Table 21.3), the mean scores for performance were all significantly lower ($P < 0.01$) than importance on all dimensions except for the company magazine. A two-dimensional action grid was plotted

Table 21.2. Comparisons between expectation and performance in holiday dimensions (SERVQUAL).

Dimensions of the holiday experience	Expectations		Performance		Pair-wise t-test	
	Mean	SD	Mean	SD	t-value	P-value
1. Brochure	4.254	0.438	3.742	0.575	−10.88	0.000
2. Waiting to go	4.144	0.427	3.640	0.715	−9.35	0.000
3. Journey	3.849	0.428	3.358	0.464	−12.20	0.000
4. Meeting the rep	4.082	0.515	3.894	0.811	−2.80	0.006
5. Transfer to accommodation	3.811	0.563	3.471	0.759	−4.93	0.000
6. Arrival at accommodation	3.767	0.521	3.582	0.871	−2.46	0.015
7. Accommodation	3.994	0.416	3.645	0.719	−5.86	0.000
8. Welcome	4.053	0.442	3.700	0.882	−4.95	0.000
9. Resort activities	4.009	0.472	3.634	0.600	−7.11	0.000
10. Skiing/snowboarding	4.230	0.493	4.208	0.538	−0.43	0.666
11. Company magazine	3.250	0.938	2.963	1.443	−2.38	0.018
12. Departure	3.954	0.484	3.784	0.830	−2.41	0.017
13. Transfer to airport	4.120	0.584	3.912	0.919	−2.59	0.011

(see Fig. 21.2), where importance values form the vertical axis while performance values form the horizontal axis. The literature on the use of IPA indicates that the selection of the crosshairs should consider management's goals for the study in question, and if possible, should force at least one attribute into each of the four quadrants (Martilla and James, 1977). However, few of the studies using IPA referred to earlier actually relate to this consideration, despite its importance. For this study, no attributes were forced into a quadrant, and the company was consulted on the position of the intersect on the action grid. Because managers were most interested in attributes that customers felt were important or extremely important, the value of 4 was chosen as the crosshair for the vertical axis. Also, placement of the crosshairs of performance at 4 reflected a desire to maintain or increase performance standards for the company. Company managers felt that any attributes perceived by

Table 21.3. Comparisons between importance and performance in holiday dimensions.

Dimensions of the holiday experience	Importance		Performance		Pair-wise t-test	
	Mean	SD	Mean	SD	t-value	P-value
1. Brochure	4.152	0.500	3.747	0.575	−8.63	0.000
2. Waiting to go	4.083	0.513	3.640	0.715	−7.49	0.000
3. Journey	3.919	0.477	3.358	0.464	−12.57	0.000
4. Meeting the rep	4.149	0.568	3.894	0.811	−3.53	0.001
5. Transfer to accommodation	4.004	0.534	3.471	0.759	−7.82	0.000
6. Arrival at accommodation	3.934	0.534	3.582	0.871	−4.88	0.000
7. Accommodation	4.038	0.437	3.645	0.719	−6.66	0.000
8. Welcome	3.941	0.541	3.700	0.882	−3.53	0.001
9. Resort activities	4.113	0.447	3.634	0.600	−9.69	0.000
10. Skiing/snowboarding	4.414	0.469	4.208	0.538	−4.77	0.000
11. Company magazine	3.083	1.069	2.963	1.443	−1.07	0.285
12. Departure	4.034	0.461	3.784	0.830	−3.82	0.000
13. Transfer to airport	4.371	0.479	3.912	0.919	−5.56	0.000

customers to be performing below good or excellent should be identified.

Figure 21.2 identifies where each of the 13 dimensions fall in terms of the four quadrants. According to the grid, only one of the dimensions – the quality of skiing and snowboarding – fell into the 'Keep Up The Good Work' area (quadrant B). Four dimensions fell within the 'Low Priority' (quadrant C) area. Holidaymakers rated these items low in performance but attached less importance to them. Significantly, the largest number of dimensions (eight) fell into the 'Concentrate Here' (quadrant A) area of the action grid. Respondents rated these attributes high in importance but low in performance. These dimensions were: the brochure; waiting to go; meeting the rep; transfer to accommodation; accommodation; resort activities; departure; and transfer to the airport.

A pair-wise t-test was conducted to measure the differences between SERVQUAL and IPA scores (see Table 21.4). There was a significant difference between 11 of the 13 dimensions ($P < 0.05$), and the IPA score was higher than the SERVQUAL gap for nine of the service quality dimensions. This was explained by the fact that importance scores were higher than expectation scores for these nine dimensions. This could be attributed to the fact that when respondents are directed to consider one attribute at a time, they are likely to inflate importance ratings of most attributes (Oh, 2001).

Service quality scores were then calculated using the formula suggested by Carman (1990) and others whereby the SERVQUAL gap is multiplied by importance. Finally, the results of performance only (SERVPERF) were analysed in order to compare with the other three formulas.

Table 21.5 indicates how each service quality dimension ranks according to the four models. It is interesting to note that factoring in importance actually makes little difference to the SERVQUAL rankings (the ranking of only four dimensions change), thereby adding little credence to Carman's formula referred to earlier. The results of calculating performance only (SERVPERF) appear to produce very different rankings to the IPA for the dimensions, most noticeably for the company magazine, which is ranked highest using IPA but lowest using SERVPERF. Similarly, SERVPERF and

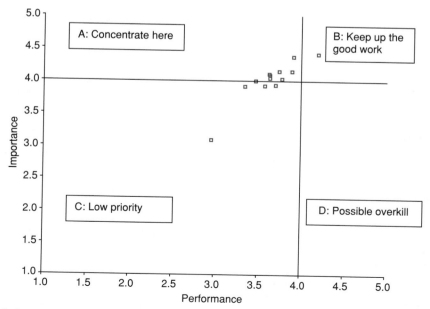

Fig. 21.2. Importance–performance grid with ratings for holiday dimensions.

Table 21.4. Comparisons between IPA and SERVQUAL.

Dimensions of the holiday experience	IPA gap		SERVQUAL gap		Pair-wise t-test	
	Mean	SD	Mean	SD	t-value	P-value
1. Brochure	−0.413	0.634	−0.507	0.617	2.64	0.009
2. Waiting to go	−0.442	0.788	−0.504	0.716	1.66	0.099
3. Journey	−0.561	0.586	−0.491	0.528	−1.83	0.069
4. Meeting the rep	−0.256	0.949	−0.188	0.883	−1.46	0.147
5. Transfer to accommodation	−0.533	0.879	−0.340	0.890	−3.64	0.000
6. Arrival at accommodation	−0.354	0.979	−0.185	1.001	−3.29	0.001
7. Accommodation	−0.393	0.802	−0.349	0.791	−1.27	0.207
8. Welcome	−0.245	0.953	−0.352	0.938	2.64	0.009
9. Resort activities	−0.485	0.675	−0.375	0.701	−2.96	0.003
10. Skiing/snowboarding	−0.214	0.587	−0.021	0.663	−4.89	0.000
11. Company magazine	−0.124	1.771	−0.286	1.585	2.13	0.035
12. Departure	−0.256	0.905	−0.170	0.930	−2.23	0.027
13. Transfer to airport	−0.455	0.982	−0.206	1.002	−5.12	0.000

SERVQUAL formulas produce differing ranks for the dimensions, although respondents show a reasonably high level of satisfaction with the overall level of performance (M = 3.65). Pearce (1991) and Hughes (1991) have argued that tourists may be satisfied even though their experiences did not fulfil their expectations. Yet, despite the many differences in rankings, the dimension skiing/snowboarding is ranked in the top two by all four tests, while the journey is ranked in the bottom three by all the tests.

As would be expected, SERVQUAL and IPA produced different rankings for the holiday dimensions. According to SERVQUAL, the largest gaps can be found in the brochure, waiting to go and the journey. Customers ranked the skiing, the departure arrangements and the arrival at accommodation as the top three in service quality. IPA on the other hand suggested that the biggest service quality problems were to be found in the journey, transfer to accommodation and resort activities, with the smallest gaps being for the magazine, the skiing and the welcome.

Expressing the data as four non-categorical, non-parametric, related groups allows Friedman's two-way ANOVA (ANalysis Of Variance between groups) test to be used to determine if there is any statistically significant difference between the four approaches to measuring satisfaction. Further, the data were

tested for internal reliability using Cronbach's alpha. The results report an alpha value of 0.8219, indicating a strong internal reliability, while the Friedman's two-way ANOVA test did not establish a significant difference between any of the four methodologies employed. In order to substantiate these findings, each methodology was individually compared with the other three, using the Wilcox Matched-Pairs Signed-Ranks Test. Once again, there was no significant statistical difference between any of the methodologies used for calculating service quality.

Implications

The findings here suggest that the service quality measurements of IPA, SERVQUAL and SERVPERF do not produce statistically different results, and that Carmen's formula for measuring service quality by factoring in importance requires more extensive field trials – an observation supported by others (Dorfman, 1979; Crompton and Love, 1995; Williams, 1998). Using SERVPERF alone does produce relatively high levels of satisfaction, but many researchers argue that performance ratings alone may not lead to the same practical applications as difference scores. For example, looking at the

Table 21.5. Ranking service quality dimensions according to the four models (1 = top service quality score; 13 = lowest service quality score).

Ranking	SERVQUAL (P–E)	IPA (P–I)	SERVQUAL × Importance (P–E)(I)	SERVPERF P only
1	Skiing/snowboarding	Company magazine	Skiing/snowboarding	Skiing/snowboarding
2	Departure	Skiing/snowboarding	Departure	Transfer to airport
3	Arrival at accommodation	Welcome	Arrival at accommodation	Meeting the rep
4	Meeting the rep	Meeting the rep	Transfer to airport	Departure
5	Transfer to airport	Departure	Meeting the rep	Brochure
6	Company magazine	Arrival at accommodation	Company magazine	Welcome
7	Transfer to accommodation	Accommodation	Transfer to accommodation	Waiting to go
8	Accommodation	Brochure	Welcome	Accommodation
9	Welcome	Transfer to airport	Accommodation	Resort activities
10	Resort activities	Waiting to go	Resort activities	Arrival at accommodation
11	Journey	Resort activities	Journey	Transfer to accommodation
12	Waiting to go	Transfer to accommodation	Waiting to go	Journey
13	Brochure	Journey	Brochure	Company magazine

SERVPERF scores in Table 21.5, the company magazine ranked last in terms of service quality, and would therefore warrant a commitment of resources to rectify the situation if SERVPERF was used in isolation. However, the IPA scores indicate that the company magazine was the least important variable as far as consumers were concerned, and it was clearly positioned in the 'Low Priority' quadrant in Fig. 21.2. This example highlights the diagnostic potential of using alternative measures to performance only.

Furthermore, despite the lack of a statistically significant difference between the methodologies, if the company used SERVQUAL only, they may commit resources to solving problems identified by IPA as 'Low Priority'. For example, the 'welcome' given in the resort produced a significant negative service gap according to SERVQUAL ($P < 0.001$), whereas IPA suggests that this factor is relatively unimportant to customers. Spending time and money on improving this factor may prove worthless.

But the results do not support the contention that practitioners should consider administering a range of instruments to measure service quality, rather than just one (Williams, 1998). Instead, one could argue that with no statistical difference between the tests, any can be used to measure satisfaction. Such a finding would enable managers to employ the most straightforward test of satisfaction, so there would be justification in measuring performance only. Performance bears a pre-eminent role in the formation of customer satisfaction because it is the main feature of the consumption experience. SERVPERF, therefore, would be a straightforward and convenient measurement to use in when time and cost are constrained. But although the perceptions format offers the most predictive power – a finding that has consistently emerged in the literature – it offers little diagnostic potential and, indeed, may result in inappropriate priorities being established (Childress and Crompton, 1997).

From a managerial perspective, it would seem important to track trends of the extent to which expectations are met over time as well as trends in performance. The use of difference scores gives managers a better understanding of whether increasing expectations or diminishing performance might be responsible for declining service quality and customer satisfaction. An examination of minimum expectations may also be fruitful. Similarly, disregarding importance may mean losing useful insights. Without considering attribute importance, one has no indication of the relative importance that respondents attach to particular aspects of service performance. In addition, the fact that IPA is easily interpreted by managers, could be of critical value for managers who do not use sophisticated software packages.

Despite the methodological implications, managers should be concerned that there were negative service quality gaps produced by the SERVQUAL or IPA instruments on all the dimensions measured. Several studies have examined the association between service quality and more specific behavioural intentions, and there is a positive and significant relationship between customers' perceptions of service quality and their willingness to recommend the company or destination (Zeithaml *et al.*, 1996). Likewise, research on service quality and retaining customers suggests that willingness to purchase again falls considerably, once services are rated below good (Gale, 1992).

As mentioned previously, all of the techniques used to measure service quality have limitations. Each methodology has its strengths and weaknesses, and, as Silverman (1993, p. 2) has suggested, methodologies 'cannot be true or false, only more or less useful'. But the results of the research are likely to support the contention that research can be made to provide evidence for either side of a debate. Thus a marketing manager could use SERVQUAL, IPA or SERVPERF to justify decisions according to his or her own preferences. Perhaps the flexibility of interpretation of these techniques is a strength that will encourage their further usage in the tourism industry amongst operators. The results of this research indicate that managers should have confidence in using any of the methodologies for measuring satisfaction. Yet, what is needed is further research to validate this finding, and the development of a clear body of research that identifies if any measure of customer satisfaction provides greater validity.

References

Alberty, S. and Mihalik, B.J. (1989) The use of importance–performance analysis as an evaluative technique in adult education. *Evaluation Review* 13(1), 33–44.

Babakus, E. and Mangold, W. (1989) Adapting SERVQUAL scale to health care environment: an empirical assessment. In: Bloom *et al.* (eds) *Enhancing Knowledge Development in Marketing*. American Marketing Association, Chicago, Illinois.

Baker, K., Hozier, G.C. Jr and Rogers, R.D. (1994) Marketing research theory and methodology and the tourism industry: a nontechnical discussion. *Journal of Travel Research* 32(3), 3–11.

Bowen, D. (2001) Research on tourist satisfaction and dissatisfaction: overcoming the limitations of a positivist and quantitative approach. *Journal of Vacation Marketing* 7(1), 31–40.

Brady, M.K. and Cronin, J.J. (2001) Some new thoughts on conceptualizing perceived service quality: a hierarchical approach. *Journal of Marketing* 65(3), 34–49.

Brown, S.W. and Swartz, T.A. (1989) A gap analysis of professional service quality. *Journal of Marketing* 53, 92–98.

Bush, R.P. and Ortinau, D.J. (1986) Discriminating first time and repeat patrons of a retail service hotel complex: a case study. In: King, R.L. (ed.) *Marketing in an Environment of Change*. Southern Marketing Association Proceedings, Atlanta, Georgia, 12–15 November, pp. 281–285.

Carman, J. (1990) Consumer perceptions of service quality: an assessment of the SERVQUAL dimensions. *Journal of Retailing* 66(1), 33–55.

Caruana, A., Ewing, M.T. and Ramaseshan, B. (2000) Assessment of the three-column format SERVQUAL: an experimental approach. *Journal of Business Research* 49, 57–65.

Chadee, D.D. and Mattsson, J. (1996) An empirical assessment of customer satisfaction in tourism. *The Service Industries Journal* 16(3), 305–320.

Childress, R.D. and Crompton, J. (1997) A comparison of alternative direct and discrepancy approaches to measuring quality of performance at a festival. *Journal of Travel Research* 36(2), 43–57.

Crompton, J. and Love, J.L. (1995) The predictive validity of alternative approaches to evaluating quality of a festival. *Journal of Travel Research* 34(1), 11–24.

Crompton, J. and MacKay, K.J. (1988) A conceptual model of consumer evaluation of recreation service quality. *Leisure Studies* 7, 41–49.

Crompton, J., MacKay, K.J. and Fesenmaier, D.R. (1991) Identifying dimensions of service quality in public recreation. *Journal of Park and Recreation Administration* 9, 15–27.

Cronin, J. and Taylor, S. (1992) Measuring service quality: a reexamination and extension. *Journal of Marketing* 56(3), 55–68.

Cronin, J. and Taylor, S. (1994) SERVPERF versus SERVQUAL: reconciling performance based and perception-minus-expectations measurement of service quality. *Journal of Marketing* 58(1), 125–131.

Cunningham, M.A. and Gaeth, G.J. (1989) Using importance–performance analysis to assess patients decisions to seek care in a dental school clinic. *Journal of Dental Education* 53(10), 584–586.

Dolinsky, A.L. (1991) Considering the competition in strategy development: an extension of importance–performance analysis. *Journal of Health Care Marketing* 11(1), 31–36.

Dorfman, P.W. (1979) Measurement and meaning of recreation satisfaction: a case study in camping. *Environment and Behavior* 11(4), 483–510.

Easingwood, C.J. and Arnott, D.C. (1991) Priorities in services marketing. *International Journal of Service Industry Management* 2(2), 59–75.

Ennew, C.T., Reed, G.V. and Binks, M.R. (1993) Importance–performance analysis and the measurement of service quality. *European Journal of Marketing* 27(2), 59–70.

Evans, M.R. and Chon, K. (1990) Formulating and evaluating tourism policy using importance–performance analysis. *Hospitality Education and Research Journal* 1, 203–213.

Fick, G.R. and Ritchie, J.R.B. (1991) Measuring service quality in the travel and tourism industry. *Journal of Travel Research* 30(2), 2–9.

Finn, D. and Lamb, C. (1991) An evaluation of the SERVQUAL scales in a retailing setting. *Advances in Consumer Research* 18, 483–490.

Gale, B. (1992) Monitoring customer satisfaction and market-perceived quality. *American Marketing Association Worth Repeating Series, No. 922CSO 1.* American Marketing Association, Chicago, Illinois.

Hamilton, J.A., Crompton, J. and More, T.A. (1991) Identifying dimensions of service quality in a park context. *Journal of Environmental Management* 32, 211–220.

Heung, V.C.S., Wong, M.Y. and Hailin, Q. (2000) Airport-restaurant service quality in Hong Kong: an application of SERVQUAL. *Cornell Hotel and Restaurant Administration Quarterly* 41(3), 86–97.

Hudson, S. and Shephard, G. (1998) Measuring service quality at tourist destinations: an application of importance–performance analysis to an Alpine ski resort. *Journal of Travel and Tourism Marketing* 7(3), 61–77.

Hughes, K. (1991) Tourist satisfaction: a guided tour in North Queensland. *Australian Psychologist* 26(3), 168.

Koelemeijer, K. (1991) Perceived customer service quality: issues on theory and management. *Sixth World Conference on Research in the Distributive Trades,* The Hague, The Netherlands, 4–5 July.

Llosa, S., Chandon, J.L. and Orsingher, C. (1998) An empirical study of SERVQUAL's dimensionality. *The Services Industries Journal* 18(2), 16–44.

Martilla, J.A. and James, J.C. (1977) Importance–performance analysis. *Journal of Marketing* 41(1), 13–17.

Martin, D.W. (1995) An importance/performance analysis of service providers. *Perception of Quality Service in the Hotel Industry* 3(1), 5–17.

McDougall, G. and Levesque, T. (1992) The measurement of service quality: some methodology issues. *2eme Seminaire International de Recherche en Management des Activites de Service.* l'Agelonde, France, pp. 411–430.

McIntosh, R.W., Goeldner, C.R. and Ritchie, J.R.B. (1995) *Tourism: Principles, Practices, Philosophies*, 7th edn. John Wiley & Sons, New York.

Morrison, A. (2002) Hospitality research: a pause for reflection. *International Journal of Tourism Research* 4, 161–169.

Nitse, P.S. and Bush, R.P. (1993) An examination of retail dental practices versus private dental practices using an importance–performance analysis. *Health Marketing Quarterly* 11(1/2), 207–221.

Oh, H. (2001) Revisiting importance–performance analysis. *Tourism Management* 22, 617–627.

Parasuraman, A., Zeithaml, V.A. and Berry, L.L. (1985) A conceptual model of service quality and its implications for future research. *Journal of Marketing* 49(4), 41–50.

Parasuraman, A., Zeithaml, V.A. and Berry, L.L. (1993) Research note: more on improving service quality measurement. *Journal of Retailing* 69(1), 140–147.

Parasuraman, A., Zeithaml, V.A. and Berry, L.L. (1994) Alternative scales for measuring service quality: a comparative assessment based on psychometric and diagnostic criteria. *Journal of Retailing* 70, 201–230.

Pearce, P.L. (1991) Introduction to tourist psychology. *Australian Psychologist* 26(3), 145–146.

Silverman, D. (1993) *Interpreting Qualitative Data – Methods for Analyzing, Talk, Text and Interaction.* Sage, London.

Slack, N. (1994) The importance–performance matrix as a determinant of improvement priority. *International Journal of Operations and Production Management* 14(5), 59–75.

Tribe, J. and Snaith, T. (1997) From SERVQUAL to HOLSTAT: holiday satisfaction in Varadero, Cuba. *Tourism Management* 19(1), 25–33.

Yuksel, A. and Rimmington, M. (1998) Customer-satisfaction measurement. *Cornell Hotel and Restaurant Administration Quarterly* 39(6), 60–71.

Weber, K. (1997) Assessment of tourist satisfaction using the expectancy disconfirmation theory: A study of the German travel market in Australia. *Pacific Tourism Review* 1, 35–45.

Williams, C. (1998) Is the SERVQUAL model an appropriate management tool for measuring service delivery quality in the UK leisure industry? *Managing Leisure* 3, 98–110.

Zeithaml, V.A., Berry, L.L. and Parasuraman, A. (1988) Communication and control processes in the delivery of service quality. *Journal of Marketing* 52, 35–48.

Zeithaml, V.A., Berry, L.L. and Parasuraman, A. (1996) The behavioral consequences of service quality. *Journal of Marketing* 60, 31–46.

22   Service Quality at the Cellar Door: A Lesson in Services Marketing from Western Australia's Wine-tourism Sector

Martin O'Neill[1*] and Steve Charters[2]

[1]Auburn University, Alabama, USA; [2]Edith Cowan University, Australia

Introduction

Wine tourism is now acknowledged as a growing area of special interest tourism in Australia, and is an increasingly significant component of the regional and rural tourism product of Western Australia. With its wide range of benefits including foreign-exchange earnings, the creation of both full- and part-time jobs and the generation of secondary economic activity, wine tourism is emerging as a very lucrative industry sector with the ability to generate and sustain substantial long-term wealth and growth. Not surprisingly, support for and investment in the wine-tourism sector is now regarded as an essential regional economic development strategy by government and the wine and tourism industries throughout Western Australia.

Against this background, this chapter seeks to address four key issues – first, the emergence of the wine-tourism phenomenon within Australia and the importance of the service quality issue to the future development and success of this sector. Secondly, the difficulties faced by cellar door operators in their efforts to continually exceed consumer expectations of a quality wine-tourism experience. Thirdly, and in an effort to show how operators are coping with these difficulties, examine

the perceptions of cellar door visitors at a number of Western Australian wineries. Finally, to provide a detailed insight into how one of Western Australia's leading wine-tourism operators – Vasse Felix – faces up to the service quality challenge.

The growth in Australian wine tourism

Wine tourism has emerged as a strong and growing area of special interest tourism throughout the world, and is now seen as an increasingly significant component of the regional and rural tourism product of many wine-producing countries, especially in the New World (Dodd and Bigotte, 1997; Carlsen, 1998; Macionis, 1998). Given its excellent climate, developing viticultural expertise and suitable soil conditions, Australia has recently emerged as both a premium quality wine producer and a serious destination choice for wine tourists. Indeed, Australia is perceived to be in the midst of what has been described as a wine-tourism boom.

Wine tourism, thus, is a relatively infant tourism activity and despite optimistic growth forecasts and expectations, a range of critical development issues confronts it, which have the potential to adversely affect its sustainability and longer-term profitability. One such

---

*Contact author

©CAB International 2006. *Managing Tourism and Hospitality Services: Theory and International Applications* (eds Bruce Prideaux, Gianna Moscardo and Eric Laws)

issue is that of visitor perceptions of the service quality experienced at the cellar door and its impact upon consumer satisfaction, future purchase intentions and brand loyalty. This has led to a heightened concern by Australian producers and consumers for the quality of services being offered.

Service quality and the cellar door experience

In wine tourism as with all aspects of tourism activity, the consumer's perception of service quality is critical, with many commentators now suggesting clear and direct links with customer satisfaction (Gabott and Hogg, 1997; Gwynne et al., 1998), future behavioural intention and long-term customer loyalty (Donovan and Samler, 1994; Heskett et al., 1997).

However, there are a number of conceptual issues that distinguish wine tourism from other forms of service activity. Wine tourism involves customers visiting a vineyard where experience of both the service processes and the tangible product (the wine) are important elements of the benefit from a visit. It is the latter benefit (wine tasting) which many vineyard operators focus on, and many see cellar door visits as a means of promoting their product and introducing new customers to it, rather than the quality of service. Many visitors to wineries may be on vacation with little likelihood of short-term repeat visits. However, benefit to the winery may derive from visitors seeking out the winery's wine when they get back home, and through word-of-mouth (WOM) referral (O'Neill et al., 2002). Indeed, high levels of service can encourage the development of relationship marketing strategies as currently interpreted (e.g. through the use of mailing lists and targeted incentives), as well as a relationship to the brand in a more traditional sense (Fig. 22.1).

Understanding the current awareness of service quality and its importance to cellar door sales is therefore essential. For the winery owner, visits to the cellar door offer three benefits: (i) distribution at a low marginal cost; (ii) the development of brand equity; and (iii) a chance to add value.

Thus it is evident that the cellar door involves a lot more than merely showcasing the winery's output. It is unique because it provides the visitor with a complete profile of the winery and its wines, as well as presenting an opportunity for wineries to develop long-term relationships with customers if planned and managed correctly.

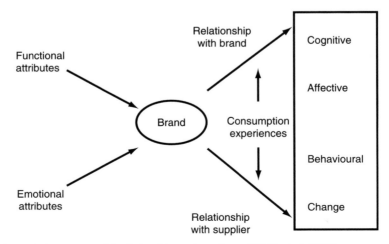

Fig. 22.1. Elements in a successful relationship strategy (from O'Neill et al., 2002).

The difficulty with cellar door service

Understanding what the wine tourist demands and their perceptions of actual delivery is vital for those who wish to succeed in the wine-tourism sector. As with most tourism services, however, delivery is complicated by the very nature of the service act, with the unique characteristics of the service offered posing problems for operators, not normally faced in their more traditional role as agriculturalists. The intangible nature of the cellar door experience, combined with the complicating real-time presence of the customer at the cellar door are factors that have been seen to create difficulties when trying to deliver a quality cellar door experience. These factors in combination with the highly 'progressive nature' of the service act have led to a number of major difficulties in consistently meeting customer requirements. It is the synthesis of these characteristics, which create the special operational and marketing environment of the wine-tourism business. It is essential, therefore, that those professing to manage in the wine-tourism field gain an appreciation of these particular characteristics and the problems they can create. This is complicated at the winery cellar door by the fact that the product being offered is both a tangible good (the wine) and a service. This complication in turn becomes more problematical because many smaller wine producers have gone into business specifically because of fascination with the product itself – rather than for any desire to engage directly with the public and offer a high-quality service experience.

Callan (1993) suggested that the quintessence of any service is its intangibility, with the customer being prevented from assessing it prior to purchase. In turn, this leads to greater uncertainty and perceived risk in the purchase/visitation decision, a fact that is heightened all the more for the first-time visitor. In practical terms, this means that customers become much more reliant on the reputation of the particular operator and opinions and views from their immediate social and/or working environment are more widely canvassed. Closely associated here is the perishable nature of the service act and the fact that as service is delivered in real time, it is almost impossible to accurately forecast and therefore plan for demand.

A further difficulty relates to the actual presence of the customer within the system and the fact that this presence must be managed from both a production and a consumption point of view. In essence this relates to the fact that services provided to the cellar door visitor cannot be separated from the provider. The service provider is present and visible to the consumer. Thus both provider and recipient may be an integral part of the production process. Unlike the manufacture of a physical product which is first produced, then distributed and then sold, the service received as part of the cellar door experience can only be produced and consumed in the presence of the customer. This requires a dual focus on the part of the winery operator in terms of both the service encounter and the more physical and tangible elements of the environment within which the service takes place.

The heterogeneous nature of the service act presents further problems for the winery operator. This implies variance and a lack of uniformity in the standard of the service. No two customers are the same and individually each enters the service setting with their own set of prior service expectations. Similarly, each customer leaves the service setting with a completely different set of perceptions. Consequently, it is frequently impossible to produce a standardized uniform service for all customers. Certain operations attempt to counter the effects of this variance by presenting a uniform product through precise production and operation methodologies, but these prescriptions in the main are only successful for the more technical elements of the service act which present themselves as being more controllable. As soon as the customer is introduced to the system, however, the possibility of providing a truly standardized service disappears. This necessitates attention to detail on staff training and first-rate customer contact personnel, as it is only through sound investment in the human resource that management of services can attempt to control quality in the service encounter, albeit indirectly.

Combined, these factors pose a number of very serious problems for wine-tourism operators, which, if left unchecked, could lead to pressure on an otherwise outstanding brand and/or reputation for quality produce. In order to counter this threat, winery operators have been forced to adopt a more integrated approach to the management of the marketing function incorporating the areas of marketing, operations and human resource management. In turn this should lead to a greater understanding of how the wine-tourism experience is created, delivered and/or perceived by the wine tourist.

Taking on the mantle of service managers, winery operators must seek answers to the following questions:

1. How may a quality service be defined – what factors influence the customer's experience and how may these factors be identified?
2. How may the winery deliver a consistent level of service quality given the heterogeneous nature of the service act?
3. How may performance or delivery of the service be measured or monitored given the intangible nature of service?

The Perceptions of Cellar Door Visitors

Methodological issues

Details of customer perceptions of cellar door service in the following case study result from research at 12 wineries in the Margaret River region in 2002.[1] Respondents were asked to rate their perceptions of both the (general) importance of elements of the cellar door experience and the performance of the specific winery that they had visited. The sample was drawn from visitors to 12 participating wineries in the Margaret River wine region over a 4-day period in April 2002. The region has some 130 wineries, of which just over 60 offer a cellar door operation. Six hundred questionnaires were administered, of which 458 were returned, representing a response rate of approximately 76%.

[1] Full details of the methodology of the study, including comprehensive demographics and the statistical process used, are available from the authors.

Scales used were based on the importance/performance paradigm (Ennew et al., 1993; Ford et al., 1999) and took the form of a multiple-item self-completion questionnaire that visitors were asked to complete immediately prior to departing each winery. For each item, respondents were asked to rate their perceptions on a 5-point Likert scale anchored at 1 (strongly disagree) and 5 (strongly agree). In addition, respondents were asked to weight the level of importance attributed to each of the items on a similar scale anchored at 1 (low importance) to 5 (high importance). Scale items were based on the 22 items of the original SERVQUAL (Parasuraman et al., 1985). The scale has been widely replicated and the factor structure found to be appropriate to a wide range of consumer services, of which cellar door operations are typical.

While the overriding goal of the study was to address the issue of visitors' time-elapsed perceptions of service quality, it proved useful to test the dimensionality of the service quality construct within the particular service setting, i.e. the cellar door operation.

Zeithaml et al. (1990) defined service in terms of the five 'RATER' dimensions: reliability, assurance, tangibles, empathy and responsiveness. While visitors were asked to complete the perception and importance sections of the questionnaire, only the perception (direct disconfirmation) scores from the 22-item scale were used to operationalize the service quality construct. The analysis revealed a rather complex factor structure with three principal components being extracted. From the analysis, extracted component 1 is reflective of a combination of the responsiveness, assurance and empathy dimensions from the original SERVQUAL instrument. Viewed in the context of the cellar door experience, component 1 seems to relate to the contact issue (CONTACT) and the moment of truth. This factor seems to revolve about the organization's ability to quickly allay any fears that first-time visitors might have, on being introduced to what is for many, a new and potentially intimidating environment. To an extent, this dimension is also reflective of the winery's ability to deliver its cellar door services on time and as expected. Component 2 is reflective of the tangible (TANGIBLE) dimension of the original SERVQUAL and relates to the more physical and/or firmer aspects of the service encounter, e.g. the setting, decor, appearance of staff, etc. Component 3 is reflective of the responsiveness (RESPONSIVENESS) dimension of the original SERVQUAL and relates to the more time-related aspects of the service encounter.

Visitor perceptions

Almost 94% (429) of visitors stated that they would revisit the wineries surveyed. This is concurrent with the relatively high mean performance values recorded for all attributes of the cellar door experience (Table 22.1). In addition, almost 94% (430) of respondents stated that they would be happy to recommend the wineries visited to others and 51% of

customers surveyed reported that they had purchased wine during their visit. This supports the view from the literature that the majority of cellar door customers are genuine buyers (Spawton, 1986). Almost 62% (283) of those surveyed stated that they had come across, tasted or purchased the wines sampled on a previous occasion and 41% (186) stated that they had heard of the respective wineries based upon personal recommendation and other WOM sources.

The next stage of the analysis was to examine the sample responses across the 22-item attributes to assess visitor perceptions of service quality and the relative importance assigned by visitors to each. This information is presented in Table 22.1, where mean scores are shown for importance and performance for each of the 22 attributes.

Table 22.1. Importance–performance means.

Quality attribute	Mean importance	Mean performance	Performance minus importance	t-value	Sig. (2-tailed)
Facilities for visitors	3.03	3.94	0.91	6.79	0.001
Décor of the winery	2.83	4.19	1.36	9.12	0.001
Winery staff appeared neat	2.75	4.18	1.43	14.41	0.001
Brochures and signposting	2.59	3.81	1.22	8.07	0.001
Range of wines	2.99	3.94	0.95	9.07	0.001
Problem solving	2.69	3.62	0.93	6.90	0.001
Ethos of right first time	2.64	3.68	1.04	6.68	0.001
Actual service right first time	2.78	3.57	0.79	7.93	0.001
Convenience of tasting times	3.01	4.13	1.12	8.23	0.001
Quality of wine tasted	3.21	4.00	0.79	7.40	0.001
Knowledgeable staff	3.02	4.13	1.11	7.13	0.001
No excessive waiting time	3.10	4.32	1.22	6.52	0.001
Staff always willing to help guests	3.08	4.13	1.05	9.68	0.001
Never too busy to respond to guests	3.13	4.12	0.99	9.68	0.001
Behaviour of staff gave confidence	3.03	4.10	1.07	10.44	0.001
Staff made customers feel secure	2.91	4.07	1.16	11.38	0.001
Staff consistently courteous	3.16	4.22	1.06	10.38	0.001
Knowledge to answer guest questions	3.09	4.09	1.00	9.76	0.001
Made to feel like a special individual	2.75	3.77	1.02	8.71	0.001
Visitors' best interests at heart	3.08	3.75	0.67	3.53	0.001
Understood the specific needs of guests	2.89	3.75	0.86	6.41	0.001
Individualized attention to guests	3.01	3.96	0.95	9.15	0.001

Analysis of Table 22.1 reveals that the relative mean scores of the quality items are skewed towards the positive end of the scale with a mean score of $m = 2.94$ for perceived importance and $m = 3.98$ for perceived performance for all operators. Once again, the results of a paired samples significance test reveal this average difference to be significant at the level of 1% ($t = 11.26; P < 0.001$).

These results paint a remarkably good picture of cellar door service provision in the area, with mean perception scores far and away exceeding visitor expectations in all instances. Positive scores are indicative of the fact that given the importance of these items to visitors, actual performance was well above expectation. These differences were found to be significant in all cases at the level of 1% ($P < 0.001$).

Positioning quality attributes

The next stage in the analysis examined the relative positioning of the individual service

quality attributes in relation to overall mean performance and importance for operators. One of the advantages of importance–performance analysis is that attributes can be plotted graphically on a matrix and this can assist in quick and efficient interpretation of the results. Figure 22.2 highlights the relative positioning of a number of the attributes in matrix format.

The matrix is represented by the importance values on the horizontal axis, while performance values are on the vertical axis. The skewed nature of the results forced the researchers to use mean values to represent the crosshairs of the matrix and this helped to identify the stronger and weaker attributes more clearly.

When presented in matrix format (Fig. 22.2) the results present operators with a number of strategic alternatives.

Quadrant A is reflective of a misuse of the operator's resources. While judged to be performing well above average in relation to the provision of the particular service attributes, customers in their assessment of the

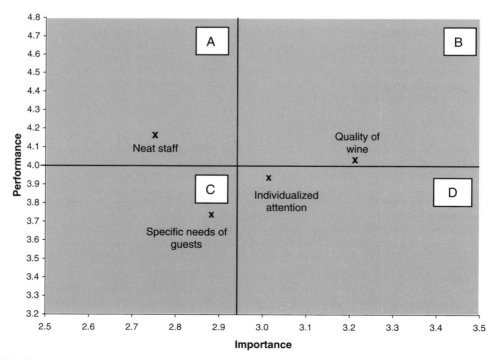

Fig. 22.2. Importance–performance matrix of individual service attributes

overall cellar door experience have deemed these same attributes relatively unimportant. It is unlikely, therefore, that any further investment and/or improvement in this area will lead to a greater perception of quality on the part of the consumer.

Quadrant B is reflective of a level of optimal performance in that operators are perceived to be performing well above average in relation to the delivery of those service attributes deemed most important by customers.

Quadrant C is reflective of the fact that certain aspects of the cellar door experience are not performing to their full service potential. When viewed in the context of the corresponding importance weighting, however, any pertaining improvement effort would have to be questioned.

Quadrant D is where the greatest of improvement effort is required. The matrix illustrates quite clearly that attributes that fall into this category are deemed to be of great importance to customers in their overall evaluation of the service experience, yet are underperforming in the customers' eyes. It is essential that company improvement efforts be prioritized in this area.

The final stage of analysis was to concentrate on the service quality dimensions.

As with the preceding variable analysis, Table 22.2 illustrates that operators are performing well above average in relation to each of the dimensions listed. Operators do seem to be experiencing some difficulty though with respect to the issue of 'responsiveness', which may be indicative of the waiting time issue during tastings. Analysis reveals that, as a whole 'contact' rated highest in terms of overall importance to visitors (m = 2.99) followed by 'tangibles' and 'responsiveness'. This is an interesting finding, and certainly does reinforce the importance of having good people operate

the cellar door. The corresponding performance scores illustrate that operators have also performed best in relation to the 'contact' dimension (m = 4.02), which is, of course, an excellent result given the level of ascribed importance recorded for this dimension. Cellar door visitors are clearly delighted with the various wineries' performance in this respect, which is clearly good news for all concerned. But to what do they owe this success? Similarly, why is it that those from a non-traditional service background continue to excel in the area of exceeding visitor expectations at the cellar door? In an attempt to answer these questions attention shall now turn to an in-depth analysis of the cellar door practices of one of the regions leading exponents of the wine-tourism experience, Vasse Felix.

The Vasse Felix factor: a lesson in cellar door tourism

Celebrating its 35th anniversary in 2002, Vasse Felix is Margaret River's original winery, with a worldwide reputation for consistent and award-winning quality. Vines were first planted here in 1967. The winery was purchased by the Holmes, a Court family in 1987 and as a result of their direct efforts, now offers one of Western Australia's best wine-tourism experiences. Vasse Felix is one of the few Margaret River wineries to achieve SQF (safe quality food) accreditation, all of which makes the cellar door visit all the more enjoyable (Vasse Felix, 2003). The winery has a carefully converted underground barrel store as its cellar door, and a restaurant that has twice won the Australian *Gourmet Traveller* magazine restaurant guide's highest rating – in 2002 and 2003. The company offers catered evening functions and has a modern public art gallery

Table 22.2. Importance/performance scores for service quality dimensions.

SERVQUAL Dimension	Mean importance	Mean performance	Performance minus importance	t-value	Sig. (2-tailed)
Contact	2.99	4.02	1.03	10.66	0.001
Tangibles	2.88	4.02	1.14	10.56	0.001
Responsiveness	2.82	3.79	0.97	10.08	0.001

and a performing arts facility. Against this background, it quickly becomes clear that Vasse Felix has a clear understanding of the importance of the service quality issue to both the future success of its cellar door operation and the longer-term growth. Vasse Felix takes a long-term relational approach to all of its activities aiming to become the 'ultimate wine-tourism experience'. It recognizes the value of every customer and views each service encounter as an opportunity to grow the company and its reputation for excellence. This is reflected in all elements of the Vasse Felix experience and its approach to harvesting life-time customer relationships and extends beyond the wine tourist, to all those involved in helping Vasse Felix to maintain its positioning.

While many wineries still base their marketing decisions around the four elements of the more traditional marketing mix – product, price, place and promotion – Vasse Felix has grasped the need for an extended approach to the management of its customer relationships. In turn, this has led the winery to invest heavily in a number of additional areas around its services marketing and management practice, focusing on its people, physical service environment and the various process elements of its service offer. Each of these elements shall now be addressed in the context of the Vasse Felix experience.

People

Given the face-to-face, real-time nature of the wine-tourism experience, Vasse Felix has placed additional emphasis on the management of winery staff. They recognize fully that customers are not solely the people who visit the cellar door, but also their staff. This has led to the development of an internal service culture where winery employees are viewed as customers in their own right and an almost direct inversion of the traditional organizational hierarchy. Instead the front-line employee is regarded as central to the company's continual pursuit of excellence. This is reflected in all elements of the winery's approach to people management, namely, recruitment, selection, ongoing training and development, empowerment, staff motivation and reward. The principal objectives are customer satisfaction and retention through the removal of barriers to improved employee performance. To this end the company recruits for expertise and attitude and upon joining the Vasse Felix family, invests continually in the ongoing education, training and development of its staff. This relates not solely to the areas of wine production and appreciation, but also customer-service training and relationship marketing.

Perhaps one of the more interesting facts about Vasse Felix is that when it comes to its cellar door it actively recruits people who do not have a traditional background in wine. Coming from backgrounds, as broad ranging as leisure, retail and interior decoration and design, management believes that this serves to strengthen and enrich the overall customer experience. Indeed, the cellar door team is looked upon as one of the most vital marketing tools that the organization has employed. Staff are encouraged to take their time with patrons and to allow the visitor to dictate the pace of service delivery. Unlike the highly scripted service approach of many other wineries in the region, Vasse Felix staff are permitted to follow the customers' lead in relation to the cellar door experience.

The company's management also understands that, while it is almost always the front-line service employee who will carry the wine-tourism experience to its logical conclusion (satisfaction or dissatisfaction), the process of delivering quality service begins much further back than the front line. They firmly believe that it is not simply enough for front-line staff to understand their obligations to the external customer and encourage staff to consider their obligations to their colleagues and associates and to view them as customers in their own right. They stress the point that every employee has a role to play in providing quality service to the cellar door visitor. The important point, of course, is that of dependency, which refers to the quality, timeliness and costliness of employee outputs, which then become inputs to the next link in what might be termed the Vasse Felix supply chain. All employee actions and reactions are thus seen as vital to the attainment of customer satisfaction and competitive market positioning.

Staff are encouraged to spend time in all of the major functional areas of the winery, thereby gaining a broader appreciation and much more holistic view of the operation. Weekly sharing of ideas and experiences is encouraged at Friday evening sundowners, otherwise known as fellowship hour. Loyalty to the organization is also rewarded on an annual basis by the winery's owners the Holmes, a Court family, at an annual staff Christmas function, which takes place on the winery grounds. The very simple gesture of awarding a service pin to staff for longevity of service is something that is looked forward to and received with pride.

Physical environment

Given the largely intangible nature of the service exchange, Vasse Felix pays extra special attention to the more physical aspects of the wine-tourism experience. This relates not solely to the actual cellar door counter, but to each tangible element on show at the winery, including signposting, entrance roads, staff presentation and grooming, production and bottling plant, viticultural machinery, display of testimonials and awards, surrounding gardens and vineyards, parking facilities and children's play areas. Just as the service delivery system relies upon the quality efforts of every employee in order to deliver a consistent quality service, so too Vasse Felix relies upon the input of the more tangible attributes of the winery and its ancillary services. While the quality of the wine on offer for tasting is undoubtedly at the forefront of most visitors' minds, the Vasse Felix team understands that there is great potential for the physical surroundings and other tangible cues to have a profound effect on the perceptions patrons form about the service they receive. Vasse Felix understands fully the issue of risk and has invested and continues to invest heavily in the more tangible side of the operation.

This, of course, has the added advantage of communicating a quality image that supports the wine that is being showcased and this is apparent from the moment one turns on to the vineyard drive to the moment of departure. An attractive tree-lined driveway, ready parking and clear signposting are crucial. Attention is paid to ambience, and the aim is a saturation of the senses with a 'cultural feast of fine art, fine dining and the finest Vasse Felix wines'.

The winery offers an attractively appealing underground cellar, which presently accounts for 8% of all case sales, a figure in advance of any other winery or cellar door operation in the region. The cellar provides an excellent opportunity to showcase the pedigree of the wine not only in tasting form but also through the display of Vasse's many awards and trophies, which can be viewed throughout the cellar. The actual tasting counter is well appointed and wines and glasses are stacked neatly for tasting, with wine labels and the Vasse Felix logo (a peregrine falcon) always facing forward toward the visitor. The cellar also serves as an outlet for the sale company merchandise and accounts for more than 20% of turnover.

Process

While Vasse Felix relies heavily upon the quality and loyalty of its people, it is not foolish enough to believe that a service-oriented attitude alone will assure good service. It recognizes that front-line staff must be supported by an appropriate service infrastructure that enables them to succeed. This has led to the design and implementation of effective systems and procedures to ensure that the services it provides are constantly focused on meeting the customer's needs. Similarly, all delivery systems are designed with the convenience of the customer in mind, and are constantly reviewed and encourage customer feedback with a view to continual improvement. This relates to all aspects of the wine-tourism offering and to all company relationships, whether with wine tourists or local suppliers and partners in the broader wine-tourism sector.

As problems arise, there is a no-blame, continual improvement approach taken to their resolution. Staff are encouraged to accept immediate responsibility and take ownership of any emerging problems and to work with the customer, whether internal or external, to find a resolution. This is followed by a subsequent diagnosis, with a view to identifying and eliminating all actual and/or potential root causes. Indeed, the right first time, prevention rather than cure ideal is very much a pillar of the organizational culture.

Similarly, the Vasse Felix approach is one that encourages flexibility with respect to the delivery of the wine-tourism experience. The idea being to view every customer as an opportunity to further the organization's reputation for excellence and to do whatever it takes to satisfy his or her requirements. One story in particular, as recounted by the Cellar Door Manager, Adrian Sapsford, highlights the potential benefits of such an approach. Normal hours of cellar door operation extend from 10.00 a.m. to 5.00 p.m., and while this is well advertised at the entrance to the cellar door, from time to time, customers still arrive after close down. While it is often tempting to simply ignore or turn visitors away after-hours, Vasse Felix staff are encouraged to be flexible and where possible offer these late arrivals a full tasting. On one occasion, which lasted no more than 15 min after-hours, this led to a AUS$10,000 order – clearly a great way to end any sales day.

Conclusion

The chapter has highlighted the importance of the service quality issue to the future success of the wine-tourism industry. It has shown that success depends not only on the quality of the wine being offered but also on the way it is offered for sale within the cellar door environment. It points out clearly that while winery operators, like many within the agricultural sector, may be considered a more product-oriented business they are also – at least at the cellar door – running a service organization. Many small-scale producers enter the wine industry in order to make wine – not to delight their visitors. However, it is the favourable memories of the more relational elements of the service encounter that rate highly with customers. Clearly their estimation of these more personal factors – seen as equally important as the wine tasted – must have an impact on the winery operators' approach to what they are giving their consumers. Indeed it may be surmised that the perceived level of service quality, and not merely of wine quality, may in fact be a vital antecedent to any purchase being made. Good business practice may require a reorientation of operator attitudes to their organizational focus.

Connected with this is the critical factor of developing good 'relationship marketing'; an efficient cellar door should generate a number of one-off sales to visitors, using finely honed sales techniques. An effective cellar door may generate lower immediate sales but – by placing emphasis on factors like contact and responsiveness – generate very strong subsequent brand loyalty, at far greater profit to the winery in the longer term. Winery operators need to understand this rather than focusing on the short-term high-profit margins generated by the distribution advantages of cellar door sales.

References

Callan, R. (1993) Defining services: a review. *International Association of Hospitality Management Schools' Annual Conference on the Theme of Service Quality.* IAHMS, Gothenburg, Sweden, 13–15 May.

Carlsen, J. (1998) Strategic issues in Australian wine tourism. *Wine Tourism – Perfect Partners, Proceedings of the First Australian Wine Tourism Conference.* Bureau of Tourism Research, Canberra, pp. 99–100.

Dodd, T. and Bigotte, V. (1997) Perceptual differences among visitor groups to wineries. *Journal of Travel Research,* Winter, 46–51.

Donovan, P. and Samler, T. (1994) *Delighting Customers: How to Build a Customer-Driven Organisation.* Chapman & Hall, New York.

Ennew, C., Reed, C. and Binks, M. (1993) Importance–performance analysis and the measurement of service quality. *European Journal of Marketing* 27(2), 59–70.

Ford, J.B., Joseph, M. and Joseph, B. (1999) Importance–performance analysis as a strategic tool for service marketers: the case of service quality perceptions of business students in New Zealand and the USA. *The Journal of Services Marketing* 13(2), 171–186.

Gabott, M. and Hogg, G. (1997) *Contemporary Services Marketing Management: A Reader.* The Dryden Press, London.

Gwynne, A.L., Devlin, J. and Ennew, C.T. (1998) Service quality and customer satisfaction: a longitudinal analysis. *The British Academy of Marketing Annual Conference.* Sheffield Hallam University, UK, 8–10 July, pp. 186–191.

Heskett, J.L., Jones, T.O., Loveman, G.W., Sasser, W.E. and Schlesinger, L.A. (1997) Putting the service profit chain to work. In: Lovelock, C.H., Patterson, P.G. and Walker, R.H. (eds) *Services Marketing.* Prentice Hall, Upper Saddle River, New Jersey.

Macionis, N. (1998) Wineries and tourism: perfect partners or dangerous liaisons. *Wine Tourism – Perfect Partners, Proceedings of the First Australian Wine Tourism Conference.* Bureau of Tourism Research, Canberra, pp. 35–50.

O'Neill, M.A., Palmer, A. and Charters, S. (2002) Wine production as a service experience – the effects of service quality on wine sales. *Journal of Services Marketing* 16(4), 342–362.

Parasuraman, A., Zeithaml, V.A. and Berry, L.L. (1985) A conceptual model of service quality and its implications for future research, *Journal of Marketing* 49(Fall), 41–50.

Spawton, T. (1986) Understanding wine purchasing: knowing how the wine buyer behaves can increase your sales. *The Australian and New Zealand Wine Industry Journal* 1(2), 54–57.

Vasse Felix (2003) *Margaret River's Enduring Symbol of Quality.* Vasse Felix Winery, Western Australia.

Zeithaml, V.A., Parasuraman, A. and Berry, L. (1990) *Delivering Quality Service: Balancing Customer Perceptions and Expectations.* Free Press, New York.

23 Using the Critical Incidents Technique to Understand Service Quality in Tourist Accommodation

Gianna Moscardo
James Cook University, Australia

Introduction

Despite its widespread use, service is an ambiguous term. It is sometimes used to refer to what service industries do (i.e. a service as proposed to a product), and sometimes to refer to particular activities provided by a company (e.g. wake-up calls and ticket bookings). Some definitions see service as an encounter between a customer and an employee, while others believe it to be the sum of all the encounters between a customer and the company (Dagger and Lawley, 2003). There is, however, general agreement on the importance of service quality for customer satisfaction and business success, the importance of customer perceptions for understanding service quality and the importance of ongoing staff training to improve service quality. This chapter studies one particular method for examining and improving customer perceptions of service quality: the critical incidents technique (CIT). In particular, the chapter reviews the use of CIT in tourism and hospitality and presents the results of a study of critical incidents reported by guests for a range of tourist accommodation types. The chapter concludes with an examination of the benefits of the technique for various aspects of hotel operations.

Approaches to Understanding Service Quality

Service dimensions

The most commonly used approaches to understanding service quality are the expectations disconfirmation models of Gronroos (1984) and Parasuraman *et al.* (1985, 1991). Of these, the SERVQUAL model of Parasuraman *et al.* (1985) is arguably the most widely used service quality measurement system. The SERVQUAL model proposes that there are five key dimensions (reduced from ten dimensions in earlier versions of the system) or factors that make up service quality:

- **Reliability** – the ability of an organization to continuously deliver goods and services as promised.
- **Assurance** – a sense of trust inspired by polite, knowledgeable and competent staff.
- **Tangibles** – the physical facilities, features and appearance of an organization's buildings, products and employees.
- **Empathy** – where customers feel as though their needs are understood and important to

the organization and that they have been given personal attention.

• **Responsiveness** – employees' willingness to help and provide prompt attention to customers.

In this system, service quality is seen as resulting from an organization's ability to meet or exceed customers' expectations on all these dimensions. This expectation disconfirmation model assumes that customers have clear expectations and measure performance of the organization against those expectations on each of the five SERVQUAL dimensions. Service quality is the sum of these mental calculations and is an overall impression based on multiple points of contact between the customer and the organization. To improve service quality, an organization must measure the importance of these dimensions for customers and use these importance scores to weight their perceptions of the organization's performance on these dimensions. If the organization also measures staff and management perceptions of customers' responses, a series of service quality gaps can be identified and used to direct change and improvement in the organization (see Parasuraman *et al.*, 1991; Knutson, 2001; O'Neill, 2001; Dagger and Lawley, 2003; Gabbott, 2003, for more details on SERVQUAL models).

Despite the widespread use of SERVQUAL in academic studies, a number of criticisms have been raised. According to Dagger and Lawley (2003) these criticisms fall into three main categories: (i) disputes over the number and range of dimensions that should be included in the system; (ii) concerns over the role of expectations; and (iii) charges of being overly complex. Of these three types of criticism, the latter two are more challenging as they question core assumptions of the model.

Several authors have argued that there is substantial semantic confusion over what the word 'expectation' actually means (Ekinci *et al.*, 2001; Gabbott, 2003). In the area of tourism there are those who argue that tourists may not always have clear expectations and thus would find it difficult to assess performance against expectations (Gyimothy, 1999). If customers or tourists do not measure performance against expectations, then alternative

processes for evaluating service performance are necessary.

Concerns over the complexity of the system include criticisms of the assumption that customers make an overall performance judgement for an organization on each SERVQUAL dimension, which sums up their experiences of multiple encounters (Gabbott, 2003). This raises the issue of how customers combine multiple encounters to produce an overall impression. At a more concrete level there are also limitations in that the system requires substantial knowledge of survey sampling and analysis to conduct, making it difficult for managers to use on an ongoing basis (O'Neill, 2001).

Service encounters

An alternative theme in the service quality literature has focused on individual interaction episodes between customers and staff referred to as service encounters (Johns and Mattsson, 2003). This alternative perspective argues that service quality perceptions can be heavily influenced by a single interaction between customers and an organization, particularly interactions between customers and employees. These service encounters are also sometimes referred to as 'moments of truth' (Bitner *et al.*, 1994). This simpler approach to understanding service quality emphasizes the importance of analysing service encounters and identifying the factors that contribute to their success or failure (Lee-Ross, 2001; Johns and Mattsson, 2003). Many authors have argued that the approach is practical and easy for managers to use (Lockwood, 1994; Lazer and Layton, 1999; Lee-Ross, 2001; Johns and Mattsson, 2003). According to Johns and Mattsson (2003, p. 191), for example, 'the service encounter concept is sufficiently flexible to provide a practical understanding of tourist experience at the micro level ... and provides a timely aid for tourism academics and managers seeking to understand service management in the tourism area'. A core methodological tool for studying service encounters is the CIT (Bitner *et al.*, 1994; Johns and Mattsson, 2003).

The Critical Incidents Technique

Critical incidents – definitions and methodological considerations

CIT was first described and used by Flanagan in 1954 as tool for investigating applied problems in psychology and for seeking insights into complex phenomena that had not previously been studied. Thus this qualitative method had both practical applications in terms of being used to identify operational and procedural problems and theoretical applications in its use to explore complex phenomena to identify key factors for further study. According to Flanagan (1954, p. 327), an incident could be defined as 'any observable human activity that is sufficiently complete in itself to permit inferences and predictions to be made about the person performing the act'. He further stated that 'to be critical, an incident must occur in a situation where the purpose or intent of the act seems fairly clear to the observer and where its consequences are sufficiently definite to leave little doubt concerning its effects' (Flanagan, 1954, p. 327).

Descriptions of critical incidents can be generated by participant observation, or from interviews with target respondents (Chell, 1998). In interview and survey approaches respondents are usually asked to describe a worst or best incident, or an incident that they believed was critical to the overall outcome of an experience. The power of the technique lies in the direction of attention to critical episodes that are easily remembered and described by respondents (Chell, 1998), and which often have already been examined for causes and outcomes by the respondents (Flanagan, 1954).

Once the information describing the incidents has been gathered it is content analysed to identify major themes relevant to the aims of the study. Researchers search through the descriptions identifying and listing words or phrases that indicate factors or processes of interest. These themes are then often categorized according to causes and consequences where the focus is an applied one or according to pre-existing conceptual frameworks for more exploratory research (Knutson, 2001; O'Neill, 2001; Gabbott, 2003).

The most common criticisms of the technique include those more generally associated with content analysis in general. It is argued, for example, that the content analysis of the incidents is subject to the biases and expectations of the coders (Gabbott, 2003). The responses to such challenges are those that would normally accompany studies using content analyses – the use of clear coding schemes and the checking of inter-coder reliability (Cavana et al., 2001).

Critical incidents research in tourism and hospitality

There is a small but growing body of literature in tourism and hospitality based on the use of CIT. Table 23.1 provides a summary of a selection of published studies in this style. The selection includes those most commonly referred to, such as the work by Bitner et al. (1994) and Edvardsson and Strandvik (2000), as well as more recently published material. In the area of service quality research in tourism and hospitality, CIT studies are usually based on verbal or written descriptions of incidents of bad or exemplary service collected in interviews and/or with survey questionnaires. As can be seen in Table 23.1 the technique has been used mostly to examine aspects of service quality in airlines and hotels, although from a variety of perspectives with a range of different research foci.

These studies highlight two important potential contributions of CIT to understanding and improving service quality in tourism and hospitality. The first is in the exploration of service quality dimensions for tourist accommodation. Although there may be differences of opinion over whether one or multiple service encounters contribute to perceived service quality, both approaches to service quality are based on service encounters. A more detailed examination of service encounters can provide insight into the validity of proposed service quality dimensions such as those listed in the SERVQUAL model.

The second potential contribution is in the examination of operational procedures and problems. Because of its simplicity CIT could

Table 23.1. Summary of selected critical incidents technique studies in tourism and hospitality.

Researcher	Sample	Major focus
Bejou *et al.* (1996)	Customers and employees of Swedish and US airlines	Identified factors from negative incidents and classified them into causes, processes and results
Bitner *et al.* (1990)	Customers of airlines, hotels and restaurants	Identified major groups of employee behaviours that contribute to the outcome of service encounters
Bitner *et al.* (1994)	Staff in tourism and hospitality businesses	Used role and script theory to analyse incidents
Callan (1998)	Guests in UK accommodation	Grouped incident themes according to operational categories
Chell and Pittaway (1998)	Business owners in restaurants and cafes	Identified actions associated with successful entrepreneurial activity in restaurants
Chung and Hoffman (1998)	Guests in hotels	Grouped negative incidents according to operational categories
Edvardsson and Strandvik (2000)	Guests in hotels	Examined outcomes of critical incidents in hotels
Gilbert and Morris (1995)	Business travellers and hotels and airlines	Listed themes contributing to dis/satisfaction
Johns and Lee-Ross (1997)	Guests in small hotels	Coded episodes using existing lists of service quality dimensions
Johnson (2002)	Gamblers	Used themes in incidents to suggest service quality factors for gaming establishments
Liden and Skalen (2003)	Customers in hotels	Examined the impact of service incidents and service guarantees on customer behaviour
Rutherford and Umbreit (2002)	Meeting planners perceptions of hotels	Identified key themes associated with positive interaction between meeting planners and hotel staff
Wang *et al.* (2000)	Tourist perceptions of package tours	Identified operational factors associated with positive and negative group tour incidents
Woods and Moscardo (2003)	Tourist perceptions of wildlife encounters	Measuring the extent to which tourists list features related to the social psychological theory of mindfulness

be a valuable tool for tourism and hospitality managers to use on a regular basis to monitor service quality problems and to improve operational procedures. This aspect of CIT application has been discussed in more detail by Lazer and Layton (1999) and Lockwood (1994), in their descriptions of the use of studies of service encounters to improve service quality assurance systems. A third potential application in the area of staff training has also been suggested (see Lee-Ross, 2001; George, 1989, for more details).

A Study of Critical Service Incidents in Tourist Accommodation

Service quality is often described as an increasingly important source of competitive advantage for tourist accommodation businesses (Kandampully, 1999; Roberts, 2001; Johns and Mattsson, 2003). The present study was conducted to explore the potential of CIT studies to contribute to our understanding of service quality both at the operational level of the individual establishment and more generally for developing conceptual frameworks to explain and predict service quality perceptions.

Method

The critical incidents for the present study were collected through a teaching exercise with two undergraduate hotel management classes. Members of the classes were asked to complete a semi-structured questionnaire themselves and to get one other adult acquaintance (not a university student) to complete a questionnaire. The questionnaire collected information on respondents' gender, age and travel experience before asking them to describe their best and worst experiences of service at any form of tourist accommodation. The overall aim of the exercise was to gather information to allow students to explore aspects of guest perceptions of hotel service and to use the incidents to develop ideas for improving hotel management processes to enhance service quality. The snowball sampling technique was considered adequate for this particular aim as the key issue for the exercise was to explore a wide range of incidents rather than to describe the relative frequency of occurrence of any one particular type of service problem. According to Cavana *et al.* (2001, p. 137) non-probability sampling methods including snowball sampling 'have the distinct advantage of quickly accessing participants who are most likely to provide rich information'.

Sample of respondents

The method described in the previous section resulted in a total sample of 100 respondents, made up of 50 students and 50 non-students. The age of the respondents ranged from 18 to 80 years with a mean age of 29 years (SD = 11). Nearly half of the respondents were aged less than 25 years consistent with the proportion of students and non-students. The sampling procedure favoured females who made up 68% of the respondents. Virtually all of the respondents had been on a domestic trip in the previous 12 months (only 6 had not), with

48% having been on between 1 and 3 trips and 44% having been on between 4 and 10 trips. More than half of the sample (68%) had not, however, been on an international trip in the previous 12 months, with 17% having been on one overseas trip and 9% twice.

Sample of incidents

In many forms of qualitative research, including CIT, the most important sample to consider is that of the episodes or incidents that are described. Table 23.2 provides a profile of key characteristics of the incidents described in the present study. The results in Table 23.2 indicate that there was a wide range of locations and types of accommodation involved in both the negative and the positive critical incidents described. The other category for accommodation types included bed and breakfast places, wilderness lodges, farm-stays and self-contained cottages and units. The sample of incidents offered substantial variety in both place and type.

Results

The 100 critical incidents were coded according to the content analysis procedures outlined by Cavana *et al.* (2001). This involved reading through the positive and negative incident descriptions and summarizing the main themes identified in the incidents. This first step in the coding was then repeated by another coder and inter-coder reliability was checked, with the two coders agreeing in 97% of the cases. The themes were then further grouped into larger categories based on common characteristics or elements related to different aspects of accommodation operational procedures. The results of this first stage in the content analysis are presented in the two sections immediately following this one.

An alternative coding system was also applied to the critical incidents. In this second stage of the content analysis an a priori coding scheme was developed using the five key dimensions of the SERVQUAL model. In this case, a set of target phrases and words was

Table 23.2. Key characteristics of the critical incidents.

Characteristics	% of positive incidents	% of negative incidents
Location of the incident (if listed)		
• Local area	8	10
• Other Australia	51	62
• Asia	12.5	8
• Europe	8	8
• South Pacific	8	2
• Africa	8	4
• Central/South America	3	2
• North America	1.5	3
Type of accommodation		
• Hotel	38	26
• Luxury hotel	4	7
• Resort	15	9
• Motel	4	10
• Caravan park	4	9
• Backpackers' hostel	3	6
• Other	32	33

specified to reflect the dimensions (listed in Table 23.5) and incidents were scanned to identify these words and phrases. The outcomes of this stage of the content analysis are presented in the last section of the results.

The major themes in positive incidents

The first step in the coding of the positive critical incidents identified 38 individual themes that are listed in Table 23.3. As can be seen in Table 23.3, these individual themes were further classified into five main groups. The most commonly reported themes were those relating to 'staff attitudes', making up 55% of all the responses coded. The second category to emerge was 'staff actions'. In this category were staff behaviours that were noted by the respondents as being out of the ordinary, or beyond what was expected.

'Service recovery' was the third category identified and consisted of incidents where a problem or service failure occurred, but was then corrected in a way that the guests saw as indicating good service. The fourth category was called the 'basics' as the guest reporting these incidents noted simply that the accommodation met the standards expected. The

final category, or 'unexpected extras' was used to classify examples where additional services or facilities were provided free of charge.

The major themes in negative incidents

The first step in the content analysis of the worst service encounters resulted in 41 individual themes as listed in Table 23.4. In order to facilitate comparisons between aspects of accommodation operations that contribute to positive and negative service encounters, the coders attempted to classify the individual themes into categories that matched those used for the positive incidents. This was possible for four out of the six categories. The most commonly reported themes were those in the category labelled 'basics not met'. In this category were incidents related to the cleanliness, security and basic functioning of the accommodation facilities. The next largest category was that of 'staff attitudes' where negative staff approaches were described. The other two categories that matched those used in the positive incidents analysis were 'unexpected extras', which in the negative case referred to a limited number of cases where guests encountered hidden costs and charges, and

Table 23.3. Major themes in positive incidents.

Categories	Themes	Examples
Staff attitudes ($n = 109$, 55% of responses)[a]	Committed to good service Helpful and friendly Knowledgeable and informative	Staff members did every thing correctly and were very efficient. Some staff went out of their way to satisfy my needs.
Staff actions ($n = 20$, 10% of responses)	Helped celebrate special occasion Walked guest to restaurant at night Helped with tour planning Organized indoor activities in poor weather Opened restaurant for latecomers Assisted with recovery of stolen items Allowed dog to stay even though advertised no pets policy Personal service from manager	I spent my birthday by myself at a hotel. I told a staff member expecting nothing in return. About half an hour later I heard a knock on my door. Three staff members entered. One had a bunch of flowers, another one had cake and the last one sang happy birthday to me. My bags were lost at airport and one of the hotel staff drove me back to the airport to get them.
Service recovery ($n = 11$, 5.5% of responses)	Apologized for a problem Provided compensation for a problem	Hotel courtesy bus to the airport was late. When they arrived they apologized to me repeatedly and they bought me a present and a card to say they are sorry.
Basics ($n = 34$, 17.5% of responses)	Very clean Wide selection of food and beverage Economical Catered to dietary needs Facilities for children Well-organized Good food in restaurant Good security systems Good quality linen Exactly as advertised	Rooms were well serviced, clean and children were catered for. Large variety of cuisine offered, rooms so comfortable. Good, clean modern facilities. Very local and personal, felt safe. Food was good, room was clean.
Unexpected extras ($n = 24$, 12% of responses)	Room upgrade Free stay from loyalty programme Free extras Great location Free transport for drinking party Late checkout Free Internet use Local tour guides Complimentary breakfast Free activities Heated outdoor spa Included animal park Chocolates on bed Spacious rooms Had organized guest activities Entertainment every night	The nicest thing that happened was the owner gave us a free bottle of wine with dinner. When my boyfriend and I arrived at the hotel we got the chance to upgrade the room without paying any extra. We were happy to get a room with free cable TV. It made our stay even better. Received a complimentary breakfast in a nice restaurant.

[a]Multiple themes were possible within a single incident.

Table 23.4. Major themes in negative incidents.

Categories	Themes	Examples
Staff attitudes (n = 39, 21% of responses)[a]	Not willing to help guests Rude and/or abusive	When the lady heard our accents she treated us very rudely, screaming at us until we left. Many problems but the staff seemed very reluctant to help.
No service recovery (n = 22, 12% of responses)	No response to problems No apologies Blames guest No compensation	Room entry cards constantly not working properly – frequent visits to reception to fix the problem where I was made to feel like a constant hassle to the staff.
Basics not met (n = 89, 47% of responses)	Dirty/smelly Damaged/broken facilities Facilities not as advertised Room/hotel not secure/safe Cockroaches/rodents Noisy Cold showers No toilet paper Limited car-parking Small room Difficult to locate No greeting on arrival	Having a cockroach crawl over me when I was in bed. Overall facilities were dirty and unpleasant. The hotel was extremely noisy which made it hard to sleep. I was charged for someone else's meal.
Operational problems (n = 28, 15% of responses)	Overbooking/booking mistakes Long wait for room for check-in Transport failure Woken by housekeepers Slow check-in Room bed configuration wrong Slow room service People still in room when entered Failed wake-up call Lost luggage Understaffed Room cards wouldn't work Lost safe key and so guests couldn't access valuables Theft by housekeepers Fire alarms went off and no communication from staff Staff member backed into car Generally disorganized	I slept late knowing that check-out time was 11.00. Surprisingly the hotel cleaners woke me up at 8.00 saying it was time to clean the rooms. The airport but when I arrived I was told an employee had made a mistake and the rooms were full, I then had to find another room in the middle of the night. I hope no one ever goes there again. My worst experience was getting a key from reception, walking to the room and unlocking it to find two people still in bed who had not checked out yet. Then we had to walk all the way back to the reception area where we had to wait 3 hours for a room to be ready.
Unexpected extras (n = 5, 2% of responses)	Hidden costs Extra charges for basics such as linen	There were hidden costs, which increased the price and blew my budget.
Other (n = 6, 3% of responses)	Other guests Staff smoking in rooms Bad weather No hotel actually there on arrival	Two other guests were fighting outside the room – they did not care about how others might feel.

[a]Multiple themes were possible within a single incident.

'no service recovery' where guests reported a lack of service recovery effort as the prime factor in the incident.

Two categories unique to the negative incidents were also used and these were an 'other' category for themes that seemed only indirectly related to the service provided by the accommodation itself, and 'operational problems'. These 'operational problems' were incident themes that described a breakdown in some aspect of the hotel's processes and procedures including things like a lack of communication between front office and housekeeping, unreliable courtesy buses and slow or inefficient service.

The incidents and SERVQUAL dimensions

The second stage of the content analysis of the critical incidents examined the use of words or phrases that were indicative of the five main SERVQUAL dimensions. Table 23.5 provides a summary of the outcomes of this content analysis approach and a comparison of the relative contributions of the different dimensions to the positive and negative incidents. The results suggested that assurance, tangibles, responsiveness and empathy were all potential aspects of positive service encounters. Only a very few positive incidents could be coded on the reliability dimension. Incidents related to a lack of reliability were, however, more common in the negative examples. Themes related to tangibles were also much more likely to be included in the negative incidents, while a lack of empathy was reported only once as the key contributor to a worst accommodation service experience.

Implications and Conclusions

The first major finding from the CIT analysis that staff attitudes are an important component of positive service encounters was not unexpected. In the SERVQUAL model, for example, four of the five key service dimensions are related to staff attitudes. The second major group of factors that contributed to pos-

itive incidents were staff actions that were seen as beyond the expected. This is a finding consistent with some other CIT studies (Bitner et al., 1990; Johnson, 2002), but not all. Callan (1998), for example, concluded that positive incidents based on extra effort from staff were rare. In addition, few other reported CIT studies identified the category of expected extra service and facilities. These results suggest that accommodation managers could develop policies that encourage staff to think about extras that could be given to customers for little or minimal cost. For example, on low occupancy nights, it would cost very little to offer the guests that do arrive an upgraded room. These two categories of unexpected extras and staff actions highlight the value of staff empowerment as a tool for enhancing service quality. In many of the positive incidents reported in this study staff took the initiative to offer something extra or to do something out of the ordinary to enhance the experience and or the self-esteem of the guest.

The final set of factors that contributed to the positive service incidents described by this group of guests has not been previously reported in the academic literature. This was the category labelled 'basics'. It is noteworthy that so many guests felt that a best accommodation service experience was one where they received nothing more than was advertised or than a clean, comfortable room. This suggests that at least for this sample, negative experiences where such basics are missing are common. This is consistent with the factors identified in the negative incidents. Basics such as cleanliness, security and maintenance dominated the negative service encounters that were described.

The other common category of negative incident themes were those related to operational problems or what Bitner et al. (1990, 1994) refer to as delivery systems failures. More specifically for hotel managers, the common failures identified were problems with room booking procedures, communications between front desk and housekeeping about customers checking out and systems for identifying and acting on maintenance problems. Each of these specific service systems failures can be corrected with management attention to the relevant policies and procedures.

Table 23.5. Critical incidents coded by SERVQUAL dimensions.

SERVQUAL dimension	Words/phrases/actions used to categorize incidents	Number of positive incidents and examples	Number of negative incidents and examples
Reliability	Service given as promised Dependable/reliable	(n = 4, 3% of responses) It looked good in the brochure and it was good in reality. There were no false impressions given.	(n = 28, 14% of responses) We asked to have a wake-up call and they never woke us up.
Assurance	Knowledgeable and courteous employees	(n = 30, 21% of responses) Frequently asked questions and inquiries were handled professionally and without hassles – knowledgeable staff helped with tour planning.	(n = 39, 19% of responses) There was little contact with staff, we were given the keys and expected to find our own rooms. Staff were unfriendly and rude.
Tangibles	Facilities, equipment, appearance of personnel	(n = 37, 26% of responses) Not only was the room clean and air conditioned, but it also had pay TV, pools, spa, gymnasium and tennis courts.	(n = 88, 44% of responses) I found the hygiene below standard, the room very small and cleanliness left a lot to be desired.
Responsiveness	Willingness to help	(n = 34, 24% of responses) No matter what we asked for the staff were willing to help.	(n = 46, 23% of responses) I complained to the person at the front desk and they would not help – they just said – it's too late at night to do anything, you will just have to live with it.
Empathy	Individual attention, understanding customer needs	(n = 36, 26% of responses) Personally approached by the manager who had a quiet conversation and a quick drink before he moved on to all the other guests to inquire of their needs.	(Only one instance where the target words/phrases were used) Staff were very ignorant and chose not to tend to our needs and concerns.

The present set of service encounters in tourist accommodation also highlighted the importance of service failure recovery for enhancing guests' service quality perceptions. Just over 10% of the negative incidents specifically noted that staff failed to attempt to recover from a service failure, while 6% of the positive incidents were descriptions of the opposite situation. In these descriptions of service recovery the guests often mentioned the recovery as evidence of the organization's commitment to high service standards. Effective service recovery then is not simply about avoiding negative outcomes but can actively contribute to positive outcomes for the organization.

According to proponents of the CIT approach, this technique offers the opportunity to link the more general quality dimensions from systems like SERVQUAL to particular actions and processes relevant to a specific context (Bitner et al., 1990; Wang et al., 2000). The present study highlights this particular benefit in that it generated information on service quality factors specific to tourist accommodation. Important tangibles in this context include safe and secure rooms and clean beds. Few other tangibles were noted in the incidents described. Reliability in hotels means finding the room set out as expected and having courtesy transport that arrives on time, and assurance can be enhanced by staff with knowledge about the local area and the ability to advise on activities and tour options.

Finally, not only do critical incidents provide a specific direction for improving tourist accommodation operations, but they also have a vividness and immediacy that gives them the power to persuade staff and managers of the need to change and improve (Johns and Lee-Ross, 1997). Personal stories have long been recognized as powerful tools in persuasive communication and education (Moscardo, 1999) and the CIT provides a simple way for guests to tell their stories.

Acknowledgements

The author would like to acknowledge the assistance provided by students enrolled in Hotel Management in 2002 and 2003 at James Cook University in collecting the critical incidents reported in this study. Several students also provided food for thought in their discussion of the major themes in, and implications of, their individual assessments of the critical incidents they collected.

References

Bejou, D., Edvardsson, B. and Rakowski, J.P. (1996) A critical incident approach to examining the effects of service failures on customer relationships: the case of Swedish and US airlines. *Journal of Travel Research* 35(10), 35–40.

Bitner, M.J., Booms, B.H. and Tetreault, M.S. (1990) The service encounter: diagnosing favorable and unfavorable incidents. *Journal of Marketing* 54, 71–84.

Bitner, M.J., Booms, B.H. and Mohr, L.A. (1994) Critical service encounters: the employee's viewpoint. *Journal of Marketing* 58(4), 95–106.

Callan, R. (1998) The critical incident technique in hospitality research: an illustration form the UK lodge sector. *Tourism Management* 19(1), 93–98.

Cavana, R.Y., Delahaye, B.L. and Sekaran, U. (2001) *Applied Business Research: Qualitative and Quantitative Methods.* John Wiley & Sons, Brisbane.

Chell, E. (1998) Critical incident technique. In: Symon, G. and Cassell, C. (eds) *Qualitative Methods and Analysis in Organizational Research.* Sage, London, pp. 51–72.

Chell, E. and Pittaway, L. (1998) A study of entrepreneurship in the restaurant and café industry: exploratory work using the critical incident technique as a methodology. *Hospitality Management* 17, 23–32.

Chung, B. and Hoffman, K.D. (1998) Critical incidents: service failures that matter most. *Cornell Hotel and Restaurant Administration Quarterly* 39(2), 66–71.

Dagger, T. and Lawley, M. (2003) Service quality. In: McColl-Kennedy, J.R. (ed.) *Services Marketing: A Managerial Approach.* John Wiley & Sons, Brisbane, pp. 72–100.

Edvardsson, B. and Strandvik, T. (2000) Is a critical incident critical for a customer relationship? *Managing Service Quality* 10(2), 82–91.

Ekinci, Y., Riley, M. and Chen, J.S. (2001) A review of comparison standards used in service quality and customer satisfaction studies: some emerging issues for hospitality and tourism research. In: Mazanec, J.A., Crouch, G.I., Ritchie, J.R.B. and Woodside, G.A. (eds) *Consumer Psychology of Tourism, Hospitality and Leisure,* Vol. 2. CAB International, Wallingford, UK, pp. 321–332.

Flanagan, J.C. (1954) The critical incident technique. *Psychological Bulletin* 51(4), 327–358.

Gabbott, M. (2003) Services research. In: McColl-Kennedy, J.R. (ed.) *Services Marketing: A Managerial Approach.* John Wiley & Sons, Brisbane, pp. 168–189.

George, R.T. (1989) Learning by example: the critical-incident technique. *Cornell Hotel and Restaurant Administration Quarterly* 30(2), 58–60.

Gilbert, D.C. and Morris, L. (1995) The relative importance of hotels and airlines to the business traveller. *International Journal of Contemporary Hospitality Management* 7(6), 19–23.

Gronroos, C. (1984) A service quality model and its marketing implications. *European Journal of Marketing* 18(4), 36–44.

Gyimothy, S. (1999) Visitors' perceptions of holiday experiences and service providers. *Journal of Travel and Tourism Marketing* 8(2), 57–74.

Johns, N. and Lee-Ross, D. (1997) A study of service quality in small hotels and guesthouses. *Progress in Tourism and Hospitality Research* 3, 351–363.

Johns, N. and Mattsson, J. (2003) Managing the service encounters in tourism. In: Kusluvan, S. (ed.) *Managing Employee Attitudes and Behaviors in the Tourism and Hospitality Industry.* Nova Science, New York, pp. 173–200.

Johnson, L. (2002) An application of the critical incident technique in gaming research. *Journal of Travel and Tourism Marketing* 12(2/3), 45–63.

Kandampully, J. (1999) Creating and maintaining a competitive advantage. In: Lee-Ross, D. (ed.) *HRM in Tourism and Hospitality.* Cassell, London, pp. 37–47.

Knutson, B.J. (2001) Service quality monitoring and feedback systems. In: Kandampully, J., Mok, C. and Sparks, B. (eds) *Service Quality Management in Hospitality, Tourism, and Leisure.* Haworth Press, New York, pp. 143–158.

Lazer, W. and Layton, R. (1999) Quality of hospitality service: a challenge for the millennium. Available at: http://www.hotel-online.com/Trends/EI/EI_ServiceChallenge.html

Lee-Ross, D. (2001) Understanding the role of the service encounter in tourism, hospitality, and leisure services. In: Kandampully, J., Mok, C. and Sparks, B. (eds) *Service Quality Management in Hospitality, Tourism, and Leisure.* Haworth Press, New York, pp. 85–95.

Liden, S.B. and Skalen, P. (2003) The effect of service guarantees on service recovery. *International Journal of Service Industry Management* 14(1), 36–58.

Lockwood, A. (1994) Using service incidents to identify quality improvement points. *International Journal of Contemporary Hospitality Management* 6(1/2), 75–80.

Moscardo, G. (1999) *Making Visitors Mindful.* Sagamore, Champaign, Illinois.

O'Neill, M. (2001) Measuring service quality and customer satisfaction. In: Kandampully, J., Mok, C. and Sparks, B. (eds) *Service Quality Management in Hospitality, Tourism, and Leisure.* Haworth Press, New York, pp. 159–191.

Parasuraman, A., Zeithaml, V. and Berry, L. (1985) A conceptual model of service quality and its implications for future research. *Journal of Marketing* 49(Fall), 41–50.

Parasuraman, A., Zeithaml, V. and Berry, L. (1991) Refinement and reassessment of the SERVQUAL scale. *Journal of Retailing* 64 (Winter), 42–450.

Roberts, C. (2001) Competitive advantages of service quality in hospitality, tourism, and leisure services. In: Kandampully, J., Mok, C. and Sparks, B. (eds) *Service Quality Management in Hospitality, Tourism, and Leisure.* Haworth Press, New York, pp. 111–122.

Rutherford, D.G. and Umbreit, W.T. (2002) Improving interactions between meeting planners and hotel employees. In: Rutherford, D.G. (ed.) *Hotel Management and Operations,* 3rd edn. John Wiley & Sons, New York, pp. 339–357.

Wang, K.-C., Hsieh, A.-T. and Huan, T.-C. (2000) Critical service features in group package tour: an exploratory research. *Tourism Management* 12(2), 177–189.

Woods, B. and Moscardo, G. (2003) Enhancing wildlife education through mindfulness. *Australian Journal of Environmental Education* 19, 97–108.

24 Factors of Satisfaction: A Case Study of Explore Park

Muzaffer Uysal
Virginia Polytechnic Institute and State University, USA

Introduction

Managers of public and private outdoor recreational areas need confirmation from the visiting public that the facilities, services and programmes generally provided are satisfactory (Noe, 1999; Schofield, 2000). The objective of this study is to understand site-specific satisfaction with services, programmes and maintenance factors. The objective is achieved by testing whether instrumental and expressive attributes are distinct behavioural indicators that could better predict visitor satisfaction. Expressive indicators involve core experiences representing the major intent of an act (e.g. exhibits, interpretation of programmes offered, experiences with recreation activities), while instrumental indicators serve to act as facilitators towards achieving that desired end (e.g. parking, rental services, restrooms) (Noe, 1987). Although these distinctions will be used to specifically define characteristics of a recreational situation that may affect satisfaction, the visitor, through past exposure or unfulfilled expectations, may also significantly alter judgements of satisfaction about that situation.

The guiding proposition of this study is based on the work conducted by Herzberg et al. (1959) and subsequently adapted to the recreation and leisure field by Howard and Crompton (1980). The original work by Herzberg et al. (1959) focused on a series of experiments in work motivation and satisfaction. Based on the data, the authors developed a theory that consisted of two qualitatively different groups of factors which motivated the employees. The first set of factors included mainly tangible items that were associated with the job content. It was concluded that such attributes as salary, tangible fringe benefits, company policies, working conditions and interpersonal relationship with others in the workplace created dissatisfaction if they were absent. Their presence may not deeply affect job satisfaction. These attributes are termed maintenance or hygiene factors by the authors. The second set of factors, termed satisfiers or motivators centred on the job content and lead to psychological benefits and intrinsic rewards from the job performed. These attributes included mainly intangible benefits such as recognition, achievement, intellectual challenge and self-actualization. Howard and Crompton (1980) adapted these concepts to explain factors in visitors' satisfaction with experiences in recreation facilities. The same analogy found fertile ground in tourism and outdoor recreation settings with the terms of instrumental attributes corresponding to maintenance factors and expressive attributes corresponding to psychological benefits and/or intrinsic rewards (Noe, 1987; Noe and Uysal, 1997; Crompton,

---

2003). However, these factors are not necessarily mutually exclusive. The challenge for resource managers is to be able to capture the extent to which these factors interact and affect visitor experience and satisfaction.

The development of a working model is based upon an outgrowth of earlier research by Noe (1987). This model assumes a direct approach for determining satisfaction and makes a theoretical distinction between instrumental and expressive indicators of satisfaction. In a subsequent study, Noe and Uysal (1997) also examined the theoretical distinction between instrumental and expressive indicators of satisfaction with respect to different outdoor settings. One of the major conclusions of their study was that the relative importance of both instrumental and expressive indicators might show variation from site to site. In marketing, Swan and Combs (1976) define instrumental performance as the means to an end or the evaluation of the physical product while the expressive attribute was the end in itself or the psychological interpretation of a product. In social action theory, both concepts are treated as necessary for human action. Both are goal-directed with the instrumental being more cognitively oriented whereas the expressive is more emotional or feeling oriented (Noe, 1999). Swan and Combs (1976) also assert that satisfaction can be produced only through the expressive activities. The evaluative mode of behaviour is also associated with expressive acts within the context of social action theory. On the other hand, Noe (1987) found that expressive indicators of satisfaction forming core recreational experiences were more salient in explaining general satisfaction. Czepiel and Rosenberg (1974) would consider these as factors which 'truly motivate and contribute to satisfaction', while the instrumental are maintenance factors which, if absent, create dissatisfaction. From this argument, it is clear that facilities and attractions may possess the duality of expressive and instrumental roles that may complementarily produce satisfaction. For example, in analysing the effects of the instrumental and expressive attributes on satisfaction, a LISREL path model was applied to analyse the variables so as to best select 'the richest and most parsimonious model . . . to explain the satisfaction process' (Jurowski et al., 1995–1996, p. 56). In testing the efficacy of the various models, the final model resulting from this research implies that instrumental and expressive satisfiers work together to produce overall satisfaction. In another study, Uysal and Williams (2004) examined whether visitor types based on motivation for travel moderate the relationship between instrumental and expressive attributes. Their study revealed that types of visitors based on motivation for travel moderated the relationship between the two constructs.

In short, expressive indicators involve core experiences representing the major intent of an act, in this case seeking a satisfactory outdoor experience in a park (e.g. sightseeing, camping, hiking a natural trail, floating a river). Instrumental indicators serve as actions or behaviours towards facilitating that desired end (e.g. rental services, restrooms, concession services) (Uysal and Noe, 2002). In our testing of the expressive–instrumental model, it is still reasonable to speculate that instrumental factors could also contribute to satisfaction since so few studies have measured these attributes.

Perceived disconfirmation, included in the marketing literature as a type of contrast theory, describes the discrepancy between actual participation and expectations as perceived by the user (Oliver and Oliver, 1981; Oliver, 1997). It is measured with a question that asks how close the product or service comes to what the respondent expected (Ryan, 1995). In all probability, previous use and expectations are probably modified by the actual experience and differ from the initial impressions in part because of dissonance reduction and assimilation. In order to avoid this confounding situation, perceptions of post experiences were measured. In measuring expectations, the 'disconfirmation' possibility was emphasized by attempting to assess whether 'more' or 'fewer' services, facilities or programmes could possibly be made available or reduced as perceived by the public.

Balance theory also justifies factoring into the explanation differences in the level of use

of a site that may function to reduce dissonance and modify expectations (Yi, 1990).
Consequently, a measure of PASTUSE was
included in the model to examine if a previous
visit to the same site enters into the determination of overall satisfaction. The current
working model describes overall satisfaction as
a function of instrumental and expressive preferences, expectations plus PASTUSE. The
major question raised in this research asks to
what extent do the above attributes, expectations and incidence of PASTUSE relate to
overall satisfaction. The hypothesized model
can be written as

$$SAT = f(INST, EXPRES, EXP, PASTUSE)$$

where:
SAT = satisfaction score with amenities;
INST = instrumental factors (e.g. restrooms,
   parking, personnel, restaurant);
EXPRES = expressive factors (e.g. exhibits,
   types of programmes offered);
EXP = expectation items;
PASTUSE = number of visits in the past.

Research Methods

Study site

The study site encompassed Virginia's Explore
Park that began operation in 1994 as a
public–private partnership between the
Virginia Recreational Facilities Authority and
the River Foundation. A 1.5-mile spur road
connects the Blue Ridge Parkway to Virginia's
Explore Park. The park is an 1100-acre outdoor living history museum and Recreation
Park that offers opportunities for leisure activity, learning and fun. The popular historic district is home to costumed interpreters who
teach visitors about life in western Virginia
from the precontact Native American to colo-
nial frontiers-people to the settlement of
Virginia. A recent addition to the 19th-century
area includes a working batteau on the
Roanoke River, which highlights river culture
during that era and the life of the freed
African-American slave. The Arthur Taubman
Welcome Center is located at the terminus of
the Roanoke River Parkway and serves as a

gateway for park visitors and a rest station for
weary Parkway motorists. Adjacent to the
Welcome Center is historic Brugh Tavern
restaurant, where diners can enjoy a delicious
meal in an upscale, historic ambience.

Sample survey

A walk-in survey at the Welcome Center was
conducted during the summer of 2001.
Respondents were both Explore Park and Blue
Ridge Parkway visitors and tested after their
park experiences at both places. Since the
data were collected at the Welcome Center of
Explore Park, visitors whose visits included
Explore Park only were omitted from the data
collection process. Through this sampling
approach, the general park users were simply
asked to complete a four-page questionnaire.
After almost 6 weeks of data collection, this
semi-structured approach to collecting data
yielded 122 usable questionnaires. There was
no attempt made to contact the respondents at
certain time intervals of the day. Visitors as
respondents were simply invited to complete
the questionnaire. For the analysis, missing
values were replaced with mean scores. It is
also important to mention that this particular
study represents one of the four possible sites
in Virginia along the Blue Ridge Parkway for
which data collection was initiated.

Variables/questionnaire

The questionnaire was organized into five distinct sections. In the first section, respondents
were asked to rate the facilities, services and
programmes that were provided at Explore
Park. Since perceived product performance is
a key predictor in explaining variance in satisfaction, a 5-point Likert scale for perceived
service performance that allowed park users to
rate the site attributes from poor to excellent
was developed. The final question in this section asked the respondents to rate their overall
impression of service and satisfaction with
their visit to Explore Park. Expectations were
measured by determining when the park
respondents felt more or less services were
expected than were actually being provided or

offered. Respondents were tested after their park experience rather than in a before–after test design, because in the post hoc situation the respondent was already exposed to what actually existed at the site offering a more realistic base of comparison for meeting an expectation. And finally, PASTUSE was gauged by calculating times frequented at the parks over a 12-month period.

Analysis

The analysis of this study consisted of three major steps. First, instrumental and expressive measures were formed for Explore Park based on its offerings. The grouping of these measurements was based on the previous relevant literature review and adapted to the test site (Table 24.1). The grouping was not intended to be totally exhaustive. However, it represents examples of theoretically based elements (features) that describe instrumental and expressive factors as discussed in the paper and present at the site. Second, the 23 expectation statements were factor analysed using a varimax rotation procedure (Table 24.2). After removing double loadings and items that did not contribute much to factor groupings on the basis of intercorrelations and variance explained, the factor analysis resulted in two factor groupings that accounted for more than 66% of the variance. The first expectation factor grouping contained such items as park guides to explain things, rangers to inform us, indoor lodging, developed campsites, picnic areas with toilets, a road providing enough parking space, a road with convenient stops, signs indicating a place to get fuel and food and a clear view from the road. These items were mostly consistent with instrumental (maintenance) factors and the second factor consisted of items (e.g. exhibits, books about the region and southern mountains, live demonstration projects) that were expressive in nature. It is also important to mention that since the site visit took place as a result of the trip to Blue Ridge Parkway, the items included in the expectation scale were directed at the Park. These factor groupings were then used as independent factors in the satisfaction model. In the final step, the above delineated

Table 24.1. Instrumental and expressive measures for the study site.

Instrumental factors	Expressive factors
Museum store	Church
Restaurant	Museum
Welcome centre	Hiking trails
Picnic pavilion	Biking trails
Parking	Tavern
Restrooms	Exhibits
Personnel	Fishing
	Environmental programmes
	Native American programmes
	18th century programmes
	19th century programmes

Note: The grouping of these measures was determined based on relevant literature review and expert assessment. The grouping was not intended to be mutually exclusive, nor exhaustive. However, it represents examples of theoretically based elements that describe instrumental and expressive factors for the site in question. Measures were rated on a 5-point Likert type scale, ranging from 1 (poor) to 5 (excellent).

and operationalized independent factors that were hypothesized to influence satisfaction were analysed using ordinary least squares. Initially, the factors that estimate satisfaction were introduced progressively into the model to obtain the most satisfactory results.

Findings

The results of the Pearson correlation analysis revealed that overall satisfaction was correlated most highly with instrumental ratings of the site ($r = -0.36$) and expressive ratings of the expectation scale ($r = -0.32$). There seemed to be almost no significant correlation between the PASTUSE and overall satisfaction. The results of the correlation matrix indicated that a relationship did exist between overall satisfaction and both the instrumental rating factors of the site and one of the two expectation factor groupings. All of the factors in the original model were then regressed against the overall satisfaction element. Table 24.3 presents the results of the final model. This final model does

Table 24.2. Factor analysis of expectations.

	Loading	Variance (%)	Eigen-value	Alpha
Expectation Factor 1		53.87	10.24	0.921
Park guides to explain things	0.882			
Rangers to inform us	0.875			
Indoor lodging	0.859			
Developed campsites	0.848			
Picnic area with toilets	0.832			
A road providing enough parking space	0.811			
Self-guided hikes	0.802			
A road with convenient stops	0.777			
Signs indicating where services are located	0.766			
A place to get fuel and food	0.697			
A road with nicely designed guard rails, shoulders, bridges and tunnels	0.635			
A clear view from the road	0.627			
Expectation Factor 2		12.61	2.39	0.853
Variety of exhibits	0.963			
Books about region and southern mountains	0.850			
Live demonstration projects	0.749			
Visible ranger patrol	0.699			
Aggressive enforcement of safety	0.686			
Total variance explained		66.48		

Note: Measures were rated on a 5-point Likert type scale, ranging from 1 (strongly disagreed) to 5 (strongly agreed).

not include the PASTUSE as an independent variable. The analysis of the results of the simple correlation coefficients and a stepwise regression procedure produced the final model, which was significant at the 0.00 probability level. The coefficient of determination indicates that almost 17% of the variation in overall satisfaction was explained by the variables included in the model. The corollary analysis indicated that several of these vari-

ables are important in determining the overall satisfaction level. The beta coefficients indicate that expressive and instrumental factors are stronger predictors of overall satisfaction or dissatisfaction. For example, the variable (INST) of instrumental factor ratings has a negative beta value of −0.544, suggesting that a poor rating of instrumental factors at the study site may influence overall satisfaction negatively. However, a positive rating of the

Table 24.3. Results of regression analysis.

	Std error	Standardized beta coefficients	t-value	Significance level
(Constant)	0.168		11.015	0.000
INST	0.081	−0.544	−2.810	0.006
EXPRES	0.68	−0.061	−0.331	0.741
EXP1	0.040	0.112	1.206	0.230
EXP2	0.045	0.351	3.407	0.001

Note: The model has the following statistics: Adjusted R^2 = 0.187; F = 7.916; Sig. 00;
INST = instrumental rating factors; EXPRES = expressive rating factors; EXP1 = expectation factor grouping 1; and EXP2 = expectation factor grouping 2.

expressive part (EXP2) of expectation items about the trip on the Blue Ridge Parkway seemed to affect overall satisfaction positively.

Conclusion

The results of the correlation and ordinary least squares analysis revealed partial support for the existence of dual satisfaction factors. These findings are also consistent with the results reported by Noe (1987), Floyd (1993), Jurowski et al. (1995) and Noe and Uysal (1997). It appears the factors representing a judgement about facilities and services are not as important to overall satisfaction for those seeking an outdoor recreational experience as they are for the casual sightseer. In this current study, the instrumental factors appear to be more important than expressive elements for the site visitor. The poor performance of site-specific instrumental factors affects satisfaction negatively, while the expressive part of expectations from a site may affect satisfaction positively. Thus, the expressive part of expectations may also contribute to overall satisfaction. These results imply that visitor satisfaction at sites designed for outdoor experiences would not necessarily depend upon expressive elements such as hiking, interpretive programmes while visitor satisfaction in areas designed for sightseeing (historical attractions) is somewhat more dependent on the provision of instrumental

elements such as restrooms and shelters. This observation suggests that further research is also needed to examine the effect of development stages of sites on satisfaction. Table 24.4 provides a summary of findings with respect to the variables used in the case study.

The advantage of approaching satisfaction from the perspective of instrumental and expressive factors along with other relevant variables is that the researcher could provide information that would allow resource managers and planners to understand the relative importance of satisfaction factors and the degree to which they could have control over these factors. The information that could be obtained from such an approach to satisfaction would allow managers not to tolerate the poor performance of instrumental factors. Because of the tangibility nature of instrumental factors, planners and managers would be able to develop appropriate amenities and maintain them at the performance level that will be expected. This approach also implies that managers and planners should examine tourist destinations and natural areas from the perspective of a systems approach. In its simplest form, the main elements of satisfaction – expressive and instrumental attributes – represent two major components of the market place, namely, demand and supply. Some expressive attributes are the behavioural results of inner emotional state and pose opportunities for interaction and participation. These attributes are the essence of travel motivation in the first place, representing the demand side of the equation. Thus, potential

Table 24.4. Summary of key findings.

Instrumental factors	Expressive factors	Expectations	Past use
Absence or poor performance of maintenance factors reduced satisfaction.	Ratings of perceived performance of site-specific expressive factors of the experience were not significant in this study.	The place exceeds visitors' expectations; both the instrumental and expressive dimensions of expectations were positively correlated with overall satisfaction. However, expressive ones were statistically significant contributors to satisfaction.	Not significant and dropped from the model.

and actual visitors are the ones who seem to have more control over these attributes. The responses to demand side or expressive attributes, including benefits-sought at the destinations would then naturally represent the supply side of travel experience. Therefore, the instrumental are maintenance attributes without which one may not achieve some degree of satisfaction on a measurement scale from the experience. It is clear from the study reported that instrumental attributes also influence satisfaction along with the expressive. As Laws (2002) points out that the appropriateness of the technical design delivery systems and product offerings along with an understanding of the meaning to customers of their experiences would be of great help to managers seeking to develop competitive position, then, maintain the advantages gained. The quality and availability of tourism supply resources are a critical element in meeting the needs of the ever-changing and growing tourism market. It is important that destinations monitor visitors' satisfaction with facilities, programmes and services in order to maintain a sustained and expanding business. Empirical studies of this nature may be of help to destination marketeers and planners to understand the complexity of satisfaction as one of the elements of visitation behaviour. Actual and potential markets can use these types of studies to develop appropriate communication materials that would incorporate the relative importance of destination features as perceived.

Acknowledgement

The author thanks the staff members of Explore Park who facilitated a walk-in survey at the Welcome Center of Explore Park during the summer of 2001.

References

Crompton, J.L. (2003) Adapting Herzberg: a conceptualization of the effects of hygiene and motivator attributes on perceptions of event quality. *Journal of Travel Research* 41(4), 305–310.

Czepiel, J.A. and Rosenberg, L.J. (1974) The study of consumer satisfaction. *AMA Educators' Proceedings*. American Marketing Association, Chicago, Illinois, pp. 119–123.

Floyd, M. (1993) *Recreation Research Survey of Cape Lookout National Seashore*. Final Report Submitted to the National Park Service. Texas A&M University, College Station, Texas.

Herzberg, F., Mausner, B. and Snyderman, B. (1959) *The Motivation to Work*. John Wiley & Sons, New York.

Howard, D.R. and Crompton, L.J. (1980) *Financing, Managing and Marketing Recreation and Park Resources*. William C. Brown, Dubuque, Iowa.

Jurowski, C., Cumbow, M., Uysal, M. and Noe, F. (1995) The effects of instrumental and expressive factors on overall satisfaction in a park environment. *Journal of Environmental Systems* 24(1), 47–67.

Laws, E. (ed.) (2002) *Tourism Marketing: Quality and Service Management Perspectives*. Continuum, London.

Noe, F. (1987) Measurement specification and leisure satisfaction. *Leisure Sciences* 9(3), 163–172.

Noe, F. (1999) *Tourist Service Satisfaction: Hotel, Transportation, and Recreation*. Sagamore Publishing, Champaign, Illinois.

Noe, F. and Uysal, M. (1997) Evaluation of outdoor recreational settings: a problem of measuring user satisfaction. *Journal of Retailing and Consumer Services* 4(4), 223–230.

Oliver, R.L. (1997) *Satisfaction: A Behavioral Perspective on the Consumer*. McGraw-Hill, London.

Oliver, R.L. and Oliver, G.L. (1981) Effects of satisfaction and its antecedents on consumer preference and intention. In: Monroe, K.B. (ed.) *Advances in Consumer Research*. Association for Consumer Research, Ann Arbor, Michigan, pp. 88–93.

Ryan, C. (1995) *Researching Tourist Satisfaction: Issues, Concepts, and Problems*. Routledge, London.

Schofield, P. (2000) Evaluating Castlefield Urban Heritage Park from the consumer perspective: destination attribute importance, visitor perception, and satisfaction. *Tourism Analysis* 5(2–4), 183–189.

Swan, J. and Combs, L. (1976) Product performance and consumer satisfaction. *Journal of Marketing Research* 40(April), 25–33.

Uysal, M. and Noe, F.P. (2002) Satisfaction in outdoor recreation and tourism settings. In: Laws, E. (ed.) *Tourism Marketing, Quality and Service Management Perspectives.* Continuum, London, pp. 140–151.

Uysal, M. and Williams, J. (2004) The role of expressive and instrumental factors in measuring visitors satisfaction. In: Crouch, G.I., Perdue, R.R., Timmermans, H.J.P. and Uysal, M. (eds) *Consumer Psychology of Tourism, Hospitality and Leisure,* Vol. 3. CAB International, Wallingford, UK, pp. 227–235.

Yi, Y.K. (1990) A critical review of consumer satisfaction. In: Zeithaml, V. (ed.) *Review of Marketing.* American Marketing Association, Chicago, Illinois.

25 The Value of a Benchmarking Approach for Assessing Service Quality Satisfaction in Environmental Tourism

Philip L. Pearce
James Cook University, Australia

Introduction

In 1965 Mick Jagger of the Rolling Stones lamented that in the growing consumer society he could not 'get no satisfaction'. Their grammar was less than perfect but the Rolling Stones' assertion of the importance of satisfaction in popular culture was a statement for its time. It may simply be coincidental, or it may reflect a Zeitgeist in Western consumer societies, but the studies of satisfaction in the business and tourism literature largely arise in and follow this mid-1960s period (Fishbein, 1967; Uhl and Schoner, 1969; Swan and Combs, 1976; Martilla and James, 1977). Concerns with satisfaction in consumer society, as well as the Rolling Stones themselves, are still very much with us four decades later.

The focus on satisfaction in this chapter is specific. It addresses satisfaction issues, including effective measurement and interpretation. It does this in the context of tourism and particularly environmental tourism businesses. It is argued that this specific satisfaction focus on tourism experiences is needed because the broader and voluminous consumer-satisfaction literature has some inherent assumptions and perspectives which can be inappropriate or misleading in the tourism context. For example, most of the consumer-satisfaction litera-

ture emphasizes repeat business and repeat purchase behaviour (Fuchs, 2002). This repeat purchasing may be highly relevant to products such as cigarettes, cars and electrical goods but is less applicable to once-in-a-lifetime tourism journeys and adventures (Pearce and Moscardo, 2001). Additionally, the very basis of tourism studies as an emerging discipline in the field of knowledge is built on the view that the purchasing of experiences which are planned for in advance, accessed in unique social and physical settings and enjoyed in retrospect, sometimes for decades after completion, requires that researchers and analysts produce distinctive frameworks of understanding (Gunn, 1994).

A distinction can be made between satisfaction and enjoyment. The latter term is largely used in leisure studies while satisfaction is employed more in business and tourism research (Ryan, 1995; Veal, 1997). These terms are not, however, simply synonyms. The enjoyment concept focuses more on the realization of social, self-esteem and fulfilment motives and less on fundamental needs and concerns. In the satisfaction literature, Noe (1999) outlines a distinction between expressive needs in satisfaction and instrumental needs. This two-part approach to satisfaction, particularly as it relates to tourist environment

©CAB International 2006. *Managing Tourism and Hospitality Services: Theory and International Applications* (eds Bruce Prideaux, Gianna Moscardo and Eric Laws)

settings, distinguishes the adequacy of basic setting features (e.g. toilets, physical comfort of the location) and expressive features (scenic qualities, atmosphere and a sense of place). Since Noe's formulation captures much of the concept of enjoyment by emphasizing the expressive component of place experiences, enjoyment as used in the leisure and recreation literature can be embraced as a part of this discussion rather than requiring separate analysis.

The status of the term satisfaction also needs clarification. In the spaghetti of terms which characterize tourist appraisal of settings and which include perception, attitudes, values, expectations, benefits, enjoyment and satisfaction, it can be asserted quite simply that satisfaction is an attitude. It is a post-experience or post-consumption attitude as it is an evaluative orientation towards a product or service that can be measured (Czepiel and Rosenberg, 1977; Pearce et al. 1998; Noe, 1999). In this view, satisfaction is a special kind of attitude because it cannot exist prior to the purchase or consumption of the attitude object.

In psychology research, attitudes have three components: (i) knowledge; (ii) affective (emotional); and (iii) implicit behavioural predisposition. There is expanding speculation and debate on the possible sequence in which these components of attitude arise as well as their relative importance (Mano and Oliver, 1993; Oliver, 1993, 1997; Bagozzi et al., 1999; Zins, 2002). There is a distinct possibility that in some circumstances cognitive components precede affective elements while in other settings affective elements guide the cognitive components (cf. Zins, 2002). The recognition of affective, cognitive and behavioural elements as intertwined elements of the satisfaction concept, even if the psychological sequencing shaping these elements remains uncertain, should alert researchers to the pivotal issues of the wording of satisfaction questions. Some expressions, it can be argued, will favour affective components while others will emphasize cognitive or implicit behavioural components. This theme will be explored further in the section on methodological and measurement issues.

Core Issues

There are several fundamental issues in organizing and advancing the discussion of satisfaction in tourist environments. First, it is valuable to consider the potential roles and purposes of satisfaction research. Subsequently, consideration will be given to quality measures of satisfaction as well as the neatly labelled 'satisfaction trap' in consumer studies. The dominant traditions in understanding satisfaction will be reviewed and a critique of the major prevailing approach will be undertaken. Once these core issues are addressed the discussion will outline some original work on a benchmarking approach in tourist environments.

The purpose of satisfaction research

There are multiple purposes for satisfaction studies. Direct satisfaction comparisons can be used for competitive advantage. For example, in countries where the law permits such explicit comparisons, promotional materials from one company can assert that more people like their product than that of a competitor, thus establishing a positive selling point while weakening the competitor's appeal (Ryan, 1995).

A second use of satisfaction studies is to assess performance targets. Many companies and many public sector organizations including National Parks have specific performance targets. An example of this approach is reported by McCarthur (2000) who notes that one destination in South Australia, Kangaroo Island, has produced a tourism plan with the specific target of having 85% of its visitors very satisfied with the destination. An allied performance-based use of satisfaction measures lies in a company's internal use of the scores. Different work teams may be assessed for their effect on customer satisfaction thus establishing motivation and incentive systems within a hotel, theme park or tourism business. Similarly, seasonality differences in the company's performance can be monitored by assessing satisfaction scores over the months of the year (Baum and Lundtorp, 2001).

Sometimes the performance targets of business and environmental management agencies are included within the framework of an integrated management plan such as a total quality management system or a learning organization framework. Frequently, satisfaction measures are integral to such larger management approaches. Hockings *et al.* (2000), for example, include visitor-satisfaction measures as a major item for evaluation in their report for the International Union for the Conservation of Nature outlining a systems-based management of protected areas.

A further use of satisfaction measures, which lies beyond individual business advantages and natural environment-management targets, resides in holistic sustainability tourism assessments. The World Tourism Organization (1998) has produced a guide for local authorities on developing sustainable tourism which includes measures of visitor satisfaction. This use of destination-based satisfaction measures is likely to become more widespread, as the satisfaction measures can be used as indicators interconnecting business performance, environmental quality and community acceptance (Payne, 1993; Ritchie *et al.*, 2000).

These larger issues in satisfaction measurement have recently been extended with the view that satisfaction measures can have a future-oriented value. Kristensen *et al.* (2000) suggest that customer satisfaction can be a forward looking measure. They report evidence from a number of European studies which demonstrate that high customer satisfaction levels were able to predict subsequent successful business performance. More specifically, the work being undertaken on a pan-European customer-satisfaction measurement instrument suggests that, at least across a range of businesses, there is mounting evidence that a rise in customer satisfaction will produce a rise in return on investment. Even more specifically, there is tentative evidence that broadly based consumer satisfaction scores have impacts on the overall stock market within 3–4 months (Ittner and Larcker, 1996; Anderson *et al.*, 1997). These kinds of links between customer satisfaction and tourism environment businesses have not yet been established. Nevertheless, this initial evidence from Europe tends to confirm the working assumption of many organizations that customer satisfaction measures are much more than historical accounts and are indeed guides to action.

A final but not trivial use of the customer satisfaction measures is to enhance the satisfaction of company employees and managers. Even though there are a number of measurement issues producing inflated or overly positive satisfaction scores, nevertheless it is rewarding to the staff of organizations to know that customers are reporting positively on their interactions and experiences. When this positive feedback is converted into bonuses, prizes, awards and company incentives, the ego-based use of satisfaction measures is even more noteworthy.

Criteria for quality measures of satisfaction

There are at least eight criteria which help to define quality satisfaction measures. The eight attributes are listed in Table 25.1 with a brief commentary.

Two concepts frequently mentioned in the literature on this topic and which are embedded in Table 25.1 deserve further attention. There is some reference in existing satisfaction studies on what has been described as the satisfaction trap (Noe, 1999). This issue, explored briefly in Table 25.1 under the heading 'Relevant', focuses on the mistake of thinking of visitor satisfaction as an end in itself rather than being one of a number of critical outcome measures. For business, what matters is not how well satisfied their customers are, but the profitability accruing from a certain number of adequately satisfied customers. A more extreme example of the satisfaction trap arises in a natural environment or heritage setting. Here, placing total priority on customer satisfaction and falling into the satisfaction trap may be particularly problematic if that customer satisfaction comes at the expense of wilful or even unwitting damage to the resource through biophysical impacts such as erosion, accretion and stress.

A second concept of note identified briefly in Table 25.1 is the commonly reported positivity bias in tourist satisfaction studies. Measures of

Table 25.1. Attributes necessary for quality satisfaction measures.

Attribute	Characteristics
Relevant	The measure of satisfaction and its importance have to fit within the total goals of the organization. Example: Satisfaction of visitors may matter less to the clergy caretaking an English cathedral than it does to a commercial theme park.
Measurable	The satisfaction measure must be clear and unambiguous. Question wording is critical and always needs close attention in design and in interpreting outcomes. Example: Assessing satisfaction by asking visitors if a location is better or worse than other places they have visited produces a shifting basis for comparison and ultimately ambiguous results. It is much better to ask for known comparisons, or direct assessments of performance.
Sensitive	The measure must be sensitive to changes as the responses of visitors change. The positivity bias, the tendencies to offer overly positive responses, is important here. Example: The measure must not have an artificial ceiling preventing the assessment of improvement such as a limited 4-point scale. This offers no room for improvement and creates a blunt measuring instrument.
Timely	The assessment of satisfaction must be timely in two senses: (a) produced quickly for rapid management action, and (b) linked to known, established phases of the operation such as the time of the day, personnel being evaluated, weather conditions and immediate contextual factors such as operational problems.
Accessible	Greater power is generated for the satisfaction measure if it is easy to understand and interpret. Example: Information presented in accessible formats both graphically and with written text evaluations or labels rather than numerically may assist widespread acceptance.
Cost effective	The collection of information should be balanced against the potential value of implementing the information. Example: Surveys of every guest may be intrusive but a random sampling of guests every month may be an effective monitoring activity. Additionally biased small samples may not be worth the effort as they have no consequences for implementation.
Public support	The measures must be seen by key stakeholders as useful, and the actions and consequences of the assessment clearly grasped.
Conceptually based	The adequacy of a satisfaction measure will be enhanced if it is linked to a system of explanation which identifies the forces acting on the visitors' experiences.

satisfaction in general typically tend to be distributed towards the positive pole of the ratings (e.g. on a 1–10 scale of satisfaction, a bias towards the top end of the scale will be obtained with many people giving 7, 8, 9 or 10) (cf. Ryan, 1995). One explanation for this kind of result is ego or self-esteem protection. When a visitor purchases a product, typically they do not want to admit they have made a bad choice. In particular, since leisure tourism and holiday activities are frequently chosen freely by the participant and reflect personal values and even status concerns, it reflects badly on the individual's decision making and personal credibility if the selection proves to be a poor one.

The difficulty with the positivity bias issue for businesses is that it becomes difficult to gauge or detect problems because, as indicated in Table 25.1, the satisfaction measure becomes insensitive; in short, it evolves into an expensive and blunt instrument. The solution to this issue lies in creating a diversity of measures and expanded scales to differentiate customer responses more adequately.

The final section of Table 25.1 presents the perspective that satisfaction studies are of greater value when they are linked to one of the organizing frameworks in satisfaction research. This view is adopted because connecting individual studies to existing traditions of research allows researchers and businesses to benefit from the cumulative experience of other analysts. The following section considers the adequacy of these existing approaches in the context of tourists and the natural environments they visit.

Understanding satisfaction: existing approaches

The dominant tradition in understanding satisfaction is labelled the expectancy/confirmation/disconfirmation or EDP model (Oliver, 1980). This approach states that customers compare actual product and service performance to their prior expectations. If the expectations are met or exceeded the customer is satisfied or highly satisfied. If the expectations are not met, dissatisfaction follows. Such a perspective is relatively common in the satisfaction literature (cf. Schofield, 2000). Assessments of satisfaction based on this approach are frequently seen in hotels, restaurants and other tourism linked service sectors. The mission statements of many companies incorporate the approach into their slogans such as 'We aim to exceed our customers' expectations' or 'We meet your expectations and then some' (cf. Hanan and Karp, 1989).

There are some limitations to the adequacy of this approach. Expectations vary in clarity and relevance. In some circumstances expectations for, say a hotel room, can be seen as establishing a normative standard which can act as a basis for evaluation. As Hughes (1991) and Fornell et al. (1996) point out expectations are not so relevant when the good or service varies greatly, when it is purchased infrequently, or when extra additional factors take over (e.g. weather, other people).

For example, in adventure tourism settings Hughes notes that visitors may still be satisfied despite expectations not being met because unanticipated positive factors intervened such as forming an unexpected close friendship.

The EDP model also generates a number of measurement issues. Teas (1993) notes that when using assumed interval levels of measurement such as rating scales to assess satisfaction and expectation, a performance expectation discrepancy of -1 can be achieved in non-equivalent ways. Specifically, a difference score of -1 can be achieved with a performance score of 6 and an expectation score of 7 or with a performance score of 1 and an expectation score of 2. The question being asked here is: are you more satisfied with a product which comes close to a high expectation or a product which comes close to or equals your low expectations? The answer is probably the former but the EDP model does not make such a distinction.

Additionally there are further difficulties. Expectations are generally rated very high (Babakus and Boller, 1992). Here, respondents may be motivated or influenced by another kind of self-protection or self-presentation issue. An implicit statement of the type 'I am a discerning, quality seeking person' may lie behind high expectation scores. One of the more bizarre suggestions which arises from this specific issue is the recommendation that companies could reduce expectations and hence promote satisfaction by 'underpromising', that is, suggesting their product is adequate rather than brilliant (cited in Noe, 1999). This extension of the theory may be logical but it is questionable whether in practice tourist settings are likely to start promoting themselves as ordinary or basic in order to suppress visitors' initial expectations.

Several researchers have commented on the reactivity of measurement issues in the EDP model. By turning attention to expectations in the not-very-natural process of asking people what they are anticipating an experience will be like, the researcher may be changing or even creating expectations. And further, once people have rated expectations this task may influence their experience of the product by drawing attention to features they would not have spontaneously considered (Pearce, 1988).

These reactivity points, it has been argued, are particularly relevant when people say they have no expectations or where expectations are tentative, uncertain or superficial (Mazursky, 1989; Crompton and Love, 1995). In these circumstances it appears to be very problematic to use the EDP model to inform satisfaction research.

A further issue of assessing satisfaction by reflective measurement can be raised. At times, some companies and researchers suggest measuring satisfaction after the service experience or simultaneously with the service experience. For example, questions of this type are: 'What were your expectations of this trip before joining the tour?' or 'Does this (environmental site) meet your expectations?' Again this is likely to produce a confused and distorted reply since the experience itself may have reorganized earlier thoughts and anticipatory responses. The argument which is sometimes offered here is that there is not a problem because respondents do complete the questions. This argument is unsound. Respondents may be able to fill in some answers and do so out of courtesy to the researchers, but in fact they are likely to be 'telling more than they can know' (cf. Nisbett and Wilson, 1977).

Kozak (2001) contributes some further valuable observations to the assessment of EDP theory. He notes, and elaborates on the point in a critical review of the consumer-satisfaction field, that the expectation performance approach is really a family of approaches differing marginally in its names and titles from researcher to researcher. Allied to the EDP approach are the following family members: contrast theory, aspiration theory, gap analysis, adaptation level, disconfirmation approach and the importance–performance approach (Kozak, 2001). The importance–performance approach is of particular interest. In some of the EDP approaches little attention is paid to how significant, valuable or important an attribute is for the total assessment of satisfaction. So, for example, how important is the handling ability of a motor vehicle compared to fuel economy, safety, comfort and other variables? The contribution made by Fishbein, a major attitude theorist, and people following and extending his work in the importance–

performance model was to ensure that the relative significance of such component attributes was included in the confirmation–disconfirmation and performance measures (Fishbein, 1967; Olshavsky and Miller, 1972; Barsky, 1992).

Kozak's critical review (2001) also discusses the second of the two dominant approaches to satisfaction assessment. He labels the second set of approaches, the Nordic School, in contrast to the 'American' EDP school discussed above. The Nordic School approach may be seen as a performance-only perspective on customer satisfaction where the customer's perception of the quality of the performance product or experience is what really matters in satisfaction research. Crompton and Love (1995) report that a performance-only approach was superior to an EDP approach in assessing visitor satisfaction at festivals. Other support for the performance-only approach comes from Prakash (1984) who noted the superiority of performance-only measures for predicting future behaviour. The approach is also consistent with that adopted by many Australian researchers including Pearce (1988), Hughes (1991), Black and Rutledge (1996), Kim and Lee (1998) and Greenwood and Moscardo (1999). Not surprisingly some of the EDP advocates (e.g. Parasuraman et al., 1985, 1994) reject the performance-only approach arguing that the relationship between expectations and performance provides valuable information. The rebuttal to this criticism is, of course, only valuable if the expectations measures are meaningful, a concern which was raised in the previous critique.

Directions for satisfaction research

Many reviews of existing approaches in this area produce a cautious and indeterminate set of conclusions. It is frequently suggested for example that researchers should be 'aware of these issues', that they should 'consider the methodological weaknesses of previous research' or more commonly 'that further research is needed to improve our understanding' (Schofield, 2000; Kozak, 2001). Such caution is understandable because there are indeed complex and unresolved matters in the satisfaction field.

It is possible, however, to suggest the continued use of both existing traditions and to develop the performance-only approach further. It can be suggested from the preceding review that the EDP family of approaches may continue to be applicable even in tourism and leisure research for frequently purchased, standardized products familiar to the consumer. The measurement of satisfaction and performance in such contexts should be both prior to and post the purchase experience, avoiding reflective questions. There may be considerable advantages in operational terms and without comprising research standards to have large independent but closely matched samples providing the expectations and performance measures. This will reduce the reactivity issue and avoid subject mortality or drop-out rates comprising the research design. A critical part of EDP approaches should be the assessment of the importance of attributes in relation to expectations and performances.

For many tourism situations where satisfaction measures are concerned with the more expressive rather than instrumental aspects of the experience, a performance-only approach can be recommended. The particular advantages of this strategy include the clarity of the task for the respondent and a consequential confidence by the researcher in the meaning of the response. It can also be strongly suggested that when attribute or component parts of the experience are being assessed, importance ratings are also assessed.

In order to enhance the suggested performance-only approach to satisfaction measurement, two additional lines of inquiry can be blended into the 'Nordic School' system. The first consideration is that of benchmarking. One of the criticisms of the performance-only approach is that when analysts and stakeholders obtain a set of scores from the post hoc satisfaction procedure they may have difficulty in interpreting or understanding the meaning of the obtained values. There are two kinds of benchmarking that can help to resolve this interpretation issue.

Benchmarking may take two forms: (i) internal benchmarking, where satisfaction scores are retained by an organization and compared over time or across departments; and (ii) external benchmarking, where the satisfaction-based performances of competitors constitute the frame of reference. In both these styles of benchmarking Fuchs (2002, p. 154) claims that the benchmarking challenge is as follows: 'what counts is not so much a measure of the absolute but the relative satisfaction level'. An understanding of the exact semantics of satisfaction is itself a research issue and while Fuchs' emphasis on comparative judgements is valuable it would be foolish to ignore the actual absolute values (Veal, 1997). For the external benchmarking approach in particular, Fuchs also notes that the aim of the business should be to establish a customer value which exceeds that of rival offerings. The inclusion of this benchmarking approach in the performance-only customer satisfaction approach will be illustrated in this chapter with examples drawn from environmentally based tourist settings.

The second amplification of the basic performance-only approach lies in developing a guide concerning what can be measured in satisfaction studies. While the work of Parasuraman et al. (1994) and Cottle (1990) is conceived within the tradition of the EDP model, their detailed attention to the content of satisfaction measures can be applied to other models. Accordingly, a rich expansion of the basic satisfaction questions often asked in performance-only studies is possible by including ideas from the SERVQUAL and RATER models developed by the above authors. Some suggestions arising from this approach include a consideration of the reliability of the service, competence and knowledge of the staff, all the tangible elements of the setting, and the care and responsiveness to the customers' needs. These directions need to be supplemented by advising that researchers should also add holistic and expressive questions to the total framework since the RATER and SERVQUAL traditions place greater emphasis on instrumental and social interaction or service-linked elements.

While benchmarking may have many advantages congruent with the desirable practices for satisfaction reported in Table 25.1 there are some pragmatic issues in obtaining truly comparative data. These kinds of problems as well as the opportunities for effective benchmarking are illustrated in the following case study.

Satisfaction with natural environments: a case study

A selection of studies featuring visitor satisfaction with a range of natural environments was compiled for the purposes of exploring benchmarking. They include a diversity of studies from different continents and feature such settings as zoos, national parks, campgrounds, attractions, environmental activities and scenery.

The studies are grouped in order of the mean ranking of the satisfaction scores and according to the number of scale points used in the assessment. Some of the work comes from a search of the *Annals of Tourism Research*, *Journal of Travel Research*, *Journal of Leisure Research*, *Leisure Sciences* and *Tourism Management*. Additionally, some postgraduate research from James Cook University is included.

The material contained in Table 25.2 illustrates a number of issues and raises questions for benchmarking-based approaches to satisfaction.

It is apparent from Table 25.2 that the satisfaction measures used are mixed. They vary in

Table 25.2. Example of benchmarking appropriate to satisfaction.

Scale (original)	Score	Situation/setting	People/participant	Reference
1–3	2.69	Magnetic Island, visit satisfaction	Post respondents (n = N/A)	Kingchan (1998)
1–3	2.52	Chain Lakes, campground satisfaction	Campers (n = 41)	Foster and Jackson (1979)
1–3	2.44	Jarvis Bay, campground satisfaction	Campers (n = 72)	Foster and Jackson (1979)
1–3	2.38	Moonshine Lake, campground satisfaction	Campers (n = 64)	Foster and Jackson (1979)
1–3	2.32	Beauvais Lake, campground satisfaction	Campers (n = 41)	Foster and Jackson (1979)
1–3	2.22	Alberta Provincial Park, satisfaction of total campgrounds	Campers (n = 438)	Foster and Jackson (1979)
1–3	2.13	Pigeon Lake, campground satisfaction	Campers (n = 68)	Foster and Jackson (1979)
1–3	2.11	Alberta Provincial Park, satisfaction of total campgrounds by campground design (random)	Campers (n = 221)	Foster and Jackson (1979)
1–3	1.99	Williamson, campground satisfaction	Campers (n = 66)	Foster and Jackson (1979)
1–3	1.57	Aspen Beach, campground satisfaction	Campers (n = 86)	Foster and Jackson (1979)
1–5	5.00	Australia, natural scenic beauty	Korean visitors to Australia	Kim (1997)
	–		(highly satisfied group based on satisfaction score index) (n = 34)	–
	–			–

Table 25.2. *Continued*

Scale (original)	Score	Situation/setting	People/participant	Reference
1–5	5.00	Quanzhou, natural scenery	Tourists ($n = 80$)	Xiao (1997)
1–5	5.00	Xiamen, natural scenery	Tourists ($n = 98$)	Xiao (1997)
1–5	4.59	Adventure tour variable (weather)	Backpackers ($n = 266$)	Derry (1996)
1–5	4.53	Level of satisfaction of the train trip	Gulf train users ($n = 291$)	Bell (1996)
1–5	4.46	Australia, wildlife and nature	Korean visitors to Australia	Kim (1997)
		–	(satisfied group based on satisfaction score index)	–
		–	($n = 48$)	–
1–5	4.38	Australia, clean and less polluted	Korean visitors to Australia	Kim (1997)
		–	(highly satisfied group based on	–
		–	satisfaction score) index ($n = 34$)	–
1–5	4.30	The Great Green Way, quality of attractions	Visitors ($n = 227$)	Ware (1998)
1–5	4.26	The Great Green Way, overall satisfaction	Visitors ($n = 227$)	Ware (1998)
1–5	4.21	The North Carolina Zoo Park, satisfaction (view animals)	Vacationer ($n = $ N/A)	Andereck and Caldwell (1994)
1–5	4.19	The Great Green Way, ease of finding attractions	Visitors ($n = 227$)	Ware (1998)
1–5	4.18	The North Carolina Zoo Park, satisfaction (view animals)	Non-vacationer ($n = $ N/A)	Andereck and Caldwell (1994)
1–5	4.05	The North Carolina Zoo Park, overall satisfaction	Out-of-state visitors ($n = $ N/A)	Andereck and Caldwell (1994)
1–5	4.02	The North Carolina Zoo Park, enjoyment variable (zoo environment)	Out-of-state visitors ($n = $ N/A)	Andereck and Caldwell (1994)
1–5	4.00	The Great Green Way, information displayed	Visitors ($n = 227$)	Ware (1998)
1–5	4.00	Quanzhou, natural scenery	Locals ($n = 73$)	Xiao (1997)
1–5	3.98	The North Carolina Zoo Park, enjoyment variable (zoo environment)	Vacationer ($n = $ N/A)	Andereck and Caldwell (1994)
1–5	3.91	The North Carolina Zoo Park, enjoyment variable (zoo environment)	Non-vacationer r ($n = $ N/A)	Andereck and Caldwell (1994)
1–5	3.91	The North Carolina Zoo Park, enjoyment variable (zoo environment)	North Carolina visitors ($n = $ N/A)	Andereck and Caldwell (1994)

Table 25.2. *Continued*

Scale (original)	Score	Situation/setting	People/participant	Reference
1–5	3.61	Kuranda, resultant satisfaction of the motive to be close to nature (for peace and harmony)	Visitors (n = N/A)	Montesanti (1999)
1–5	3.56	Kuranda, resultant satisfaction of the motive to improve one's knowledge of rainforest	Visitors (n = N/A)	Montesanti (1999)
1–5	3.54	The North Carolina Zoo Park, enjoyment variable (animals)	Out-of-state visitors (n = N/A)	Andereck and Caldwell (1994)
1–5	3.47	The North Carolina Zoo Park, enjoyment variable (animals)	Vacationer (n = N/A)	Andereck and Caldwell (1994)
1–5	3.28	The North Carolina Zoo Park, enjoyment variable (animals)	Non-vacationer (n = N/A)	Andereck and Caldwell (1994)
1–5	3.27	The North Carolina Zoo Park, enjoyment variable (animals)	North Carolina visitors (n = N/A)	Andereck and Caldwell (1994)
1–5	3.15	The North Carolina Zoo Park, enjoyment variable (being outdoors)	Non-vacationer (n = N/A)	Andereck and Caldwell (1994)
1–5	3.14	The North Carolina Zoo Park, enjoyment variable (being outdoors)	North Carolina visitors (n = N/A)	Andereck and Caldwell (1994)
1–5	3.13	Australia, different environment (seasonality) based on satisfaction score index (n = 48)	Korean visitors to Australia (satisfied group)	Kim (1997)
1–5	3.09	The North Carolina Zoo Park, enjoyment variable (being outdoors)	Out-of-state visitors (n = N/A)	Andereck and Caldwell (1994)
1–5	3.06	The North Carolina Zoo Park, enjoyment variable (being outdoors)	Vacationer (n = N/A)	Andereck and Caldwell (1994)
1–5	3.00	Xiamen, natural scenery	Locals (n = 65)	Xiao (1997)
1–5	2.10	Satisfaction with the Cairns region	Backpackers (n = 383)	Day (1997)
5–1	2.61	Satisfaction of 'enjoy wonders of nature' (swimming)	General USA female residents (n = 603)	Hawes (1978)
5–1	2.43	Satisfaction of 'enjoy wonders of nature' (swimming)	General USA male residents (n = 512)	Hawes (1978)
5–1	2.35	National park rangers	Participants and spectators of the	Noe (1987)

Table 25.2. *Continued*

Scale (original)	Score	Situation/setting	People/participant	Reference
			Chattahoochee River Raft Race (*n* = 872)	
5–1	1.99	Satisfaction of 'enjoy wonders of nature' (gardening, lawn care, landscaping)	General USA male residents (*n* = 512)	Hawes (1978)
5–1	1.83	Satisfaction of 'enjoy wonders of nature' (picnicking)	General USA female residents (*n* = 603)	Hawes (1978)
5–1	1.68	Satisfaction of 'enjoy wonders of nature' (fishing or hunting)	General USA female residents (*n* = 603)	Hawes (1978)
5–1	1.65	Satisfaction of 'enjoy wonders of nature' (fishing or hunting)	General USA male residents (*n* = 512)	Hawes (1978)
5–1	1.59	Satisfaction of 'enjoy wonders of nature' (gardening, lawn care, landscaping)	General USA female residents (*n* = 603)	Hawes (1978)
5–1	1.56	Satisfaction of 'enjoy wonders of nature' (driving around for pleasure)	General USA male residents (*n* = 512)	Hawes (1978)
5–1	1.27	Satisfaction of 'enjoy wonders of nature' (camping by trailer, camper, motor home)	General USA female residents (*n* = 603)	Hawes (1978)
1–6	5.38	Forsythe National Refuge, satisfaction ratings for visitors	Low ID score group (*n* = 49)	Applegate and Clarke (1987)
1–6	5.05	Forsythe National Refuge, satisfaction ratings for visitors	All participants (*n* = 92)	Applegate and Clarke (1987)
1–6	5.00	Rogue River, trip satisfaction	1977 participants (*n* = 89)	Shelby and Shindler (1995)
1–6	4.77	Forsythe National Refuge, satisfaction ratings for visitors	High ID score group (*n* = 43)	Applegate and Clarke (1987)
1–6	4.74	Non-consumptive recreational activities	Based on data collected in 12 separate studies (*n* = 5871)	Vaske *et al.* (1982)
1–6	4.70	Rogue River, trip satisfaction	1991 participants (*n* = 89)	Shelby and Shindler (1995)
1–6	3.56	Consumptive recreational activities (successful users)	Based on data collected in 12 separate studies (*n* = 352)	Vaske *et al.* (1982)
1–6	2.60	Consumptive recreational activities (unsuccessful users)	Based on data collected in 12 separate studies (*n* = 984)	Vaske *et al.* (1982)

Table 25.2. *Continued*

Scale (original)	Score	Situation/setting	People/participant	Reference
6–1	2.60	Overall rating on experience during the raft-race activities	Participants and spectators of the Chattahoochee River Raft Race ($n = 866$)	Noe (1987)
6–1	2.10	Overall self-enjoyment on raft-race day	Participants and spectators of the Chattahoochee River Raft Race ($n = 872$)	Noe (1987)
1–7	6.13	Bareboating experience in Whitsundays, overall satisfaction	Bareboat charterers ($n = 133$)	Howe (1998)
1–9	7.49	Central Illinois, catching fish	Recreational fishermen ($n = 428$)	Buchanan (1983)
1–9	6.36	Central Illinois, experiencing nature	Recreational fishermen ($n = 428$)	Buchanan (1983)
1–9	3.37	Psychological outcome from wilderness recreation experience	Users of Rawah wilderness ($n = 264$) (the smells, sights and sounds of nature)	Brown and Haas (1980)
1–9	3.24	Psychological outcome from wilderness recreation experience	Users of Rawah wilderness ($n = 264$) (being where things are natural)	Brown and Haas (1980)
1–9	3.07	Psychological outcome from wilderness recreation experience (gaining a greater appreciation of nature)	Users of Rawah wilderness ($n = 264$)	Brown and Haas (1980)
1–9	2.75	Psychological outcome from wilderness recreation experience (living in harmony with nature)	Users of Rawah wilderness ($n = 264$)	Brown and Haas (1980)
1–9	2.30	Psychological outcome from wilderness recreation experience (challenging nature with your skills)	Users of Rawah wilderness ($n = 264$)	Brown and Haas (1980)
0–10	9	Magnetic Island, satisfaction of Balding Bay	Visitors to Balding Bay ($n = 70$)	Smith (1998)
0–10	8.98	Cape Tribulation/Daintree, visitor rating of tour guide	Visitors on large tours ($n = 57$)	Jones (1993)
0–10	8.65	Cape Tribulation/Daintree, visitor rating of tour guide	Visitors on small tours ($n = 35$)	Jones (1993)
0–10	8.5	Magnetic Island, satisfaction of Alma Bay	Visitors to Alma Bay ($n = 103$)	Smith (1998)
0–10	8.35	Cape Tribulation/Daintree, visitor satisfaction	Visitors on small tours ($n = 35$)	Jones (1993)

Table 25.2. *Continued*

Scale (original)	Score	Situation/setting	People/participant	Reference
0–10	8.05	How enjoyable was the reef or beach walk?	Low Isle visitors (n = 99)	Johnson (1994)
0–10	8.03	How enjoyable was the reef or beach walk?	Heron Island visitors (n = 102)	Johnson (1994)
0–10	7.61	Cape Tribulation/ Daintree, visitor satisfaction	Visitors on large tours (n = 57)	Jones (1993)
0–10	7.3	Magnetic Island, satisfaction of Horseshoe Bay	Visitors to Horseshoe Bay (n = 90)	Smith (1998)
0–10	7.02	How enjoyable was the reef or beach walk?	Magnetic Island visitors (n = 49)	Johnson (1994)
0–10	2.6	Magnetic Island, satisfaction of Florence Bay	Visitors to Balding Bay (n = 74)	Smith (1998)
1–10	8.90	Great Barrier Reef, mean rating of enjoyment in introductory scuba dive	Males (n = 178)	Wilkins (1992)
1–10	8.69	Great Barrier Reef, mean rating of enjoyment in introductory scuba dive	All (n = 294)	Wilkins (1992)
1–10	8.63	Overall satisfaction of dive trip to Cairns	Divers – female (n = 29)	Sivoro (1998)
1–10	8.39	Overall satisfaction of dive trip to Cairns	Divers (n = 130)	Sivoro (1998)
1–10	8.37	Great Barrier Reef, mean rating of enjoyment in introductory scuba dive	Females (n = 116)	Wilkins (1992)
1–10	8.33	Overall satisfaction of dive trip to Cairns	Divers – male (n = 29)	Sivoro (1998)
1–10	7.60	Vermont rivers, satisfaction	Recreationists (n = 866)	Manning and Charles (1980)

Note: The first mentioned number, e.g. 1 in 1–5 represents the low end of the satisfaction scale employed.

terms of exactly how the questions are asked, what is actually being assessed in the satisfaction framework and the kinds of scales employed. In considering this material the possibility of attempting algebraic conversions of the scales to a common standard was considered. This approach was abandoned simply because standardizing 4-point, 7-point and 11-point rating scales raises difficulties of properly adjusting for ceiling and floor effects. It is there-fore necessary to consider only the blocks of data resulting from scales with the same range. Within this limitation some of the studies in Fig. 25.1 do provide comparative information, particularly those deriving from the same author and related to a range of similar settings.

The cross-national data reported in Fig. 25.1 raise the question of how do respondents from different nationalities use scales – there may be, for example, a tendency for

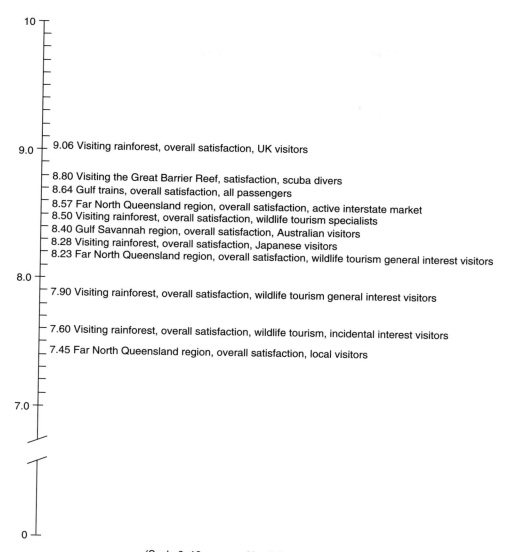

(Scale 0–10 was used in all the assessments)

Fig. 25.1. Comparing regional satisfaction scores: evidence from reef and rainforest studies. (Scale 0–10 was used in all the assessments.) Source: adapted from Black and Clark (1998); Pearce and Moscardo (1998, 1999). It is built on technical reports prepared for the Reef and Rainforest Cooperative Research Centres.

some Asian visitors to provide maximum scores (cf. Xiao, 1997) while Western visitors tend to be more constrained in their use of extreme scales. These points relate to long-standing issues in the psychometric literature (Cronbach, 1970) but are worth reintroducing to tourism studies when cross-national comparisons of guest satisfaction are being compared

(Kim and Lee, 1998; Greenwood and Moscardo, 1999). As an extension of the material presented in Table 25.2 a more localized benchmarking appraisal for natural environments can be presented by considering a set of studies conducted in Northern Australia. This work prepared for and published largely in technical reports and conference presentations to the reef and rainforest operators of the region is outlined in Fig. 25.1.

What benefits can be obtained from the kind of benchmarked satisfaction data reported in Fig. 25.1? It is noteworthy that most of the data reported in the table reflect core sample sizes of over 1000 respondents. At first glance it might seem there is little difference, for example, in a score of 8.0 and 8.1 on an 11-point satisfaction score. If, however, one considers the semantics of satisfaction with a sample size of 1000 people, the shift in scores is actually considerable. If all the 1000 people give a score of 8.0, the mean will of course be 8.0. If 100 give the higher score of 9 instead of 8, the new mean will be 8.1. Effectively a small change in the mean scores such as indicated represents 10% of the respondents moving their scale from a verbal equivalent of quite satisfied to very satisfied, a valuable additional compliment to the tourism environment business.

From the data provided in Fig. 25.1 managers of the region and local businesses might reflect on the lower satisfaction scores of Japanese and local visitors. Such indicators of relatively lower scores might prompt attention to information marketing and customer care. The scores for individual businesses are not included in Fig. 25.1 but for those ecotourism operations receiving scores above 8.5 they may take some comfort in the adequacy of their current satisfaction scores. The work of Hanan and Karp (1989) reinforces the view that scores above 8.5 are meritorious. In their US-based assessments of reactions to natural environments they report that high levels of satisfaction occur when 85–90% of the respondents provide a score of either 8, 9 or 10 on such scales. A medium or moderate satisfaction outcome occurs when 70–80% of respondents provide a score of 8, 9 or 10 and a lower satisfaction rating would be an appropriate label if 60% or less provided the top three ratings. When these percentages are

translated into mean score assessments, ratings above 7.8 are good, between 7.1 and 7.8 moderate and below 7.1 less than satisfactory. As already suggested there may be cross-national and context differences in these kinds of numerical applications of the benchmarking approach. Nevertheless, the promise of some specificity in appraising the satisfaction ratings measured in the same way in a similar region promises to fulfil the more grandiose goals of satisfaction identified by Ritchie et al. (2000) and others earlier in this chapter.

There are a number of additional technical and substantive issues that need to be developed to promote more insightful satisfaction studies. Hazelrigg and Hardy (2000), for example, argue that more attention should be given to the language of satisfaction (including the meanings of modifiers such as extremely satisfied, very satisfied and somewhat satisfied). They provide evidence that there are some subtle differences in the meaning of these terms in different life domains, such as assessing one's health or one's friends. A potentially important implication of this issue in the tourism domain is the adequacy of translated questionnaires in conveying the satisfaction modifiers to visitors from different sources. Additionally there remain vexed questions in this technical aspect of satisfaction studies as to whether the collected data should be treated as interval or ordinal or indeed simply used to classify more and less satisfied visitors. A particular advantage of the benchmarking approach is that, unlike the EDP approach, it makes few assumptions of this sort and it is only when analysts build multivariate explanatory models that the issue surfaces. Satisfaction research and studies of tourist satisfaction are an active and substantial area of scholarly and practitioner interest. Understanding satisfaction, providing satisfaction and getting satisfaction remain interconnected goals for analysts, managers and visitors.

References

Andereck, K.L. and Caldwell, L.L. (1994) Variable selection in tourism market segmentation models. *Journal of Travel Research* 33(Fall), 40–46.

Anderson, E.W., Fornell, C. and Rust, R.T. (1997) Customer satisfaction, productivity and profitability: differences between goods and services. *Marketing Science* 16(2), 129–145.

Applegate, J.F. and Clarke, K.E. (1987) Satisfaction levels of birdwatchers: an observation on the consumptive–nonconsumptive continuum. *Leisure Sciences* 21, 81–102.

Babakus, E. and Boller, G.W. (1992) An empirical assessment of SERVQUAL. *Journal of Business Research* 24(3), 253–268.

Bagozzi, R.P., Gopinath, M. and Nyer, P.W. (1999) The role of emotions in marketing. *Journal of the Academy of Marketing Sciences* 27(2), 184–206.

Barsky, J.D. (1992) Customer satisfaction in the hotel industry: meaning and management. *Hospitality Research Journal* 16(1), 51–73.

Baum, T. and Lundtorp, S. (eds) (2001) *Seasonality in Tourism*. Pergamon, Oxford.

Bell, J.M. (1996) A critical evaluation of tourism in the Gulf Savannah: a study of the gulf trains, savannah guides and tourism operators of the region. Thesis, Tourism Department, James Cook University, Townsville, Australia.

Black, N. and Clark, A. (1998) *Tourism in Northwest Queensland*. Tropical Savannahs CRC, James Cook University, Townsville, Australia.

Black, N. and Rutledge, J. (1996) *Outback Tourism*. Tourism Department, James Cook University, Townsville, Australia.

Brown, P.J. and Haas, G.E. (1980) Wilderness recreation experience, Rahwah experience. *Journal of Leisure Research* 12(3), 229–241.

Buchanan, T. (1983) Toward an understanding of variability in satisfactions within activities. *Journal of Leisure Research* 15(1), 39–51.

Cottle, D.W. (1990) *Client-Centered Service: How to Keep Them Coming Back for More*. John Wiley & Sons, New York.

Crompton, J. and Love, L.L. (1995) The predictive validity of alternate approaches to evaluating quality of a festival. *Journal of Travel Research* 34(1), 11–25.

Cronbach, L. (1970) *Essentials of Psychological Testing*. Harper & Row, New York.

Czepiel, J.A. and Rosenberg, L.J. (1977) The study of consumer satisfaction, addressing the 'So what?' question. In: Hunt, H.K. (ed.) *Conceptualization and Measurement of Consumer Satisfaction and Dissatisfaction*. Marketing Science Institute, Cambridge, Massachusetts, pp. 92–119.

Day, K. (1997) Understanding backpackers and their travel movements: a case study of backpackers travelling within the Cairns region. Honours thesis, Tourism Department, James Cook University, Townsville, Australia.

Derry, J. (1996) Gender divisions in adventure tourism: an assessment of guide and tourist interaction on one-day adventure operations. Honours thesis, Tourism Department, James Cook University, Townsville, Australia.

Fishbein, M. (1967) A behaviour theory approach to the relations between beliefs about an object and the attitude towards the object. In: Fishbein, M. (ed.) *Readings in Attitude Theory and Measurement*. John Wiley & Sons, New York, pp. 289–400.

Fornell, C., Johnson, M.D., Anderson, E.W., Cha, J. and Bryant, B. (1996) The American customer satisfaction index: nature, purpose and findings. *Journal of Marketing* 60, 7–18.

Foster, R.J. and Jackson, E.L. (1979) Factors associated with camping satisfaction in Alberta Provincial Park campgrounds. *Journal of Leisure Research* 11(4), 292–306.

Fuchs, M. (2002) Benchmarking indicator systems and their potential for tracking guest satisfaction. *Tourism* 50(2), 141–155.

Greenwood, T. and Moscardo, G. (1999) Australian and North American coastal and marine tourists: what do they want? In: Saxena, N. (ed.) *Recent Advances in Marine Science and Technology, 98*. Korea Ocean Research and Development Institute, Seoul, pp. 253–260.

Gunn, C.A. (1994) *Tourism Planning: Basics, Concepts, Cases*, 3rd edn. Taylor & Francis, New York.

Hanan, M. and Karp, P. (1989) *Customer Satisfaction*. Amacom, New York.

Hawes, D.K. (1978) Satisfactions derived from leisure-time pursuits: an exploratory nationwide survey. *Journal of Leisure Research* 10(4), 247–264.

Hazelrigg, L.E. and Hardy, M.A. (2000) Scaling the semantics of satisfaction. *Social Indicators Research* 49, 147–180.

Hockings, M., Stolton, S. and Dudley, N. (2000) *Evaluating Effectiveness: A Framework for Assessing the Management of Protected Areas*. IUCN – The World Conservation Union, Cambridge, UK.

Howe, S. (1998) Bareboating in the Whitsundays: the importance of interpretation and its role in the preservation of the Great Barrier Reef. Honours thesis, Tourism Department, James Cook University, Townsville, Australia.

Hughes, K. (1991) Tourist satisfaction: a guided cultural tour in North Queensland. *Australian Psychologist* 26(3), 166–171.

Ittner, C.D. and Larcker, D.F. (1996) Measuring the impact of quality initiatives on firm financial performance. In: Fedor, D.F. and Ghosh, S. (eds) *Advances in the Management of Organizational Quality*, Vol. 1. JAI Press, Greenwich, Connecticut, pp. 1–37.

Johnson, V.Y. (1994) Reef walking on the Great Barrier Reef: a study of visitor experiences. Honours thesis, Tourism Department, James Cook University, Townsville, Australia.

Jones, K. (1993) Ecotourism operator guidelines – a case study of the Cape Tribulation/Daintree section of the Wet Tropics World Heritage Area. Honours thesis, Tourism Department, James Cook University, Townsville, Australia.

Kim, E. and Lee, D. (1998) Japanese tourists' attitudes towards natural environments in the North Queensland Region – Reef experience. In: *Proceedings of the Fourth Asia Pacific Tourism Association Conference 'The Role of Tourism: National and Regional Perspectives'* (Series A), Korea, 18–21 August, pp. 331–344.

Kim, Y.J. (1997) Korean inbound tourism in Australia. PhD thesis, Tourism Department, James Cook University, Townsville, Australia.

Kingchan, K. (1998) Tourist satisfaction in relation to a holiday in Thailand. Master's thesis, Tourism Department, James Cook University, Townsville, Australia.

Kozak, M. (2001) A critical review of approaches to measure satisfaction with tourist destinations. In: Mazanec, J.A., Crouch, G., Brent Ritchie, J.R. and Woodside, A.R. (eds) *Consumer Psychology of Tourism, Hospitality and Leisure*, Vol. 2. CAB International, Wallingford, UK, pp. 321–332.

Kristensen, K., Martensen, A. and Gromholdt, L. (2000) Measuring customer satisfaction: a key dimension of business performance. *International Journal of Business Performance Management* 2, 157–170.

Manning, R.E. and Charles, P.C. (1980) Recreation density user satisfaction: a further exploration of the satisfaction model. *Journal of Leisure Research* 12(4), 329–345.

Mano, H. and Oliver, R.L. (1993) Assessing the dimensionality and structure of the consumption experience: evaluation scaling and satisfaction. *Journal of Consumer Research* 20, 451–466.

Martilla, J. and James, J. (1977) Importance–performance analysis. *Journal of Marketing* 41, 77–79.

Mazursky, D. (1989) Past experience and future tourism decisions. *Annals of Tourism Research* 16, 333–344.

McCarthur, S. (2000) Beyond carrying capacity: introducing a model to monitor and manage visitor activity in forests. In: Font, X. and Tribe, J. (eds) *Forest Tourism and Recreation: Case Studies in Environmental Management*. CAB International, Wallingford, UK, pp. 259–278.

Montesanti, V. (1999) An investigation into visitor satisfaction with the Kuranda village experience. Honours thesis, Tourism Department, James Cook University, Townsville, Australia.

Nisbett, R.E. and Wilson, T.D. (1977) Telling more than we can know: verbal reports on mental processes. *Psychological Review* 84, 231–259.

Noe, F.P. (1987) Measurement specification and leisure satisfaction. *Leisure Sciences* 9, 163–172.

Noe, F.P. (1999) *Tourism Service Satisfaction: Hotel, Transportation, and Recreation*. Sagamore, Champaign, Illinois.

Oliver, R.L. (1980) A cognitive model of the antecedents and consequences of satisfaction decisions. *Journal of Marketing Research* 17(November), 460–469.

Oliver, R.L. (1993) A conceptual model of service quality and service satisfaction; compatible goals, different concepts. In: Swartz, T.A., Bowen, D.E. and Brown, S.W. (eds) *Advances in Services Marketing and Management*, Vol. 2. JAI Press, Greenwich, Connecticut, pp. 65–85.

Oliver, R.L. (1997) *Satisfaction: A Behavioural Perspective on the Consumer*. McGraw-Hill, New York.

Olshavsky, R.W. and Miller, J.A. (1972) Consumer expectations product performance and perceived product quality. *Journal of Marketing Research* 9, 19–21.

Parasuraman, A., Zeithmal, V.A. and Berry, L.L. (1985) A conceptual model of service quality and its implications for future research. *Journal of Marketing* 49, 41–50.

Parasuraman, A., Zeithmal, V.A. and Berry, L.L. (1994) Reassessment of expectations as a comparison standard in measuring service quality: implications for further research. *Journal of Marketing* 58, 11–124.

Payne, R. (1993) Sustainable tourism: suggested indicators and monitoring techniques. In: Nelson, J.G. Butler, R. and Wall, G. (eds) *Tourism and Sustainable Development: Monitoring, Planning, Managing.* University of Waterloo, London, Ontario, pp. 249–253.

Pearce, P.L. (1988) *The Ulysses Factor: Evaluating Visitors in Tourist Settings.* Springer-Verlag, New York.

Pearce, P.L. and Moscardo, G. (1998) The role of interpretation in influencing visitor satisfaction: a rainforest case study. In: Faulkner, W., Tideswell, C. and Weaver, D. (eds) *Progress in Tourism and Hospitality Research,* Proceedings of the Eighth Australian Tourism and Hospitality Research Conference. Bureau of Tourism Research, Canberra, pp.259–308.

Pearce, P.L. and Moscardo, G. (1999) Understanding ethnic tourists. *Annals of Tourism Research* 26(2), 416–434.

Pearce, P.L. and Moscardo, G. (2001) 'Been already and done it before': understanding visitors repeating trips to the Great Barrier Reef. In: Pforr, C. and Janeczko, B. (eds) *CAUTHE 2001: Capitalising on Research,* Proceedings of the Eleventh Australian Tourism and Hospitality Research Conference, 7–10 February, University of Canberra, Canberra, pp. 268–280.

Pearce, P.L., Morrison, A. and Rutledge, J. (1998) *Tourism: Bridges Across Continents.* McGraw-Hill, Sydney, Australia.

Prakash, V. (1984) Validity and reliability of the confirmation of expectations paradigm as a determinant of consumer satisfaction. *Journal of the Academy of Marketing Science* 12(4), 63–76.

Ritchie, J.R.B., Crouch, G.I. and Hudson, S. (2000) Developing operational measures for the components of a destination competitiveness/sustainability model: consumer versus managerial perspectives. In: Mazanec, J.A., Crouch, G.I., Ritchie, J.R.B. and Woodside, A.G. (eds) *Consumer Psychology of Tourism, Hospitality and Leisure.* CAB International, Wallingford, UK, pp. 1–17.

Ryan, C. (1995) *Researching Tourist Satisfaction.* Routledge, London.

Schofield, P. (2000) Deciphering day-trip destination choice using a tourist expectation/satisfaction construct. In: Woodside, A., Crouch, G., Mazanec, J., Oppermann, M. and Sakai, M. (eds) *Consumer Psychology of Tourism, Hospitality and Leisure.* CAB International, Wallingford, UK, pp. 269–294.

Shelby, B. and Shindler, B. (1995) Product shift in recreation settings: findings and implications from panel research. *Leisure Sciences* 17, 91–107.

Sivoro, B.J. (1998) Toward the ecologically sustainable development of the Solomon Islands dive tourism industry. Honours thesis, Tourism Department, James Cook University, Townsville, Australia.

Smith, P.K. (1998) Planning for the tourist and recreational use of the bays of Magnetic Island. Honours thesis, Tourism Department, James Cook University, Townsville, Australia.

Swan, J.E. and Combs, L.J. (1976) Product performance and consumer satisfaction: a new concept. *Journal of Marketing* 40, 25–33.

Teas, R.K. (1993) Consumer expectations and the measurement of perceived service quality. *Journal of Professional Services Marketing* 8(2), 33–53.

Uhl, K.P. and Schoner, B. (1969) *Marketing Research: Information Systems and Decision Marking.* John Wiley & Sons, New York.

Vaske, J.J., Donnelly, M.P., Heberlein, T.A. and Shelby, B. (1982) Differences in reported satisfaction ratings by consumptive and nonconsumptive recreationists. *Journal of Leisure Research* 14(3), 195–206.

Veal, A.J. (1997) *Research Methods for Leisure and Tourism,* 2nd edn. Financial Times/Prentice-Hall, London.

Ware, C. (1998) The Great Green Way: road to regional tourism prosperity. Honours thesis, Tourism Department, James Cook University, Townsville, Australia.

Wilkins, J. (1992) Introductory scuba diving on the Great Barrier Reef. *Australian Parks and Recreation* 14(6), 18–23.

World Tourism Organization (1998) *Guide for Local Authorities on Developing Sustainable Tourism.* WTO, Madrid.

Xiao, H. (1997) Tourism and leisure in China: a tale of two cities. *Annals of Tourism Research* 24(2), 357–370.

Zins, A.H. (2002) Consumption emotions, experience quality and satisfaction: a structural analysis for complainers and non-complainers. *Journal of Travel and Tourism Marketing* 12(2), 3–18.

26 The Development and Tracking of a Branding Campaign for Brisbane

Noel Scott[1] and Stephen Clark[2]

[1]University of Queensland, Australia; [2]Tourism Queensland, Australia

Introduction

The study of destination management and destination branding in the tourism literature has been the focus for tourism research over the last 10 years. In this area, destinations are seen as tourism products and the process of marketing of other products is applied to them (Moutinho, 1999). The application of branding and marketing theory to destinations as products, however, provides a different context for use of these theories than the large company, fast moving consumer goods context in which they originated.

While useful in theory, the literature of marketing has some difficulty in direct application to a tourism destination context. The literature of marketing is primarily derived from a study of the marketing of large corporations (Low and Fullerton, 1994) rather than the small business cooperative context of destinations. This difference in context leads to a number of problems in the direct application to tourism of the methods of branding research and application found in the literature of marketing.

In particular, the problems of direct application of marketing knowledge to tourism destination marketing discussed in this case study are the importance of inclusion of important stakeholder organizations and the availability of relevant research data on existing markets. Other problems discussed are more general and include the importance of development of a research programme to maximize the effectiveness of research studies rather than disjointed one of research projects. While there is literature on strategic planning for tourism (Soteriou and Roberts, 1998) and on the linkages among these various research approaches, the implementation of these approaches in a unified research programme has not been discussed in the tourism literature. Instead the focus is on adapting and collating existing information sources (Ritchie and Ritchie, 2002).

The availability of research data is problematic for many destinations. The research data traditionally available in many destinations are statistical in nature and designed for identification of the number of visitors and certain other demographic characteristics. This limits the usefulness of the information for branding. The simple rationale underlying the concept of branding is that a product's image is as important as its physical attributes. Creating the right image can mean the difference between success and failure of a new product. According to Keller (1993) a brand is a name, term, sign, symbol or design which is intended to identify the product or service of one seller or a group of sellers and to differentiate them from those of competitors. A variety of other definitions are available (de Chernatony and Riley, 1998). The theory behind branding is that consumers perceive the sum total of the branded product or service to be greater than the sum of its tangible assets. Branding provides intangible personality that adds value to the product.

Developing brands requires information about the motivational and internal thoughts of visitors. The critical question to be answered when deciding on the usefulness of research information is: 'How is it used?' It is often the case that more information is collected than is analysed and used. The wrong information may be collected and therefore does not provide insight into the problem under examination. Alternatively, the right information may be collected but not be timely or accurate enough. A number of examples of each drawn from the author's experiences are given in Table 26.1.

There are three general types of research: (i) pure, (ii) strategic, and (iii) tactical. In the pure research situation, the aim is to generate new ways of thinking about a particular problem. In the strategic research, the objective is to set direction and objectives at the broadest level. In the tactical research, the aim is performance measurement or process improvement when the objectives and problem context are already known. Examples of these three types of research are given in Table 26.2.

Table 26.1. Examples of problems with research information.

Wrong information	Not timely or accurate enough
Information is collected on visitor numbers rather than visitor expenditure	Statistics on overseas arrivals available to a year after the collection period
Aggregate customer satisfaction data are used rather than exploring reasons for dissatisfaction	Statistical information on change in visitor numbers to small regions is reported but confidence intervals are not provided

In many destinations, the same statistically based data collections are used to address all three research problems usually due to issues of convenience or budgetary constraints. The alternative is to develop different approaches and types of research but ensure that these different projects are constructed in such a way as to ensure they all contribute effectively to the overall problem of destination marketing and branding.

Additionally, relevant information about the reasons why tourists visit a destination useful for strategic research purposes may be available to individual operators but they may be disinclined to share what is perceived to be a valuable resource. This arises both from their own research in origin markets and with their own customer research. Further, the research and information collected by individual operators will typically vary in utility due to problems with differing data collection standards and intentions. This can lead to a lack of availability of comparable data for amalgamation into a destination wide perspective and hence compromise the tactical research task. In turn, this can lead to confusion and lack of commonality in the overall positioning and branding of a destination. While 'visioning' programmes within a destination have been suggested as a way of obtaining a common position and brand for a destination (Ritchie, 1999), this does not eliminate the need for knowledge and research. In fact, a 'visioning' programme should be based on the use of objective knowledge and research or else it runs the risk of becoming an exercise of power rather than a commonly accepted direction.

Importantly, information collected and used for positioning is often not used in a systematic way both to position a destination and to track performance of a destination programme directly. Thus there is a literature individually on developing the positioning, tracking of marketing programmes indirectly (Wicks and Schuett, 1991), and these typically involve stand-alone research that does not integrate well.

This chapter describes the process of branding Brisbane, the capital city of Queensland, Australia, from a strategic research perspective. The process described is seen as an

Table 26.2. Three general types of research.

Type	Outcome	Example
Pure research	Change in how a problem is thought about	Defining the eco-tourism market from a consumer perspective
Strategic research	Direction setting	Collection of market share and volume
Tactical research	Performance measurement	Advertising awareness tracking

integrated whole linked across the strategic planning, branding tracking, marketing evaluation and programme evaluation processes.

Tourism Queensland and Regional Branding

For many years, Australia has been marketed as a brand. The Australian Tourist Commission (ATC), the federal government body responsible for marketing of Australia, had adopted a strategy of promotion of Australia as a brand in the international market called Brand Australia. In 1995, the ATC had developed a new strategy of 'sub-branding regions within Brand Australia'. This meant that instead of marketing only 'Australia' as a destination they have begun to promote particular destinations within Australia such as Cairns in Far North Queensland (FNQ). However, in order to avoid confusion in the marketplace and competition between sub-brands, there was a clear necessity to ensure that these regional sub-brands were consistent in market image and positioning with Brand Australia.

One of the first destinations in Australia to be involved in the sub-branding process was Cairns. The growth of Cairns in the international market had been driven in large part by increasing numbers of Japanese visitors. The opening of an international airport in Cairns and the building of a number of new international standard hotels had led to increasing popularity of the destination in international and domestic markets. The attractions of the destinations were the Great Barrier Reef and Daintree Rainforest. These attractions differed markedly from the traditional sun and sand

image of Queensland based around the surf beaches of the Gold Coast in the south of the state.

In 1995, concern was raised over a decline in the number of visitors from Japan and an investigation was conducted into the image of the destination in the international and domestic markets. This became the first sub-branding process. While originally the project involved the international market, it soon became clear that there was a need to consider the domestic image of Cairns as part of the project. This became the BrandFNQ project and was a joint initiative of the ATC Tourism Queensland (TQ) and the Far North Queensland Promotion Board (Noakes et al., 1996). The investigation led to a major positioning and image study of the destination. It involved a review of existing international market research data and a major new research study in the interstate markets of New South Wales and Victoria. The process undertaken was then adopted in other states, one example of its application is the sub-branding of Western Australia, described by Crockett and Wood (2002).

TQ, previously the Queensland Tourist and Travel Corporation (QTTC), is a Queensland Government-owned enterprise. The role of TQ is defined by an act of Parliament as 'promotion of Queensland as a tourist destination'. TQ is controlled by the Government of Queensland and State Department of Tourism through the ministerial appointment of a Chairman and Board. Established in 1979, TQ has a history of proactive marketing and product development. In 1991, after a controversial involvement in failed resort developments in central and northern coastal Queensland, a series of changes were made in the structure of the organization. The product development functions of TQ (then QTTC) were transferred to the Department of Tourism. At the same time the research department was effectively disbanded. As a result, the role of TQ was restricted to promotion of Queensland.

The TQ retained a variety of promotional-related tasks including advertising, public relations and publicity outside Queensland in the interstate and international markets. In addition, TQ operated two self-funded commercial operations, SUNLOVER (a wholesaler of Queensland holiday product) and the Queensland Government Travel Centres (a chain of retail travel agents). These operations provide access to the distribution systems for a wider variety of 'holiday product' than otherwise would be available. Additionally, they performed an information provision role for potential visitors to Queensland. These commercial organizations provide a significant ability to convey both brand and product advertising to the domestic market.

In 1995, TQ also began the process of developing a new domestic promotional advertisement for leisure tourism in Queensland. This was prompted by calls from industry for a review of the QTTC 'Live it Up' advertising campaign. This advertisement, in line with past advertising strategy, was a key promotional tool and was based around a 'fun, sun and sand' image. In 1994, a research officer was appointed to TQ and limited statistical data analysis undertaken. In 1995, a market research function was added to this officer's duties. As a result, the testing of possible marketing images for this new campaign was undertaken using innovative consumer research techniques.

The actual technique used was to show a test audience of consumers, a number of partly completed advertisements. Four different advertisements were shown to groups of 60 Australian consumers in Sydney and Melbourne. The results indicated that each of the advertisements were associated with a different destination in the state. Slower, more relaxed tempo advertisements were associated with Cairns and the tropical north of the state while faster paced more exciting advertising was associated with the Gold Coast beach destination. These results had a far-reaching effect on the marketing strategy used by TQ.

These market research results appeared around the time that the 'sub-branding' project was beginning in Cairns. As a result, it was decided to combine the international and domestic repositioning exercises into the one BrandFNQ project and to conduct a major domestic market research project to determine the appropriate target market and positioning. In 1996, this market research was let by tender to a market research company, Brian Sweeney and Associates. The research involved a series of four focus groups and a telephone survey of 600 respondents in the key domestic markets of Brisbane, Sydney and Melbourne.

The result was the relaunch of the region around Cairns as a destination in its own right called 'Tropical North Queensland' in both the domestic and international markets. For the domestic market, it was realized that Tropical North Queensland had developed its own image as a 'reef and rainforest' destination distinct from the 'sun and sand' beaches of the Gold Coast. As a result, there was a shift in the marketing strategy of TQ from the promotion of Queensland as one image to the development of a 'destination' portfolio. In 1997, TQ undertook to move from promotion of Queensland overall to promotion of destinations within Queensland.

A Research-driven Marketing Programme

The outcome of the research and marketing analysis conducted for Tropical North Queensland was a call for similar studies to be done in other destinations in Queensland. However, it soon became clear that some criteria were necessary to limit the number of branding campaigns conducted. This led to an examination of various statistical and other tourism sources of data to profile the 14 tourism regions of Queensland. One particularly useful source identified at this time was the Roy Morgan Holiday Tracking Study Database (HTS). The HTS is part of the Roy Morgan Single Source omnibus survey. This omnibus survey includes questions that track preferences, intentions and actual travel behaviour. Questions are directed to a base survey sample of over 50,000 people aged 14 years and over per year. Data are collected on: advertising awareness of holiday destinations in Australia; where people would prefer to go for short and long trips; and intention of taking such trips as well as media usage and many other respondent characteristics.

Consideration of the information available from this source highlighted a significant difference in the destination awareness and desirability levels for various regions of Queensland. As a result, four other destinations were considered to have sufficient desirability amongst the Australian public to benefit from brand advertising: The Whitsundays, Sunshine Coast, Brisbane and Gold Coast. These were termed developed destinations and considered to be places tourists wanted to visit. A developed destination was defined as one with an existing awareness of the destination in origin markets and a sufficiently large interstate market for promotion to be effective (see Fig. 26.1).

Underpinning the planning process and development of the brand (Pritchard and Morgan, 1998; Hall et al., 1999; Cai, 2002) was the use of a simple model based on the effects of advertising (Rossiter and Percy, 1996). In this model, the steps in the decision-making process for holidays are related to the different advertising objectives. The decision-making process consists of five steps: a recognition of the need for a holiday, awareness of a destination, a desire to visit, the intention to book a holiday and the decision to purchase. Advertising and other communication may be targeted at each of these steps. The appropriate communication effect for each stage is shown in Table 26.3. Each particular destination may require a different focus for advertising. Thus a destination may be well known and desirable but not actually visited. The primary communication task then becomes a focus on creation intention to book and actual purchase.

In the case examined here, destinations were selected for promotion that had high awareness in the Australian market and additionally had some level of desirability. The branding process, however, reinforced this and additionally ensured the most attractive attributes of the destination were used as the basis for promotion.

While such a simple model of advertising effects may be criticized, notably because of the complexity of the travel decision-making process (Dellaert et al., 1998; Maser and Weiermair, 1998), it provided a useful framework in this case. Its usefulness was primarily in providing a clear communication of the purposes of branding for the tourism operators. Moreover, the model had been previously used to collect data on awareness, interest and desirability of different destinations in Australia. Thus the theory was able to be linked to, and illustrated by, existing data available from the Roy Morgan Holiday Tracking Study. This data became central to the developing research programme and enabled the analysis and selection of target markets to be related to media selection decisions.

The planning framework used

There is some discussion in the literature regarding the approach adopted to planning for a destination. Some authors suggest that formal marketing planning confers several benefits such as more systematic thinking and better coordination of efforts, which lead to improved performance (Kotler et al., 1993). Others suggest that a destination strategy is crafted and that the 'design school' approach to strategy formulation is misdirected (Mintzberg, 1990; Ritchie, 1999).

In this case, however, one of the strengths of the approach was to introduce a strong methodology and format for planning as suggested by other authors (Heath and Wall, 1992). This model generally follows a strategic marketing approach and involved the nine steps shown in Table 26.4. Research has a role in each one of these steps.

This rational approach was chosen with a clear intent to allow decisions on targets for each destination to be based on consumer research and consensus decisions involving stakeholders in each destination. As a result of this consultation, the tourism industry in each region committed to cooperative funding for the establishment and maintenance of the brands. These agreements reflected the tourism industry's involvement and endorsement of the new marketing direction.

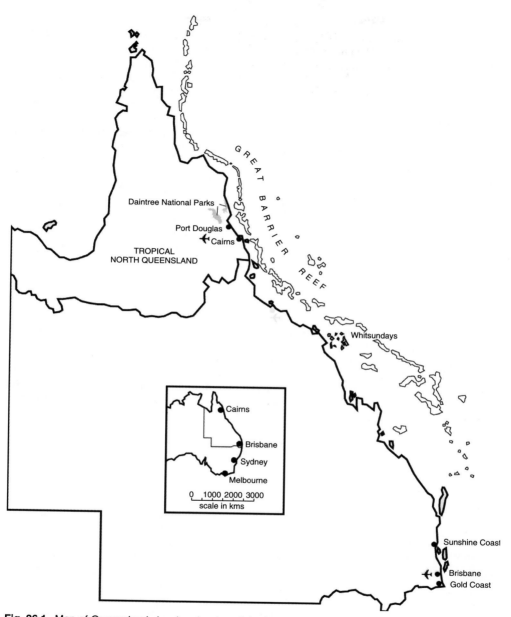

Fig. 26.1. Map of Queensland showing developed destinations.

An integrated research and marketing programme for Brisbane

Brisbane had a population of around 1.7 million in 2003. It is the third largest and the fastest growing city in Australia (Australian Bureau of Statistics, 2004). Brisbane is a major gateway for tourists entering Queensland with international and domestic air terminals and other transport infrastructure. In 2003, some 750,000 international visitors travelled to Brisbane and spent over 8.4 million visitor

Table 26.3. Relationship between stage of decision and communication effect.

Decision	Communication effect	Definition
Need for a holiday	Category need	Buyer's acceptance that the category (a product or service) is to remove or satisfy a perceived discrepancy between the current motivational state and the desired motivational state.
Awareness of destination	Brand awareness	Buyer's ability to identify (recognize or recall) the brand, within the category, in sufficient detail to make a purchase.
Desire to visit a destination	Brand attitude	Buyer's evaluation of the brand with respect to its perceived ability to meet a currently relevant motivation.
Intention to book	Brand purchase intention	Buyer's self-instruction to purchase the brand or to take purchase related action.
Purchase	Purchase facilitation	Buyer's assurance that other marketing factors will not hinder purchase.

Source: adapted from Rossiter and Percy (1996).

nights making it the largest tourism region in Queensland (Bureau of Tourism Research, 2004). Tourism is a significant contributor to the economy of Brisbane (AUS$690 million) with significant business and visiting friends and relatives segments (Queensland Tourist and Travel Corporation, 1997).

It is located on the Brisbane River and to the north and south are the major tourism destinations of the Sunshine Coast and Gold Coast. These are two of the other regions branded in the process described here. At the time of the case study, the holiday market though significant was underdeveloped

Table 26.4. Strategic marketing step and corresponding research task.

Strategic marketing step	Research task
Create a stakeholder project team.	Identify stakeholder
Analyse the available secondary data and conduct primary research.	Collect and reanalyse data
Identify the regions 'distinctive competence' or 'competitive advantage'.	Conduct 'positioning' study
Select primary target markets which will shape the brand.	Segmentation analysis
Clearly define a brand which optimizes the match between the distinctive competence and the motivations of the target markets.	Target market focus groups to determine key benefits
Maximize the utilization of the brand by all those involved in the promotion of the region.	Activity analysis of target markets to determine product usage
Facilitate this by developing brand collateral and making this widely available.	Communication research and testing
Provide the region with the foundations of a marketing plan to implement and manage the brand.	Liaison with marketing specialists and destination managers
Evaluate and track marketing and modify as required.	Evaluation research

compared to surrounding destinations such as the Gold Coast and Sunshine Coast.

Stakeholder involvement

A *stakeholder* is any person, group or institution that has an interest in a development activity, project or programme. This definition includes intended beneficiaries and intermediaries, winners and losers, and those involved or excluded from decision-making processes (Social Development Division, 1995).

Stakeholders can be divided into three broad groups:

- Key stakeholders are those who can significantly influence the project, or are most important if the project's objectives are to be met. Both primary and secondary stakeholders may be key stakeholders.
- Primary stakeholders are those who are ultimately affected, i.e. who expect to benefit from or be adversely affected by a project.
- Secondary stakeholders are those with some intermediary role. In an enterprise project these might include government departments, trade unions, banks, export promotion agencies, business service providers, etc.

In this case, a working party was developed involving key stakeholders including industry operators, the Regional Tourism Association (Brisbane Tourism), representatives from the Brisbane City Council as well as TQ, an advertising agency and an external facilitator.

Segmentation and targeting

Market segmentation is one of the basic tools of marketing and can be performed at a number of levels. Segmentation aims to find a group of people with similar characteristics who are likely to buy a product. Segmentation on demographics alone (one of the most basic levels of segmentation) allows for broad planning on destinations. It provides direction for products that should appeal to target markets – a destination's attributes. The research conducted as part of the 'rebranding' of FNQ was

innovative for TQ in the segmentation criteria used. Previous research conducted by TQ in 1988 (The Domestic Market Segmentation Study or DMSS) provided a number of *post hoc* segments derived from cluster analysis of activities and demographics. The DMSS resulted in categories such as active families, stimulus seekers and luxury seekers. A later study again based on *post hoc* factor and cluster analysis (called the holiday traveller study) provided another series of segments based on activity.

In Brisbane, it was found that the existing market that could be influenced to travel to Brisbane more frequently lived within a 400-km radius. These visitors travelled for purposes such as special occasion, special purpose, special events/festivals, pro-sport, cultural activities, shopping and city experiences. This target market was of particular interest to major accommodation providers in the city as they were likely to visit on weekends when the occupancy rates were lower. Brisbane city hotels derived much of their income from business travellers during the working week and the idea of developing leisure business for the weekend was attractive to them.

An additional research project was undertaken by a market research company (Brian Sweeney and Associates, 1997) involving a series of focus groups to investigate why people did not come to Brisbane, what they thought of the city and how to stimulate overnight travel. Interstate markets were found to have poor images of Brisbane as a tourism destination especially compared to the capital cities of Sydney and Melbourne.

Positioning research advertisement development

This research conducted among current and potential visitors indicated a number of key concerns centring on a lack of knowledge about or interest in 'what there was to do in Brisbane'. This perception was a key barrier to improving the economic impact of tourism in Brisbane. Overall, there appeared to be a lack of a common positive image for Brisbane. An analysis of the positive reasons for travel to Brisbane among the 400-km drive market indicated a significant 'entertainment and event' base. Brisbane's most appealing aspects were the attractions it offers which the local town does not offer. A common reason for visitors to travel to Brisbane was to engage in some form of activity which could not be enjoyed at the same level as in their own home towns. These include:

- live international shows and concerts;
- sporting events such as football, rugby, cricket;
- exhibitions and events;
- shopping opportunities and range of shopping.

There was a possibility of increasing the length of stay of this existing market but there was a need to develop a stronger communication of what there was to do in Brisbane.

Visitors identified three main sources used to gain information about Brisbane:

- word of mouth;
- television;
- newspapers.

An examination of the existing attractive features and images known to travellers indicated the subtropical climate and relaxed atmosphere were distinctive and appealing. The atmosphere and pace of Brisbane were considered appealing when compared with other capital cities. Brisbane was classified as:

- friendly;
- safe;
- clean;
- warm;
- relaxing;
- outgoing;
- casual.

Additionally, comparison with competitor city destinations indicated the positionings for nightlife and entertainment (Sydney) and culture and sophistication and major events (Melbourne) were already taken. As a result, a primary target market was identified as the short break drive market – families and couples focused on special events and interests. In developing the destination image for Brisbane, it was important to distinguish the two possible target markets: residents and visitors. The position was:

> Brisbane city is a modern and diverse subtropical metropolis. As Queensland's capital city, Brisbane offers visitors a stimulating city experience in a warm, friendly and relaxed environment.

(Tourism Queensland, 2003)

This positioning was then taken by the advertising agency retained by TQ and a campaign developed. The expression of the position was 'City of Sun Days'. This expression encapsulated the relaxed leisure atmosphere required and also evoked the idea that the weekend was a great time to visit the city.

A 30-s commercial was tested with focus group participants. Qualitative results indicated that the participants found the advertisement communicated the brand values and no significant distractions were identified. In 1997, TQ and Brisbane Tourism launched the Brisbane City of Sun Days Domestic Leisure Marketing Strategy. An extensive marketing programme was developed and implemented and most importantly monitored over 1997. The total marketing investment was AUS$2.4 million. The level of industry investment, a tangible indicator of support for the campaign, amounted to around AUS$1.2 million.

Programme evaluation

An advertising tracking study was undertaken annually since June 1997 (and biannually in 1997 and 2000) to measure changes in visitation, advertising awareness and perceptions of Brisbane (Brisbane Advertising Tracking, NFS Market Research, 1997–2003). The study was conducted in Brisbane's primary source markets and key advertising.

Table 26.5 shows the level of agreement with a range of statements about Brisbane. The figure shown is the average score. The scale used was −2 (strongly disagree) and +2 (strongly agree). Table 26.5 shows that perceptions of Brisbane amongst the primary source market have continued to improve since 1997.

Given the advertising campaign is targeted to bring people from the surrounding

Table 26.5. Level of agreement with statements about Brisbane among target market.

People's opinions of Brisbane	June 1997	October 1997	October 1998	June 1999	March 2000	May 2000	June 2001	June 2002	June 2003
Is a place for shopping	1.3	1.4	1.5	1.3	1.4	1.3	1.4	1.4	1.6
Is a place for entertainment	1.3	1.4	1.4	1.3	1.5	1.4	1.5	1.5	1.5
Is a place for cultural arts and activities	1.2	1.3	1.2	1.3	1.3	1.4	1.4	1.4	1.4
Is a place for attending special events	1.2	1.3	1.3	1.2	1.4	1.5	1.4	1.4	1.4
Is a place for watching professional sporting events	1.1	1.2	1.3	1.3	1.3	1.3	1.4	1.5	1.5
Offers lots to see and do	1.1	1.2	1.2	1.2	1.3	1.3	1.3	1.4	1.4
Is an attractive city to visit	1.0	1.2	1.1	1.1	1.3	1.1	1.2	1.3	1.4
Is a friendly and hospitable city	1.0	1.0	1.1	1.2	1.3	1.2	1.3	1.3	1.4
Is an interesting place to visit	1.0	1.1	1.0	1.1	1.2	1.1	1.1	1.2	1.3
Is a lively place to visit	0.9	0.9	1.0	1.0	1.0	1.0	1.0	1.2	1.2
Is a place for attending festivals	0.9	0.9	0.9	1.0	1.0	1.1	1.1	1.2	1.3
Is a place for tours and attractions	0.7	0.8	0.6	0.7	0.9	0.7	0.8	1.0	1.2
Is a short break destination	0.7	0.7	0.9	0.8	1.0	1.0	1.0	1.0	1.0
Is a place for a weekend of indulgence	0.7	0.8	0.8	0.7	0.8	0.8	0.8	1.0	1.1
Is a place for a special occasion or a celebration	0.6	0.7	0.7	0.7	0.8	0.8	0.8	0.8	1.0
Is a place for romantic getaways	0.0	0.0	0.0	0.2	0.3	0.3	0.3	0.4	0.8
Is a place for relaxation and leisure	0.0	0.1	0.3	0.5	0.6	0.5	0.6	0.6	0.6

areas into the city on weekends using hotels, one critical tracking concern is the type of accommodation used. The results found are that over a 6-year period there has been a trend to increasing usage of hotels by the target market as shown in Fig. 26.2.

Modification – involving the Brisbane City Council

Early into the branding process, the involvement of the Brisbane City Council (BCC) became an issue. The BCC is an important contributor to the marketing of the City of Brisbane. Research had indicated that residents of the city played an important role in communicating the attractions and features of the city to potential visitors often by word of mouth. The residents of Brisbane were an important target market for the BCC which had numerous channels of communication to them. Prior to the branding campaign the BCC considered the Brisbane River was an 'iconic' feature. It was also a policy of the BCC to promote the clean up of the Brisbane River. This led the BCC to develop a 'River City' advertising campaign for the city. This advertising focused on the attractive features of the Brisbane River as a focus for improving the favourable impression of Brisbane among residents.

At issue was the conflict between a campaign targeted at residents and one that targeted potential visitors in the surrounding regions. While both the 'River City' campaign targeted at Brisbane residents and the 'City of Sun Days' campaign targeted at surrounding residents had similar objectives, the lack of coordination between the campaigns meant that neither was as effective as it could have been. Both campaigns sought to reverse negative perceptions of Brisbane as a leisure destination amongst their target market. However, while the BCC was involved in the development of 'City of Sun Days', the necessary coordination was not possible.

In June 1998, a project was initiated by TQ in an effort to investigate the perceptions that Brisbane residents had of their city. Previous research had identified the views of the past and potential tourists; however, there existed a lack of knowledge regarding Brisbane residents. The TQ commissioned a market research to conduct the study. Three hundred and one telephone interviews were conducted with randomly selected male and female residents of Brisbane. TQ and NFS Market Research jointly developed the questionnaire. These results found that the Brisbane River was one feature of the city among many others and was not particularly associated with leisure and recreation. Subsequently, the BCC changed its advertising but this still remained separate from that of the 'City of Sun Days' campaign. This less than ideal situation continues and reflects interorganizational politics and priorities.

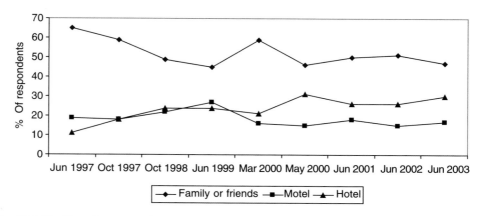

Fig. 26.2. Tracking of accommodation used on most recent visit to Brisbane among target market.

Examining the marketing mix

A 'brand health review' commissioned by TQ highlighted the successes of the campaign and recommended a development of the creative aspects to enhance brand positioning, personality and meaning. As a result of this report, television and print media were reviewed resulting in refreshed print elements and images and a new television commercial.

Important elements of the marketing programme were continually examined. The Where Else But Brisbane Events and Entertainment Guide (formerly known as the Showbriz Guide) is a quarterly seasonal feature appearing in regional newspapers. The circulation through these newspapers is around 220,000 per edition. The guide is also distributed through the travel agents and direct mail to a qualified list of events subscribers. Currently 14,000 copies of the guide are distributed via direct mail. A further 2000 guides are distributed in the Brisbane CBD.

The results of the survey of the target market for these publications were conducted in 2002 and 2003. The aim of this research was to identify the effect of these marketing pieces. The results shown in Table 26.6 indicate that in 2003, nearly three quarters (73%) of respondents kept the guide for further reference rather than throwing it away. This was a lower retention rate in 2003, with just under one half (49%) keeping the guide.

Respondents who had either kept the guide or passed it on to someone else were asked how long they kept the guide themselves. While a proportion kept the guide for at least a few months (32% in 2002, 46% in 2003), most kept it for a month or less.

The majority of respondents used the guide to get general information and ideas on what was happening in Brisbane (69% in 2002, 74% in 2003) as shown in Table 26.7. A significant proportion also uses the guide to plan weekends/short breaks to Brisbane (33% in 2002, 56% in 2003) and/or to plan daytrips to Brisbane (29% in 2002, 33% in 2003).

These and other results provided useful feedback about the performance of the guide and also allowed its effectiveness to be increased over time by modifying both the content and distribution.

Table 26.6. Processing of entertainment guide.

Upon receiving the entertainment guide what best describes what you did with it?	2002 (%)	2003 (%)
Read it in detail and keep it	39	30
Read it in detail and then throw it away	8	26
Read it in detail and then pass it to someone else	5	6
Browse through it and keep it	34	19
Browse through it and then throw it away	10	17
Browse through it and then pass it to someone else	3	3

Festival product development

Other elements of importance in a marketing plan for improving the economic benefit of tourism to Brisbane include product development, i.e. improving the visitor/resident experience through development of tourism 'product' such as tours, accommodation, events, attractions and infrastructure. The other research conducted for TQ has highlighted the potential for Special Events and Festivals in Brisbane. In particular the research indicates there is potential for an event in Brisbane that focuses on gar-

Table 26.7. Use of guide for holidays.

Which of the following do you use the guide for?	2002 (%)	2003 (%)
To plan daytrips to Brisbane	29	33
To plan weekends away to Brisbane or short breaks of 1–2 nights	33	56
To plan breaks of more than 2 nights	13	15
To get general information and ideas on what is happening	69	74
Not planning to use it/have not used it	2	5

Note: multiple responses accepted.

dening, with a significant proportion of people who express a desire to visit Brisbane being interested in gardening (nearly 60% of Brisbane preferrers had worked in the garden in the last 3 months). Brisbane locals are also big gardening participants, with just under 60% having done some gardening in the last 4 weeks. This local interest further boosts the potential of a gardening event.

A garden event is a good 'fit' with Brisbane's positioning as a cosmopolitan capital city with restaurants, cafes, shopping, entertainment and events (e.g. exhibitions, concerts, shows, pro-sports) offering a subtropical climate and lifestyle. A garden event would take advantage of the climate and lifestyle appeals of Brisbane. This product concept is currently being developed further.

This case has examined a research programme conducted over several years and involving close liaison and coordination between the destination marketing and research tasks. The integrated nature of the research programme has led to a number of advantages for the destination stakeholders. These include enhanced coordination between stakeholders and a better ability to target and track marketing activity.

Discussion

This case study has examined the importance of a systematic approach to research and marketing over many years. It highlights the importance of a clear strategy for research and marketing for a destination and also the need to include stakeholders in the process. The use of research

in developing a culture of knowledge-based decisions is an underlying theme.

In examining this case study, the importance of a programme of research that builds over time is important. Research conducted over the years moved from strategic to tactical outcomes. The initial research provided the platform of a target market and positioning from which refinements and developments in marketing could be developed over time.

The case highlights the need for specialist skills in the development and marketing of destinations. These skills certainly include the areas of marketing and advertising research, project management over extended periods of time and also importantly in research management.

Equally the case suggests the importance of a sufficient budget to ensure that adequate research is undertaken. In many situations, it has been noted that there is a tendency to trade research off for marketing in situations of budget constraints. In fact, in Brisbane the opposite has been observed. A commitment to research and evaluation has led in most cases better cooperation and funding of the marketing programme since results are readily available.

However, no marketing programme works perfectly. The problem of gaining acceptance of research findings by all stakeholders in Brisbane has been a continuing deficiency. Despite strong research evidence about the advantages of cooperative marketing, the objectives of organizations do differ and in this case has led to less than optimum outcomes. It may be possible to reconcile these objectives but this is beyond the scope of research by itself.

References

Australian Bureau of Statistics (2004) *Regional Population Growth, Australia and New Zealand (cat. no. 3218.0)*. Commonwealth Government of Australia, Canberra.
Brian Sweeney and Associates (1997) *Brisbane Segmentation Study*. Queensland Tourism and Travel Corporation, Brisbane.
Bureau of Tourism Research (2004) *International Visitor Survey*. Bureau of Tourism Research, Canberra.
Cai, L.A. (2002) Cooperative branding for rural destinations. *Annals of Tourism Research* 29(3), 720–742.
Crockett, S.R. and Wood, L. (2002) Brand Western Australia: 'holidays of an entirely different nature'. In: Morgan, N., Prichard, A. and Pride, R. (eds) *Destination Branding: Creating the Unique Destination Proposition*. Butterworth–Heinemann, Oxford, pp. 124–147.
de Chernatony, L. and Riley, F.D.O. (1998) Defining a brand: beyond the literature with experts. *Journal of Marketing Management* 14(4/5), 417–443.

Dellaert, B.G., Ettema, D. and Lindh, C. (1998) Multifaceted tourist travel decisions: a constraints-based conceptual framework to describe tourists sequential choices of travel components. *Tourism Management* 19(4), 313–320.

Hall, D., Morgan, N. and Pritchard, A. (1999) Destination branding, niche marketing and national image projection in Central and Eastern Europe. *Journal of Vacation Marketing* 5(3), 227–237.

Heath, E. and Wall, G. (1992) *Marketing Tourism Destinations: A Strategic Planning Approach*. John Wiley & Sons, Ontario, Canada.

Keller, K.L. (1993) Conceptualising, measuring, and managing customer-based brand equity. *Journal of Marketing* 57, 1–22.

Kotler, P., Haider, D.H. and Rein, I. (1993) *Marketing Places: Attracting Investments, Industry, and Tourism to Cities, States and Nations*. Free Press, New York.

Low, G.S. and Fullerton, R.A. (1994) Brands, brand management and the brand management system: a critical-historical evaluation. *Journal of Marketing Research* 31(May), 173–190.

Maser, B. and Weiermair, K. (1998) Travel decision making: from the vantage point of perceived risk and information preference. *Journal of Travel and Tourism Marketing* 7(4), 107–121.

Mintzberg, H. (1990) The design school: reconsidering the basic premise of strategic management. *Strategic Management Journal* 11(3), 171–195.

Moutinho, L. (1999) Segmentation, targeting, positioning and strategic marketing. In *Strategic Management in Tourism*. CAB International, Wallingford, UK, pp. 121–166.

Noakes, S., Scott, N., Mallam, J. and Valerio, P. (1996) *The Branding of Far North Queensland*. Far North Queensland Promotion Board, Cairns, Australia.

Pritchard, A. and Morgan, N. (1998) 'Mood Marketing' – The new destination branding strategy: a case study of 'Wales' The Brand. *Journal of Vacation Marketing* 4(3), 215–229.

Queensland Tourist and Travel Corporation (1997) *Queensland Visitor Survey Executive Summary 1996/97*. Queensland Tourist & Travel Corporation, Brisbane.

Ritchie, J.R.B. (1999) Crafting a value-driven vision for a national tourism treasure. *Tourism Management* 20(3), 273–282.

Ritchie, R. and Ritchie, J.R.B. (2002) A framework for an industry supported destination marketing information system. *Tourism Management* 23, 439–454.

Rossiter, J.R. and Percy, L. (1996) *Advertising Communication and Promotion Management*, 2nd edn. McGraw-Hill, Sydney.

Social Development Division (1995) *Stakeholder Participation & Analysis*. UK Department for International Development, London.

Soteriou, E.C. and Roberts, C. (1998) The strategic planning process in national tourism organisations. *Journal of Travel Research* 37(August), 21–29.

Tourism Queensland (2003) *Brisbane Regional Summary 2003*. Tourism Queensland, Brisbane.

Wicks, B.E. and Schuett, M.A. (1991) Examining the role of tourism promotion through the use of brochures. *Tourism Management* 12(4), 301–312.

27 The Rasch Model Applied to Customer Satisfaction in Marbella

José L. Santos-Arrebola

Catedràtico de Universidad, University of Malaga, Spain

Introduction

The growing recognition of the importance of customer satisfaction in tourism is leading to a substantial increase in research into the process of judging satisfaction or dissatisfaction. Researchers, marketing and political experts, and businessmen are all concerned with deepening their understanding of this concept and improving its measurement.

This chapter describes one such tool that has proved to be highly useful for measuring customer satisfaction, in this case applied to the holiday resort of Marbella (Spain), a top destination where the local administration has spent a great deal of money modernizing the town and therefore wishes to measure the response of tourists to these improvements.

For many authors the paradigm of satisfaction/dissatisfaction is the result of a comparative process between generated and perceived expectations. According to Cardozo (1965), it is an evaluative judgement of an occasional purchase. Hunt (1977) sees satisfaction as an affective state that is at the same time a function of expectations and results. Oliver (1980) understands consumer satisfaction as being an emotional reaction to consumption. Last but not least, satisfaction can be seen as a psychological result in which certain variables other than service quality inter-

vene, variables beyond the control of the person rendering the service (Crompton and Love, 1995).

In the literature, a handful of comparisons between expectations have been proposed. Miller (1977), for instance, states that, 'the standard expectation is an ideal', while Zeithaml *et al*. (1991) describe four types of expectations: (i) expected; (ii) desired; (iii) adequate; and (iv) perceived. With the 'Model Based on the Norms of Experience', Woodruff *et al*. (1983) suggest that satisfaction occurs when the result coincides with the norm. Morris (1977) maintains that there are cultural norms that consumers use to evaluate satisfaction. Lastly, to determine the level of satisfaction, Haywood and Muller (1988), Whipple and Tmach (1988) and Mazursky (1989) focus on experience-based norms.

Satisfaction in Tourism and the Rasch Model

The satisfaction of tourists with a destination is a concept that many researchers have difficulty in defining. A tourist destination is a package of amenities and services composed of a number of multidimensional attributes, which together determine the capacity of a destination to fulfil the needs of visitors.

According to Hu and Ritchie (1993), these attributes reflect the feelings, beliefs and opinions that an individual has on a given destination. Goodrich (1977) examines the benefits that tourists wish to obtain during their holidays – scenic beauty, pleasant attitude of the locals, appropriate accommodation, rest and relaxation, amongst others – as these benefits have a direct effect on their overall satisfaction. For Lounsbury and Hoopes (1985), holiday satisfaction is measured in terms of numerous aspects from the surroundings, climate, accommodation, spending budget, rest and relaxation, through opportunities to practise favourite pastimes, socializing with other people and 'letting one's hair down', to certain variables such as the individual's personal situation: age, sex, education, work, income, marital status, the number of accompanying children and so on. In the opinion of Moutinho (1987), satisfaction is influenced by a large number of natural, social and motivational attributes, including service quality, perceptions, the predisposition of the tourist and the availability of alternative trips to different destinations, while Ritchie et al. (1978) underline the importance of general factors including nature, culture, sports, recreational and shopping facilities, infrastructure, prices, the locals' attitude towards tourists, the accessibility of the region, and social and cultural elements such as history, architecture, language, gastronomy, art and music.

The Rasch Model was first used in psychometric studies. Owing greatly to its simplicity it later became one of the most popular subsets of the Item Response Theory (IRT), which may be defined as the study of test and item scores based on assumptions concerning the mathematical relationship between abilities (or other hypothesized traits) and item responses.

According to this model, tourist satisfaction is a latent variable defined by a series of items determining the level of satisfaction of tourists visiting a specific destination, in this case Marbella. The model – within the framework of IRT – not only focuses on the overall results of the questionnaire but also on the interaction between the individual and the items. In other words, it is perceived as a continuum along which the individual's responses to the items are situated, with the level of satisfaction as the sole dimension. After classifying the items in terms of more or less satisfaction the results obtained are presented in table format.

The Rasch Model

The level of satisfaction in Marbella can be considered a latent variable defined by a series of items, which are the attributes determining the level of satisfaction. Latent variable theory takes into account the measurement of a series of underlying traits belonging to the subject, which are unobservable and condition the reply to each item.

For Wright (1977), the situation in which a person endeavours to give a reply to an item is potentially complicated. Results may be influenced in many ways – for instance, the physical characteristics and attitude of the person conducting the survey, the mood of the person taking part in the survey, amongst other factors – which when a person gives a reply to an item latent variable models try to measure.

According to Hambleton and Cook (1977), the relationship between the 'observable performance' in the questionnaire and the 'unobservable' trait, which is assumed to underlie the evaluation of the questionnaire, indicates a specific latent variable model.

Latent variable models are mathematical models that try to explain the process of how a reply to an item is obtained. These models focus attention not only on the overall result of the questionnaire but also on the interaction between a person and an item. According to Wright (1977, pp. 97–116), the Rasch Model is the most representative model of latent variable theory to which the IRT is applied, a model that functions with only two parameters: parameter β for each individual and parameter δ for each item. A more detailed description of the Rasch Model is given later.

Developed by the Danish mathematician Rasch (1980), the model was used in his study of psychometrics. Subsequently, it received a lot of attention especially from Wright and

Stone (1979). As mentioned earlier, this model is the one to which the IRT is mainly applied chiefly because of the simplicity of its logic, which can be seen later.

If the difference $(\beta_n - \delta_i)$, called 'logit' by Wright (1977), is used as basic exponent e, then

$$0 \le e^{(\beta_n - \delta_i)} \le \infty$$

Carrying out the corresponding calculations and applying limits, one can obtain the following expression between intervals 0 and 1:

$$0 \le \left(\frac{e^{(\beta_n - \delta_i)}}{1 + e^{(\beta_n - \delta_i)}} \right) \le 1$$

Given parameters β_n and δ_i, this formula is an estimate of the probability that tourist n will give item i a score of 1. The relationship can be expressed as proposed by Rasch (1980):

$$P\{X_{ni} = 1/\beta_n \delta_i\} = \frac{e^{(\beta_n - \delta_i)}}{1 + e^{(\beta_n - \delta_i)}}$$

This is the formula that Rasch obtained by developing the Theory of Latent Variables. The complementary probability for $X_{ni} = 0$ is

$$\{PX_{ni} = 0/\beta_n \delta_i\} = 1 - P\{X_{ni} = 1/\beta_n \delta_i\} =$$

$$1 - \frac{e^{(\beta_n - \delta_i)}}{1 + e^{(\beta_n - \delta_i)}}$$

Rasch's formula for the degree of satisfaction that does not give the probability that tourist n will give item i a score of x, where x has a value between 1 and 4, can be expressed in the following way:

$$P(X_{ni} = X) = \frac{e^{(\beta_n - \delta_i)}}{1 + e^{(\beta_n - \delta_i)}}$$

For each of the different categories, parameters β_n and δ_i are estimated by the maximum probability method using algorithms PROX and UCON (Wright and Linacre, 1992).

According to this model, the level of satisfaction is conceived as a continuum, along which the items and tourists are situated, with a sole dimension: the level of satisfaction. The variable makes it possible to visualize satisfaction as a measure located at a given point along a line (Fig. 27.1).

For Wright and Stone (1979) the purpose of giving a person a test is to estimate the posi-

tion on the line that is implied by the said test. The level of satisfaction is conceived as a line along which the items and tourists are situated with the point of least satisfaction on the extreme left and that of greatest satisfaction on the extreme right. The items are represented by the symbols $\delta_1, \delta_2, ..., \delta_i$, and tourist satisfaction by $\beta_1, \beta_2, ..., \beta_i$.

Figure 27.2 represents the way in which the satisfaction of tourist β_n with items δ can be plotted along the satisfaction continuum according to the position of the latter. The measure of tourist β has an expected result of 3, which means, as can be seen in Fig. 27.2, that he or she is satisfied with items δ_1, δ_2 and δ_3, because his or her measure is greater than the measure for these three items. Nevertheless, the tourist is not satisfied with item δ_4 because his or her measure is lower than the measure for this item.

Measurement and analysis using the Rasch Model

To measure the level of satisfaction, the Rasch Model was applied to the 150 completed questionnaires, using the BIGSTEPS computer program created by Wright and Linacre (1992), the results of which are shown in Tables 27.1 and 27.3.

Table 27.1 shows the order of the 32 items arranged from those with the lowest measure to those with highest. The columns contain the following information:

- *Entry no.* The number identifying each item according to the order in which it was introduced into the program.
- *Raw score.* The total number of points given to each item (this is not a measure but an appraisal that is made by the program in terms of the scores and the number of people replying to each item).
- *Count.* The total number of guests who filled in the questionnaire.
- *Measure.* The computer program BIGSTEPS, created by Wright and Linacre, was used to calculate the results.
- *Standard error.* This is the standard error that accompanies the specific measure, i.e.

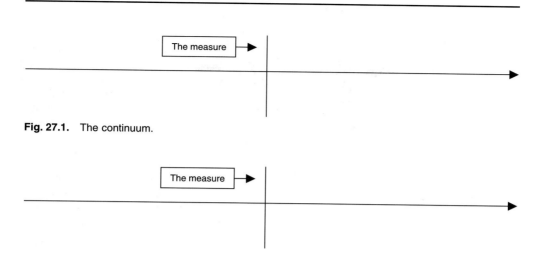

Fig. 27.1. The continuum.

Fig. 27.2. The tourist satisfaction continuum. Source: adapted from Wright and Stone (1979).

the precision with which the estimate has been obtained.

- *Infit and outfit.* These columns contain unexpected appraisals, based on the standardization of MNSQ relative to the count with a mean of 0 and a deviation of 1 (ZSTD). Both are 'fit' statistics and in a Rasch context they indicate how accurately or predictably data fit the model. Infit means inlier-sensitive or information-weighted fit. This is more sensitive to the pattern of responses to items targeted on the person, and vice versa. For example, infit reports overfit for Guttman patterns, underfit for alternative curricula or idiosyncratic clinical groups. These patterns can be hard to diagnose and remedy. Outfit means outlier-sensitive fit. This is more sensitive to responses to items with difficulty far from a person, and vice versa. For example, outfit reports overfit for imputed responses, underfit for lucky guesses and careless mistakes. These are usually easy to diagnose and remedy.
- *PTBIS* (compute point-biserial correlations). The correlation between the total raw score and the measure.

Methods

The survey described here was carried out in five stages: (i) selecting the items; (ii) determining the latent variable; (iii) preparing the questionnaire; (iv) conducting fieldwork; and (v) measuring and analysing the results using the Rasch Model.

In a pilot survey, a questionnaire containing 80 items was given to a sample of ten people who were chosen at random with the sole objective of checking the structure of the questionnaire's items. As a result it was discovered that many of the items gave the same measure, which in turn made it possible to group them together in more global item categories with the object of minimizing information loss and shortening the questionnaire to the 32 items (see Table 27.2). For instance, the original items 'folklore festivals', 'concerts' and 'miscellaneous cultural activities' were grouped together as one item 'concerts and festivals'. Likewise, the items 'historical importance', 'artistic and architectonic characteristics' and 'archaeological remains' were grouped together as 'town centre of Marbella'.

Table 27.1. Tourist statistics: measure order.

Entry no.	Raw score	Count	Measure	Error	Infit MNSQ	ZSTD	Outfit MNSQ	ZSTD	PTBIS	Tourist
146	73	25	71.3	3.4	1.20	0.3	2.26	1.0	-0.17	DC.5*.2.H.POR.LIB.1W.CA.UNIV.1
16	68	24	66.9	2.5	1.37	0.7	1.94	1.2	-0.25	GU.4*.5.M.ESP.JUB.3W.CA.PRIM.0
149	68	24	66.8	2.5	0.67	-0.8	0.44	-1.2	0.63	DC.5*.3.H.KUW.EMP.2W.CA.UNI.+3
105	89	32	65.9	2.0	1.81	1.9	0.96	-0.1	0.58	LM.5*.3.M.ESP.LIB.2W.CA.UNIV.0
37	70	26	64.1	1.9	2.08	2.4	1.77	1.5	0.33	EF.4*.5.H.ESP.AUT.2W.CA.UNIV.0
31	78	29	64.0	1.8	1.58	1.6	1.11	0.3	0.56	EF.4*.5.M.ESP.FUN.3W.CA.UNI.+3
116	73	27	63.5	1.9	0.75	-0.8	0.71	-0.8	0.51	PR.5*.3.M.U.K.OTR.2W.SO.SECU.0
144	80	30	63.4	1.7	1.43	1.2	1.26	0.7	0.43	DC.5*.3.M.LUX.OTR.2W.CA.SECU.2
80	69	26	62.9	1.9	1.38	1.0	1.96	2.0	0.14	CB.4*.2.M.ESP.OTR.2W.SE.UNIV.0
118	66	25	62.8	1.9	2.12	2.6	1.73	1.6	0.26	PR.5*.3.M.POR.LIB.1W.CA.SECU.2
36	71	27	62.5	1.8	0.80	-0.7	0.69	-1.0	0.62	EF.4*.2.H.ESP.EMP.2W.CA.UNIV.2
139	71	27	62.2	1.8	0.85	-0.5	1.07	0.2	0.34	DC.5*.4.M.ESP.OTR.2W.CA.SECU.1
136	69	27	61.4	1.7	0.83	-0.6	0.85	-0.5	0.36	DC.5*.4.M.ESP.OTR.1W.CA.SECU.1
6	82	32	61.4	1.5	0.99	0.0	0.86	-0.5	0.51	AP.4*.4.M.ESP.OTR.3W.VI.UNIV.0
115	67	26	61.3	1.7	0.89	-0.4	0.80	-0.7	0.65	PR.5*.1.M.ITA.EST.1M.SO.UNIV.1
107	62	24	61.3	1.8	0.80	-0.6	0.75	-0.8	0.59	PR.5*.3.H.ESP.EMP.1W.CA.UNIV.1
64	74	29	61.2	1.6	1.67	2.0	1.20	0.6	0.67	MD.4*.3.H.ESP.OTR.2W.CA.SECU.2
4	63	25	60.7	1.7	1.61	1.7	1.83	2.1	0.07	AP.4*.3.M.ESP.EJE.2W.CA.UNIV.2
41	74	29	60.6	1.6	0.89	-0.4	0.87	-0.5	0.27	EF.4*.3.M.U.K.AUT.2W.CA.SECU.2
97	75	30	60.5	1.5	1.20	0.7	0.96	-0.1	0.56	LM.5*.2.H.ESP.EJE.3W.CA.UNIV.1
117	59	23	60.4	1.8	1.21	0.6	1.21	0.6	0.21	PR.5*.2.H.JAP.EMP.1W.CA.UNIV.1
30	75	30	60.2	1.5	1.36	1.2	1.44	1.4	0.11	GU.4*.2.M.MEX.EMP.2W.CA.SECU.1
40	73	29	60.1	1.5	1.00	0.0	0.97	-0.1	0.12	EF.4*.3.H.U.K.EJE.2W.CA.SECU.2
5	65	26	59.6	1.6	1.08	0.3	0.93	-0.3	0.72	AP.4*.2.H.ESP.FUN.1W.CA.SECU.0
7	65	26	59.6	1.6	1.08	0.3	0.93	-0.3	0.72	AP.4*.1.M.ESP.FUN.1W.CA.SECU.0
52	68	28	59.5	1.5	1.48	1.5	1.22	-0.8	0.73	RA.4*.1.M.ESP.OTR.3W.SO.UNIV.0
98	78	32	59.5	1.4	1.68	2.2	1.59	1.9	0.34	LM.5*.1.H.ESP.EJE.1M.SO.UNIV.0
109	68	28	59.5	1.5	1.15	0.5	1.00	0.0	0.54	PR.5*.3.H.USA.EMP.2W.CA.UNIV.0
142	70	29	59.3	1.5	1.01	0.0	1.01	0.0	0.35	DC.5*.5.H.ESP.EMP.2W.CA.SECU.1
96	66	27	59.3	1.5	0.91	-0.3	0.99	0.0	0.50	LM.5*.3.H.ESP.LIB.1W.CA.UNIV.3
14	75	31	59.3	1.4	0.84	-0.6	0.89	-0.4	0.22	AP.4*.1.M.U.K.EJE.2W.CA.SECU.1
38	53	30	52.1	1.2	1.00	0.0	1.04	0.2	0.24	EF.4*.3.H.ALE.EJE.2W.CA.UNIV.0

46	47	27	52.0	1.3	1.01	0.0	0.94	-0.2	0.40	RA.4*.1.M.ESP.EST.2W.SO.UNIV.0
26	48	27	52.0	1.3	1.28	1.0	1.25	0.9	0.44	GU.4*.2.H.ESP.LIB.2W.CA.UNIV.0
15	53	31	51.7	1.2	1.29	1.1	1.28	1.1	0.70	AP.4*.5.H.U.K.JUB.1M.CA.UNIV.0
143	46	27	51.7	1.3	0.87	-0.5	0.91	-0.4	0.69	DC.5*.5.H.ESP.EMP.2W.CA.SECU.1
69	43	25	51.6	1.3	0.96	-0.2	0.96	-0.1	0.73	MD.4*.3.M.ALE.EJE.3W.CA.SECU.0
88	40	23	51.6	1.4	1.22	0.8	1.24	0.8	0.49	CB.4*.3.H.USA.LIB.2W.CA.UNIV.2
75	47	28	51.6	1.2	1.81	2.6	1.77	2.5	0.28	MD.4*.1.M.SUI.OTR.2W.SO.SECU.0
60	43	24	51.6	1.3	0.80	-0.8	0.81	-0.7	0.45	RA.4*.2.H.U.K.LIB.1W.CA.SECU.2
55	43	25	51.5	1.3	0.69	-1.3	0.73	-1.1	0.52	RA.4*.3.M.POR.OTR.1W.CA.UNIV.1
56	50	29	51.4	1.2	1.61	2.1	1.69	2.3	0.29	RA.4*.3.H.FRA.AUT.1W.CA.UNIV.1
134	46	28	51.3	1.2	0.85	-0.6	0.87	-0.5	0.65	DP.5*.1.H.ESP.EMP.3W.SO.SECU.0
104	36	21	51.1	1.4	2.20	3.1	2.21	3.1	0.14	LM.5*.2.M.USA.EMP.1W.CA.UNIV.0
2	48	29	51.1	1.2	0.20	-5.0	0.21	-4.9	0.80	AP.4*.2.M.ESP.EMP.2W.CA.UNIV.0
9	48	29	51.0	1.2	1.88	2.9	1.88	2.9	0.28	AP.4*.1.H.U.K.EST.1W.SO.UNIV.0
130	33	19	50.9	1.5	0.24	-3.7	0.24	-3.7	0.76	DP.5*.4.H.FRA.EMP.2W.SO.UNIV.0
126	35	21	50.6	1.4	0.57	-1.8	0.62	-1.5	0.56	DP.5*.4.H.ALE.LIB.2W.CA.UNIV.0
58	48	30	50.4	1.2	0.99	0.0	0.96	-0.2	0.53	RA.4*.1.H.U.K.EST.2W.SO.UNIV.0
57	50	32	50.3	1.1	0.74	-1.2	0.74	-1.2	0.53	RA.4*.1.M.U.K.EST.2W.SO.UNIV.0
43	43	28	50.1	1.2	0.97	-0.1	0.96	-0.1	0.52	EF.4*.3.M.U.K.EJE.2W.CA.SECU.1
87	36	23	49.9	1.3	0.74	-1.0	0.75	-1.0	0.60	CB.4*.2.H.JAP.OTR.1W.CA.UNIV.0
84	41	27	49.7	1.2	0.14	-5.6	0.15	-5.6	0.88	CB.4*.3.H.ESP.EMP.2W.CA.UNIV.1
133	21	13	48.7	1.8	0.24	-3.0	0.23	-3.1	0.69	DP.5*.3.H.U.K.EJE.1W.CA.UNIV.0
3	39	29	48.6	1.2	0.69	-1.5	0.70	-1.4	0.70	AP.4*1.M.ESP.EST.1W.CA.UNIV.0
12	34	25	47.9	1.3	1.36	1.2	1.44	1.5	0.28	AP.4*.3.H.POR.EMP.1W.CA.SECU.1
147	35	29	46.9	1.2	1.35	1.3	1.35	1.3	0.50	DC.5*.3.H.CAN.AUT.2W.CA.SECU.2
71	22	15	46.5	1.6	1.11	0.3	1.12	0.4	0.25	MD.4*.1.H.BELL.LIB.1W.CA.SECU.1
19	30	26	46.2	1.2	1.03	0.1	1.05	0.2	0.38	GU.4*.5.H.ESP.JUB.3W.CA.UNIV.0
73	21	15	45.9	1.6	0.85	-0.5	0.86	-0.4	0.26	MD.4*.1.M.BELL.LIB.1W.CA.SECU.1
Mean	56	27	55.7	1.4	1.02	-0.2	1.01	-0.2		
SD	12	3	4.3	0.3	0.44	1.6	0.43	1.6		

Table 27.2. The 32 items included in the questionnaire.

1. Natural surroundings
2. Climate
3. Town centre of Marbella
4. Puerto Banús (Marina)
5. Street cleanliness
6. Street safety
7. Hawkers
8. Begging
9. Traffic congestion
10. Parking
11. Concerts and festivals
12. Quality of hotel service
13. Quality of restaurant service
14. Quality of beach restaurant service
15. Quality of café service
16. Hotel prices
17. Restaurant prices
18. Beach restaurant prices
19. Café prices
20. Taxi tariffs
21. Entertainment and nightlife in Marbella
22. Facilities for playing golf
23. Facilities for playing tennis
24. Facilities for practising water sports
25. Cleanliness of the seawater
26. Cleanliness of beaches
27. Pleasant attitude of the locals
28. Restful atmosphere
29. Prestige of the destination
30. Satisfaction with Marbella as it is
31. Satisfaction with Marbella as it was 5 years ago
32. Satisfaction with improvements carried out by the town council

Tourist satisfaction has a fairly important psychological component, which is the result of comparing generated expectations with those perceived, thus producing a series of underlying characteristics in each individual, which are 'unobservable' and which determine his or her way of responding to the items. This is known as the latent variable.

In latent variable theory, it is assumed that there exists a variable – in this study, level of customer satisfaction – and a probabilistic relationship between this variable and each one of the items used. The score of an individual, i.e. his or her position on the scale of the variable, is not determined by measurement but estimated from the response of the said individual to a series of items.

For Hambleton and Cook (1977), a latent variable model specifies a relationship between the observable performance in the test and the unobservable characteristic that is supposed to underlie the test's evaluation. The relationship between 'observable' and 'unobservable' quantities is described by a mathematical function. Wherefore, latent variable models and 'mathematical models' try to explain the response process to the item. These latent variable models focus not only on the overall result of the tests but also on the interaction between a person and an item. The properties of the items, as a measurement tool, are described in terms of the individuals to whom they are applied.

In the case under study, the latent variable was determined by the level of satisfaction of tourists staying at 4- and 5-star hotels in Marbella. The items chosen to measure this contained all the indicators that, in the opinion of the author, described the level of satisfaction of tourists visiting the resort.

The Rasch Model provides misfits with the two parameters: items and people. The columns 'infit' and 'outfit' contain these misfits, which in the case of the Rasch Model have a standard deviation greater or less than 3. Positive value indicates that the items have been overrated by the people taking part in the survey, and negative indicates that they have been underrated, which signifies that in evaluating the items the tourists disagreed with each other. High misfits indicate a discrepancy between the score given by each person and the score each item should receive in relation to the scores for the rest of the items, according to the estimation of the parameters. 'Infit' evaluates how the questions are answered most suitably and 'outfit' measures the consistency with which tourists answer the questions. It must be noted that the misfits are not eliminated but analysed individually. Likewise, the misfits help to discover whether the people taking part in the survey answered the questions seriously or not. Hence, it is possible to conduct a more in-depth study of their socio-demographic profile by analysing the causes of the misfits.

As regards items, misfits included Puerto Banús, climate, parking, cleanliness of seawater, Marbella as it was 5 years ago, and golf. Out of the 150 tourists taking part in the survey, 17 gave misfitting answers to some of the questions.

The final questionnaire was written in Spanish and English, all other languages having been discarded since most of the hotel guests spoke the latter. The four possible replies to each item were as follows: (i) bad; (ii) average; (iii) good; and (iv) very good. These four categories were chosen as it was assumed that they corresponded to the levels of satisfaction with the items and because they coincided with the categories used in the questionnaires with which the reception desks at the hotels used in the survey were provided.

The fieldwork involved asking 150 national and foreign tourists to fill in a questionnaire, and was carried out during the first 2 weeks of August 1996 at a number of 4- and 5-star hotels in Marbella. The 5-star hotels were Puente Romano (PR), Los Monteros (LM), Don Pepe (DP) and Don Carlos (DC) and the 4-star hotels, Andalucía Plaza (AP), Coral Beach (CB), El Fuerte (EF), Guadalmina (GU), Marbella Dinamar (MD) and Rincón Andaluz (RA).

The Sample

The sample distribution was carried out by proportional allocation to the sizes of the hotels of both categories. Over a period of 2 weeks, 150 guests – based on previous studies, the proportion of Spanish and foreign tourists was 54% and 46%, respectively – were chosen randomly on arrival at the reception desk of the hotels used in the survey and were asked to fill in the questionnaire. In the event that a guest refused to do so, the next random number was chosen using a coherent apportionment criterion in all the hotels involved. There were no open-ended questions, so if a person taking part in the survey gave an anomalous answer, i.e. when he or she answered in jest, the Rasch Model classified it in the section called 'misfits' (see the aforementioned explanation). In any event, the Rasch Model provides the measure of each item.

Results

Item order

The Rasch Model makes it possible to arrange all the items (Table 27.1) from those with the lowest measure to those with the highest. As mentioned earlier, the least satisfying items are located at the top of the list and the most satisfying at the bottom. The explanation for this is that the items with lower measures are located at the beginning of the line and are exceeded by the greatest number of subjects taking part in the survey, thereby giving them satisfaction.

The climate is the most satisfying item of all followed by street safety and cleanliness, both the responsibility of Marbella Town Council. Next on the list are golf and the quality of hotel service. The three items related to strong holiday motivations are restful atmosphere, nightlife and facilities for playing tennis.

The elimination of bothersome features such as begging and hawking satisfied the tourists taking part in the survey, as did those concerning the attractiveness of the town such as the natural surroundings, the town centre with all its improvements, Puerto Banús, pleasant attitude of the locals and Marbella.

As has been already mentioned, unsatisfactory items include parking and traffic congestion, which reveal the need to reduce traffic and provide more parking spaces to meet the needs of a greater number of tourists travelling by car. Two more items that cause a lot of dissatisfaction are the beaches and the seawater; the quality of the latter has suffered from the population increase and the full sanitation of the Costa del Sol has yet to be completed. According to these appraisals, keeping the seawater and beaches clean are the two problems that should be tackled as soon as possible in order to increase tourist satisfaction.

Another group of items that causes great dissatisfaction is prices. In Marbella, café prices cause most dissatisfaction followed by taxi tariffs, beach restaurant and restaurant prices, and lastly hotel prices. Those taking part in the survey voiced the need for hotel owners to control existing price levels in Marbella in order to increase tourist satisfaction.

With reference to the items concerning service quality, people taking part in the survey were dissatisfied with the service in cafés and beach restaurants. Lastly, it is worth noting that the items dealing with concerts and festivals, as well as with water sports, were deemed unsatisfactory. Promoting cultural activities and water sports with the organization of events aimed at palliating this problem should be a future objective.

Tourist order

Using the Rasch Model, it is possible to arrange tourists by the measure obtained by them by means of proportional analysis. In Table 27.3, the tourists taking part in the survey are arranged from top to bottom in order of their satisfaction. Those above the median are the most satisfied and those below, the least. Due to shortage of space, only the first 30 and the last 30 tourists are included.

The satisfied tourists have been grouped by hotel category and name, length of stay and socio-demographic profile (hotel, category, age, sex, nationality, profession, duration of stay, marital status, academic qualifications, number of children). For example, the personal data for the first guest in the tourist column is as follows: DC (Hotel Don Carlos), 5* (maximum category, e.g. 5-star ranking), 2 (age group), M (male), POR (Portuguese/nationality), LIB (liberal/profession), 1W (1 week/duration of stay), MA (married/marital status), UNIV (university degree/academic qualifications), 1 (number of children).

For the proportion analysis, according to the measure order, the following data can be obtained from Table 27.3. As regards the duration of their holiday, the most satisfied tourists are those whose stay lasted 3 weeks (67%), followed by those who stayed a fortnight (51%). The level of satisfaction as regards stays lasting 1 and 4 weeks was 48% and 45%, respectively. On the subject of the demographic profile of the tourists, women were more satisfied (53%) with their holiday in Marbella than men (47%). The most satisfied age group was 51–60 (79%). For the under 30s, 41–50 and the over 50s age groups satisfaction was 45%. The Spanish were the most satisfied (60%), with all foreigners being less satisfied (38%). As regards profession, miscellaneous professions (55%), freelancers (55%), businessmen (53%), liberal professions and executives (48%) were the most satisfied, students and pensioners (75%) being the least satisfied. In relation to marital status, married couples were the most satisfied (54%), single tourists being less so (41%). Tourists with a university degree were less satisfied (48%) than those without a university education (55%). Finally, married couples with children were more satisfied (61%) than childless couples (52%).

This analysis shows the utility of the Rasch Model. On the one hand, all the items have been classified and analysed, revealing those tourists who were most satisfied with their holiday in Marbella. On the other hand, all the tourists have been classified according to certain characteristics that will be extremely useful in future analyses. Bearing in mind that the results were analysed as a whole and that with future research it would be possible to

Table 27.3. Tourist statistics: measure order.

Entry no.	Raw score	Count	Measure	Error	Infit MNSQ	Infit ZSTD	Outfit MNSQ	Outfit ZSTD	PTBIS	Tourist
146	73	25	71.3	3.4	1.20	0.3	2.26	1.0	-0.17	DC.5*.2.M.POR.LIB.1W.MA.UNIV.1
16	68	24	66.9	2.5	1.37	0.7	1.94	1.2	-0.25	GU.4*.5.F.SP.PEN.3W.MA.PRIM.0
149	68	24	66.8	2.5	0.67	-0.8	0.44	-1.2	0.63	DC.5*.3.M.KUW.EMP.2W.MA.UNI.+3
105	89	32	65.9	2.0	1.81	1.9	0.96	-0.1	0.58	LM.5*.3.F.SP.LIB.2W.MA.UNIV.2
37	70	26	64.1	1.9	2.08	2.4	1.77	1.5	0.33	EF.4*.5.M.SP.FREE.2W.MA.UNIV.0
31	78	29	64.0	1.8	1.58	1.6	1.11	0.3	0.56	EF.4*.5.F.SP.BUR.3W.MA.UNI.+3
116	73	27	63.5	1.9	0.75	-0.8	0.71	-0.8	0.51	PR.5*.3.F.UK.OTH.2W.SIN.SECO.0
144	80	30	63.4	1.7	1.43	1.2	1.26	0.7	0.43	DC.5*.3.F.LUX.OTH.2W.MA.SECO.2
80	69	26	62.9	1.9	1.38	1.0	1.96	2.0	0.14	CB.4*.2.F.SP.OTH.2W.SEP.UNIV.0
118	66	25	62.8	1.9	2.12	2.6	1.73	1.6	0.26	PR.5*.3.F.POR.LIB.1W.MA.SECO.2
36	71	27	62.5	1.8	0.80	-0.7	0.69	-1.0	0.62	EF.4*.2.M.SP.EMP.2W.MA.UNIV.2
139	71	27	62.2	1.8	0.85	-0.5	1.07	0.2	0.34	DC.5*.4.F.SP.OTH.2W.MA.SECO.1
136	69	27	61.4	1.7	0.83	-0.6	0.85	-0.5	0.36	DC.5*.4.F.SP.OTH.1W.MA.SECO.1
6	82	32	61.4	1.5	0.99	0.0	0.86	-0.5	0.51	AP.4*.4.F.SP.OTH.3W.WID.UNIV.0
115	67	26	61.3	1.7	0.89	-0.4	0.80	-0.7	0.65	PR.5*.1.F.ITA.ST.1M.SIN.UNIV.1
107	62	24	61.3	1.8	0.80	-0.6	0.75	-0.8	0.59	PR.5*.3.M.SP.EMP.1W.MA.UNIV.1
64	74	29	61.2	1.6	1.67	2.0	1.20	0.6	0.67	MD.4*.3.M.SP.OTH.2W.MA.SECO.2
4	63	25	60.7	1.7	1.61	1.7	1.83	2.1	0.07	AP.4*.3.F.SP.EXE.2W.MA.UNIV.2
41	74	29	60.6	1.6	0.89	-0.4	0.87	-0.5	0.27	EF.4*.3.F.UK.FREE.2W.MA.SECO.2
97	75	30	60.5	1.5	1.20	0.7	0.96	-0.1	0.56	LM.5*.2.M.SP.EXE.3W.MA.UNIV.1
117	59	23	60.4	1.8	1.21	0.6	1.21	0.6	0.21	PR.5*.2.M.JAP.EMP.1W.MA.UNIV.1
30	75	30	60.2	1.5	1.36	1.2	1.44	1.4	0.11	GU.4*.2.F.MEX.EMP.2W.MA.SECO.1
40	73	29	60.1	1.5	1.00	0.0	0.97	-0.1	0.12	EF.4*.3.M.UK.EXE.2W.MA.SECO.2
5	65	26	59.6	1.6	1.08	0.3	0.93	-0.3	0.72	AP.4*.2.M.SP.BUR.1W.MA.SECO.0
7	65	26	59.6	1.6	1.08	0.3	0.93	-0.3	0.72	AP.4*.1.F.SP.BUR.1W.MA.SECO.0
52	68	28	59.5	1.5	1.48	1.5	1.22	-0.8	0.73	RA.4*.1.F.SP.OTH.3W.SIN.UNIV.0
98	78	32	59.5	1.4	1.68	2.2	1.59	1.9	0.34	LM.5*.1.M.SP.EXE.1M.SIN.UNIV.0
109	68	28	59.5	1.5	1.15	0.5	1.00	0.0	0.54	PR.5*.3.M.USA.EMP.2W.MA.UNIV.0
142	70	29	59.3	1.5	1.01	0.0	1.01	0.0	0.35	DC.5*.5.M.SP.EMP.2W.MA.SECO.1
96	66	27	59.3	1.5	0.91	-0.3	0.99	0.0	0.50	LM.5*.3.M.SP.LIB.1W.MA.UNIV.3
14	75	31	59.3	1.4	0.84	-0.6	0.89	-0.4	0.22	AP.4*.1.F.UK.EXE.2W.MA.SECO.1
38	53	30	52.1	1.2	1.00	0.0	1.04	0.2	0.24	EF.4*.3.M.GER.EXE.2W.MA.UNIV.0

Continued

Table 27.3. Continued

Entry no.	Raw score	Count	Measure	Error	Infit MNSQ	ZSTD	Outfit MNSQ	ZSTD	PTBIS	Tourist
46	47	27	52.0	1.3	1.01	0.0	0.94	-0.2	0.40	RA.4*.1.F.SP.ST.2W.SIN.UNIV.0
26	48	27	52.0	1.3	1.28	1.0	1.25	0.9	0.44	GU.4*.2.M.SP.LIB.2W.MA.UNIV.0
15	53	31	51.7	1.2	1.29	1.1	1.28	1.1	0.70	AP.4*.5.M.UK.PEN.1M.MA.UNIV.0
143	46	27	51.7	1.3	0.87	-0.5	0.91	-0.4	0.69	DC.5*.5.M.SP.EMP.2W.MA.SECO.1
69	43	25	51.6	1.3	0.96	-0.2	0.96	-0.1	0.73	MD.4*.3.F.GER.EXE.3W.MA.SECO.0
88	40	23	51.6	1.4	1.22	0.8	1.24	0.8	0.49	CB.4*.3.M.USA.LIB.2W.MA.UNIV.2
75	47	28	51.6	1.2	1.81	2.6	1.77	2.5	0.28	MD.4*.1.F.SWIT.OTH.2W.SIN.SECU.0
60	43	24	51.6	1.3	0.80	-0.8	0.81	-0.7	0.45	RA.4*.2.M.UK.LIB.1W.MA.SECO.2
55	43	25	51.5	1.3	0.69	-1.3	0.73	-1.1	0.52	RA.4*.3.F.POR.OTH.1W.MA.UNIV.1
56	50	29	51.4	1.2	1.61	2.1	1.69	2.3	0.29	RA.4*.3.M.FRA.FREE.1W.MA.UNIV.1
134	46	28	51.3	1.2	0.85	-0.6	0.87	-0.5	0.65	DP.5*.1.M.SP.EMP.3W.SIN.SECO.0
104	36	21	51.1	1.4	2.20	3.1	2.21	3.1	0.14	LM.5*.2.F.USA.EMP.1W.MA.UNIV.0
2	48	29	51.1	1.2	0.20	-5.0	0.21	-4.9	0.80	AP.4*.2.F.SP.EMP.2W.MA.UNIV.0
9	48	29	51.0	1.2	1.88	2.9	1.88	2.9	0.28	AP.4*.1.M.UK.ST.1W.SIN.UNIV.0
130	33	19	50.9	1.5	0.24	-3.7	0.24	-3.7	0.76	DP.5*.4.M.FRA.EMP.2W.SIN.UNIV.0
126	35	21	50.6	1.4	0.57	-1.8	0.62	-1.5	0.56	DP.5*.4.M.GER.LIB.2W.MA.UNIV.0
58	48	30	50.4	1.2	0.99	0.0	0.96	-0.2	0.53	RA.4*.1.M.UK.STU.2W.SIN.UNIV.0
57	50	32	50.3	1.1	0.74	-1.2	0.74	-1.2	0.53	RA.4*.1.F.UK.ST.2W.SIN.UNIV.0
43	43	28	50.1	1.2	0.97	-0.1	0.96	-0.1	0.52	EF.4*.3.F.UK.EXE.2W.MA.SECO.1
87	36	23	49.9	1.3	0.74	-1.0	0.75	-1.0	0.60	CB.4*.2.M.JAP.OTH.1W.MA.UNIV.0
84	41	27	49.7	1.2	0.14	-5.6	0.15	-5.6	0.88	CB.4*.3.M.SP.EMP.2W.MA.UNIV.1
133	21	13	48.7	1.8	0.24	-3.0	0.23	-3.1	0.69	DP.5*.3.M.UK.EXE.1W.MA.UNIV.0
3	39	29	48.6	1.2	0.69	-1.5	0.70	-1.4	0.70	AP.4*.1.F.SP.ST.1W.MA.UNIV.0
12	34	25	47.9	1.3	1.36	1.2	1.44	1.5	0.28	AP.4*.3.M.POR.EMP.1W.MA.SECO.1
147	35	29	46.9	1.2	1.35	1.3	1.35	1.3	0.50	DC.5*.3.M.CAN.FREE.2W.MA.SECO.2
71	22	15	46.5	1.6	1.11	0.3	1.12	0.4	0.25	MD.4*.1.M.BEL.LIB.1W.MA.SECO.1
19	30	26	46.2	1.2	1.03	0.1	1.05	0.2	0.38	GU.4*.5.M.SP.PEN.3W.MA.UNIV.0
73	21	15	45.9	1.6	0.85	-0.5	0.86	-0.4	0.26	MD.4*.1.F.BEL.LIB.1W.MA.SECO.1
Mean	56	27	55.7	1.4	1.02	-0.2	1.01	-0.2		
SD	12	3	4.3	0.3	0.44	1.6	0.43	1.6		

compile additional information, some very valuable data were obtained regarding the profiles of satisfied tourists.

Conclusions

The processing and analysis of the information underlying the data processed using the Rasch Model is an innovation that is being applied to the tourist sector for the first time. This measure of the level of satisfaction reveals that the model is both viable and suitable for measuring this latent variable. The empirical method used for analysing the results provides a measure for the users (tourists) and another for the items. The study of misfits facilitates a methodology for determining the causes of the abnormal behaviour of items and tourists alike.

The analysis of the results revealed that the most satisfying items in order of importance were: climate, street safety, golf, quality of hotel service, relaxing atmosphere, etc. The ranking of least satisfying items was as follows: parking, cleanliness of beaches, traffic congestion, cleanliness of seawater, café prices, etc.

Regarding the tourist profile and taking into account the information contained in both tables, it is possible to arrive at the following conclusions:

- The most satisfied tourists are Spanish.
- Women are more satisfied than men.
- The most satisfied age group is 51–60.
- Married couples are more satisfied than single tourists.
- Married couples with children are more satisfied than those without children.
- Tourists who stay 3 weeks are the most satisfied.

- Tourists without higher education are more satisfied than those with a university degree.
- Professionals, freelancers and businessmen are the most satisfied.
- Tourists staying in 5-star hotels are the most satisfied.

Hotel directors and tourism managers could use studies of this sort to segment markets, identify customer typologies by their level of satisfaction, and define market objectives at which to aim their marketing strategies. Likewise, the local authorities could use the study results to improve services that tourists have been perceived as unsatisfactory – in the case of Marbella, parking, cleanliness of beaches, traffic congestion, prices, etc.

This survey opens up new lines of research involving successive analyses of each tourist typology in terms of the hotel in which they stay, their nationality and sociodemographic profile, and checking the different order of the items for each one of them. The study of the measure order of the items for each analysis would determine the most relevant items in each case.

This model differs from other methods, for instance, ANOVA, factorial analysis, discriminating analysis, to the extent that it is possible to discriminate each one of the items by means of the measure, discovering which items are the most and the least valued, and taking specific measures of each item. Likewise, it is possible to analyse the profile of visitors according to their order, measured by their degree of satisfaction, and to segment the market by hotel choice, duration of stay, sex, nationality, profession, marital status, academic qualifications and number of children.

References

Cardozo, R.N. (1965) An experimental study of customer effort, expectation and satisfaction. *Journal of Marketing Research* 24, 305–314.

Crompton, R.L. and Love, L.L. (1995) The predictive validity of alternative approach to evaluating quality of a festival. *Journal of Travel Research* (Summer), 11–24.

Goodrich, J.N. (1977) Benefit bundle analysis: an empirical study of international travellers. *Journal of Travel Research* 3, 6–9.

Hambleton, R.K. and Cook, L.L. (1977) Latent trait models and their use in the analysis of educational test data. *Journal of Educational Measurement* 14(2), 75–95.

Haywood, M.K. and Muller, T.E. (1988) The urban tourist experience evaluating satisfaction. *Hospitality Education and Research Journal*, 453–458.

Hu, J. and Ritchie, J.N. (1993) Measuring destination attractiveness: a contextual approach. *Journal of Travel Research* (Fall), 25–34.

Hunt, H.K. (1977) *Conceptualisation and Measurement of Consumer Satisfaction and Dissatisfaction*. Proceedings of Conference Conducted by the Marketing Science Institute. MSI Report No. 77–103.

Lounsbury, J.W. and Hoopes, L. (1985) An investigation of factors associated with vacation satisfaction. *Journal of Leisure Research* 17(1), 1–13.

Mazursky, D. (1989) Past experience and future tourism decisions. *Annals of Tourism Research* 16, 333–344.

Miller, J.A. (1977) Studying satisfaction, modifying models, eliciting expectations, posing problems and making meaningful measurements. In: *Conceptualisation and Measurement of Consumer Satisfaction and Dissatisfaction*. Proceedings of the Conference Conducted by the Marketing Science Institute. MSI May Report No. 77–103, pp. 72–91.

Morris, E.W. (1977) A normative deficit approach to consumer satisfaction. In: *Conceptualisation and Measurement of Consumer Satisfaction and Dissatisfaction*. Proceedings of the Conference Conducted by the Marketing Science Institute. MSI May Report No. 77–103, pp. 240–270.

Moutinho, L. (1987) Consumer behaviour in tourism. *European Journal of Marketing,* 1–44.

Oliver, R. (1980) A cognitive model of the antecedents and consequences of satisfaction decisions. *Journal of Marketing Research* 17 (November), 460–469.

Rasch, G. (1980) *Probabilistic Models for Some Intelligence and Attainment Test*. MESA Press, University of Chicago, Chicago, Illinois.

Ritchie, J.R. Brent and Zins, M. (1978) Culture as determinant of the attractiveness of a tourism region. *Annals of Tourism Research* 5, 252–267.

Whipple, T. and Tmach, S. (1988) Group tour management: does good service produce satisfied customers? *Journal of Travel Research* (Fall), 16–21.

Woodruff, R., Cadotte, E. and Jenkins, R. (1983) Modelling consumer satisfaction processes using experience-based norms. *Journal of Marketing Research* 20, 296–304.

Wright, B.D. (1977) Solving measurement problems with the Rasch model. *Journal of Educational Measurement* 14(2), 97–116.

Wright, B.D. and Linacre, M. (1992) *A User's Guide to BIGSTEPS*. MESA Press, University of Chicago, Chicago, Illinois.

Wright, B.D. and Stone, M.H. (1979) *Best Test Design. Rasch Measurement*. MESA Press, University of Chicago, Chicago, Illinois.

Zeithaml, V.A., Parasuraman, A. and Berry, L.L. (1991) The nature and determinants of customer expectations of service. *Marketing Science Institute*. MSI May Report No. 91–113, pp. 1–28.

28 Researching and Managing Tourism and Hospitality Service: Challenges and Conclusions

Gianna Moscardo, Bruce Prideaux and Eric Laws
James Cook University, Australia

Introduction

There are a number of strengths and weaknesses associated with edited volumes that need to be acknowledged and addressed and this concluding chapter seeks to do this in relation to the contributions compiled in the present book. A brief analysis of the comments made in reviews of edited books published in the last 5 years of the *Annals of Tourism Research* suggests two main issues to be addressed in this concluding chapter. The first and most commonly reported of these was that a major strength of many edited books was having a diversity of contributions that allowed for the stimulation of new research questions and highlighted tensions and challenges in the area. The second issue relates to the use of a concluding chapter to present the common themes, gaps and issues, and future directions for research that arise from a diverse collection of chapters. In particular, the development of overall framework to bring together the various contributions can be seen as a valuable addition to an edited book.

In consideration of these review comments, the aim of this concluding chapter is to set out a descriptive concept map of the main elements of tourist satisfaction and to use this to consolidate and summarize the contributions in the book. This conclusion also hopes to highlight the major themes that can be identified from the chapters. In addition to describing these major themes, this chapter also attempts to identify some of the challenges raised by the research reported in the contributions, as well as some of the gaps in the coverage of the book as a whole. Finally, the chapter concludes with some suggested future research directions in this area.

A Concept Map of Tourist Satisfaction

Figure 28.1 provides a concept map that sets out the main components related to satisfaction in tourism and hospitality services and suggests relationships or links between key variables. This figure is derived from both the chapters in this book and the broader literature on service quality and satisfaction in tourism and hospitality settings. At the centre of this concept map lies the core concept of satisfaction. According to Pearce (Chapter 25) satisfaction can be defined as a post-experience attitude with a strong emphasis on the evaluative component of this attitude. This is consistent with Dagger and Lawley's (2003) and O'Neill's (2001) reviews, which stressed both the post-experience nature and evaluative elements of the concept of satisfaction.

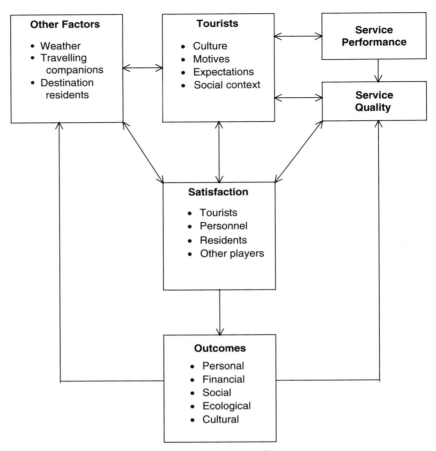

Fig. 28.1. Concept map of satisfaction in tourism and hospitality.

A long-standing tradition in the tourism and hospitality literature is to limit the use of the term satisfaction, to refer to the post-consumption judgements of tourists. As noted in the contributions of Scott (Chapter 5) and Cooper and Erfurt (Chapter 18), tourism is a complex phenomenon involving many players in addition to the tourists themselves. Within the hospitality literature there has been some recognition of this with increasing attention given to tourism and hospitality staff perceptions and judgements of service encounters (see Johns and Mattson, 2003; Anderson, Chapter 15; Prideaux and Kim, Chapter 19; Laws, Chapter 20). On the whole though, discussions of satisfaction in tourism have focused on the tourist alone. There exists, however, a substantial literature on destination residents' post-experience judgements of encounters with tourists and the tourism system – the area of social and cultural impacts of tourism. The reader is directed to Archer and Cooper (1998) and Pearce and Moscardo (1999) for major reviews of this area.

This narrow focus on tourist satisfaction has also resulted in a narrow focus on the outcomes of satisfaction in tourism contexts. Generally tourist satisfaction is linked to repeat purchase, positive word-of-mouth promotion and, through these, increased revenue. See Dagger and Lawley (2003), Deery and Jago (Chapter 2), Kandampully and Kandampully

(Chapter 9), and Pearce (Chapter 25) for more details on these links. A more extensive view of the outcomes of satisfying experiences for tourists and other players would include consideration of the link between satisfaction and the development of positive conservation attitudes which may contribute to fewer negative ecological and other impacts for the host destination (Moscardo, 1999).

Research into the impacts of tourism on destination communities also provides evidence that well-planned and managed tourist–host interactions can contribute to improvements in the social and cultural lives of hosts (Pearce and Moscardo, 1999). A consideration of enhancements to the quality of life of hosts leads to the consideration of the long-term benefits of satisfying tourism experiences for the guests. The existing tourist satisfaction literature has been almost exclusively concerned with the outcomes of tourist satisfaction for tourism and hospitality businesses. An examination of the research into the benefits of leisure for participants (Mannell and Kleiber, 1997) could be a useful extension of tourist satisfaction research.

The concept map in Fig. 28.1 has three sets of elements that contribute to satisfaction: Service Quality, the Tourist, and Other Factors. This use of three elements builds upon Noe's (1999) distinction between instrumental and expressive attributes of tourist experiences (see Uysal, Chapter 24, for more details on this approach). Instrumental attributes are defined as 'the means used by the tourist to achieve some desired end' and expressive attributes 'are the psychological or social benefits derived by participating' (Noe, 1999, p. 77). Thus instrumental attributes include all the elements or variables that are often seen as dimensions of service quality and that to some extent can be influenced by tourism managers. Expressive attributes emerge, however, from the interaction between the tourists and their motives and the opportunities offered by the tourism setting to achieve motives. In this approach, a tourist's level of satisfaction may be due to factors or incidents that have little to do with the service performance of relevant tourism organizations.

The concept map also includes a number of interactions between these elements recognizing several important processes. The link

between satisfaction and service quality, for example, indicates that perceived service quality can contribute to overall satisfaction. It is also, however, possible that high satisfaction derived from an expressive element can contribute to an enhanced perception of service quality (Soutar, 2001). In other words, a tourist whose satisfying experience is based mainly on spending time with a rewarding social companion in pleasant weather in a beautiful setting may be predisposed to positively evaluate other aspects of the experience including the service performance.

The links between the tourist and all the other elements in the concept map acknowledge that service encounters, perceptions of service quality and of satisfaction are all influenced by characteristics and actions of the tourists themselves. See Santos-Arrebola (Chapter 27) and Moscardo (Chapter 4) for examples of the influence of tourist variables on satisfaction. Most definitions of service quality, for example, involve the idea that this is the result of tourists' comparing performance against expectations (O'Neill, 2001; Dagger and Lawley, 2003). In such definitions it would seem that the outcome depends as much upon the tourist and their expectations as upon the actual service performance. In addition to the expectations, culture has also been identified as an important variable in service performance encounters and service quality judgements (Prideaux and Kim, Chapter 19).

The 'other factors' component includes all those context elements that can intervene in a tourist's experience but which are not directly under the control of either the tourists or the tourism personnel. These could include the weather, the behaviour of travelling companions and other tourists and interactions with local residents not employed by tourism organizations. In addition this component could include broader contextual factors such as alliances and practices associated with airline deregulation (Rhoades et al., Chapter 8), destination branding (Scott and Clark, Chapter 26) and restaurant co-branding (Khan, Chapter 7).

Finally, the concept map includes two feedback loops connecting the outcomes of satisfaction back to service performance and to other factors. In the case of service performance several mechanisms can be described. The positive financial outcomes for tourism businesses that derive from satisfied customers, for example, can contribute to enhanced service performance through investment in upgraded facilities and equipment and staff training. Another possible mechanism lies with increased effort from staff who find service encounters rewarding. In a similar fashion, destination residents who are satisfied with their tourism encounters may be more friendly in future encounters. This is an example of the feedback loop between outcomes and other factors.

Contributions of this Book to the Concept Map of Tourist Satisfaction

It is argued here that much of the existing academic attention in the area of tourist satisfaction and service management has been focused on tourists alone. Further, this attention has concentrated heavily on the links between service performance, service quality and satisfaction. One of the contributions of this book is to broaden this focus to include a wider range of issues and factors. Table 28.1 provides a simple classification of the chapters in the book that can be used to examine these contributions in more detail.

Factors that Influence Satisfaction

The present book provides information on a wider range of tourist settings than has been typically found in discussions of tourism and hospitality service management. It also provides a greater focus on satisfaction as the core variable of interest allowing for the identification of a wider range of variables that can be related to service management. Moscardo's study of wildlife-based tourism (Chapter 4) for example, found that a number of variables related to the wildlife themselves, such as the variety and number seen and their response to the presence of humans, were significantly related to tourist satisfaction. Getz and Carlsen's study (Chapter 13) of a surfing event noted that the size of the waves at the time of

the competition was a potential determinant of visitor satisfaction. Tourists describing their satisfaction with Marbella rated the climate as the most satisfying element of their experience (Santos-Arrebola, Chapter 27). All these examples highlight the potential importance of factors other than those usually examined in studies of service performance and quality.

The Role of Staff in Service Encounters

Several of the chapters in the present book analysed aspects of the role of staff and staff perceptions of service encounters. Pegg and Suh (Chapter 3), for example, explored hospitality manager attitudes towards service recovery systems, while Anderson (Chapter 15) described the emotional coping strategies of front-line service staff in several tourism sectors. Several chapters reinforced the importance of empowerment as a tool for enhancing service performance (Kandampully and Kandampully, Chapter 9; Anderson, Chapter 15; Pegg and Suh, Chapter 3). Komppulla (Chapter 11) and Varini and Diamantis (Chapter 17) describe the importance of staff skills and training for service performance. In these areas of staff perspectives on, and involvement in, service performance the chapters in this book confirm existing arguments (Kandampully, 1999; Chernish, 2001; Johns and Mattson, 2003).

Cross-cultural Influences on Tourist and Hospitality Service and Satisfaction

Prideaux and Kim (Chapter 19) identified the importance of cross-cultural perceptions of service performance. This chapter begins an exploration of an area that has been only rarely considered in detail in tourist service and satisfaction research (Mok, 2001). According to Mok the limited research evidence that is available demonstrates that cultural groups differ on all the components of satisfaction and service quality set out in the concept map in this chapter. Such arguments

Table 28.1. Summary of key characteristics of the chapters.

Main focus	Author(s)	Chapter	Sample	Method style
Satisfaction with a destination	Scott	5	N/A	N/A
	Cooper and Erfurt	18	Tourists	Quantitative
	Scott and Clark	26	Tourists	Quantitative
	Santos-Arrebola	27	Tourists	Quantitative
Satisfaction with a particular type of tourism	Deery and Jago	2	Conference delegates	Mixture
	Moscardo	4	Tourists	Quantitative
	Getz and Carlsen	13	Visitors to a surfing event	Mixture
	Yu and Weiler	16	Industry representatives, tour guides, Chinese tour participants	Mixture
	Hudson, Miller and Hudson	21	Tour operator clients	Quantitative
	O'Neill and Charters	22	Tourists	Quantitative
	Uysal	24	Tourists	Quantitative
Service quality	Pegg and Suk	3	Managers in a variety of businesses	Qualitative
	Anderson	15	Accommodation, information centre and transport staff and managers	Qualitative
	Prideaux and Kim	19	Korean airline cabin crew	Quantitative
Tools for improving service performance	Buhalis, Karcher and Brown	6	N/A	N/A
	Krebs and Wall	10	Tourists	Mixture
	Kamppula	11	N/A	N/A
	LePelley and Pettit	14	N/A	N/A
	Kandampully and Kandampully	9	N/A	N/A
	Laws	20	N/A	N/A
Impact of tourism trends on service performance/ service quality	Khan	7	N/A	N/A
	Rhoades	8	US airline passengers	Quantitative
	Varini and Diamantis	17	Swiss hotel managers	Quantitative
	Williams and Macleod (styles of development)	12	Visitors, business organizations in 6 European regions	Quantitative
Research methods	Hudson, Miller and Hudson	21	Tour operator clients	Quantitative
	Pearce	25	Multiple	Quantitative (meta-analytic)
	Moscardo (CIT)	23	Accommodation guests	Qualitative
	Santos-Arrebola	27	Tourists	Quantitative

Note: N/A is an abbreviation for not applicable. Mixture refers to the use of both quantitative and qualitative methods.

are also made by Weiermair (2000) who provides an even more detailed framework for analysing and understanding the role of culture in service perceptions.

New Technology and Service Performance

Another area that the chapters in this book contribute to is that of understanding the actual and potential effects of new technological systems on service performance. Buhalis *et al.* (Chapter 6) and Krebs and Wall (Chapter 10) provide critical analyses of the use of internet technology to promote destinations and provide information to tourists. Growing tourist use of these forms of communication and promotion requires a better understanding of tourist evaluations of the value and effectiveness of these new media. Varini and Diamantis (Chapter 17) researched a different use of technology and its impact on service quality – the use of yield management systems in hotels. In this study, the authors report that hotel managers' perceptions of the potential negative impacts of such systems on guests' evaluations of service performance are a critical factor in the adoption of such systems.

Impacts of Major Trends on Service Quality

The increasing use of computer and information technologies reported in the previous section is just one of a number of major trends that have been identified as impacting on tourism in general. Several other major trends and their connections to service quality and satisfaction are explored across various chapters in this book. Khan (Chapter 7) and Rhoades *et al.* (Chapter 8) provide analyses of the service performance and service quality implications of restaurant co-branding and airline deregulation, respectively. Williams and MacLeod (Chapter 12) introduce sustainability themes with an analysis of the links between styles of development and tourist satisfaction and Cooper and Erfurt (Chapter 18) extend this with a discussion of tourist satisfaction and sustainability in a World Heritage Area.

Gaps and Challenges

While it was argued earlier that one of the strengths of this volume is that the contributions provide a broad and eclectic view of this area, not all areas of the concept map in Fig. 28.1 have been given attention in this book and there is value in identifying some of the gaps in coverage. For instance, Scott (Chapter 5) and Cooper and Erfurt (Chapter 18) suggest that the satisfaction of players other than tourists is important. But while these contributors highlight this issue, the primary focus of most of the chapters in the present book is on the tourist. There is also little attention paid to the outcomes of tourist and hospitality experiences other than the tourists' intention to repeat, return or recommend their experiences.

At least two chapters, Moscardo (Chapter 4) and Pearce (Chapter 25), raise concerns about the role of expectations in the determination of service quality and satisfaction. Such concerns about expectations have been raised elsewhere (Gyimothy, 1999; Ekinci *et al.*, 2001; Gabbott, 2003) presenting a challenge for those who base their service quality and service satisfaction research on expectation–disconfirmation models such as SERVQUAL. While some of the chapters in this book are based on SERVQUAL or similar approaches, most chapters do not explicitly acknowledge the use of any conceptual model or theory. Three exceptions are the use of mindfulness theory from cognitive psychology (Moscardo, Chapter 4), role theory from sociology (Yu and Weiler, Chapter 16) and Rasch's model from psychometrics (Santos-Arrebola, Chapter 27).

Only one chapter (Prideaux and Kim, Chapter 19) discusses in detail the importance of cross-cultural interactions and differences for understanding and managing service. While a number of different national and ethnic groups are included in the various samples described in the research chapters in the book, the analyses in these are not directed towards understanding culture as a variable of concern. It could also be argued that most of these chapters assume homogeneity in tourists with only a few offering analyses of difference among tourists in both their satisfaction and perceptions of service quality (see Moscardo,

Chapter 4; Santos-Arrebola, Chapter 27). An examination of the last column of Table 28.1 reveals that quantitative methods dominate in those chapters that report on research studies. A greater use of qualitative methods to examine emic perspectives on these phenomena might result in greater attention to individual differences in perceptions of service quality and satisfaction. Such approaches could also suggest some different theoretical avenues to explore.

Future Research Directions

The gaps and challenges identified in the previous section offer some directions for future research effort. Specifically, to improve our understanding and management of tourism and hospitality of service and satisfaction, we need:

- more analysis of variables related to the tourists themselves, especially culture;
- more analysis of the nature and role of expectations;
- to evaluate the applicability of a broader range of theories;
- to expand the range of players and outcomes that are studied.

In addition to these topics, the chapters on satisfaction with tourist experiences and destinations suggest a wider variety of variables that can influence perceptions of service quality. This is consistent with existing criticisms of the application of SERVQUAL in tourism and hospitality that argue that the SERVQUAL dimensions do not incorporate all the relevant attributes of service encounters in these contexts (Fick and Ritchie, 1991; Johns, 1993; Johns and Lee-Ross, 1997). An alternative way to look at this issue is to ask if there are some attributes or dimensions that apply to all tourism contexts or sectors. It seems likely that a hierarchy of service attributes could exist with:

- some attributes that matter in all tourist and hospitality contexts;
- some attributes that matter only in certain types or sectors of tourism and hospitality, such as conference tourism or wildlife-based tourism;
- some attributes that matter for certain types of tourist;
- some attributes that are site specific.

Meta-analytic studies, such as that provided by Pearce (Chapter 25), offer one way to examine and develop such a hierarchy.

References

Archer, B. and Cooper, C. (1998) The positive and negative impacts of tourism. In: Theobald, W.F. (ed.) *Global Tourism*, 2nd edn. Butterworth–Heinemann, Oxford, pp. 63–81.

Chernish, W.N. (2001) Empowering service personnel to deliver quality service. In: Kandampully, J., Mok, C. and Sparks, B. (eds) *Service Quality Management in Hospitality, Tourism, and Leisure*. Haworth Press, New York, pp. 223–237.

Dagger, T. and Lawley, M. (2003) Service quality. In: McColl-Kennedy, J.R. (ed.) *Services Marketing: A Managerial Approach*. John Wiley & Sons, Brisbane, pp. 72–100.

Ekinci, Y., Riley, M. and Chen, J.S. (2001) A review of comparison standards used in service quality and customer satisfaction studies: some emerging issues for hospitality and tourism research. In: Mazanec, J.A., Crouch, G.I., Ritchie, J.R.B. and Woodside, G.A. (eds) *Consumer Psychology of Tourism, Hospitality and Leisure*, Vol. 2. CAB International, Wallingford, UK, pp. 321–332.

Fick, G. and Ritchie, J. (1991) Measuring service quality in the travel and tourism industry. *Journal of Travel Research* 30(2), 2–9.

Gabbott, M. (2003) Services research. In: McColl-Kennedy, J.R. (ed.) *Services Marketing: A Managerial Approach*. John Wiley & Sons, Brisbane, pp. 168–189.

Gyimothy, S. (1999) Visitors' perceptions of holiday experiences and service providers. *Journal of Travel and Tourism Marketing* 8(2), 57–74.

Johns, N. (1993) Quality management in the hospitality industry: part 3 – recent developments. *International Journal of Contemporary Hospitality Management* 5(1), 10–15.

Johns, N. and Lee-Ross, D. (1997) A study of service quality in small hotels and guesthouses. *Progress in Tourism and Hospitality Research* 3, 351–363.

Johns, N. and Mattsson, J. (2003) Managing the service encounters in tourism. In: Kusluvan, S. (ed.) *Managing Employee Attitudes and Behaviors in the Tourism and Hospitality Industry.* Nova Science, New York, pp. 173–200.

Kandampully, J. (1999) Creating and maintaining a competitive advantage. In: Lee-Ross, D. (ed.) *HRM in Tourism and Hospitality.* Cassell, London, pp. 37–47.

Mannell, R.C. and Kleiber, D.A. (1997) *A Social Psychology of Leisure.* Venture Publishing, State College, Pennsylvania.

Mok, C. (2001) Cross-cultural issues in service quality. In: Kandampully, J., Mok, C. and Sparks, B. (eds) *Service Quality Management in Hospitality, Tourism, and Leisure.* Haworth Press, New York, pp. 269–280.

Moscardo, G. (1999) *Making Visitors Mindful.* Sagamore, Champaign, Illinois.

Noe, F. (1999) *Tourist Service Satisfaction: Hotel, Transportation, and Recreation.* Sagamore, Champaign, Illinois.

O'Neill, M. (2001) Measuring service quality and customer satisfaction. In: Kandampully, J., Mok, C. and Sparks, B. (eds) *Service Quality Management in Hospitality, Tourism, and Leisure.* Haworth Press, New York, pp. 159–191.

Pearce, P.L. and Moscardo, G. (1999) Tourism community analysis: asking the right questions. In: Pearce, D.G. and Butler, R.W. (eds) *Contemporary Issues in Tourism Development.* Routledge, London, pp. 31–51.

Soutar, G.N. (2001) Service quality, customer satisfaction, and value: an examination of their relationships. In: Kandampully, J., Mok, C. and Sparks, B. (eds) *Service Quality Management in Hospitality, Tourism, and Leisure.* Haworth Press, New York, pp. 97–110.

Weiermair, K. (2000) Tourists' perceptions towards and satisfaction with service quality in the cross-cultural service encounter: implications for hospitality and tourism management. *Managing Service Quality* 10(6), 397–409.

Index